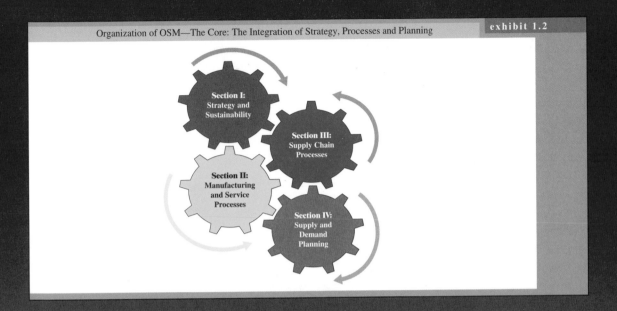

Organization of OSM—The Core: The Integration of Strategy, Processes and Planning

exhibit 1.2

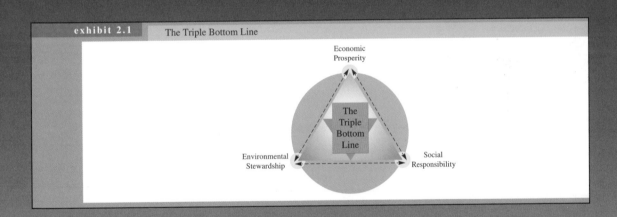

exhibit 2.1 The Triple Bottom Line

Operations and Supply Management: The Core

Operations and Decision Sciences

OPERATIONS MANAGEMENT

Beckman and Rosenfield
Operations, Strategy: Competing in the 21st Century
First Edition

Benton
Purchasing and Supply Chain Management
Second Edition

Bowersox, Closs, and Cooper
Supply Chain Logistics Management
Third Edition

Brown and Hyer
Managing Projects: A Team-Based Approach
First Edition

Burt, Petcavage, and Pinkerton
Supply Management
Eighth Edition

Cachon and Terwiesch
Matching Supply with Demand: An Introduction to Operations Management
Second Edition

Finch
Interactive Models for Operations and Supply Chain Management
First Edition

Fitzsimmons and Fitzsimmons
Service Management: Operations, Strategy, Information Technology
Sixth Edition

Gehrlein
Operations Management Cases
First Edition

Larson and Gray
Project Management: The Managerial Process
Fifth Edition

Harrison and Samson
Technology Management
First Edition

Hayen
SAP R/3 Enterprise Software: An Introduction
First Edition

Hill
Manufacturing Strategy: Text & Cases
Third Edition

Hopp
Supply Chain Science
First Edition

Hopp and Spearman
Factory Physics
Third Edition

Jacobs and Chase
Operations and Supply Management: The Core
Second Edition

Jacobs, Chase, and Aquilano
Operations and Supply Management
Twelfth Edition

Jacobs and Whybark
Why ERP?
First Edition

Leenders, Johnson, Flynn, and Fearon
Purchasing and Supply Management
Thirteenth Edition

Nahmias
Production and Operations Analysis
Sixth Edition

Olson
Introduction to Information Systems Project Management
Second Edition

Schroeder, Goldstein, Rungtusanatham
Operations Management: Contemporary Concepts and Cases
Fifth Edition

Seppanen, Kumar, and Chandra
Process Analysis and Improvement
First Edition

Simchi-Levi, Kaminsky, and Simchi-Levi
Designing and Managing the Supply Chain: Concepts, Strategies, Case Studies
Third Edition

Sterman
Business Dynamics: Systems Thinking and Modeling for Complex World
First Edition

Swink, Melnyk, Cooper, and Hartley
Managing Operations Across the Supply Chain
First Edition

Thomke
Managing Product and Service Development: Text and Cases
First Edition

Ulrich and Eppinger
Product Design and Development
Fourth Edition

Vollmann, Berry, Whybark, and Jacobs
Manufacturing Planning & Control for Supply Chain Management
Sixth Edition

Zipkin
Foundations of Inventory Management
First Edition

QUANTITATIVE METHODS AND MANAGEMENT SCIENCE

Hillier and Hillier
Introduction to Management Science: A Modeling and Case Studies Approach with Spreadsheets
Fourth Edition

Stevenson and Ozgur
Introduction to Management Science with Spreadsheets
First Edition

Operations and Supply Management: The Core

second edition

F. Robert Jacobs
Indiana University

Richard B. Chase
University of Southern California

McGraw-Hill
Irwin

OPERATIONS AND SUPPLY MANAGEMENT: THE CORE

Published by McGraw-Hill/Irwin, a business unit of The McGraw-Hill Companies, Inc., 1221 Avenue of the Americas, New York, NY, 10020. Copyright © 2010, 2008 by The McGraw-Hill Companies, Inc. All rights reserved. No part of this publication may be reproduced or distributed in any form or by any means, or stored in a database or retrieval system, without the prior written consent of The McGraw-Hill Companies, Inc., including, but not limited to, in any network or other electronic storage or transmission, or broadcast for distance learning.

Some ancillaries, including electronic and print components, may not be available to customers outside the United States.

This book is printed on acid-free paper.

1 2 3 4 5 6 7 8 9 0 DOW/DOW 0 9

ISBN: 978-0-07-340333-5
MHID: 0-07-340333-4

Vice president and editor-in-chief: *Brent Gordon*
Publisher: *Tim Vertovec*
Editorial director: *Stewart Mattson*
Executive editor: *Richard T. Hercher, Jr.*
Director of development: *Ann Torbert*
Managing development editor: *Gail Korosa*
Vice president and director of marketing: *Robin J. Zwettler*
Marketing manager: *Sankha Basu*
Vice president of editing, design and production: *Sesha Bolisetty*
Lead project manager: *Christine A. Vaughan*
Senior production supervisor: *Debra R. Sylvester*
Lead designer: *Matthew Baldwin*
Senior photo research coordinator: *Jeremy Cheshareck*
Photo researcher: *Allison Grimes*
Media project manager: *Jennifer Lohn*
Cover design: *Evan Modesto*
Cover image: *©Getty Images*
Typeface: *10/12 Times*
Compositor: *MPS Limited*
Printer: *R. R. Donnelley*

Library of Congress Cataloging-in-Publication Data

Jacobs, F. Robert.
   Operations and supply management : the core / F. Robert Jacobs, Richard B. Chase.—2nd ed.
     p. cm.—(The McGraw-Hill/Irwin series operations and decision sciences)
     Includes index.
  ISBN-13: 978-0-07-340333-5 (alk. paper)
  ISBN-10: 0-07-340333-4 (alk. paper)
  1. Production management. I. Chase, Richard B. II. Title.

TS155.J27 2010
658.5—dc22

                        2009034501

www.mhhe.com

To Harriet and the Kids—Laurie,
Andy, Glenn, Rob, Christine, and Eloy
and
To Jennifer and Suzy

PREFACE

The goal of this book is to provide you with the essential information that every manager needs to know about operations and supply–related activities in a firm. Times have changed dramatically over the last few years. Organization structures are now much flatter, and rather than being functionally organized, companies often are organized by customer and product groups. Today's manager cannot ignore how the real work of the organization is done. This book is all about how to get the real work done effectively. It makes little difference if you are officially in finance, marketing, accounting, or operations: The value-added work, the process of creating and delivering products, needs to be completed in a manner that is both high-quality and maximally efficient. Many of the things you do, or will do, in your job are repetitive, even some of the most creative and high-profile activities. You should think of this course as preparing you to be your most productive and helping you help your organization be its most productive.

We can consider the importance of the material in the book on many levels, but let's focus on three. First, consider your role as a business unit manager with people working under your supervision. Next, in the longer term, you probably have aspirations to become a senior executive with responsibility for multiple businesses or products. Finally, you may decide to specialize in operations and supply management as a long-term career.

In your role as a manager with people working under your supervision, one of your major duties will be to organize the way work is done. There needs to be some structure to the work process, including how information is captured and analyzed, as well as how decisions and changes and improvements are made. Without a logical or structured approach, even a small group may be subject to errors, ineffiencies, and even chaos.

Designing efficient process flows is an important element of getting a group to work together. If your group is involved in creative activities such as designing cars, buildings, or even stock portfolios, there still needs to be structure to how the work is done, who is responsible for what, and how progress is reported. The concepts of project management, manufacturing and service process design, capacity analysis, and quality in this text are all directly related to the knowledge you will need to be a great supervisor in your organization, and getting your group to work productively and efficiently will lead to success and more responsibility for you.

Next, think about becoming a senior executive. Making acquisitions, planning mergers, and buying and selling divisions will get your name and picture in business magazines. Deals are easily explained to boards, shareholders, and the media. They are newsworthy and offer the prospect of nearly immediate gratification, and being a deal maker is consistent with the image of the modern executive as someone who focuses on grand strategy and leaves operations details to others. Unfortunately, the majority of deals are unsuccessful. The critical element of success, even with the grandest deals, can still be found most often in the operational details.

Real success happens when operational processes can be improved. Productivity improvements from things such as sharing customer service processes, purchasing systems, distribution and manufacturing systems, and other processes can lead to great synergies and success. Operations accounts for 60 to 80 percent of the direct expenses that limit the profit of most firms. Without these operations synergies, designed and implemented by executives with a keen understanding of the concepts in this book, companies are often left with expensive debt, disappointed customers and shareholders, and pressure on the bottom line—on earnings.

Finally, you may be interested in a career in operations. Well, you are not alone. Professional organizations such as the Association for Operations Management, the Institute for Supply Management, and the Council of Supply Chain Management Professionals have well over 200,000 members participating in regular monthly meetings, annual conferences, and certification programs. Entry-level jobs might be as a forecast strategist, project manager, inventory control manager, production supervisor, purchasing manager, logistics manager, or warehouse specialist. In addition, top operations students may obtain their initial jobs with consulting firms, working as business process analysts and system design specialists.

We encourage you to talk to your instructor about what you want to get out of the course. What are your career aspirations, and how do they relate to the material in this course? Write your instructor a short e-mail describing what you want to do in the future—this is invaluable information for tailoring the material in the course to your needs. As you work through the text share your experiences and insights with the class. Being an active student is guaranteed to make your experience more valuable and interesting.

ACKNOWLEDGMENTS

Special thanks to Rex Cutshall, Indiana University, for countless contributions to creating this text as well as authoring the ScreenCam tutorials; William Berry, Queens College, for preparing the Test Bank; Christopher Kelly, University of Indianapolis, for accuracy checking the text and preparing the Solutions Manual; Ronny Richardson, Southern Polytechnic State University, for revising the PowerPoint slides and preparing the narrated solutions to the examples in the text; Patrick Johanns, Purdue University, for creating the Excel templates; and Laura Meade, Texas Christian University, for accuracy checking the text and Solutions Manual.

We also wish to thank the following reviewers, focus group, and survey participants for their many thoughtful suggestions for this text:

REVIEWERS

Cuneyt Altinoz, *East Carolina University;* Antonio Arreola-Risa, *Texas A&M University;* Greg Bier, *University of Missouri;* Jennifer Blackhurst, *Iowa State University;* Carolyn Borne, *Louisiana State University;* Karen Eboch, *Bowling Green State University;* Brian Fugate, *Lehigh University;* Ralph Janaro, *Clarkson University;* Hale Kaynak, *University of Texas, Pan American;* Anita Lee-Post, *University of Kentucky;* Rod Lievano, *University of Minnesota, Duluth;* Steve Lyman, *Ferris State University;* Daniel Marrone, *Farmingdale State College;* Marie Matta, *George Washington University;* Samuel McDowell, *University of Vermont;* Laura Meade, *Texas Christian University;* Holmes Miller, *Muhlenberg College;* John Nicholas, *Loyola University, Chicago;* Peter Salzarulo, *Miami University of Ohio;* Kimberlee Snyder, *Winona State University;* Young K. Son, *Baruch College;* James Stewart, *University of Maryland;* Peter Swan, *Penn State University, Harrisburg;* Rajesh Tyagi, *DePaul University;* Harish Verma, *Wayne State University;* Robert Vokurka, *Texas A&M University, Corpus Christi;* and Edward Waston, *Louisiana State University.*

FOCUS GROUPS

Yasemin Aksoy, *Strategic Operations Alignment, LLC;* Gerald Aase, *Northern Illinois University;* Ajay Das, *Baruch College;* Ray deMatta, *University of Iowa;* Tej Dhakar, *Southern New Hampshire University;* Steven Dickstein, *The Ohio State University;* Arthur Duhaime, *Nichols College;* Karen Chinander Dye, *Florida Atlantic University;* Richard Franza, *Kennesaw State University;* Harold Fraser, *Cal State, Fullerton;* Lawrence Fredendall, *Clemson University;* Steven Harrod, *University of Dayton;* James Ho, *University of Illinois, Chicago;* Apurva Jain, *University of Washington;* Rahul Kale, *University of North Florida;* Rhonda Lummus, *Indiana University;* Laura Meade, *Texas Christian University;*

Nagesh Murthy, *University of Oregon;* Philip Musa, *University of Alabama, Birmingham;* Fariborz Partovi, *Drexel University;* Eddy Patuwo, *Kent State University;* Bharatendra Rai, *University of Massachusetts, Dartmouth;* Cesar Rego, *University of Mississippi;* Kaushik Sengupta, *Hofstra University;* Carlo Smith, *Missouri State University;* Don Smith, *California State University, Fullerton;* Gilvan Souza, *University of Maryland;* and Elizabeth Trybus, *California State University;* Peter Wagner, *Northridge University of Dayton.*

We would also like to thank the many reviewers of the first edition for their contributions.

SURVEY PARTICIPANTS

Ajay Das, *Baruch College;* Jonatan Jelen, *Baruch College;* Mark Barrat, *Arizona State University—Tempe;* Johnny Rungtusanatham, *University of Minnesota;* William Verdini, *Arizona State University—Tempe;* Antonio Arrela-Risa, *Texas A&M University;* Matt Keblis, *Texas A&M University;* Drew Stapleton, *University of Wisconsin—Lacrosse;* David Lewis, *Brigham Young University;* Kathy Dhanda, *DePaul University;* Daniel R. Heiser, *DePaul University;* Ann Marucheck, *University of North Carolina—Chapel Hill;* Eric Svaan, *University of Michigan—Ann Arbor;* Amer Qureshi, *Columbus State University;* Mark Ippolito, *Indiana University, Purdue University—Indianapolis;* Jayanta Bandyopadhyay, *Central Michigan University;* and Rohit Verma, *Cornell University.*

Alan Cannon, *University of Texas—Arlington;* Anita Lee-Post, *University of Kentucky;* Barbara Downey, *University of Missouri;* Cesar Rego, *University of Mississippi;* Ednilson Bernardes, *Georgia Southern University;* Eng Gee, *Ngee Am Poly—Singapore;* Eric Svaan, *University of Michigan, Ann Arbor;* Fathi Sokkar, *Eastern Michigan University;* Karen Eboch, *Bowling Green State University;* Kimberlee Snyder, *Winona State University;* Kevin Watson, *University of New Orleans;* Lori Koste, *Grand Valley State University;* Mustafa Yilmaz, *Northeastern University;* Marijane Hancock, *University of Nebraska;* Renato De Matta, *University of Iowa—Iowa City;* Rick Franza, *Kennesaw State University;* Robert Szymanski, *University of Central Florida;* Seong Jong Joo, *Central Washington University;* Stephan Vachon, *Clarkson University;* Terry Harrison, *Penn State University;* Timothy McClurg, *University of Wisconsin;* Theresa Wells, *University of Wisconsin—Eau Claire;* Tomislav Mandakovic, *Florida International University—Miami;* Uttarayan Bagchi, *University of Texas, Austin.*

Thanks to the McGraw-Hill/Irwin marketing and production team who make this possible—Sankha Basu, marketing manager; Stewart Mattson, editorial director; Christine Vaughan, project manager; Debra Sylvester, production supervisor; Matt Baldwin, designer; Jeremy Cheshareck, photo research coordinator; Jennifer Lohn, media project manager; and Kerry Bowler, lead media project manager.

A special thanks to our outstanding editorial team. Gail Korosa, our amazing developmental editor, has become our passionate partner in the development of this book. Thanks for your enthusiasm, organizational skills, and patience. We love working with you.

We appreciate our executive editor, Dick Hercher. His brilliant guidance and unwavering dedication to working with us is a constant motivator. His leadership has provided the solid foundation on which the entire team associated with this book is built. It is an honor to publish another book with Dick Hercher.

Last, but certainly not least, we thank our families. We have stolen countless hours, time that would otherwise be spent with them. We sincerely appreciate your support.

F. Robert Jacobs
Richard B. Chase

A NOTE TO INSTRUCTORS

The Cover and the Title

Operations and Supply Management: The Core derives its title from a combination of ideas and trends. First, in order to be lean and focused, the book presents the important core ideas. A review by Professor Jacobs of the syllabi of over a dozen representative U.S. universities revealed that, as expected, there was a wide variety of topics covered; all of which would lead naturally to a comprehensive text such as Jacobs & Chase *Operations and Supply Management*. The topics covered in all of these sampled schools, i.e., the consistent or Core topics, is what this text includes.

In addition to that study, the authors participated in a two-session meeting chaired by Mark Berenson at the National DSI meeting in Boston in which faculty suggested that four areas ought to be considered "core" in Operations Management courses. These areas are Processes, Quality, Inventory, and Supply Chain Management, roughly similar to the sections of this text.

Finally, as is well known in the field, success for companies today requires successfully managing the entire supply flow, from the sources of the firm, through the value-added processes of the firm, and on to the customers of the firm.

The cover illustration might be considered symbolic or representative of the core as well as the supply flow.

Just as lava flows from the core of the earth, operations and supply management is the core of business. Materials must flow through supply processes to create cash output and profits.

In *Operations and Supply Management: The Core 2e,* we take students to the center of the business and focus on the core concepts and tools needed to ensure that these processes run smoothly.

Discussion of Second Edition Revisions

In developing the revisions for the second edition, we have been very careful to make the sections and chapters as modular as possible. Even though this book is designed to be covered in its entirety in a class we realize that you may want to rearrange topics and even drop some topics from the course. Our discussions concerning the current lineup of chapters were extensive, but we realize that no matter what we end up with, it is a compromise. We know from experience that the current lineup works well. Another popular way to use the book is to cover the last section first; we know this works as well.

In this second edition, we have significantly strengthened the supply chain management material. This is particularly true in the areas of purchasing and strategic sourcing, and in lean supply chain analysis. Another major emphasis is in the area of sustainability as it relates to operations and supply chain processes. Sustainability has been woven into the book in several areas including strategy, quality management and value stream mapping, purchasing and global sourcing, and lean supply chain analysis. Sustainably is a topic that fits well within operation and supply chain management due to the strong tie between being green and being efficient. This is sometimes a synergistic relationship, but often involves a difficult trade-off that needs to be considered. The reality of global customers, global suppliers, and global supply chains has made the global firm recognize the importance of being both lean and green to ensure competitiveness.

We have reorganized the book slightly, based on input from users. First, we moved out the Strategy material from the first chapter to create a new chapter focused on Strategy and Sustainability. Another change was to move Project Management from Chapter 2 to Chapter 6 and it is now part of the section on Manufacturing and Service Processes.

A major new feature is a Super Quiz included at the end of each chapter. This is designed to allow students to see how well they understand the material using a format that is similar to what they might see in an exam. The questions are designed in a short answer fill-in-the-blank format. Many of the questions are straightforward, but in each chapter we have included a few more insightful questions that require true understanding of the material. You may want to go over these questions with your students as part of a review session prior to an exam.

The following are a list of the major revisions in each chapter:

- *Chapter 1* Operations and Supply Chain Management—We refocused this chapter on understanding what Operations and Supply Chain Management is all about: its origins and how it relates to current business practice. We split the strategy material out into Chapter 2 to make room for better coverage of the basics. We introduce the SCORE "Plan, Source, Make, Deliver, Return" framework for understanding how the processes in the supply chain must integrate.
- *Chapter 2* Strategy and Sustainability—This is a new strategy chapter. The chapter has an introduction to sustainability and triple bottom-line material (people, planet, and profit). We have also included new material on the "process" for creating a strategy.
- *Chapter 3* Strategic Capacity Management—Based on reviews, we removed the Learning Curve problem from this chapter and moved it to an appendix. The Decision Tree problem is still included in the chapter.
- *Chapter 4* Production Processes—We have retitled this chapter to "Production" processes, rather than "Manufacturing." This is a subtle but important change as it generalizes the chapter. We have added material from the SCOR model (Make-Source-Deliver) and added the concept of "customer order decoupling point" to the chapter. We have added a quick example of process mapping and a clean explanation of Little's law with examples of how to do the calculations.
- *Chapter 5* Service Processes—We have added new material on virtual services and now include service blueprinting in the chapter.
- *Chapter 6* Quality Management and Six-Sigma—Here we added c-charts to the material. This was requested by a number of reviewers. Some notation was also cleaned up in the chapter.
- *Chapter 7* Projects—Based on reviews, PERT (CPM with Three Activity Time Estimates) was added to the chapter. We also reworked and improved the explanation of crashing.
- *Chapter 8* Global Sourcing and Procurement—A new introduction on "The Green Supply Chain" was added. We added information on different types of sourcing processes including Vendor Management Inventory. A Green Sourcing process that includes material on the Total Cost of Ownership with an example and new problems has also been added.
- *Chapter 9* Location, Logistics and Distribution—The chapter has been streamlined and a new puzzle-type problem called "Supply and Demand" has been added.
- *Chapter 10* Lean and Sustainability—New material on Green Supply Chains has been added and we show how this relates to being "lean." A major new section on Value Stream Mapping including examples and problems has been added to the chapter. All the "lean" material has been consolidated into this chapter including discussion of the Toyota Production System concepts, pull concepts, and developing supplier networks to support lean processes.
- *Chapter 11* Demand Management—Here we have updated CPFR and moved it up in the chapter so that it can be used to discuss the importance of an integrated process for managing demand. In terms of actual forecasting techniques, as suggested by adopters, regression is now the first technique discussed due to its general applicability.

We have also added "decomposition" techniques (seasonal indexes) to this discussion. An example and problems have been added to support this material.

- *Chapter 12* Aggregate Operations Planning—Based on requests from reviewers, we have added a Service Aggregate Planning example to the chapter.
- *Chapter 13* Inventory Control—Based on requests from reviewers, we have added the price-break model (quantity discounts) to the chapter.
- *Chapter 14* Material Requirements Planning—Here we have added enterprise resource planning (ERP) system material to the chapter. Our reviewers indicated they would like this included.

McGraw-Hill *Connect Operations Management*
Less Managing. More Teaching. Greater Learning.

 *Connect Learn Succeed™*

McGraw-Hill *Connect Operations Management* is an online assignment and assessment solution that connects students with the tools and resources they'll need to achieve success.

McGraw-Hill *Connect Operations Management* helps prepare students for their future by enabling faster learning, more efficient studying, and higher retention of knowledge.

McGraw-Hill *Connect Operations Management* features

Connect Operations Management offers a number of powerful tools and features to make managing assignments easier, so faculty can spend more time teaching. With *Connect Operations Management* students can engage with their coursework anytime and anywhere, making the learning process more accessible and efficient. *Operations Management* offers you the features described below.

Simple assignment management

With *Connect Operations Management,* creating assignments is easier than ever, so you can spend more time teaching and less time managing. The assignment management function enables you to:

- Create and deliver assignments easily with selectable end-of-chapter questions and test bank items.
- Streamline lesson planning, student progress reporting, and assignment grading to make classroom management more efficient than ever.
- Go paperless with the eBook and online submission and grading of student assignments.

Smart grading

When it comes to studying, time is precious. *Connect Operations Management* helps students learn more efficiently by providing feedback and practice material when they need it, where they need it. When it comes to teaching, your time also is precious. The grading function enables you to:

- Have assignments scored automatically, giving students immediate feedback on their work and side-by-side comparisons with correct answers.
- Access and review each response; manually change grades or leave comments for students to review.
- Reinforce classroom concepts with practice tests and instant quizzes.

Instructor library

The *Connect Operations Management* Instructor Library is your repository for additional resources to improve student engagement in and out of class. You can select and use any asset that enhances your lecture. The *Connect Operations Management* Instructor Library includes:

- PowerPoint slides
- Text Figures
- ScreenCam Tutorials
- Excel Templates and Data Files
- Instructor's Solutions Manual
- Instructor's Resource Manual
- Test Bank

Student study center

The *Connect Operations Management* Student Study Center is the place for students to access additional resources. The Student Study Center:

- Offers students quick access to study and review material.

Student progress tracking

Connect Operations Management keeps instructors informed about how each student, section, and class is performing, allowing for more productive use of lecture and office hours. The progress-tracking function enables you to:

- View scored work immediately and track individual or group performance with assignment and grade reports.
- Access an instant view of student or class performance relative to chapter headings.

Lecture capture

Increase the attention paid to lecture discussion by decreasing the attention paid to note taking. For an additional charge Lecture Capture offers new ways for students to focus on the in-class discussion, knowing they can revisit important topics later. Lecture Capture enables you to:

- Record and distribute your lecture with a click of the button.
- Record and index PowerPoint presentations and anything shown on your computer so it is easily searchable, frame by frame.

McGraw-Hill *Connect Plus Operations Management*

McGraw-Hill reinvents the textbook learning experience. *Connect Plus Operations Management* provides all of the *Connect Operations Management* features plus the following:

- An integrated eBook, allowing for anytime, anywhere access to the textbook.
- Dynamic links between the problems or questions you assign to your students and the location in the eBook where that problem or question is covered.
- A powerful search function to pinpoint and connect key concepts in a snap.

For more information about Connect, go to www.mcgrawhillconnect.com, or contact your local McGraw-Hill sales representative.

Assurance of Learning Ready

Many educational institutions today are focused on the notion of *assurance of learning*, an important element of some accreditation standards. Operations and Supply Management: The Core is designed specifically to support your assurance of learning initiatives with a simple, yet powerful solution.

Each test bank question for Operations and Supply Management: The Core maps to a specific chapter learning outcome/objective listed in the text. You can use our test bank software, EZ Test and EZ Test Online, or in *Connect Operations Management* to easily query for learning outcomes/objectives. You can then use the reporting features of EZ Test to aggregate student results making the collection and presentation of assurance of learning data simple and easy.

AACSB Statement

The McGraw-Hill Companies is a proud corporate member of AACSB International. Understanding the importance and value of AACSB accreditation, *Operations and Supply Management: The Core* Second Edition recognizes the curricula guidelines detailed in the AACSB standards for business accreditation by connecting selected questions in the test bank to the six general knowledge and skill areas in the AACSB standards Assessment of Learning Standards.

The statements contained in *Operations and Supply Management: The Core* Second Edition are provided only as a guide for the users of this textbook. The AACSB leaves content coverage and assessment within the purview of individual schools, the mission of the school, and the faculty. While *Operations and Supply Management: The Core* Second Edition and the teaching package make no claim of any specific AACSB qualification or evaluation, we have within the Test Bank for the Second Edition labeled questions according to the six general knowledge and skill areas.

McGraw-Hill Customer Care Contact Information

At McGraw-Hill, we understand that getting the most from new technology can be challenging. That's why our services don't stop after you purchase our products. You can e-mail our Product Specialists 24 hours a day to get product-training online. Or you can search our knowledge bank of Frequently Asked Questions on our support Web site. For Customer Support, call **800-331-5094,** e-mail hmsupport@mcgraw-hill.com, or visit www.mhhe.com/support. One of our Technical Support Analysts will be able to assist you in a timely fashion.

Walkthrough

The following section highlights the key features developed to provide you with the best overall text available. We hope these features give you maximum support to learn, understand, and apply operations concepts.

Chapter Opener

CHAPTER 7

PROJECTS

After reading the chapter you will:
- Explain what project management is and why it is important.
- Identify the different ways projects can be structured.
- Describe how projects are organized into major subprojects.
- Understand what a project milestone is.
- Determine the "critical path" for a project.
- Demonstrate how to "crash," or reduce the length, of a project.

179   National Aeronautics and Space Administration's Constellation Program

181   What Is Project Management?

            Project defined
            Project management defined

181   Structuring Projects
      Pure Project
      Functional Project   Pure project defined
      Matrix Project   Functional project defined
            Matrix project defined

185   Work Breakdown Structure

            Project milestone defined
            Work breakdown structure defined
            Activities defined

186   Project Control Charts
      Earned Value Management

            Gantt chart defined
            Earned value management defined

191   Network-Planning Models
      Critical Path Method (CPM)
      CPM with Three Activity Time Estimates   Critical path defined
      Time–Cost Models and Project Crashing   Immediate predecessor defined
            Slack time defined
            Early start schedule defined
            Late start schedule defined
            Time–cost models defined

203   Managing Resources
      Tracking Progress

205   Summary

Opening Vignettes

Each chapter opens with a short vignette to set the stage and help pique students' interest in the material about to be studied. A few examples include:

- The GAP, Chapter 1, page 5
- Toshiba, Chapter 4, page 65
- NASA, Chapter 7, page 179
- Top 10 "Green" Manufacturers, Chapter 10, page 271

GREEN IS THE NEW BLACK[1]
Survey Suggests that Enviro-Conscious Manufacturers are the Best Risk for Investors

Many manufacturers still have a long way to go to address the risks and opportunities posed by the push toward more environment-friendly production processes, according to a new study conducted by RiskMetrics Group, a provider of risk management services. Those risks include higher energy costs due to tighter greenhouse gas (GHG) emissions standards, and the opportunities include growing global demand for more energy-efficient products.

The report ranks large manufacturers and other companies on their effectiveness in such areas as reducing GHG emissions, energy efficiency projects, expanding renewable energy purchases, and integrating climate factors into product designs. However, perhaps reflecting the skepticism many people still have as to exactly what role, if any, manufacturing plays in global warming, many companies are largely ignoring climate change, particularly at the board and CEO level.

According to the report, which was sponsored by the Ceres Investor coalition, only 17 percent of the respondent companies say their boards

Boxes

The boxes provide examples or expansions of the topics presented by highlighting leading companies practicing new, breakthrough ways to run their operations. Examples include:

- Understanding the Global Supply Chain, Chapter 1
- J. D. Power and Associates Defines Quality, Chapter 6
- Capability Sourcing at 7-Eleven, Chapter 8
- Convenience Drives Honda Decision, Chapter 9
- It's All in the Planning, Chapter 12

Capability Sourcing at 7-Eleven

The term *capability sourcing* was coined to refer to the way companies focus on the things they do best and outsource other functions to key partners. The idea is that owning capabilities may not be as important as having control of those capabilities. This allows many additional capabilities to be outsourced. Companies are under intense pressure to improve revenue and margins because of increased competition. An area where this has been particularly intense is the convenience store industry, where 7-Eleven is a major player.

Before 1991, 7-Eleven was one of the most vertically integrated convenience store chains. When it is vertically integrated, a firm controls most of the activities in its supply chain. In the case of 7-Eleven, the firm owned its own distribution network, which delivered gasoline to each store, made its own candy and ice, and required the managers to handle store maintenance, credit card processing, store payroll, and even the in-store information technology (IT) system. For a while 7-Eleven even owned the cows that produced the milk sold in the stores. It was difficult for 7-Eleven to manage costs in this diverse set of functions.

At that time 7-Eleven had a Japanese branch that was very successful but was based on a totally different integration model. Rather than using a company-owned and vertically integrated model, the Japanese stores had partnerships with suppliers that carried out many of the day-to-day functions.

Those suppliers specialized in each area, enhancing quality and improving service while reducing cost. The Japanese model involved outsourcing everything possible without jeopardizing the business by giving competitors critical information. A simple rule said that if a partner could provide a capability more effectively than 7-Eleven could itself, that capability should be outsourced. In the United States the company eventually outsourced activities such as human resources, finance, information technology, logistics, distribution, product development, and packaging. 7-Eleven still maintains control of all vital information and handles all merchandising, pricing, positioning, promotion of gasoline, and ready-to-eat food.

The following chart shows how 7-Eleven has structured key partnerships:

Activity	Outsourcing Strategy
Gasoline	Outsourced distribution to Citgo. Maintains control over pricing and promotion. These are activities that can differentiate its stores.
Snack foods	Frito-Lay distributes its products directly to the stores. 7-Eleven makes critical decisions about order quantities and shelf placement. 7-Eleven mines extensive data on local customer purchase patterns to make these decisions at each store.

Examples with Solutions

Examples follow quantitative topics and demonstrate specific procedures and techniques. Clearly set off from the text, they help students understand the computations.

A series of detailed, worked-out solutions for every example in the text can be found on the text Web site which provides another level of detailed support for students.

Example 5.2: Equipment Selection

The Robot Company franchises combination gas and car wash stations throughout the United States. Robot gives a free car wash for a gasoline fill-up or, for a wash alone, charges $0.50. Past experience shows that the number of customers that have car washes following fill-ups is about the same as for a wash alone. The average profit on a gasoline fill-up is about $0.70, and the cost of the car wash to Robot is $0.10. Robot stays open 14 hours per day.

Robot has three power units and drive assemblies, and a franchisee must select the unit preferred. Unit I can wash cars at the rate of one every five minutes and is leased for $12 per day. Unit II, a larger unit, can wash cars at the rate of one every four minutes but costs $16 per day. Unit III, the largest, costs $22 per day and can wash a car in three minutes.

The franchisee estimates that customers will not wait in line more than five minutes for a car wash. A longer time will cause Robot to lose the gasoline sales as well as the car wash sale.

If the estimate of customer arrivals resulting in washes is 10 per hour, which wash unit should be selected?

Service

Step by Step

Excel: Queue

SOLUTION

Using unit I, calculate the average waiting time of customers in the wash line (μ for unit I = 12 per hour). From the Model 2—Constant Service Time System equations (Exhibit 5.11),

$$L_q = \frac{\lambda^2}{2\mu(\mu - \lambda)} = \frac{10^2}{2(12)(12 - 10)} = 2.08333$$

$$W_q = \frac{L_q}{\lambda} = \frac{2.08333}{10} = 0.208 \text{ hour, or } 12\tfrac{1}{2} \text{ minutes}$$

For unit II at 15 per hour,

$$L_q = \frac{10^2}{2(15)(15 - 10)} = 0.667$$

$$W_q = \frac{0.667}{10} = 0.0667 \text{ hour, or 4 minutes}$$

Global

Global icons identify
international examples and text
discussion.

Global

Supply Chain

Supply chain icons highlight
areas with a direct link to supply
chain management.

**Supply
Chain**

Services

Service icons alert students to
examples that relate to services
and service companies.

Service

Step by Step

Every example and solved
problem in the book includes
a step-by-step icon. They draw
attention to detailed, worked-out
solutions on the text Web site.

Step by Step

Excel

Excel icons point out concepts
where Excel templates are
available on the text Web site.

Excel

Tutorials

The tutorial icons highlight links
to the ScreenCam tutorials on the
text Web site.

Tutorials

Photos and Exhibits

Over sixty photos and two hundred exhibits are included in the text to enhance the visual appeal and clarify text discussions. Many of the photos illustrate additional examples of companies that utilize the operations and supply chain concepts in their business.

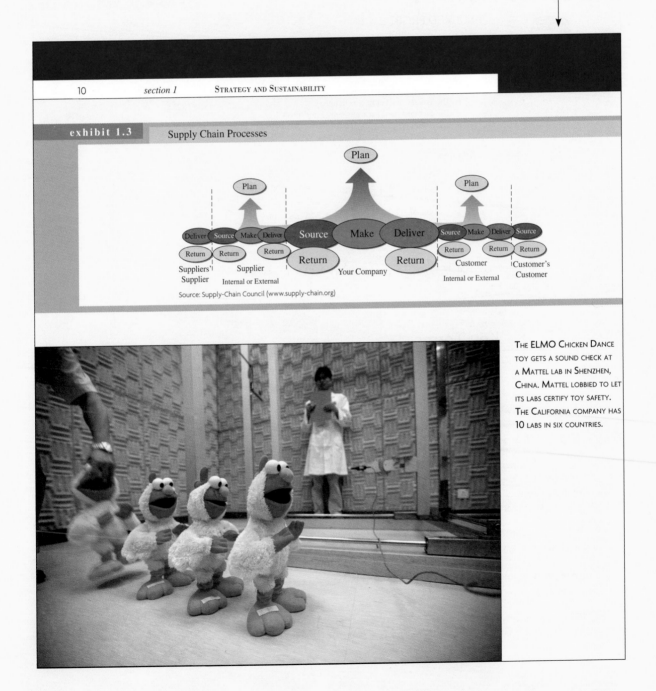

10 *section 1* STRATEGY AND SUSTAINABILITY

exhibit 1.3 Supply Chain Processes

Source: Supply-Chain Council (www.supply-chain.org)

THE ELMO CHICKEN DANCE TOY GETS A SOUND CHECK AT A MATTEL LAB IN SHENZHEN, CHINA. MATTEL LOBBIED TO LET ITS LABS CERTIFY TOY SAFETY. THE CALIFORNIA COMPANY HAS 10 LABS IN SIX COUNTRIES.

Solved Problems

Representative problems are placed at the end of appropriate chapters.
Each includes a worked-out solution giving students a review before
solving problems on their own.

Solved Problems

Excel:
Queue

SOLVED PROBLEM 1

Quick Lube Inc. operates a fast lube and oil change garage. On a typical day, customers arrive at the
rate of three per hour, and lube jobs are performed at an average rate of one every 15 minutes. The
mechanics operate as a team on one car at a time.

Assuming Poisson arrivals and exponential service, find

a. Utilization of the lube team.
b. The average number of cars in line.
c. The average time a car waits before it is lubed.
d. The total time it takes to go through the system (that is, waiting in line plus lube time).

Solution

$\lambda = 3, \mu = 4$

a. Utilization $\rho = \dfrac{\lambda}{\mu} = \dfrac{3}{4} = 75\%$.

b. $L_q = \dfrac{\lambda^2}{\mu(\mu - \lambda)} = \dfrac{3^2}{4(4 - 3)} = \dfrac{9}{4} = 2.25$ cars in line.

c. $W_q = \dfrac{L_q}{\lambda} = \dfrac{2.25}{3} = .75$ hour, or 45 minutes.

d. $W_s = \dfrac{L_s}{\lambda} = \dfrac{\lambda}{\mu - \lambda} \Big/ \lambda = \dfrac{3}{4 - 3} \Big/ 3 = 1$ hour (waiting + lube).

Key Terms

The vocabulary of *Operations and Supply Management* is highlighted in
the Key Terms section at the end of each chapter and includes definitions.

Key Terms

High and low degree of customer contact The physical
presence of the customer in the system and the percentage of
time the customer must be in the system relative to the total
time it takes to perform the service.

Service blueprint The flowchart of a service process emphasizing what is visible and what is not visible to the customer.

Poka-yokes Procedures that prevent mistakes from becoming defects.

Queuing system Consists of three major components:
(1) the source population and the way customers arrive at the

system, (2) the serving systems, and (3) how customers exit
the system.

Arrival rate The expected number of customers that arrive
each period.

Exponential distribution A probability distribution often associated with interarrival times.

Poisson distribution Probability distribution often used to
describe the number of arrivals during a given time period.

Service rate The capacity of a server measured in number of
units that can be processed over a given time period.

Formula Reviews

These lists at the end of chapters summarize formulas in one spot for easy
student access and review.

Formula Review

Exponential distribution

$$f(t) = \lambda e^{-\lambda t}$$ [5.1]

Poisson distribution

$$P_T(n) = \frac{(\lambda T)^n e^{-\lambda T}}{n!}$$ [5.2]

Model 1 (See Exhibit 5.11.)

$$L_q = \frac{\lambda^2}{\mu(\mu - \lambda)} \qquad W_q = \frac{L_q}{\lambda} \qquad P_n = \left(1 - \frac{\lambda}{\mu}\right)\left(\frac{\lambda}{\mu}\right)^n \qquad P_o = \left(1 - \frac{\lambda}{\mu}\right)$$

$$L_s = \frac{\lambda}{\mu - \lambda} \qquad W_s = \frac{L_s}{\lambda} \qquad \rho = \frac{\lambda}{\mu}$$ [5.3]

Model 2

$$L_q = \frac{\lambda^2}{2\mu(\mu - \lambda)} \qquad W_q = \frac{L_q}{\lambda}$$

$$L_s = L_q + \frac{\lambda}{\mu} \qquad W_s = \frac{L_s}{\lambda}$$ [5.4]

Model 3

$$L_s = L_q + \lambda/\mu \qquad\qquad W_s = L_s/\lambda$$

$$W_q = L_q/\lambda \qquad\qquad P_w = L_q\left(\frac{S_\mu}{\lambda} - 1\right)$$ [5.5]

Exhibit 5.12 provides the value of L_q given λ/μ and the number of servers S.

Super Quiz

Designed to allow students to see how well they understand the material using a format that is similar to what they might see in an exam. The super quiz includes many straightforward review questions, but also has a selection which tests for mastery and integration/application level understanding, that is, the kind of questions that make an exam challenging. The super quizzes include short answers at the bottom so students can see how they perform.

Super Quiz

1 A strategy that is designed to meet current needs without compromising the ability of future generations to meet their needs.
2 The three criteria included in a triple bottom line.
3 It is probably most difficult to compete on this major competitive dimension.
4 Name the seven operations and supply competitive dimensions.
5 This occurs when a company seeks to match what a competitor is doing while maintaining its existing competitve position.

6 A criterion that differentiates the products or services of one firm from those of another.
7 A screening criterion that permits a firm's products to be considered as possible candidates for purchase.
8 A diagram showing the activities that support a company's strategy.
9 A measure calculated by taking the ratio of output to input.

1. Sustainable 2. Social, economic, environmental 3. Cost 4. Cost, quality, delivery speed, delivery reliability, coping with changes in demand, flexibility and new product introduction speed, other product-specific criteria 5. Straddling 6. Order winner 7. Order qualifier 8. Activity-system map 9. Productivity

Cases

At the end of each chapter, cases allow students to think critically about issues discussed in the chapter. Cases include:

Timbuk2, Chapter 2
Designing Toshiba's Notebook computer line, Chapter 4
Cell Phone Design Project, Chapter 7
Hewlett-Packard—Supplying the Deskjet Printer in Europe, Chapter 13

CASE: Designing Toshiba's Notebook Computer Line

Toshihiro Nakamura, manufacturing engineering section manager, examined the prototype assembly process sheet (shown in Exhibit 4.10) for the newest subnotebook computer model. With every new model introduced, management felt that the assembly line had to increase productivity and lower costs, usually resulting in changes to the assembly process. When a new model was designed, considerable attention was directed toward reducing the number of components and simplifying parts production and assembly requirements. This new computer was a marvel of high-tech, low-cost innovation and should give Toshiba an advantage during the upcoming fall/winter selling season.

Production of the subnotebook was scheduled to begin in 10 days. Initial production for the new model was to be at 150 units per day, increasing to 250 units per day the following week (management thought that eventually production would reach 300 units per day). Assembly lines at the plant normally were staffed by 10 operators who worked at a 14.4-meter-long assembly line. The line could accommodate up to 12 operators if there was a need. The line normally operated for 7.5 hours a day (employees worked from 8:15 A.M. to 5:00 P.M. and regular hours included 1 hour of unpaid lunch and 15 minutes of scheduled breaks). It is possible to run one, two, or three hours of overtime, but employees need at least three days' notice for planning purposes.

For Instructors

Instructor CD-ROM

The Instructor Resource CD provides a library of video clips, PowerPoint slides, text figures, and digital versions of the teaching supplements including the Test Bank (in Word) and the E-Z Test Computerized Testing System, Instructor's Solutions Manual, and Instructor's Resource Manual.

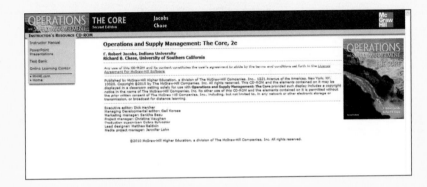

Text Web Site

Text Online Learning Center (OLC) at www.mhhe.com/jacobs2e. The text Web site includes a variety of material for instructors and students.

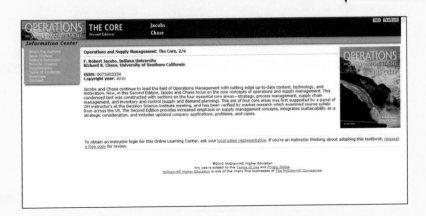

Student Web Site

Multiple-choice quizzes
Excel templates
PowerPoint slides
ScreenCam tutorials
Glossary
Narrated solutions to text examples

Instructor Site

Instructor's Resource Manual
Test Bank
Instructor PowerPoint Slides
Instructor Solutions Manual

OMC

The Operations Management Center Supersite at www.mhhe.com/pom offers a wealth of edited and organized OM resources including links to Operations Management *BusinessWeek* articles, OM Organizations, and virtual tours of operations in real companies.

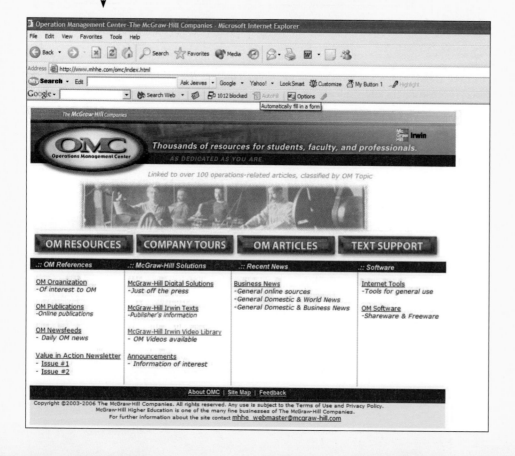

Student Operations Management Videos DVD-ROM

These videos cover topics such as service at Zappos.com, project management at Six Flags, supply chain management and supplier partnering at Ford, Burton Snowboards, and Noodles and Company, special services at FedEx, the development of Honda's new "green" Civic, and several others. This DVD can be packaged free with the text.

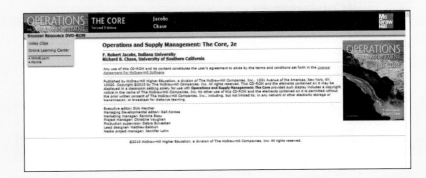

Operations Management Video Series

The 17 volume series, free to text adopters, includes professionally developed videos showing students real applications of key manufacturing and service topics in real companies. Each segment includes on site or plant footage, interviews with company managers, and focused presentation of OM applications in use to help the companies gain competitive advantage. Companies such as Zappos, FedEx, Suburu, Disney, BP, Chase Bank, DHL, Louisville Slugger, McDonalds, Noodles, and Honda are featured.

ScreenCam Tutorials

These screen "movies" and voice over tutorials demonstrate chapter content using Excel and other software platforms.

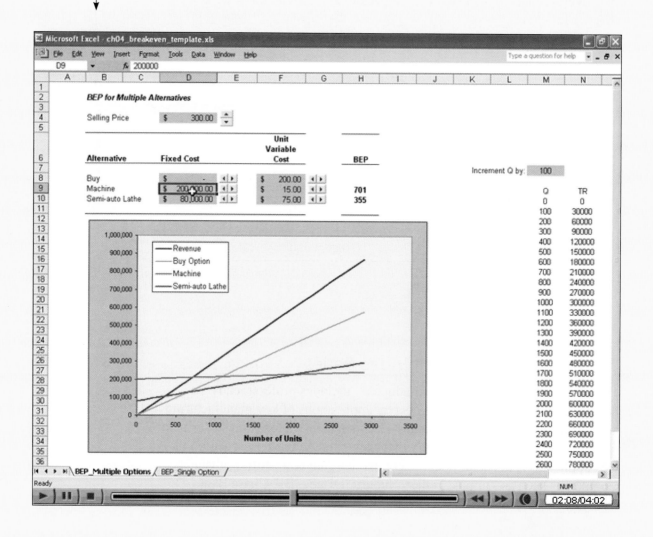

CONTENTS IN BRIEF

SECTION ONE

STRATEGY AND SUSTAINABILITY

1 Operations and Supply Chain Management 4

2 Strategy and Sustainability 22

SECTION TWO

MANUFACTURING AND SERVICE PROCESSES

3 Strategic Capacity Management 42

4 Production Processes 64

5 Service Processes 98

6 Quality Management and Six Sigma 132

7 Projects 178

SECTION THREE

SUPPLY CHAIN PROCESSES

8 Global Sourcing and Procurement 222

9 Location, Logistics, and Distribution 248

10 Lean and Sustainable Supply Chains 270

SECTION FOUR

SUPPLY AND DEMAND PLANNING

11 Demand Management and Forecasting 304

12 Sales and Operations Planning 354

13 Inventory Control 384

14 Material Requirements Planning 430

APPENDICES

A Linear Programming Using the Excel Solver 461

B Learning Curves 483

C Answers to Selected Problems 494

D Present Value Table 496

E Negative Exponential Distribution: Values of e^{-x^1} 497

F Areas of the Cumulative Standard Normal Distribution 498

PHOTO CREDITS 499

NAME INDEX 501

SUBJECT INDEX 503

CONTENTS

SECTION ONE

STRATEGY AND SUSTAINABILITY

1 OPERATIONS AND SUPPLY CHAIN MANAGEMENT 4
Quick Supply Chains Enable Retailers to Get Fashions to Market Quickly 5
What Is Operations and Supply Management? 6
Operations and Supply Processes 9
Differences between Services and Goods 11
 The Goods–Services Continuum 11
 Servitization Strategies 12
Efficiency, Effectiveness, and Value 12
Careers in Operations and Supply Management 14
 Chief Operating Officer 15
Historical Development of Operations and Supply Management 15
Current Issues in Operations and Supply Management 18

Key Terms 19 Review and Discussion Questions 19 Internet Exercise: Harley-Davidson Motorcycles 19 Super Quiz 20 Selected Bibliography 20 Footnotes 21

2 STRATEGY AND SUSTAINABILITY 22
How IKEA Designs Its Sexy Prices 23
A Sustainable Strategy 24
What Is Operations and Supply Strategy? 25
 Competitive Dimensions 27
 The Notion of Trade-Offs 29
 Order Winners and Order Qualifiers: The Marketing–Operations Link 30
Strategic Fit: Fitting Operational Activities to Strategy 30
Productivity Measurement 32
How Does Wall Street Evaluate Operations Performance? 33
Summary 34

Key Terms 35 Solved Problem 35 Review and Discussion Questions 35 Problems 36 Case: The Tao of Timbuk2 38 Selected Bibliography 39 Super Quiz 39 Footnote 39

SECTION TWO

MANUFACTURING AND SERVICE PROCESSES

3 STRATEGIC CAPACITY MANAGEMENT 42
Shouldice Hospital: Hernia Surgery Innovation 43
Capacity Management in Operations 44
Capacity Planning Concepts 45
 Economies and Diseconomies of Scale 45
 Capacity Focus 46
 Capacity Flexibility 46
Capacity Planning 47
 Considerations in Changing Capacity 47
 Determining Capacity Requirements 48
 Using Decision Trees to Evaluate Capacity Alternatives 51
Planning Service Capacity 54
 Capacity Planning in Service versus Manufacturing 54
 Capacity Utilization and Service Quality 55
Summary 56

Key Terms 57 Formula Review 57 Solved Problem 57 Review and Discussion Questions 58 Problems 59 Case: Shouldice Hospital—A Cut Above 60 Super Quiz 62 Selected Bibliography 63

4 PRODUCTION PROCESSES 64
Toshiba: Producer of the First Notebook Computer 65
Production Processes 66
 Production Process Mapping and Little's Law 69
How Production Processes Are Organized 72
Break-Even Analysis 73
Designing a Production System 75
 Project Layout 75
 Workcenters 75
 Manufacturing Cell 76
 Assembly Line and Continuous Process Layouts 76
Assembly-Line Design 78
 Splitting Tasks 82
 Flexible and U-Shaped Line Layouts 82
 Mixed-Model Line Balancing 82
Summary 85

Key Terms 85 Formula Review 86 Solved Problems 86 Review and Discussion Questions 89 Problems 90 Advanced Problem 93 Case: Designing Toshiba's

Notebook Computer Line 93   Super Quiz 96   Selected Bibliography 97

5 SERVICE PROCESSES 98

Supply Chain Services at DHL 99
An Operational Classification of Services 100
Designing Service Organizations 101
Structuring the Service Encounter: Service-System Design Matrix 101
   Virtual Service: The New Role of the Customer 103
Service Blueprinting and Fail-Safing 103
Economics of the Waiting Line Problem 106
   The Practical View of Waiting Lines 106
The Queuing System 107
   Customer Arrivals 108
   Distribution of Arrivals 109
   The Queuing System: Factors 112
   Exiting the Queuing System 115
Waiting Line Models 115
Computer Simulation of Waiting Lines 122
Summary 122

Key Terms 123   Formula Review 123   Solved Problems 124   Review and Discussion Questions 125   Problems 125   Case: Community Hospital Evening Operating Room 130   Super Quiz 130   Selected Bibliography 131   Footnote 131

6 QUALITY MANAGEMENT AND SIX SIGMA 132

GE Six-Sigma Supply Chain Processes 133
Total Quality Management 134
Quality Specifications and Quality Costs 136
   Developing Quality Specifications 136
   Cost of Quality 138
ISO 9000 and ISO 14000 140
Six-Sigma Quality 141
   Six-Sigma Methodology 142
   Analytical Tools for Six Sigma 142
Statistical Quality Control 146
   Variation Around Us 148
   Process Capability 149
Process control Procedures 154
   Process Control with Attribute Measurements: Using p-Charts 156
   Process Control with Attribute Measurements: Using c-Charts 157
   Process Control with Variable Measurements: Using $\bar{X}$- and R-Charts 158
   How to Construct $\bar{X}$- and R-Charts 160

Acceptance Sampling 162
   Design of a Single Sampling Plan for Attributes 162
   Operating Characteristic Curves 165
Summary 166

Key Terms 166   Formula Review 167   Solved Problems 168   Review and Discussion Questions 169   Problems 170   Advanced Problem 174   Case: Hank Kolb, Director of Quality Assurance 174   Footnotes 176   Super Quiz 176   Selected Bibliography 177

7 PROJECTS 178

National Aeronautics and Space Administration's Constellation Program May Land Men on the Moon By 2020 179
What Is Project Management? 181
Structuring Projects 181
   Pure Project 182
   Functional Project 182
   Matrix Project 184
Work Breakdown Structure 185
Project Control Charts 186
   Earned Value Management (EVM) 188
Network-Planning Models 191
   Critical Path Method (CPM) 192
   CPM with Three Activity Time Estimates 196
   Time–Cost Models and Project Crashing 199
Managing Resources 203
   Tracking Progress 205
Summary 205

Key Terms 205   Formula Review 206   Solved Problems 207   Review and Discussion Questions 211   Problems 211   Advanced Problem 217   Case: Cell Phone Design Project 217   Super Quiz 218   Selected Bibliography 219   Footnote 219

SECTION THREE ▬▬

SUPPLY CHAIN PROCESSES

8 GLOBAL SOURCING AND PROCUREMENT 222

The World Is Flat 223
   Flattener 5: Outsourcing 223
   Flattener 6: Offshoring 223
Strategic Sourcing 224
   The Bullwhip Effect 226
Outsourcing 230
Green Sourcing 235
Total Cost of Ownership 238
Measuring Sourcing Performance 241

Summary 243

*Key Terms 243   Formula Review 243
Review and Discussion Questions 244
Problems 244   Case: Pepe Jeans 246
Footnotes 247   Super Quiz 247   Selected
Bibliography 247*

**9 LOCATION, LOGISTICS, AND
DISTRIBUTION 248**

FedEx: A Leading Global Logistics
Company 249
Logistics 250
Decisions Related to Logistics 251
Cross-Docking 252
Issues in Facility Location 253
Plant Location Methods 255
*Factor-Rating Systems 256
Transportation Method of Linear
Programming 256
Centroid Method 260*
Locating Service Facilities 261
Summary 263

*Key Terms 264   Formula Review 264   Solved
Problem 264   Review and Discussion
Questions 265   Problems 265   Case:
Applichem—The Transportation
Problem 267   Footnote 268   Super
Quiz 268   Selected Bibliography 269*

**10 LEAN AND SUSTAINABLE SUPPLY
CHAINS 270**

Green Is the New Black 271
*Survey Suggests that Enviro-Conscious
Manufacturers are the Best Risk for
Investors 271*
Lean Production 272
Lean Logic 273
The Toyota Production System 274
*Elimination of Waste 274
Respect for People 274*
Lean Supply Chains 275
Value Stream Mapping 278
Lean Supply Chain Design Principles 280
*Lean Layouts 281
Lean Production Schedules 284
Lean Supply Chains 288*
Lean Services 289
Summary 291

*Key Terms 291   Formula Review 292
Solved Problem 1 292   Solved Problem 2 292
Review and Discussion Questions 296
Problems 296   Case: Quality Parts
Company 297   Case: Value Stream
Mapping 298   Case: Pro Fishing Boats—A
Value Stream Mapping Exercise 300
Super Quiz 300   Selected Bibliography 301
Footnotes 301*

SECTION FOUR ▬▬▬▬

SUPPLY AND DEMAND PLANNING

**11 DEMAND MANAGEMENT AND
FORECASTING 304**

Walmart's Data Warehouse 305
Demand Management 307
Types of Forecasting 308
Components of Demand 308
Time Series Analysis 310
*Linear Regression Analysis 311
Decomposition of a Time Series 314
Simple Moving Average 321
Weighted Moving Average 323
Exponential Smoothing 324
Forecast Errors 328
Sources of Error 328
Measurement of Error 328*
Causal Relationship Forecasting 331
Multiple Regression Analysis 332
Qualitative Techniques in
Forecasting 333
*Market Research 333
Panel Consensus 334
Historical Analogy 334
Delphi Method 334*
Web-Based Forecasting: Collaborative
Planning, Forecasting, and Replenishment
(CPFR) 335
SUMMARY 336

*Key Terms 337   Formula Review 338   Solved
Problems 339   Review and Discussion
Questions 343   Problems 343   Case: Altavox
Electronics 352   Super Quiz 352   Selected
Bibliography 353   Footnotes 353*

12 SALES AND OPERATIONS PLANNING 354

What Is Sales and Operations
Planning? 356
Overview of Sales and Operations
Planning Activities 356
The Aggregate Operations Plan 358
*Production Planning Environment 359
Relevant Costs 361*
Aggregate Planning Techniques 362
*A Cut-and-Try Example: The JC
Company 363
Aggregate Planning Applied to Services:
Tucson Parks and Recreation
Department 367*
Level Scheduling 370
Yield Management 372
*Operating Yield Management
Systems 373*
Summary 374

Key Terms 374　Solved Problem 375　Review and Discussion Questions 378　Problems 378　Case: Bradford Manufacturing—Planning Plant Production 381　Super Quiz 382　Selected Bibliography 383　Footnotes 383

13 INVENTORY CONTROL 384
Direct to Store—The UPS Vision 385
　The UPS Direct Approach 386
Definition of Inventory 389
Purposes of Inventory 389
Inventory Costs 390
Independent versus Dependent Demand 391
Inventory Systems 392
　A Single-Period Inventory Model 393
　Multiperiod Inventory Systems 396
Fixed—Order Quantity Models 398
　Establishing Safety Stock Levels 401
　Fixed—Order Quantity Model with Safety Stock 402
Fixed—Time Period Models 405
　Fixed—Time Period Model with Safety Stock 405
Inventory Control and Supply Chain Management 407
Price-Break Models 408
ABC Inventory Planning 410
　ABC Classification 411
Inventory Accuracy and Cycle Counting 412
Summary 414

Key Terms 415　Formula Review 415　Solved Problems 417　Review and Discussion Questions 418　Problems 419　Case: Hewlett-Packard—Supplying the DeskJet Printer in Europe 425　Super Quiz 428　Selected Bibliography 429　Footnotes 429

14 MATERIAL REQUIREMENTS PLANNING 430
From Push to Pull 431
Master Production Scheduling 433
　Time Fences 434
Where MRP Can Be Used 435
Material Requirements Planning System Structure 436
　Demand for Products 436
　Bill of Materials 438
　Inventory Records 439
　MRP Computer Program 440
An Example Using MRP 441
　Forecasting Demand 441
　Developing a Master Production Schedule 442
　Bill of Materials (Product Structure) 442
　Inventory Records 443
　Performing the MRP Calculations 444
Lot Sizing in MRP Systems 447
　Lot-for-Lot 447
　Economic Order Quantity 448
　Least Total Cost 448
　Least Unit Cost 450
　Choosing the Best Lot Size 451
Summary 451

Key Terms 451　Solved Problems 452　Review and Discussion Questions 453　Problems 453　Case: Brunswick Motors, Inc.—An Introductory Case for MRP 457　Super Quiz 458　Selected Bibliography 459

APPENDICES

A Linear Programming Using the Excel Solver 461

B Learning Curves 483

C Answers to Selected Problems 494

D Present Value Table 496

E Negative Exponential Distribution: Values of e^{-x^1} 497

F Areas of the Cumulative Standard Normal Distribution 498

PHOTO CREDITS 499

NAME INDEX 501

SUBJECT INDEX 503

Operations and Supply Management: The Core

STRATEGY AND SUSTAINABILITY

1. Operations and Supply Chain Management

2. Strategy and Sustainability

TWENTY-FIRST-CENTURY OPERATIONS AND SUPPLY MANAGEMENT

Managing a modern supply chain involves specialists in manufacturing, purchasing, and distribution. However, today it is also vital to the work of chief financial officers, chief information officers, operations and customer service executives, and chief executive officers. Changes in operations and supply management have been truly revolutionary, and the pace of progress shows no sign of moderating. In our increasingly interconnected and interdependent global economy, the process of delivering supplies and finished goods from one place to another is accomplished by means of mind-boggling technological innovation, clever new applications of old ideas, seemingly magical mathematics, powerful software, and old-fashioned concrete, steel, and muscle.

In the first section of *Operations and Supply Management: The Core* we lay a foundation for understanding the dynamic field of operations and supply management. This book is about designing and operating processes that deliver a firm's goods and services in a manner that matches customers' expectations. Really successful firms have a clear and unambiguous idea of how they intend to make money. Be it high-end products or services that are custom-tailored to the needs of a single customer or generic inexpensive commodities that are bought largely on the basis of cost, competitively producing and distributing these products is a great challenge. In this section we show the critical link between the processes used to deliver goods and services and customers' expectations. Customers make a choice between different suppliers based on key attributes of the product or service. Aligning the processes used to deliver the product or service is important to success. If, for example, cost is the key customer order winning attribute, the firm must do everything it can to design processes that are as efficient as possible. Competing on the basis of cost alone can be a brutal way to do business, and so many firms today move into other market segments by offering products

with innovative services and features that attract a loyal customer following.

Take, for example, the U.S. motorcycle manufacturer Harley-Davidson. Customers pay top dollar for a unique and classic motorcycle that can be individualized by each customer through the selection of dealer-installed options. Further, the firm has developed a highly profitable line of clothing, memorabilia, and other accessories to complete the Harley-Davidson concept. Processes needed to support that concept certainly need to be efficient, but even more important is the ready availability of the options and accessories that are often purchased on impulse or for gifts.

CHAPTER 1

OPERATIONS AND SUPPLY CHAIN MANAGEMENT

After reading this chapter you will:

- Understand why it is important to study operations and supply chain management.
- Define efficient and effective operations.
- Categorize operations and supply chain processes.
- Contrast differences between services and goods producing processes.
- Identify operations and supply chain management career opportunities.
- Describe how the field has developed over time.

5   Quick Supply Chains Enable Retailers to Get Fashions to Market Quickly

6   What Is Operations and Supply Management?
     Operations and supply management (OSM) defined

9   Operations and Supply Processes

11   Differences between Services and Goods
     The Goods–Services Continuum
     Servitization Strategies   Servitization defined

12   Efficiency, Effectiveness, and Value
     Efficiency defined
     Effectiveness defined
     Value defined

14   Careers in Operations and Supply Management
     Chief Operating Officer

15   Historical Development of Operations and Supply Management
     Mass customization defined

18   Current Issues in Operations and Supply Management
     Sustainability defined
     Triple bottom line defined

19   Internet Exercise: Harley-Davidson Motorcycles

20   Super Quiz

QUICK SUPPLY CHAINS ENABLE RETAILERS TO GET FASHIONS TO MARKET QUICKLY

Retailers now know that to keep earnings high they need to get the latest fashions into their stores as quickly as possible. Chains ranging from JC Penney to J. Crew scramble to make their orders more precise, so they can stock just enough of the hottest styles for today's increasingly fickle and tight-fisted consumers. Advances in software and technology allow stores to offer the latest trends weeks or even months faster than before and give these retailers more stable profitability. The analysts at Piper Jaffray, a consulting company, say that profit margins have improved at such retailers as Abercrombie & Fitch, Gap, Aéropostale, and Kohl's due to these technology advances.

Efficient logistics have taken on a whole new level of importance. Until recently, many stores were still using the phone and fax machines to place big orders, a very manual and slow, error-prone process. Now, software lets designers, buyers, and manufacturers view the same fabric swatch or color at the same time, thereby eliminating the need to fly designers around the globe or to send overnight packages. By quickly moving the most desirable items into stores, retailers can also ease their reliance on price markdowns, which cut into earnings. They can also order less merchandise and order more often. This lets them adjust orders more easily once certain styles or sizes fail to sell.

The goal is to have the right product at the right place at the right time. In these competitive times, fashion retailers, in particular, need to be agile and flexible. They cannot afford to carry excess inventory, and the ability to react to what is selling is as important as customers demand the most innovative and current products. So today's leading retailers are using operations and supply chain management techniques to match supply and demand as closely and quickly as possible. They refer to the strategy as minimizing "concept-to-cash" time and work to minimize the time between the appearance of a fashion concept and the time they start receiving revenue from the sales of that concept.

Source: Adapted from Jayne O'Donnell, "Stores Get Fashions to Market Lickety-Split," *USA Today*, May 29, 2008, p. 1B.

WHAT IS OPERATIONS AND SUPPLY MANAGEMENT?

Operations and supply management (OSM)

Service

Operations and supply management (OSM) is defined as the design, operation, and improvement of the systems that create and deliver the firm's primary products and services. Like marketing and finance, OSM is a functional field of business with clear line management responsibilities. OSM is concerned with the management of the entire system that produces a good or delivers a service. Producing a product such as the Men's Nylon Supplex Parka or providing a service such as a cellular phone account involves a complex series of transformation processes.

Exhibit 1.1 shows a supply network for a Men's Nylon Supplex Parka sold on Web sites such as L.L. Bean or Land's End. We can understand the network by looking at the four color-coded paths. The blue path traces the activities needed to produce the Polartec insulation material used in the parkas. Polartec insulation is purchased in bulk, processed to get the proper finish, and then dyed prior to being checked for consistency—or grading—and color. It is then stored in a warehouse. The red path traces the production of the nylon Supplex used in the parkas. Using petroleum-based polymer, the nylon is extruded and drawn into a yarnlike material. From here the green path traces the many steps required to fabricate the clothlike Supplex used to make the parkas. The yellow path shows the Supplex and Polartec material coming together and used to assemble the lightweight and warm parka. The completed parkas are sent to a warehouse and then on to the retailer's distribution center. The parkas are then picked and packed for shipment to individual customers. Think of the supply network as a pipeline through which material and information flows. There are key locations in the pipeline where material and information is stored for future use: Polartec is stored near the end of the blue pipeline; Supplex is stored near the end of the red pipeline. In both cases, fabric is cut prior to merging with the yellow pipeline. At the beginning of the yellow path, bundles of Supplex and Polartec are stored prior to their use in the fabrication of the parkas. At the end of the yellow path are the distribution steps which involve storing to await orders, picking according to actual customer order, packing, and finally shipping to the final customer.

Networks such as this can be constructed for any product or service. Typically each part of the network is controlled by different companies including the nylon Supplex producer, the Polartec producer, the parka manufacturer, and the catalog sales retailer. All of the material is moved using transportation providers, ships and trucks in this case. The network also has a global dimension with each entity potentially located in a different country. Trace the origin of a Toyota car in the box titled "Understanding the Global Supply Chain." For a successful transaction, all of these steps need to be coordinated and operated to keep costs low and to minimize waste. OSM manages all of these individual processes as effectively as possible.

exhibit 1.1

Process Steps for Men's Nylon Supplex Parka

Understanding the Global Supply Chain

Supply Chain

At an iron-ore mine in Western Australia, I once stood and watched as a young man worked an excavator to claw bucketfuls of deep-red ore from the ground. For a project, I wanted to follow the ore on its journey from raw material to finished product. So I went on a train that took it to a port, then traveled on the Chinese ship that carried it to Japan. There it was refined into steel ingots, which were sent to a factory outside Tokyo and fashioned into a Toyota Corolla. Next I got on a mighty ship carrying thousands of Toyota imports across the Pacific Ocean to Seattle.

The car made from my ore—small, red, sporty—was unloaded in Washington and put on a truck. I rode with it to a dealer in San Francisco, where I bought the car. Then I drove it to a port and put it, and me as well, onto a Norwegian passenger liner bound for Australia. Ten days later, I unloaded and drove the car to the cliff face and the young excavator operator.

"Here," I said to him, pointing at the car. "This is what your bucketful of iron ore made." He was astonished. Astonished that I had come back to see him. Astonished that his pile of ore had been made into a car. But most astonished of all to learn that so many people—Chinese, Japanese, American, Norwegian—from so many countries had been involved in the process. "I guess we are all linked," he said. "Even if we never think we are."

Source: Adapted from Simon Winchester, "How America Can Maintain Its Edge," *Parade*, December 21, 2008, p. 8.

Success in today's global markets requires a business strategy that matches the preferences of customers with the realities imposed by complex supply networks. A sustainable strategy that meets the needs of shareholders and employees, and preserves the environment is critical. Concepts related to developing this type of strategy is the topic of Section I (see Exhibit 1.2).

In the context of our discussion, the terms *operations* and *supply* take on special meaning. *Operations* refers to manufacturing and service processes that are used to transform the resources employed by a firm into products desired by customers. These processes are covered in Section II. For example, a manufacturing process would produce some type of physical product such as an automobile or a computer. A service process would produce an intangible product such as a call center that provides information to customers stranded on the highway or a hospital that services accident victims in an emergency room.

Service

Supply Chain

Supply refers to supply chain processes that move information and material to and from the manufacturing and service processes of the firm. These include the logistics processes that physically move product and the warehousing and storage processes that position products for quick delivery to the customer. Supply in this context refers to providing goods and service to plants and warehouses at the input end, and also the supply of goods and service to the customer on the output end of the supply chain. These processes are covered in Section III.

Another element of OSM is the supply and demand planning needed to manage and coordinate the manufacturing, service, and supply chain processes. These involve forecasting

exhibit 1.2

Organization of OSM—The Core: The Integration of Strategy, Processes and Planning

demand, making intermediate term plans for how demand will be met, controlling different types of inventory, and detailed weekly scheduling of processes. Topics related to this are covered in Section IV.

We consider the topics included in this book the foundation or "core" material. Many other topics could be included, but these cover the basic concepts. All managers should understand these basic principles that guide the design of transformation processes. This includes understanding how different types of processes are organized, how to determine the capacity of a process, how long it should take a process to make a unit, how the quality of a process is monitored, and how planning information systems are used to coordinate these processes.

The field of operations and supply management is ever changing due to the dynamic nature of competing in global business and the constant evolution of information technology. So while many of the basic concepts have been around for many years, their application in new and innovative ways is exciting. Internet technology has made the sharing of reliable real-time information inexpensive. Capturing information directly from the source through such systems as point-of-sale, radio-frequency identification tags, bar-code scanners, and automatic recognition has changed the focus to one of understanding what all the information is saying and how good decisions can be made using it.

OPERATIONS AND SUPPLY PROCESSES

Operations and supply processes can be conveniently categorized, particularly from the view of a producer of consumer products and services, as planning, sourcing, making, delivering, and returning. Exhibit 1.3 depicts where the processes are used in different

exhibit 1.3   Supply Chain Processes

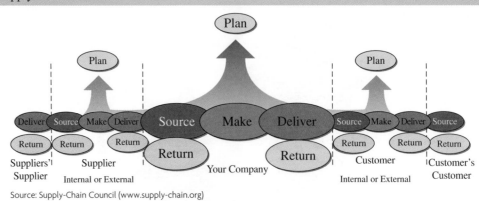

Source: Supply-Chain Council (www.supply-chain.org)

parts of a supply chain. The following describes the work involved in each type of process.

1. **Planning** consists of the processes needed to operate an existing supply chain strategically. Here a firm must determine how anticipated demand will be met with available resources. A major aspect of planning is developing a set of metrics to monitor the supply chain so that it is efficient and delivers high quality and value to customers.
2. **Sourcing** involves the selection of suppliers that will deliver the goods and services needed to create the firm's product. A set of pricing, delivery, and payment processes are needed together with metrics for monitoring and improving the relationships between partners of the firm. These processes include receiving shipment, verifying them, transferring them to manufacturing facilities, and authorizing supplier payments.
3. **Making** is where the major product is produced or the service provided. The step requires scheduling processes for workers and the coordination of material and other critical resources such as equipment to support producing or providing the service. Metrics that measure speed, quality, and worker productivity are used to monitor these processes.
4. **Delivering** is also referred to as logistics processes. Carriers are picked to move products to warehouses and customers, coordinate and schedule the movement of goods and information through the supply network, develop and operate a network of warehouses, and run the information systems that manage the receipt of orders from customers, and invoicing systems to collect payments from customers.
5. **Returning** involves the processes for receiving worn-out, defective, and excess products back from customers and support for customers who have problems with delivered products. In the case of services, this may involve all types of follow-up activities that are required for after-sales support.

Service

To understand the topic it is important to consider the many different players that need to coordinate work in a typical supply chain. The aforementioned steps of planning, sourcing, making, delivering, and returning are fine for manufacturing and can also be used for the many processes that do not involve the discrete movement and production of parts. In the case of a service firm such as a hospital, for example, supplies are typically delivered on a daily basis from drug and health care suppliers and require coordination between drug companies, local warehouse operations, local delivery services, and hospital receiving. Patients need to be scheduled into the services provided by the hospital such as operations and blood tests. Other areas, such as the emergency room, need to be staffed to provide service on demand. The orchestration of all of these activities is critical to providing quality service at a reasonable cost.

DIFFERENCES BETWEEN SERVICES AND GOODS

Service

There are five essential differences between services and goods. The first is that a service is an *intangible* process that cannot be weighed or measured, whereas a good is a tangible output of a process that has physical dimensions. This distinction has important business implications since a service innovation, unlike a product innovation, cannot be patented. Thus, a company with a new concept must expand rapidly before competitors copy its procedures. Service intangibility also presents a problem for customers since, unlike with a physical product, they cannot try it out and test it before purchase.

The second is that a service requires some degree of *interaction with the customer* for it to be a service. The interaction may be brief, but it must exist for the service to be complete. Where face-to-face service is required, the service facility must be designed to handle the customer's presence. Goods, on the other hand, are generally produced in a facility separate from the customer. They can be made according to a production schedule that is efficient for the company.

The third is that services, with the big exception of hard technologies such as ATMs and information technologies such as answering machines and automated Internet exchanges, are inherently *heterogeneous*—they vary from day to day and even hour by hour as a function of the attitudes of the customer and the servers. Thus, even highly scripted work such as found in call centers can produce unpredictable outcomes. Goods, in contrast, can be produced to meet very tight specifications day-in and day-out with essentially zero variability. In those cases where a defective good is produced, it can be reworked or scrapped.

The fourth is that services as a process are *perishable and time dependent,* and unlike goods, they can't be stored. You cannot "come back last week" for an air flight or a day on campus.

And fifth, the specifications of a service are defined and evaluated as a *package of features* that affect the five senses. These features are

- Supporting facility (location, decoration, layout, architectural appropriateness, supporting equipment).
- Facilitating goods (variety, consistency, quantity of the physical goods that go with the service; for example, the food items that accompany a meal service).
- Explicit services (training of service personnel, consistency of service performance, availability and access to the service, and comprehensiveness of the service).
- Implicit services (attitude of the servers, atmosphere, waiting time, status, privacy and security, and convenience).

The Goods–Services Continuum

Service

Most any product offering is a combination of goods and services. In Exhibit 1.4, we show this arrayed along a continuum of "pure goods" to "pure services." The continuum

exhibit 1.4

The Goods–Services Continuum

Pure Goods	Core Goods	Core Services	Pure Services
Food products	Appliances	Hotels	Teaching
Chemicals	Data storage systems	Airlines	Medical advice
Book publishing	Automobiles	Internet service providers	Financial consulting

Goods ◄──► Services

Source: Anders Gustofsson and Michael D. Johnson, *Competing in a Service Economy* (San Francisco Jossey-Bass, 2003), p. 7.

captures the main focus of the business and spans from firms that just produce products to those that only provide services. Pure goods industries have become low-margin commodity businesses, and in order to differentiate, they are often adding some services. Some examples are providing help with logistical aspects of stocking items, maintaining extensive information databases, and providing consulting advice.

Core goods providers already provide a significant service component as part of their businesses. For example, automobile manufacturers provide extensive spare parts distribution services to support repair centers at dealers.

Core service providers must integrate tangible goods. For example, your cable television company must provide cable hookup and repair services and also high-definition cable boxes. Pure services, such as may be offered by a financial consulting firm, may need little in the way of facilitating goods, but what they do use—such as textbooks, professional references, and spreadsheets—are critical to their performance.

Servitization Strategies

Servitization refers to a company building service activities into its product offerings for its current users, that is, its installed base. Such services include maintenance, spare part provisioning, training, and in some cases, total systems design and R&D. A well-known pioneer in this area is IBM, which treats its business as a service business and views physical goods as a small part of the "business solutions" it provides its customers. Companies that are most successful in implementing this strategy start by drawing together the service aspects of the business under one roof in order to create a consolidated service organization. The service evolves from a focus on enhancing the product's performance to developing systems and product modifications that support the company's move up the "value stream" into new markets. A servitization strategy might not be the best approach for all product companies, however. A recent study found that while servitized firms generate higher revenues, they tend to generate lower profits as a percent of revenues when compared to focused firms. This is because they are often unable to generate revenues or margins high enough to cover the additional investment required to cover service-related costs.

Servitization

Service

EFFICIENCY, EFFECTIVENESS, AND VALUE

Compared with most of the other ways managers try to stimulate growth—technology investments, acquisitions, and major market campaigns, for example—innovations in operations are relatively reliable and low cost. As a business student, you are perfectly

Understand Operations

Efficiency: It's the Details That Count

Getting passengers on a plane quickly can greatly affect an airline's costs. Southwest says that if its boarding times increased by 10 minutes per flight, it would need 40 more planes at a cost of $40 million each to run the same number of flights it does currently.

Not all the innovation in the airline industry is from Southwest. US Airways, working with researchers at Arizona State University, has developed an innovative boarding system called "reverse pyramid." The first economy-class passengers to get on the plane are those with window seats in the middle and rear of the plane. Then US Airways gradually fills in the plane, giving priority to those with window or rear seats, until it finally boards those seated along aisles in the front. This is in contrast to the approach used by many airlines of just boarding all seats starting from the back of the plane and working forward.

The time it takes for passengers to board has more than doubled since 1970, according to studies by Boeing Co. A study in the mid-1960s found that 20 passengers boarded the plane per minute. Today that figure is down to nine per minute as passengers bring along heftier carry-on luggage. Both Boeing and Airbus, the two top commercial-aircraft makers, are working on improving boarding time as a selling point to airlines.

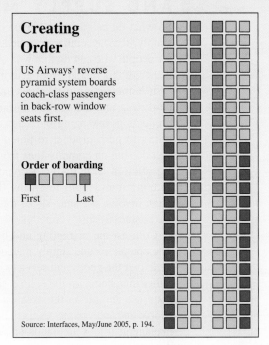

Creating Order

US Airways' reverse pyramid system boards coach-class passengers in back-row window seats first.

Order of boarding

First   Last

Source: Interfaces, May/June 2005, p. 194.

---

positioned to come up with innovative operations-related ideas. You understand the big picture of all the processes that generate the costs and support the cash flow essential to the firm's long-term viability.

Through this book, you will become aware of the concepts and tools now being employed by companies around the world as they craft efficient and effective operations. **Efficiency** means doing something at the lowest possible cost. Later in the book we define this more thoroughly, but roughly speaking the goal of an efficient process is to produce a good or provide a service by using the smallest input of resources. **Effectiveness** means doing the right things to create the most value for the company. Often maximizing effectiveness and efficiency at the same time creates conflict between the two goals. We see this trade-off every day in our lives. At the customer service counter at a local store or bank, being efficient means using the fewest people possible at the counter. Being effective, though, means minimizing the amount of time customers need to wait in line. Related to efficiency and effectiveness is the concept of **Value**, which can be metaphorically defined as quality divided by price. If you can provide the customer with a better car without changing price, value has gone up. If you can give the customer a better car at a *lower* price, value goes way up. A major objective of this book is to show how smart management can achieve high levels of value.

Efficiency

Effectiveness

Service

Value

CAREERS IN OPERATIONS AND SUPPLY MANAGEMENT

So what do people who pursue careers in operations and supply management do? Quite simply, they specialize in managing the production of goods and services. Jobs abound for people who can do this well since every organization is dependent on effective performance of this fundamental activity for its long-term success.

It is interesting to contrast entry-level jobs in operations and supply management to marketing and finance jobs. Many marketing entry-level jobs focus on actually selling products or managing the sales of products. These individuals are out on the front line trying to push product to potential customers. Often a significant part of your income will depend on commissions from these sales. Entry-level finance (and accounting) jobs are often in large public accounting firms. These jobs often involve working at a desk auditing transactions to ensure the accuracy of financial statements. Other assignments often involve the analysis of transactions to better understand the costs associated with the business.

Contrast the marketing and finance jobs to operations and supply management jobs. The operations and supply manager is out working with people to figure out the best way to deliver the goods and services of the firm. Sure, they work with the marketing folks, but rather than being on the selling side, they are on the buying side: trying to select the best materials and hiring the greatest talent. They will use the data generated by the finance people and analyze processes to figure out the best way to do things. Operations and supply management jobs are hands-on, working with people and figuring out the best way to do things.

The following are some typical management and staff jobs in operations and supply management:

- Plant manager—Oversees the workforce and physical resources (inventory, equipment, and information technology) required to produce the organization's product.
- Hospital administrator—Oversees human resource management, staffing, and finances at a health care facility.
- Branch manager (bank)—Oversees all aspects of financial transactions at a branch.
- Department store manager—Oversees all aspects of staffing and customer service at a store.
- Call center manager—Oversees staffing and customer service activities at a call center.
- Supply chain manager—Negotiates contracts with vendors and coordinates the flow of material inputs to the production process and the shipping of finished products to customers.
- Purchasing manager—Manages the day-to-day aspects of purchasing such as invoicing and follow-up.
- Business process improvement analyst—Applies the tools of lean production to reduce cycle time and eliminate waste in a process.
- Quality control manager—Applies techniques of statistical quality control such as acceptance sampling and control charts to the firm's products.
- Lean improvement manager—Trains organizational members in lean production and continuous improvement methods.
- Project manager—Plans and coordinates staff activities such as new-product development, new-technology deployment, and new-facility location.

- Production control analyst—Plans and schedules day-to-day production.
- Facilities manager—Assures that the building facility design, layout, furniture, and other equipment are operating at peak efficiency.

Chief Operating Officer

So how far can you go in a career in operations and supply management? One goal would be to become the chief operating officer of a company. The chief operating officer (COO) works with the CEO and company president to determine the company's competitive strategy. The COO's ideas are filtered down through the rest of the company. COOs determine an organization's location, its facilities, which vendors to use, and how the hiring policy will be implemented. Once the key decisions are made, lower-level operations personnel carry them out. Operations personnel work to find solutions and then set about fixing the problems.

Managing the supply chain, service, and support are particularly challenging aspects of a chief operating officer's job. Career opportunities in operations and supply management are plentiful today as companies strive to improve profitability by improving quality and productivity and reducing costs. The hands-on work of managing people is combined with great opportunities to leverage the latest technologies in getting the job done at companies around the world. No matter what you might do for a final career, your knowledge of operations and supply management will prove to be a great asset.

HISTORICAL DEVELOPMENT OF OPERATIONS AND SUPPLY MANAGEMENT

Our purpose in this section is not to go through all the details of OSM; that would require us to recount the entire Industrial Revolution. Rather, the focus is on major operations-related concepts that have been popular since the 1980s. Where appropriate, how a supposedly new idea relates to an older idea is discussed. (We seem to keep rediscovering the past.)

Lean Manufacturing, JIT, and TQC   The 1980s saw a revolution in the management philosophies and technologies by which production is carried out. Just-in-time (JIT) production was the major breakthrough in manufacturing philosophy.

Pioneered by the Japanese, JIT is an integrated set of activities designed to achieve high-volume production using minimal inventories of parts that arrive at the workstation exactly when they are needed. The philosophy—coupled with total quality control (TQC), which aggressively seeks to eliminate causes of production defects—is now a cornerstone in many manufacturers' production practices, and the term "lean manufacturing" is used to refer to the set of concepts.

Of course, the Japanese were not the first to develop a highly integrated, efficient production system. In 1913, Henry Ford developed an assembly line to make the Model-T automobile. Ford developed a system for making the Model-T that was constrained only by the capabilities of the workforce and existing technology. Quality was a critical prerequisite for Ford: The line could not run steadily at speed without consistently good components. On-time delivery was also critical for Ford; the desire to keep workers and machines busy with materials flowing constantly made scheduling critical. Product, processes, material, logistics, and people were well integrated and balanced in the design and operation of the plant.[1]

Manufacturing Strategy Paradigm The late 1970s and early 1980s saw the development of the manufacturing strategy paradigm by researchers at the Harvard Business School. This work by professors William Abernathy, Kim Clark, Robert Hayes, and Steven Wheelwright (built on earlier efforts by Wickham Skinner) emphasized how manufacturing executives could use their factories' capabilities as strategic competitive weapons. Central to their thinking was the notion of factory focus and manufacturing trade-offs. They argued that because a factory cannot excel on all performance measures, its management must devise a focused strategy, creating a focused factory that performs a limited set of tasks extremely well. This required trade-offs among such performance measures as low cost, high quality, and high flexibility in designing and managing factories. Ford seems to have realized this about 60 years before the Harvard professors.

Service

Service Quality and Productivity The great diversity of service industries—ranging from airlines to zoos, with many different types in between—precludes identifying any single pioneer or developer that has made a major impact in these areas. However, McDonald's unique approach to quality and productivity has been so successful that it stands as a reference point in thinking about how to deliver high-volume standardized services.

Global

Total Quality Management and Quality Certification Another major development was the focus on total quality management (TQM) in the late 1980s and 1990s. All operations executives are aware of the quality message put forth by the so-called quality gurus: W. Edwards Deming, Joseph M. Juran, and Philip Crosby. It's interesting that these individuals were students of Shewhart, Dodge, and Romig in the 1930s (sometimes it takes a generation for things to catch on). Helping the quality movement along is the Baldrige National Quality Award, which was started in 1987 under the direction of the National Institute of Standards and Technology. The Baldrige Award recognizes companies each year for outstanding quality management systems.

The ISO 9000 certification standards, created by the International Organization for Standardization, now plays a major role in setting quality standards for global manufacturers. Many European companies require that their vendors meet these standards as a condition for obtaining contracts.

Business Process Reengineering The need to become lean to remain competitive in the global economic recession in the 1990s pushed companies to seek innovations in the processes by which they run their operations. The flavor of business process reengineering (BPR) is conveyed in the title of Michael Hammer's influential article in *Harvard Business Review:* "Reengineering Work: Don't Automate, Obliterate." The approach seeks to make revolutionary changes as opposed to evolutionary changes (which are commonly advocated in TQM). It does this by taking a fresh look at what the organization is trying to do in all its business processes, and then eliminating non–value-added steps and computerizing the remaining ones to achieve the desired outcome.

Hammer actually was not the first consultant to advocate eliminating non–value-added steps and reengineering processes. In the early 1900s, Frederick W. Taylor developed principles of scientific management that applied scientific analysis to eliminating wasted effort from manual labor. Around the same time, Frank and Lillian Gilbreth used the new technology of the time, motion pictures, to analyze such diverse operations as bricklaying and medical surgery procedures. Many of the innovations this husband-and-wife team developed, such as time and motion study, are widely used today.

Six-Sigma Quality   Originally developed in the 1980s as part of total quality management, six-sigma quality in the 1990s saw a dramatic expansion as an extensive set of diagnostic tools was developed. These tools have been taught to managers as part of "Green and Black Belt Programs" at many corporations. The tools are now applied to not only the well-known manufacturing applications, but also to nonmanufacturing processes such as accounts receivable, sales, and research and development. Six-sigma has been applied to environmental, health, and safety services at companies and is now being applied to research and development, finance, information systems, legal, marketing, public affairs, and human resources processes.

Supply Chain Management   The central idea of supply chain management is to apply a total system approach to managing the flow of information, materials, and services from raw material suppliers through factories and warehouses to the end customer. Recent trends such as outsourcing and **mass customization** are forcing companies to find flexible ways to meet customer demand. The focus is on optimizing core activities to maximize the speed of response to changes in customer expectations.

Mass customization

Supply Chain

Electronic Commerce   The quick adoption of the Internet and the World Wide Web during the late 1990s was remarkable. The term *electronic commerce* refers to the use of the Internet as an essential element of business activity. The Internet is an outgrowth of a government network called ARPANET, which was created in 1969 by the Defense Department of the U.S. government. The use of Web pages, forms, and interactive search engines has changed the way people collect information, shop, and communicate. It has changed the way operations managers coordinate and execute production and distribution functions.

Service Science   A direct response to the growth of services is the development of a major industry and university program called Service Science Management and Engineering (SSME). SSME aims to apply the latest concepts in information technology to continue to improve service productivity of technology-based organizations. An interesting question raised by Jim Spohrer, leader of the IBM team that started the effort, is where will the labor go, once productivity improves in the service sector? "The short answer is new service sector industries and business—recall the service sector is very diverse and becoming more so every day. Consider the growth of retail (franchises, ecommerce, Amazon, eBay), communication (telephones, T-Mobile, Skype), transportation (airlines, FedEx), financial (discount ebrokers, Schwab), as well as information (television, CNN, Google) services. Not to mention all the new services in developing nations of the world. The creative capacity of the service sector for new industries and business has scarcely been tapped."[2]

Service

CURRENT ISSUES IN OPERATIONS AND SUPPLY MANAGEMENT

Operations and supply management is a dynamic field, and challenges presented by global enterprise present exciting new issues for operations managers. Looking forward to the future, we believe the major challenges in the field will be as follows:

1. **Coordinating the relationships between mutually supportive but separate organizations.** Recently there has been a dramatic surge in the outsourcing of parts and services that had previously been produced internally. This has been encouraged by the availability of fast, inexpensive communications. A whole new breed of *contract manufacturers* that specialize in performing focused manufacturing activities now exists. The success of this kind of traditional outsourcing has led companies to consider outsourcing other major corporate functions such as information systems, product development and design, engineering services, packaging, testing, and distribution. The ability to coordinate these activities is a significant challenge for the operations manager of the future.

Global

2. **Optimizing global supplier, production, and distribution networks.** The implementation of global enterprise resource planning systems, now common in large companies, has challenged managers to use all of this information. This requires a careful understanding of where control should be centralized and where autonomy is important, among other issues. Companies have only begun to truly take advantage of the information from these systems to optimally control such resources as inventory, transportation, and production equipment.

3. **Managing customer touch points.** As companies strive to become superefficient, they often scrimp on customer support personnel (and training) required to effectively staff service departments, help lines, and checkout counters. This leads to the frustrations we have all experienced such as being placed in call-center limbo seemingly for hours, getting bad advice when finally interacting with a company rep, and so on. The issue here is to recognize that making resource utilization decisions must capture the implicit costs of lost customers as well as the direct costs of staffing.

4. **Raising senior management awareness of operations as a significant competitive weapon.** As we stated earlier, many senior executives entered the organization through finance, strategy, or marketing and built their reputations on work in these areas, and as a result often take operations for granted. As we will demonstrate in this book, this can be a critical mistake when we realize how profitable companies such as Toyota, Dell, Taco Bell, and Southwest Airlines are. These are companies where executives have creatively used operations management for competitive advantage.

Sustainability
Triple bottom line

5. **Sustainability and the triple bottom line. Sustainability** is the ability to maintain balance in a system. Management must now consider the mandates related to the ongoing economic, employee, and environmental viability of the firm (the triple bottom line). Economically the firm must be profitable. Employee job security, positive working conditions, and development opportunities are essential. Nonpolluting and nonresource depleting products and processes bring new challenges to operations and supply managers.

Key Terms

Operations and supply management (OSM) Design, operation, and improvement of the systems that create and deliver the firm's primary products and services.

Servitization Building service activities to support a firm's product offerings.

Efficiency Doing something at the lowest possible cost.

Effectiveness Doing the right things to create the most value for the company.

Value Ratio of quality to price paid. Competitive "happiness" is being able to increase quality and reduce price while maintaining or improving profit margins. (This is a way that operations can directly increase customer retention and gain market share.)

Mass customization Producing products to order in lot sizes of one.

Sustainability The ability to maintain balance in a system.

Triple bottom line Relates to the economic, employee, and environmental impact of the firm's strategy.

Review and Discussion Questions

1 Look at the want ads in *The Wall Street Journal* and evaluate the opportunities for an OSM major with several years of experience.
2 What factors account for the resurgence of interest in OSM today?
3 Using Exhibit 1.3 as a model, describe the source-make-deliver-return relationships in the following systems:
   a. An airline.
   b. An automobile manufacturer.
   c. A hospital.
   d. An insurance company.
4 Define the service package of your college or university. What is its strongest element? Its weakest one?
5 What service industry has impressed you the most with its innovativeness?
6 What are value-added services and what are the benefits to external customers?
7 What is the difference between a service and a good?
8 Recent outsourcing of parts and services that had previously been produced internally is addressed by which current issue facing operation management today?

Internet Exercise: Harley-Davidson Motorcycles

Harley-Davidson has developed a Web site that allows potential customers to customize their new motorcycles. Working from a "basic" model, the customer can choose from an assortment of bags, chrome covers, color schemes, exhausts, foot controls, mirrors, and other accessories. The Web-based application is set up so that the customer cannot only select from the extensive list of accessories but also see exactly what the motorcycle will look like. These unique designs can be shared with friends and family by printing the final picture or transferring it via e-mail. What a slick way to sell motorcycles!

Go to the Harley-Davidson (HD) Web site (www.Harley-Davidson.com). From there select "Accessories and Apparel" and "Genuine Motor Accessories," then select "Your Guide to Customization." This should get you into the application.

1   How many different bike configurations do you think are possible? Could every customer have a different bike? To make this a little simpler, what if HD had only two types of bikes, three handle bar choices, four saddlebag combinations, and two exhaust pipe choices? How many combinations are possible in this case?

2   To keep things simple, HD has the dealer install virtually all these options. What would be the trade-off involved if HD installed these options at the factory instead of having the dealers install the options?

3   How important is this customization to HD's marketing strategy? Concisely describe HD's operations and supply strategy.

Super Quiz

1   The pipelinelike movement of the materials and information needed to produce a good or service.

2   A strategy that meets the needs of shareholders, employees, and preserves the environment.

3   The processes needed to determine the set of future actions required to operate an existing supply chain.

4   The selection of suppliers.

5   A type of process where the major product is produced or service provided.

6   A type of process that moves products to warehouses or customers.

7   Processes that involve the receiving of wornout, defective, and excess products back from customers and support for customers who have problems.

8   A business where the major product is intangible that cannot be weighed or measured.

9   Refers to when a company builds service activities into its product offerings.

10   Means doing something at the lowest possible cost.

11   Means doing the right things to create the most value for the company.

12   Metaphorically defined as quality divided by price.

13   A philosophy which aggressively seeks to eliminate causes of production defects.

14   An approach that seeks to make revolutionary changes as opposed to evolutionary changes (which is advocated by total quality management).

15   An approach that combines TQM and JIT.

16   Tools that are taught to managers in "Green and Black Belt Programs."

17   A program to apply the latest concepts in information technology to improve service productivity.

1. Supply (chain) network 2. Triple bottom line strategy 3. Planning 4. Sourcing 5. Making 6. Delivery 7. Returning 8. Service 9. Servitization 10. Efficiently 11. Effectively 12. Value 13. Total quality control 14. Business process reengineering 15. Lean manufacturing 16. Six-Sigma Quality 17. Service science management and engineering.

Selected Bibliography

APICS The Association for Operations Management. www.APICS.org.

Journal of Operations Management. Washington, DC: American Production and Inventory Control Society, 1980–current.

Manufacturing & Service Operations Management: M&SOM. Linthicum, MD: Institute for Operations Research and the Management Sciences, 1999–current.

Neely, A. (2007) "The Servitization of Manufacturing: An Empirical analysis of Global Trends," unpublished, Cranfield School of Management.

Nersesian, R. L. *Trends and Tools for Operations Management: An Updated Guide for Executives and Managers.* Westport, CT: Quorum, 2000.

Production and Operations Management: An International Journal of the Production and Operations Management Society/POMS. Baltimore: Production and Operations Management Society, 1992–current.

Production and Operations Management Society. www.poms.org.

Slack, N., ed. *The Blackwell Encyclopedia Dictionary of Operations Management.* Cambridge, MA: Blackwell, 2006.

Footnotes

1 See J. Wilson, "Henry Ford: A Just-in-Time Pioneer," *Production & Inventory Management Journal* 37 (1996), pp. 26–31.

2 Jim Spohrer, "Service Science, Management, and Engineering (SSME): A Next Frontier in Education, Employment, Innovation, and Economic Growth," IBM India, teleconference to India from Santa Clara, CA, December 2006.

CHAPTER 2

STRATEGY AND SUSTAINABILITY

After reading the chapter you will:

- Compare how operations and supply chain strategy relates to marketing and finance.
- Understand the competitive dimensions of operations and supply chain strategy.
- Identify order winners and order qualifiers.
- Understand the concept of strategic fit.
- Describe how productivity is measured and how it relates to operations and supply chain processes.
- Explain how the financial markets evaluate a firm's operations and supply chain performance.

23	How IKEA Designs Its Sexy Prices	
24	A Sustainable Strategy	Triple bottom line defined
25	What Is Operations and Supply Strategy?	Operations and supply strategy defined
	Competitive Dimensions	
	The Notion of Trade-Offs	Straddling defined
	Order Winners and Order Qualifiers:	Order winner defined
	The Marketing–Operations Link	Order qualifier defined
30	Strategic Fit: Fitting Operational Activities to Strategy	Activity-system maps defined
32	Productivity Measurement	Productivity defined
33	How Does Wall Street Evaluate Operations Performance?	
34	Summary	
38	Case: The Tao of Timbuk2	
39	Super Quiz	

HOW IKEA DESIGNS ITS SEXY PRICES

Global

Competitive strategy is about being different. It means deliberately choosing a different set of activities to deliver a unique mix of value. IKEA, the Swedish retailer of home products, dominates markets in 43 countries, and is poised to conquer North America.

Above all else, one factor accounts for IKEA's success: good quality at a low price. IKEA sells household items that are cheap but not cheapo, with prices that typically run 30 to 50 percent below those of the competition. While the price of other companies' products tends to rise over time, IKEA says it has reduced its retail prices by a total of about 20 percent during the last four years. At IKEA the process of driving down costs starts the moment a new item is conceived and continues relentlessly throughout the life of the product.

IKEA has always had a 50-cent coffee mug. Prior to the new TROFÉ mug, the company offered the "Bang" mug, which had been redesigned three times, in ways to maximize the

number of mugs that could be stored on a pallet. Originally, only 864 mugs would fit. A redesign added a rim such as you would find on a flowerpot so that each pallet could hold 1,280 mugs. Another redesign created a shorter mug with a new handle, allowing 2,024 to squeeze onto a pallet. These changes reduced shipping costs by 60 percent.

The latest version of the 50-cent coffee mug has been made even more useful with a simple notch on the bottom that prevents water from pooling up around the base during a dishwasher run. Further refinements have optimized the speed at which the cup can pass through the machines forming the cups and enable IKEA to fit the maximum number into kilns, saving on the expensive firing process. Simple changes in the shape of the mug have reduced the cost to produce the mug significantly while creating more value for customers purchasing this simple 50-cent coffee mug.

This is the essence of operations management: creating great value to the customer while reducing the cost of delivering the good or service.

A SUSTAINABLE STRATEGY

Strategy should describe how a firm intends to create and sustain value for its current share-holders. By adding "sustainability" to the concept, we add the requirement to meet these current needs without compromising the ability of future generations to meet their own needs. *Shareholders* are those individuals or companies that legally own one or more shares of stock in the company. Many companies today have expanded the scope of their strategy to include stakeholders. *Stakeholders* are those individuals or organizations who are influenced, either directly or indirectly, by the actions of the firm. This expanded view means that the scope of the firm's strategy must not only focus on the economic viability of its share-holders but should also consider the environmental and social impact on key stakeholders.

Triple bottom line

To capture this expanded view the phrase **triple bottom line** has been coined.[1] The triple bottom line, Exhibit 2.1, considers evaluating the firm against social, economic, and environmental criteria. Many companies have developed this expanded view through goals that relate to sustainability along each of these dimensions. Some alternative phrases for the same concept are "People, Planet, and Profit" used by Shell Oil Company, and "Folk, Work, and Place" which originated with the 20th century writer Patrick Geddes. The following expands on the meaning of each dimension of the triple bottom line framework.

- **Social** Pertains to fair and beneficial business practices toward labor, the community, and the region in which a firm conducts its business. A triple bottom line company seeks to benefit its employees, the community, and other social entities that are impacted by the firm's existence. A company should not use child labor, should pay fair salaries to its workers, maintain a safe work environment with tolerable working hours, and not otherwise exploit a community or its labor force. A business can also give back by contributing to the strength and growth of its community through health care, education and other special programs.
- **Economic** The firm is obligated to compensate shareholders who provide capital through stock purchases and other financial instruments via a competitive return on investment. Company strategies should promote growth and grow long-term value to this group in the form of profit. Within a sustainability framework, this dimension goes beyond just profit for the firm but also provides lasting economic benefit to society.
- **Environmental** This refers to the firm's impact on the environment. The company should protect the environment as much as possible—or at least cause no harm.

exhibit 2.1   The Triple Bottom Line

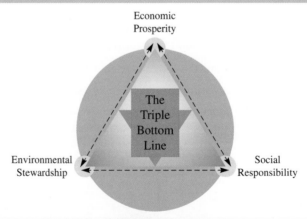

Managers should move to reduce a company's ecological footprint by carefully managing its consumption of natural resources and by reducing waste, as well as ensuring that the waste is less toxic before disposing of it in a safe and legal manner. Many businesses now conduct "cradle-to-grave" assessments of products to determine what the true environmental costs are—from processing the raw material to manufacture to distribution to eventual disposal by the final customer.

Conventional strategy focuses on the economic part of this framework. Because many of the processes that fall under the domain of operations and supply management have social and environment impact, it is important these criteria be considered as well. Some proponents argue that in many ways European Union countries are more advanced due to the standardized reporting of ecological and social losses that came with the adoption of the euro.

Although many company planners agree with the goals of improving society and preserving the environment, many others disagree. Dissenting arguments relate to the potential loss of efficiency due to the focus on conflicting criteria. Others argue that these goals may be appropriate for rich societies who can afford to contribute to society and the environment. A company in a poor or developing society/nation must focus on survival. The economic benefit derived from the use of abundant local resources may be viewed as worth their destruction.

In this chapter we take a customer-centered focus; issues associated with people and the environment are left to an individual case approach. Depending on the country, industry, and scope of the firm, these other issues vary widely and it would be difficult to provide a general approach for analysis. The issues and their relationship to operations and supply management are very real however, and we anticipate they will become even more important relevant in the future.

WHAT IS OPERATIONS AND SUPPLY STRATEGY?

Operations and supply strategy is concerned with setting broad policies and plans for using the resources of a firm and must be integrated with corporate strategy. So, for example, if the high-level corporate strategy includes goals related to the environment and social responsibility, then the operations and supply strategy must consider this. A major focus to the operations and supply strategy is operations effectiveness. *Operations effectiveness* relates to the core business processes needed to run the business. The processes span all the business functions from taking customer orders, handling return, manufacturing, managing the updating of the Web site, to shipping products. Operational effectiveness is reflected directly in the costs associated with doing business. Strategies associated with operational effectiveness, such as quality assurance and control initiatives, process redesign, planning and control systems, and technology investments, can show quick near-term (12 to 24 months) results.

Operations and supply strategy can be viewed as part of a planning process that coordinates operational goals with those of the larger organization. Since the goals of the larger organization change over time, the operations strategy must be designed to anticipate

Operations and supply strategy

future needs. A firm's operations and supply capabilities can be viewed as a portfolio best suited to adapt to the changing product and/or service needs of the firm's customers.

Planning strategy is a process just like making a product or delivering a service. The process involves a set of activities that are repeated at different intervals over time. Just as products are made over and over, the strategy planning activities are repeated. A big difference is that these activities are done by executives in the board room!

Exhibit 2.2 shows the major activities of a typical strategic planning process. Activity 1 is performed at least yearly and is where the overall strategy is developed. A key part of this step is the "strategic analysis," which involves looking out and forecasting how business conditions that impact the firm's strategy are going to change in the future. Here such things as changes in customer preferences, the impact of new technologies, changes in population demographics, and the anticipation of new competitors are considered. A successful strategy will anticipate change and formulate new initiatives in response. "Initiatives" are the major steps that need to be taken to drive success in the firm. Many of these initiatives are repeated from year to year such as the updating of existing product designs and the operation of manufacturing plants in different regions of the world. New initiatives that innovatively respond to market dynamics are extremely important to company success. Initiatives that develop innovative new products or open new markets, for example, drive future revenue growth. Other initiatives that reduce costs directly impact the profitability of the firm. Companies with triple bottom line strategies may have initiatives that reduce waste or enhance the welfare of the local communities.

exhibit 2.2   Closed-Loop Strategy Process

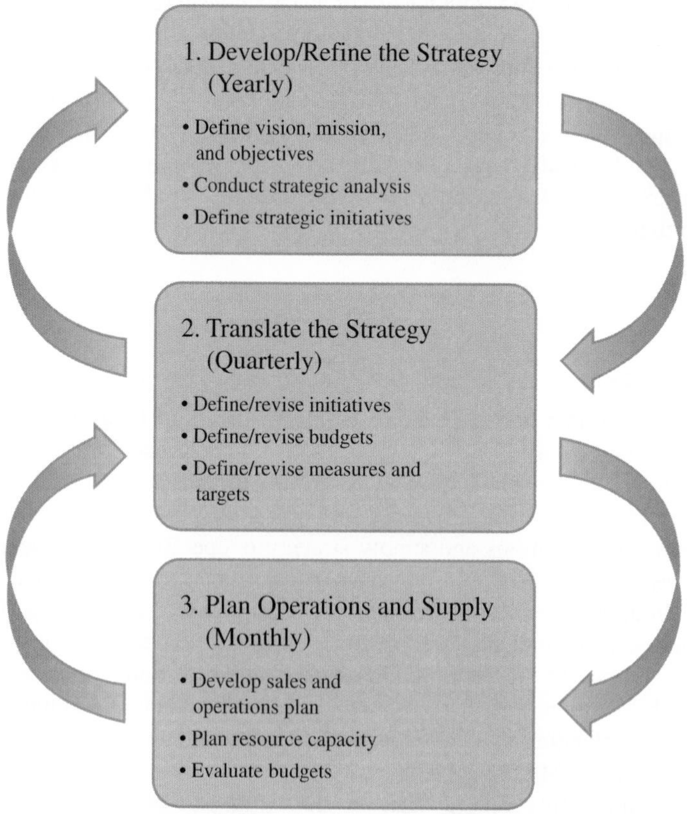

1. Develop/Refine the Strategy (Yearly)
   - Define vision, mission, and objectives
   - Conduct strategic analysis
   - Define strategic initiatives

2. Translate the Strategy (Quarterly)
   - Define/revise initiatives
   - Define/revise budgets
   - Define/revise measures and targets

3. Plan Operations and Supply (Monthly)
   - Develop sales and operations plan
   - Plan resource capacity
   - Evaluate budgets

Activity 2 in Exhibit 2.2 is where the overall strategy is refined and updated as often as four times a year. Here each initiative is evaluated and appropriate budget estimates for the next year or more are developed. Measures that relate to the performance of each initiative are needed so that success or failure can be gauged in an unbiased and objective way. Because of the quickly changing nature of global business, many businesses must revise plans several times per year.

The operations and supply planning activity shown in the third box is where operational plans that relate to functional areas such as marketing, manufacturing, warehousing, transportation, and purchasing are coordinated for six months up to a year and a half. The functional areas involved in the coordination can vary greatly depending on the needs of the firm. A hospital can involve coordination across the operating room, intensive care units, and auxiliary units such as radiation and chemotherapy. Similarly, the coordination for a retailer such as Walmart may be very different compared to an automobile manufacturer such as Ford. These coordination efforts are largely focused on adjusting capacity and resource availability based on anticipated demand scenarios.

In the next section, we focus on integrating operations and supply strategy with a firm's operations capabilities. This involves decisions that relate to the design of the processes and infrastructure needed to support these processes. Process design includes the selecting the appropriate technology, sizing the process over time, determining the role of inventory in the process, and locating the process. The infrastructure decisions involve the logic associated with the planning and control systems, quality assurance and control approaches, work payment structure, and organization of the operations and supply functions. A firm's operations capabilities can be viewed as a portfolio best suited to adapt to the changing product and/or service needs of a firm's customers.

Competitive Dimensions

Given the choices customers face today, how do they decide which product or service to buy? Different customers are attracted by different attributes. Some customers are interested primarily in the cost of a product or service and, correspondingly, some companies attempt to position themselves to offer the lowest prices. The major competitive dimensions that form the competitive position of a firm include the following.

Cost or Price: "Make the Product or Deliver the Service Cheap"

Within every industry, there is usually a segment of the market that buys solely on the basis of low cost. To successfully compete in this niche, a firm must be the low-cost producer, but even this does not always guarantee profitability and success. Products and services sold strictly on the basis of cost are typically commodity-like; in other words, customers cannot distinguish the product or service of one firm from those of another. This segment of the market is frequently very large, and many companies are lured by the potential for significant profits, which they associate with the large unit volumes. As a consequence, however, competition in this segment is fierce—and so is the failure rate. After all, there can be only one low-cost producer, who usually establishes the selling price in the market.

Price, however, is not the only basis on which a firm can compete (although many economists appear to assume it is!). Other companies, such as BMW, seek to attract those who want *higher quality*—in terms of performance, appearance, or features—than that available in competing products and services, even though accompanied by a higher price.

Quality: "Make a Great Product or Deliver a Great Service"

There are two characteristics of a product or service that define quality: design quality and process quality. Design quality relates to the set of features the product or service

contains. This relates directly to the design of the product or service. Obviously a child's first two-wheel bicycle is of significantly different quality than the bicycle of a world-class cyclist. The use of special aluminum alloys and special lightweight sprockets and chains is important to the performance needs of the advanced cyclist. These two types of bicycle are designed for different customers' needs. The higher-quality cyclist product commands a higher price in the marketplace due to its special features. The goal in establishing the proper level of design quality is to focus on the requirements of the customer. Overdesigned products and services with too many or inappropriate features will be viewed as prohibitively expensive. In comparison, underdesigned products and services will lose customers to products that cost a little more but are perceived by customers as offering greater value.

Process quality, the second characteristic of quality, is critical because it relates directly to the reliability of the product or service. Regardless of whether the product is a child's first two-wheeler or a bicycle for an international cyclist, customers want products without defects. Thus, the goal of process quality is to produce defect-free products and services. Product and service specifications, given in dimensional tolerances and/or service error rates, define how the product or service is to be made. Adherence to these specifications is critical to ensure the reliability of the product or service as defined by its intended use.

Delivery Speed: "Make the Product or Deliver the Service Quickly" In some markets, a firm's ability to deliver more quickly than its competitors is critical. A company that can offer an on-site repair service in only 1 or 2 hours has a significant advantage over a competing firm that guarantees service only within 24 hours.

Service

Delivery Reliability: "Deliver It When Promised" This dimension relates to the firm's ability to supply the product or service on or before a promised delivery due date. For an automobile manufacturer, it is very important that its supplier of tires provide the needed quantity and types for each day's car production. If the tires needed for a particular car are not available when the car reaches the point on the assembly line where the tires are installed, the whole assembly line may have to be shut down until they arrive. For a service firm such as Federal Express, delivery reliability is the cornerstone of its strategy.

Coping with Changes in Demand: "Change Its Volume" In many markets, a company's ability to respond to increases and decreases in demand is important to its ability to compete. It is well known that a company with increasing demand can do little wrong. When demand is strong and increasing, costs are continuously reduced due to economies of scale, and investments in new technologies can be easily justified. But scaling back when demand decreases may require many difficult decisions about laying off employees and related reductions in assets. The ability to effectively deal with dynamic market demand over the long term is an essential element of operations strategy.

Flexibility and New-Product Introduction Speed: "Change It" Flexibility, from a strategic perspective, refers to the ability of a company to offer a wide variety of products to its customers. An important element of this ability to offer different products is the time required for a company to develop a new product and to convert its processes to offer the new product.

Other Product-Specific Criteria: "Support It" The competitive dimensions just described are certainly the most common. However, other dimensions often relate to specific products or situations. Notice that most of the dimensions listed next are primarily service in nature. Often special services are provided to augment the sales of manufactured products.

1. **Technical liaison and support.** A supplier may be expected to provide technical assistance for product development, particularly during the early stages of design and manufacturing.
2. **Meeting a launch date.** A firm may be required to coordinate with other firms on a complex project. In such cases, manufacturing may take place while development work is still being completed. Coordinating work between firms and working simultaneously on a project will reduce the total time required to complete the project.
3. **Supplier after-sale support.** An important competitive dimension may be the ability of a firm to support its product after the sale. This involves availability of replacement parts and, possibly, modification of older, existing products to new performance levels. Speed of response to these after-sale needs is often important as well.
4. **Environmental impact.** A dimension related to criteria such as carbon dioxide emissions, use of non-renewable resources, or other factors that relate to sustainability.
5. **Other dimensions.** These typically include such factors as colors available, size, weight, location of the fabrication site, customization available, and product mix options.

The Notion of Trade-Offs

Central to the concept of operations and supply strategy is the notion of operations focus and trade-offs. The underlying logic is that an operation cannot excel simultaneously on all competitive dimensions. Consequently, management has to decide which parameters of performance are critical to the firm's success and then concentrate the resources of the firm on these particular characteristics.

For example, if a company wants to focus on speed of delivery, it cannot be very flexible in its ability to offer a wide range of products. Similarly, a low-cost strategy is not compatible with either speed of delivery or flexibility. High quality also is viewed as a trade-off to low cost.

A strategic position is not sustainable unless there are compromises with other positions. Trade-offs occur when activities are incompatible so that more of one thing necessitates less of another. An airline can choose to serve meals—adding cost and slowing turnaround time at the gate—or it can choose not to, but it cannot do both without bearing major inefficiencies.

Straddling occurs when a company seeks to match the benefits of a successful position while maintaining its existing position. It adds new features, services, or technologies onto the activities it already performs. The risky nature of this strategy is shown by Continental Airlines' ill-fated attempt to compete with Southwest Airlines. While maintaining its position as a full-service airline, Continental set out to match Southwest on a number of point-to-point routes. The airline dubbed the new service Continental Lite. It eliminated meals and first-class service, increased departure frequency, lowered fares, and shortened gate turnaround time. Because Continental remained a full-service airline on other routes, it continued to use travel agents and its mixed fleet of planes and to provide baggage checking and seat assignments.

Straddling

Service

Trade-offs ultimately grounded Continental Lite. The airline lost hundreds of millions of dollars, and the chief executive officer lost his job. Its planes were delayed leaving congested hub cities or slowed at the gate by baggage transfers. Late flights and cancellations generated a thousand complaints a day. Continental Lite could not afford to compete on price and still pay standard travel agent commissions, but neither could it do without agents for its full-service business. The airline compromised by cutting commissions for all Continental flights. Similarly, it could not afford to offer the same frequent-flier benefits to travelers paying the much lower ticket prices for Lite service. It compromised again by lowering the rewards of Continental's entire frequent-flier program. The results: angry travel agents and full-service customers. Continental tried to compete in two ways at once and paid an enormous straddling penalty.

Order Winners and Order Qualifiers: The Marketing–Operations Link

Global

A well-designed interface between marketing and operations is necessary to provide a business with an understanding of its markets from both perspectives. The terms *order winner* and *order qualifier* describe marketing-oriented dimensions that are key to competitive success. An **order winner** is a criterion that differentiates the products or services of one firm from those of another. Depending on the situation, the order-winning criterion may be the cost of the product (price), product quality and reliability, or any of the other dimensions developed earlier. An **order qualifier** is a screening criterion that permits a firm's products to even be considered as possible candidates for purchase. Oxford Professor Terry Hill states that a firm must "requalify the order qualifiers" every day it is in business.

It is important to remember that the order-winning and order-qualifying criteria may change over time. For example, when Japanese companies entered the world automobile markets in the 1970s, they changed the way these products won orders, from predominantly price to product quality and reliability. American automobile producers were losing orders through quality to the Japanese companies. By the late 1980s, product quality was raised by Ford, General Motors, and Chrysler; today they are "qualified" to be in the market. Consumer groups continually monitor the quality and reliability criteria, thus requalifying the top-performing companies. Today the order winners for automobiles vary greatly depending on the model. Customers know the set of features they want (such as reliability, design features, and gas mileage), and they want to purchase a particular combination at the lowest price, thus maximizing value.

STRATEGIC FIT: FITTING OPERATIONAL ACTIVITIES TO STRATEGY

Service

All the activities that make up a firm's operation relate to one another. To make these activities efficient, the firm must minimize its total cost without compromising customers' needs. IKEA targets young furniture buyers who want style at a low cost. IKEA has chosen to perform activities differently from its rivals.

Consider the typical furniture store, where showrooms display samples of the merchandise. One area may contain many sofas, another area displays dining tables, and there are many other areas focused on particular types of furniture. Dozens of books displaying fabric swatches or wood samples or alternative styles offer customers thousands of product varieties from which to choose. Salespeople escort customers through the store, answering questions and helping them navigate through the maze of choices. Once a customer decides what he or she wants, the order is relayed to a third-party manufacturer. With a lot of luck, the furniture will be delivered to the customer's home within six to eight weeks. This is a supply chain that maximizes customization and service but does so at a high cost.

In contrast, IKEA serves customers who are happy to trade service for cost. Instead of using sales associates, IKEA uses a self-service model with roomlike displays where furniture is shown in familiar settings. Rather than relying on third-party manufacturers, IKEA designs its own low-cost, modular, ready-to-assemble furniture. In the store there is a warehouse section with the products in boxes ready for delivery. Customers do their own picking from inventory and delivery. Much of its low-cost operation comes from having customers service themselves, yet IKEA offers extra services such as in-store child care and extended hours. Those services align well with the needs of its customers, who are young, not wealthy, and likely to have children, and who need to shop at odd hours.

Exhibit 2.3 shows how IKEA's strategy is implemented through a set of activities designed to deliver it. **Activity-system maps** such as the one for IKEA show how a

Activity-system maps

Mapping Activity Systems

exhibit 2.3

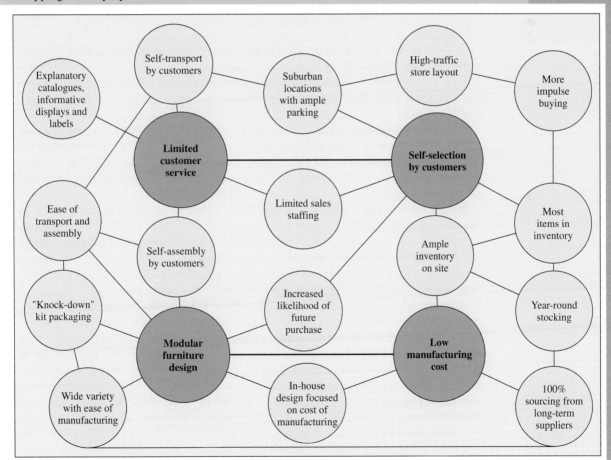

Activity-system maps, such as this one for IKEA, show how a company's strategic position is contained in a set of tailored activities designed to deliver it. In companies with a clear strategic position, a number of higher-order strategic themes (in darker green circles) can be identified and implemented through clusters of tightly linked activities (in lighter circles).

Source: M. E. Porter, *On Competition* (Boston: HBS, 1998), p. 50.

company's strategy is delivered through a set of tailored activities. In companies with a clear strategy, a number of higher-order strategic themes (in darker green) can be identified and implemented through clusters of tightly linked activities. This type of map can be useful in understanding how good the fit is between the system of activities and the company's strategy. Competitive advantage comes from the way a firm's activities fit with and reinforce one another.

PRODUCTIVITY MEASUREMENT

Productivity

Productivity is a common measure of how well a country, industry, or business unit is using its resources (or factors of production). Since operations and supply management focuses on making the best use of the resources available to a firm, productivity measurement is fundamental to understanding operations-related performance. In this section, we define various measures of productivity. Throughout the rest of the book, many other performance measures will be defined as they relate to the material.

In its broadest sense, productivity is defined as

$$\text{Productivity} = \frac{\text{Outputs}}{\text{Inputs}}$$

To increase productivity, we want to make this ratio of outputs to inputs as large as practical.

Productivity is what we call a *relative measure*. In other words, to be meaningful, it needs to be compared with something else. For example, what can we learn from the fact that we operate a restaurant and that its productivity last week was 8.4 customers per labor hour? Nothing!

Productivity comparisons can be made in two ways. First, a company can compare itself with similar operations within its industry, or it can use industry data when such data are available (e.g., comparing productivity among the different stores in a franchise). Another approach is to measure productivity over time within the same operation. Here we would compare our productivity in one time period with that in the next.

As Exhibit 2.4 shows, productivity may be expressed as partial measures, multifactor measures, or total measures. If we are concerned with the ratio of output to a single input, we have a *partial productivity measure*. If we want to look at the ratio of output to a group of inputs (but not all inputs), we have a *multifactor productivity measure*. If we want to express the ratio of all outputs to all inputs, we can use a *total factor measure of productivity* to describe the productivity of an entire organization or even a nation.

A numerical example of productivity appears in Exhibit 2.4. The data reflect quantitative measures of input and output associated with the production of a certain product. Notice that for the multifactor and partial measures, it is not necessary to use total output as the numerator. Often it is desirable to create measures that represent productivity as it relates to some particular output of interest. For example, as in Exhibit 2.4, total units might be the output of interest to a production control manager, whereas total output may be of key interest to the plant manager. This process of aggregation and disaggregation of productivity measures provides a means of shifting the level of the analysis to suit a variety of productivity measurement and improvement needs.

Exhibit 2.4 shows all units in dollars. Often, however, management can better understand how the company is performing when units other than dollars are used. In these cases, only partial measures of productivity can be used, as we cannot combine dissimilar units such as labor hours and pounds of material. Examples of some commonly used partial measures of productivity are presented in Exhibit 2.5. Such partial measures of productivity give managers information in familiar units, allowing them to easily relate these measures to the actual operations.

Examples of Productivity Measures

exhibit 2.4

Partial measure	$\dfrac{\text{Output}}{\text{Labor}}$ or $\dfrac{\text{Output}}{\text{Capital}}$ or $\dfrac{\text{Output}}{\text{Materials}}$ or $\dfrac{\text{Output}}{\text{Energy}}$
Multifactor measure	$\dfrac{\text{Output}}{\text{Labor + Capital + Energy}}$ or $\dfrac{\text{Output}}{\text{Labor + Capital + Materials}}$
Total measure	$\dfrac{\text{Output}}{\text{Inputs}}$ or $\dfrac{\text{Goods and services produced}}{\text{All resources used}}$

INPUT AND OUTPUT PRODUCTION DATA ($)		PRODUCTIVITY MEASURE EXAMPLES

OUTPUT

1. Finished units	$10,000
2. Work in process	2,500
3. Dividends	1,000
4. Bonds	
5. Other income	
Total output	$13,500

Total measure

$$\frac{\text{Total output}}{\text{Total input}} = \frac{13,500}{15,193} = 0.89$$

Multifactor measures:

$$\frac{\text{Total output}}{\text{Human + Material}} = \frac{13,500}{3,153} = 4.28$$

$$\frac{\text{Finished units}}{\text{Human + Material}} = \frac{10,000}{3,153} = 3.17$$

INPUT

1. Human	$ 3,000
2. Material	153
3. Capital	10,000
4. Energy	540
5. Other expenses	1,500
Total input	$ 15,193

Partial measures:

$$\frac{\text{Total output}}{\text{Energy}} = \frac{13,500}{540} = 25$$

$$\frac{\text{Finished units}}{\text{Energy}} = \frac{10,000}{540} = 18.52$$

**Excel:
Productivity Measures**

Partial Measures of Productivity

exhibit 2.5

BUSINESS	PRODUCTIVITY MEASURE
Restaurant	Customers (meals) per labor hour
Retail store	Sales per square foot
Chicken farm	Lb. of meat per lb. of feed
Utility plant	Kilowatts per ton of coal
Paper mill	Tons of paper per cord of wood

HOW DOES WALL STREET EVALUATE OPERATIONS PERFORMANCE?

Comparing firms from an operations view is important to investors since the relative cost of providing a good or service is essential to high earnings growth. When you think about it, earnings growth is largely a function of the firm's profitability and profit can be increased through higher sales and/or reduced cost. Highly efficient firms usually shine when demand drops during recession periods since they often can continue to make a profit due to their low-cost structure. These operations-savvy firms may even see a recession as an opportunity to gain market share as their less-efficient competitors struggle to remain in business.

exhibit 2.6 Efficiency Measures Used by Wall Street

		A COMPARISON OF AUTOMOBILE COMPANIES			
MANAGEMENT EFFICIENCY MEASURE	TOYOTA	FORD	GENERAL MOTORS	CHRYSLER	INDUSTRY
Income per employee	$40,000	$8,000	$10,000	$8,000	$15,000
Revenue per employee	$663,000	$535,000	$597,000	$510,000	$568,000
Receivables turnover	4.0	1.5	1.0	2.2	2.1
Inventory turnover	12.0	11.5	11.7	5.9	11.0
Asset turnover	0.8	0.6	0.4	0.8	0.8

Take a look at the automobile industry, where efficiency has been such an important factor. Exhibit 2.6 shows a comparison of some of the major companies. These ratios reflect late 2008 performance, prior to the restructuring of General Motors and Chrysler in 2009. As you can see, Toyota dominates the group. Toyota's net income per employee is five times greater than that of Ford and Chrysler, truly an amazing accomplishment. Toyota also shines in receivables turnover, inventory turnover, and asset turnover. Ford and General Motors have worked hard at implementing the inventory management philosophy that was pioneered by Toyota in Japan. True efficiency goes beyond inventory management and requires an integrated product development, sales, manufacturing, and supply system. Toyota is very mature in its approach to these activities, and that clearly shows on its bottom line.

Each summer, *USA Today* publishes annual reports of productivity gains by the largest U.S. firms. Productivity has been on the rise for the past few years, which is very good for the economy. Productivity often increases in times of recession; as workers are fired, those remaining are expected to do more. Increases also come from technological advances. Think of what the tractor did for farm productivity.

When evaluating the largest productivity winners and losers, it is important to look for unusual explanations. For example, energy companies have had big productivity gains due almost exclusively to higher oil prices, which boosted the companies' revenue without forcing them to add employees. Pharmaceutical companies such as Merck and Pfizer have not done well recently. Their productivity plunges were due primarily to one-time events, Merck because it spun off a company and Pfizer because it bought a company. Such one-time quirks create a lot of noise for anybody who wants to know how well companies are run. It is best to examine multiyear productivity patterns.

SUMMARY

In this chapter we have stressed the importance of the link between operations and supply management and the competitive success of the firm. The topics in this book include those that all managers should be familiar with. The operations and supply activities of the firm need to strategically support the competitive priorities of the firm. IKEA's entire integrated process, including the design of products, design of the packaging, manufacturing, distribution, and retail outlets, is carefully wired toward delivering functionally innovative products at the lowest cost possible.

In this chapter we show how the overall strategy of the firm can be tied to operations and supply strategy. Important concepts are the operational competitive dimensions, order winner and qualifiers, and strategic fit. The ideas apply to virtually any business and are critical to the firm's ability to sustain a competitive advantage. For a firm to remain competitive, all of the operational activities must buttress the firm's strategy. Wall Street analysts are constantly monitoring how efficient companies are from an operations view. Companies that are strong operationally are able to generate more profit for each dollar of sales, thus making them attractive investments.

Key Terms

Triple bottom line A business strategy that includes social, economic, and environmental criteria.

Operations and supply strategy Setting broad policies and plans for using the resources of a firm to best support the firm's long-term competitive strategy.

Straddling Occurs when a firm seeks to match what a competitor is doing by adding new features, services, or technologies to existing activities. This often creates problems if certain trade-offs need to be made.

Order winner A dimension that differentiates the products or services of one firm from those of another.

Order qualifier A dimension used to screen a product or service as a candidate for purchase.

Activity-system maps A diagram that shows how a company's strategy is delivered through a set of supporting activities.

Productivity A measure of how well resources are used.

Solved Problem

A furniture manufacturing company has provided the following data. Compare the labor, raw materials and supplies, and total productivity of 2009 and 2010.

		2009	2010
Output:	Sales value of production	$22,000	$35,000
Input:	Labor	10,000	15,000
	Raw materials and supplies	8,000	12,500
	Capital equipment depreciation	700	1,200
	Other	2,200	4,800

Solution

	2009	2010
Partial productivities		
Labor	2.20	2.33
Raw materials and supplies	2.75	2.80
Total productivity	1.05	1.04

Review and Discussion Questions

1   Can a factory be fast, dependable, and flexible; produce high-quality products; and still provide poor service from a customer's perspective?
2   Why should a service organization worry about being world-class if it does not compete outside its own national border? What impact does the Internet have on this?

3   What are the major priorities associated with operations strategy? How has their relationship to one another changed over the years?
4   Find examples where companies have used features related to environmental sustainability to "win" new customers.
5   For each priority in question 3, describe the unique characteristics of the market niche with which it is most compatible.
6   A few years ago, the dollar showed relative weakness with respect to foreign currencies such as the yen, euro, and pound. This stimulated exports. Why would long-term reliance on a lower-valued dollar be at best a short-term solution to the competitiveness problem?
7   In your opinion, do business schools have competitive priorities?
8   Why does the "proper" operations strategy keep changing for companies that are world-class competitors?
9   What is meant by the expressions *order winners* and *order qualifiers*? What was the order winner(s) for your last major purchase of a product or service?
10   What do we mean when we say productivity is a "relative" measure?

Problems *

1   As operations manager, you are concerned about being able to meet sales requirements in the coming months. You have just been given the following production report.

	JAN	FEB	MAR	APR
Units produced	2300	1800	2800	3000
Hours per machine	325	200	400	320
Number of machines	3	5	4	4

Find the average monthly productivity (units per hour).

2   Sailmaster makes high-performance sails for competitive windsurfers. Below is information about the inputs and outputs for one model, the Windy 2000.

Units sold	1,217
Sale price each	$1,700
Total labor hours	46,672
Wage rate	$12/hour
Total materials	$60,000
Total energy	$4,000

Calculate the productivity in **sales revenue/labor expense.**

3   *Acme Corporation* received the data below for its rodent cage production unit. Find the **total** productivity.

OUTPUT	INPUT	
50,000 cages	Production time	620 labor hours
Sales price: $3.50 per unit	Wages	$7.50 per hour
	Raw materials (total cost)	$30,000
	Component parts (total cost)	$15,350

*Special thanks to Bill Ruck of Arizona State University for the problems in this section.

4   Two types of cars (Deluxe and Limited) were produced by a car manufacturer in 2008. Quantities sold, price per unit, and labor hours follow. What is the labor productivity for each car? Explain the problem(s) associated with the labor productivity.

	QUANTITY	$/UNIT
Deluxe car	4,000 units sold	$8,000/car
Limited car	6,000 units sold	$9,500/car
Labor, Deluxe	20,000 hours	$12/hour
Labor, Limited	30,000 hours	$14/hour

5   A U.S. manufacturing company operating a subsidiary in an LDC (less developed country) shows the following results:

	U.S.	LDC
Sales (units)	100,000	20,000
Labor (hours)	20,000	15,000
Raw materials (currency)	$20,000	FC 20,000
Capital equipment (hours)	60,000	5,000

   a. Calculate partial labor and capital productivity figures for the parent and subsidiary. Do the results seem misleading?
   b. Compute the multifactor productivity figures for labor and capital together. Are the results better?
   c. Calculate raw material productivity figures (units/$ where $1 = FC 10). Explain why these figures might be greater in the subsidiary.

6   Various financial data for 2009 and 2010 follow. Calculate the total productivity measure and the partial measures for labor, capital, and raw materials for this company for both years. What do these measures tell you about this company?

		2009	2010
Output:	Sales	$200,000	$220,000
Input:	Labor	30,000	40,000
	Raw materials	35,000	45,000
	Energy	5,000	6,000
	Capital	50,000	50,000
	Other	2,000	3,000

7   An electronics company makes communications devices for military contracts. The company just completed two contracts. The navy contract was for 2,300 devices and took 25 workers two weeks (40 hours per week) to complete. The army contract was for 5,500 devices that were produced by 35 workers in three weeks. On which contract were the workers more productive?

8   A retail store had sales of $45,000 in April and $56,000 in May. The store employs eight full-time workers who work a 40-hour week. In April the store also had seven part-time workers at 10 hours per week, and in May the store had nine part-timers at 15 hours per week (assume four weeks in each month). Using sales dollars as the measure of output, what is the percentage change in productivity from April to May?

9   A parcel delivery company delivered 103,000 packages in 2009, when its average employment was 84 drivers. In 2010 the firm handled 112,000 deliveries with 96 drivers. What was the percentage change in productivity from 2009 to 2010?

10   A fast-food restaurant serves hamburgers, cheeseburgers, and chicken sandwiches. The restaurant counts a cheeseburger as equivalent to 1.25 hamburgers and chicken sandwiches as

0.8 hamburger. Current employment is five full-time employees who work a 40-hour week. If the restaurant sold 700 hamburgers, 900 cheeseburgers, and 500 chicken sandwiches in one week, what is its productivity? What would its productivity have been if it had sold the same number of sandwiches (2,100) but the mix was 700 of each type?

CASE: The Tao of Timbuk2*

"Timbuk2 is more than a bag. It's more than a brand. Timbuk2 is a bond. To its owner, a Timbuk2 bag is a dependable, everyday companion. We see fierce, emotional attachments form between Timbuk2 customers and their bags all the time. A well-worn Timbuk2 bag has a certain patina—the stains and scars of everyday urban adventures. Many Timbuk2 bags are worn daily for a decade, or more, accompanying the owner through all sorts of defining life events. True to our legend of 'indestructibility,' it's not uncommon for a Timbuk2 bag to outlive jobs, personal relationships, even pets. This is the Tao of Timbuk2."

What makes Timbuk2 so unique? Visit their Web site at www.timbuk2.com and see for yourself. Each bag is custom designed by the customer on their Web site. After the customer selects the basic bag configuration and size, colors for each of the various panels are presented; various lines, logos, pockets, and straps are selected so that the bag is tailored to the exact specifications of the customer. A quick click of the mouse and the bag is delivered directly to the customer in only two days. How do they do this?

This San Francisco based company is known for producing high-quality custom and classic messenger bags direct to customer order. They have a team of approximately 25 hardworking cutters and sewers in their San Francisco plant. Over the years, they have fine-tuned their production line to make it as efficient as possible while producing the highest-quality messenger bags available.

The local manufacturing is focused on the custom messenger bag. For these bags, orders are taken over the Internet. The customers are given many configuration, size, color, pocket, and strap options. The bag is tailored to the exact specifications of the customer on the Timbuk2 assembly line in San Francisco and sent via overnight delivery directly to the customer.

Recently, Timbuk2 has begun making some of its new products in China, which is a concern to some of its long-standing customers. The company argues that it has designed its new products to provide the best possible features, quality, and value at reasonable prices and stresses that these new products are designed in San Francisco. Timbuk2 argues that

the new bags are much more complex to build and require substantially more labor and a variety of very expensive machines to produce. They argue that the San Francisco factory labor cost alone would make the retail price absurdly high. After researching a dozen factories in China, Timbuk2 found one that it thinks is up to the task of producing these new bags. Much as in San Francisco, the China factory employs a team of hardworking craftspeople who earn good wages and an honest living. Timbuk2 visits the China factory every four to eight weeks to ensure superior quality standards and working conditions.

On the Timbuk2 Web site, the company argues they are the same hardworking group of bag fanatics designing and making great bags, and supporting our local community and increasingly competitive global market. The company reports that demand is still strong for the custom messenger bags made in San Francisco and that the new laptop bags sourced from China are receiving rave reviews. The additional business is allowing them to hire more people in all departments at the San Francisco headquarters—creating even more jobs locally.

*Special thanks to Kyle Cattani of Indiana University for this case.

Questions

1 Consider the two categories of products that Timbuk2 makes and sells. For the custom messenger bag, what are the key competitive dimensions that are driving sales? Are their competitive priorities different for the new laptop bags sourced in China?

2 Compare the assembly line in China to that in San Francisco along the following dimensions: (1) volume or rate of production, (2) required skill of the workers, (3) level of automation, and (4) amount of raw materials and finished goods inventory.

3 Draw two diagrams, one depicting the supply chain for those products sourced in China and the other depicting the bags produced in San Francisco. Show all the major steps, including raw material, manufacturing, finished goods, distribution inventory, and transportation. Other than manufacturing cost, what other costs should Timbuk2 consider when making the sourcing decision?

Selected Bibliography

Blamchard, David. *Supply Chain Management Best Practices*. New York: John Wiley & Sons, 2006.

Hayes, Robert; Gary Pisano; David Upton; and Steven Wheelwright. *Operations, Strategy, and Technology: Pursuing the Competitive Edge*. New York: John Wiley & Sons, 2004.

Hill, T. J. *Manufacturing Strategy—Text and Cases*. Burr Ridge; IL: Irwin/McGraw-Hill, 2000.

Slack, N., and M. Lewis. *Operations Strategy*. Harlow, England, and New York: Prentice Hall, 2002.

Super Quiz

1 A strategy that is designed to meet current needs without compromising the ability of future generations to meet their needs.

2 The three criteria included in a triple bottom line.

3 It is probably most difficult to compete on this major competitive dimension.

4 Name the seven operations and supply competitive dimensions.

5 This occurs when a company seeks to match what a competitor is doing while maintaining its existing competitve position.

6 A criterion that differentiates the products or services of one firm from those of another.

7 A screening criterion that permits a firm's products to be considered as possible candidates for purchase.

8 A diagram showing the activities that support a company's strategy.

9 A measure calculated by taking the ratio of output to input.

1. Sustainable 2. Social, economic, environmental 3. Cost 4. Cost, quality, delivery speed, delivery reliability, coping with changes in demand, flexibility and new product introduction speed, other product-specific criteria 5. Straddling 6. Order winner 7. Order qualifier 8. Activity-system map 9. Productivity

Footnote

[1] Elkington, J. "Toward the Sustainable Corporation: Win-win-win Business Strategies for Sustainable Development." *California Management Review* 36, no. 2: 90–100.

MANUFACTURING AND SERVICE PROCESSES

3. Strategic Capacity Management

4. Production Processes

5. Service Processes

6. Quality Management and Six-Sigma

7. Projects

PROCESSES

The second section of *Operations and Supply Management: The Core* is centered on the design and analysis of business processes. Maybe becoming an efficiency expert is not your dream, but it is important to learn the fundamentals. Have you ever wondered why you always have to wait in line at one store but another one seems to be on top of the crowds? The key to serving customers well, whether with products or with services, is having a great process.

We use processes to do most things. You probably have a regular process that you use every morning to get to work or school. What are the tasks associated with your process? Do you brush your teeth, take a shower, dress, make coffee, and read the paper? Have you ever thought about how the tasks should be ordered or what is the best way to execute each task? In making these decisions, you are allocating your own personal capacity.

This section is about designing efficient processes and allocating capacity for all types of businesses. Companies also need to develop a quality philosophy and integrate it into their processes. Actually, quality and process efficiency are closely related. Have you ever done something but then had to do it again because it was not done properly the first time? This section considers these subjects in both manufacturing and service industries.

THE ORIGINAL VERSION OF THE MOVIE *CHEAPER BY THE DOZEN* MADE IN THE 1950S WAS BASED UPON THE LIFE OF FRANK GILBRETH WHO INVENTED MOTION STUDY IN THE 1900S. GILBRETH WAS SO CONCERNED WITH PERSONAL EFFICIENCY THAT HE DID A STUDY OF WHETHER IT WAS FASTER AND MORE ACCURATE TO BUTTON ONE'S SEVEN BUTTON VEST FROM THE BOTTOM UP OR THE TOP DOWN. (ANSWER: BOTTOM UP!)

CHAPTER 3

STRATEGIC CAPACITY MANAGEMENT

After reading the chapter you will:

- Recognize the concept of capacity and how important it is to "manage" capacity.
- Explain the impact of economies of scale on the capacity of a firm.
- Understand how to use decision trees to analyze alternatives when faced with the problem of adding capacity.
- Describe the differences in planning capacity between manufacturing firms and service firms.

43   Shouldice Hospital: Hernia Surgery Innovation

44   Capacity Management in Operations
Strategic capacity planning defined

45   Capacity Planning Concepts
Capacity defined
Best operating level defined
Capacity utilization rate defined
Economies and Diseconomies of Scale   Economies of scale defined
Capacity Focus   Focused factory defined
Plant within a plant (PWP) defined
Capacity Flexibility   Economies of scope defined

47   Capacity Planning
Considerations in Changing Capacity
Determining Capacity Requirements   Capacity cushion defined
Using Decision Trees to Evaluate Capacity Alternatives

54   Planning Service Capacity
Capacity Planning in Service versus Manufacturing
Capacity Utilization and Service Quality

56   Summary

60   Case: Shouldice Hospital—A Cut Above

62   Super Quiz

SHOULDICE HOSPITAL: HERNIA SURGERY INNOVATION

During World War II, Dr. Edward Earle Shouldice, a major in the army, found that many young men willing to serve their country had to be denied enlistment because they needed surgical treatment to repair hernias before they could be pronounced physically fit for military training. In 1940, hospital space and doctors were scarce, especially for a nonemergency surgery that normally took three weeks of hospitalization. So, Dr. Shouldice resolved to do what he could to alleviate the problem. Contributing his services at no fee, he performed an innovative method of surgery on 70 of those men, speeding their induction into the army.

The recruits made their success stories known, and by the war's end, more than 200 civilians had contacted the doctor and were awaiting surgery. The limited availability of hospitals beds, however, created a major problem. There was only one solution: Dr. Shouldice decided to open his own hospital.

In July 1945, Shouldice Hospital, with a staff consisting of a nurse, a secretary, and a cook, opened its doors to its waiting patients. In a single operating room, Dr. Shouldice repaired two hernias per day. As requests for this surgery increased, Dr. Shouldice extended the facilities, located on Church Street in Toronto, by eventually buying three adjacent buildings and increasing the staff accordingly. In 1953, he purchased a country estate in Thornhill, where a second hospital was established.

Today all surgery takes place in Thornhill. Repeated development has culminated in the present 90-bed facility. Shouldice Hospital has been dedicated to the repair of hernias for over 55 years, using the "Shouldice Technique." The "formula," although not a secret, extends beyond the skill of surgeons and their ability to perform to the Shouldice standard. Shouldice Hospital is a total environment. Study the capacity problems with this special type of hospital in the case at the end of this chapter.

Source: Summarized from www.shouldice.com.

Manufacturing and service capacity investment decisions can be very complex. Consider some of the following difficult questions that need to be addressed:

- How long will it take to bring new capacity on stream? How does this match with the time that it takes to develop a new product?
- What will be the impact of not having sufficient capacity in the supply chain for a promising product?
- How large a facility should we build?
- When and how much capacity should we add to our existing facility?
- Should the firm use third-party contract manufacturers? How much of a premium will the contract manufacturer charge for providing flexibility in manufacturing volume?

In this chapter, we look at these tough strategic capacity decisions. We begin by discussing the nature of capacity from an OM perspective.

CAPACITY MANAGEMENT IN OPERATIONS

Service

A dictionary definition of capacity is "the ability to hold, receive, store, or accommodate." In a general business sense, it is most frequently viewed as the amount of output that a system is capable of achieving over a specific period of time. In a service setting, this might be the number of customers that can be handled between noon and 1:00 P.M. In manufacturing, this might be the number of automobiles that can be produced in a single shift.

When looking at capacity, operations managers need to look at both resource inputs *and* product outputs. For planning purposes, real (or effective) capacity depends on what is to be produced. For example, a firm that makes multiple products inevitably can produce more of one kind than of another with a given level of resource inputs. Thus, while the managers of an automobile factory may state that their facility has 6,000 production hours available per year, they are also thinking that these hours can be used to make either 150,000 two-door models or 120,000 four-door models (or some mix of the two- and four-door models). This reflects their knowledge of what their current technology and labor force inputs can produce and the product mix that is to be demanded from these resources.

An operations management view also emphasizes the time dimension of capacity. That is, capacity must also be stated relative to some period of time. This is evidenced in the common distinction drawn between long-range, intermediate-range, and short-range capacity planning.

Capacity planning is generally viewed in three time durations:

Long range—greater than one year. Where productive resources (such as buildings, equipment, or facilities) take a long time to acquire or dispose of, long-range capacity planning requires top management participation and approval.

Intermediate range—monthly or quarterly plans for the next 6 to 18 months. Here, capacity may be varied by such alternatives as hiring, layoffs, new tools, minor equipment purchases, and subcontracting.

Short range—less than one month. This is tied into the daily or weekly scheduling process and involves making adjustments to eliminate the variance between planned and actual output. This includes alternatives such as overtime, personnel transfers, and alternative production routings.

Although there is no one person with the job title "capacity manager," there are several managerial positions charged with the effective use of capacity. *Capacity* is a relative term; in an operations management context, it may be defined as *the amount of resource inputs available relative to output requirements over a particular period of time.*

The objective of **strategic capacity planning** is to provide an approach for determining the overall capacity level of capital-intensive resources—facilities, equipment, and overall labor force size—that best supports the company's long-range competitive strategy. The capacity level selected has a critical impact on the firm's response rate, its cost structure, its inventory policies, and its management and staff support requirements. If capacity is inadequate, a company may lose customers through slow service or by allowing competitors to enter the market. If capacity is excessive, a company may have to reduce prices to stimulate demand; underutilize its workforce; carry excess inventory; or seek additional, less profitable products to stay in business.

Strategic capacity planning

CAPACITY PLANNING CONCEPTS

The term **capacity** implies an attainable rate of output, for example, 480 cars per day, but says nothing about how long that rate can be sustained. Thus, we do not know if this 480 cars per day is a one-day peak or a six-month average. To avoid this problem, the concept of **best operating level** is used. This is the level of capacity for which the process was designed and thus is the volume of output at which average unit cost is minimized. Determining this minimum is difficult because it involves a complex trade-off between the allocation of fixed overhead costs and the cost of overtime, equipment wear, defect rates, and other costs.

Capacity

Best operating level

An important measure is the **capacity utilization rate**, which reveals how close a firm is to its best operating level:

Capacity utilization rate

$$Capacity\ utilization\ rate = \frac{Capacity\ used}{Best\ operating\ level} \qquad \textbf{[3.1]}$$

So, for example, if our plant's *best operating level* were 500 cars per day and the plant was currently operating at 480 cars per day, the *capacity utilization rate* would be 96 percent.

$$Capacity\ utilization\ rate = \frac{480}{500} = .96\ or\ 96\%$$

The capacity utilization rate is expressed as a percentage and requires that the numerator and denominator be measured in the same units and time periods (such as machine hours/day, barrels of oil/day, dollars of output/day).

Economies and Diseconomies of Scale

The basic notion of **economies of scale** is that as a plant gets larger and volume increases, the average cost per unit of output drops. This is partially due to lower operating and capital cost, because a piece of equipment with twice the capacity of another piece typically does not cost twice as much to purchase or operate. Plants also gain efficiencies when they become large enough to fully utilize dedicated resources (people and equipment) for information technology, material handling, and administrative support.

Economies of scale

At some point, the size of a plant becomes too large and diseconomies of scale become a problem. These diseconomies may surface in many different ways. For example, maintaining the demand required to keep the large facility busy may require significant discounting of the product. The U.S. automobile manufacturers continually face this problem. Another typical example involves using a few large-capacity pieces of equipment. Minimizing

Global

equipment downtime is essential in this type of operation. M&M Mars, for example, has highly automated, high-volume equipment to make M&Ms. A single packaging line moves 2.6 million M&Ms each hour. Even though direct labor to operate the equipment is very low, the labor required to maintain the equipment is high.

In many cases, the size of a plant may be influenced by factors other than the internal equipment, labor, and other capital expenditures. A major factor may be the cost to transport raw materials and finished product to and from the plant. A cement factory, for example, would have a difficult time serving customers more than a few hours from its plant. Similarly, automobile companies such as Ford, Honda, Nissan, and Toyota have found it advantageous to locate plants within specific international markets. The anticipated size of these intended markets will largely dictate the size and capacity of the plants.

Jaguar, the luxury automobile producer, recently found they had too many plants. Jaguar was employing 8,560 workers in three plants that produced 126,122 cars, about 14 cars per employee. In comparison, Volvo's plant in Torslanda, Sweden, was more than twice as productive, building 158,466 cars with 5,472 workers, or 29 cars per employee. By contrast, BMW AG's Mini unit made 174,000 vehicles at a single British plant with just 4,500 workers (39 cars per employee).

Capacity Focus

Focused factory

The concept of a **focused factory** holds that a production facility works best when it focuses on a fairly limited set of production objectives. This means, for example, that a firm should not expect to excel in every aspect of manufacturing performance: cost, quality, delivery speed and reliability, changes in demand, and flexibility to adapt to new products. Rather, it should select a limited set of tasks that contribute the most to corporate objectives. Typically the focused factory would produce a specific product or related group of products. A focused factory allows capacity to be focused on producing those specific items.

Plant within a plant (PWP)

The capacity focus concept can be operationalized through the mechanism of **plant within a plant**—or **PWP**. A focused factory (see Exhibit 3.1) may have several PWPs, each of which may have separate suborganizations, equipment and process policies, workforce management policies, production control methods, and so forth for different products—even if they are made under the same roof. This, in effect, permits finding the best operating level for each department of the organization and thereby carries the focus concept down to the operating level.

Capacity Flexibility

Capacity flexibility means having the ability to rapidly increase or decrease production levels, or to shift production capacity quickly from one product or service to another. Such flexibility is achieved through flexible plants, processes, and workers, as well as through strategies that use the capacity of other organizations. Increasingly, companies are taking the idea of flexibility into account as they design their supply chains. Working with suppliers, they can build capacity into their whole systems.

exhibit 3.1

Focused Factories—Plant-Within-Plant

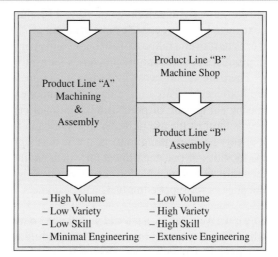

A FACILITY THAT IS ILL-DESIGNED, ATTEMPTS TOO MUCH OR IS OPTIMIZED FOR THE WRONG TASK AND CAN BE A MILLSTONE.

FACILITY PLANNING CAN HELP ADDRESS THIS STRATEGIC ISSUE USING THE "PLANT-WITHIN-PLANT" CONCEPT.

HERE, THE PLANT LAYOUT HAS REGIONS THAT BECOME, ESSENTIALLY, STANDALONE FACTORIES. EACH HAS (AT LEAST SUBSTANTIALLY) ITS OWN AREA AND INFRASTRUCTURE SUCH AS MAINTENANCE, PURCHASING AND ENGINEERING.

THE FIGURE ILLUSTRATES THIS WITH AN EXAMPLE. TWO MAJOR PRODUCT LINES HAD CONFLICTING DEMANDS FROM CUSTOMERS AND CONFLICTING DEMANDS ON THE FACTORY'S INFRASTRUCTURE. IN ADDITION, ONE OF THE PRODUCT LINES HAD HIGHLY DISSIMILAR PROCESSES. THE FACTORY WAS SPLIT INTO THREE FOCUSED FACTORIES, AS SHOWN.

Flexible Plants Perhaps the ultimate in plant flexibility is the *zero-changeover-time* plant. Using movable equipment, knockdown walls, and easily accessible and reroutable utilities, such a plant can quickly adapt to change. An analogy to a familiar service business captures the flavor well: a plant with equipment "that is easy to install and easy to tear down and move—like the Ringling Bros.–Barnum and Bailey Circus in the old tent-circus days."

Flexible Processes Flexible processes are epitomized by flexible manufacturing systems on the one hand and simple, easily set up equipment on the other. Both of these technological approaches permit rapid low-cost switching from one product to another, enabling what are sometimes referred to as **economies of scope**. (By definition, economies of scope exist when multiple products can be combined and produced at one facility, at a lower cost than they can be produced separately.)

Economies of scope

Flexible Workers Flexible workers have multiple skills and the ability to switch easily from one kind of task to another. They require broader training than specialized workers and need managers and staff support to facilitate quick changes in their work assignments.

CAPACITY PLANNING

Considerations in Changing Capacity

Many issues must be considered when adding or decreasing capacity. Three important ones are maintaining system balance, frequency of capacity additions or reductions, and the use of external capacity.

Maintaining System Balance In a perfectly balanced plant, the output of stage 1 provides the exact input requirement for stage 2. Stage 2's output provides the exact input requirement for stage 3, and so on. In practice, however, achieving such a "perfect" design is usually both impossible and undesirable. One reason is that the best operating levels for each stage generally differ. For instance, department 1 may operate most efficiently over a range of 90 to 110 units per month, whereas department 2, the next stage in the process, is most efficient at 75 to 85 units per month, and department 3 works best over a range of 150 to 200 units per month. Another reason is that variability in product demand and the processes themselves may lead to imbalance.

There are various ways of dealing with imbalance. One is to add capacity to stages that are bottlenecks. This can be done by temporary measures such as scheduling overtime, leasing equipment, or purchasing additional capacity through subcontracting. A second way is through the use of buffer inventories in front of the bottleneck stage to ensure that it always has something to work on. A third approach involves duplicating or increasing the facilities of one department on which another is dependent. All these approaches are increasingly being applied to supply chain design. This supply planning also helps reduce imbalances for supplier partners and customers.

Supply Chain

Frequency of Capacity Additions There are two types of costs to consider when adding capacity: the cost of upgrading too frequently and that of upgrading too infrequently. Upgrading capacity too frequently is expensive. Direct costs include removing and replacing old equipment and training employees on the new equipment. In addition, the new equipment must be purchased, often for considerably more than the selling price of the old. Finally, there is the opportunity cost of idling the plant or service site during the changeover period.

Conversely, upgrading capacity too infrequently is also expensive. Infrequent expansion means that capacity is purchased in larger chunks. Any excess capacity that is purchased must be carried as overhead until it is utilized. (Exhibit 3.2 illustrates frequent versus infrequent capacity expansion.)

External Sources of Operations and Supply Capacity In some cases, it may be cheaper to not add capacity at all, but rather to use some existing external source of capacity. Two common strategies used by organizations are outsourcing and sharing capacity. An example of outsourcing is Dell Computer using a Chinese company to assemble their notebook computers. An example of sharing capacity is two domestic airlines flying different routes with different seasonal demands exchanging aircraft (suitably repainted) when one's routes are heavily used and the other's are not. A new twist is airlines sharing routes—using the same flight number even though the airline company may change through the route. Outsourcing is covered in more depth in Chapter 8.

Decreasing Capacity Although we normally think in terms of expansions, shedding capacity in response to decreased demand can create significant problems for a firm. Temporary strategies such as scheduling fewer hours or scheduling an extended shutdown period are often used. More permanent reductions in capacity would typically require the sale of equipment or possibly even the liquidation of entire facilities.

Determining Capacity Requirements

In determining capacity requirements, we must address the demands for individual product lines, individual plant capabilities, and allocation of production throughout the plant network. Typically this is done according to the following steps:

1. Use forecasting techniques (see Chapter 11) to predict sales for individual products within each product line.

exhibit 3.2

Frequent versus Infrequent Capacity Expansion

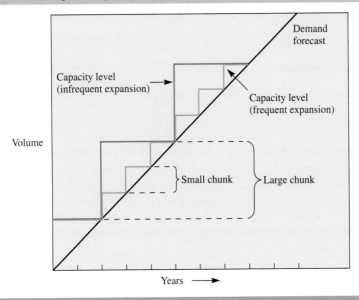

2. Calculate equipment and labor requirements to meet product line forecasts.
3. Project labor and equipment availabilities over the planning horizon.

Often the firm then decides on some **capacity cushion** that will be maintained between the projected requirements and the actual capacity. A capacity cushion is an amount of capacity in excess of expected demand. For example, if the expected annual demand on a facility is $10 million in products per year and the design capacity is $12 million per year, it has a 20 percent capacity cushion. A 20 percent capacity cushion equates to an 83 percent utilization rate (100%/120%).

When a firm's design capacity is less than the capacity required to meet its demand, it is said to have a negative capacity cushion. If, for example, a firm has a demand of $12 million in products per year but can produce only $10 million per year, it has a negative capacity cushion of 16.7 percent.

We now apply these three steps to an example.

Capacity cushion

Example 3.1: Determining Capacity Requirements

The Stewart Company produces two flavors of salad dressings: Paul's and Newman's. Each is available in bottles and single-serving plastic bags. Management would like to determine equipment and labor requirements for the next five years.

Step by Step

SOLUTION

Step 1. Use forecasting techniques to predict sales for individual products within each product line. The marketing department, which is now running a promotional campaign for Newman's dressing, provided the following forecast demand values (in thousands) for the next five years. The campaign is expected to continue for the next two years.

	YEAR				
	1	2	3	4	5
PAUL'S					
Bottles (000s)	60	100	150	200	250
Plastic bags (000s)	100	200	300	400	500
NEWMAN'S					
Bottles (000s)	75	85	95	97	98
Plastic bags (000s)	200	400	600	650	680

Step 2. Calculate equipment and labor requirements to meet product line forecasts. Currently, three machines that can package up to 150,000 bottles each per year are available. Each machine requires two operators and can produce bottles of both Newman's and Paul's dressings. Six bottle machine operators are available. Also, five machines that can package up to 250,000 plastic bags each per year are available. Three operators are required for each machine, which can produce plastic bags of both Newman's and Paul's dressings. Currently, 20 plastic bag machine operators are available.

Total product line forecasts can be calculated from the preceding table by adding the yearly demand for bottles and plastic bags as follows:

Excel: Capacity

	YEAR				
	1	2	3	4	5
Bottles (000s)	135	185	245	297	348
Plastic bags (000s)	300	600	900	1,050	1,180

We can now calculate equipment and labor requirements for the current year (year 1). Because the total available capacity for packaging bottles is 450,000/year (3 machines × 150,000 each), we will be using 135/450 = 0.3 of the available capacity for the current year, or 0.3 × 3 = 0.9 machine. Similarly, we will need 300/1,250 = 0.24 of the available capacity for plastic bags for the current year, or 0.24 × 5 = 1.2 machines. The number of crew required to support our forecast demand for the first year will consist of the crew required for the bottle and the plastic bag machines.

The labor requirement for year 1's bottle operation is

$$0.9 \text{ bottle machine} \times 2 \text{ operators} = 1.8 \text{ operators}$$
$$1.2 \text{ bag machines} \times 3 \text{ operators} = 3.6 \text{ operators}$$

Step 3. Project labor and equipment availabilities over the planning horizon. We repeat the preceding calculations for the remaining years:

	YEAR				
	1	2	3	4	5
PLASTIC BAG OPERATION					
Percentage capacity utilized	24	48	72	84	94
Machine requirement	1.2	2.4	3.6	4.2	4.7
Labor requirement	3.6	7.2	10.8	12.6	14.1
BOTTLE OPERATION					
Percentage capacity utilized	30	41	54	66	77
Machine requirement	.9	1.23	1.62	1.98	2.31
Labor requirement	1.8	2.46	3.24	3.96	4.62

A positive capacity cushion exists for all five years because the available capacity for both operations always exceeds the expected demand. The Stewart Company can now begin to develop the

$450,000 over the next three years. Which alternative should we select and what is the expected value of the expansion? Assume a 10 percent interest rate.

8 In a service process such as the checkout counter in a discount store, a good target for capacity utilization is about this percent.

1. Best operating level 2. 85% 3. Economies of scale 4. Focused factory 5. Economies of scope 6. Capacity cushion 7. Alternative 1 Present Value = 500,000 × (.909 + .826 + .751) − 1,000,000 = $243,000, Alternative 2 Present Value = 450,000 × (.909 + .826 + .751) − 800,000 = $318,700, Alternative 2 is best 8. 70 percent

Selected Bibliography

Wright, T. P. "Factors Affecting the Cost of Airplanes." *Journal of Aeronautical Sciences,* February 1936, pp. 122–128.

Yu-Lee, R. T. *Essentials of Capacity Management.* New York: Wiley, 2002.

CHAPTER 4

PRODUCTION PROCESSES

After reading the chapter, you will:

- Understand the idea of production process mapping.
- Define Little's law.
- Demonstrate how production processes are organized.
- Explain the trade-offs that need to be considered when designing production processes.
- Describe the product-process matrix.
- Recognize how break-even analysis is just as important in operations and supply chain management as it is in other functional areas.
- Understand how to design and analyze an assembly line.

65	Toshiba: Producer of the First Notebook Computer	
66	Production Processes	
		Lead time defined
		Customer order decoupling point defined
		Make-to-stock defined
		Assemble-to-order defined
		Make-to-order defined
		Engineer-to-order defined
		Lean manufacturing defined
	Production Process Mapping	Total average value of inventory defined
	and Little's Law	Inventory turn defined
		Days-of-supply defined
		Little's law defined
		Throughput defined
		Flow time defined
72	How Production Processes Are Organized	
		Project layout defined
		Workcenter defined
		Manufacturing cell defined
		Assembly line defined
		Continuous process defined
		Product–process matrix defined

73   Break-Even Analysis

75   Designing a Production System
        Project Layout
        Workcenters
        Manufacturing Cell
        Assembly Line and Continuous Process Layouts

78   Assembly-Line Design
        Splitting Tasks   Workstation cycle time defined
        Flexible and U-Shaped Line Layouts   Assembly-line balancing defined
        Mixed-Model Line Balancing   Precedence relationship defined

85   Summary

93   Case: Designing Toshiba's Notebook Computer Line

96   Super Quiz

TOSHIBA: PRODUCER OF THE FIRST NOTEBOOK COMPUTER

Tokyo Shibaura Denki (Tokyo Shibaura Electric Co. Ltd) was formed in 1939 by a merger of two highly innovative Japanese companies: Shibaura Seisaku-sho (Shibaura Engineering Works), which manufactured transformers, electrical motors, hydroelectric generators, and x-ray tubes, and Tokyo Electric Company, which produced lightbulbs, radio receivers, and cathode-ray tubes. The company was soon after known as "Toshiba," which became its official name in 1978. Toshiba became the first company in Japan to make fluorescent lamps (1940), radar (1942), broadcasting equipment (1952), and digital computers (1954). Toshiba also

became the first in the world to produce the powerful 1-megabit DRAM chip and the first laptop computer, the T3100, both in 1985.

Toshiba has built its strength in the notebook PC market by beating its competitors to the market with aggressively priced, technologically innovative products. Competition in the notebook PC market is fierce, and Toshiba can retain its position as a market leader only by relentlessly improving its manufacturing processes and lowering its costs.

Dell Computer is a formidable competitor and seeks to minimize its costs by assembling to order and selling directly to customers. Toshiba has some significant advantages over Dell that stem largely from huge investments in technologies such as thin-film transistor (TFT) color displays, hard disk drives, lithium-ion batteries, and DVD drives. In addition, by forming partnerships and joint ventures with other industry giants, Toshiba can share the risk of developing expensive new technologies.

Put yourself in the position of Toshihiro Nakamura, the production supervisor at Toshiba's Ome Works plant. Production of Toshiba's latest subnotebook computer is scheduled to begin in only 10 days. As he wends his way through a maze of desks, heading to the factory floor, he wonders if it is really feasible to get the line designed in time.

Read the details related to designing the new assembly line in the case at the end of this chapter titled "Designing Toshiba's Notebook Computer Line."

Global

Source: Adapted from *Toshiba: Ome Works,* Harvard Business School (9-696-059) and www.toshiba.co.jp/worldwide/about/history.html.

PRODUCTION PROCESSES

In this chapter we consider how processes used to make tangible goods are designed. Production processes are used to make everything that we buy ranging from the apartment building in which we live to the ink pens with which we write. The high-level view of what is required to make something can be divided into three simple steps. The first step is sourcing the parts we need, followed by actually making the item, and then sending the item to the customer. As discussed in Chapter 1, a supply chain view of this may involve a complex series of players where subcontractors feed suppliers, suppliers feed manufacturing plants, manufacturing plants feed warehouses, and finally warehouses feed retailers. Depending on the item being produced, the supply chain can be very long with subcontractors and manufacturing plants spread out over the globe (such as an automobile or computer manufacturer) or short where parts are sourced and the product made locally (such as a house builder).

Consider Exhibit 4.1, which illustrates the Source step where parts are procured from one or more suppliers, the Make step where manufacturing takes place, and the Deliver step where the product is shipped to the customer. Depending on the strategy of the firm, the capabilities of manufacturing, and the needs of customers, these activities are organized to minimize cost while meeting the competitive priorities necessary to attract customer orders. For example, in the case of consumer products such as DVDs or clothes, customers normally want these products "on-demand" for quick delivery from a local department store. As a manufacturer of these products, we build them ahead of time in anticipation of demand and ship them to the retail stores where they are carried in inventory until they are sold. At the other end of the spectrum are custom products, such as military airplanes, that are ordered with very specific uses in mind and that need to be designed and then built to

exhibit 4.1

Positioning Inventory in the Supply Chain

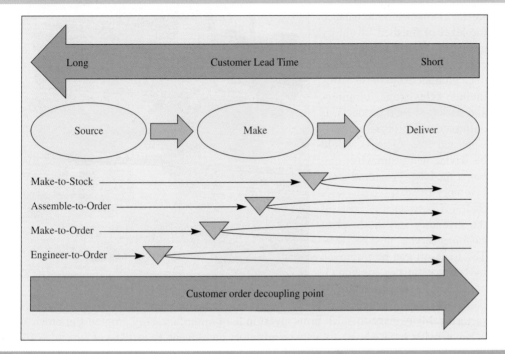

the design. In the case of an airplane, the time needed to respond to a customer order, called the **lead time**, could easily be years compared to only a few minutes for the DVD.

A key concept in production processes is the **customer order decoupling point** which determines where inventory is positioned to allow processes or entities in the supply chain to operate independently. For example, if a product is stocked at a retailer, the customer pulls the item from the shelf and the manufacturer never sees a customer order. Inventory acts as a buffer to separate the customer from the manufacturing process. Selection of decoupling points is a strategic decision that determines customer lead times and can greatly impact inventory investment. The closer this point is to the customer, the quicker the customer can be served. Typically, there is a trade-off where quicker response to customer demand comes at the expense of greater inventory investment because finished goods inventory is more expensive than raw material inventory. An item in finished goods inventory typically contains all the raw materials needed to produce the item. So from a cost view it includes the cost of the material plus the cost to fabricate the finished item.

Positioning of the customer order decoupling point is important to understanding production environments. Firms that serve customers from finished goods inventory are known as **make-to-stock** firms. Those that combine a number of preassembled modules to meet a customer's specifications are called **assemble-to-order** firms. Those that make the customer's product from raw materials, parts, and components are **make-to-order** firms. An **engineer-to-order** firm will work with the customer to design the product, and then make it from purchased materials, parts, and components. Of course, many firms serve a combination of these environments and a few will have all simultaneously. Depending on the environment and the location of the customer order decoupling point, one would expect inventory concentrated in finished goods, work-in-process (this is inventory in the manufacturing process), manufacturing raw material, or at the supplier as shown in Exhibit 4.1.

Lead time
Customer order decoupling point

Make-to-stock
Assemble-to-order
Make-to-order
Engineer-to-order

The essential issue in satisfying customers in the make-to-stock environment is to balance the level of finished inventory against the level of service to the customer. Examples of products produced by these firms include televisions, clothing, and packaged food products. If unlimited inventory were possible and free, the task would be trivial. Unfortunately, that is not the case. Providing more inventory increases costs, so a trade-off between the costs of the inventory and the level of customer service must be made. The trade-off can be improved by better estimates (or knowledge) of customer demand, by

more rapid transportation alternatives, by speedier production, and by more flexible manu-

Lean manufacturing   facturing. Many make-to-stock firms invest in **lean manufacturing** programs in order to achieve higher service levels for a given inventory investment. Regardless of the trade-offs involved, the focus in the make-to-stock environment is on providing finished goods where and when the customers want them.

In the assemble-to-order environment, a primary task is to define a customer's order in terms of alternative components and options since it is these components that are carried in inventory. A good example is the way Dell Computer makes their desktop computers. The number of combinations that can be made may be nearly infinite (although some might not be feasible). One of the capabilities required for success in the assemble-to-order environment is an engineering design that enables as much flexibility as possible in combining components, options, and modules into finished products. Similar to make-to-stock, many assemble-to-order companies have applied lean manufacturing principles to dramatically decrease the time required to assemble finished goods. By doing so they are delivering customers' order so quickly that they appear to be make-to-stock firms from the perspective of the customer.

When assembling-to-order there are significant advantages from moving the customer order decoupling point from finished goods to components. The number of finished products is usually substantially greater than the number of components that are combined to produce the finished product. Consider, for example, a computer for which there are four processor alternatives, three hard disk drive choices, four DVD alternatives, two speaker systems, and four monitors available. If all combinations of these 17 components are valid, they can be combined into a total of 384 different final configurations. This can be calculated as follows:

If N_i is the number of alternatives for component I, the total number of combinations of n components (given all are viable) is:

$$\text{Total number of combinations} = N_1 \times N_2 \times \cdots \times N_n \qquad \textbf{[4.1]}$$
$$\text{Or } 384 = 4 \times 3 \times 4 \times 2 \times 4 \text{ for this example.}$$

It is much easier to manage and forecast the demand for 17 components than for 384 computers.

In the make-to-order and engineer-to-order environments the customer order decoupling point could be in either raw materials at the manufacturing site or possibly even with the supplier inventory. Boeing's process for making commercial aircraft is an example of make-to-order. The need for engineering resources in the engineer-to-order case is somewhat different than make-to-order since engineering determines what materials will be required, and what steps will be required in manufacturing. Depending on how similar the products are it might not even be possible to pre-order parts. Rather than inventory, the emphasis in these environments may be more toward managing capacity of critical resources such as engineering and construction crews. Lockheed Martin's Satellite division uses an engineer-to-order strategy.

Production Process Mapping and Little's Law

Supply Chain

Next, we look at how to quickly develop a high-level map of a supply chain process, which can be useful to understand how material flows and where inventory is held. The approach used here should be the first step in analyzing the flow of material through a production process. This idea will be further developed in "Value Stream Mapping" in Chapter 9.

Consider a simple system that might be typical of many make-to-stock companies. As shown in Exhibit 4.2, material is purchased from a set of suppliers and initially staged in raw material inventory. The material is used in a manufacturing process where the product is fabricated (different types of manufacturing processes are discussed in the next section, "How Production Processes Are Organized"). After fabrication, the product is put into finished goods inventory and from here it is shipped according to orders received from customers.

Focusing on the Make part of the process, it is useful to analyze how this step operates using performance measures that relate to the inventory investment and also how quickly material flows through the process. A simplified way of thinking about material in a process is that it is in one of two states. The first state is where material is moving or "in-transit." The second state is material that is sitting in inventory and acting as a "buffer" waiting to be used.

In the first state, material is moving in the process. This is material that is in-transit between entities in the process, for example, between the vendor and the raw material inventory at the manufacturer. Material that is in a manufacturing process in a factory can also be considered in-transit. Actually, we refer to this material as "work-in-process" inventory. In the second state, material is held in a storage area and waits until it is needed. In the case of raw material inventory, the need is dependent on the factory usage of the item. This "buffer" inventory allows different entities in the process to operate relatively independently.

A common measure is the **total average value of inventory** in the process. From an accounting view this would be the sum of the value (at cost) of the raw material,

Total average value of inventory

Make-to-Stock Process Map

exhibit 4.2

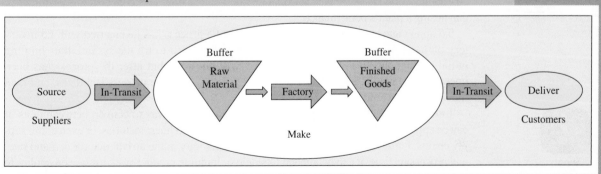

Inventory turn

work-in-process, and finished goods inventory. This is commonly tracked in accounting systems and reported in the firm's financial statements. In addition to the total value of this inventory, another measure is the firm's **inventory turn**, which is the cost of goods sold divided by the average inventory value. Although useful for accounting purposes, these measures are not particularly useful for evaluating the performance of a process. Consider the total average value of inventory. What is better, a firm that has $2 million worth of inventory on average or one that has $4 million? This depends greatly on the size of the firm, the type of strategy being used (make-to-order or make-to-stock, for example), and the relative cost of the product being produced.

A better measure than the total value of inventory is inventory turn. Since inventory turn scales the amount of inventory by dividing by the cost of goods sold, this provides a relative measure that has some comparability, at least across similar firms. For two similar consumer products manufacturers, an inventory turn of six times per year is certainly much

Days-of-supply

better than a firm turning inventory two times per year. A measure directly related is **days-of-supply**, which is the inverse of inventory turn scaled to days. For example, if a firm turns inventory six times per year, the days of supply is equal to one-sixth times per year or approximately every 61 days (this is calculated as 1/6 year × 365 days/year = 60.8 days).

Little's law

Simple systems can be analyzed quickly using a principle known as **Little's law**. Little's law says there is a long-term relationship between the inventory, throughput, and flow time of a production system in steady state. The relationship is:

$$Inventory = Throughput\ rate \times Flow\ time \qquad \textbf{[4.2]}$$

Throughput
Flow time

Throughput is the long term average rate that items are flowing through the process. **Flow time** is the time that it takes a unit to flow through the process from beginning to end. Consider the Factory process in Exhibit 4.2. Raw material is brought into the factory and is transformed and then stored in finished goods inventory. The analysis assumes that the process is operating in "steady state," meaning that over a long enough period of time the amount that is produced by the factory is equal to the amount shipped to customers. The throughput rate of the process is equal to average demand, and the process is not producing any excess or shortage. If this was not true and the amount produced by the manufacturing process was greater than demand, for example, the finished goods inventory would build over time. So if demand averages 1,000 units per day and if it takes 20 days for a unit to flow through the factory, then the expected work-in-process in the factory would be 20,000 units.

We can think of Little's law as a relationship between units and time. Inventory is measured in pieces, flow time in days, and throughput in pieces per day. Therefore, if we divide inventory by throughput we get flow time. For example, 20,000 units divided by 1,000 units per day is 20 days. We can also take inventory and divide by flow time and get throughput rate. Here 20,000 units divided by 20 days is equal to 1,000 units a day. This conversion is useful when diagnosing a plant's performance.

To appreciate a major limitation, suppose that a process has just started with no inventory on hand. Some of the initial production will be used to fill the system, thus limiting initial throughput. In this case Little's law will not hold, but after the process has been operating for awhile, and there is inventory at every step, the process stabilizes, and then the relationship holds.

Little's law is actually much more general than a simple way to convert between units. It can be applied to single work stations, multistep production lines, factories, or even entire supply chains. Further, it applies to processes with variability in the arrival rate (or demand rate) and processing time. It can be applied to single or multiple product systems. It even applies to nonproduction systems where inventory represents people, financial orders, or other entities.

**Supply
Chain**

For our factory, it is common for accounting systems to capture average work-in-process in terms of the value (at cost) of the inventory that is being worked on in the factory. For our example, say that work-in-process averages $200,000 and that each unit is valued at cost at $10.00. This would imply that there are 20,000 units in the factory (calculated $200,000 ÷ $10.00 per unit = 20,000 units).

The following example shows how these concepts can be applied to quickly analyze simple processes.

Example 4.1

An automobile company assembles cars in a plant and purchases batteries from a vendor in China. The average cost of each battery is $45. The automobile company takes ownership of the batteries when they arrive at the plant. It takes exactly 12 hours to make a car in the plant and the plant assembles 200 cars per 8 hour shift (currently the plant operates one shift per day). Each car uses one battery. The company holds on average 8,000 batteries in raw material inventory at the plant as a buffer. Assignment: Find the total number of batteries in the plant on average (in work-in-process at the plant and in raw material inventory). How much are these batteries worth? How many days of supply are held in raw material inventory on average?

Global

Step by Step

SOLUTION

We can split this into two inventories, work-in-process and raw material. For the work-in-process, Little's law can be directly applied to find the amount of work-in-process inventory:

$$Inventory = Throughput \times Flow\ time$$

Throughput is the production rate of the plant, 200 cars per 8 hour shift or 25 cars per hour. Since we use one battery per car, our throughput rate for the batteries is 25 per hour. Flow time is 12 hours, so the work-in-process is:

$$Work\text{-}in\text{-}process\ inventory = 25\ batteries/hour \times 12\ hours = 300\ batteries$$

We know from the problem there are 8,000 batteries in raw material inventory, so the total number of batteries in the pipeline on average is:

$$Total\ inventory = 8,000 + 300 = 8,300\ batteries$$

These batteries are worth 8,300 × $45 = $373,500.

The days of supply in raw material inventory in the "flow time" for a battery in raw material inventory (or the average amount of time that a battery spends in raw material inventory). Here, we need to assume that they are used in the same order they arrive. Rearranging our Little's law formula:

$$Flow\ time = Inventory/Throughput$$

So, Flow time = 8,000 batteries/(200 batteries/day) = 40 days which represents a 40 day supply of inventory.

In the next section, we look at how the production processes are organized in different environments. This is largely dependent on the variety of products being produced and on the volume. How a company produces airplanes is very different when compared to building computers or making ink pens.

HOW PRODUCTION PROCESSES ARE ORGANIZED

Process selection refers to the strategic decision of selecting which kind of production processes to use to produce a product or provide a service. For example, in the case of Toshiba notebook computers, if the volume is very low, we may just have a worker manually assemble each computer by hand. In contrast, if the volume is higher, setting up an assembly line is appropriate.

The formats by which a facility is arranged are defined by the general pattern of work flow; there are five basic structures (project, workcenter, manufacturing cell, assembly line, and continuous process).

Project layout

In a **project layout**, the product (by virtue of its bulk or weight) remains in a fixed location. Manufacturing equipment is moved to the product rather than vice versa. Construction sites (houses and bridges) and movie shooting lots are examples of this format. Items produced with this type of layout are typically managed using the project management techniques described in Chapter 7. Areas on the site will be designated for various purposes, such as material staging, subassembly construction, site access for heavy equipment, and a management area.

Workcenter

A **workcenter** layout, sometimes referred to as a job shop, is where similar equipment or functions are grouped together, such as all drilling machines in one area and all stamping machines in another. A part being worked on travels, according to the established sequence of operations, from workcenter to workcenter, where the proper machines are located for each operation.

Manufacturing cell

A **manufacturing cell** layout is a dedicated area where products that are similar in processing requirements are produced. These cells are designed to perform a specific set of processes, and the cells are dedicated to a limited range of products. A firm may have many different cells in a production area, each set up to produce a single product or a similar group of products efficiently. These cells typically are scheduled to produce "as needed" in response to current customer demand.

Assembly line

An **assembly line** is where work processes are arranged according to the progressive steps by which the product is made. The path for each part is, in effect, a straight line. Discrete products are made by moving from workstation to workstation at a controlled rate, following the sequence needed to build the product. Examples include the assembly of toys, appliances, and automobiles.

Continuous process

A **continuous process** is similar to an assembly line in that production follows a predetermined sequence of steps, but the flow is continuous such as with liquids, rather than discrete. Such structures are usually highly automated and, in effect, constitute one integrated "machine" that may operate 24 hours a day to avoid expensive shutdowns and start-ups. Conversion and processing of undifferentiated materials such as petroleum, chemicals, and drugs are good examples.

Product–process matrix

The relationship between layout structures is often depicted on a **product–process matrix** similar to the one shown in Exhibit 4.3. Two dimensions are shown. The first dimension relates to the volume of a particular product or group of standardized products. Standardization is shown on the vertical axis and refers to variations in the product that is produced. These variations are measured in terms of geometric differences, material differences, and so on. Standardized products are highly similar from a manufacturing processing point of view, whereas low standardized products require different processes.

Exhibit 4.3 shows the processes approximately on a diagonal. In general, it can be argued that it is desirable to design processes along the diagonal. For example, if we produce nonstandard products at relatively low volumes, workcenters should be used. A highly

exhibit 4.3

Product–Process Matrix: Framework Describing Layout Strategies

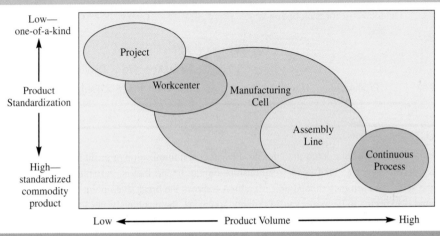

standardized product (commodity) produced at high volumes should be produced using an assembly line or a continuous process, if possible. As a result of the advanced manufacturing technology available today, we see that some of the layout structures span relatively large areas of the product–process matrix. For example, manufacturing cells can be used for a very wide range of applications, and this has become a popular layout structure that often is employed by manufacturing engineers.

BREAK-EVEN ANALYSIS

The choice of which specific equipment to use in a process often can be based on an analysis of cost trade-offs. In the product–process matrix (Exhibit 4.3) there is often a trade-off between more and less specialized equipment. Less specialized equipment is referred to as "general-purpose," meaning that it can be used easily in many different ways if it is set up in the proper way. More specialized equipment, referred to as "special-purpose," is often available as an alternative to a general-purpose machine. For example, if we need to drill holes in a piece of metal, the general-purpose option may be to use a simple hand drill. An alternative special-purpose drill is a drill press. Given the proper setup, the drill press can drill holes much quicker than the hand drill can. The trade-offs involve the cost of the equipment (the manual drill is inexpensive, and the drill press expensive), the setup time (the manual drill is quick, while the drill press takes some time), and the time per unit (the manual drill is slow, and the drill press quick).

A standard approach to choosing among alternative processes or equipment is *break-even analysis*. A break-even chart visually presents alternative profits and losses due to the number of units produced or sold. The choice obviously depends on anticipated demand. The method is most suitable when processes and equipment entail a large initial investment and fixed cost, and when variable costs are reasonably proportional to the number of units produced.

Example 4.2: Break-Even Analysis

Suppose a manufacturer has identified the following options for obtaining a machined part: It can buy the part at $200 per unit (including materials); it can make the part on a numerically controlled semiautomatic lathe at $75 per unit (including materials); or it can make the part on a machining

**Tutorial:
Breakeven
Analysis**

center at $15 per unit (including materials). There is negligible fixed cost if the item is purchased; a semiautomatic lathe costs $80,000; and a machining center costs $200,000.

The total cost for each option is

Step by Step

$$\text{Purchase cost} = \$200 \times \text{Demand}$$
$$\text{Produce-using-lathe cost} = \$80,000 + \$75 \times \text{Demand}$$
$$\text{Produce-using-machining-center cost} = \$200,000 + \$15 \times \text{Demand}$$

SOLUTION

Whether we approach the solution to this problem as cost minimization or profit maximization really makes no difference as long as the relationships remain linear: that is, variable costs and revenue are the same for each incremental unit. Exhibit 4.4 shows the break-even point for each process. If demand is expected to be more than 2,000 units (point A), the machine center is the best choice because this would result in the lowest total cost. If demand is between 640 (point B) and 2,000 units, the semiautomatic lathe is the cheapest. If demand is less than 640 (between 0 and point B), the most economical course is to buy the product.

The break-even point A calculation is

$$\$80,000 + \$75 \times \text{Demand} = \$200,000 + \$15 \times \text{Demand}$$
$$\text{Demand (point A)} = 120,000/60 = 2,000 \text{ units}$$

The break-even point B calculation is

$$\$200 \times \text{Demand} = \$80,000 + \$75 \times \text{Demand}$$
$$\text{Demand (point B)} = 80,000/125 = 640 \text{ units}$$

Consider the effect of revenue, assuming the part sells for $300 each. As Exhibit 4.4 shows, profit (or loss) is the distance between the revenue line and the alternative process cost. At 1,000 units, for

exhibit 4.4   Break-Even Chart of Alternative Processes

Excel: Breakeven Analysis

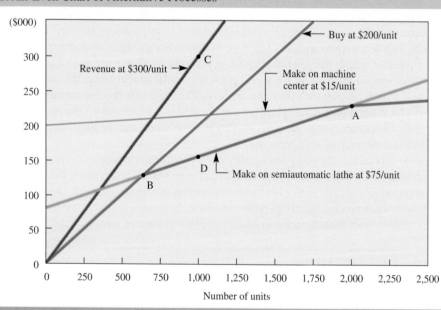

example, maximum profit is the difference between the $300,000 revenue (point C) and the semiautomatic lathe cost of $155,000 (point D). For this quantity the semiautomatic lathe is the cheapest alternative available. The optimal choices for both minimizing cost and maximizing profit are the lowest segments of the lines: origin to B, to A, and to the right side of Exhibit 4.4 as shown in green. ●

DESIGNING A PRODUCTION SYSTEM

There are many techniques available to determine the actual layouts of the production process. This section gives a quick overview of how the problems are addressed. For each of the layout types, descriptions are given of how the layouts are represented and the main criteria used. The next section takes an in-depth look at the assembly line balancing problem.

Project Layout

In developing a project layout, visualize the product as the hub of a wheel, with materials and equipment arranged concentrically around the production point in the order of use and movement difficulty. Thus, in building commercial aircraft, for example, rivets that are used throughout construction would be placed close to or in the fuselage; heavy engine parts, which must travel to the fuselage only once, would be placed at a more distant location; and cranes would be set up close to the fuselage because of their constant use.

PROJECT LAYOUT

In a project layout, a high degree of task ordering is common. To the extent that this task ordering, or precedence, determines production stages a project layout may be developed by arranging materials according to their assembly priority. This procedure would be expected in making a layout for a large machine tool, such as a stamping machine, where manufacturing follows a rigid sequence; assembly is performed from the ground up, with parts being added to the base in almost a building-block fashion.

Workcenters

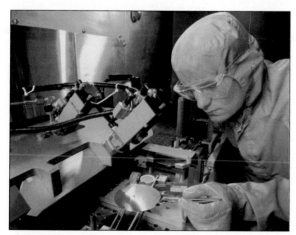

WORKCENTER

The most common approach to developing this type of layout is to arrange workcenters in a way that optimizes the movement of material. A workcenter sometimes is referred to as a department and is focused on a particular type of operation.

Examples include a workcenter for drilling holes, one for performing grinding operations, and a painting area. The workcenters in a low-volume toy factory might consist of shipping and receiving, plastic molding and stamping, metal forming, sewing, and painting. Parts for the toys are fabricated in these workcenters and then sent to the assembly workcenter, where they are put together. In many installations, optimal placement often means placing workcenters with large amounts of interdepartmental traffic adjacent to each other.

Manufacturing Cell

A manufacturing cell is formed by allocating dissimilar machines to cells that are designed to work on products that have similar shapes and processing requirements. Manufacturing cells are widely used in metal fabricating, computer chip manufacture, and assembly work.

The process used to develop a manufacturing cell is depicted in Exhibit 4.5. It can be broken down into three distinct steps:

1. Group parts into families that follow a common sequence of steps. This requires classifying parts by using some type of coding system. In practice, this can often be quite complex and can require a computerized system. For the purpose of the example shown in Exhibit 4.5A, four "part families" have already been defined and are identified by unique arrow designs. This part of the exhibit shows

MANUFACTURING CELL

the routing of parts when a conventional workcenter-based layout is used. Here parts are routed through the individual workcenters to be produced.
2. Next, dominant flow patterns are identified for each part family. This will be used as the basis for reallocating equipment to the manufacturing cells (see Exhibit 4.5B).
3. Finally, machines and the associated processes are physically regrouped into cells (see Exhibit 4.5C). Often there will be parts that cannot be associated with a family and specialized machinery that cannot be placed in any single cell because of its general use. These unattached parts and machinery are placed in a "remainder cell."

Assembly Line and Continuous Process Layouts

An assembly line is a layout design for the special purpose of building a product by going through a progressive set of steps. The assembly steps are done in areas referred to as "stations," and typically the stations are linked by some form of material handling device. In

ASSEMBLY LINE

Development of Manufacturing Cell

exhibit 4.5

A. Original workcenter layout

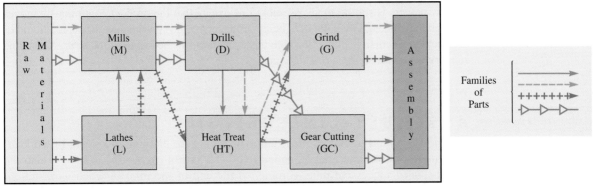

Source: Adapted from D. Fogarty and T. Hoffman, *Production and Inventory Management* (Cincinnati: South-Western Publishing, 1983), p. 472.

B. Routing matrix based upon flow of parts

Raw Materials	Part Family	Lathes	Mills	Drills	Heat Treating	Grinders	Gear Cutting	To	Assembly
---→			X	X	X	X		---→	
▷▷			X	X			X	▷▷	
——→		X	X	X	X		X	——→	
+++▶		X	X		X	X		+++▶	

C. Reallocating machines to form cells according to part family processing requirements

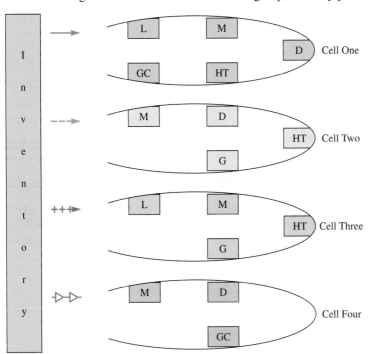

addition, usually there is some form of pacing by which the amount of time allowed at each station is managed. Rather than develop the process for designing assembly at this time, we will devote the entire next section of this chapter to the topic of assembly-line design since these designs are used so often by manufacturing firms around the world. A continuous or flow process is similar to an assembly line except that the product continuously moves through the process. Often the item being produced by the continuous process is a liquid or chemical that actually "flows" through the system; this is the origin of the term. A gasoline refinery is a good example of a flow process.

ASSEMBLY-LINE DESIGN

workstation cycle time

The most common assembly line is a moving conveyor that passes a series of workstations in a uniform time interval called the **workstation cycle time** (which is also the time between successive units coming off the end of the line). At each workstation, work is performed on a product either by adding parts or by completing assembly operations. The work performed at each station is made up of many bits of work, termed *tasks*.

Assembly-line balancing

The total work to be performed at a workstation is equal to the sum of the tasks assigned to that workstation. The **assembly-line balancing** problem is one of assigning all tasks to a series of workstations so that each workstation has no more than can be done in the work station cycle time, and so that the unassigned (that is, idle) time across all workstations is minimized. The problem is complicated by the relationships among tasks imposed by product design and process technologies. This is called the **precedence relationship**, which specifies the order in which tasks must be performed in the assembly process.

Precedence relationship

What's It Like Working on an Assembly Line?

Ben Hamper, the infamous "Rivethead" working for General Motors, describes his new job on the Chevy Suburban assembly line with the following:

> The whistle blew and the Rivet Line began to crawl. I took a seat up on the workbench and watched the guy I was replacing tackle his duties. He'd grab one end of a long rail and, with the help of the worker up the line from him, flip it over on its back. CLAAAANNNNNNGGGG! He then raced back to the bench and grabbed a four-wheel-drive spring casting and a muffler hanger. He would rivet the pieces onto the rail. With that completed, he'd jostle the rail back into an upright position and grab a cross member off the overhanging feeder line that curled above the bench. Reaching up with his spare arm, he'd grab a different rivet gun while fidgeting to get the cross member firmly planted so that it

aligned with the proper set of holes. He then inserted the rivets and began squashing the cross member into place. Just watching this guy go at it made my head hurt.

> "How about takin' a stab at it?" the guy asked me after a while. "You're not gonna get the feel of the job sittin' up there on the bench."

> I politely declined. I didn't want to learn any portion of this monster maze before it was absolutely necessary. Once the bossman thought you had a reasonable grasp of the setup, he was likely to step in and turn you loose on your own. I needed to keep delaying in order to give Art some time to reel me back up to Cab Shop.

> "Well, you've got three days," the guy replied. "After that, this baby's all yours."

Excerpt from B. Hamper's *Rivethead: Tales from the Assembly Line* (New York: Warner Books, 1992), p. 90.

The steps in balancing an assembly line are straightforward:

1. Specify the sequential relationships among tasks using a precedence diagram. The diagram consists of circles and arrows. Circles represent individual tasks; arrows indicate the order of task performance.
2. Determine the required workstation cycle time (C), using the formula

$$C = \frac{\text{Production time per day}}{\text{Required output per day (in units)}} \quad \textbf{[4.3]}$$

3. Determine the theoretical minimum number of workstations (N_t) required to satisfy the workstation cycle time constraint using the formula (note that this must be rounded up to the next highest integer)

$$N_t = \frac{\text{Sum of task times } (T)}{\text{Cycle time } (C)} \quad \textbf{[4.4]}$$

4. Select a primary rule by which tasks are to be assigned to workstations, and a secondary rule to break ties.
5. Assign tasks, one at a time, to the first workstation until the sum of the task times is equal to the workstation cycle time, or no other tasks are feasible because of time or sequence restrictions. Repeat the process for Workstation 2, Workstation 3, and so on until all tasks are assigned.
6. Evaluate the efficiency of the balance derived using the formula

$$\text{Efficiency} = \frac{\text{Sum of task times } (T)}{\text{Actual number of workstations } (N_a) \times \text{Workstation cycle time } (C)} \quad \textbf{[4.5]}$$

7. If efficiency is unsatisfactory, rebalance using a different decision rule.

Example 4.3: Assembly-Line Balancing

The Model J Wagon is to be assembled on a conveyor belt. Five hundred wagons are required per day. Production time per day is 420 minutes, and the assembly steps and times for the wagon are given in Exhibit 4.6. Assignment: Find the balance that minimizes the number of workstations, subject to cycle time and precedence constraints.

**Tutorial:
Line
Balancing**

Step by Step

SOLUTION

1. Draw a precedence diagram. Exhibit 4.7 illustrates the sequential relationships identified in Exhibit 4.6. (The length of the arrows has no meaning.)
2. Determine workstation cycle time. Here we have to convert to seconds because our task times are in seconds.

$$C = \frac{\text{Production time per day}}{\text{Output per day}} = \frac{60 \text{ sec.} \times 420 \text{ min.}}{500 \text{ wagons}} = \frac{25,200}{500} = 50.4$$

3. Determine the theoretical minimum number of workstations required (the actual number may be greater):

$$N_t = \frac{T}{C} = \frac{195 \text{ seconds}}{50.4 \text{ seconds}} = 3.87 = 4 \text{ (rounded up)}$$

4. Select assignment rules. Research has demonstrated that some rules are better than others for certain problem structures. In general, the strategy is to use a rule assigning tasks that either have many followers or are of long duration because they effectively limit the balance achievable. In this case, we use the following as our primary rule:

exhibit 4.6	Assembly Steps and Times for Model J Wagon

TASK	TASK TIME (IN SECONDS)	DESCRIPTION	TASKS THAT MUST PRECEDE
A	45	Position rear axle support and hand fasten four screws to nuts.	—
B	11	Insert rear axle.	A
C	9	Tighten rear axle support screws to nuts.	B
D	50	Position front axle assembly and hand fasten with four screws to nuts.	—
E	15	Tighten front axle assembly screws.	D
F	12	Position rear wheel #1 and fasten hubcap.	C
G	12	Position rear wheel #2 and fasten hubcap.	C
H	12	Position front wheel #1 and fasten hubcap.	E
I	12	Position front wheel #2 and fasten hubcap.	E
J	8	Position wagon handle shaft on front axle assembly and hand fasten bolt and nut.	F, G, H, I
K	9	Tighten bolt and nut.	J
	195		

exhibit 4.7	Precedence Graph for Model J Wagon

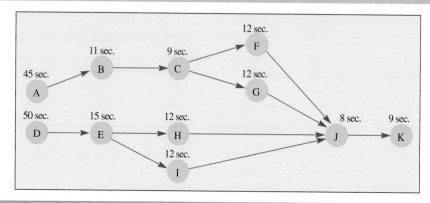

a. Prioritize tasks in order of the largest number of following tasks.

TASK	NUMBER OF FOLLOWING TASKS
A	6
B or D	5
C or E	4
F, G, H, or I	2
J	1
K	0

exhibit 4.8

A. Balance Made According to Largest-Number-of-Following-Tasks Rule

	TASK	TASK TIME (IN SECONDS)	REMAINING UNASSIGNED TIME (IN SECONDS)	FEASIBLE REMAINING TASKS	TASK WITH MOST FOLLOWERS	TASK WITH LONGEST OPERATION TIME
Station 1	A	45	5.4 idle	None		
Station 2	D	50	0.4 idle	None		
Station 3	B	11	39.4	C, E	C, E	E
	E	15	24.4	C, H, I	C	
	C	9	15.4	F, G, H, I	F, G, H, I	F, G, H, I
	F*	12	3.4 idle	None		
Station 4	G	12	38.4	H, I	H, I	H, I
	H*	12	26.4	I		
	I	12	14.4	J		
	J	8	6.4 idle	None		
Station 5	K	9	41.4 idle	None		

*Denotes task arbitrarily selected where there is a tie between longest operation times.

B. Precedence Graph for Model J Wagon

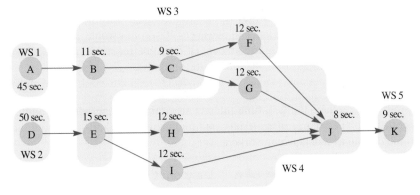

C. Efficiency Calculation

$$\text{Efficiency} = \frac{T}{N_a C} = \frac{195}{(5)(50.4)} = .77, \text{ or } 77\%$$

Our secondary rule, to be invoked where ties exist from our primary rule, is

b. Prioritize tasks in order of longest task time (shown in Exhibit 4.8). Note that D should be assigned before B, and E assigned before C due to this tiebreaking rule.

5. Make task assignments to form Workstation 1, Workstation 2, and so forth until all tasks are assigned. The actual assignment is given in Exhibit 4.8A and is shown graphically in Exhibit 4.8B. It is important to meet precedence and cycle time requirements as the assignments are made.

6. Calculate the efficiency. This is shown in Exhibit 4.8C.

7. Evaluate the solution. An efficiency of 77 percent indicates an imbalance or idle time of 23 percent (1.0−.77) across the entire line. From Exhibit 4.8A we can see that there are 57 total seconds of idle time, and the "choice" job is at Workstation 5.

Is a better balance possible? In this case, yes. Try balancing the line with rule *b* and breaking ties with rule *a*. (This will give you a feasible four-station balance.) ●

Splitting Tasks

Often the longest required task time forms the shortest workstation cycle time for the production line. This task time is the lower time bound unless it is possible to split the task into two or more workstations.

Consider the following illustration: Suppose that an assembly line contains the following task times in seconds: 40, 30, 15, 25, 20, 18, 15. The line runs for $7\frac{1}{2}$ hours per day and demand for output is 750 per day.

The workstation cycle time required to produce 750 per day is 36 seconds ([$7\frac{1}{2}$ hours $\times$ 60 minutes $\times$ 60 seconds]/750). Our problem is that we have one task that takes 40 seconds. How do we deal with this task?

There are several ways that we may be able to accommodate the 40-second task in a 36-second cycle. Possibilities are

1. **Split the task.** Can we split the task so that complete units are processed in two workstations?
2. **Share the task.** Can the task somehow be shared so an adjacent workstation does part of the work? This differs from the split task in the first option because the adjacent station acts to assist, not to do some units containing the entire task.
3. **Use parallel workstations.** It may be necessary to assign the task to two workstations that would operate in parallel.
4. **Use a more skilled worker.** Because this task exceeds the workstation cycle time by just 11 percent, a faster worker may be able to meet the 36-second time.
5. **Work overtime.** Producing at a rate of one every 40 seconds would create 675 per day, 75 short of the needed 750. The amount of overtime required to produce the additional 75 is 50 minutes (75 $\times$ 40 seconds/60 seconds).
6. **Redesign.** It may be possible to redesign the product to reduce the task time slightly.

Other possibilities to reduce the task time include an equipment upgrade, a roaming helper to support the line, a change of materials, and multiskilled workers to operate the line as a team rather than as independent workers.

Flexible and U-Shaped Line Layouts

As we saw in the preceding example, assembly-line balances frequently result in unequal workstation times. Flexible line layouts such as those shown in Exhibit 4.9 are a common way of dealing with this problem. In our toy company example, the U-shaped line with work sharing at the bottom of the figure could help resolve the imbalance.

Mixed-Model Line Balancing

Mixed-model line balancing involves scheduling several different models to be produced over a given day or week on the same line in a cyclical fashion. This approach is used by JIT manufacturers such as Toyota. Its objective is to meet the demand for a variety of products and to avoid building high inventories.

Step by Step

Example 4.4: Mixed-Model Line Balancing

To illustrate how this is done, suppose our toy company has a fabrication line to bore holes in its Model J wagon frame and its Model K wagon frame. The time required to bore the holes is different for each wagon type.

Assume that the final assembly line downstream requires equal numbers of Model J and Model K wagon frames. Assume also that we want to develop a cycle time for the fabrication line that is balanced for the production of equal numbers of J and K frames. Of course, we could produce Model

exhibit 4.9

Flexible Line Layouts

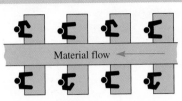

Bad: Operators caged. No chance
to trade elements of work
between them.
(Subassembly line layout
common in American plants.)

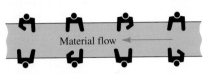

Better: Operators can trade elements of
work. Can add and subtract
operators. Trained ones can
nearly self-balance at different
output rates.

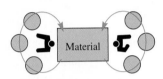

Bad: Operators birdcaged. No
chance to increase output
with a third operator.

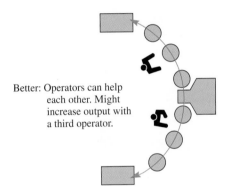

Better: Operators can help
each other. Might
increase output with
a third operator.

Bad: Straight line difficult to balance.

Better: One of several advantages
of U-line is better operator
access. Here, five operators
were reduced to four.

Source: R. W. Hall, *Attaining Manufacturing Excellence* (Homewood, IL: Dow Jones-Irwin, 1987), p. 125. Copyright
© 1987 McGraw-Hill Companies Inc.

J frames for several days and then produce Model K frames until an equal number of frames have
been produced. However, this would build up unnecessary work-in-process inventory.

   If we want to reduce the amount of in-process inventory, we could develop a cycle mix that greatly reduces inventory buildup while keeping within the restrictions of equal numbers of J and K wagon frames.

   Process times: 6 minutes per J and 4 minutes per K.
   The day consists of 480 minutes (8 hours × 60 minutes).

SOLUTION

$$6J + 4K = 480$$

Because equal numbers of J and K are to be produced (or J = K), produce 48J and 48K per day, or
6J and 6K per hour.

The following shows one balance of J and K frames.

Balanced Mixed-Model Sequence

Model sequence	J J	K K K	J J	J J	K K K	
Operation time	66	444	66	66	444	Repeats
Minicycle time	12	12	12	12	12	8 times per day

Total cycle time   60

This line is balanced at 6 frames of each type per hour with a minicycle time of 12 minutes.

Another balance is J K K J K J, with times of 6, 4, 4, 6, 4, 6. This balance produces 3J and 3K every 30 minutes with a minicycle time of 10 minutes (JK, KJ, KJ). ●

The simplicity of mixed-model balancing (under conditions of a level production schedule) is seen in Yasuhiro Mondon's description of Toyota Motor Corporation's operations:

> Final assembly lines of Toyota are mixed product lines. The production per day is averaged by taking the number of vehicles in the monthly production schedule classified by specifications, and dividing by the number of working days.
>
> In regard to the production sequence during each day, the cycle time of each different specification vehicle is calculated. To have all specification vehicles appear at their own cycle time, different specification vehicles are ordered to follow each other.

SUMMARY

Designing a customer-pleasing product is an art. Building that product is a science. Moving the product from design to the customer is management. World-class manufacturers excel in the speedy and flexible integration of these processes. Effective manufacturing process design requires a clear understanding of what the factory can and cannot do relative to process structures. Many plants use a combination of the layouts identified in this chapter: workcenters for some parts, assembly operations for others. Frequently a choice exists as to when demand seems likely to favor a switch from one to the other. Making such decisions also requires understanding the nuances of each process choice to determine whether the process really fits new product specifications.

Key Terms

Lead time The time needed to respond to a customer order.

Customer order decoupling point The place where inventory is positioned to allow processes or entities in the supply chain to operate independently.

Make-to-stock A production environment where the customer is served "on-demand" from finished goods inventory.

Assemble-to-order A production environment where preassembled components, subassemblies, and modules are put together in response to a specific customer order.

Make-to-order A production environment where the product is built directly from raw materials and components in response to a specific customer order.

Engineer-to-order Here the firm works with the customer to design the product, which is then made from purchased materials, parts, and components.

Lean manufacturing The attempt to achieve high customer service with minimum levels of inventory investment.

Total average value of inventory The total average investment in raw material, work-in-process, and finished goods inventory. This is valued at the cost to the firm.

Inventory turn The cost of goods sold divided by the total average value of inventory.

Days-of-supply The number of days of inventory of an item. If an item were not replenished, this would be the numbers of days until the firm would run out of the item (on average). Also, the inverse of inventory turn expressed in days.

Little's law A mathematical expression that relates inventory, throughput, and flow time.

Throughput The long-term average rate that items flow through a process.

Flow time The time it takes a unit to flow through a process from beginning to end.

Project layout The product, because of its sheer bulk or weight, remains fixed in a location. Equipment is moved to the product rather than vice versa.

Workcenter A process structure suited for low-volume production of a great variety of nonstandard products. Workcenters sometimes are referred to as departments and are focused on a particular type of operation.

Manufacturing cell An area where simple items that are similar in processing requirements are produced.

Assembly line A process structure designed to make discrete parts. Parts are moved through a set of specially designed workstations at a controlled rate.

Continuous process An often automated process that converts raw materials into a finished product in one continuous process.

Product–process matrix Shows the relationships between different production units and how they are used depending on product volume and the degree of product standardization.

Workstation cycle time The time between successive units coming off the end of an assembly line.

Assembly-line balancing The problem of assigning all the tasks to a series of workstations so that each workstation has no more than can be done in the workstation cycle time and so that idle time across all workstations is minimized.

Precedence relationship The order in which tasks must be performed in the assembly process.

Formula Review

$$\text{Total number of combinations} = N_1 \times N_2 \times \cdots \times N_n \qquad [4.1]$$
$$\text{Or } 384 = 4 \times 3 \times 4 \times 2 \times 4 \text{ for this example.}$$

$$Inventory = Throughput\ rate \times Flow\ time \qquad [4.2]$$

$$C = \frac{\text{Production time per day}}{\text{Required output per day (in units)}} \qquad [4.3]$$

$$N_t = \frac{\text{Sum of task times } (T)}{\text{Cycle time } (C)} \qquad [4.4]$$

$$Efficiency = \frac{\text{Sum of task times } (T)}{\text{Actual number of workstations } (N_a) \times \text{Workstation cycle time } (C)} \qquad [4.5]$$

Solved Problems

SOLVED PROBLEM 1

Step by Step

Suppose we schedule shipments to our customers so that we expect each shipment to wait for two days in finished goods inventory (in essence we add two days to when we expect to be able to ship). We do this as protection against system variability to ensure a high on-time delivery service. If we ship approximately 2,000 units each day, how many units do we expect to have in finished goods inventory due to allowing this extra time? If the item is valued at $4.50 each, what is the expected value of this inventory?

Solution

Using Little's law the expected finished goods inventory is:

$$\text{Inventory} = 2,000 \text{ units per day} \times 2 \text{ days} = 4,000 \text{ units}$$

This would be valued at 4,000 units × $4.50 per unit = $18,000

SOLVED PROBLEM 2

A company is considering adding a new feature that will increase unit sales by 6 percent and product cost by 10 percent. Profit is expected to increase by 16 percent of the increased sales. Initially the product cost incurred by the company was 63 percent of the sales price. Should the new feature be added?

Solution

Let the sales be $100 M.
Sales increase by 6% = $100 M × 6% = $6 M.

Benefits: Profits increase by 16% of the increased sales = $6 M × 16% = $0.96 M.
Cost: Increase product cost by 10% = ($100 M × 63%) × 10% = $6.3 M.

Because costs exceed benefits, the new feature should not be added.

SOLVED PROBLEM 3

An automobile manufacturer is considering a change in an assembly line that should save money due to a reduction in labor and material cost. The change involves the installation of four new robots that will automatically install windshields. The cost of the four robots, including installation and initial programming, is $400,000. Current practice is to amortize the initial cost of robots over two years on a straight-line basis. The process engineer estimates that one full-time technician will be needed to monitor, maintain, and reprogram the robots on an ongoing basis. This person will cost approximately $60,000 per year. Currently, the company uses four full-time employees on this job and each makes about $52,000 per year. One of these employees is a material handler, and this person will still be needed with the new process. To complicate matters, the process engineer estimates that the robots will apply the windshield sealing material in a manner that will result in a savings of $0.25 per windshield installed. How many automobiles need to be produced over the next two years to make the new robots an attractive investment? Due to the relatively short horizon, do not consider the time value of money.

Solution

Cost of the current process over the next two years is just the cost of the four full-time employees.

$$\$52,000 \text{ per employee} \times 4 \text{ employees} \times 2 \text{ years} = \$416,000$$

The cost of the new process over the next two years, assuming the robot is completely costed over that time, is the following:

$$(\$52,000 \text{ per material handler} + \$60,000 \text{ per technician}) \times 2 + \$400,000 \text{ per robot} - \$0.25 \times \text{autos}$$

Equating the two alternatives:

$$\$416,000 = \$624,000 - \$0.25 \times \text{autos}$$

Solving for the break-even point:

$$-\$208,000/-\$0.25 = 832,000 \text{ autos}$$

This indicates that to break even, 832,000 autos would need to be produced with the robots over the next two years.

SOLVED PROBLEM 4

The following tasks must be performed on an assembly line in the sequence and times specified:

Task	Task Time (Seconds)	Tasks That Must Precede
A	50	——
B	40	——
C	20	A
D	45	C
E	20	C
F	25	D
G	10	E
H	35	B, F, G

a. Draw the schematic diagram.
b. What is the theoretical minimum number of stations required to meet a forecast demand of 400 units per eight-hour day?
c. Use the longest-task-time rule and balance the line in the minimum number of stations to produce 400 units per day.

Solution

a.

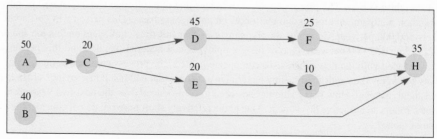

b.   The theoretical minimum number of stations to meet $D = 400$ is

$$N_t = \frac{T}{C} = \frac{245 \text{ seconds}}{\left(\dfrac{60 \text{ seconds} \times 480 \text{ minutes}}{400 \text{ units}}\right)} = \frac{245}{72} = 3.4 \text{ stations}$$

c.

	TASK	TASK TIME (SECONDS)	REMAINING UNASSIGNED TIME	FEASIBLE REMAINING TASK
Station 1	A	50	22	C
	C	20	2	None
Station 2	D	45	27	E,F
	F	25	2	None
Station 3	B	40	32	E
	E	20	12	G
	G	10	2	None
Station 4	H	35	37	None

SOLVED PROBLEM 5

The manufacturing engineers at Suny Manufacturing were working on a new remote-controlled toy Monster Truck. They hired a production consultant to help them determine the best type of production process to meet the forecasted demand for this new product. The consultant recommended that they use an assembly line. He told the manufacturing engineers that the line must be able to produce 600 Monster Trucks per day to meet the demand forecast. The workers in the plant work eight hours per day. The task information for the new monster truck is given below:

TASK	TASK TIME (SECONDS)	TASK THAT MUST PRECEDE
A	28	——
B	13	——
C	35	B
D	11	A
E	20	C
F	6	D,E
G	23	F
H	25	F
I	37	G
J	11	G,H
K	27	I,J
Total	236	

a. Draw the schematic diagram.

b. What is the required cycle time to meet the forecasted demand of 600 trucks per day based on an eight-hour work day?

c. What is the theoretical minimum number of workstations given the answer in part *b*?

d. Use longest task time with alphabetical order as the tie breaker and balance the line in the minimum number of stations to produce 600 trucks per day.

e. Use the largest number of following tasks and as a tie breaker use the shortest task time, to balance the line in the minimum number of stations to produce 600 trucks per day.

Solution

a.

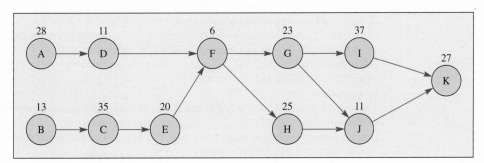

b. $C = \dfrac{\text{Production time per day}}{\text{Output per day}} = \dfrac{60 \text{ seconds} \times 480 \text{ minutes}}{600 \text{ trucks}} = \dfrac{28{,}800}{600} = 48 \text{ seconds}$

c. $N_t = \dfrac{T}{C} = \dfrac{236 \text{ seconds}}{48 \text{ seconds}} = 4.92 = 5 \text{ (rounded up)}$

d.

	FEASIBLE TASKS	TASK	TASK TIME (SECONDS)	REMAINING UNASSIGNED TIME
Station 1	A,B	A	28	20
	B,D	B	13	7
Station 2	C,D	C	35	13
	D	D	11	2
Station 3	E	E	20	28
	F	F	6	22
Station 4	G,H	G	23	25
	H,I	H	25	0
Station 5	I,J	I	37	11
	J	J	11	0
Station 6	K	K	27	21

e. Solution same as above.

Review and Discussion Questions

1 What kind of layout is used in a physical fitness center?

2 What is the objective of assembly-line balancing? How would you deal with a situation in which one worker, although trying hard, is 20 percent slower than the other 10 people on a line?

3 How do you determine the idle time percentage from a specific assembly-line balance?

4 What is the essential requirement for mixed-model lines to be practical?

5 Why might it be difficult to develop a manufacturing cell?

6   How would you characterize the most important difference for the following issues when comparing a facility organized with workcenters versus a continuous process?

ISSUE	WORKCENTERS	CONTINUOUS PROCESS
Number of changeovers		
Labor content of product		
Flexibility		

7   A certain custom engraving shop has traditionally had orders for between 1 and 50 units of whatever a customer orders. A large company has contacted this shop about engraving "reward" plaques (which are essentially identical to each other). It wants the shop to place a bid for this order. The expected volume is 12,000 units per year and will most likely last four years. To successfully bid (low enough price) for such an order, what will the shop likely have to do?

8   The product–process matrix is a convenient way of characterizing the relationship between product volumes (one-of-a-kind to continuous) and the processing system employed by a firm at a particular location. In the boxes presented below, describe the nature of the intersection between the type of shop (column) and process dimension (row).

	WORKCENTERS	CONTINUOUS PROCESS
Engineering emphasis		
General workforce skill		
Statistical process control		
Facility layout		
WIP inventory level		

9   For each of the following variables, explain the differences (in general) as one moves from a workcenter process to a continuous process environment.
    a. Throughput time (time to convert raw material into product).
    b. Capital/labor intensity.
    c. Bottlenecks.

Problems

1   You are in a line at the bank drive through and 10 cars are in front of you. You estimate that the clerk is taking about five minutes per car to serve. How long do you expect to wait in line?

2   A firm has redesigned its production process so that it now takes 10 hours for a unit to be made. Using the old process, it took 15 hours to make a unit. If the process makes one unit each hour on average and each unit is worth $1,500, what is the reduction in work-in-process value?

3   A book publisher has fixed costs of $300,000 and variable costs per book of $8.00. The book sells for $23.00 per copy.
    a. How many books must be sold to break even?
    b. If the fixed cost increased, would the new break-even point be higher or lower?
    c. If the variable cost per unit decreased, would the new break-even point be higher or lower?

(Continued)

exhibit 4.10

STATION	OPN. #	TIME (SEC)	DESCRIPTION OF OPERATIONS
7	49	18	Place protective seal on LCD display
108 sec	50	10	Place brand name seal on LCD mask
	51	11	Place brand name seal on outside of cover
	52	8	Connect cable to DVD drive
	53	33	Install DVD on base
	54	22	Install cover on DVD
	55	6	Put screws for Opns 56, 57 in foam tray
8	56	58	Turn over machine and put screws in base
93 sec	57	8	Put in grounding screw
	58	8	Install connector protective flap
	59	8	Install DVD assembly
	60	6	Install battery cover on battery pack
	61	5	Install battery cover
9	62	31	Insert memory card for hardware test and start software
310 sec	63	208	Software load (does not require operator)
	64	71	Test DVD, LCD, keyboard, and pointer; remove memory
10	65	5	Place unit on shock test platform
105 sec	66	75	Perform shock test
	67	10	Scan bar codes
	68	15	Place unit on rack for burn-in

Source: Adapted from : *Toshiba: Ome Works,* Harvard Business School (9-696-059).

The Assembly Line

At the head of the assembly line, a computer displayed the daily production schedule, consisting of a list of model types and corresponding lot sizes scheduled to be assembled on the line. The models were simple variations of hard disk size, memory, and battery power. A typical production schedule included seven or eight model types in lot sizes varying from 10 to 100 units. The models were assembled sequentially: All the units of the first model were assembled, followed by all the units of the second, and so on. This computer screen also indicated how far along the assembly line was in completing its daily schedule, which served as a guide for the material handlers who supplied parts to the assembly lines.

The daily schedules were shared with the nearby Fujihashi Parts Collection and Distribution Center. Parts were brought from Fujihashi to the plant within two hours of when they were needed. The material supply system was very tightly coordinated and worked well.

The assembly line consisted of a 14.4-meter conveyor belt that carried the computers, separated at 1.2-meter intervals by white stripes on the belt. Workers stood shoulder to shoulder on one side of the conveyor and worked on the units as they moved by. In addition to 10 assembly workers,

a highly skilled worker, called a "supporter," was assigned to each line. The supporter moved along the line, assisting workers who were falling behind and replacing workers who needed to take a break. Supporters also made decisions about what to do when problems were encountered during the assembly process (such as a defective part). The line speed and the number of workers varied from day to day, depending on production demand and the workers' skills and availability. Although the assembly line was designed for 10 workers, the number of workers could vary between 8 and 12.

Exhibit 4.10 provides details of how the engineers who designed the new subnotebook computer felt that the new line should be organized. These engineers design the line assuming that one notebook is assembled every two minutes by 10 line workers. In words, the following is a brief description of what each operator does:

1   The first operator lays out the major components of a computer between two white lines on the conveyor.
2   The second operator enters the bar codes on those components into a centralized computer system by scanning the bar codes with a hand-held scanning wand. On a shelf above the conveyor, portable

computers display the operations that are performed at each station.

3 The next six steps of the assembly process involve a large number of simple operations performed by hand or with simple tools, such as electric screwdrivers. Typical operations involve snapping connectors together or attaching parts with small screws. All tools are hung by a cable above the operators, within easy reach. Although the individual operations are simple, they require manual dexterity and speed.

4 The last two operations are the hardware and shock tests. To prepare for the hardware test, an operator inserts a memory card into the USB port containing software designed to test different components of the computer circuitry. Because it takes nearly four minutes to load the testing software, the cycle time of this operation is longer than the other cycle times on the line. To achieve a lower cycle time for the line, the hardware test is performed in parallel on three different units. The units remain on the moving conveyor, and the tests are staggered so that they can be performed by a single operator. The shock test (the last operation on the assembly line) tests the ability of the computer to withstand vibrations and minor impacts.

The computers are moved to a burn-in area after the assembly line shock test. Here computers are put in racks for a 24-hour 25°C "burn-in" of the circuit components. After burn-in, the computer is tested again, software is installed, and the finished notebook computer is packaged and placed on pallets.

Tweaking the Initial Assembly-Line Design

From past experience Toshihiro has found that the initial assembly-line design supplied by the engineers often needs to be tweaked. Consider the following questions that Toshihiro is considering:

1 What is the daily capacity of the assembly line designed by the engineers?
2 When it is running at maximum capacity, what is the efficiency of the line?
3 How should the line be redesigned to operate at the target 300 units per day, assuming that no overtime will be used? What is the efficiency of your new design?
4 What other issues might Toshihiro consider when bringing the new assembly line up to speed?

Super Quiz

1 A firm that makes predesigned products directly to fill customer orders has this type of production environment.
2 A point where inventory is positioned to allow the production process to operate independently of the customer order delivery process.
3 A firm that designs and builds products from scratch according to customer specifications would have this type of production environment.
4 If a production process makes a unit every two hours and it takes 42 hours for the unit to go through the entire process, then the expected work-in-process is equal to this.
5 A finished goods inventory on average contains 10,000 units. Demand averages 1,500 units per week. Given that the process runs 50 weeks a year, what is the expected inventory turn for the inventory? Assume

that each item held in inventory is valued at about the same amount.
6 This is a production layout where similar products are made. Typically it is scheduled on an as-needed basis in response to current customer demand.
7 The relationship between how different layout structures are best suited depending on volume and product variety characteristics is depicted on this type of graph.
8 A firm is using an assembly line and needs to produce 500 units during an eight-hour day. What is the required cycle time in seconds?
9 What is the efficiency of an assembly line that has 25 workers and a cycle time of 45 seconds? Each unit produced on the line has 16 minutes of work that needs to be completed based on a time study completed by engineers at the factory.

1. Make-to-order 2. Customer order decoupling point 3. Engineer-to-order 4. 21 units = 42/2 5. 7.5 turns = (1500 × 50)/10000 6. Manufacturing cell 7. Product-process matrix 8. 57.6 seconds = (8 × 60 × 60)/500 9. 85% = (16 × 60)/(25 × 45)

Selected Bibliography

Heragu, S. *Facilities Design*. Boston: PWS Publishing, 1997.

Hyer, N., and U. Wemmerlöv. *Reorganizing the Factory: Competing through Cellular Manufacturing*. Portland, OR: Productivity Press, 2002.

Tompkins, J. A., and J. A. While. *Facilities Planning*. New York: John Wiley & Sons, 2003.

CHAPTER 5

SERVICE PROCESSES

After reading the chapter, you will:

- Describe the characteristics of service processes and how they differ from manufacturing processes.
- Classify service processes.
- Explain service blueprinting.
- Understand waiting line (queuing) analysis.
- Model some common waiting line situation and estimate server utilization, the length of a waiting line, and average customer wait time.

99   Supply Chain Services at DHL

100   An Operational Classification of Services
                            High and low degree of customer contact defined

101   Designing Service Organizations

101   Structuring the Service Encounter:
        Service-System Design Matrix
                Virtual Service: The New Role of the Customer

103   Service Blueprinting and Fail-Safing
                                            Service blueprint defined
                                            Poka-yokes defined

106   Economics of the Waiting Line Problem
                The Practical View of Waiting Lines

107   The Queuing System
                Customer Arrivals   Queuing system defined
                Distribution of Arrivals   Arrival rate defined
                The Queuing System: Factors   Exponential distribution defined
                Exiting the Queuing System   Poisson distribution defined
                                                        Service rate defined

115   Waiting Line Models

122   Computer Simulation of Waiting Lines

122   Summary

130   Case: Community Hospital Evening Operating Room

130   Super Quiz

SUPPLY CHAIN SERVICES AT DHL

Supply
Chain

To entice people to buy their mainstream products, companies often offer extensive additional services to their customers. Consider DHL, a global delivery company that ships everything from flowers to industrial freight all over the world. With over 6,500 offices around the world, DHL operates over a network with 240 gateways and more than 450 hubs, warehouses, and terminals. Using its fleet of over 420 aircraft and over 76,200 vehicles, DHL serves some 4.1 million customers worldwide.

DHL offers customers a variety of value-added supply chain–related services that extend beyond delivering packages, improving efficiencies and reducing costs. These services allow DHL customers to outsource much of the work required to coordinate their supply chain processes. The following is a quick list of some of the services offered by DHL:

Order management: Receipt, management, execution, sequencing, and dispatch of orders in a timely manner.

Call center management: Manages orders, monitors sales activities, provides customer services, and functions as a help desk.

Global inventory management: DHL gives the customer a global view of inventory, thus enabling informed decisions about the disposition of stock.

Consolidated billing services: The creation of a consolidated and categorized invoice, based on all services performed in a specific period by more than one service provider.

Freight and customs solutions: DHL's experience servicing over 220 countries and territories with international trade requirements and formalities, combined with the European Competence Centre and country expertise, gives customers a leading edge in service, quality, and management in cross-border transactions.

AN OPERATIONAL CLASSIFICATION OF SERVICES

Service

Service organizations are generally classified according to who the customer is, for example, individuals or other businesses, and to the service they provide (financial services, health services, transportation services, and so on). These groupings, though useful in presenting aggregate economic data, are not particularly appropriate for OSM purposes because they tell us little about the process. Manufacturing, by contrast, has fairly evocative terms to classify production activities (such as assembly lines and continuous processes); when applied to a manufacturing setting, they readily convey the essence of the process. Although it is possible to describe services in these same terms, we need one additional item of information to reflect the fact that the customer is involved in the production system. That item, which we believe operationally distinguishes one service system from another in its production function, is the extent of customer contact in the creation of the service.

Customer contact refers to the physical presence of the customer in the system, and *creation of the service* refers to the work process involved in providing the service itself. *Extent of contact* here may be roughly defined as the percentage of time the customer must be in the system relative to the total time it takes to perform the customer service. Generally speaking, the greater the percentage of contact time between the service system and the customer, the greater the degree of interaction between the two during the production process.

High and low degree of customer contact

From this conceptualization, it follows that service systems with a **high degree of customer contact** are more difficult to control and more difficult to rationalize than those with a **low degree of customer contact**. In high-contact systems, the customer can affect the time of demand, the exact nature of the service, and the quality, or perceived quality, of service because the customer is involved in the process.

Mayo Clinic Design Improves the Patient–Provider Experience

Mayo Clinic invited IDEO to help turn an internal medicine wing into a laboratory for improving the patient–provider experience. The team devised a simple and flexible design that allows for more informative, comfortable, and guided interactions among staff and patients. There are four areas through which patients proceed: Service Home Base; Visitor-Facing Hub; Preparation Service area; and Innovation Central.

There can be tremendous diversity of customer influence and, hence, system variability within high-contact service systems. For example, a bank branch offers both simple services such as cash withdrawals that take just a minute or so and complicated services such as loan application preparation that can take in excess of an hour. Moreover, these activities may range from being self-service through an ATM, to coproduction where bank personnel and the customer work as a team to develop the loan application.

DESIGNING SERVICE ORGANIZATIONS

In designing service organizations we must remember one distinctive characteristic of services: We cannot inventory services. Unlike manufacturing, where we can build up inventory during slack periods for peak demand and thus maintain a relatively stable level of employment and production planning, in services we must (with a few exceptions) meet demand as it arises. Consequently, in services capacity becomes a dominant issue. Think about the many service situations you find yourself in—for example, eating in a restaurant or going to a Saturday night movie. Generally speaking, if the restaurant or the theater is full, you will decide to go someplace else. So, an important design parameter in services is "What capacity should we aim for?" Too much capacity generates excessive costs. Insufficient capacity leads to lost customers. In these situations, of course, we seek the assistance of marketing. This is one reason we have discount airfares, hotel specials on weekends, and so on. This is also a good illustration of why it is difficult to separate the operations management functions from marketing in services.

Service

Waiting line models, which are discussed in this chapter, provide a powerful mathematical tool for analyzing many common service situations. Questions such as how many tellers we should have in a bank or how many computer servers we need in an Internet service operation can be analyzed with these models. These models can be easily implemented using spreadsheets.

STRUCTURING THE SERVICE ENCOUNTER: SERVICE-SYSTEM DESIGN MATRIX

Service encounters can be configured in a number of different ways. The service-system design matrix in Exhibit 5.1 identifies six common alternatives.

Service

The top of the matrix shows the degree of customer/server contact: the *buffered core,* which is physically separated from the customer; the *permeable system,* which is penetrable by the customer via phone or face-to-face contact; and the *reactive system,* which is both penetrable and reactive to the customer's requirements. The left side of the matrix shows what we believe to be a logical marketing proposition, namely, that the greater the amount of contact, the greater the sales opportunity; the right side shows the impact on production efficiency as the customer exerts more influence on the operation.

The entries within the matrix list the ways in which service can be delivered. At one extreme, service contact is by mail; customers have little interaction with the system. At the other extreme, customers "have it their way" through face-to-face contact. The remaining four entries in the exhibit contain varying degrees of interaction.

As one would guess, production efficiency decreases as the customer has more contact (and therefore more influence) on the system. To offset this, the face-to-face contact

exhibit 5.1   Service-System Design Matrix

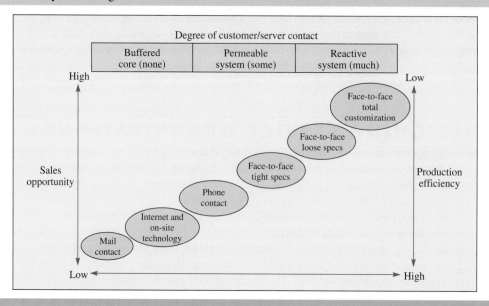

provides high sales opportunity to sell additional products. Conversely, low contact, such as mail, allows the system to work more efficiently because the customer is unable to significantly affect (or disrupt) the system. However, there is relatively little opportunity for additional product sales.

There can be some shifting in the positioning of each entry. For our first example, consider the "Internet and on-site technology" entry in the matrix. The Internet clearly buffers the company from the customer, but interesting opportunities are available to provide relevant information and services to the customer. Because the Web site can be programmed to intelligently react to the inputs of the customer, significant opportunities for new sales may be possible. In addition, the system can be made to interface with real employees when the customer needs assistance that goes beyond the programming of the Web site. The Internet is truly a revolutionary technology when applied to the services that need to be provided by a company.

Another example of shifting in the positioning of an entry can be shown with the "face-to-face tight specs" entry in Exhibit 5.1. This entry refers to those situations where there is little variation in the service process—neither customer nor server has much discretion in creating the service. Fast-food restaurants and Disneyland come to mind. Face-to-face loose specs refers to situations where the service process is generally understood but there are options in how it will be performed or in the physical goods that are part of it. A full-service restaurant and a car sales agency are examples. Face-to-face total customization refers to service encounters whose specifications must be developed through some interaction between the customer and server. Legal and medical services are of this type, and the degree to which the resources of the system are mustered for the service determines whether the system is reactive, possibly to the point of even being proactive, or merely permeable. Examples would be the mobilization of an advertising firm's resources in preparation for an office visit by a major client, or an operating team scrambling to prepare for emergency surgery.

Exhibit 5.2 extends the design matrix. It shows the changes in workers, operations, and types of technical innovations as the degree of customer/service system contact changes. For worker requirements, the relationships between mail contact and clerical skills, Internet

exhibit 5.2

Characteristics of Workers, Operations, and Innovations Relative to the Degree of Customer/Server Contact

Degree of customer/server contact

Low ←   → High

Worker requirements	Clerical skills	Helping skills	Verbal skills	Procedural skills	Trade skills	Diagnostic skills
Focus of operations	Paper handling	Demand management	Scripting calls	Flow control	Capacity management	Client mix
Technological innovations	Office automation	Routing methods	Computer databases	Electronic aids	Self-serve	Client/worker teams

technology and helping skills, and phone contact and verbal skills are self-evident. Face-to-face tight specs require procedural skills in particular, because the worker must follow the routine in conducting a generally standardized, high-volume process. Face-to-face loose specs frequently call for trade skills (bank teller, draftsperson, maître d', dental hygienist) to finalize the design for the service. Face-to-face total customization tends to call for diagnostic skills of the professional to ascertain the needs or desires of the client.

Virtual Service: The New Role of the Customer

The service system design matrix was developed from the perspective of the production system's utilization of company resources. With the advent of virtual services through the Internet, we need to account not just for customer's interactions with a business, but for his or her interaction with other customers as well. As suggested by BYU Professor Scott Sampson, we have two categories of contact: *pure virtual customer contact* where companies such as eBay and Second Life enable customers to interact with one another in an open environment; and *mixed virtual and actual customer contact* where customers interact with one another in a server-moderated environment such as product discussion groups, YouTube, and WikiPedia. In these environments the operations management challenge is to keep the technology functioning and up to date, and to provide a policing function through monitoring the encounters that take place.

SERVICE BLUEPRINTING AND FAIL-SAFING

Just as is the case with manufacturing process design, the standard tool for service process design is the flowchart. Recently, the service gurus have begun calling the flowchart a **service blueprint** to emphasize the importance of process design. A unique feature of the service blueprint is the distinction made between the high customer contact aspects of the service (the parts of the process that the customer sees) and those activities that the customer does not see. This distinction is made with a "line of visibility" on the flowchart.

Exhibit 5.3 is a blueprint of a typical automobile service operation. Each activity that makes up a typical service encounter is mapped into the flowchart. To better show the entity that controls the activities, levels are shown in the flowchart. The top level consists of activities that are under the control of the customer. Next are those activities performed by the service manager in handling the customer. The third level is the repair activities performed in the garage; the lowest level is the internal accounting activity.

Service blueprint

Service

exhibit 5.3   Fail-Safing an Automotive Service Operation

FAILURE: CUSTOMER FORGETS THE NEED FOR SERVICE.
POKA-YOKE: SEND AUTOMATIC REMINDERS WITH A 5 PERCENT DISCOUNT.

FAILURE: CUSTOMER CANNOT FIND SERVICE AREA, OR DOES NOT FOLLOW PROPER FLOW.
POKA-YOKE: CLEAR AND INFORMATIVE SIGNAGE DIRECTING CUSTOMERS.

FAILURE: CUSTOMER HAS DIFFICULTY COMMUNICATING PROBLEM.
POKA-YOKE: JOINT INSPECTION—SERVICE ADVISER REPEATS HIS/HER UNDERSTANDING OF THE PROBLEM FOR CONFIRMATION OR ELABORATION BY THE CUSTOMER.

FAILURE: CUSTOMER DOES NOT UNDERSTAND THE NECESSARY SERVICE.
POKA-YOKE: PREPRINTED MATERIAL FOR MOST SERVICES, DETAILING WORK, REASONS, AND POSSIBLY A GRAPHIC REPRESENTATION.

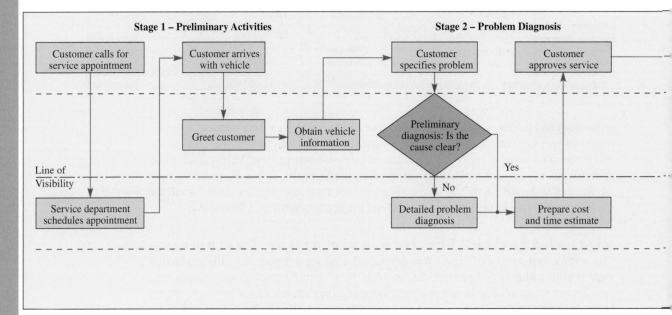

FAILURE: CUSTOMER ARRIVAL UNNOTICED.
POKA-YOKE: USE A BELL CHAIN TO SIGNAL ARRIVALS.

FAILURE: CUSTOMERS NOT SERVED IN ORDER OF ARRIVAL.
POKA-YOKE: PLACE NUMBERED MARKERS ON CARS AS THEY ARRIVE.
FAILURE: VEHICLE INFORMATION INCORRECT AND PROCESS IS TIME-CONSUMING.
POKA-YOKE: MAINTAIN CUSTOMER DATABASE AND PRINT FORMS WITH HISTORICAL INFORMATION.

FAILURE: INCORRECT DIAGNOSIS OF THE PROBLEM.
POKA-YOKE: HIGH-TECH CHECKLISTS, SUCH AS EXPERT SYSTEMS AND DIAGNOSTIC EQUIPMENT.

FAILURE: INCORRECT ESTIMATE.
POKA-YOKE: CHECKLISTS ITEMIZING COSTS BY COMMON REPAIR TYPES.

Poka-yokes

Basic blueprinting describes the features of the service design but does not provide any direct guidance for how to make the process conform to that design. An approach to this problem is the application of **poka-yokes**—procedures that block the inevitable mistake from becoming a service defect.[1] Poka-yokes (roughly translated from the Japanese as "avoid mistakes") are common in factories and consist of such things as fixtures to ensure that parts can be attached only in the right way, electronic switches that automatically shut off equipment if a mistake is made, kitting of parts prior to assembly to make sure the right quantities are used, and checklists to ensure that the right sequence of steps is followed.

There are many applications of poka-yokes to services as well. These can be classified into warning methods, physical or visual contact methods, and by what we call the *Three T's*—the Task to be done (Was the car fixed right?), the Treatment accorded to the customer (Was the service manager courteous?), and the Tangible or environmental features of the service facility (Was the waiting area clean and comfortable?). Finally (unlike in

FAILURE: CUSTOMER NOT LOCATED.
POKA-YOKE: ISSUE BEEPERS TO CUSTOMERS WHO WISH TO LEAVE FACILITY.

FAILURE: BILL IS ILLEGIBLE.
POKA-YOKE: TOP COPY TO CUSTOMER, OR PLAIN PAPER BILL.

FAILURE: FEEDBACK NOT OBTAINED.
POKA-YOKE: CUSTOMER SATISFACTION POSTCARD GIVEN TO CUSTOMER WITH KEYS TO VEHICLE.

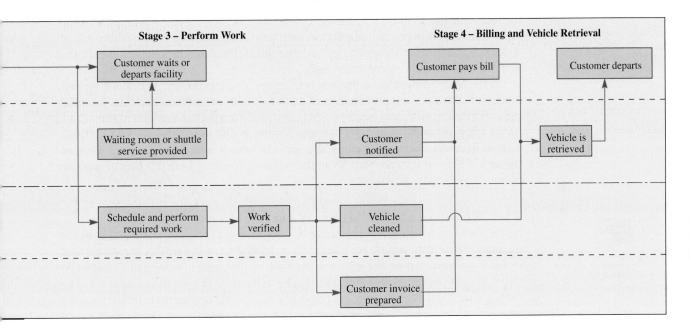

FAILURE: SERVICE SHUTTLE IS INCONVENIENT.
POKA-YOKE: SEATING IN AVAILABLE SHUTTLES IS ALLOCATED WHEN SCHEDULING APPOINTMENTS. LACK OF FREE SPACE INDICATES THAT CUSTOMERS NEEDING SHUTTLE SERVICE SHOULD BE SCHEDULED FOR ANOTHER TIME.
FAILURE: PARTS ARE NOT IN STOCK.
POKA-YOKE: LIMIT SWITCHES ACTIVATE SIGNAL LAMPS WHEN PART LEVEL FALLS BELOW ORDER POINT.

FAILURE: VEHICLE NOT CLEANED CORRECTLY.
POKA-YOKE: PERSON RETRIEVING VEHICLE INSPECTS, ORDERS A TOUCH-UP IF NECESSARY, AND REMOVES FLOOR MAT IN PRESENCE OF CUSTOMER.

FAILURE: VEHICLE TAKES TOO LONG TO ARRIVE.
POKA-YOKE: WHEN CASHIER ENTERS CUSTOMER'S NAME TO PRINT THE BILL, INFORMATION IS ELECTRONICALLY SENT TO RUNNERS WHO RETRIEVE VEHICLE WHILE THE CUSTOMER IS PAYING.

manufacturing), service poka-yokes often must be applied to fail-safing the actions of the customer as well as the service worker.

Poka-yoke examples include height bars at amusement parks; indented trays used by surgeons to ensure that no instruments are left in the patient; chains to configure waiting lines; take-a-number systems; turnstiles; beepers on ATMs to warn people to take their cards out of the machine; beepers at restaurants to make sure customers do not miss their table calls; mirrors on telephones to ensure a "smiling voice"; reminder calls for appointments; locks on airline lavatory doors that activate lights inside; small gifts in comment card envelopes to encourage customers to provide feedback about a service; and pictures of what "a clean room" looks like for kindergarten children.

Exhibit 5.3 illustrates how a typical automobile service operation might be fail-safed using poka-yokes. As a final comment, although these procedures cannot guarantee the level of error protection found in the factory, they still can reduce such errors in many service situations.

ECONOMICS OF THE WAITING LINE PROBLEM

Service

A central problem in many service settings is the management of waiting time. The manager must weigh the added cost of providing more rapid service (more traffic lanes, additional landing strips, more checkout stands) against the inherent cost of waiting.

Frequently, the cost trade-off decision is straightforward. For example, if we find that the total time our employees spend in the line waiting to use a copying machine would otherwise be spent in productive activities, we could compare the cost of installing one additional machine to the value of employee time saved. The decision could then be reduced to dollar terms and the choice easily made.

On the other hand, suppose that our waiting line problem centers on demand for beds in a hospital. We can compute the cost of additional beds by summing the costs for building construction, additional equipment required, and increased maintenance. But what is on the other side of the scale? Here we are confronted with the problem of trying to place a dollar figure on a patient's need for a hospital bed that is unavailable. While we can estimate lost hospital income, what about the human cost arising from this lack of adequate hospital care?

Service

The Practical View of Waiting Lines

Before we proceed with a technical presentation of waiting line theory, it is useful to look at the intuitive side of the issue to see what it means. Exhibit 5.4 shows arrivals at a service facility (such as a bank) and service requirements at that facility (such as tellers and loan officers). One important variable is the number of arrivals over the hours that the service system is open. From the service delivery viewpoint, customers demand varying amounts of service, often exceeding normal capacity. We can control arrivals in a variety of ways. For example, we can have a short line (such as a drive-in at a fast-food restaurant with only several spaces), we can establish specific hours for specific customers, or we can run specials. For the server, we can affect service time by using faster or slower servers, faster or slower machines, different tooling, different material, different layout, faster setup time, and so on.

The essential point is waiting lines are *not* a fixed condition of a productive system but are to a very large extent within the control of the system management and design.

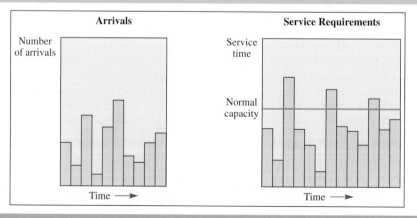

Useful suggestions for managing queues based on research in the banking industry are the following:

- **Segment the customers.**   If a group of customers need something that can be done very quickly, give them a special line so that they do not have to wait for the slower customers.
- **Train your servers to be friendly.**   Greeting the customer by name or providing another form of special attention can go a long way toward overcoming the negative feeling of a long wait. Psychologists suggest that servers be told when to invoke specific friendly actions such as smiling when greeting customers, taking orders, and giving change (for example, in a convenience store). Tests using such specific behavioral actions have shown significant increases in the perceived friendliness of the servers in the eyes of the customer.
- **Inform your customers of what to expect.**   This is especially important when the waiting time will be longer than normal. Tell them why the waiting time is longer than usual and what you are doing to alleviate the wait.
- **Try to divert the customer's attention when waiting.**   Providing music, a video, or some other form of entertainment may help distract the customers from the fact that they are waiting.
- **Encourage customers to come during slack periods.**   Inform customers of times when they usually would not have to wait; also tell them when the peak periods are—this may help smooth the load.

THE QUEUING SYSTEM

The **queuing system** consists essentially of three major components: (1) the source population and the way customers arrive at the system, (2) the servicing system, and (3) the condition of the customers exiting the system (back to source population or not?), as seen in Exhibit 5.5. The following sections discuss each of these areas.

Queuing system

Service

exhibit 5.5   Components of a Queuing System

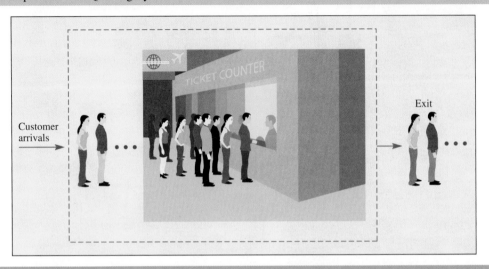

Customer Arrivals

Arrivals at a service system may be drawn from a *finite* or an *infinite* population. The distinction is important because the analyses are based on different premises and require different equations for their solution.

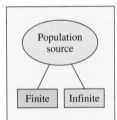

Finite Population A *finite population* refers to the limited-size customer pool that will use the service and, at times, form a line. The reason this finite classification is important is that when a customer leaves its position as a member for the population (a machine breaking down and requiring service, for example), the size of the user group is reduced by one, which reduces the probability of the next occurrence. Conversely, when a customer is serviced and returns to the user group, the population increases and the probability of a user requiring service also increases.

SIX FLAGS' FAST LANE USERS PURCHASE LOW-TECH, GO-TO-THE-HEAD-OF-THE-LINE PAPER TICKETS OR A HIGH-TECH, ELECTRONIC "Q-BOT" DEVICE. Q-BOTS ARE BEEPERS THAT SERVE AS VIRTUAL PLACEHOLDERS. THEY VIBRATE AND FLASH A TEXT MESSAGE WHEN IT'S TIME TO REPORT TO THE RIDE.

This finite class of problems requires a separate set of formulas from that of the infinite population case.

As an example, consider a group of six machines maintained by one repairperson. When one machine breaks down, the source population is reduced to five, and the chance of one of the remaining five breaking down and needing repair is certainly less than when six machines were operating. If two machines are down with only four operating, the probability of another breakdown is again changed. Conversely, when a machine is repaired and returned to service, the machine population increases, thus raising the probability of the next breakdown.

Infinite Population An *infinite population* is large enough in relation to the service system so that the population size caused by subtractions or additions to the population (a customer needing service or a serviced customer returning to the population) does not significantly affect the system probabilities. If, in the preceding finite explanation, there were 100 machines instead of 6, then if one or two machines broke down, the probabilities for the next breakdowns would not be very different and the assumption could be made without a great deal of error that the population (for all practical purposes) was infinite. Nor would the formulas for "infinite" queuing problems cause much error if applied to a physician with 1,000 patients or a department store with 10,000 customers.

Distribution of Arrivals

When describing a waiting system, we need to define the manner in which customers or the waiting units are arranged for service.

Waiting line formulas generally require an **arrival rate**, or the number of units per period (such as an average of one every six minutes). A *constant* arrival distribution is periodic, with exactly the same time between successive arrivals. In productive systems, the only arrivals that truly approach a constant interval period are those subject to machine control. Much more common are *variable* (random) arrival distributions.

Arrival rate

In observing arrivals at a service facility, we can look at them from two viewpoints: First, we can analyze the time between successive arrivals to see if the times follow some statistical distribution. Usually we assume that the time between arrivals is exponentially distributed. Second, we can set some time length (T) and try to determine how many arrivals might enter the system within T. We typically assume that the number of arrivals per time unit is Poisson distributed.

Exponential Distribution In the first case, when arrivals at a service facility occur in a purely random fashion, a plot of the interarrival times yields an **exponential distribution** such as that shown in Exhibit 5.6. The probability function is

Exponential distribution

$$f(t) = \lambda e^{-\lambda t} \qquad \text{[5.1]}$$

where λ is the mean number of arrivals per time period.

The cumulative area beneath the curve in Exhibit 5.6 is the summation of equation (5.1) over its positive range, which is $e^{-\lambda t}$. This integral allows us to compute the probabilities of arrivals within a specified time. For example, for the case of single arrivals to a waiting line ($\lambda = 1$), the following table can be derived either by solving $e^{-\lambda t}$ or by using Appendix E. Column 2 shows the probability that it will be more than t minutes until the next arrival.

exhibit 5.6   Exponential Distribution

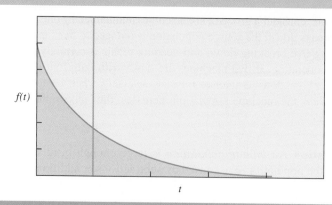

Column 3 shows the probability of the next arrival within t minutes (computed as 1 minus column 2)

(1)	(2)	(3)
	PROBABILITY THAT THE NEXT ARRIVAL WILL OCCUR IN	PROBABILITY THAT THE NEXT ARRIVAL WILL OCCUR IN
t	t MINUTES OR MORE (FROM	t MINUTES OR LESS
(MINUTES)	APPENDIX D OR SOLVING e^{-t})	[1 − COLUMN (2)]
0	1.00	0
0.5	0.61	0.39
1.0	0.37	0.63
1.5	0.22	0.78
2.0	0.14	0.86

Poisson Distribution In the second case, where one is interested in the number of arrivals during some time period T, the distribution appears as in Exhibit 5.7 and is obtained by finding the probability of exactly n arrivals during T. If the arrival process is **Poisson distribution**   random, the distribution is the **Poisson**, and the formula is

$$P_T(n) = \frac{(\lambda T)^n e^{-\lambda T}}{n!}$$ **[5.2]**

Equation (5.2) shows the probability of exactly n arrivals in time T. For example, if the mean arrival rate of units into a system is three per minute ($\lambda = 3$) and we want to find the probability that exactly five units will arrive within a one-minute period ($n = 5$, $T = 1$), we have

$$P_1(5) = \frac{(3 \times 1)^5 e^{-3 \times 1}}{5!} = \frac{3^5 e^{-3}}{120} = 2.025 e^{-3} = 0.101$$

That is, there is a 10.1 percent chance that there will be five arrivals in any one-minute interval.

Although often shown as a smoothed curve, as in Exhibit 5.7, the Poisson is a discrete distribution. (The curve becomes smoother as n becomes large.) The distribution is discrete because n refers, in our example, to the number of arrivals in a system, and this must be an integer. (For example, there cannot be 1.5 arrivals.)

Also note that the exponential and Poisson distributions can be derived from one another. The mean and variance of the Poisson are equal and denoted by λ. The mean of the

exhibit 5.7

Poisson Distribution for $\lambda T = 3$

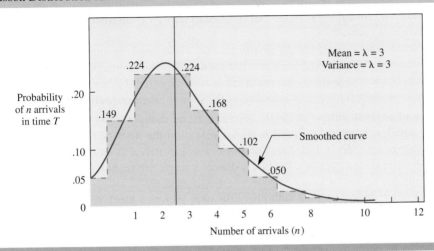

Mean = λ = 3
Variance = λ = 3

Probability of n arrivals in time T

.224 .224
.168
.149
.102
Smoothed curve
.050

Number of arrivals (n)

exponential is $1/\lambda$ and its variance is $1/\lambda^2$. (Remember that the time between arrivals is exponentially distributed and the number of arrivals per unit of time is Poisson distributed.)

Other arrival characteristics include arrival patterns, size of arrival units, and degree of patience. (See Exhibit 5.8.)

Arrival patterns. The arrivals at a system are far more controllable than is generally recognized. Barbers may decrease their Saturday arrival rate (and supposedly shift it to other days of the week) by charging an extra $1 for adult haircuts or charging adult

exhibit 5.8

Customer Arrivals in Queues

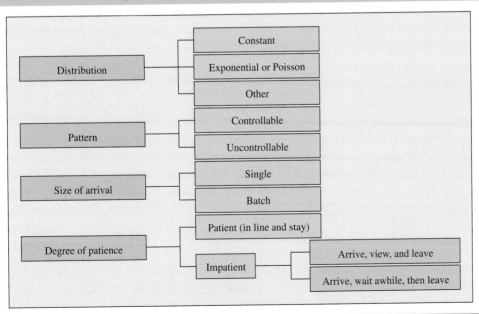

Distribution — Constant / Exponential or Poisson / Other

Pattern — Controllable / Uncontrollable

Size of arrival — Single / Batch

Degree of patience — Patient (in line and stay) / Impatient — Arrive, view, and leave / Arrive, wait awhile, then leave

prices for children's haircuts. Department stores run sales during the off-season or hold one-day-only sales in part for purposes of control. Airlines offer excursion and off-season rates for similar reasons. The simplest of all arrival-control devices is the posting of business hours.

Some service demands are clearly uncontrollable, such as emergency medical demands on a city's hospital facilities. But even in these situations, arrivals at emergency rooms in specific hospitals are controllable to some extent by, say, keeping ambulance drivers in the service region informed of the status of their respective host hospitals.

Size of arrival units.   A *single arrival* may be thought of as one unit. (A unit is the smallest number handled.) A single arrival on the floor of the New York Stock Exchange (NYSE) is 100 shares of stock; a single arrival at an egg-processing plant might be a dozen eggs or a flat of 2½ dozen; a single arrival at a restaurant is a single person.

A *batch arrival* is some multiple of the unit, such as a block of 1,000 shares on the NYSE, a case of eggs at the processing plant, or a party of five at a restaurant.

Degree of patience.   A *patient* arrival is one who waits as long as necessary until the service facility is ready to serve him or her. (Even if arrivals grumble and behave impatiently, the fact that they wait is sufficient to label them as patient arrivals for purposes of waiting line theory.)

There are two classes of *impatient* arrivals. Members of the first class arrive, survey both the service facility and the length of the line, and then decide to leave. Those in the second class arrive, view the situation, join the waiting line, and then, after some period of time, depart. The behavior of the first type is termed *balking,* while the second is termed *reneging.* To avoid balking and reneging companies that provide high service levels typically try to target server utilization levels (the percent of time busy) at no more than 70 to 80 percent.

The Queuing System: Factors

Service

The queuing system consists primarily of the waiting line(s) and the available number of servers. Here we discuss issues pertaining to waiting line characteristics and management, line structure, and service rate. Factors to consider with waiting lines include the line length, number of lines, and queue discipline.

Length.   In a practical sense, an infinite line is simply one that is very long in terms of the capacity of the service system. Examples of *infinite potential length* are a line of vehicles backed up for miles at a bridge crossing and customers who must form a line around the block as they wait to purchase tickets at a theater.

Gas stations, loading docks, and parking lots have *limited line capacity* caused by legal restrictions or physical space characteristics. This complicates the waiting line problem not only in service system utilization and waiting line computations but also in the shape of the actual arrival distribution. The arrival denied entry into the line because of lack of space may rejoin the population for a later try or may seek service elsewhere. Either action makes an obvious difference in the finite population case.

Number of lines.   A single line or single file is, of course, one line only. The term *multiple lines* refers to the single lines that form in front of two or more servers or to single lines that converge at some central redistribution point. The disadvantage of multiple lines in a busy facility is that arrivals often shift lines if several previous services have been of short duration or if those customers currently in other lines appear to require a short service time.

Queue discipline. A queue discipline is a priority rule or set of rules for determining the order of service to customers in a waiting line. The rules selected can have a dramatic effect on the system's overall performance. The number of customers in line, the average waiting time, the range of variability in waiting time, and the efficiency of the service facility are just a few of the factors affected by the choice of priority rules.

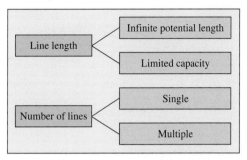

Probably the most common priority rule is first come, first served (FCFS). This rule states that customers in line are served on the basis of their chronological arrival; no other characteristics have any bearing on the selection process. This is popularly accepted as the fairest rule, although in practice it discriminates against the arrival requiring a short service time.

Reservations first, emergencies first, highest-profit customer first, largest orders first, best customers first, longest waiting time in line, and soonest promised date are other examples of priority rules. There are two major practical problems in using any

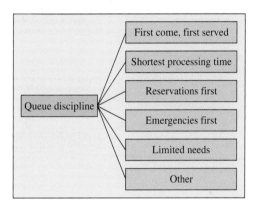

rule: One is ensuring that customers know and follow the rule. The other is ensuring that a system exists to enable employees to manage the line (such as take-a-number systems).

Service Time Distribution Another important feature of the waiting structure is the time the customer or unit spends with the server once the service has started. Waiting line formulas generally specify **service rate** as the capacity of the server in number of units per time period (such as 12 completions per hour) and *not* as service time, which might average five minutes each. A constant service time rule states that each service takes exactly the same time. As in constant arrivals, this characteristic is generally limited to machine-controlled operations.

Service rate

When service times are random, they can be approximated by the exponential distribution. When using the exponential distribution as an approximation of the service times, we will refer to μ as the average number of units or customers that can be served per time period.

Line Structures As Exhibit 5.9 shows, the flow of items to be serviced may go through a single line, multiple lines, or some mixture of the two. The choice of format depends partly on the volume of customers served and partly on the restrictions imposed by sequential requirements governing the order in which service must be performed.

1. **Single channel, single phase.** This is the simplest type of waiting line structure, and straightforward formulas are available to solve the problem for standard distribution patterns of arrival and service. When the distributions are nonstandard, the

exhibit 5.9   Line Structures

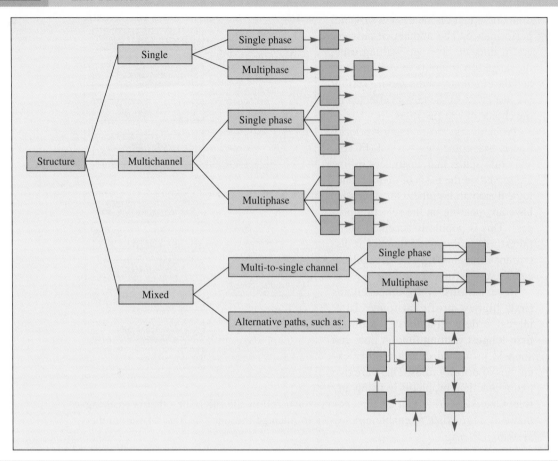

problem is easily solved by computer simulation. A typical example of a single-channel, single-phase situation is the one-person barbershop.

2. **Single channel, multiphase.** A car wash is an illustration because a series of services (vacuuming, wetting, washing, rinsing, drying, window cleaning, and parking) is performed in a fairly uniform sequence. A critical factor in the single-channel case with service in series is the amount of buildup of items allowed in front of each service, which in turn constitutes separate waiting lines.

3. **Multichannel, single phase.** Tellers' windows in a bank and checkout counters in high-volume department stores exemplify this type of structure. The difficulty with this format is that the uneven service time given each customer results in unequal speed or flow among the lines. This results in some customers being served before others who arrived earlier, as well as in some degree of line shifting. Varying this structure to ensure the servicing of arrivals in chronological order would require forming a single line, from which, as a server becomes available, the next customer in the queue is assigned.

The major problem of this structure is that it requires rigid control of the line to maintain order and to direct customers to available servers. In some

instances, assigning numbers to customers in order of their arrival helps alleviate this problem.

4. **Multichannel, multiphase.** This case is similar to the preceding one except that
two or more services are performed in sequence. The admission of patients in a
hospital follows this pattern because a specific sequence of steps is usually followed: initial contact at the admissions desk, filling out forms, making identification tags, obtaining a room assignment, escorting the patient to the room, and so
forth. Because several servers are usually available for this procedure, more than
one patient at a time may be processed.

5. **Mixed.** Under this general heading we consider two subcategories: (1)
multiple-to-single channel structures and (2) alternative path structures. Under
(1), we find either lines that merge into one for single-phase service, as at a bridge
crossing where two lanes merge into one, or lines that merge into one for multiphase service, such as subassembly lines feeding into a main line. Under (2), we
encounter two structures that differ in directional flow requirements. The first is
similar to the multichannel–multiphase case, except that (a) there may be switching from one channel to the next after the first service has been rendered and
(b) the number of channels and phases may vary—again—after performance of
the first service.

Exiting the Queuing System

Once a customer is served, two exit fates are possible: (1) The customer may return to
the source population and immediately become a competing candidate for service again
or (2) there may be a low probability of reservice. The first case can be illustrated by a
machine that has been routinely repaired and returned to duty but may break down again;
the second can be illustrated by a machine that has been overhauled or modified and has
a low probability of reservice over the near future. In a lighter vein, we might refer to
the first as the "recurring-common-cold case" and to the second as the "appendectomy-
only-once case."

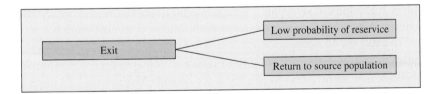

It should be apparent that when the population source is finite, any change in the service
performed on customers who return to the population modifies the arrival rate at the service
facility. This, of course, alters the characteristics of the waiting line under study and necessitates reanalysis of the problem.

WAITING LINE MODELS

In this section we present three sample waiting line problems followed by their solutions.
Each has a slightly different structure (see Exhibit 5.10) and solution equation (see
Exhibit 5.11). There are more types of models than these three, but the formulas and

exhibit 5.10

Properties of Some Specific Waiting Line Models

MODEL	LAYOUT	SERVICE PHASE	SOURCE POPULATION	ARRIVAL PATTERN	QUEUE DISCIPLINE	SERVICE PATTERN	PERMISSIBLE QUEUE LENGTH	TYPICAL EXAMPLE
1. Simple System	Single channel	Single	Infinite	Poisson	FCFS	Exponential	Unlimited	Drive-in teller at bank; one-lane toll bridge
2. Constant Service Time System	Single channel	Single	Infinite	Poisson	FCFS	Constant	Unlimited	Roller coaster rides in amusement park
3. Multichannel System	Multichannel	Single	Infinite	Poisson	FCFS	Exponential	Unlimited	Parts counter in auto agency

Excel: Queue_Models

solutions become quite complicated, and those problems are generally solved using computer simulation. Also, in using these formulas, keep in mind that they are steady-state formulas derived on the assumption that the process under study is ongoing. Thus, they may provide inaccurate results when applied to processes where the arrival rates and/or service rates change over time. The Excel Spreadsheet QueueModels.xls included on the DVD-ROM, can be used to solve these problems.

Here is a quick preview of our three problems to illustrate each of the three waiting line models in Exhibits 5.10 and 5.11.

Service

Problem 1: Customers in line.   A bank wants to know how many customers are waiting for a drive-in teller, how long they have to wait, the utilization of the teller, and what the service rate would have to be so that 95 percent of the time there will not be more than three cars in the system at any time.

Problem 2: Equipment selection.   A franchise for Robot Car Wash must decide which equipment to purchase out of a choice of three. Larger units cost more but wash cars faster. To make the decision, costs are related to revenue.

Problem 3: Determining the number of servers.   An auto agency parts department must decide how many clerks to employ at the counter. More clerks cost more money, but there is a savings because mechanics wait less time.

Service

Step by Step

Example 5.1: Customers in Line

Western National Bank is considering opening a drive-through window for customer service. Management estimates that customers will arrive at the rate of 15 per hour. The teller who will staff the window can service customers at the rate of one every three minutes or 20 per hour.

Part 1   Assuming Poisson arrivals and exponential service, find

1. Utilization of the teller.
2. Average number in the waiting line.
3. Average number in the system.

Notations for Equations

INFINITE QUEUING NOTATION: MODELS 1–3

λ = Arrival rate

μ = Service rate

$\dfrac{1}{\mu}$ = Average service time

$\dfrac{1}{\lambda}$ = Average time between arrivals

ρ = Ratio of total arrival rate to service rate for a single server $\left(\dfrac{\lambda}{\mu}\right)^*$

L_q = Average number waiting in line

L_s = Average number in system (including any being served)

W_q = Average time waiting in line
W_s = Average total time in system (including time to be served)
n = Number of units in the system
S = Number of identical service channels
P_n = Probability of exactly n units in system
P_w = Probability of waiting in line

EQUATIONS FOR SOLVING THREE MODEL PROBLEMS

Model 1

$$L_q = \frac{\lambda^2}{\mu(\mu - \lambda)} \qquad W_q = \frac{L_q}{\lambda} \qquad P_n = \left(1 - \frac{\lambda}{\mu}\right)\left(\frac{\lambda}{\mu}\right)^n \qquad P_n = \left(1 - \frac{\lambda}{\mu}\right)$$

$$L_s = \frac{\lambda}{\mu - \lambda} \qquad W_s = \frac{L_s}{\lambda} \qquad \rho = \frac{\lambda}{\mu}$$

(5.3)

Model 2

$$L_q = \frac{\lambda^2}{2\mu(\mu - \lambda)} \qquad W_q = \frac{L_q}{\lambda}$$

$$L_s = L_q + \frac{\lambda}{\mu} \qquad W_s = \frac{L_s}{\lambda}$$

(5.4)

Model 3

$$L_s = L_q + \lambda/\mu \qquad W_s = L_s/\lambda$$

$$W_q = L_q/\lambda \qquad P_w = L_q\left(\frac{S\mu}{\lambda} - 1\right)$$

(5.5)

(Exhibit 5.12 provides the value of L_q given λ/μ and the number of servers S.)

*For single-server queues, this is equivalent to utilization.

4. Average waiting time in line.
5. Average waiting time in the system, including service.

SOLUTION—Part 1

1. The average utilization of the teller is (using Model 1—Simple System)

$$\rho = \frac{\lambda}{\mu} = \frac{15}{20} = 75 \text{ percent}$$

2. The average number in the waiting line is

$$L_q = \frac{\lambda^2}{\mu(\mu - \lambda)} = \frac{(15)^2}{20(20 - 15)} = 2.25 \text{ customers}$$

3. The average number in the system is

$$L_s = \frac{\lambda}{\mu - \lambda} = \frac{15}{20 - 15} = 3 \text{ customers}$$

Excel Queue

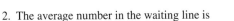

4. Average waiting time in line is

$$W_q = \frac{L_q}{\lambda} = \frac{2.25}{15} = 0.15 \text{ hour, or 9 minutes}$$

5. Average waiting time in the system is

$$W_s = \frac{L_s}{\lambda} = \frac{3}{15} = 0.2 \text{ hour, or 12 minutes}$$

Part 2   Because of limited space availability and a desire to provide an acceptable level of service, the bank manager would like to ensure, with 95 percent confidence, that no more than three cars will be in the system at any time. What is the present level of service for the three-car limit? What level of teller use must be attained and what must be the service rate of the teller to ensure the 95 percent level of service?

SOLUTION—Part 2

The present level of service for three or fewer cars is the probability that there are 0, 1, 2, or 3 cars in the system. From Model 1, Exhibit 5.11,

$$P_n = \left(1 - \frac{\lambda}{\mu}\right)\left(\frac{\lambda}{\mu}\right)^n$$

at $n = 0$, $P_0 = (1 - 15/20)$ $(15/20)^0 = 0.250$
at $n = 1$, $P_1 = (1/4)$ $(15/20)^1 = 0.188$
at $n = 2$, $P_2 = (1/4)$ $(15/20)^2 = 0.141$
at $n = 3$, $P_3 = (1/4)$ $(15/20)^3 = \underline{0.105}$
                                            0.684   or   68.4 percent

The probability of having more than three cars in the system is 1.0 minus the probability of three or fewer cars ($100 - 68.4 = 31.6$ percent).

For a 95 percent service level of three or fewer cars, this states that $P_0 + P_1 + P_2 + P_3 = 95$ percent.

$$0.95 = \left(1 - \frac{\lambda}{\mu}\right)\left(\frac{\lambda}{\mu}\right)^0 + \left(1 - \frac{\lambda}{\mu}\right)\left(\frac{\lambda}{\mu}\right)^1 + \left(1 - \frac{\lambda}{\mu}\right)\left(\frac{\lambda}{\mu}\right)^2 + \left(1 - \frac{\lambda}{\mu}\right)\left(\frac{\lambda}{\mu}\right)^3$$

$$0.95 = \left(1 - \frac{\lambda}{\mu}\right)\left[1 + \frac{\lambda}{\mu} + \left(\frac{\lambda}{\mu}\right)^2 + \left(\frac{\lambda}{\mu}\right)^3\right]$$

We can solve this by trial and error for values of λ/μ. If $\lambda/\mu = 0.50$,

$$0.95 \stackrel{?}{=} 0.5(1 + 0.5 + 0.25 + 0.125)$$
$$0.95 \neq 0.9375$$

With $\lambda/\mu = 0.45$,

$$0.95 \stackrel{?}{=} (1 - 0.45)(1 + 0.45 + 0.203 + 0.091)$$
$$0.95 \neq 0.96$$

With $\lambda/\mu = 0.47$,

$$0.95 \stackrel{?}{=} (1 - 0.47)(1 + 0.47 + 0.221 + 0.104) = 0.9512$$
$$0.95 \approx 0.95135$$

Therefore, with the utilization $\rho = \lambda/\mu$ of 47 percent, the probability of three or fewer cars in the system is 95 percent.

To find the rate of service required to attain this 95 percent service level, we simply solve the equation $\lambda/\mu = 0.47$, where λ = number of arrivals per hour. This gives $\mu = 32$ per hour. That is, the teller must serve approximately 32 people per hour (a 60 percent increase over the original 20-per-hour capability) for 95 percent confidence that not more than three cars will be in the system. Perhaps service may be speeded up by modifying the method of service, adding another teller, or limiting the types of transactions available at the drive-through window. Note that with the condition of 95 percent confidence that three or fewer cars will be in the system, the teller will be idle 53 percent of the time. ●

Example 5.2: Equipment Selection

The Robot Company franchises combination gas and car wash stations throughout the United States. Robot gives a free car wash for a gasoline fill-up or, for a wash alone, charges $0.50. Past experience shows that the number of customers that have car washes following fill-ups is about the same as for a wash alone. The average profit on a gasoline fill-up is about $0.70, and the cost of the car wash to Robot is $0.10. Robot stays open 14 hours per day.

Robot has three power units and drive assemblies, and a franchisee must select the unit preferred. Unit I can wash cars at the rate of one every five minutes and is leased for $12 per day. Unit II, a larger unit, can wash cars at the rate of one every four minutes but costs $16 per day. Unit III, the largest, costs $22 per day and can wash a car in three minutes.

The franchisee estimates that customers will not wait in line more than five minutes for a car wash. A longer time will cause Robot to lose the gasoline sales as well as the car wash sale.

If the estimate of customer arrivals resulting in washes is 10 per hour, which wash unit should be selected?

Service

Step by Step

Excel:
Queue

SOLUTION

Using unit I, calculate the average waiting time of customers in the wash line (μ for unit I = 12 per hour). From the Model 2—Constant Service Time System equations (Exhibit 5.11),

$$L_q = \frac{\lambda^2}{2\mu(\mu - \lambda)} = \frac{10^2}{2(12)(12 - 10)} = 2.08333$$

$$W_q = \frac{L_q}{\lambda} = \frac{2.08333}{10} = 0.208 \text{ hour, or } 12\tfrac{1}{2} \text{ minutes}$$

For unit II at 15 per hour,

$$L_q = \frac{10^2}{2(15)(15 - 10)} = 0.667$$

$$W_q = \frac{0.667}{10} = 0.0667 \text{ hour, or 4 minutes}$$

If waiting time is the only criterion, unit II should be purchased. But before we make the final decision, we must look at the profit differential between both units.

With unit I, some customers would balk and renege because of the $12\tfrac{1}{2}$-minute wait. And, although this greatly complicates the mathematical analysis, we can gain some estimate of lost sales with unit I by increasing $W_q = 5$ minutes or $\frac{1}{12}$ hour (the average length of time customers will wait) and solving for λ. This would be the effective arrival rate of customers:

$$W_q = \frac{L_q}{\lambda} = \left(\frac{\lambda^2/2\mu(\mu - \lambda)}{\lambda} \right)$$

$$W_q = \frac{\lambda}{2\mu(\mu - \lambda)}$$

$$\lambda = \frac{2W_q \mu^2}{1 + 2W_q \mu} = \frac{2\left(\frac{1}{12}\right)(12)^2}{1 + 2\left(\frac{1}{12}\right)(12)} = 8 \text{ per hour}$$

Therefore, because the original estimate of λ was 10 per hour, an estimated 2 customers per hour will be lost. Lost profit of 2 customers per hour $\times$ 14 hours $\times \frac{1}{2}$($0.70 fill-up profit + $0.40 wash profit) = $15.40 per day.

Because the additional cost of unit II over unit I is only $4 per day, the loss of $15.40 profit obviously warrants installing unit II.

The original five-minute maximum wait constraint is satisfied by unit II. Therefore unit III is not considered unless the arrival rate is expected to increase.●

Service

Step by Step

Excel:
Queue

Example 5.3: Determining the Number of Servers

In the service department of the Glenn-Mark Auto Agency, mechanics requiring parts for auto repair or service present their request forms at the parts department counter. The parts clerk fills a request while the mechanic waits. Mechanics arrive in a random (Poisson) fashion at the rate of 40 per hour, and a clerk can fill requests at the rate of 20 per hour (exponential). If the cost for a parts clerk is $6 per hour and the cost for a mechanic is $12 per hour, determine the optimum number of clerks to staff the counter. (Because of the high arrival rate, an infinite source may be assumed.)

SOLUTION

First, assume that three clerks will be used because having only one or two clerks would create infinitely long lines (since $\lambda = 40$ and $\mu = 20$). The equations for Model 3—Multichannel System from Exhibit 5.11 will be used here. But first we need to obtain the average number in line using the table of Exhibit 5.12. Using the table and values $\lambda/\mu = 2$ and $S = 3$, we obtain $L_q = 0.8888$ mechanic.

At this point, we see that we have an average of 0.8888 mechanic waiting all day. For an eight-hour day at $12 per hour, there is a loss of mechanic's time worth 0.8888 mechanic $\times$ $12 per hour $\times$ 8 hours = $85.32.

Our next step is to reobtain the waiting time if we add another parts clerk. We then compare the added cost of the additional employee with the time saved by the mechanics. Again, using the table of Exhibit 5.12 but with $S = 4$, we obtain

$$L_q = 0.1730 \text{ mechanic in line}$$

0.1730 $\times$ $12 $\times$ 8 hours = $16.61 cost of a mechanic waiting in line

Value of mechanics' time saved is $85.32 − $16.61	= $68.71
Cost of an additional parts clerk is 8 hours $\times$ $6/hour	= 48.00
Cost of reduction by adding fourth clerk	= $20.71

exhibit 5.12

Expected Number of People Waiting in Line (L_q) for Various Values of S and λ/μ

NUMBER OF SERVICE CHANNELS, S

λ/μ	1	2	3	4	5	6	7	8	9	10	11	12	13	14	15
0.10	0.0111														
0.15	0.0264	0.0006													
0.20	0.0500	0.0020													
0.25	0.0833	0.0039													
0.30	0.1285	0.0069													
0.35	0.1884	0.0110													
0.40	0.2666	0.0166													
0.45	0.3681	0.0239	0.0019												
0.50	0.5000	0.0333	0.0030												
0.55	0.6722	0.045	0.0043												
0.60	0.9090	0.0593	0.0061												
0.65	1.2071	0.0767	0.0084												
0.70	1.6333	0.0976	0.0112												
0.75	2.2500	0.1227	0.0147												
0.80	3.2000	0.1523	0.0189												
0.85	4.8165	0.1873	0.0239	0.0031											
0.90	8.1000	0.2285	0.0300	0.0041											
0.95	18.0500	0.2767	0.0371	0.0053											
1.0		0.3333	0.0454	0.0067											
1.2		0.6748	0.0940	0.0158											
1.4		1.3449	0.1778	0.0324	0.0059										
1.6		2.8441	0.3128	0.0604	0.0121										
1.8		7.6731	0.5320	0.1051	0.0227	0.0047									
2.0			0.8888	0.1730	0.0390	0.0090									
2.2			1.4907	0.2770	0.066	0.0158									
2.4			2.1261	0.4205	0.1047	0.0266	0.0065								
2.6			4.9322	0.6581	0.1609	0.0425	0.0110								
2.8			12.2724	1.0000	0.2411	0.0659	0.0180								
3.0				1.5282	0.3541	0.0991	0.0282	0.0077							
3.2				2.3855	0.5128	0.1452	0.0427	0.0122							
3.4				3.9060	0.7365	0.2085	0.0631	0.0189							
3.6				7.0893	1.0550	0.2947	0.0912	0.0283	0.0084						
3.8				16.9366	1.5181	0.4114	0.1292	0.0412	0.0127						
4.0					2.2164	0.5694	0.1801	0.0590	0.0189						
4.2					3.3269	0.7837	0.2475	0.0827	0.0273	0.0087					
4.4					5.2675	1.0777	0.3364	0.1142	0.0389	0.0128					
4.6					9.2885	1.4857	0.4532	0.1555	0.0541	0.0184					
4.8					21.6384	2.0708	0.6071	0.2092	0.0742	0.0260					
5.0						2.9375	0.8102	0.2785	0.1006	0.0361	0.0125				
5.2						4.3004	1.0804	0.3680	0.1345	0.0492	0.0175				
5.4						6.6609	1.4441	0.5871	0.1779	0.0663	0.0243	0.0085			
5.6						11.5178	1.9436	0.6313	0.2330	0.0683	0.0330	0.0119			
5.8						26.3726	2.6481	0.8225	0.3032	0.1164	0.0443	0.0164			
6.0							3.6878	1.0707	0.3918	0.1518	0.0590	0.0224			
6.2							5.2979	1.3967	0.5037	0.1964	0.0775	0.0300	0.0113		
6.4							8.0768	1.8040	0.6454	0.2524	0.1008	0.0398	0.0153		
6.6							13.7992	2.4198	0.8247	0.3222	0.1302	0.0523	0.0205		
6.8							31.1270	3.2441	1.0533	0.4090	0.1666	0.0679	0.0271	0.0105	
7.0								4.4471	1.3471	0.5172	0.2119	0.0876	0.0357	0.0141	
7.2								6.3133	1.7288	0.6521	0.2677	0.1119	0.0463	0.0187	
7.4								9.5102	2.2324	0.8202	0.3364	0.1420	0.0595	0.0245	0.0097
7.6								16.0379	2.9113	1.0310	0.4211	0.1789	0.0761	0.0318	0.0129
7.8								35.8956	3.8558	1.2972	0.5250	0.2243	0.0966	0.0410	0.0168
8.0									5.2264	1.6364	0.6530	0.2796	0.1214	0.0522	0.0220
8.2									7.3441	2.0736	0.8109	0.3469	0.1520	0.0663	0.0283
8.4									10.9592	2.6470	1.0060	0.4288	0.1891	0.0834	0.0361
8.6									18.3223	3.4160	1.2484	0.5236	0.2341	0.1043	0.0459
8.8									40.6824	4.4805	1.5524	0.6501	0.2885	0.1208	0.0577
9.0										6.0183	1.9366	0.7980	0.3543	0.1603	0.0723
9.2										8.3869	2.4293	0.9788	0.4333	0.1974	0.0899
9.4										12.4183	3.0732	1.2010	0.5267	0.2419	0.1111
9.6										20.6160	3.9318	1.4752	0.5437	0.2952	0.1367
9.8										45.4769	5.1156	1.8165	0.7827	0.3699	0.16731
10											6.8210	2.2465	0.9506	0.4352	0.2040

Excel: Expected Length

This problem could be expanded to consider the addition of runners to deliver parts to mechanics; the problem then would be to determine the optimal number of runners. This, however, would have to include the added cost of lost time caused by errors in parts receipts. For example, a mechanic would recognize a wrong part at the counter and obtain immediate correction, whereas the parts runner might not. ●

Service

COMPUTER SIMULATION OF WAITING LINES

Some waiting line problems that seem simple on first impression turn out to be extremely difficult or impossible to solve. Throughout this chapter we have been treating waiting line situations that are independent; that is, either the entire system consists of a single phase, or else each service that is performed in a series is independent. (This could happen if the output of one service location is allowed to build up in front of the next one so that this, in essence, becomes a calling population for the next service.) When a series of services is performed in sequence where the output rate of one becomes the input rate of the next, we can no longer use the simple formulas. This is also true for any problem where conditions do not meet the requirements of the equations, as specified in Exhibit 5.10. The technique best suited to solving this type of problem is computer simulation.

Service

SUMMARY

This chapter has shown how service businesses are in many ways very similar to manufacturing businesses. In both types of businesses there is a need to make trade-offs in developing a focus. Just as in manufacturing, a service business cannot be all things to all people.

The service-system design matrix is in many ways similar to the product–process matrix we used to categorize manufacturing operations. Services are, however, very different from manufacturing when we consider the high degree of personalization often required, the speed of delivery needed, the direct customer contact, and the inherent variability of service encounters. The buffering and scheduling mechanisms that we have available to smooth the demand placed on a manufacturing operation is often not available to a service operation. Services generally require much higher levels of capacity relative to demand. In addition, they impose a greater need for flexibility on the workers involved in providing the services.

Waiting line analysis is relevant to many service situations. The basic objective is to balance the cost of waiting with the cost of adding more resources. For a service system this means that the utilization of a server may be quite low to provide a short waiting time to the customer. Many queuing problems appear simple until an attempt is made to solve them. This chapter has dealt with the simpler problems. When situations become more complex, when there are multiple phases, or when services are performed only in a particular sequence, computer simulation is necessary.

Key Terms

High and low degree of customer contact The physical presence of the customer in the system and the percentage of time the customer must be in the system relative to the total time it takes to perform the service.

Service blueprint The flowchart of a service process emphasizing what is visible and what is not visible to the customer.

Poka-yokes Procedures that prevent mistakes from becoming defects.

Queuing system Consists of three major components: (1) the source population and the way customers arrive at the system, (2) the serving systems, and (3) how customers exit the system.

Arrival rate The expected number of customers that arrive each period.

Exponential distribution A probability distribution often associated with interarrival times.

Poisson distribution Probability distribution often used to describe the number of arrivals during a given time period.

Service rate The capacity of a server measured in number of units that can be processed over a given time period.

Formula Review

Exponential distribution

$$f(t) = \lambda e^{-\lambda t} \tag{5.1}$$

Poisson distribution

$$P_T(n) = \frac{(\lambda T)^n e^{-\lambda T}}{n!} \tag{5.2}$$

Model 1 (See Exhibit 5.11.)

$$L_q = \frac{\lambda^2}{\mu(\mu - \lambda)} \qquad W_q = \frac{L_q}{\lambda} \qquad P_n = \left(1 - \frac{\lambda}{\mu}\right)\left(\frac{\lambda}{\mu}\right)^n \qquad P_o = \left(1 - \frac{\lambda}{\mu}\right)$$

$$L_s = \frac{\lambda}{\mu - \lambda} \qquad W_s = \frac{L_s}{\lambda} \qquad \rho = \frac{\lambda}{\mu} \tag{5.3}$$

Model 2

$$L_q = \frac{\lambda^2}{2\mu(\mu - \lambda)} \qquad W_q = \frac{L_q}{\lambda}$$

$$L_s = L_q + \frac{\lambda}{\mu} \qquad W_s = \frac{L_s}{\lambda} \tag{5.4}$$

Model 3

$$L_s = L_q + \lambda/\mu \qquad W_s = L_s/\lambda$$

$$W_q = L_q/\lambda \qquad P_w = L_q\left(\frac{S_\mu}{\lambda} - 1\right) \tag{5.5}$$

Exhibit 5.12 provides the value of L_q given λ/μ and the number of servers S.

Solved Problems

Excel:
Queue

SOLVED PROBLEM 1

Quick Lube Inc. operates a fast lube and oil change garage. On a typical day, customers arrive at the rate of three per hour, and lube jobs are performed at an average rate of one every 15 minutes. The mechanics operate as a team on one car at a time.

Assuming Poisson arrivals and exponential service, find

    a. Utilization of the lube team.
    b. The average number of cars in line.
    c. The average time a car waits before it is lubed.
    d. The total time it takes to go through the system (that is, waiting in line plus lube time).

Solution

$\lambda = 3, \mu = 4$

    a. Utilization $\rho = \dfrac{\lambda}{\mu} = \dfrac{3}{4} = 75\%$.

    b. $L_q = \dfrac{\lambda^2}{\mu(\mu - \lambda)} = \dfrac{3^2}{4(4 - 3)} = \dfrac{9}{4} = 2.25$ cars in line.

    c. $W_q = \dfrac{L_q}{\lambda} = \dfrac{2.25}{3} = .75$ hour, or 45 minutes.

    d. $W_s = \dfrac{L_s}{\lambda} = \dfrac{\lambda}{\mu - \lambda} \bigg/ \lambda = \dfrac{3}{4 - 3} \bigg/ 3 = 1$ hour (waiting + lube).

Excel:
Queue

SOLVED PROBLEM 2

American Vending Inc. (AVI) supplies vended food to a large university. Because students often kick the machines out of anger and frustration, management has a constant repair problem. The machines break down on an average of three per hour, and the breakdowns are distributed in a Poisson manner. Downtime costs the company $25/hour per machine, and each maintenance worker gets $4 per hour. One worker can service machines at an average rate of five per hour, distributed exponentially; two workers working together can service seven per hour, distributed exponentially; and a team of three workers can do eight per hour, distributed exponentially.

What is the optimal maintenance crew size for servicing the machines?

Solution

Case I—One worker:
    $\lambda = 3$/hour Poisson, $\mu = 5$/hour exponential
There is an average number of machines in the system of

$$L_s = \frac{\lambda}{\mu - \lambda} = \frac{3}{5 - 3} = \frac{3}{2} = 1.5 \text{ machines}$$

Downtime cost is $25 \times 1.5 = \$37.50$ per hour; repair cost is $4.00 per hour; and total cost per hour for 1 worker is $37.50 + $4.00 = $41.50.

Downtime (1.5 × $25) = $37.50
Labor (1 worker × $4) =   4.00
                $41.50

Case II—Two workers:
   $\lambda = 3, \mu = 7$

$$L_s = \frac{\lambda}{\mu - \lambda} = \frac{3}{7 - 3} = .75 \text{ machine}$$

Downtime (.75 × $25)   = $18.75
Labor (2 workers × $4.00) =   8.00
                              $26.75

Case III—Three workers:
   $\lambda = 3, \mu = 8$

$$L_s = \frac{\lambda}{\mu - \lambda} = \frac{3}{8 - 3} = \frac{3}{5} = .60 \text{ machine}$$

Downtime (.60 × $25)   = $15.00
Labor (3 workers × $4) =   12.00
                           $27.00

Comparing the costs for one, two, or three workers, we see that Case II with two workers is the optimal decision.

Review and Discussion Questions

1. Why should a manager of a bank home office be evaluated differently than a manager of a bank branch?
2. Identify the high-contact and low-contact operations of the following services:
   a. A dental office.
   b. An airline.
   c. An accounting office.
   d. An automobile agency.
   e. Amazon.com
3. Take a visit to secondlife.com. Where do sales opportunities exist?

Problems

1. Place the following hospital activities/relationships on the service design matrix: physician/patient, nurse/patient, billing, medical records, lab tests, admissions, diagnostic tests (such as X-rays).
2. Perform a quick service audit the next time you go shopping at a department store. Evaluate the three T's of service: the Task, the Treatment, and the Tangible features of the service on a scale of 1 (poor), 3 (average), and 5 (excellent). Remember that the tangible features include the environment, layout, and appearance of the store, not the goods you purchased.
3. SYSTEM DESCRIPTION EXERCISE
   The beginning step in studying a productive system is to develop a description of that system. Once a system is described, we can better determine why the system works well or poorly and recommend production-related improvements. Because most of us are familiar

with fast-food restaurants, try your hand at describing the production system employed at, say, a McDonald's. In doing so, answer the following questions:

a. What are the important aspects of the service package?

b. Which skills and attitudes are needed by the service personnel?

c. How can customer demand be altered?

d. Provide a rough-cut blueprint of the delivery system. (It is not necessary to provide execution times. Just diagram the basic flow through the system.) Critique the blueprint. Are there any unnecessary steps or can failure points be eliminated?

e. Can the customer/provider interface be changed to include more technology? More self-serve?

f. Which measures are being used to evaluate the service? Which could be used?

4   What are the differences between high and low customer contact service (CCS) businesses, in general, for the dimensions listed below? (Example—Facility Layout: in a high CCS, the facility would be designed to enhance the feelings and comfort of the customer while in a low CCS, the facility would be designed for efficient processing.)

	LOW CCS BUSINESSES	HIGH CCS BUSINESSES
Worker skill		
Capacity utilization		
Level of automation		

5   Students arrive at the Administrative Services Office at an average of one every 15 minutes, and their requests take on average 10 minutes to be processed. The service counter is staffed by only one clerk, Judy Gumshoes, who works eight hours per day. Assume Poisson arrivals and exponential service times.

a. What percentage of time is Judy idle?

b. How much time, on average, does a student spend waiting in line?

c. How long is the (waiting) line on average?

d. What is the probability that an arriving student (just before entering the Administrative Services Office) will find at least one other student waiting in line?

6   The managers of the Administrative Services Office estimate that the time a student spends waiting in line costs them (due to goodwill loss and so on) $10 per hour. To reduce the time a student spends waiting, they know that they need to improve Judy's processing time (see Problem 5). They are currently considering the following two options:

a. Install a computer system, with which Judy expects to be able to complete a student request 40 percent faster (from 2 minutes per request to 1 minute and 12 seconds, for example).

b. Hire another temporary clerk, who will work at the same rate as Judy.

If the computer costs $99.50 to operate per day, while the temporary clerk gets paid $75 per day, is Judy right to prefer the hired help? Assume Poisson arrivals and exponential service times.

7   Sharp Discounts Wholesale Club has two service desks, one at each entrance of the store. Customers arrive at each service desk at an average of one every six minutes. The service rate at each service desk is four minutes per customer.

a. How often (what percentage of time) is each service desk idle?

b. What is the probability that both service clerks are busy?

c. What is the probability that both service clerks are idle?

d. How many customers, on average, are waiting in line in front of each service desk?

e. How much time does a customer spend at the service desk (waiting plus service time)?

8   Sharp Discounts Wholesale Club is considering consolidating its two service desks (see Problem 7) into one location, staffed by two clerks. The clerks will continue to work at the same individual speed of four minutes per customer.

a. What is the probability of waiting in line?

b. How many customers, on average, are waiting in line?

c. How much time does a customer spend at the service desk (waiting plus service time)?

d. Do you think the Sharp Discounts Wholesale Club should consolidate the service desks?

9 Burrito King (a new fast-food franchise opening up nationwide) has successfully automated burrito production for its drive-up fast-food establishments. The Burro-Master 9000 requires a constant 45 seconds to produce a batch of burritos. It has been estimated that customers will arrive at the drive-up window according to a Poisson distribution at an average of one every 50 seconds. To help determine the amount of space needed for the line at the drive-up window, Burrito King would like to know the expected average time in the system, the average line length (in cars), and the average number of cars in the system (both in line and at the window).

10 The Bijou Theater in Hermosa Beach, California, shows vintage movies. Customers arrive at the theater line at the rate of 100 per hour. The ticket seller averages 30 seconds per customer, which includes placing validation stamps on customers' parking lot receipts and punching their frequent watcher cards. (Because of these added services, many customers don't get in until after the feature has started.)

a. What is the average customer time in the system?

b. What would be the effect on customer time in the system of having a second ticket taker doing nothing but validations and card punching, thereby cutting the average service time to 20 seconds?

c. Would system waiting time be less than you found in *b* if a second window was opened with each server doing all three tasks?

11 To support National Heart Week, the Heart Association plans to install a free blood pressure testing booth in El Con Mall for the week. Previous experience indicates that, on the average, 10 persons per hour request a test. Assume arrivals are Poisson from an infinite population. Blood pressure measurements can be made at a constant time of five minutes each. Assume the queue length can be infinite with FCFS discipline.

a. What average number in line can be expected?

b. What average number of persons can be expected to be in the system?

c. What is the average amount of time that a person can expect to spend in line?

d. On the average, how much time will it take to measure a person's blood pressure, including waiting time?

e. On weekends, the arrival rate can be expected to increase to over 12 per hour. What effect will this have on the number in the waiting line?

12 A cafeteria serving line has a coffee urn from which customers serve themselves. Arrivals at the urn follow a Poisson distribution at the rate of three per minute. In serving themselves, customers take about 15 seconds, exponentially distributed.

a. How many customers would you expect to see on the average at the coffee urn?

b. How long would you expect it to take to get a cup of coffee?

c. What percentage of time is the urn being used?

d. What is the probability that three or more people are in the cafeteria?

e. If the cafeteria installs an automatic vendor that dispenses a cup of coffee at a constant time of 15 seconds, how does this change your answers to *a* and *b*?

13 L. Winston Martin (an allergist in Chicago) has an excellent system for handling his regular patients who come in just for allergy injections. Patients arrive for an injection and fill out a name slip, which is then placed in an open slot that passes into another room staffed by one or two nurses. The specific injections for a patient are prepared, and the patient is called through a speaker system into the room to receive the injection. At certain times during the day, patient load drops and only one nurse is needed to administer the injections.

Let's focus on the simpler case of the two—namely, when there is one nurse. Also assume that patients arrive in a Poisson fashion and the service rate of the nurse is exponentially distributed. During this slower period, patients arrive with an interarrival time of approximately three minutes. It takes the nurse an average of two minutes to prepare the patients' serum and administer the injection.

a. What is the average number you would expect to see in Dr. Martin's facilities?

b. How long would it take for a patient to arrive, get an injection, and leave?

  c. What is the probability that there will be three or more patients on the premises?

  d. What is the utilization of the nurse?

  e. Assume three nurses are available. Each takes an average of two minutes to prepare the patients' serum and administer the injection. What is the average total time of a patient in the system?

14 The Judy Gray Income Tax Service is analyzing its customer service operations during the month prior to the April filing deadline. On the basis of past data it has been estimated that customers arrive according to a Poisson process with an average interarrival time of 12 minutes. The time to complete a return for a customer is exponentially distributed with a mean of 10 minutes. Based on this information, answer the following questions:

  a. If you went to Judy, how much time would you allow for getting your return done?

  b. On average, how much room should be allowed for the waiting area?

  c. If Judy stayed in the office 12 hours per day, how many hours on average, per day, would she be busy?

  d. What is the probability that the system is idle?

  e. If the arrival rate remained unchanged but the average time in system must be 45 minutes or less, what would need to be changed?

15 Benny the Barber owns a one-chair shop. At barber college, they told Benny that his customers would exhibit a Poisson arrival distribution and that he would provide an exponential service distribution. His market survey data indicate that customers arrive at a rate of two per hour. It will take Benny an average of 20 minutes to give a haircut. Based on these figures, find the following:

  a. The average number of customers waiting.

  b. The average time a customer waits.

  c. The average time a customer is in the shop.

  d. The average utilization of Benny's time.

16 Benny the Barber (see problem 15) is considering the addition of a second chair. Customers would be selected for a haircut on a FCFS basis from those waiting. Benny has assumed that both barbers would take an average of 20 minutes to give a haircut, and that business would remain unchanged with customers arriving at a rate of two per hour. Find the following information to help Benny decide if a second chair should be added:

  a. The average number of customers waiting.

  b. The average time a customer waits.

  c. The average time a customer is in the shop.

17 Customers enter the camera department of a store at the average rate of six per hour. The department is staffed by one employee, who takes an average of six minutes to serve each arrival. Assume this is a simple Poisson arrival exponentially distributed service time situation.

  a. As a casual observer, how many people would you expect to see in the camera department (excluding the clerk)? How long would a customer expect to spend in the camera department (total time)?

  b. What is the utilization of the clerk?

  c. What is the probability that there are more than two people in the camera department (excluding the clerk)?

  d. Another clerk has been hired for the camera department who also takes an average of six minutes to serve each arrival. How long would a customer expect to spend in the department now?

18 Cathy Livingston, bartender at the Los Gactos Racquet Club, can serve drinks at the rate of one every 50 seconds. During a hot evening recently, the bar was particularly busy and every 55 seconds someone was at the bar asking for a drink.

  a. Assuming that everyone in the bar drank at the same rate and that Cathy served people on a first-come, first-served basis, how long would you expect to have to wait for a drink?

    b. How many people would you expect to be waiting for drinks?

    c. What is the probability that three or more people are waiting for drinks?

    d. What is the utilization of the bartender (how busy is she)?

    e. If the bartender is replaced with an automatic drink dispensing machine (with a constant service time), how would this change your answer in part *a*?

19   An office employs several clerks who originate documents and one operator who enters the document information in a word processor. The group originates documents at a rate of 25 per hour. The operator can enter the information with average exponentially distributed time of two minutes. Assume the population is infinite, arrivals are Poisson, and queue length is infinite with FCFS discipline.

    a. Calculate the percentage utilization of the operator.

    b. Calculate the average number of documents in the system.

    c. Calculate the average time in the system.

    d. Calculate the probability of four or more documents being in the system.

    e. If another clerk were added, the document origination rate would increase to 30 per hour. What would this do to the word processor workload? Show why.

20   A study-aid desk staffed by a graduate student has been established to answer students' questions and help in working problems in your OSM course. The desk is staffed eight hours per day. The dean wants to know how the facility is working. Statistics show that students arrive at a rate of four per hour, and the distribution is approximately Poisson. Assistance time averages 10 minutes, distributed exponentially. Assume population and line length can be infinite and queue discipline is FCFS.

    a. Calculate the percentage utilization of the graduate student.

    b. Calculate the average number of students in the system.

    c. Calculate the average time in the system.

    d. Calculate the probability of four or more students being in line or being served.

    e. Before a test, the arrival of students increases to six per hour on the average. What does this do to the average length of the line?

21   At the California border inspection station, vehicles arrive at the rate of 10 per minute in a Poisson distribution. For simplicity in this problem, assume that there is only one lane and one inspector, who can inspect vehicles at the rate of 12 per minute in an exponentially distributed fashion.

    a. What is the average length of the waiting line?

    b. What is the average time that a vehicle must wait to get through the system?

    c. What is the utilization of the inspector?

    d. What is the probability that when you arrive there will be three or more vehicles ahead of you?

22   The California border inspection station (see Problem 21) is considering the addition of a second inspector. The vehicles would wait in one lane and then be directed to the first available inspector. Arrival rates would remain the same (10 per minute) and the new inspector would process vehicles at the same rate as the first inspector (12 per minute).

    a. What would be the average length of the waiting line?

    b. What would be the average time that a vehicle must wait to get through the system? If a second lane was added (one lane for each inspector):

    c. What would be the average length of the waiting line?

    d. What would be the average time that a vehicle must wait to get through the system?

23   During the campus Spring Fling, the bumper car amusement attraction has a problem of cars becoming disabled and in need of repair. Repair personnel can be hired at the rate of $20 per hour, but they only work as one team. Thus, if one person is hired, he or she works alone; two or three people work together on the same repair.

    One repairer can fix cars in an average time of 30 minutes. Two repairers take 20 minutes, and three take 15 minutes. While these cars are down, lost income is $40 per hour. Cars tend to break down at the rate of two per hour.

    How many repairers should be hired?

24   A toll tunnel has decided to experiment with the use of a debit card for the collection of tolls. Initially, only one lane will be used. Cars are estimated to arrive at this experimental lane at the rate of 750 per hour. It will take exactly four seconds to verify the debit card.

   a. In how much time would you expect the customer to wait in line, pay with the debit card, and leave?

   b. How many cars would you expect to see in the system?

CASE: Community Hospital Evening Operating Room

The American College of Surgeons has developed criteria for determining operating room standards in the United States. Level I and II trauma centers are required to have in-house operating room (OR) staff 24 hours per day. So a base level of a single OR team available 24 hours a day is mandatory. During normal business hours, a hospital will typically have additional OR teams available since surgery is scheduled during these times and these additional teams can be used in an emergency. An important decision, though, must be made concerning the availability of a backup team during the evening hours.

A backup team is needed during the evening hours if the probability of having two or more cases simultaneously is significant. "Significant" is difficult to judge, but for the purposes of this case assume that a backup OR team should be employed if the expected probability of two or more cases occurring simultaneously is greater than 1 percent.

A real application was recently studied by doctors at the Columbia University College of Physicians and Surgeons in Stamford, CT.* The doctors studied emergency OR patients that arrived after 11 P.M. and before 7 A.M. during a one year period. During this time period there were 62 patients that required OR treatment. The average service time was 80.79 minutes.

In analyzing the problem think about this as a single-channel, single-phase system with Poisson arrivals and Exponential service times.

1   Calculate the average customer arrival rate and service rate per hour.

2   Calculate the probability of zero patients in the system (P0), probability of one patient (P1), and the probability of two or more patients simultaneously arriving during the night shift.

3   Using a criterion that if the probability is greater than 1 percent, a backup OR team should be employed, make a recommendation to hospital administration.

* Tucker, J.B., Barone, J.E., Cecere, J., Blabey, R.G., Rha, C.K. "Using Queuing Theory to Determine Operating Room Staffing Needs," *Journal of Trauma,* Vol. 46(1), pp. 71–79.

Super Quiz

1   Service systems can be generally categorized according to this characteristic that relates to the customer.

2   A framework that relates to the customer service system encounter.

3   This is the key feature that distinguishes a service blueprint from a normal flowchart.

4   This is done to make a system mistake proof.

5   The queuing models assume that customers are served in what order?

6   Consider two queuing systems identical except for the service time distribution. In the first system the service time is random and distributed according to a Poisson distribution. The service time is constant in the second system. How would the waiting time differ in the two systems?

7   What is the average utilization of the servers in a system that has three servers? On average, 15 customers arrive every 15 minutes. It takes a server exactly three minutes to wait on each customer.

8   What is the expected waiting time for the system described in question 6?

9   Firms that desire high service levels where customers have short wait times should target server utilization levels at no more than this percent.

10   If a firm increases its service capacity by 10 percent it would expect waiting times to be reduced by what percent? Assume customer arrivals and service times are random.

1. Degree of customer contact 2. Service-system design matrix 3. Line of visibility 4. Poka-yoke
5. First come first served 6. Waiting time in the first system is two times the second 7. 100%
8. Infinite 9. 70–80% 10. Greater than 10%

Selected Bibliography

Fitzsimmons, J. A., and M. J. Fitzsimmons. *Service Management,* 4th ed. New York: Irwin/McGraw-Hill, 2003.

Gross, D., and C. M. Harris. *Fundamentals of Queuing Theory.* New York: Wiley, 1997.

Hillier, F. S., et al. *Queuing Tables and Graphs.* New York: Elsevier–North Holland, 1981.

Kleinrock, L., and R. Gail. *Queuing Systems: Problems and Solutions.* New York: Wiley, 1996.

Winston, W. L., and S. C. Albright. *Practical Management Science: Spreadsheet Modeling and Application.* New York: Duxbury, 2000.

Footnote

1 R. B. Chase and D. M. Stewart, "Make Your Service Fail-Safe," *Sloan Management Review,* Spring 1994, pp. 35–44.

CHAPTER 6
QUALITY MANAGEMENT AND SIX SIGMA

After reading the chapter, you will:

- Understand total quality management.
- Discuss how quality is measured and be aware of the different dimensions of quality.
- Explain the define, measure, analyze, improve, and control (DMAIC) quality improvement process.
- Show how to calculate the capability of a process.
- Describe how processes are monitored with control charts.
- Understand acceptance sampling concepts.

133   GE Six-Sigma Supply Chain Processes

134   Total Quality Management

Total quality management defined
Malcolm Baldrige National Quality Award defined

136   Quality Specifications and Quality Costs

Developing Quality Specifications   Design quality defined
Cost of Quality   Conformance quality defined
Quality at the source defined
Dimensions of quality defined
Cost of quality defined

140   ISO 9000 and ISO 14000

141   Six-Sigma Quality

Six-Sigma Methodology   Six Sigma defined
Analytical Tools for Six Sigma   DPMO defined
DMAIC defined

146   Statistical Quality Control

Variation Around Us   Assignable variation defined
Process Capability   Common variation defined
Upper and lower specification limits defined
Capability index (C_{pk}) defined

154   Process Control Procedures

Process Control with Attribute
  Measurements: Using p-Charts

Process Control with Attribute Measurements:
  Using c-Charts

Process Control with Variable
  Measurements: Using $\bar{X}$- and R-Charts

How to Construct $\bar{X}$- and R-Charts

Statistical process control (SPC) defined

Attributes defined

Variables defined

162   Acceptance Sampling

Design of a Single Sampling Plan for Attributes

Operating Characteristic Curves

166   Summary

174   Case: Hank Kolb, Director of Quality Assurance

176   Super Quiz

GE SIX-SIGMA SUPPLY CHAIN PROCESSES

General Electric (GE) has been a major advocate of Six Sigma for over 10 years. Jack Welch, the legendary and now retired CEO, declared that "the big myth is that Six Sigma is about quality control and statistics. It is that—but it's much more. Ultimately, it drives leadership to be better by providing tools to think through tough issues. At Six Sigma's core is an idea that can turn a company inside out, focusing the organization outward on the customer." GE's commitment to quality centers on Six Sigma. Six Sigma is defined on the GE Web site as follows:

First, What is Six Sigma? First, what it is not. It is not a secret society, a slogan or a cliché. Six Sigma is a highly disciplined process that helps us focus on developing and delivering near-perfect products and services. Why "Sigma"? The word is a statistical term that measures how far a given process deviates from perfection. The central idea behind Six Sigma is that if you can measure how many "defects" you have in a process, you can systematically figure out how to eliminate them and get as close to "zero defects" as possible. To achieve Six Sigma Quality, a process must produce no more than 3.4 defects per million opportunities. An "opportunity" is defined as a chance for nonconformance, or not meeting the required specifications. This means we need to be nearly flawless in executing our key processes.

At its core, Six Sigma revolves around a few key concepts.

Critical to Quality:	Attributes most important to the customer
Defect:	Failing to deliver what the customer wants
Process Capability:	What your process can deliver
Variation:	What the customer sees and feels
Stable Operations:	Ensuring consistent, predictable processes to improve what the customer sees and feels
Design for Six Sigma:	Designing to meet customer needs and process capability.

TOTAL QUALITY MANAGEMENT

Total quality management

Total quality management may be defined as "managing the entire organization so that it excels on all dimensions of products and services that are important to the customer." It has two fundamental operational goals, namely

1. Careful design of the product or service.
2. Ensuring that the organization's systems can consistently produce the design.

These two goals can only be achieved if the entire organization is oriented toward them—hence the term *total* quality management. TQM became a national concern in the United States in the 1980s primarily as a response to Japanese quality superiority in manufacturing

Baldrige Quality Award

The Baldrige Quality Award is given to organizations that have demonstrated outstanding quality in their products and processes. Four awards may be given annually in each of these categories: manufacturing, service, small business, education and health care, and not-for-profit.

Candidates for the award must submit an application of up to 75 pages that details the approach, deployment, and results of their quality activities under seven major categories: Leadership, Strategic Planning, Customer and Market Focus, Information and Analysis, Human Resource Focus, Process Management, and Business Results. These applications are scored on total points out of 1,000 by examiners and judges. Those who score above roughly 650 are selected for site visits. Winners selected from this group are then honored at an annual meeting in Washington, DC. A major benefit to all applicants is feedback from the examiners, which is essentially an audit of their practices. Many states have used the Baldrige Criteria as the basis of their own quality award programs. A report, *Building on Baldrige: American Quality for the 21st Century,* by the private Council on Competitiveness, said, "More than any other program, the Baldrige Quality Award is responsible for making quality a national priority and disseminating best practices across the United States."

automobiles and other durable goods such as room air conditioners. A widely cited study of Japanese and U.S. air-conditioning manufacturers showed that the best-quality American products had *higher* average defect rates than those of the poorest Japanese manufacturers.[1] So severe was the quality shortfall in the United States that improving it throughout industry became a national priority, with the Department of Commerce establishing the Malcolm Baldrige National Quality Award in 1987 to help companies review and structure their quality programs. Also gaining major attention at this time was the requirement that suppliers demonstrate that they are measuring and documenting their quality practices according to specified criteria, called ISO standards, if they wished to compete for international contracts. We will have more to say about this later.

Malcolm Baldrige National Quality Award

The philosophical leaders of the quality movement, notably Philip Crosby, W. Edwards Deming, and Joseph M. Juran—the so-called Quality Gurus—had slightly different definitions of what quality is and how to achieve it (see Exhibit 6.1), but they all had the same

The Quality Gurus Compared

exhibit 6.1

	CROSBY	DEMING	JURAN
Definition of quality	Conformance to requirements	A predictable degree of uniformity and dependability at low cost and suited to the market	Fitness for use (satisfies customer's needs)
Degree of senior management responsibility	Responsible for quality	Responsible for 94% of quality problems	Less than 20% of quality problems are due to workers
Performance standard/ motivation	Zero defects	Quality has many "scales"; use statistics to measure performance in all areas; critical of zero defects	Avoid campaigns to do perfect work
General approach	Prevention, not inspection	Reduce variability by continuous improvement; cease mass inspection	General management approach to quality, especially human elements
Structure	14 steps to quality improvement	14 points for management	10 steps to quality improvement
Statistical process control (SPC)	Rejects statistically acceptable levels of quality [wants 100% perfect quality]	Statistical methods of quality control must be used	Recommends SPC but warns that it can lead to tool-driver approach
Improvement basis	A process, not a program; improvement goals	Continuous to reduce variation; eliminate goals without methods	Project-by-project team approach; set goals
Teamwork	Quality improvement teams; quality councils	Employee participation in decision making; break down barriers between departments	Team and quality circle approach
Costs of quality	Cost of nonconformance; quality is free	No optimum; continuous improvement	Quality is not free; there is not an optimum
Purchasing and goods received	State requirements; supplier is extension of business; most faults due to purchasers themselves	Inspection too late; sampling allows defects to enter system; statistical evidence and control charts required	Problems are complex; carry out formal surveys
Vendor rating	Yes; quality audits useless	No, critical of most systems	Yes, but help supplier improve

general message: To achieve outstanding quality requires quality leadership from senior management, a customer focus, total involvement of the workforce, and continuous improvement based upon rigorous analysis of processes. Later in the chapter, we will discuss how these precepts are applied in the latest approach to TQM—Six Sigma. We will now turn to some fundamental concepts that underlie any quality effort: quality specifications and quality costs.

QUALITY SPECIFICATIONS AND QUALITY COSTS

Fundamental to any quality program is the determination of quality specifications and the costs of achieving (or *not* achieving) those specifications.

Developing Quality Specifications

The quality specifications of a product or service derive from decisions and actions made relative to the quality of its design and the quality of its conformance to that design.

Design quality

Design quality refers to the inherent value of the product in the marketplace and is thus a strategic decision for the firm. The dimensions of quality are listed in Exhibit 6.2. These dimensions refer to features of the product or service that relate directly to design issues. A firm designs a product or service to address the need of a particular market.

A firm designs a product or service with certain performance characteristics and features based on what the intended market expects. Materials and manufacturing process attributes can greatly impact the reliability and durability of a product. Here the company attempts to design a product or service that can be produced or delivered at reasonable cost. The serviceability of the product may have a great impact on the cost of the product or service to the customer after the initial purchase is made. It also may impact the warranty and repair cost to the firm. Aesthetics may greatly impact the desirability of the product or service, in particular consumer products. Especially when a brand name is involved, the design often represents the next generation of an ongoing stream of products or services. Consistency in the relative performance of the product compared to the state of the art, for example, may have a great impact on how the quality of the product is perceived. This may be very important to the long-run success of the product or service.

exhibit 6.2   The Dimensions of Design Quality

DIMENSION	MEANING
Performance	Primary product or service characteristics
Features	Added touches, bells and whistles, secondary characteristics
Reliability/durability	Consistency of performance over time, probability of failing, useful life
Serviceability	Ease of repair
Aesthetics	Sensory characteristics (sound, feel, look, and so on)
Perceived quality	Past performance and reputation

J. D. Power and Associates Initial Quality Study of New Cars

J. D. Power and Associates uses concepts similar to those discussed in this section to measure the quality of new automobiles during the first 90 days of ownership. The study is run each year on newly designed vehicles produced by manufacturers from around the world. Each year results from the study are published at http://www.jdpower.com. The study captures problems experienced by owners in two distinct categories—design-related problems and defects and malfunctions. The following is a list of their measures:

Powertrain Quality—Design: This score is based on problems with the engine or transmission as well as problems that affect the driving experience (i.e., ride smoothness, responsiveness of the steering system and brakes, and handling/stability).

Body and Interior Quality—Design: This score is based on problems with the front-/rear-end styling, the appearance of the interior and exterior, and the sound of the doors when closing.

Features and Accessories Quality—Design: This score is based on problems with the seats, stereo/navigation system, heater, air conditioner, and sunroof.

Overall Quality—Mechanical: This score is based on problems that have caused a complete breakdown or malfunction of any component, feature, or item (i.e., components that stop working or trim pieces that break or come loose).

Body and Interior Quality—Mechanical: This score is based on problems with wind noise, water leaks, poor interior fit/finish, paint imperfection, and squeaks/rattles.

Features and Accessories Quality—Mechanical: This score is based on problems with the seats, windshield wipers, navigation system, rear-seat entertainment system, heater, air conditioner, stereo system, sunroof, and trip computer.

Source: http://www.jdpower.com

Conformance quality refers to the degree to which the product or service design specifications are met. The activities involved in achieving conformance are of a tactical, day-to-day nature. It should be evident that a product or service can have high design quality but low conformance quality, and vice versa.

Conformance quality

Quality at the source is frequently discussed in the context of conformance quality. This means that the person who does the work takes responsibility for making sure that his or her output meets specifications. Where a product is involved, achieving the quality specifications is typically the responsibility of manufacturing management; in a service firm, it is usually the responsibility of the branch operations management. Exhibit 6.3 shows two examples of the **dimensions of quality**. One is a laser printer that meets the pages-per-minute and print density standards; the second is a checking account transaction in a bank.

Quality at the source

Dimensions of quality

Both quality of design and quality of conformance should provide products that meet the customer's objectives for those products. This is often termed the product's *fitness for use,* and it entails identifying the dimensions of the product (or service) that the customer wants (that is, the voice of the customer) and developing a quality control program to ensure that these dimensions are met.

exhibit 6.3   Examples of Dimensions of Quality

	MEASURES	
DIMENSION	PRODUCT EXAMPLE: LASER PRINTER	SERVICE EXAMPLE: CHECKING ACCOUNT AT A BANK
Performance	Pages per minute Print density	Time to process customer requests
Features	Multiple paper trays Color capability	Automatic bill paying
Reliability/ durability	Mean time between failures Estimated time to obsolescence Expected life of major components	Variability of time to process requests Keeping pace with industry trends
Serviceability	Availability of authorized repair centers Number of copies per print cartridge Modular design	Online reports Ease of getting updated information
Aesthetics	Control button layout Case style Courtesy of dealer	Appearance of bank lobby Courtesy of teller
Perceived quality	Brand name recognition Rating in *Consumer Reports*	Endorsed by community leaders

Cost of Quality

Cost of quality

Although few can quarrel with the notion of prevention, management often needs hard numbers to determine how much prevention activities will cost. This issue was recognized by Joseph Juran, who wrote about it in 1951 in his *Quality Control Handbook*. Today, cost of quality (COQ) analyses are common in industry and constitute one of the primary functions of QC departments.

There are a number of definitions and interpretations of the term *cost of quality*. From the purist's point of view, it means all of the costs attributable to the production of quality that is not 100 percent perfect. A less stringent definition considers only those costs that are the difference between what can be expected from excellent performance and the current costs that exist.

How significant is the cost of quality? It has been estimated at between 15 and 20 percent of every sales dollar—the cost of reworking, scrapping, repeated service, inspections, tests, warranties, and other quality-related items. Philip Crosby states that the correct cost for a well-run quality management program should be under 2.5 percent.[2]

Three basic assumptions justify an analysis of the costs of quality: (1) failures are caused, (2) prevention is cheaper, and (3) performance can be measured.

The costs of quality are generally classified into four types:

1. **Appraisal costs.** Costs of the inspection, testing, and other tasks to ensure that the product or process is acceptable.
2. **Prevention costs.** The sum of all the costs to prevent defects, such as the costs to identify the cause of the defect, to implement corrective action to eliminate the cause, to train personnel, to redesign the product or system, and to purchase new equipment or make modifications.
3. **Internal failure costs.** Costs for defects incurred within the system: scrap, rework, repair.

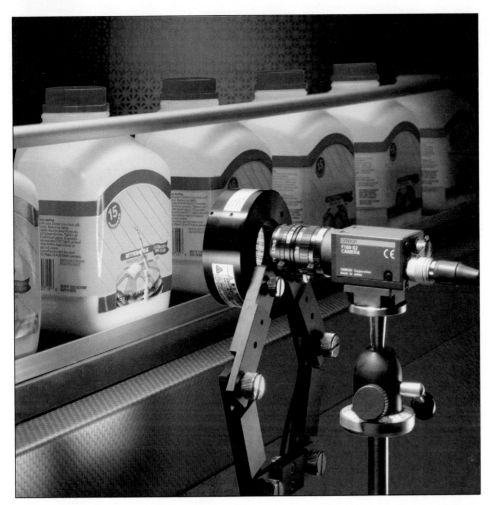

PRODUCTS WITH TORN OR IMPROPERLY POSITIONED LABELS REFLECT POORLY ON THE BRAND AND BRING INTO QUESTION THE QUALITY OF THE CONTENTS. USING A VISION SENSOR PLACED AFTER LABELING A BEFORE THE BOTTLES ARE PLACED INTO CARTONS PREVENTS IMPERFECTLY LABELED PRODUCTS FROM GETTING IN THE SUPPLY CHAIN.

4. **External failure costs.** Costs for defects that pass through the system: customer warranty replacements, loss of customers or goodwill, handling complaints, and product repair.

Exhibit 6.4 illustrates the type of report that might be submitted to show the various costs by categories. Prevention is the most important influence. A rule of thumb says that for every dollar you spend in prevention, you can save $10 in failure and appraisal costs.

Often increases in productivity occur as a by-product of efforts to reduce the cost of quality. A bank, for example, set out to improve quality and reduce the cost of quality and found that it had also boosted productivity. The bank developed this productivity measure for the loan processing area: the number of tickets processed divided by the resources required (labor cost, computer time, ticket forms). Before the quality improvement program, the productivity index was 0.2660 [2,080/($11.23 × 640 hours + $0.05 × 2,600 forms + $500 for systems costs)]. After the quality improvement project was completed, labor time fell to 546 hours and the number of forms rose to 2,100, for a change in the index to 0.3088, an increase in productivity of 16 percent.

Service

exhibit 6.4   Quality Cost Report

	CURRENT MONTH'S COST	PERCENTAGE OF TOTAL
Prevention costs		
Quality training	$ 2,000	1.3%
Reliability consulting	10,000	6.5
Pilot production runs	5,000	3.3
Systems development	8,000	5.2
Total prevention	25,000	16.3
Appraisal costs		
Materials inspection	6,000	3.9
Supplies inspection	3,000	2.0
Reliability testing	5,000	3.3
Laboratory testing	25,000	16.3
Total appraisal	39,000	25.5
Internal failure costs		
Scrap	15,000	9.8
Repair	18,000	11.8
Rework	12,000	7.8
Downtime	6,000	3.9
Total internal failure	51,000	33.3
External failure costs		
Warranty costs	14,000	9.2
Out-of-warranty repairs and replacement	6,000	3.9
Customer complaints	3,000	2.0
Product liability	10,000	6.5
Transportation losses	5,000	3.3
Total external failure	38,000	24.9
Total quality costs	$153,000	100.0%

ISO 9000 AND ISO 14000

Global

ISO 9000 and ISO 14000 are international standards for quality management and assurance. The standards are designed to help companies document that they are maintaining an efficient quality system. The standards were originally published in 1987 by the International Organization for Standardization (ISO), a specialized international agency recognized by affiliates in more than 160 countries. ISO 9000 has become an international reference for quality management requirements in business-to-business dealing, and ISO 14000 is primarily concerned with environmental management.

The idea behind the standards is that defects can be prevented through the planning and application of *best practices* at every stage of business—from design through manufacturing and then installation and servicing. These standards focus on identifying criteria by which any organization, regardless of whether it is manufacturing or service oriented, can ensure that product leaving its facility meets the requirements of its customers. These standards ask a company first to document and implement its systems for quality management and then to verify, by means of an audit conducted by an independent accredited third party, the compliance of those systems with the requirements of the standards.

Service

The ISO 9000 standards are based on eight quality management principles. These principles focus on business processes related to different areas in the firm. These areas include (1) customer focus, (2) leadership, (3) involvement of people, (4) process approach, (5) system approach to management, (6) continual improvement, (7) factual approach to decision making, and (8) mutually beneficial supplier relationships. The ISO documents provide detailed requirements for meeting the standards and describe standard tools that are used for improving quality in the firm. These documents are intended to be generic and applicable to any organization producing products or services.

The ISO 14000 family of standards on environmental management addresses the need to be environmentally responsible. The standards define a three-pronged approach for dealing with environmental challenges. The first is the definition of more than 350 international standards for monitoring the quality of air, water, and soil. For many countries, these standards serve as the technical basis for environmental regulation. The second part of ISO 14000 is a strategic approach by defining the requirements of an environmental management system that can be implemented using the monitoring tools. Finally, the environmental standard encourages the inclusion of environment aspects in product design and encourages the development of profitable environment-friendly products and services.

SIX-SIGMA QUALITY

Six Sigma refers to the philosophy and methods companies such as General Electric and Motorola use to eliminate defects in their products and processes. A defect is simply any component that does not fall within the customer's specification limits. Each step or activity in a company represents an opportunity for defects to occur and Six-Sigma programs seek to reduce the variation in the processes that lead to these defects. Indeed, Six-Sigma advocates see variation as the enemy of quality, and much of the theory underlying Six Sigma is devoted to dealing with this problem. A process that is in Six-Sigma control will produce no more than two defects out of every billion units. Often, this is stated as four defects per million units, which is true if the process is only running somewhere within 1.5 sigma of the target specification.

Six Sigma

One of the benefits of Six-Sigma thinking is that it allows managers to readily describe the performance of a process in terms of its variability and to compare different processes using a common metric. This metric is **defects per million opportunities (DPMO)**. This calculation requires three pieces of data:

DPMO

1. **Unit.** The item produced or being serviced.
2. **Defect.** Any item or event that does not meet the customer's requirements.
3. **Opportunity.** A chance for a defect to occur.

A straightforward calculation is made using the following formula:

$$\text{DPMO} = \frac{\text{Number of defects}}{\text{Number of opportunities for error per unit} \times \text{Number of units}} \times 1,000,000$$

Example 6.1

The customers of a mortgage bank expect to have their mortgage applications processed within 10 days of filing. This would be called a *critical customer requirement,* or CCR, in Six-Sigma terms. Suppose all defects are counted (loans in a monthly sample taking more than 10 days to process), and it is determined that there are 150 loans in the 1,000 applications processed last month that don't meet this customer requirement. Thus, the DPMO = 150/1000 × 1,000,000, or 150,000 loans out of

Service

Step by Step

every million processed that fail to meet a CCR. Put differently, it means that only 850,000 loans out of a million are approved within time expectations. Statistically, 15 percent of the loans are defective and 85 percent are correct. This is a case where all the loans processed in less than 10 days meet our criteria. Often there are upper and lower customer requirements rather than just a single upper requirement as we have here. ●

There are two aspects to Six-Sigma programs: the methodology side and the people side. We will take these up in order.

Six-Sigma Methodology

DMAIC

While Six Sigma's methods include many of the statistical tools that were employed in other quality movements, here they are employed in a systematic project-oriented fashion through the define, measure, analyze, improve, and control (**DMAIC**) cycle. The overarching focus of the methodology is understanding and achieving what the customer wants, since that is seen as the key to profitability of a production process. In fact, to get across this point, some use the DMAIC as an acronym for "Dumb Managers Always Ignore Customers."

The standard approach to Six-Sigma projects is the DMAIC methodology developed by General Electric, described below:[3]

1. Define (D)
   - Identify customers and their priorities.
   - Identify a project suitable for Six-Sigma efforts based on business objectives as well as customer needs and feedback.
   - Identify CTQs (critical-to-quality characteristics) that the customer considers to have the most impact on quality.
2. Measure (M)
   - Determine how to measure the process and how it is performing.
   - Identify the key internal processes that influence CTQs and measure the defects currently generated relative to those processes.
3. Analyze (A)
   - Determine the most likely causes of defects.
   - Understand why defects are generated by identifying the key variables that are most likely to create process variation.
4. Improve (I)
   - Identify means to remove the causes of defects.
   - Confirm the key variables and quantify their effects on the CTQs.
   - Identify the maximum acceptance ranges of the key variables and a system for measuring deviations of the variables.
   - Modify the process to stay within an acceptable range.
5. Control (C)
   - Determine how to maintain the improvements.
   - Put tools in place to ensure that the key variables remain within the maximum acceptance ranges under the modified process.

Analytical Tools for Six Sigma

The analytical tools of Six Sigma have been used for many years in traditional quality improvement programs. What makes their application to Six Sigma unique is the integration of these tools in a corporatewide management system. The tools common to all quality efforts are flowcharts, run charts, Pareto charts, histograms, checksheets, cause-and-effect diagrams, and control charts. Examples of these, along with an opportunity flow diagram, are shown in Exhibit 6.5, arranged according to DMAIC categories where they commonly appear.

Flowcharts.   There are many types of flowcharts. The one shown in Exhibit 6.5 depicts the process steps as part of a SIPOC (supplier, input, process, output, customer) analysis. SIPOC in essence is a formalized input-output model, used in the define stage of a project.

Run charts.   They depict trends in data over time, and thereby help to understand the magnitude of a problem at the define stage. Typically, they plot the median of a process.

Pareto charts.   These charts help to break down a problem into the relative contributions of its components. They are based on the common empirical finding that a large percentage of problems are due to a small percentage of causes. In the example, 80 percent of customer complaints are due to late deliveries, which are 20 percent of the causes listed.

Checksheets.   These are basic forms that help standardize data collection. They are used to create histograms such as shown on the Pareto chart.

Cause-and-effect diagrams.   Also called *fishbone diagrams,* they show hypothesized relationships between potential causes and the problem under study. Once the C&E diagram is constructed, the analysis would proceed to find out which of the potential causes were in fact contributing to the problem.

Opportunity flow diagram.   This is used to separate value-added from non-value-added steps in a process.

Process control charts.   These are time-sequenced charts showing plotted values of a statistic including a centerline average and one or more control limits. It is used to assure that processes are in statistical control.

Other tools that have seen extensive use in Six-Sigma projects are failure mode and effect analysis (FMEA) and design of experiments (DOE).

Failure mode and effect analysis.   This is a structured approach to identify, estimate, prioritize, and evaluate risk of possible failures at each stage of a process. It begins with identifying each element, assembly, or part of the process and listing the potential failure modes, potential causes, and effects of each failure. A risk priority number (RPN) is calculated for each failure mode. It is an index used to measure the rank importance of the items listed in the FMEA chart. See Exhibit 6.6. These conditions include the probability that the failure takes place (occurrence), the damage resulting from the failure (severity), and the probability of detecting the failure in-house (detection). High RPN items should be targeted for improvement first. The FMEA suggests a recommended action to eliminate the failure condition by assigning a responsible person or department to resolve the failure by redesigning the system, design, or process and recalculating the RPN.

Design of experiments (DOE).   DOE, sometimes referred to as *multivariate testing,* is a statistical methodology used for determining the cause-and-effect relationship between process variables (X's) and the output variable (Y). In contrast to standard statistical tests, which require changing each individual variable to determine the most influential one, DOE permits experimentation with many variables simultaneously through carefully selecting a subset of them.

exhibit 6.5

Analytical Tools for Six Sigma and Continuous Improvement

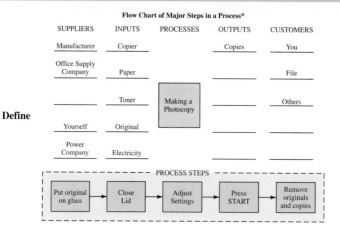

Flow Chart of Major Steps in a Process*

SUPPLIERS	INPUTS	PROCESSES	OUTPUTS	CUSTOMERS
Manufacturer	Copier		Copies	You
Office Supply Company	Paper			File
	Toner	Making a Photocopy		Others
Yourself	Original			
Power Company	Electricity			

Define

PROCESS STEPS

Put original on glass → Close Lid → Adjust Settings → Press START → Remove originals and copies

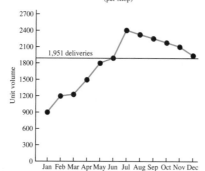

Run Chart**
Average monthly volume of deliveries
(per shop)

1,951 deliveries

Unit volume

Jan Feb Mar Apr May Jun Jul Aug Sep Oct Nov Dec

Measure

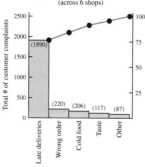

Pareto Chart**
Types of customer complaints
Total = 2520 October–December
(across 6 shops)

(1890) (220) (206) (117) (87)

Late deliveries | Wrong order | Cold food | Taste | Other

Total # of customer complaints

Illustration note: Delivery time was defined
by the total time from when the order was
placed to when the customer received it.

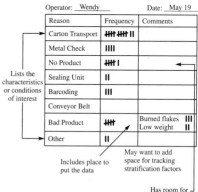

DATA COLLECTION FORMS*

Checksheets are basic forms that help standardize data collection
by providing specific spaces where people should record data.

Defines what data → **Machine Downtime**
are being collected **(Line 13)**

Operator: Wendy   Date: May 19

Reason	Frequency	Comments
Carton Transport	‖‖‖ ‖‖‖ ‖	
Metal Check	‖‖‖‖	
No Product	‖‖‖ ‖	←
Sealing Unit	‖	
Barcoding	‖‖	
Conveyor Belt		
Bad Product	‖‖‖	Burned flakes ‖‖‖ / Low weight ‖
Other	‖	

Lists the characteristics or conditions of interest

Includes place to put the data

May want to add space for tracking stratification factors

Has room for comments

*Source: Rath & Strong, *Rath & Strong's Six Sigma Pocket Guide,* 2001.

**Source: From *The Memory Jogger*™II, 2001. Used with permission of GOAL/QPC.

C & E/Fishbone Diagram*
Reasons for late pizza deliveries

Analyze

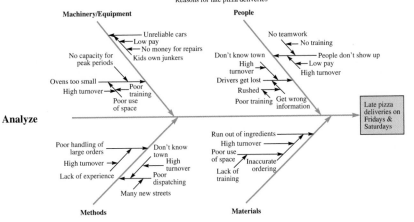

Improve

Opportunity Flow Diagram*
Organized to separate value-added steps from non-value-added steps.

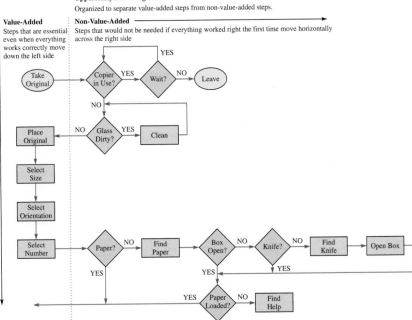

Control

Process Control Chart Features*

Basic features same as a time plot

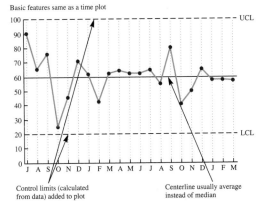

exhibit 6.6

FMEA Form

FMEA Analysis

Project: _____

Date: _____(original)

Team: _____

_____(revised)

Item or Process Step	Potential Failure Mode	Potential Effects of Failure	Severity	Potential Cause(s)	Occurrence	Current Controls	Detection	RPN	Recommended Action	Responsibility and Target Date	"After" ⟶ Action Taken	Severity	Occurrence	Detection	RPN
	Total Risk Priority Number:									"After" Risk Priority Number:					

Source: Rath & Strong, *Rath & Strong's Six Sigma Pocket Guide*: 2001, p. 31.

STATISTICAL QUALITY CONTROL

This section on statistical quality control (SQC) covers the quantitative aspects of quality management. In general, SQC is a number of different techniques designed to evaluate quality from a conformance view. That is, how well are we doing at meeting the specifications that have been set during the design of the parts or services that we are providing? Managing quality performance using SQC techniques usually involves periodic sampling of a process and analysis of these data using statistically derived performance criteria.

As you will see, SQC can be applied to logistics, manufacturing, and service processes. Here are some examples of situations where SQC can be applied:

- How many paint defects are there in the finish of a car? Have we improved our painting process by installing a new sprayer?
- How long does it take to execute market orders in our Web-based trading system? Has the installation of a new server improved the service? Does the performance of the system vary over the trading day?
- How well are we able to maintain the dimensional tolerance on our three-inch ball bearing assembly? Given the variability of our process for making this ball bearing, how many defects would we expect to produce per million bearings that we make?
- How long does it take for customers to be served from our drive-through window during the busy lunch period?

Service

Processes that provide goods and services usually exhibit some variation in their output. This variation can be caused by many factors, some of which we can control and others that are inherent in the process. Variation that is caused by factors that can be clearly iden-

Assignable variation

tified and possibly even managed is called **assignable variation**. For example, variation caused by workers not being equally trained or by improper machine adjustment is assign-

Common variation

able variation. Variation that is inherent in the process itself is called **common variation**.

Common variation is often referred to as *random variation* and may be the result of the type of equipment used to complete a process, for example.

As the title of this section implies, this material requires an understanding of very basic statistics. Recall from your study of statistics involving numbers that are normally distributed the definition of the mean and standard deviation. The mean ($\overline{X}$) is just the average value of a set of numbers. Mathematically this is

$$\overline{X} = \sum_{i=1}^{N} x_i/N \qquad \textbf{[6.1]}$$

where:

x_i = Observed value
N = Total number of observed values

The standard deviation is

$$\sigma = \sqrt{\frac{\sum_{i=1}^{N} (x_i - \overline{X})^2}{N}} \qquad \textbf{[6.2]}$$

In monitoring a process using SQC, samples of the process output would be taken and sample statistics calculated. The distribution associated with the samples should exhibit the same kind of variability as the actual distribution of the process, although the actual variance of the sampling distribution would be less. This is good because it allows the quick detection of changes in the actual distribution of the process. The purpose of sampling is to find when the process has changed in some nonrandom way, so that the reason for the change can be quickly determined.

In SQC terminology, *sigma* is often used to refer to the sample standard deviation. As you will see in the examples, sigma is calculated in a few different ways, depending on the underlying theoretical distribution (i.e., a normal distribution or a Poisson distribution).

Variation Around Us

It is generally accepted that as variation is reduced, quality is improved. Sometimes that knowledge is intuitive. If a train is always on time, schedules can be planned more precisely. If clothing sizes are consistent, time can be saved by ordering from a catalog. But rarely are such things thought about in terms of the value of low variability. With engineers, the knowledge is better defined. Pistons must fit cylinders, doors must fit openings, electrical components must be compatible, and boxes of cereal must have the right amount of raisins—otherwise quality will be unacceptable and customers will be dissatisfied.

However, engineers also know that it is impossible to have zero variability. For this reason, designers establish specifications that define not only the target value of something but also acceptable limits about the target. For example, if the aim value of a dimension is 10 inches, the design specifications might then be 10.00 inches ±0.02 inch. This would tell the manufacturing department that, while it should aim for exactly 10 inches, anything between 9.98 and 10.02 inches is OK. These design limits are often referred to as the **upper and lower specification limits**.

Upper and lower specification limits

A traditional way of interpreting such a specification is that any part that falls within the allowed range is equally good, whereas any part falling outside the range is totally bad. This is illustrated in Exhibit 6.7. (Note that the cost is zero over the entire specification range, and then there is a quantum leap in cost once the limit is violated.)

Genichi Taguchi, a noted quality expert from Japan, has pointed out that the traditional view illustrated in Exhibit 6.7 is nonsense for two reasons:

1. From the customer's view, there is often practically no difference between a product just inside specifications and a product just outside. Conversely, there is a far greater difference in the quality of a product that is the target and the quality of one that is near a limit.
2. As customers get more demanding, there is pressure to reduce variability. However, Exhibit 6.7 does not reflect this logic.

Taguchi suggests that a more correct picture of the loss is shown in Exhibit 6.8. Notice that in this graph the cost is represented by a smooth curve. There are dozens of illustrations

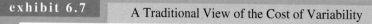

exhibit 6.7   A Traditional View of the Cost of Variability

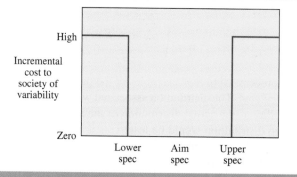

exhibit 6.8

Taguchi's View of the Cost of Variability

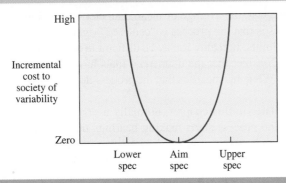

of this notion: the meshing of gears in a transmission, the speed of photographic film, the temperature in a workplace or department store. In nearly anything that can be measured, the customer sees not a sharp line, but a gradation of acceptability away from the "Aim" specification. Customers see the loss function as Exhibit 6.8 rather than Exhibit 6.7.

Of course, if products are consistently scrapped when they are outside specifications, the loss curve flattens out in most cases at a value equivalent to scrap cost in the ranges outside specifications. This is because such products, theoretically at least, will never be sold so there is no external cost to society. However, in many practical situations, either the process is capable of producing a very high percentage of product within specifications and 100 percent checking is not done, or if the process is not capable of producing within specifications, 100 percent checking is done and out-of-spec products can be reworked to bring them within specs. In any of these situations, the parabolic loss function is usually a reasonable assumption.

Service

Process Capability

Taguchi argues that being within specification is not a yes/no decision, but rather a continuous function. The Motorola quality experts, on the other hand, argue that the process used to produce a good or deliver a service should be so good that the probability of generating a defect should be very, very low. Motorola made process capability and product design famous by adopting Six-Sigma limits. When a part is designed, certain dimensions are specified to be within the upper and lower specification limits.

As a simple example, assume engineers are designing a bearing for a rotating shaft—say an axle for the wheel of a car. There are many variables involved for both the bearing and the axle—for example, the width of the bearing, the size of the rollers, the size of the axle, the length of the axle, how it is supported, and so on. The designer specifies limits for each of these variables to ensure that the parts will fit properly. Suppose that initially a design is selected and the diameter of the bearing is set at 1.250 inches ±0.005 inch. This means that acceptable parts may have a diameter that varies between 1.245 and 1.255 inches (which are the lower and upper specification limits).

Next, consider the process in which the bearing will be made. Consider that many different processes for making the bearing are available. Usually there are trade-offs that need to be considered when designing a process for making a part. The process, for example, might be fast but not consistent, or alternatively it might be slow but consistent. The consistency of a process for making the bearing can be measured by the standard deviation of the diameter measurement. A test can be run by making, say, 100 bearings and measuring the diameter of each bearing in the sample.

After running the test, the average or mean diameter is found to be 1.250 inches. Another way to say this is that the process is "centered" right in the middle of the upper and lower specification limits. In reality it may be difficult to have a perfectly centered process like this example. Consider that the diameter values have a standard deviation or sigma equal to 0.002 inch. What this means is that the process does not make each bearing exactly the same size.

As is discussed later in this chapter, normally a process is monitored using control charts such that if the process starts making bearings that are more than three standard deviations ($\pm$0.006 inch) above or below 1.250 inches, the process is stopped. This means that the process will produce parts that vary between 1.244 (this is $1.250 - 3 \times .002$) and 1.256 (this is $1.250 + 3 \times .002$) inches. The 1.244 and 1.256 are referred to as the upper and lower process limits. Be careful and do not get confused with the terminology here. The "process" limits relate to how consistent the process is for making the bearing. The goal in managing the process is to keep it within plus or minus three standard deviations of the process mean. The "specification" limits are related to the design of the part. Recall that, from a design view, acceptable parts have a diameter between 1.245 and 1.255 inches (which are the lower and upper specification limits).

As can be seen, process limits are slightly greater than the specification limits given by the designer. This is not good since the process will produce some parts that do not meet specifications. Companies with Six-Sigma processes insist that a process making a part be capable of operating so that the design specification limits are six standard deviations away from the process mean. For the bearing process, how small would the process standard deviation need to be for it to be Six-Sigma capable? Recall that the design specification was 1.250 inches plus or minus 0.005 inch. Consider that the 0.005 inch must relate to the variation in the process. By dividing 0.005 inch by 6, which equals 0.00083, to determine the process standard deviation for a Six-Sigma process. So for the process to be Six-Sigma capable, the mean diameter produced by the process would need to be exactly 1.250 inches and the process standard deviation would need to be less than or equal to 0.00083 inch.

We can imagine that some of you are really confused at this point with the whole idea of Six Sigma. Why doesn't the company, for example, just check the diameter of each bearing and throw out the ones with a diameter less than 1.245 or greater than 1.255? This could certainly be done and for many, many parts 100 percent testing is done. The problem is for a company that is making thousands of parts each hour, testing each critical dimension of each part made can be very expensive. For the bearing, there could easily be 10 or more additional critical dimensions in addition to the diameter. These would all need to be checked. Using a 100 percent testing approach, the company would spend more time testing than it takes to actually make the part! This is why a company uses small samples to periodically check that the process is in statistical control. We discuss exactly how this statistical sampling works later in the chapter.

We say that a process is *capable* when the mean and standard deviation of the process are operating such that the upper and lower control limits are acceptable relative to the upper and lower specification limits. Consider diagram A in Exhibit 6.9. This represents the distribution of the bearing diameter dimension in our original process. The average or mean value is 1.250 and the lower and upper design specifications are 1.245 and 1.255 respectively. Process control limits are plus and minus three standard deviations (1.244 and 1.256). Notice that there is a probability (the purple areas) of producing defective parts.

If the process can be improved by reducing the standard deviation associated with the bearing diameter, the probability can be reduced. Diagram B in Exhibit 6.9 shows a new

Process Capability

exhibit 6.9

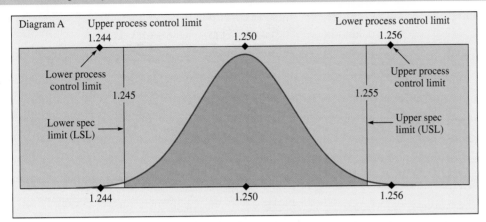

Diagram A

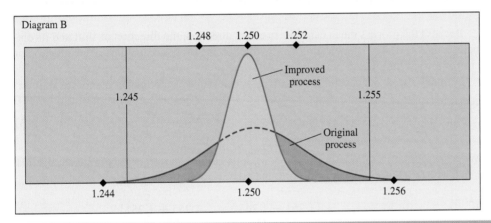

Diagram B

process where the standard deviation has been reduced to 0.00083 (the orange area). Even though we cannot see it in the diagram, there is some probability that a defect could be produced by this new process, but that probability is very, very small.

Suppose that the central value or mean of the process shifts away from the mean. Exhibit 6.10 shows the mean shifted one standard deviation closer to the upper specification limit. This, of course, causes a slightly higher number of expected defects, but we can see that this is still very, very good. The *capability index* is used to measure how well our process is capable of producing relative to the design specifications. A description of how to calculate this index is in the next section.

Capability Index (C_{pk}) The capability index (C_{pk}) shows how well the parts being produced fit into the range specified by the design specification limits. If the specification limits are larger than the three sigma allowed in the process, then the mean of the process can be allowed to drift off-center before readjustment, and a high percentage of good parts will still be produced.

Referring to Exhibits 6.9 and 6.10, the capability index (C_{pk}) is the position of the mean and tails of the process relative to design specifications. The more off-center, the greater the chance to produce defective parts.

Capability index (C_{pk})

**Excel:
SPC
DONE**

exhibit 6.10

Process Capability with a Shift in the Process Mean

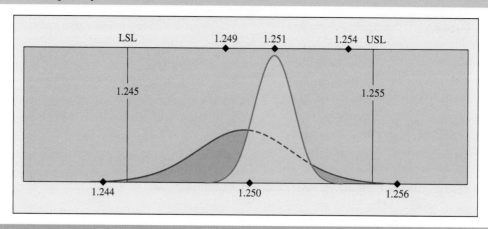

Because the process mean can shift in either direction, the direction of shift and its distance from the design specification set the limit on the process capability. The direction of shift is toward the smaller number.

Formally stated, the capability index (C_{pk}) is calculated as the smaller number as follows:

$$C_{pk} = \min \left[\frac{\overline{\overline{X}} - \text{LSL}}{3\sigma} \quad \text{or} \quad \frac{\text{USL} - \overline{\overline{X}}}{3\sigma} \right] \qquad \textbf{[6.3]}$$

Working with our example in Exhibit 6.10, let's assume our process is centered at 1.251 and $\sigma = 0.00083$ (σ is the symbol for standard deviation).

$$C_{pk} = \min \left[\frac{1.251 - 1.245}{3(.00083)} \quad \text{or} \quad \frac{1.255 - 1.251}{3(.00083)} \right]$$

$$= \min \left[\frac{.006}{.00249} \quad \text{or} \quad \frac{.004}{.00249} \right]$$

$$C_{pk} = \min [2.4 \quad \text{or} \quad 1.6]$$

$C_{pk} = 1.6$, which is the smaller number. This is a pretty good capability index.

This tells us that the process mean has shifted to the right similar to Exhibit 6.10, but parts are still well within design specification limits.

At times it is useful to calculate the actual probability of producing a defect. Assuming that the process is producing with a consistent standard deviation, this is a fairly straightforward calculation, particularly when we have access to a spreadsheet. The approach to use is to calculate the probability of producing a part outside the lower and upper design specification limits given the mean and standard deviation of the process.

Working with our example, where the process is not centered, with a mean of 1.251 inch, $\sigma = .00083$, LSL = 1.245, and USL = 1.255, we first need to calculate the Z score associated with the upper and lower specification limits. Recall from your study of statistics that the Z score is the standard deviations either to the right or to the left of zero in a probability distribution.

$$Z_{\text{LSL}} = \frac{\text{LSL} - \overline{\overline{X}}}{\sigma} \qquad Z_{\text{USL}} = \frac{\text{USL} - \overline{\overline{X}}}{\sigma}$$

For our example,

$$Z_{\text{LSL}} = \frac{1.245 - 1.251}{.00083} = -7.2289 \quad Z_{\text{USL}} = \frac{1.255 - 1.251}{.00083} = 4.8193$$

An easy way to get the probabilities associated with these Z values is to use the NORMSDIST function built into Excel (you also can use the table in Appendix E). The format for this function is NORMSDIST(Z), where Z is the Z value calculated above. Excel returns the following values. (We have found that you might get slightly different results from those given here, depending on the version of Excel you are using.)

NORMSDIST(-7.2289) = 2.43461E-13   and   NORMSDIST(4.8193) = .99999928

Interpreting this information requires understanding exactly what the NORMSDIST function is providing. NORMSDIST is giving the cumulative probability to the left of the given Z value. Since $Z = -7.2289$ is the number of standard deviations associated with the lower specification limit, the fraction of parts that will be produced lower than this is 2.43461E-13. This number is in scientific notation and that E-13 at the end means we need to move the decimal over 13 places to get the real fraction defective. So the fraction defective is .00000000000024361, which is a very small number! Similarly, we see that approximately .99999928 of our parts will be below our upper specification limit. What we are really interested in is the fraction that will be above this limit since these are the defective parts. This fraction defective above the upper spec is $1 - .99999928 = .00000082$ of our parts.

Adding these two fraction defective numbers together we get .00000082000024361. We can interpret this to mean that we only expect about .82 parts per million to be defective. Clearly, this is a great process. You will discover as you work the problems at the end of the chapter that this is not always the case.

Example 6.2

The quality assurance manager is assessing the capability of a process that puts pressurized grease in an aerosol can. The design specifications call for an average of 60 pounds per square inch (psi) of pressure in each can with an upper specification limit of 65 psi and a lower specification limit of 55 psi. A sample is taken from production and it is found that the cans average 61 psi with a standard deviation of 2 psi. What is the capability of the process? What is the probability of producing a defect?

Step by Step

SOLUTION

Step 1—Interpret the data from the problem

$$\text{LSL} = 55 \quad \text{USL} = 65 \quad \overline{\overline{X}} = 61 \quad \sigma = 2$$

Step 2—Calculate the C_{pk}

$$C_{pk} = \min\left[\frac{\overline{\overline{X}} - \text{LSL}}{3\sigma}, \frac{\text{USL} - \overline{\overline{X}}}{3\sigma}\right]$$

$$C_{pk} = \min\left[\frac{61 - 55}{3(2)}, \frac{65 - 61}{3(2)}\right]$$

$$C_{pk} = \min\,[1, .6667] = .6667$$

This is not a very good capability index.

Step 3—Calculate the probability of producing a defect

Probability of a can with less than 55 psi

$$Z = \frac{X - \overline{\overline{X}}}{\sigma} = \frac{55 - 61}{2} = -3$$

NORMSDIST(−3) = 0.001349898

Probability of a can with more than 65 psi

$$Z = \frac{X - \overline{X}}{\sigma} = \frac{65 - 61}{2} = 2$$

1 − NORMSDIST(2) = 1 − 0.977249868 = 0.022750132

Probability of a can less than 55 psi or more than 65 psi

Probability = 0.001349898 + 0.022750132 = .024100030

Or approximately 2.4 percent of the cans will be defective. ●

The following table is a quick reference for the fraction of defective units for various design specification limits (expressed in standard deviations). This table assumes that the standard deviation is constant and that the process is centered exactly between the design specification limits.

DESIGN LIMITS	DEFECTIVE PARTS	FRACTION DEFECTIVE
$\pm 1\sigma$	317 per thousand	.3173
$\pm 2\sigma$	45 per thousand	.0455
$\pm 3\sigma$	27 per thousand	.0027
$\pm 4\sigma$	63 per million	.000063
$\pm 5\sigma$	574 per billion	.000000574
$\pm 6\sigma$	2 per billion	.000000002

Motorola's design specification limit of six sigma with a shift of the process off the mean by 1.5σ ($C_{pk} = 1.5$) gives 3.4 defects per million. If the mean is exactly in the center ($C_{pk} = 2$), then 2 defects per *billion* are expected, as the table above shows.

PROCESS CONTROL PROCEDURES

Process control is concerned with monitoring quality *while the product or service is being produced*. Typical objectives of process control plans are to provide timely information on whether currently produced items are meeting design specifications and to detect shifts in the process that signal that future products may not meet specifications. **Statistical process control (SPC)** involves testing a random sample of output from a process to determine whether the process is producing items within a preselected range.

Statistical process control (SPC)

The examples given so far have all been based on quality characteristics (or *variables*) that are measurable, such as the diameter or weight of a part. **Attributes** are quality characteristics that are classified as either conforming or not conforming to specification. Goods or services may be observed to be either good or bad, or functioning or malfunctioning.

Attributes

For example, a lawnmower either runs or it doesn't; it attains a certain level of torque and horsepower or it doesn't. This type of measurement is known as sampling by attributes. Alternatively, a lawnmower's torque and horsepower can be measured as an amount of deviation from a set standard. This type of measurement is known as sampling by variables. The following section describes some standard approaches to controlling processes: first an approach useful for attribute measures and then an approach for variable measures. Both of these techniques result in the construction of control charts. Exhibit 6.11 shows some examples for how control charts can be analyzed to understand how a process is operating.

Process Control Chart Evidence for Investigation

exhibit 6.11

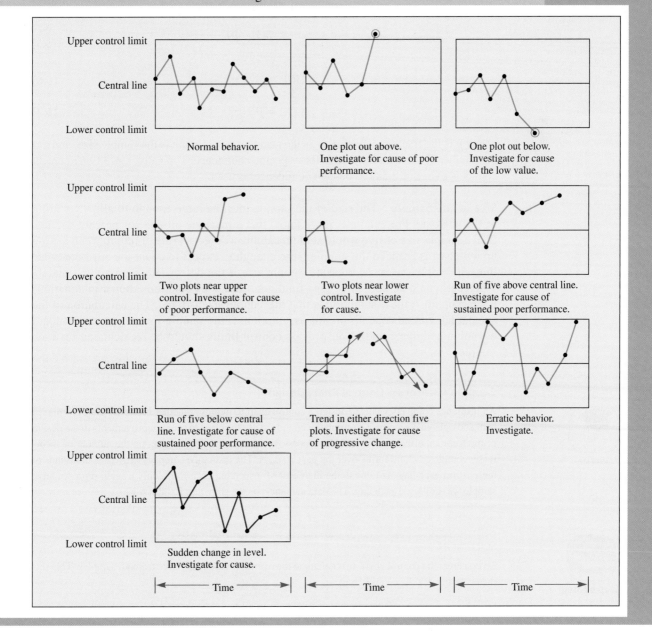

Process Control with Attribute Measurements: Using *p*-Charts

Tutorial: SPC

Measurement by attributes means taking samples and using a single decision—the item is good or it is bad. Because it is a yes or no decision, we can use simple statistics to create a *p* chart with an upper process control limit (UCL) and a lower process control limit (LCL). We can draw these control limits on a graph and then plot the fraction defective of each individual sample tested. The process is assumed to be working correctly when the samples, which are taken periodically during the day, continue to stay between the control limits.

$$\bar{p} = \frac{\text{Total number of defects from all samples}}{\text{Number of samples} \times \text{Sample size}} \qquad \textbf{[6.4]}$$

$$s_p = \sqrt{\frac{\bar{p}(1 - \bar{p})}{n}} \qquad \textbf{[6.5]}$$

$$\text{UCL} = \bar{p} + zs_p \qquad \textbf{[6.6]}$$

$$\text{LCL} = \bar{p} - zs_p \qquad \textbf{[6.7]}$$

where $\bar{p}$ is the fraction defective, s_p is the standard deviation, n is the sample size, and z is the number of standard deviations for a specific confidence. Typically, $z = 3$ (99.7 percent confidence) or $z = 2.58$ (99 percent confidence) is used.

Size of the Sample   The size of the sample must be large enough to allow counting of the attribute. For example, if we know that a machine produces 1 percent defects, then a sample size of five would seldom capture a defect. A rule of thumb when setting up a *p*-chart is to make the sample large enough to expect to count the attribute twice in each sample. So an appropriate sample size if the defect rate were approximately 1 percent would be 200 units. One final note: In the calculations shown in equations 6.4 through 6.7, the assumption is that the sample size is fixed. The calculation of the standard deviation depends on this assumption. If the sample size varies, the standard deviation and upper and lower process control limits should be recalculated for each sample.

Example 6.3: Process Control Chart Design

Service

An insurance company wants to design a control chart to monitor whether insurance claim forms are being completed correctly. The company intends to use the chart to see if improvements in the design of the form are effective. To start the process, the company collected data on the number of incorrectly completed claim forms over the past 10 days. The insurance company processes thousands of these forms each day, and due to the high cost of inspecting each form, only a small representative sample was collected each day. The data and analysis are shown in Exhibit 6.12.

Step by Step

SOLUTION

To construct the control chart, first calculate the overall fraction defective from all samples. This sets the centerline for the control chart.

$$\bar{p} = \frac{\text{Total number of defects from all samples}}{\text{Number of samples} \times \text{Sample size}} = \frac{91}{3000} = .03033$$

Insurance Company Claim Form

exhibit 6.12

SAMPLE	NUMBER INSPECTED	NUMBER OF FORMS COMPLETED INCORRECTLY	FRACTION DEFECTIVE
1	300	10	0.03333
2	300	8	0.02667
3	300	9	0.03000
4	300	13	0.04333
5	300	7	0.02333
6	300	7	0.02333
7	300	6	0.02000
8	300	11	0.03667
9	300	12	0.04000
10	300	8	0.02667
Totals	3000	91	0.03033
Sample standard deviation			0.00990

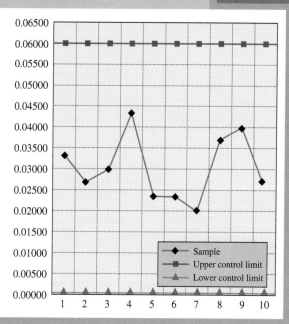

Next calculate the sample standard deviation:

$$s_p = \sqrt{\frac{\bar{p}(1-\bar{p})}{n}} = \sqrt{\frac{.03033(1-.03033)}{300}} = .00990$$

Finally, calculate the upper and lower process control limits. A z-value of 3 gives 99.7 percent confidence that the process is within these limits.

$$\text{UCL} = \bar{p} + 3s_p = .03033 + 3(.00990) = .06003$$
$$\text{LCL} = \bar{p} - 3s_p = .03033 - 3(.00990) = .00063$$

The calculations in Exhibit 6.12, including the control chart, are included in the spreadsheet SPC.xls. ●

**Excel:
SPC
DONE**

Process Control with Attribute Measurements: Using c-Charts

In the case of the *p*-chart, the item was either good or bad. There are times when the product or service can have more than one defect. For example, a board sold at a lumber yard may have multiple knotholes and, depending on the quality grade, may or may not be defective. When it is desired to monitor the number of defects per unit, the *c*-chart is appropriate.

The underlying distribution for the *c*-chart is the Poisson, which is based on the assumption that defects occur randomly on each unit. If c is the number of defects for a particular unit, then $\bar{c}$ is the average number of defects per unit, and the standard deviation is $\sqrt{\bar{c}}$. For

the purposes of our control chart we use the normal approximation to the Poisson distribution and construct the chart using the following control limits.

$$\bar{c} = \text{Average number of defects per unit} \qquad \text{[6.8]}$$

$$s_p = \sqrt{\bar{c}} \qquad \text{[6.9]}$$

$$\text{UCL} = \bar{c} + z\sqrt{\bar{c}} \qquad \text{[6.10]}$$

$$\text{LCL} = \bar{c} - z\sqrt{\bar{c}} \text{ or 0 if less than 0} \qquad \text{[6.11]}$$

Just as with the *p*-chart, typically $z = 3$ (99.7 percent confidence) or $z = 2.58$ (99 percent confidence) is used.

Step by Step

Example 6.4

The owners of a lumber yard want to design a control chart to monitor the quality of 2 × 4 boards that come from their supplier. For their medium quality boards they expect an average of four knotholes per 8 foot board. Design a control chart for use by the person receiving the boards using three-sigma (standard deviation) limits.

SOLUTION

For this problem, $\bar{c} = 4$, $s_p = \sqrt{\bar{c}} = 2$

$$\text{UCL} = \bar{c} + z\sqrt{\bar{c}} = 4 + 3(2) = 10$$

$$\text{LCL} = \bar{c} - z\sqrt{\bar{c}} = 4 - 3(2) = -2 \rightarrow 0$$

Process Control with Variable Measurements: Using $\bar{X}$- and R-Charts

$\bar{X}$- and R- (range) charts are widely used in statistical process control.

Variables

In attribute sampling, we determine whether something is good or bad, fits or doesn't fit—it is a go/no-go situation. In **variables** sampling, however, we measure the actual weight, volume, number of inches, or other variable measurements, and we develop control charts to determine the acceptability or rejection of the process based on those measurements. For example, in attribute sampling, we might decide that if something is over 10 pounds we will reject it and under 10 pounds we will accept it. In variable sampling, we measure a sample and may record weights of 9.8 pounds or 10.2 pounds. These values are used to create or modify control charts and to see whether they fall within the acceptable limits.

There are four main issues to address in creating a control chart: the size of the samples, number of samples, frequency of samples, and control limits.

Size of Samples   For industrial applications in process control involving the measurement of variables, it is preferable to keep the sample size small. There are two main reasons. First, the sample needs to be taken within a reasonable length of time; otherwise,

A FOREMAN AND TEAM COACH EXAMINE PROCESS CONTROL CHARTS AT THE FORD FIESTA ASSEMBLY LINE IN COLOGNE-NIEHL, GERMANY.

the process might change while the samples are taken. Second, the larger the sample, the more it costs to take.

Sample sizes of four or five units seem to be the preferred numbers. The *means* of samples of this size have an approximately normal distribution, no matter what the distribution of the parent population looks like. Sample sizes greater than five give narrower process control limits and thus more sensitivity. For detecting finer variations of a process, it may be necessary, in fact, to use larger sample sizes. However, when sample sizes exceed 15 or so, it would be better to use $\overline{X}$-charts with standard deviation σ rather than $\overline{X}$-charts with the range R as we use in Example 6.4.

Number of Samples   Once the chart has been set up, each sample taken can be compared to the chart and a decision can be made about whether the process is acceptable. To set up the charts, however, prudence and statistics suggest that 25 or so samples be taken.

Frequency of Samples   How often to take a sample is a trade-off between the cost of sampling (along with the cost of the unit if it is destroyed as part of the test) and the benefit of adjusting the system. Usually, it is best to start off with frequent sampling of a process and taper off as confidence in the process builds. For example, one might start with a sample of five units every half hour and end up feeling that one sample per day is adequate.

Control Limits   Standard practice in statistical process control for variables is to set control limits three standard deviations above the mean and three standard deviations below. This means that 99.7 percent of the sample means are expected to fall within these process control limits (that is, within a 99.7 percent confidence interval). Thus, if one sample mean falls outside this obviously wide band, we have strong evidence that the process is out of control.

How to Construct $\bar{X}$- and R-Charts

If the standard deviation of the process distribution is known, the $\bar{X}$-chart may be defined:

$$\text{UCL}_{\bar{X}} = \bar{\bar{X}} + zS_{\bar{X}} \quad \text{and} \quad \text{LCL}_{\bar{X}} = \bar{\bar{X}} - zS_{\bar{X}} \qquad \textbf{[6.12]}$$

where

$\quad S_{\bar{X}} = s/\sqrt{n} =$ Standard deviation of sample means

$\quad s =$ Standard deviation of the process distribution

$\quad n =$ Sample size

$\quad \bar{\bar{X}} =$ Average of sample means or a target value set for the process

$\quad z =$ Number of standard deviations for a specific confidence level (typically, $z = 3$)

An $\bar{X}$-chart is simply a plot of the means of the samples that were taken from a process. $\bar{\bar{X}}$ is the average of the means.

In practice, the standard deviation of the process is not known. For this reason, an approach that uses actual sample data is commonly used. This practical approach is described in the next section.

An R-chart is a plot of the range within each sample. The range is the difference between the highest and the lowest numbers in that sample. R values provide an easily calculated measure of variation used like a standard deviation. An $\bar{R}$-chart is the average of the range of each sample. More specifically defined, these are

$$\bar{X} = \frac{\sum\limits_{i=1}^{n} X_i}{n} \qquad \textbf{[Same as 6.1]}$$

where

$\quad \bar{X} =$ Mean of the sample

$\quad i =$ Item number

$\quad n =$ Total number of items in the sample

$$\bar{\bar{X}} = \frac{\sum\limits_{j=1}^{m} \bar{X}_j}{m} \qquad \textbf{[6.13]}$$

where

$\quad \bar{\bar{X}} =$ The average of the means of the samples

$\quad j =$ Sample number

$\quad m =$ Total number of sample

$$\bar{R} = \frac{\sum\limits_{j=1}^{m} R_j}{m} \qquad \textbf{[6.14]}$$

Factor for Determining from $\bar{R}$ the Three-Sigma Control Limits for $\bar{X}$- and R-Charts

exhibit 6.13

NUMBER OF OBSERVATIONS IN SUBGROUP n	FACTOR FOR $\bar{X}$-CHART A_2	FACTORS FOR R-CHART	
		LOWER CONTROL LIMIT D_3	UPPER CONTROL LIMIT D_4
2	1.88	0	3.27
3	1.02	0	2.57
4	0.73	0	2.28
5	0.58	0	2.11
6	0.48	0	2.00
7	0.42	0.08	1.92
8	0.37	0.14	1.86
9	0.34	0.18	1.82
10	0.31	0.22	1.78
11	0.29	0.26	1.74
12	0.27	0.28	1.72
13	0.25	0.31	1.69
14	0.24	0.33	1.67
15	0.22	0.35	1.65
16	0.21	0.36	1.64
17	0.20	0.38	1.62
18	0.19	0.39	1.61
19	0.19	0.40	1.60
20	0.18	0.41	1.59

Upper control limit for $\bar{X} = \text{UCL}_{\bar{X}} = \bar{\bar{X}} + A_2\bar{R}$
Lower control limit for $\bar{X} = \text{LCL}_{\bar{X}} = \bar{\bar{X}} - A_2\bar{R}$
Upper control limit for $R = \text{UCL}_R = D_4\bar{R}$
Lower control limit for $R = \text{LCL}_R = D_3\bar{R}$

Note: All factors are based on the normal distribution.

Excel: SPC DONE

where

R_j = Difference between the highest and lowest measurement in the sample
$\bar{R}$ = Average of the measurement differences R for all samples

E. L. Grant and R. Leavenworth computed a table (Exhibit 6.13) that allows us to easily compute the upper and lower control limits for both the $\bar{X}$-chart and the R-chart.[4] These are defined as

$$\text{Upper control limit for } \bar{X} = \bar{\bar{X}} + A_2\bar{R} \qquad \textbf{[6.15]}$$

$$\text{Lower control limit for } \bar{X} = \bar{\bar{X}} - A_2\bar{R} \qquad \textbf{[6.16]}$$

$$\text{Upper control limit for } R = D_4\bar{R} \qquad \textbf{[6.17]}$$

$$\text{Lower control limit for } R = D_3\bar{R} \qquad \textbf{[6.18]}$$

Example 6.5: $\bar{X}$- and R-Charts

We would like to create $\bar{X}$- and R-charts for a process. Exhibit 6.14 shows measurements for all 25 samples. The last two columns show the average of the sample $\bar{X}$ and the range R.

Step by Step

exhibit 6.14

Measurements in Samples of Five from a Process

SAMPLE NUMBER	EACH UNIT IN SAMPLE					AVERAGE $\overline{X}$	RANGE R
1	10.60	10.40	10.30	9.90	10.20	10.28	.70
2	9.98	10.25	10.05	10.23	10.33	10.17	.35
3	9.85	9.90	10.20	10.25	10.15	10.07	.40
4	10.20	10.10	10.30	9.90	9.95	10.09	.40
5	10.30	10.20	10.24	10.50	10.30	10.31	.30
6	10.10	10.30	10.20	10.30	9.90	10.16	.40
7	9.98	9.90	10.20	10.40	10.10	10.12	.50
8	10.10	10.30	10.40	10.24	10.30	10.27	.30
9	10.30	10.20	10.60	10.50	10.10	10.34	.50
10	10.30	10.40	10.50	10.10	10.20	10.30	.40
11	9.90	9.50	10.20	10.30	10.35	10.05	.85
12	10.10	10.36	10.50	9.80	9.95	10.14	.70
13	10.20	10.50	10.70	10.10	9.90	10.28	.80
14	10.20	10.60	10.50	10.30	10.40	10.40	.40
15	10.54	10.30	10.40	10.55	10.00	10.36	.55
16	10.20	10.60	10.15	10.00	10.50	10.29	.60
17	10.20	10.40	10.60	10.80	10.10	10.42	.70
18	9.90	9.50	9.90	10.50	10.00	9.96	1.00
19	10.60	10.30	10.50	9.90	9.80	10.22	.80
20	10.60	10.40	10.30	10.40	10.20	10.38	.40
21	9.90	9.60	10.50	10.10	10.60	10.14	1.00
22	9.95	10.20	10.50	10.30	10.20	10.23	.55
23	10.20	9.50	9.60	9.80	10.30	9.88	.80
24	10.30	10.60	10.30	9.90	9.80	10.18	.80
25	9.90	10.30	10.60	9.90	10.10	10.16	.70
						$\overline{\overline{X}} = 10.21$	$\overline{R} = .60$

Excel:
SPC
DONE

Values for A_2, D_3, and D_4 were obtained from Exhibit 6.13.

Upper control limit for $\overline{X} = \overline{\overline{X}} + A_2\overline{R} = 10.21 + .58(.60) = 10.56$

Lower control limit for $\overline{X} = \overline{\overline{X}} - A_2\overline{R} = 10.21 - .58(.60) = 9.86$

Upper control limit for $R = D_4\overline{R} = 2.11(.60) = 1.27$

Lower control limit for $R = D_3\overline{R} = 0(.60) = 0$

SOLUTION

Exhibit 6.15 shows the $\overline{X}$-chart and R-chart with a plot of all the sample means and ranges of the samples. All the points are well within the control limits, although sample 23 is close to the $\overline{X}$ lower control limit. ●

ACCEPTANCE SAMPLING

Design of a Single Sampling Plan for Attributes

Acceptance sampling is performed on goods that already exist to determine what percentage of products conform to specifications. These products may be items received from another company and evaluated by the receiving department, or they may be components

exhibit 6.15

$\bar{X}$-Chart and R-Chart

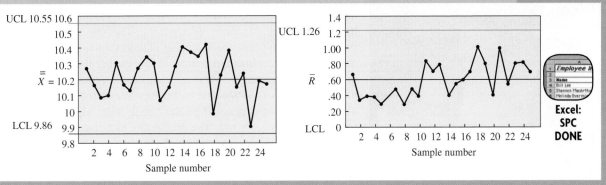

Excel:
SPC
DONE

that have passed through a processing step and are evaluated by company personnel either in production or later in the warehousing function. Whether inspection should be done at all is addressed in the following example.

Acceptance sampling is executed through a sampling plan. In this section we illustrate the planning procedures for a single sampling plan—that is, a plan in which the quality is determined from the evaluation of one sample. (Other plans may be developed using two or more samples. See J. M. Juran and F. M. Gryna's *Quality Planning and Analysis* for a discussion of these plans.)

Example 6.6: Costs to Justify Inspection

Total (100 percent) inspection is justified when the cost of a loss incurred by not inspecting is greater than the cost of inspection. For example, suppose a faulty item results in a $10 loss and the average percentage defective of items in the lot is 3 percent.

Step by Step

SOLUTION

If the average percentage of defective items in a lot is 3 percent, the expected cost of faulty items is $0.03 \times \$10$, or $0.30 each. Therefore, if the cost of inspecting each item is less than $0.30, the economic decision is to perform 100 percent inspection. Not all defective items will be removed, however, because inspectors will pass some bad items and reject some good ones.

The purpose of a sampling plan is to test the lot to either (1) find its quality or (2) ensure that the quality is what it is supposed to be. Thus, if a quality control supervisor already knows the quality (such as the 0.03 given in the example), he or she does not sample for defects. Either all of them must be inspected to remove the defects or none of them should be inspected, and the rejects pass into the process. The choice simply depends on the cost to inspect and the cost incurred by passing a reject. ●

A single sampling plan is defined by n and c, where n is the number of units in the sample and c is the acceptance number. The size of n may vary from one up to all the items in the lot (usually denoted as N) from which it is drawn. The acceptance number c denotes the maximum number of defective items that can be found in the sample before the lot is rejected. Values for n and c are determined by the interaction of four factors (AQL, α, LTPD, and β) that quantify the objectives of the product's producer and its consumer.

ALUMINUM SHEETS ARE EXAMINED UNDER QUALITY CONTROL LIGHTS ON THE ALUMINUM PRODUCTION LINE AT THE ALCOA SZÉKESFEHÉRVÁR, HUNGARY, EXTRUSION PLANT.

The objective of the producer is to ensure that the sampling plan has a low probability of rejecting good lots. Lots are defined as high quality if they contain no more than a specified level of defectives, termed the *acceptable quality level (AQL)*.[5] The objective of the consumer is to ensure that the sampling plan has a low probability of accepting bad lots. Lots are defined as low quality if the percentage of defectives is greater than a specified amount, termed *lot tolerance percent defective (LTPD)*. The probability associated with rejecting a high-quality lot is denoted by the Greek letter alpha (α) and is termed the *producer's risk*. The probability associated with accepting a low-quality lot is denoted by the letter beta (β) and is termed the *consumer's risk*. The selection of particular values for AQL, α, LTPD, and β is an economic decision based on a cost trade-off or, more typically, on company policy or contractual requirements.

There is a humorous story supposedly about Hewlett-Packard during its first dealings with Japanese vendors, who place great emphasis on high-quality production. HP had insisted on 2 percent AQL in a purchase of 100 cables. During the purchase agreement, some heated discussion took place wherein the Japanese vendor did not want this AQL specification; HP insisted that they would not budge from the 2 percent AQL. The Japanese vendor finally agreed. Later, when the box arrived, there were two packages inside. One contained 100 good cables. The other package had 2 cables with a note stating: "We have sent you 100 good cables. Since you insisted on 2 percent AQL, we have enclosed 2 defective cables in this package, though we do not understand why you want them."

The following example, using an excerpt from a standard acceptance sampling table, illustrates how the four parameters—AQL, α, LTPD, and β—are used in developing a sampling plan.

Step by Step

Example 6.7: Values of *n* and *c*

Hi-Tech Industries manufactures Z-Band radar scanners used to detect speed traps. The printed circuit boards in the scanners are purchased from an outside vendor. The vendor produces the boards to an AQL of 2 percent defectives and is willing to run a 5 percent risk (α) of having lots of this level or fewer defectives rejected. Hi-Tech considers lots of 8 percent or more defectives (LTPD) unacceptable and wants to ensure that it will accept such poor-quality lots no more than 10 percent of the time (β). A large shipment has just been delivered. What values of *n* and *c* should be selected to determine the quality of this lot?

SOLUTION

The parameters of the problem are AQL = 0.02, α = 0.05, LTPD = 0.08, and β = 0.10. We can use Exhibit 6.16 to find *c* and *n*.

First, divide LTPD by AQL (0.08 ÷ 0.02 = 4). Then, find the ratio in column 2 that is equal to or just greater than that amount (4). This value is 4.057, which is associated with *c* = 4.

Finally, find the value in column 3 that is in the same row as *c* = 4, and divide that quantity by AQL to obtain *n* (1.970 ÷ 0.02 = 98.5).

The appropriate sampling plan is *c* = 4, *n* = 99. ●

exhibit 6.16

Excerpt from a Sampling Plan Table for $\alpha = 0.05$, $\beta = 0.10$

c	LTPD ÷ AQL	$n \cdot$ AQL	c	LTPD ÷ AQL	$n \cdot$ AQL
0	44.890	0.052	5	3.549	2.613
1	10.946	0.355	6	3.206	3.286
2	6.509	0.818	7	2.957	3.981
3	4.890	1.366	8	2.768	4.695
4	4.057	1.970	9	2.618	5.426

Operating Characteristic Curves

While a sampling plan such as the one just described meets our requirements for the extreme values of good and bad quality, we cannot readily determine how well the plan discriminates between good and bad lots at intermediate values. For this reason, sampling plans are generally displayed graphically through the use of operating characteristic (OC) curves. These curves, which are unique for each combination of n and c, simply illustrate the probability of accepting lots with varying percentages of defectives. The procedure we have followed in developing the plan, in fact, specifies two points on an OC curve: one point defined by AQL and $1-\alpha$ and the other point defined by LTPD and β. Curves for common values of n and c can be computed or obtained from available tables.[6]

Shaping the OC Curve   A sampling plan discriminating perfectly between good and bad lots has an infinite slope (vertical) at the selected value of AQL. In Exhibit 6.17,

exhibit 6.17

Operating Characteristic Curve for AQL = 0.02, $\alpha = 0.05$, LTPD = 0.08, $\beta = 0.10$

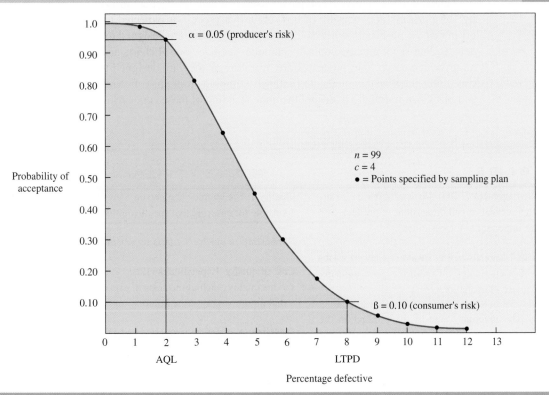

any percentage defective to the left of 2 percent would always be accepted, and those to the right, always rejected. However, such a curve is possible only with complete inspection of all units and thus is not a possibility with a true sampling plan.

An OC curve should be steep in the region of most interest (between the AQL and the LTPD), which is accomplished by varying n and c. If c remains constant, increasing the sample size n causes the OC curve to be more vertical. While holding n constant, decreasing c (the maximum number of defective units) also makes the slope more vertical, moving closer to the origin.

The Effects of Lot Size The size of the lot that the sample is taken from has relatively little effect on the quality of protection. Consider, for example, that samples—all of the same size of 20 units—are taken from different lots ranging from a lot size of 200 units to a lot size of infinity. If each lot is known to have 5 percent defectives, the probability of accepting the lot based on the sample of 20 units ranges from about 0.34 to about 0.36. This means that as long as the lot size is several times the sample size, it makes little difference how large the lot is. It seems a bit difficult to accept, but statistically (on the average in the long run) whether we have a carload or box full, we'll get about the same answer. It just seems that a carload should have a larger sample size. Of course, this assumes that the lot is randomly chosen and that defects are randomly spread through the lot.

SUMMARY

Companies now expect employees to understand the Six-Sigma improvement methodology. DMAIC, the acronym for define, measure, analyze, improve, and control, is a process fundamental to the approach companies use to guide improvement projects. The "capability" of a process is a measure of how often that process is expected to produce a defect given that the process is in control. Six-Sigma processes are designed to produce very few defects. Statistical process control techniques include control charts and acceptance sampling, which ensure that processes are operating as they are designed to operate. World-class companies have implemented extensive training programs (often referred to as "green and black belt training") to ensure the understanding of these concepts.

Key Terms

Total quality management (TQM) Managing the entire organization so that it excels on all dimensions of products and services that are important to the customer.

Malcolm Baldrige National Quality Award An award established by the U.S. Department of Commerce given annually to companies that excel in quality.

Design quality The inherent value of the product in the marketplace.

Conformance quality The degree to which the product or service design specifications are met.

Quality at the source The person who does the work is responsible for ensuring that specifications are met.

Dimensions of quality Criteria by which quality is measured.

Cost of quality Expenditures related to achieving product or service quality, such as the costs of prevention, appraisal, internal failure, and external failure.

Six Sigma A statistical term to describe the quality goal of no more than four defects out of every million units. Also refers to a quality improvement philosophy and program.

DPMO (defects per million opportunities) A metric used to describe the variability of a process.

DMAIC An acronym for the **D**efine, **M**easure, **A**nalyze, **I**mprove, and **C**ontrol improvement methodology followed by companies engaging in Six-Sigma programs.

Assignable variation Deviation in the output of a process that can be clearly identified and managed.

Common variation Deviation in the output of a process that is random and inherent in the process itself.

Upper and lower specification limits The range of values in a measure associated with a process that are allowable given the intended use of the product or service.

Capability index (C_{pk}) The ratio of the range of values produced by a process divided by the range of values allowed by the design specification.

Statistical process control (SPC) Techniques for testing a random sample of output from a process to determine whether the process is producing items within a prescribed range.

Attributes Quality characteristics that are classified as either conforming or not conforming to specification.

Variables Quality characteristics that are measured in actual weight, volume, inches, centimeters, or other measure.

Formula Review

Mean or average

$$\overline{X} = \sum_{i=1}^{N} x_i / N \qquad [6.1]$$

Standard deviation

$$\sigma = \sqrt{\frac{\sum_{i=1}^{N}(x_i - \overline{X})^2}{N}} \qquad [6.2]$$

Capability index

$$C_{pk} = \min\left[\frac{\overline{\overline{X}} - \text{LSL}}{3\sigma}, \frac{\text{USL} - \overline{\overline{X}}}{3\sigma}\right] \qquad [6.3]$$

Process control charts using attribute measurements

$$\overline{p} = \frac{\text{Total number of defects from all samples}}{\text{Number of samples} \times \text{Sample size}} \qquad [6.4]$$

$$s_p = \sqrt{\frac{\overline{p}(1 - \overline{p})}{n}} \qquad [6.5]$$

$$\text{UCL} = \overline{p} + zs_p \qquad [6.6]$$

$$\text{LCL} = \overline{p} - zs_p \qquad [6.7]$$

$$\overline{c} = \text{Average number of defects per unit} \qquad [6.8]$$

$$s_p = \sqrt{\overline{c}} \qquad [6.9]$$

$$\text{UCL} = \overline{c} + z\sqrt{\overline{c}} \qquad [6.10]$$

$$\text{LCL} = \overline{c} - z\sqrt{\overline{c}} \text{ or 0 if less then 0} \qquad [6.11]$$

$$\text{UCL}_{\overline{x}} = \overline{\overline{X}} + zS_{\overline{x}} \qquad \text{and} \qquad \text{LCL}_{\overline{x}} = \overline{\overline{X}} - zS_{\overline{x}} \qquad [6.12]$$

Process control $\overline{X}$- and R-charts

$$\overline{\overline{X}} = \frac{\sum\limits_{j=1}^{m} \overline{X}_j}{m} \qquad \text{[6.13]}$$

$$\overline{R} = \frac{\sum\limits_{j=1}^{m} R_j}{m} \qquad \text{[6.14]}$$

Upper control limit for $\overline{X} = \overline{\overline{X}} + A_2\overline{R}$ [6.15]

Lower control limit for $\overline{X} = \overline{\overline{X}} - A_2\overline{R}$ [6.16]

Upper control limit for $R = D_4\overline{R}$ [6.17]

Lower control limit for $R = D_3\overline{R}$ [6.18]

Solved Problems

SOLVED PROBLEM 1

**Excel:
SPC
DONE**

Completed forms from a particular department of an insurance company were sampled daily to check the performance quality of that department. To establish a tentative norm for the department, one sample of 100 units was collected each day for 15 days, with these results:

SAMPLE	SAMPLE SIZE	NUMBER OF FORMS WITH ERRORS	SAMPLE	SAMPLE SIZE	NUMBER OF FORMS WITH ERRORS
1	100	4	9	100	4
2	100	3	10	100	2
3	100	5	11	100	7
4	100	0	12	100	2
5	100	2	13	100	1
6	100	8	14	100	3
7	100	1	15	100	1
8	100	3			

a. Develop a p-chart using a 95 percent confidence interval ($1.96s_p$).
b. Plot the 15 samples collected.
c. What comments can you make about the process?

Solution

a. $\overline{p} = \dfrac{46}{15(100)} = .0307$

$s_p = \sqrt{\dfrac{\overline{p}(1 - \overline{p})}{n}} = \sqrt{\dfrac{.0307(1 - .0307)}{100}} = \sqrt{.0003} = .017$

$\text{UCL} = \overline{p} + 1.96s_p = .031 + 1.96(.017) = .064$

$\text{LCL} = \overline{p} - 1.96s_p = .031 - 1.96(.017) = -.00232 \text{ or zero}$

b. The defectives are plotted below.

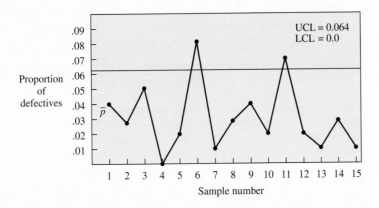

c. Of the 15 samples, 2 were out of the control limits. Because the control limits were established as 95 percent, or 1 out of 20, we would say that the process is out of control. It needs to be examined to find the cause of such widespread variation.

SOLVED PROBLEM 2

Management is trying to decide whether Part A, which is produced with a consistent 3 percent defective rate, should be inspected. If it is not inspected, the 3 percent defectives will go through a product assembly phase and have to be replaced later. If all Part A's are inspected, one-third of the defectives will be found, thus raising the quality to 2 percent defectives.

a. Should the inspection be done if the cost of inspecting is $0.01 per unit and the cost of replacing a defective in the final assembly is $4.00?

b. Suppose the cost of inspecting is $0.05 per unit rather than $0.01. Would this change your answer in *a*?

Solution

Should Part A be inspected?

.03 defective with no inspection.

.02 defective with inspection.

a. This problem can be solved simply by looking at the opportunity for 1 percent improvement.

Benefit = .01($4.00) = $0.04

Cost of inspection = $0.01

Therefore, inspect and save $0.03 per unit.

b. A cost of $0.05 per unit to inspect would be $0.01 greater than the savings, so inspection should not be performed.

Review and Discussion Questions

1 The capability index allows for some drifting of the process mean. Discuss what this means in terms of product quality output.

2 Discuss the purposes of and differences between *p* charts and $\overline{X}$- and *R*-charts.

3 In an agreement between a supplier and a customer, the supplier must ensure that all parts are within specification before shipment to the customer. What is the effect on the cost of quality to the customer?

4 In the situation described in question 3, what would be the effect on the cost of quality to the supplier?

5 Discuss the trade-off between achieving a zero AQL (acceptable quality level) and a positive AQL (such as an AQL of 2 percent).

Problems

1 A manager states that his process is really working well. Out of 1,500 parts, 1,477 were produced free of a particular defect and passed inspection. Based on Six-Sigma theory, how would you rate this performance, other things being equal?

2 A company currently using an inspection process in its material receiving department is trying to install an overall cost reduction program. One possible reduction is the elimination of one inspection position. This position tests material that has a defective content on the average of 0.04. By inspecting all items, the inspector is able to remove all defects. The inspector can inspect 50 units per hour. The hourly rate including fringe benefits for this position is $9. If the inspection position is eliminated, defects will go into product assembly and will have to be replaced later at a cost of $10 each when they are detected in final product testing.

   a. Should this inspection position be eliminated?

   b. What is the cost to inspect each unit?

   c. Is there benefit (or loss) from the current inspection process? How much?

3 A metal fabricator produces connecting rods with an outer diameter that has a $1 \pm .01$ inch specification. A machine operator takes several sample measurements over time and determines the sample mean outer diameter to be 1.002 inches with a standard deviation of .003 inch.

   a. Calculate the process capability index for this example.

   b. What does this figure tell you about the process?

4 Ten samples of 15 parts each were taken from an ongoing process to establish a *p* chart for control. The samples and the number of defectives in each are shown in the following table:

SAMPLE	*n*	NUMBER OF DEFECTS IN SAMPLE	SAMPLE	*n*	NUMBER OF DEFECTS IN SAMPLE
1	15	3	6	15	2
2	15	1	7	15	0
3	15	0	8	15	3
4	15	0	9	15	1
5	15	0	10	15	0

   a. Develop a *p*-chart for 95 percent confidence (1.96 standard deviations).

   b. Based on the plotted data points, what comments can you make?

5 Output from a process contains 0.02 defective units. Defective units that go undetected into final assemblies cost $25 each to replace. An inspection process, which would detect and remove all defectives, can be established to test these units. However, the inspector, who can test 20 units per hour, is paid $8 per hour, including fringe benefits. Should an inspection station be established to test all units?

   a. What is the cost to inspect each unit?

   b. What is the benefit (or loss) from the inspection process?

6 There is a 3 percent error rate at a specific point in a production process. If an inspector is placed at this point, all the errors can be detected and eliminated. However, the inspector is paid $8 per hour and can inspect units in the process at the rate of 30 per hour.

If no inspector is used and defects are allowed to pass this point, there is a cost of $10 per unit to correct the defect later on.

Should an inspector be hired?

7   A shirt manufacturer buys cloth by the 100 yard roll from a supplier. For setting up a control chart to manage the irregularities (e.g., loose threads and tears) the following data was collected from a sample provided by the supplier.

SAMPLE	1	2	3	4	5	6	7	8	9	10
IRREGULARITIES	3	5	2	6	5	4	6	3	4	5

a. Using these data set up a *c*-chart with $z = 2$.

b. Suppose the next five rolls from the supplier had three, two, five, three and seven irregularities. Is the supplier process under control?

8   Resistors for electronic circuits are manufactured on a high-speed automated machine. The machine is set up to produce a large run of resistors of 1,000 ohms each.

To set up the machine and to create a control chart to be used throughout the run, 15 samples were taken with four resistors in each sample. The complete list of samples and their measured values are as follows:

SAMPLE NUMBER	READINGS (IN OHMS)			
1	1010	991	985	986
2	995	996	1009	994
3	990	1003	1015	1008
4	1015	1020	1009	998
5	1013	1019	1005	993
6	994	1001	994	1005
7	989	992	982	1020
8	1001	986	996	996
9	1006	989	1005	1007
10	992	1007	1006	979
11	996	1006	997	989
12	1019	996	991	1011
13	981	991	989	1003
14	999	993	988	984
15	1013	1002	1005	992

Develop an $\bar{X}$-chart and an R-chart and plot the values. From the charts, what comments can you make about the process? (Use three-sigma control limits as in Exhibit 6.13.)

9   In the past, Alpha Corporation has not performed incoming quality control inspections but has taken the word of its vendors. However, Alpha has been having some unsatisfactory experience recently with the quality of purchased items and wants to set up sampling plans for the receiving department to use.

For a particular component, X, Alpha has a lot tolerance percentage defective of 10 percent. Zenon Corporation, from which Alpha purchases this component, has an acceptable quality level in its production facility of 3 percent for component X. Alpha has a consumer's risk of 10 percent and Zenon has a producer's risk of 5 percent.

a.   When a shipment of Product X is received from Zenon Corporation, what sample size should the receiving department test?

b.   What is the allowable number of defects in order to accept the shipment?

10   You are the newly appointed assistant administrator at a local hospital, and your first project is to investigate the quality of the patient meals put out by the food-service department. You conducted a 10-day survey by submitting a simple questionnaire to the 400 patients with each meal, asking that they simply check off that the meal was either satisfactory or

unsatisfactory. For simplicity in this problem, assume that the response was 1,000 returned questionnaires from the 1,200 meals each day. The results are as follows:

	NUMBER OF UNSATISFACTORY MEALS	SAMPLE SIZE
December 1	74	1,000
December 2	42	1,000
December 3	64	1,000
December 4	80	1,000
December 5	40	1,000
December 6	50	1,000
December 7	65	1,000
December 8	70	1,000
December 9	40	1,000
December 10	75	1,000
	600	10,000

    a. Construct a *p*-chart based on the questionnaire results, using a confidence interval of 95.5 percent, which is two standard deviations.

    b. What comments can you make about the results of the survey?

11   Large-scale integrated (LSI) circuit chips are made in one department of an electronics firm. These chips are incorporated into analog devices that are then encased in epoxy. The yield is not particularly good for LSI manufacture, so the AQL specified by that department is 0.15 while the LTPD acceptable by the assembly department is 0.40.

    a. Develop a sampling plan.

    b. Explain what the sampling plan means; that is, how would you tell someone to do the test?

12   The state and local police departments are trying to analyze crime rates so they can shift their patrols from decreasing-rate areas to areas where rates are increasing. The city and county have been geographically segmented into areas containing 5,000 residences. The police recognize that not all crimes and offenses are reported: people do not want to become involved, consider the offenses too small to report, are too embarrassed to make a police report, or do not take the time, among other reasons. Every month, because of this, the police are contacting by phone a random sample of 1,000 of the 5,000 residences for data on crime. (Respondents are guaranteed anonymity.) Here are the data collected for the past 12 months for one area:

MONTH	CRIME INCIDENCE	SAMPLE SIZE	CRIME RATE
January	7	1,000	0.007
February	9	1,000	0.009
March	7	1,000	0.007
April	7	1,000	0.007
May	7	1,000	0.007
June	9	1,000	0.009
July	7	1,000	0.007
August	10	1,000	0.010
September	8	1,000	0.008
October	11	1,000	0.011
November	10	1,000	0.010
December	8	1,000	0.008

Construct a *p*-chart for 95 percent confidence (1.96) and plot each of the months. If the next three months show crime incidences in this area as

January = 10 (out of 1,000 sampled)
February = 12 (out of 1,000 sampled)
March = 11 (out of 1,000 sampled)

what comments can you make regarding the crime rate?

13   Some citizens complained to city council members that there should be equal protection under the law against the occurrence of crimes. The citizens argued that this equal protection

should be interpreted as indicating that high-crime areas should have more police protection than low-crime areas. Therefore, police patrols and other methods for preventing crime (such as street lighting or cleaning up abandoned areas and buildings) should be used proportionately to crime occurrence.

In a fashion similar to problem 11, the city has been broken down into 20 geographic areas, each containing 5,000 residences. The 1,000 sampled from each area showed the following incidence of crime during the past month:

AREA	NUMBER OF CRIMES	SAMPLE SIZE	CRIME RATE
1	14	1,000	0.014
2	3	1,000	0.003
3	19	1,000	0.019
4	18	1,000	0.018
5	14	1,000	0.014
6	28	1,000	0.028
7	10	1,000	0.010
8	18	1,000	0.018
9	12	1,000	0.012
10	3	1,000	0.003
11	20	1,000	0.020
12	15	1,000	0.015
13	12	1,000	0.012
14	14	1,000	0.014
15	10	1,000	0.010
16	30	1,000	0.030
17	4	1,000	0.004
18	20	1,000	0.020
19	6	1,000	0.006
20	30	1,000	0.030
	300		

Suggest a reallocation of crime protection effort, if indicated, based on a *p*-chart analysis. To be reasonably certain in your recommendation, select a 95 percent confidence level (that is, $Z = 1.96$).

14 The following table contains the measurements of the key length dimension from a fuel injector. These samples of size five were taken at one-hour intervals.

SAMPLE NUMBER	OBSERVATIONS				
	1	2	3	4	5
1	.486	.499	.493	.511	.481
2	.499	.506	.516	.494	.529
3	.496	.500	.515	.488	.521
4	.495	.506	.483	.487	.489
5	.472	.502	.526	.469	.481
6	.473	.495	.507	.493	.506
7	.495	.512	.490	.471	.504
8	.525	.501	.498	.474	.485
9	.497	.501	.517	.506	.516
10	.495	.505	.516	.511	.497
11	.495	.482	.468	.492	.492
12	.483	.459	.526	.506	.522
13	.521	.512	.493	.525	.510
14	.487	.521	.507	.501	.500
15	.493	.516	.499	.511	.513
16	.473	.506	.479	.480	.523
17	.477	.485	.513	.484	.496
18	.515	.493	.493	.485	.475
19	.511	.536	.486	.497	.491
20	.509	.490	.470	.504	.512

Construct a three-sigma $\overline{X}$-chart and R-chart (use Exhibit 6.13) for the length of the fuel injector. What can you say about this process?

15 C-Spec, Inc., is attempting to determine whether an existing machine is capable of milling an engine part that has a key specification of $4 \pm .003$ inches. After a trial run on this machine, C-Spec has determined that the machine has a sample mean of 4.001 inches with a standard deviation of .002 inch.

a. Calculate the C_{pk} for this machine.

b. Should C-Spec use this machine to produce this part? Why?

Advanced Problem

16 Design specifications require that a key dimension on a product measure 100 ± 10 units. A process being considered for producing this product has a standard deviation of four units.

a. What can you say (quantitatively) regarding the process capability?

b. Suppose the process average shifts to 92. Calculate the new process capability.

c. What can you say about the process after the shift? Approximately what percentage of the items produced will be defective?

CASE: Hank Kolb, Director of Quality Assurance

Hank Kolb was whistling as he walked toward his office, still feeling a bit like a stranger since he had been hired four weeks before as director of quality assurance. All that week he had been away from the plant at a seminar given for quality managers of manufacturing plants by the corporate training department. He was now looking forward to digging into the quality problems at this industrial products plant employing 1,200 people.

Kolb poked his head into Mark Hamler's office, his immediate subordinate as the quality control manager, and asked him how things had gone during the past week. Hamler's muted smile and an "Oh, fine," stopped Kolb in his tracks. He didn't know Hamler very well and was unsure about pursuing this reply any further. Kolb was still uncertain of how to start building a relationship with him since Hamler had been passed over for the promotion to Kolb's job; Hamler's evaluation form had stated "superb technical knowledge; managerial skills lacking." Kolb decided to inquire a little further and asked Hamler what had happened; he replied, "Oh, just another typical quality snafu. We had a little problem on the Greasex line last week [a specialized degreasing solvent packed in a spray can for the high-technology sector]. A little high pressure was found in some cans on the second shift, but a supervisor vented them so that we could ship them out. We met our delivery schedule!" Because Kolb was still relatively unfamiliar with the plant and its products, he asked Hamler to elaborate; painfully, Hamler continued:

> We've been having some trouble with the new filling equipment and some of the cans were pressurized beyond the upper specification limit.

The production rate is still 50 percent of standard, about 14 cases per shift, and we caught it halfway into the shift. Mac Evans [the inspector for that line] picked it up, tagged the cases "hold," and went on about his duties. When he returned at the end of the shift to write up the rejects, Wayne Simmons, first-line supervisor, was by a pallet of finished goods finishing sealing up a carton of the rejected Greasex; the reject "hold" tags had been removed. He told Mac that he had heard about the high pressure from another inspector at coffee break, had come back, taken off the tags, individually turned the cans upside down and vented every one of them in the eight rejected cartons. He told Mac that production planning was really pushing for the stuff and they couldn't delay by having it sent through the rework area. He told Mac that he would get on the operator to run the equipment right next time. Mac didn't write it up but came in about three days ago to tell me about it. Oh, it happens every once in a while and I told him to make sure to check with maintenance to make sure the filling machine was adjusted; and I saw Wayne in the hall and told him that he ought to send the stuff through rework next time.

Kolb was a bit dumbfounded at this and didn't say much—he didn't know if this was a big deal or not. When he got to his office he thought again what Morganthal, general manager, had said when he had hired him. He warned Kolb about the "lack of quality attitude" in the plant, and said that

Kolb "should try and do something about this." Morganthal further emphasized the quality problems in the plant: "We have to improve our quality; it's costing us a lot of money, I'm sure of it, but I can't prove it! Hank, you have my full support in this matter; you're in charge of these quality problems. This downward quality–productivity–turnover spiral has to end!"

The incident had happened a week before; the goods were probably out in the customers' hands by now, and everyone had forgotten about it (or wanted to). There seemed to be more pressing problems than this for Kolb to spend his time on, but this continued to nag him. He felt that the quality department was being treated as a joke, and he also felt that this was a personal slap from manufacturing. He didn't want to start a war with the production people, but what could he do? Kolb was troubled enough to cancel his appointments and spend the morning talking to a few people. After a long and very tactful morning, he learned the following information:

1   **From personnel.**   The operator for the filling equipment had just been transferred from shipping two weeks ago. He had no formal training in this job but was being trained by Wayne, on the job, to run the equipment. When Mac had tested the high-pressure cans, the operator was nowhere to be found and had only learned of the rejected material from Wayne after the shift was over.

2   **From plant maintenance.**   This particular piece of automated filling equipment had been purchased two years ago for use on another product. It had been switched to the Greasex line six months ago and maintenance completed 12 work orders during the last month for repairs or adjustments on it. The equipment had been adapted by plant maintenance for handling the lower viscosity of Greasex, which it had not originally been designed for. This included designing a special filling head. There was no scheduled preventive maintenance for this equipment, and the parts for the sensitive filling head, replaced three times in the last six months, had to be made at a nearby machine shop. Nonstandard downtime was 15 percent of actual running time.

3   **From purchasing.**   The plastic nozzle heads for the Greasex can, designed by a vendor for this new product on a rush order, were often found to have slight burrs on the inside rim, and this caused some trouble in fitting the top to the can. An increase in application pressure at the filling head by maintenance adjustment had solved the burr application problem or had at least forced the nozzle heads on despite burrs. Purchasing agents said that they were going to talk to the sales representative of the nozzle head supplier about this the next time he came in.

4   **From product design and packaging.**   The can, designed especially for Greasex, had been contoured to allow better gripping by the user. This change, instigated by marketing research, set Greasex apart from the appearance of its competitors and was seen as significant by the designers. There had been no test of the effects of the contoured can on filling speed or filling hydrodynamics from a high-pressured filling head. Kolb had a hunch that the new design was acting as a venturi (carrier creating suction) when being filled, but the packaging designer thought that was unlikely.

5   **From the manufacturing manager.**   He had heard about the problem; in fact, Simmons had made a joke about it, bragging about how he beat his production quota to the other foremen and shift supervisors. The manufacturing manager thought Simmons was one of the "best foremen we have . . . he always got his production out." His promotion papers were actually on the manufacturing manager's desk when Kolb dropped by. Simmons was being strongly considered for promotion to shift supervisor. The manufacturing manager, under pressure from Morganthal for cost improvements and reduced delivery times, sympathetized with Kolb but said that the rework area would have vented with their pressure gauges what Wayne had done by hand. "But I'll speak with Wayne about the incident," he said.

6   **From marketing.**   The introduction of Greasex had been rushed to market to beat competitors, and a major promotional advertising campaign was under way to increase consumer awareness. A deluge of orders was swamping the order-taking department and putting Greasex high on the back-order list. Production had to turn the stuff out; even being a little off spec was tolerable because "it would be better to have it on the shelf than not there at all. Who cares if the label is a little crooked or the stuff comes out with a little too much pressure? We need market share now in that high-tech segment."

What bothered Kolb most was the safety issue of the high pressure in the cans. He had no way of knowing how much of a hazard the high pressure was or if Simmons had vented them enough to effectively reduce the hazard. The data from the can manufacturer, which Hamler had showed him, indicated that the high pressure found by the inspector was not in the danger area. But, again, the inspector had used only a sample testing procedure to reject the eight cases. Even if he could morally accept that there was no product safety hazard, could Kolb make sure that this would never happen again?

Skipping lunch, Kolb sat in his office and thought about the morning's events. The past week's seminar had talked about the role of quality, productivity and quality, creating a new attitude, and the quality challenge; but where had they told him what to do when this happened? He had left a very good job to come here because he thought the company was serious about the importance of quality, and he wanted a challenge. Kolb had demanded and received a salary equal to the manufacturing, marketing, and R&D directors, and he was one of the direct reports to the general manager. Yet he still didn't know exactly what he should or shouldn't do, or even what he could or couldn't do under these circumstances.

Questions

1   What are the causes of the quality problems on the Greasex line? Display your answer on a fishbone diagram.
2   What general steps should Hank follow in setting up a continuous improvement program for the company? What problems will he have to overcome to make it work?

Source: Copyright 1981 by President and Fellows of Harvard College, Harvard Business School. Case 681.083. This case was prepared by Frank S. Leonard as the basis for class discussion rather than to illustrate either effective or ineffective handling of an administrative situation. Reprinted by permission of the Harvard Business School.

Footnotes

1 D. A. Garvin, *Managing Quality* (New York: Free Press, 1988).

2 P. B. Crosby, *Quality Is Free* (New York: New American Library, 1979), p. 15.

3 S. Walleck, D. O'Halloran, and C. Leader, "Benchmarking World-Class Performance," *McKinsey Quarterly,* no. 1 (1991), p. 7.

4 E. L. Grant and R. S. Leavenworth, *Statistical Quality Control* (New York: McGraw-Hill, 1996).

5 There is some controversy surrounding AQLs. This is based on the argument that specifying some acceptable percentage of defectives is inconsistent with the philosophical goal of zero defects. In practice, even in the best QC companies, there is an acceptable quality level. The difference is that it may be stated in parts per million rather than in parts per hundred. This is the case in Motorola's Six-Sigma quality standard, which holds that no more than 3.4 defects per million parts are acceptable.

6 See, for example, H. F. Dodge and H. G. Romig, *Sampling Inspection Tables—Single and Double Sampling* (New York: John Wiley & Sons, 1959); and *Military Standard Sampling Procedures and Tables for Inspection by Attributes* (MIL-STD-105D) (Washington, DC: U.S. Government Printing Office, 1983).

Super Quiz

1   This refers to the inherent value of the product in the marketplace and is a strategic decision for the firm.
2   Relates to how well a product or service meets design specifications.
3   Relates to how the customer views quality dimensions of a product or service.
4   The series of international quality standards.
5   What is the enemy of good quality?
6   A Six-Sigma process that is running at the center of its control limits would expect this defect rate.
7   The standard quality improvement methodology developed by General Electric.
8   Variation that can be clearly identified and possibly managed.
9   Variation inherent in the process itself.
10   If a process has a capability index of 1 and is running normally (centered on the mean), what percent of the units would one expect to be defective?

11   An alternative to viewing a item as simply good or bad due to it falling in or out of the tolerance range.
12   Quality characteristics that are classified as either conforming or not conforming to specification.
13   A quality characteristic that is actually measured, such as the weight of an item.
14   A quality chart suitable for when an item is either good or bad.
15   A quality chart suitable for when a number of blemishes are expected on each unit, such as a spool of yarn.
16   Useful for checking quality when we periodically purchase large quantities of an item and it would be very costly to check each unit individually.
17   A chart that depicts the manufacturer's and consumer's risk associated with a sampling plan.

1. Design quality 2. Conformance quality 3. Fitness for use 4. ISO 9000 5. Variation 6. 2 parts per billion units 7. DMAIC cycle 8. Assignable variation 9. Common variation 10. Design limits are at $\pm 3\sigma$ or 2.7 defects per thousand 11. Taguchi loss function 12. Attributes 13. Variables 14. *P*-chart 15. C-chart 16. Acceptance sampling 17. Operating characteristic curve.

Selected Bibliography

Evans, James R., and William M. Lindsay. *The Management and Control of Quality,* 6th ed. Cincinnati: South-Western College Publications, 2004.

Rath & Strong. *Rath & Strong's Six Sigma Pocket Guide.* Rath & Strong, Inc., 2000.

Small, B. B. (with committee). *Statistical Quality Control Handbook.* Western Electric Co., Inc., 1956.

Zimmerman, S. M., and M. L. Icenogel. *Statistical Quality Control; Using Excel.* 2nd ed. Milwaukee, WI: ASQ Quality Press, 2002.

CHAPTER 7

PROJECTS

After reading the chapter you will:

- Explain what project management is and why it is important.
- Identify the different ways projects can be structured.
- Describe how projects are organized into major subprojects.
- Understand what a project milestone is.
- Determine the "critical path" for a project.
- Demonstrate how to "crash," or reduce the length, of a project.

179   National Aeronautics and Space Administration's
      Constellation Program

181   What Is Project Management?

                                                      Project defined
                                          Project management defined

181   Structuring Projects
      Pure Project   Pure project defined
      Functional Project   Functional project defined
      Matrix Project   Matrix project defined

185   Work Breakdown Structure

                                            Project milestone defined
                                 Work breakdown structure defined
                                               Activities defined

186   Project Control Charts
      Earned Value Management   Gantt chart defined
                                      Earned value management defined

191   Network-Planning Models
      Critical Path Method (CPM)   Critical path defined
      CPM with Three Activity Time Estimates   Immediate predecessor defined
      Time–Cost Models and Project Crashing   Slack time defined
                                           Early start schedule defined
                                            Late start schedule defined
                                             Time–cost models defined

203   Managing Resources
      Tracking Progress

205   Summary

217   Case: Cell Phone Design Project

218   Super Quiz

NATIONAL AERONAUTICS AND SPACE ADMINISTRATION'S CONSTELLATION PROGRAM MAY LAND MEN ON THE MOON BY 2020

It has been over 40 years since United States astronaut Neil Armstrong set foot on the moon on July 20, 1969. Today the United States Space Exploration Policy calls *". . . for a sustained and affordable exploration program to explore the solar system, including a return to the Moon by the end of the next decade, to establish a human presence there, and to open the path to other destinations including Mars."*

NASA's exploration activity is now in a period of transition, as the Agency works to complete the International Space Station and retire the Shuttle fleet by 2010, while developing the next generation of spacecraft to support human space flight.

To complete the goal of returning to the Moon, NASA has initiated the Constellation Program to accomplish the feat. The Constellation Program is developing and testing a set of space exploration systems that include the Orion crew exploration vehicle, the Ares I launch vehicle that is intended to propel Orion to low Earth orbit, and the Ares V,

Implementation Schedule

Project	Schedule by Fiscal Year																Phase Dates		
	Prior	08	09	10	11	12	13	14	15	16	17	18	19	20	21	22		Beg	End
Orion																	Tech		
																	Form	Nov-04	Feb-10
																	Dev	Feb-10	Sep-15
																	Ops	Oct-15	Sep-20
																	Res		
Ares I Crew Launch Vehicle (under review)																	Tech		
																	Form	Nov-04	Dec-08
																	Dev	Jan-09	Sep-15
																	Ops	Oct-15	Sep-20
																	Res		
Ares V Cargo Launch Vehicle (preliminary dates)																	Tech		
																	Form	Oct-07	Apr-13
																	Dev	May-13	Apr-20
																	Ops	May-20	
																	Res		

■ Tech & Adv Concepts (Tech)
☐ Formulation (Form)
■ Development (Dev)
☐ Operations (Ops)
■ Research (Res)
☐ Represents a period of no activity for the Project

which is intended to carry a lunar lander to low Earth orbit to dock with Orion and deliver the crew and cargo to the Moon.

The implementation schedule shows the timeline for each of the major projects within the program. The Orion, Ares I, and Ares V projects are each divided into major phases starting with Technology and Advanced concepts, Formulation, Development and Operations. NASA uses the techniques described in this chapter to organize the Constellation Program and to manage the projects within the program. It will be exciting to track this nearly trillion dollar program where man will once again have the opportunity to explore our galaxy for real.

Source: NASA 2010 Budget request. http://www.nasa.gov.

> *"The high-impact project is the gem . . . the fundamental nugget . . . the*
> *fundamental atomic particle from which the new white collar world will*
> *be constructed and/or reconstructed. Projects should be, well WOW!"*
> —Tom Peters

Although most of the material in this chapter focuses on the technical aspects of project management (structuring project networks and calculating the critical path), as we see in the opening vignette, the management aspects are certainly equally important. Success in project management is very much an activity that requires careful control of critical resources. We spend much of the time in this book focused on the management of nonhuman resources such as machines and material; for projects, however, the key resource is often our employees' time. Human resources are often the most expensive and those people involved in the projects critical to the success of the firm are often the most valuable managers, consultants, and engineers.

At the highest levels in an organization, management often involves juggling a portfolio of projects. There are many different types of projects ranging from the development of totally new products, revisions to old products, new marketing plans, and a vast array of projects for better serving customers and reducing costs.

Most companies deal with projects individually—pushing each through the pipeline as quickly and cost-effectively as possible. Many of these same companies are very good at applying the techniques described in this chapter in a manner where the myriad of tasks are executed flawlessly, but the projects just do not deliver the expected results. Worse, what often happens is the projects consuming the most resources have the least connection to the firm's strategy.

The vital big-picture decision is what mix of projects is best for the organization. A firm should have the right mix of projects that best support a company's strategy. Projects should be selected from the following types: derivative (incremental changes such as new product packaging or no-frills versions), breakthrough (major changes that create entirely

exhibit 7.1

Types of Development Projects

	Breakthrough Projects	Platform Projects	Derivative Projects
	More ⟵ Change ⟶ Less		
Product Change	New core product	Additional to product family	Product enhancement
Process Change	New core process	Process upgrade	Incremental change
Research & Development	New core technology	Technology upgrade	Incremental change
Alliance & Partnership	Outsource major activity	Select new partner	Incremental change

new markets), platform (fundamental improvements to existing products). Projects can be categorized in four major areas: product change, process change, research and development, and alliance and partnership (see Exhibit 7.1).

In this chapter we only scratch the surface in our introduction to the topic of project management. Professional project managers are individuals skilled at not only the technical aspects of calculating such things as early start and early finish time but, just as important, the people skills related to motivation. In addition, the ability to resolve conflicts as key decision points occur in the project is a critical skill. Without a doubt, leading successful projects is the best way to prove your promotability to the people who make promotion decisions. Virtually all project work is team work and leading a project involves leading a team. Your success at leading a project will spread quickly through the individuals in the team. As organizations flatten (through reengineering, downsizing, outsourcing), more will depend on projects and project leaders to get work done, work that previously was handled within departments.

WHAT IS PROJECT MANAGEMENT?

A **project** may be defined as a series of related jobs usually directed toward some major output and requiring a significant period of time to perform. **Project management** can be defined as planning, directing, and controlling resources (people, equipment, material) to meet the technical, cost, and time constraints of the project.

Project

Project management

Although projects are often thought to be one-time occurrences, the fact is that many projects can be repeated or transferred to other settings or products. The result will be another project output. A contractor building houses or a firm producing low-volume products such as supercomputers, locomotives, or linear accelerators can effectively consider these as projects.

STRUCTURING PROJECTS

Before the project starts, senior management must decide which of three organizational structures will be used to tie the project to the parent firm: pure project, functional project, or matrix project. We next discuss the strengths and weaknesses of the three main forms.

Pure Project

Tom Peters predicts that most of the world's work will be "brainwork," done in semipermanent networks of small project-oriented teams, each one an autonomous, entrepreneurial center of opportunity, where the necessity for speed and flexibility dooms the hierarchical management structures we and our ancestors grew up with. Thus, out of the three basic project organizational structures, Peters favors the **pure project** (nicknamed *skunkworks*), where a self-contained team works full time on the project.

Pure project

ADVANTAGES
- The project manager has full authority over the project.
- Team members report to one boss. They do not have to worry about dividing loyalty with a functional-area manager.
- Lines of communication are shortened. Decisions are made quickly.
- Team pride, motivation, and commitment are high.

DISADVANTAGES
- Duplication of resources. Equipment and people are not shared across projects.
- Organizational goals and policies are ignored, as team members are often both physically and psychologically removed from headquarters.
- The organization falls behind in its knowledge of new technology due to weakened functional divisions.
- Because team members have no functional area home, they worry about life-after-project, and project termination is delayed.

Functional Project

Functional project

At the other end of the project organization spectrum is the **functional project**, housing the project within a functional division.

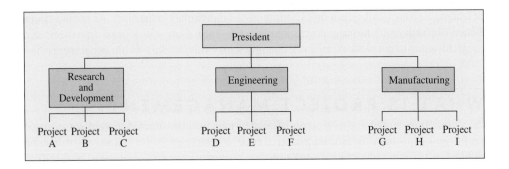

ADVANTAGES
- A team member can work on several projects.
- Technical expertise is maintained within the functional area even if individuals leave the project or organization.
- The functional area is a home after the project is completed. Functional specialists can advance vertically.
- A critical mass of specialized functional-area experts creates synergystic solutions to a project's technical problems.

exhibit 7.4

Sample of Graphic Project Reports

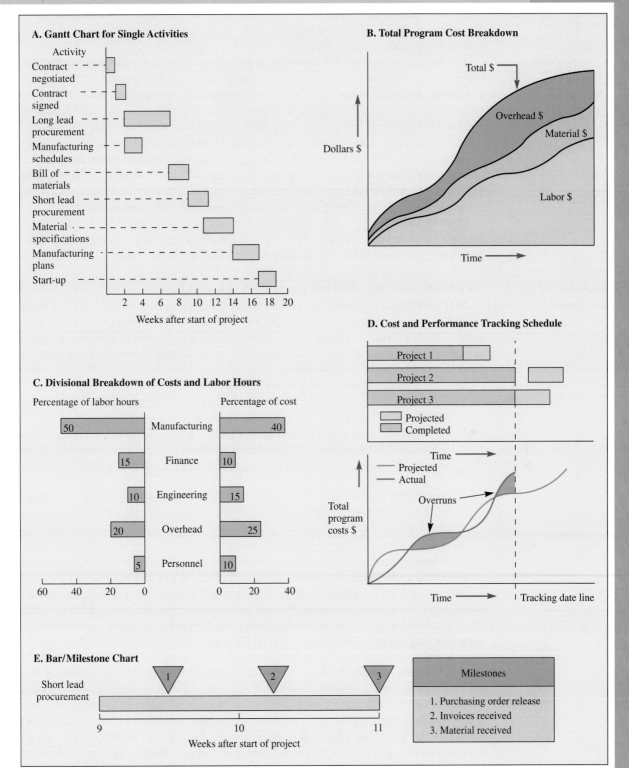

A. Gantt Chart for Single Activities

Activity
Contract negotiated
Contract signed
Long lead procurement
Manufacturing schedules
Bill of materials
Short lead procurement
Material specifications
Manufacturing plans
Start-up

2 4 6 8 10 12 14 16 18 20
Weeks after start of project

B. Total Program Cost Breakdown

Dollars $

Total $
Overhead $
Material $
Labor $

Time

C. Divisional Breakdown of Costs and Labor Hours

Percentage of labor hours   Percentage of cost

50   Manufacturing   40
15   Finance   10
10   Engineering   15
20   Overhead   25
5   Personnel   10

60 40 20 0   0 20 40

D. Cost and Performance Tracking Schedule

Project 1
Project 2
Project 3
Projected
Completed

Time
Projected
Actual
Overruns

Total program costs $

Time   Tracking date line

E. Bar/Milestone Chart

Short lead procurement

1   2   3

9   10   11
Weeks after start of project

Milestones
1. Purchasing order release
2. Invoices received
3. Material received

Exhibit 7.4C shows the percentage of the project's labor hours that comes from the various areas of manufacturing, finance, and so on. These labor hours are related to the proportion of the project's total labor cost. For example, manufacturing is responsible for 50 percent of the project's labor hours, but this 50 percent has been allocated just 40 percent of the total labor dollars charged.

The top half of Exhibit 7.4D shows the degree of completion of these projects. The dotted vertical line signifies today. Project 1, therefore, is already late because it still has work to be done. Project 2 is not being worked on temporarily, so there is a space before the projected work. Project 3 continues to be worked on without interruption. The bottom of Exhibit 7.4D compares actual total costs and projected costs. As we see, two cost overruns occurred, and the current cumulative costs are over projected cumulative costs.

Exhibit 7.4E is a milestone chart. The three milestones mark specific points in the project where checks can be made to see if the project is on time and where it should be. The best place to locate milestones is at the completion of a major activity. In this exhibit, the major activities completed were "purchase order release," "invoices received," and "material received."

Other standard reports can be used for a more detailed presentation comparing cost to progress (such as cost schedule status report—CSSR) or reports providing the basis for partial payment (such as the earned value report which we discuss next).

Earned value management

Earned Value Management (EVM)

EVM is a technique for measuring project progress in an objective manner. EVM has the ability to combine measurements of scope, schedule, and cost in a project. When properly applied, EVM provides a method for evaluating the relative success of a project at a point in time. The measures can be applied to projects focused on either "revenue generation" or "cost" depending on the type of project.

Essential features of any EVM implementation include

1. a project plan that identifies the activities to be accomplished,
2. a valuation of each activity work. In the case of a project that generates revenue this is called the Planned Value (PV) of the activity. In the case where a project is evaluated based on cost, this is called the Budgeted Cost of Work Scheduled (BCWS) for the activity, and
3. predefined "earning or costing rules" (also called metrics) to quantify the accomplishment of work, called Earned Value (EV) or Budgeted Cost of Work Performed (BCWP).

The terminology used in the features is general since the valuations could be either based on a value measure (revenue or profit) or a cost measure. EVM implementations for large or complex projects include many more features, such as indicators and forecasts of cost performance (over budget or under budget) and schedule performance (behind schedule or ahead of schedule). However, the most basic requirement of an EVM system is that it quantifies progress using PV (or BCWS) and EV (or BCWP).

Project Tracking without EVM[1] It is helpful to see an example of project tracking that does not include earned value performance management. Consider a project that has been planned in detail, including a time-phased spend plan for all elements of work. This is a case where the project is evaluated based on cost. Exhibit 7.5A shows the cumulative cost budget for this project as a function of time (the blue line, labeled BCWS). It also shows the cumulative actual cost of the project (red line) through week 8. To those unfamiliar with EVM, it might appear that this project was over budget through week 4 and then

Earned Value Management Charts

exhibit 7.5

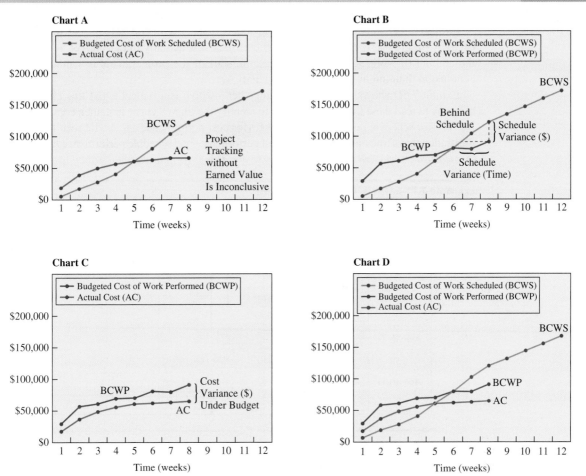

under budget from week 6 through week 8. However, what is missing from this chart is any understanding of how much work has been accomplished during the project. If the project was actually completed at week 8, then the project would actually be well under budget and well ahead of schedule. If, on the other hand, the project is only 10 percent complete at week 8, the project is significantly over budget and behind schedule. A method is needed to measure technical performance objectively and quantitatively, and that is what EVM accomplishes.

Project Tracking with EVM Consider the same project, except this time the project plan includes pre-defined methods of quantifying the accomplishment of work. At the end of each week, the project manager identifies every detailed element of work that has been completed, and sums the Budgeted Cost of Work Performed for each of these completed elements by estimating the percent complete of the activity and multiplying by the activity budgeted cost. Budgeted Cost of Work Performed (BCWP) may be accumulated monthly, weekly, or as progress is made.

Exhibit 7.5B shows the BCWS curve (in orange) along with the BCWP curve from chart C. The chart indicates that technical performance (i.e., progress) started more rapidly than planned, but slowed significantly and fell behind schedule at week 7 and 8. This chart illustrates the schedule performance aspect of EVM. It is complementary to critical path schedule management (described in the next section).

Exhibit 7.5C shows the same BCWP curve (blue) with the actual cost data from Chart A (in green). It can be seen that the project was actually under budget, relative to the amount of work accomplished, since the start of the project. This is a much better conclusion than might be derived from Chart A.

Exhibit 7.5D shows all three curves together—which is a typical EVM line chart. The best way to read these three-line charts is to identify the BCWS curve first, then compare it to BCWP (for schedule performance) and AC (for cost performance). It can be seen from this illustration that a true understanding of cost performance and schedule performance *relies first on measuring technical performance objectively.* This is the *foundational principle* of EVM.

Example 7.1:   Earned Value Management

Step by Step

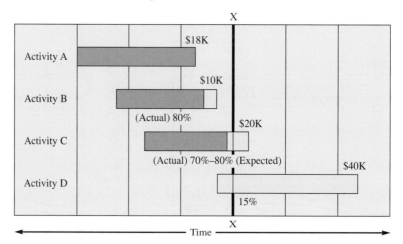

The figure above illustrates how to determine the Budgeted Cost of Work Scheduled by summing the dollar values (in $1,000s of the work scheduled for accomplishment at the end of period "X". The Budgeted Cost of Work Performed is determined by summing the earned value for the work actually accomplished, shown in red shading.

SOLUTION

From the diagram the budgeted cost of all the project work is the following: Activity A − $18K, B − $10K, C − $20K, D − $40K. This is the cost of each activity when they are 100% completed.

The project is currently at day "X" and from the diagram 100% of activity A should be completed, and it is; 100% of activity B should be completed, but only 80% is; 80% of activity C should be completed, but only 70% is; and 15% of activity D, but it has not started.

Step 1: Calculate the Budgeted Cost of Work Scheduled (BCWS) given the current state of the project. This is the value or cost of the project that is expected, given the project is at time "X":

Activity A − 100% of $18K = $18K
Activity B − 100% of $10K = $10K
Activity C − 80% of $20K = $16K
Activity D − 15% of $40K = $6K

BCWS = $18K + $10K + $16K + $6K = $50K

Step 2: Calculate the Budgeted Cost of Work Performed (BCWP) given the current state of the project. This is the actual value or cost of the project to date, given the project is at time "X":

Activity A — 100% of $18K = $18K
Activity B — 80% of $10K = $8K
Activity C — 70% of $20K = $14K
Activity D — 0% of $40K = $0

BCWP = $18K + $8K + $14K + $0K = $40K

Step 3: Obtain the Actual Cost (AC) of the work performed. This would need to be obtained from accounting records for the project. Assume that the actual cost for this project to date is $45K.

AC = $45K (Data from Acct. System)

Step 4: Calculate key performance measures for the project:

Schedule Variance: This is the difference between the Budgeted Cost of Work Performed (BCWP) and the Budgeted Cost of Work Scheduled (BCWS) for the project:

Schedule Variance = BCWP − BCWS
Schedule Variance = $40K − $50K = −$10K

Greater than 0 is generally good as it implies the project is ahead of schedule.

Schedule Performance Index: This is the ratio of the BCWP versus the BCWS for the project:

Schedule Performance Index = BCWP/BCWS
Schedule Performance Index = $40K/$50K = 0.8

Greater than 1 is generally good as it implies the project is ahead of schedule.

Cost Variance: This is the difference between BCWP and the Actual Cost (AC):

Cost Variance = BCWP − AC
Cost Variance = $40K − $45K = −$5K

Greater than zero is generally good as it implies under budget.

Cost Performance Index: This is the ratio of the BCWP versus the AC for the project to date:

Cost Performance Index = BCWP/AC
Cost Performance Index = $40K/$45K = 0.89

< 1 means the cost of completing the work is higher than planned, which is bad;
= 1 means the cost of completing the work is right on plan, which is good;
> 1 means the cost of completing the work is lower than planned, which is usually good.

That means the project is spending about $1.13 for every $1.00 of budgeted work accomplished. This is not very good as the project is over budget and tasks are not being completed on time or on budget. A Schedule Performance Index and a Cost Performance Index greater than one is desirable. ●

NETWORK-PLANNING MODELS

The two best-known network-planning models were developed in the 1950s. The Critical Path Method (CPM) was developed for scheduling maintenance shutdowns at chemical processing plants owned by Du Pont. Since maintenance projects are performed often in this industry, reasonably accurate time estimates for activities are available. CPM is based on the assumptions that project activity times can be estimated accurately and that they do

NEW ZEALAND'S TE APITI WIND FARM PROJECT CONSTRUCTED THE LARGEST WIND FARM IN THE SOUTHERN HEMISPHERE, WITHIN ONE YEAR FROM COMMISSION TO COMPLETION, ON-TIME AND WITHIN BUDGET. EMPLOYING EFFECTIVE PROJECT MANAGEMENT AND USING THE CORRECT TOOLS AND TECHNIQUES, THE MERIDIAN ENERGY COMPANY PROVIDED A VIABLE OPTION FOR RENEWABLE ENERGY IN NEW ZEALAND, AND ACTS AS BENCHMARK FOR LATER WIND FARM PROJECTS.

Critical path

not vary. The Program Evaluation and Review Technique (PERT) was developed for the U.S. Navy's Polaris missile project. This was a massive project involving over 3,000 contractors. Because most of the activities had never been done before, PERT was developed to handle uncertain time estimates. As years passed, features that distinguished CPM from PERT have diminished, so in our treatment here we just use the term CPM.

In a sense, the CPM techniques illustrated here owe their development to the widely used predecessor, the Gantt chart. Although the Gantt chart is able to relate activities to time in a usable fashion for small projects, the interrelationship of activities, when displayed in this form, becomes extremely difficult to visualize and to work with for projects that include more than 25 activities. Also, the Gantt chart provides no direct procedure for determining more than 25 activities. Also, the Gantt chart provides no direct procedure for determining the critical path, which is of great practical value to identify.

The **critical path** of activities in a project is the sequence of activities that form the longest chain in terms of their time to complete. If any one of the activities in the critical path is delayed, then the entire project is delayed. It is possible and it often happens that there are multiple paths of the same length through the network so there are multiple critical paths. Determining scheduling information about each activity in the project is the major goal of CPM techniques. The techniques calculate when an activity must start and end, together with whether the activity is part of the critical path.

Critical Path Method (CPM)

Here is a procedure for scheduling a project. In this case, a single time estimate is used because we are assuming that the activity times are known. A very simple project will be scheduled to demonstrate the basic approach.

Consider that you have a group assignment that requires a decision on whether you should invest in a company. Your instructor has suggested that you perform the analysis in the following four steps:

A Select a company.
B Obtain the company's annual report and perform a ratio analysis.
C Collect technical stock price data and construct charts.
D Individually review the data and make a team decision on whether to buy the stock.

Your group of four people decides that the project can be divided into four activities as suggested by the instructor. You decide that all the team members should be involved in selecting the company and that it should take one week to complete this activity. You will meet at the end of the week to decide what company the group will consider. During this meeting you will divide your group: two people will be responsible for the annual report and ratio analysis, and the other two will collect the technical data and construct the charts. Your group expects it to take two weeks to get the annual report and perform the ratio analysis, and a week to collect the stock price data and generate the charts. You agree that the two groups can work independently. Finally, you agree to meet as a team to make the purchase decision. Before you meet, you want to allow one week for each team member to review all the data.

This is a simple project, but it will serve to demonstrate the approach. The following are the appropriate steps.

1. **Identify each activity to be done in the project and estimate how long it will take to complete each activity.**   This is simple, given the information from your

instructor. We identify the activities as follows: A(1), B(2), C(1), D(1). The number is the expected duration of the activity.

2. **Determine the required sequence of activities and construct a network reflecting the precedence relationships.** An easy way to do this is to first identify the **immediate predecessors** associated with an activity. The immediate predecessors are the activities that need to be completed immediately before an activity. Activity A needs to be completed before activities B and C can start. B and C need to be completed before D can start. The following table reflects what we know so far:

Immediate predecessors

ACTIVITY	DESIGNATION	IMMEDIATE PREDECESSORS	TIME (WEEKS)
Select company	A	None	1
Obtain annual report and perform ratio analysis	B	A	2
Collect stock price data and perform technical analysis	C	A	1
Review data and make a decision	D	B and C	1

Here is a diagram that depicts these precedence relationships:

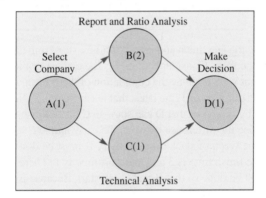

3. **Determine the critical path.** Consider each sequence of activities that runs from the beginning to the end of the project. For our simple project there are two paths: A–B–D and A–C–D. The critical path is the path where the sum of the activity times is the longest. A–B–D has a duration of four weeks and A–C–D, a duration of three weeks. The critical path, therefore, is A–B–D. If any activity along the critical path is delayed, then the entire project will be delayed.

4. **Determine the early start/finish and late start/finish schedule.** To schedule the project, find when each activity needs to start and when it needs to finish. For some activities in a project there may be some leeway in when an activity can start and finish. This is called the **slack time** in an activity. For each activity in the project, we calculate four points in time: the early start, early finish, late start, and late finish times. The early start and early finish are the earliest times that the activity can start and be finished. Similarly, the late start and late finish are the latest times the activities can start and finish. The difference between the late start time and early start time is the slack time. To help keep all of this straight, we place these numbers in special places around the nodes that represent each activity in our network diagram, as shown here.

Slack time

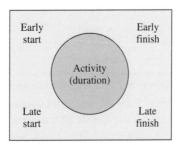

To calculate numbers, start from the beginning of the network and work to the end, calculating the early start and early finish numbers. Start counting with the current period, designated as period 0. Activity A has an early start of 0 and an early finish of 1. Activity B's early start is A's early finish or 1. Similarly, C's early start is 1. The early finish for B is 3, and the early finish for C is 2. Now consider activity D. D cannot start until both B and C are done. Because B cannot be done until 3, D cannot start until that time. The early start for D, therefore, is 3, and the early finish is 4. Our diagram now looks like this.

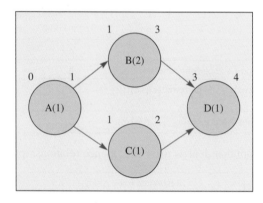

To calculate the late finish and late start times, start from the end of the network and work toward the front. Consider activity D. The earliest that it can be done is at time 4; and if we do not want to delay the completion of the project, the late finish needs to be set to 4. With a duration of 1, the latest that D can start is 3. Now consider activity C. C must be done by time 3 so that D can start, so C's late finish time is 3 and its late start time is 2. Notice the difference between the early and late start and finish times: This activity has one week of slack time. Activity B must be done by time 3 so that D can start, so its late finish time is 3 and late start time is 1. There is no slack in B. Finally, activity A must be done so that B and C can start. Because B must start earlier than C, and A must get done in time for B to start, the late finish time for A is 1. Finally, the late start time for A is 0. Notice there is no slack in activities A, B, and D. The final network looks like this. (Hopefully the stock your investment team has chosen is a winner!)

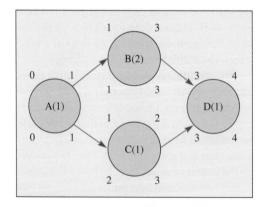

Excel: Project Management

Example 7.2: Critical Path Method

Many firms that have tried to enter the notebook computer market have failed. Suppose your firm believes that there is a big demand in this market because existing products have not been designed

Step by Step

correctly. They are too heavy, too large, or too small to have standard-size keyboards. Your intended computer will be small enough to carry inside a jacket pocket if need be. The ideal size will be no larger than 5 inches × 9½ inches × 1 inch with a folding keyboard. It should weigh no more than 15 ounces and have an LCD display, a micro disk drive, and a wireless connection. This should appeal to traveling businesspeople, but it could have a much wider market, including students. It should be priced in the $175–$200 range.

The project, then, is to design, develop, and produce a prototype of this small computer. In the rapidly changing computer industry, it is crucial to hit the market with a product of this sort in less than a year. Therefore, the project team has been allowed approximately eight months (35 weeks) to produce the prototype.

SOLUTION

The first charge of the project team is to develop a project network chart and determine if the prototype computer can be completed within the 35-week target. Let's follow the steps in the development of the network.

1. **Activity identification.** The project team decides that the following activities are the major components of the project: design of the computer, prototype construction, prototype testing, methods specification (summarized in a report), evaluation studies of automatic assembly equipment, an assembly equipment study report, and a final report summarizing all aspects of the design, equipment, and methods.

2. **Activity sequencing and network construction.** On the basis of discussion with staff, the project manager develops the precedence table and sequence network shown in Exhibit 7.6. When constructing a network, take care to ensure that the activities are in the proper order and that the logic of their relationships is maintained. For example, it would be illogical to have a situation where Event A precedes Event B, B precedes C, and C precedes A.

CPM Network for Computer Design Project

exhibit 7.6

CPM ACTIVITY DESIGNATIONS AND TIME ESTIMATES

ACTIVITY	DESIGNATION	IMMEDIATE PREDECESSORS	TIME (WEEKS)
Design	A	–	21
Build prototype	B	A	5
Evaluate equipment	C	A	7
Test prototype	D	B	2
Write equipment report	E	C, D	5
Write methods report	F	C, D	8
Write final report	G	E, F	2

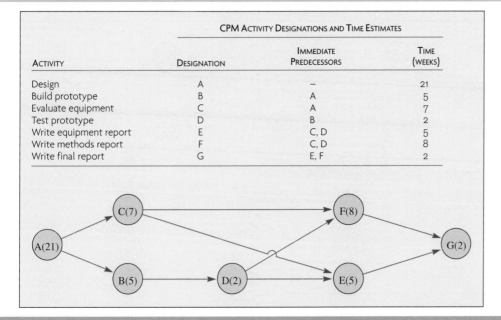

3. **Determine the critical path.**   The critical path is the longest sequence of connected activities through the network and is defined as the path with zero slack time. This network has four different paths: A–C–F–G, A–C–E–G, A–B–D–F–G, and A–B–D–E–G. The lengths of these paths are 38, 35, 38, and 35 weeks. Note that this project has two different critical paths; this might indicate that this would be a fairly difficult project to manage. Calculating the early start and late start schedules gives additional insight into how difficult this project might be to complete on time. ●

Early start schedule

Early Start and Late Start Schedules   An **early start schedule** is one that lists all of the activities by their early start times. For activities not on the critical path, there is slack time between the completion of each activity and the start of the next activity. The early start schedule completes the project and all its activities as soon as possible.

Late start schedule

A **late start schedule** lists the activities to start as late as possible without delaying the completion date of the project. One motivation for using a late start schedule is that savings are realized by postponing purchases of materials, the use of labor, and other costs until necessary. These calculations are shown in Exhibit 7.7. From this we see that the only activity that has slack is activity E. This certainly would be a fairly difficult project to complete on time.

CPM with Three Activity Time Estimates

If a single estimate of the time required to complete an activity is not reliable, the best procedure is to use three time estimates. These three times not only allow us to estimate the activity time but also let us obtain a probability estimate for completion time for the entire network. Briefly, the procedure is as follows: The estimated activity time is calculated using a weighted average of a minimum, maximum, and most likely time estimate.

exhibit 7.7   CPM Network for Computer Design Project

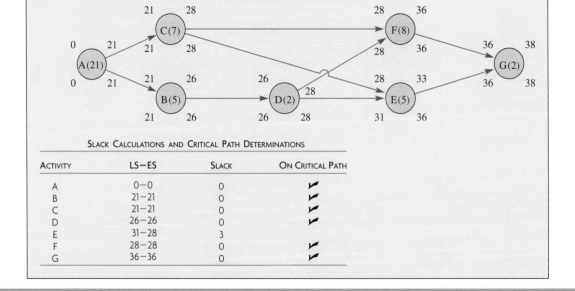

ACTIVITY	LS−ES	SLACK	ON CRITICAL PATH
A	0−0	0	✔
B	21−21	0	✔
C	21−21	0	✔
D	26−26	0	✔
E	31−28	3	
F	28−28	0	✔
G	36−36	0	✔

SLACK CALCULATIONS AND CRITICAL PATH DETERMINATIONS

The expected completion time of the network is computed using the procedure described above. Using estimates of variability for the activities on the critical path, the probability of completing the project by particular times can be estimated. (Note that the probability calculations are a distinguishing feature of the classic PERT approach.)

Example 7.3: Three Time Estimates

We use the same information as in Example 7.2 with the exception that activities have three time estimates.

Step by Step

SOLUTION

1. Identify each activity to be done in the project.
2. Determine the sequence of activities and construct a network reflecting the precedence relationships.
3. The three estimates for an activity time are

    a = Optimistic time: the minimum reasonable period of time in which the activity can be completed. (There is only a small probability, typically assumed to be 1 percent, that the activity can be completed in less time.)

    m = Most likely time: the best guess of the time required. Since m would be the time thought most likely to appear, it is also the mode of the beta distribution discussed in step 4.

    b = Pessimistic time: the maximum reasonable period of time the activity would take to be completed. (There is only a small probability, typically assumed to be 1 percent, that it would take longer.)

    Typically, this information is gathered from those people who are to perform the activity.
4. Calculate the expected time (ET) for each activity. The formula for this calculation is

$$ET = \frac{a + 4m + b}{6} \qquad \textbf{[7.1]}$$

    This is based on the beta statistical distribution and weights the most likely time (m) four times more than either the optimistic time (a) or the pessimistic time (b). The beta distribution is extremely flexible. It can take on the variety of forms that typically arise; it has finite end points (which limit the possible activity times to the area between a and b); and, in the simplified version, it permits straightforward computation of the activity mean and standard deviation.
5. Determine the critical path. Using the expected times, a critical path is calculated in the same way as the single time case.
6. Calculate the variances (σ^2) of the activity times. Specifically, this is the variance, σ^2, associated with each ET and is computed as follows:

$$\sigma^2 = \left(\frac{b - a}{6}\right)^2 \qquad \textbf{[7.2]}$$

    As you can see, the variance is the square of one-sixth the difference between the two extreme time estimates. Of course, the greater this difference, the larger the variance.
7. Determine the probability of completing the project on a given date, based on the application of the standard normal distribution. A valuable feature of using three time estimates is that it enables the analyst to assess the effect of uncertainty on project completion time. (If you

are not familiar with this type of analysis, see the box titled "Probability Analysis.") The mechanics of deriving this probability are as follows:

a. Sum the variance values associated with each activity on the critical path.

b. Substitute this figure, along with the project due date and the project expected completion time, into the Z transformation formula. This formula is

$$Z = \frac{D - T_{\mathrm{E}}}{\sqrt{\Sigma \, \sigma_{cp}^2}}$$ [7.3]

where

$$D = \text{Desired completion date for the project}$$
$$T_{\mathrm{E}} = \text{Expected completion time for the project}$$
$$\Sigma \, \sigma_{cp}^2 = \text{Sum of the variances along the critical path}$$

c. Calculate the value of Z, which is the number of standard deviations (of a standard normal distribution) that the project due date is from the expected completion time.

d. Using the value of Z, find the probability of meeting the project due date (using a table of normal probabilities such as Appendix F). The *expected completion time* is the starting time plus the sum of the activity times on the critical path.

Following the steps just outlined, we developed Exhibit 7.8 showing expected times and variances. The project network was created the same as we did previously. The only difference is that the activity times are weighted averages. We determine the critical path as before, using these values as if they were single numbers. The difference between the single time estimate and the three times (optimistic, most likely, and pessimistic) is in computing probabilities of completion. Exhibit 7.9 shows the network and critical path.

Because there are two critical paths in the network, we must decide which variances to use in arriving at the probability of meeting the project due date. A conservative approach dictates using the path with the largest total variance to focus management's attention on the activities most likely to exhibit broad variations. On this basis, the variances associated with activities A, C, F, and G would

exhibit 7.8   Activity Expected Times and Variances

Excel: Project Management

ACTIVITY	ACTIVITY DESIGNATION	TIME ESTIMATES a	m	b	EXPECTED TIMES (ET) $\frac{a + 4m + b}{6}$	ACTIVITY VARIANCES (σ^2) $\left(\frac{b - a}{6}\right)^2$
Design	A	10	22	28	21	9
Build prototype	B	4	4	10	5	1
Evaluate equipment	C	4	6	14	7	$2\frac{7}{9}$
Test prototype	D	1	2	3	2	$\frac{1}{9}$
Write report	E	1	5	9	5	$1\frac{7}{9}$
Write methods report	F	7	8	9	8	$\frac{1}{9}$
Write final report	G	2	2	2	2	0

exhibit 7.9

Computer Design Project with Three Time Estimates

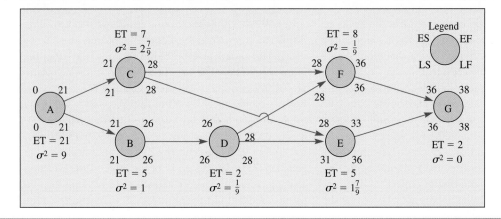

be used to find the probability of completion. Thus $\Sigma\sigma^2_{cp} = 9 + 2\frac{7}{9} + \frac{1}{9} + 0 = 11.89$. Suppose management asks for the probability of completing the project in 35 weeks. D, then, is 35. The expected completion time was found to be 38. Substituting into the Z equation and solving, we obtain

$$Z = \frac{D - T_E}{\sqrt{\Sigma\,\sigma^2_{cp}}} = \frac{35 - 38}{\sqrt{11.89}} = -0.87$$

Looking at Appendix F, we see that a Z value of –0.87 yields a probability of 0.1922, which means that the project manager has only about a 19 percent chance of completing the project in 35 weeks. Note that this probability is really the probability of completing the critical path A–C–F–G. Because there is another critical path and other paths that might become critical, the probability of completing the project in 35 weeks is actually less than 0.19. ●

Time–Cost Models and Project Crashing
In practice, project managers are as much concerned with the cost to complete a project as with the time to complete the project. For this reason, **time–cost models** have been devised. These models—extensions of the basic critical path method—attempt to develop a minimum-cost schedule for an entire project and to control expenditures during the project.

Time–cost models

Minimum-Cost Scheduling (Time–Cost Trade-Off) The basic assumption in minimum-cost scheduling, also known as "Crashing," is that there is a relationship between activity completion time and the cost of a project. "Crashing refers to the compression or shortening of the time to complete the project. On one hand, it costs money to expedite an activity; on the other, it costs money to sustain (or lengthen) the project. The costs associated with expediting activities are termed *activity direct costs* and add to the project direct cost. Some may be worker-related, such as overtime work, hiring more workers, and transferring workers from other jobs; others are resource-related, such as buying or leasing additional or more efficient equipment and drawing on additional support facilities.

The costs associated with sustaining the project are termed *project indirect costs:* overhead, facilities, and resource opportunity costs, and, under certain contractual situations,

Probability Analysis

The three-time-estimate approach introduces the ability to consider the probability that a project will be completed within a particular amount of time. The assumption needed to make this probability estimate is that the activity duration times are independent random variables. If this is true, the central limit theorem can be used to find the mean and the variance of the sequence of activities that form the critical path. The central limit theorem says that the sum of a group of independent, identically distributed random variables approaches a normal distribution as the number of random variables increases. In the case of project management problems, the random variables are the actual times for the activities in the project. (Recall that the time for each activity is assumed to be independent of other activities, and to follow a beta statistical distribution.) For this the expected time to complete the critical path activities is the sum of the activity times.

Likewise, because of the assumption of activity time independence, the sum of the variances of the activities along the critical path is the variance of the expected time to complete the path. Recall that the standard deviation is equal to the square root of the variance.

To determine the actual probability of completing the critical path activities within a certain amount of time, we need to find where on our probability distribution the time falls.

Appendix F shows the areas of the cumulative standard normal distribution for different values of Z. Z measures the number of standard deviations either to the right or to the left of zero in the distribution. The values correspond to the cumulative probability associated with each value of Z. For example, the first value in the table, −4.00, has a G(z) equal to .00003. This means that the probability associated with a Z value of −4.0 is only .003 percent. Similarly, a Z value of 1.50 has a G(z) equal to .93319 or 93.319 percent. The Z values are calculated using Equation (7.3) given in Step 7b of the "Three Time Estimates" example solution. These cumulative probabilities also can be obtained by using the NORMSDIST (Z) function built into Microsoft Excel.

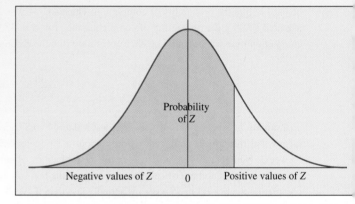

penalty costs or lost incentive payments. Because *activity direct costs and project indirect costs* are opposing costs dependent on time, the scheduling problem is essentially one of finding the project duration that minimizes their sum, or in other words, finding the optimum point in a time–cost trade-off.

The procedure for project crashing consists of the following five steps. It is explained by using the simple four-activity network shown in Exhibit 7.10. Assume that the indirect costs remain constant for eight days and then increase at the rate of $5 per day.

1. **Prepare a CPM-type network diagram.** For each activity this diagram should list
   a. Normal cost (NC): the lowest expected activity costs. (These are the lesser of the cost figures shown under each node in Exhibit 7.10.)
   b. Normal time (NT): the time associated with each normal cost.
   c. Crash time (CT): the shortest possible activity time.
   d. Crash cost (CC): the cost associated with each crash time.
2. **Determine the cost per unit of time (assume days) to expedite each activity.** The relationship between activity time and cost may be shown graphically by plotting CC and CT coordinates and connecting them to the NC and NT coordinates

Example of Time–Cost Trade-Off Procedure

exhibit 7.10

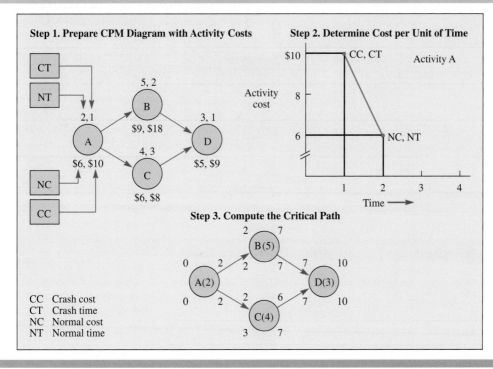

Step 1. Prepare CPM Diagram with Activity Costs

Step 2. Determine Cost per Unit of Time

Step 3. Compute the Critical Path

CC   Crash cost
CT   Crash time
NC   Normal cost
NT   Normal time

Excel: Project Management

by a concave, convex, or straight line—or some other form, depending on the actual cost structure of activity performance, as in Exhibit 7.10. For activity A, we assume a linear relationship between time and cost. This assumption is common in practice and helps us derive the cost per day to expedite because this value may be found directly by taking the slope of the line using the formula Slope = (CC − NC) ÷ (NT − CT). (When the assumption of linearity cannot be made, the cost of expediting must be determined graphically for each day the activity may be shortened.)

The calculations needed to obtain the cost of expediting the remaining activities are shown in Exhibit 7.11.

3. **Compute the critical path.**   For the simple network we have been using, this schedule would take 10 days. The critical path is A–B–D.

4. **Shorten the critical path at the least cost.**   The easiest way to proceed is to start with the normal schedule, find the critical path, and reduce the path time by one day using the lowest-cost activity. Then recompute and find the new critical path and reduce it by one day also. Repeat this procedure until the time of completion is satisfactory, or until there can be no further reduction in the project completion time. Exhibit 7.12 shows the reduction of the network one day at a time.

Working though Exhibit 7.12 might initially seem difficult. In the first line, all activities are at their normal time and costs are at their lowest value. The critical path is A–B–D, cost for completing the project is $26, and the project completion time is 10 days.

The goal in line two is to reduce the project completion time by one day. We know it is necessary to reduce the time for one or more of the activities on the

exhibit 7.11

Calculation of Cost per Day to Expedite Each Activity

ACTIVITY	CC − NC	NT − CT	$\dfrac{CC - NC}{NT - CT}$	COST PER DAY TO EXPEDITE	NUMBER OF DAYS ACTIVITY MAY BE SHORTENED
A	$10 − $6	2 − 1	$\dfrac{\$10 - \$6}{2 - 1}$	$4	1
B	$18 − $9	5 − 2	$\dfrac{\$18 - \$9}{5 - 2}$	$3	3
C	$8 − $6	4 − 3	$\dfrac{\$8 - \$6}{4 - 3}$	$2	1
D	$9 − $5	3 − 1	$\dfrac{\$9 - \$5}{3 - 1}$	$2	2

exhibit 7.12

Reducing the Project Completion Time One Day at a Time

CURRENT CRITICAL PATH(S)	REMAINING NUMBER OF DAYS ACTIVITY MAY BE SHORTENED	COST PER DAY TO EXPEDITE EACH ACTIVITY	LEAST-COST ACTIVITY TO EXPEDITE	TOTAL COST OF ALL ACTIVITIES IN NETWORK	PROJECT COMPLETION TIME
ABD	All activity times and costs are normal.			$26	10
ABD	A−1, B−3, D−2	A−4, B−3, D−2	D	28	9
ABD	A−1, B−3, D−1	A−4, B−3, D−2	D	30	8
ABD	A−1, B−3	A−4, B−3	B	33	7
ABD ACD	A−1, B−2, C−1	A−4, B−3, C−2	A*	37	6
ABD ACD	B−2, C−1	B−3, C−2	B&C†	42	5
ABD ACD	B−1	B−3	B+	45	5

*To reduce the critical path by one day, reduce either A alone or B and C together at the same time (either B or C by itself just modifies the critical path without shortening it).

†B&C must be crashed together to reduce the path by one day.

+Crashing activity B does not reduce the length of the project, so this additional cost would not be incurred.

critical path. In the second column we note that activity A can be reduced one day (from two to one day), activity B can be reduced three days (from five to two days), and activity D can be reduced two days (from three to one day). The next column tracks the cost to reduce each of the activities by a single day. For example, for activity A, it normally costs $6 to complete in two days. It could be completed in one day at a cost of $10, a $4 increase. So we indicate the cost to expedite activity A by one day is $4. For activity B, it normally costs $9 to complete in five days. It could be completed in two days at a cost of $18. Our cost to reduce B by three days is $9, or $3 per day. For C, it normally costs $5 to complete in three days. It could be completed in one day at a cost of $9; a two-day reduction would cost $4 ($2 per day). The least expensive alternative for a one-day reduction in time is to expedite

exhibit 7.13

Plot of Costs and Minimum-Cost Schedule   exhibit 7.13

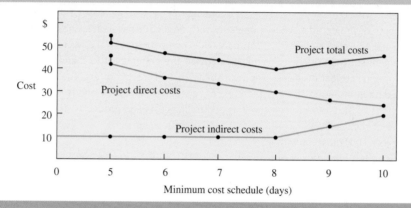

activity D at a cost of $2. Total cost for the network goes up to $28 and the project completion time is reduced to nine days.

Our next iteration starts in line three, where the goal is to reduce the project completion time to eight days. The nine-day critical path is A–B–D. We could shorten activity A by one day, B by three days, and D by one day (note D has already been reduced from three to two days). Cost to reduce each activity by one day is the same as in line two. Again, the least expensive activity to reduce is D. Reducing activity D from two to one day results in the total cost for all activities in the network going up to $30 and the project completion time coming down to eight days.

Line four is similar to line three, but now only A and B are on the critical path and can be reduced. B is reduced, which takes our cost up $3 to $33 and reduces the project completion time to seven days.

In line five (actually our fifth iteration in solving the problem), activities A, B, C, and D are all critical. D cannot be reduced, so our only options are activities A, B, and C. Note that B and C are in parallel, so it does not help to reduce B without reducing C. Our options are to reduce A alone at a cost of $4 or B and C together at a cost of $5 ($3 for B and $2 for C), so we reduce A in this iteration.

In line six, we take the B and C option that was considered in line five. Finally, in line seven, our only option is to reduce activity B. Since B and C are in parallel and we cannot reduce C, there is no value in reducing B alone. We can reduce the project completion time no further.

5. **Plot project direct, indirect, and total-cost curves and find the minimum-cost schedule.**   Exhibit 7.13 shows the indirect cost plotted as a constant $10 per day for up to eight days and increasing $5 per day thereafter. The direct costs are plotted from Exhibit 7.12, and the total project cost is shown as the total of the two costs.

Summing the values for direct and indirect costs for each day yields the project total cost curve. As you can see, this curve is at its minimum with an eight-day schedule, which costs $40 ($30 direct + $10 indirect).

MANAGING RESOURCES

In addition to scheduling each task, we must assign resources. Modern software quickly highlights overallocations—situations in which allocations exceed resources.

Project Management Information Systems

Interest in the techniques and concepts of project management has exploded in the past 10 years. This has resulted in a parallel increase in project management software offerings. Now there are over 100 companies offering project management software. For the most up-to-date information about software available, check out the Web site of the Project Management Institute (www.pmi.org). Two of the leading companies are Microsoft, with Microsoft Project, and Primavera, with Primavera Project Planner. The following is a brief review of these two programs:

The Microsoft Project program comes with an excellent online tutorial, which is one reason for its overwhelming popularity with project managers tracking midsized projects. This package is compatible with the Microsoft Office Suite, which opens all the communications and Internet integration capability that Microsoft offers. The program includes features for scheduling, allocating and leveling resources, as well as controlling costs and producing presentation-quality graphics and reports.

Finally, for managing very large projects or programs having several projects, Primavera Project Planner is often the choice. Primavera was the first major vendor of this type of software and has possibly the most sophisticated capability.

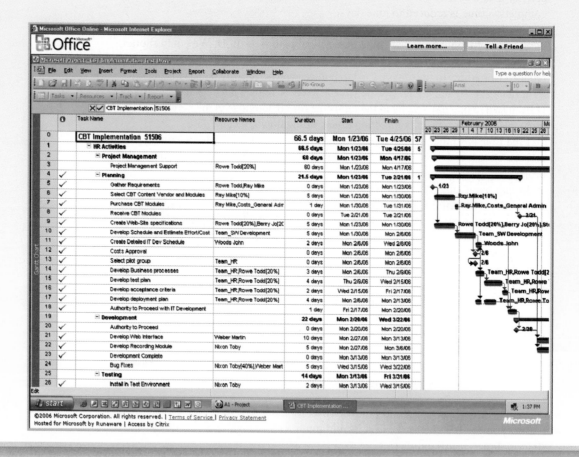

To resolve overallocations manually, you can either add resources or reschedule. Moving a task within its slack can free up resources.

Mid- to high-level project management information systems (PMIS) software can resolve overallocations through a "leveling" feature. Several rules of thumb can be used. You can specify that low-priority tasks should be delayed until higher-priority ones are complete, or that the project should end before or after the original deadline.

Tracking Progress

The real action starts after the project gets underway. Actual progress will differ from your original, or baseline, planned progress. Software can hold several different baseline plans, so you can compare monthly snapshots.

A *tracking Gantt chart* superimposes the current schedule onto a baseline plan so deviations are easily noticed. If you prefer, a spreadsheet view of the same information could be output. Deviations between planned start/finish and newly scheduled start/finish also appear, and a "slipping filter" can be applied to highlight or output only those tasks that are scheduled to finish at a later date than the planned baseline.

Management by exception also can be applied to find deviations between budgeted costs and actual costs. (See the box titled "Project Management Information Systems.")

PARAMOUNT INVESTED OVER $17 MILLION IN THIS PROJECT AT GREAT AMERICA IN SANTA CLARA. THE PROJECT INCLUDED A UNIQUE USE OF COMPUTERS FOR LAYOUT, DESIGN, AND SIMULATION IN ORDER TO COMPLY WITH RIGID SAFETY STANDARDS FOR THE WORLDS FIRST "FLYING COASTER."

SUMMARY

This chapter provides a description of the basics of managing projects. The chapter first describes how the people involved with a project are organized from a management viewpoint. The scope of the project will help define the organization. This organization spans the use of a dedicated team to a largely undedicated matrix structure. Next, the chapter considers how project activities are organized into subprojects by using the work breakdown structure. Following this, the technical details of calculating the shortest time it should take to complete a project are covered. Finally, the chapter considers how projects can be shortened through the use of "crashing" concepts.

Key Terms

Project A series of related jobs usually directed toward some major output and requiring a significant period of time to perform.

Project management Planning, directing, and controlling resources (people, equipment, material) to meet the technical, cost, and time constraints of a project.

Pure project A structure for organizing a project where a self-contained team works full time on the project.

Functional project A structure where team members are assigned from the functional units of the organization. The team members remain a part of their functional units and typically are not dedicated to the project.

Matrix project A structure that blends the functional and pure project structures. Each project uses people from different functional areas. A dedicated project manager decides what tasks need to be performed and when, but the functional managers control which people to use.

Project milestone A specific event in a project.

Work breakdown structure The hierarchy of project tasks, subtasks, and work packages.

Activities Pieces of work within a project that consume time. The completion of all the activities of a project marks the end of the project.

Gantt chart Shows in a graphic manner the amount of time involved and the sequence in which activities can be performed. Often referred to as a *bar chart*.

Earned Value Management Technique that combines measures of scope, schedule, and cost for evaluating project progress.

Critical path The sequence of activities in a project that forms the longest chain in terms of their time to complete. This path contains zero slack time. It is possible for there to be multiple critical paths in a project. Techniques used to find the critical path are called CPM or Critical Path Method techniques.

Immediate predecessor Activity that needs to be completed immediately before another activity.

Slack time The time that an activity can be delayed; the difference between the late and early start times of an activity.

Early start schedule A project schedule that lists all activities by their early start times.

Late start schedule A project schedule that lists all activities by their late start times. This schedule may create savings by postponing purchases of material and other costs associated with the project.

Time–cost models Extension of the critical path models that considers the trade-off between the time required to complete an activity and cost. This is often referred to as "crashing" the project.

Formula Review

Expected Time

$$ET = \frac{a + 4m + b}{6} \qquad [7.1]$$

Variance (σ^2) of the activity times

$$\sigma^2 = \left(\frac{b - a}{6}\right)^2 \qquad [7.2]$$

Z transformation formula

$$Z = \frac{D - T_E}{\sqrt{\Sigma \sigma_{cp}^2}} \qquad [7.3]$$

(1) 1st week: CP = A–B–D–H–I. Cheapest is A at $500. Critical path stays the same.

(2) 2nd week: A is still the cheapest at $500. Critical path stays the same.

(3) 3rd week: Because A is no longer available, the choices are B (at $3,000), D (at $2,000), H (at $2,333), or I (at $9,000). Therefore, choose D at $2,000.

Total project cost shortened three weeks is

A	$ 11,000
B	6,000
C	4,000
D	16,000
E	9,000
F	7,000
G	13,000
H	11,000
I	20,000
	$97,000

Review and Discussion Questions

1   What was the most complex project that you have been involved in? Give examples of the following as they pertain to the project: the work breakdown structure, tasks, subtasks, and work package. Were you on the critical path? Did it have a good project manager?

2   What are some reasons project scheduling is not done well?

3   Discuss the graphic presentations in Exhibit 7.4. Are there any other graphic outputs you would like to see if you were project manager?

4   Which characteristics must a project have for critical path scheduling to be applicable? What types of projects have been subjected to critical path analysis?

5   What are the underlying assumptions of minimum-cost scheduling? Are they equally realistic?

6   "Project control should always focus on the critical path." Comment.

7   Why would subcontractors for a government project want their activities on the critical path? Under what conditions would they try to avoid being on the critical path?

Problems

1   Your project to obtain charitable donations is now 30 days into a planned 40-day project. The project is divided into 3 activities. The first activity is designed to solicit individual donations. It is scheduled to run the first 25 days of the project and to bring in $25,000. Even though we are 30 days into the project, we still see that we have only 90% of this activity complete. The second activity relates to company donations and is scheduled to run for 30 days starting on day 5 and extending through day 35. We estimate that even though we should have (25/30) 83% of this activity complete, it is actually only 50% complete. This part of the project was scheduled to bring in $150,000 in donations. The final activity is for matching funds. This activity is scheduled to run the last 10 days of the project and has not started. It is scheduled to bring in an additional $50,000. So far $175,000 has actually been brought in on the project.

Calculate the schedule variance, schedule performance index, and cost (actually value in this case) performance index. How is the project going? Hint: Note that this problem is different since revenue rather than cost is the relevant measure. Use care in how the measures are interpreted.

2   A project to build a new bridge seems to be going very well since the project is well ahead of schedule and costs seem to be running very low. A major milestone has been reached

where the first two activities have been totally completed and the third activity is 60% complete. The planners were only expecting to be 50% through the third activity at this time. The first activity involves prepping the site for the bridge. It was expected that this would cost $1,420,000 and it was done for only $1,300,000. The second activity was the pouring of concrete for the bridge. This was expected to cost $10,500,000 but was actually done for $9,000,000. The third and final activity is the actual construction of the bridge superstructure. This was expected to cost a total of $8,500,000. To date they have spent $5,000,000 on the superstructure.

Calculate the schedule variance, schedule performance index, and the cost index for the project to date. How is the project going?

3   The following activities are part of a project to be scheduled using CPM:

ACTIVITY	IMMEDIATE PREDECESSOR	TIME (WEEKS)
A	——	6
B	A	3
C	A	7
D	C	2
E	B, D	4
F	D	3
G	E, F	7

a. Draw the network.
b. What is the critical path?
c. How many weeks will it take to complete the project?
d. How much slack does activity B have?

4   Schedule the following activities using CPM:

ACTIVITY	IMMEDIATE PREDECESSOR	TIME (WEEKS)
A	——	1
B	A	4
C	A	3
D	B	2
E	C, D	5
F	D	2
G	F	2
H	E, G	3

a. Draw the network.
b. What is the critical path?
c. How many weeks will it take to complete the project?
d. Which activities have slack, and how much?

5   The R&D department is planning to bid on a large project for the development of a new communication system for commercial planes. The accompanying table shows the activities, times, and sequences required:

ACTIVITY	IMMEDIATE PREDECESSOR	TIME (WEEKS)
A	—	3
B	A	2
C	A	4
D	A	4
E	B	6
F	C, D	6
G	D, F	2
H	D	3
I	E, G, H	3

a. Draw the network diagram.
b. What is the critical path?
c. Suppose you want to shorten the completion time as much as possible, and you have the option of shortening any or all of B, C, D, and G each one week. Which would you shorten?
d. What is the new critical path and earliest completion time?

6 The following represents a project that should be scheduled using CPM:

		TIMES (DAYS)		
ACTIVITY	IMMEDIATE PREDECESSORS	a	m	b
A	—	1	3	5
B	—	1	2	3
C	A	1	2	3
D	A	2	3	4
E	B	3	4	11
F	C, D	3	4	5
G	D, E	1	4	6
H	F, G	2	4	5

a. Draw the network.
b. What is the critical path?
c. What is the expected project completion time?
d. What is the probability of completing this project within 16 days?

7 There is an 82% chance the project below can be completed in X weeks or less. What is X?

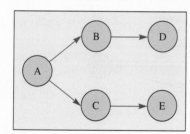

ACTIVITY	MOST OPTIMISTIC	MOST LIKELY	MOST PESSIMISTIC
A	2	5	11
B	3	3	3
C	1	3	5
D	6	8	10
E	4	7	10

8 The following table represents a plan for a project:

		TIMES (DAYS)		
JOB NO.	PREDECESSOR JOB(S)	a	m	b
1	—	2	3	4
2	1	1	2	3
3	1	4	5	12
4	1	3	4	11
5	2	1	3	5
6	3	1	2	3
7	4	1	8	9
8	5, 6	2	4	6
9	8	2	4	12
10	7	3	4	5
11	9, 10	5	7	8

a. Construct the appropriate network diagram.
b. Indicate the critical path.
c. What is the expected completion time for the project?

d. You can accomplish any one of the following at an additional cost of $1,500:
   (1) Reduce job 5 by two days.
   (2) Reduce job 3 by two days.
   (3) Reduce job 7 by two days.
   If you will save $1,000 for each day that the earliest completion time is reduced, which action, if any, would you choose?

e. What is the probability that the project will take more than 30 days to complete?

9 A construction project is broken down into the following 10 activities:

ACTIVITY	IMMEDIATE PREDECESSOR	TIME (WEEKS)
1	—	4
2	1	2
3	1	4
4	1	3
5	2, 3	5
6	3	6
7	4	2
8	5	3
9	6, 7	5
10	8, 9	7

a. Draw the network diagram.

b. Find the critical path.

c. If activities 1 and 10 cannot be shortened, but activities 2 through 9 can be shortened to a minimum of one week each at a cost of $10,000 per week, which activities would you shorten to cut the project by four weeks?

10 Here is a CPM network with activity times in weeks:

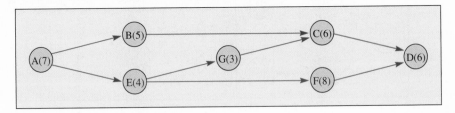

a. Determine the critical path.

b. How many weeks will the project take to complete?

c. Suppose F could be shortened by two weeks and B by one week. How would this affect the completion date?

11 Here is a network with the activity times shown in days:

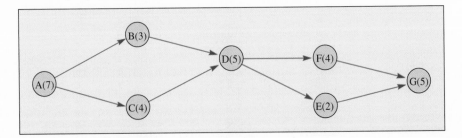

a. Find the critical path.

b. The following table shows the normal times and the crash times, along with the associated costs for each activity.

ACTIVITY	NORMAL TIME	CRASH TIME	NORMAL COST	CRASH COST
A	7	6	$7,000	$ 8,000
B	3	2	5,000	7,000
C	4	3	9,000	10,200
D	5	4	3,000	4,500
E	2	1	2,000	3,000
F	4	2	4,000	7,000
G	5	4	5,000	8,000

If the project is to be shortened by four days, show which activities, in order of reduction, would be shortened and the resulting cost.

12   The home office billing department of a chain of department stores prepares monthly inventory reports for use by the stores' purchasing agents. Given the following information, use the critical path method to determine:

a. How long the total process will take.

b. Which jobs can be delayed without delaying the early start of any subsequent activity.

	JOB AND DESCRIPTION	IMMEDIATE PREDECESSORS	TIME (HOURS)
a	Start	—	0
b	Get computer printouts of customer purchases	a	10
c	Get stock records for the month	a	20
d	Reconcile purchase printouts and stock records	b, c	30
e	Total stock records by department	b, c	20
f	Determine reorder quantities for coming period	e	40
g	Prepare stock reports for purchasing agents	d, f	20
h	Finish	g	0

13   For the network shown:

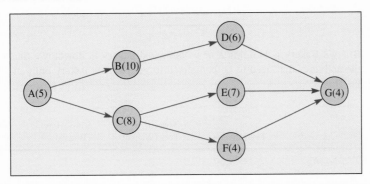

a. Determine the critical path and the early completion time in weeks for the project.

b. For the data shown, reduce the project completion time by three weeks. Assume a linear cost per week shortened, and show, step by step, how you arrived at your schedule.

ACTIVITY	NORMAL TIME	NORMAL COST	CRASH TIME	CRASH COST
A	5	$ 7,000	3	$13,000
B	10	12,000	7	18,000
C	8	5,000	7	7,000
D	6	4,000	5	5,000
E	7	3,000	6	6,000
F	4	6,000	3	7,000
G	4	7,000	3	9,000

14 The following CPM network has estimates of the normal time in weeks listed for the activities:

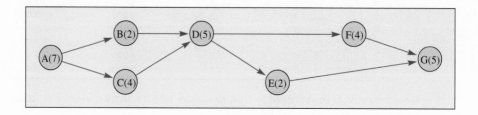

a. Identify the critical path.
b. What is the length of time to complete the project?
c. Which activities have slack, and how much?
d. Here is a table of normal and crash times and costs. Which activities would you shorten to cut two weeks from the schedule in a rational fashion? What would be the incremental cost? Is the critical path changed?

ACTIVITY	NORMAL TIME	CRASH TIME	NORMAL COST	CRASH COST
A	7	6	$7,000	$ 8,000
B	2	1	5,000	7,000
C	4	3	9,000	10,200
D	5	4	3,000	4,500
E	2	1	2,000	3,000
F	4	2	4,000	7,000
G	5	4	5,000	8,000

15 Bragg's Bakery is building a new automated bakery in downtown Sandusky. Here are the activities that need to be completed to get the new bakery built and the equipment installed.

ACTIVITY	PREDECESSOR	NORMAL TIME (WEEKS)	CRASH TIME (WEEKS)	EXPEDITING COST/WEEK
A	—	9	6	$3,000
B	A	8	5	$3,500
C	A	15	10	$4,000
D	B, C	5	3	$2,000
E	C	10	6	$2,500
F	D, E	2	1	$5,000

a. Draw the project diagram.
b. What is the normal project length?
c. What is the project length if all activities are crashed to their minimum?
d. Bragg's loses $3,500 in profit per week for every week the bakery is not completed. How many weeks will the project take if we are willing to pay crashing cost as long as it is less than $3,500?

Advanced Problem

16 Assume the network and data that follow:

ACTIVITY	NORMAL TIME (WEEKS)	NORMAL COST	CRASH TIME (WEEKS)	CRASH COST	IMMEDIATE PREDECESSORS
A	2	$50	1	$70	—
B	4	80	2	160	A
C	8	70	4	110	A
D	6	60	5	80	A
E	7	100	6	130	B
F	4	40	3	100	D
G	5	100	4	150	C, E, F

a. Construct the network diagram.

b. Indicate the critical path when normal activity times are used.

c. Compute the minimum total direct cost for each project duration based on the cost associated with each activity. Consider durations of 13, 14, 15, 16, 17, and 18 weeks.

d. If the indirect costs for each project duration are $400 (18 weeks), $350 (17 weeks), $300 (16 weeks), $250 (15 weeks), $200 (14 weeks), and $150 (13 weeks), what is the total project cost for each duration? Indicate the minimum total project cost duration.

CASE: Cell Phone Design Project

You work for Motorola in their global cell phone group. You have been made project manager for the design of a new cell phone model. Your supervisors have already scoped the project so you have a list showing the work breakdown structure and this includes major project activities. You must plan the project schedule and calculate project duration and project costs. Your boss wants the schedule and costs on his desk tomorrow morning!

You have been given the information in Exhibit 7.14. It includes all the activities required in the project and the duration of each activity. Also, dependencies between the activities have been identified. Remember that the preceding activity must be fully completed before work on the following activity can be started.

Your project is divided into five major tasks. Task "P" involves developing specifications for the new cell phone. Here decisions related to such things as battery life, size of the phone and features need to be determined. These details are based on how a customer uses the cell phone. These user specifications are redefined in terms that have meaning to the subcontractors that will actually make the new cell phone in Task "S" supplier specifications. These involve engineering details for how the product will perform. The individual components that make up the product are the focus of Task "D." Task "I" brings all the components together and a working prototype is built and tested. Finally in Task "V," vendors are selected and contracts are negotiated.

1 Draw a project network that includes all the activities.

2 Calculate the start and finish times for each activity and determine the minimum number of weeks for completing the project. Find the critical set of activities for the project.

3 Identify slack in the activities not on the project critical path.

4 Your boss would like you to suggest changes that could be made to the project that would significantly shorten it. What would you suggest?

exhibit 7.14   Work Breakdown Structure and Activities for the Cell Phone Design Project

**Excel:
Cell_Phone
Design**

MAJOR PROJECT TASKS/ACTIVITIES	ACTIVITY IDENTIFICATION	DEPENDENCY	DURATION (WEEKS)
Product specifications (P)			
Overall product specifications	P1	—	4
Hardware specifications	P2	P1	5
Software specifications	P3	P1	5
Market research	P4	P2, P3	2
Supplier specifications (S)			
Hardware	S1	P2	5
Software	S2	P3	6
Market research	S3	P4	1
Product design (D)			
Circuits	D1	S1, D7	8
Battery	D2	S1	1
Display	D3	S1	2
Outer cover	D4	S3	4
User interface	D5	S2	4
Camera	D6	S1, S2, S3	1
Functionality	D7	D5, D6	4
Product integration (I)			
Hardware	I1	D1, D2, D3, D4, D6	3
Software	I2	D7	5
Prototype Testing	I3	I1,I2	5
Subcontracting (V)			
Vendor selection	V1	D7	10
Contract negotiation	V2	I3, V1	2

Super Quiz

1 A project structured where a self-contained team works full time on the project.

2 Specific events that upon completion mark important progress toward completing a project.

3 This defines the hierarchy of project tasks, subtasks, and work packages.

4 Pieces of work in a project that consume time to complete.

5 A chart that shows both the time and sequence for completing the activities in a project.

6 Activities that in sequence form the longest chain in a project.

7 The difference between the late and early start time for an activity.

8 When activities are scheduled with probabilistic task times.

9 The procedure used to reduce project completion time by trading off time versus cost.

10 A key assumption related to the resources needed to complete activities when using the critical path method.

1. Pure project or skunkworks 2. Milestones 3. Work breakdown structure 4. Activities
5. Gantt chart 6. Critical path(s) 7. Slack 8. The Program Evaluation and Review Technique
(PERT) 9. Crashing 10. Resources are always available

Selected Bibliography

Gray, C. *Agile Project Management: How to Succeed in the Face of Changing Project Requirements*. New York: American Management Association, 2004.

Gray, C. F., and E. W. Larson. *Project Management: The Managerial Process*. New York: Irwin/McGraw-Hill, 2002.

Kerzner, H. *Project Management: A Systems Approach to Planning, Scheduling, and Controlling*. 8th ed. New York: Wiley, 2002.

Lewis, James P. *The Project Manager's Desk Reference*. New York: McGraw-Hill Professional Publishing, 1999.

Footnote

1 Based on material from Wikipedia, the free encyclopedia (http://en.wikipedia.org/wiki/Earned_value_management.

SECTION THREE

SUPPLY CHAIN PROCESSES

8. Global Sourcing and Procurement

9. Location, Logistics, and Distribution

10. Lean and Sustainable Supply Chains

THE GREEN SUPPLY CHAIN

An important part of sustainability initiatives at global organizations is the close examination of their supply chain environmental footprint. The term *environmental footprint* relates to the impact that running the supply chain has on the environment. There are complex trade-offs between sustainability goals and other business objectives such as efficiency, profitability, or improved customer service. It is essential that companies orchestrate greening efforts across all supply chain processes, starting with product development, sourcing, manufacturing, packaging, transportation, demand fulfillment, and end-of-life management.

Most companies choose to focus greening efforts on one or two processes, at least to start. The following are some activities that are commonly chosen:

- Reduce energy consumption through plant redesign and machine preventative maintenance.

- Measure and minimize the transportation carbon footprint in the distribution network.
- Work with suppliers to minimize excess packaging.
- Audit and make its maintenance, repair and operating (MRO) inventory more eco-friendly.
- Incorporate product reuse and recycling into its product development initiatives.

Managing logistics, which are transportation-related processes, is probably one of the more discussed greening efforts in supply chain management. There is a direct relationship between transportation efficiency and transportation costs. Minimizing miles traveled, using more efficient means for moving goods, and improving capacity utilization through consolidation of shipments reduces energy consumption and transportation costs, while at the same time reducing carbon emissions.

CHAPTER 8

GLOBAL SOURCING AND PROCUREMENT

After reading the chapter you will:

- Understand how important sourcing decisions go beyond simple material purchasing decisions.
- Demonstrate the "bullwhip effect" and how it is important to synchronize the flow of material between supply chain partners.
- Describe how characteristics of supply and demand have an impact on structuring supply chains.
- Know the reason for outsourcing capabilities.
- Illustrate what "green" sourcing is.
- Analyze the total cost of ownership.
- Calculate inventory turnover and days of supply.

223	**The World Is Flat**	
	Flattener 5: Outsourcing	
	Flattener 6: Offshoring	
224	**Strategic Sourcing**	
	The Bullwhip Effect	Strategic sourcing defined
		Vendor managed inventory defined
		Bullwhip effect defined
		Functional products defined
		Innovative products defined
230	**Outsourcing**	
		Outsourcing defined
		Logistics defined
235	**Green Sourcing**	
238	**Total Cost of Ownership**	
		Total cost of ownership defined

241   Measuring Sourcing Performance

Inventory turnover defined
Cost of goods sold defined
Average aggregate inventory value defined
Weeks of supply defined

243   Summary

246   Case: Pepe Jeans

247   Super Quiz

THE WORLD IS FLAT

Flattener 5: Outsourcing
Flattener 6: Offshoring

The owner of a fuel pump factory in Beijing posted the following African proverb, translated into Mandarin, on his factory floor:

> *Every morning in Africa, a gazelle wakes up.*
> *It knows it must run faster than the fastest lion or it will be killed.*
> *Every morning a lion wakes up.*
> *It knows it must outrun the slowest gazelle or it will starve to death.*
> *It doesn't matter whether you are a lion or a gazelle.*
> *When the sun comes up, you better start running.*

Global

The opening of China to the rest of the world started on December 11, 2001, when that country formally joined the World Trade Organization (WTO). Ever since China joined the WTO, both it and the rest of the world have had to run faster and faster. This is because China's membership in the WTO gave a huge boost to another form of collaboration: offshoring. Offshoring, which has been around for decades, is different from outsourcing. Outsourcing means

taking some specific but limited function that your company was doing in-house—such as research, call centers, or accounts receivable—and having another company perform the exact same function for you and then reintegrating its work back into your overall operation. Offshoring, by contrast, is when a company takes one of its factories that is operating in Canton, Ohio, and moves the whole factory offshore to Canton, China. There, it produces the very same product in the very same way, only with cheaper labor, lower taxes, subsidized energy, and lower health-care costs. Just as Y2K took India and the world to a whole new level of outsourcing, China's joining the WTO took Beijing and the world to a whole new level of offshoring, with more companies shifting production offshore and then integrating it into the global supply chain.

Adapted from: Thomas L. Friedman, *The World Is Flat* [Updated and Expanded], New York: Farrar, Straus and Giroux, 2006, p. 136.

STRATEGIC SOURCING

Strategic sourcing

Supply Chain

Strategic sourcing is the development and management of supplier relationships to acquire goods and services in a way that aids in achieving the immediate needs of the business. In the past the term *sourcing* was just another term for purchasing, a corporate function that financially was important but strategically was not the center of attention. Today, as a result of globalization and inexpensive communications technology, the basis for competition is changing. A firm is no longer constrained by the capabilities it owns; what matters is its ability to make the most of available capabilities, whether they are owned by the firm or not. Outsourcing is so sophisticated that even core functions such as engineering, research and development, manufacturing, information technology, and marketing can be moved outside the firm.

Sourcing activities can vary greatly and depend on the item being purchased. Exhibit 8.1 maps different processes for sourcing or purchasing an item. The term *sourcing* implies a more complex process suitable for products that are strategically important. Purchasing processes that span from a simple "spot" or one-time purchase to a long-term strategic

exhibit 8.1   The Sourcing/Purchasing Design Matrix

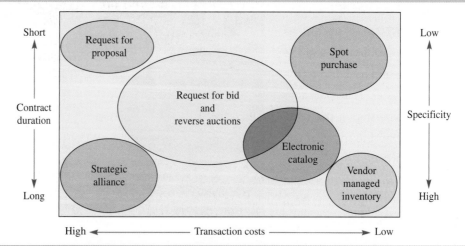

alliance are depicted on the diagram. The diagram positions a purchasing process according to the specificity of the item, contract duration, and intensity of transaction costs.

Specificity refers to how common the item is and, in a relative sense, how many substitutes might be available. For example, blank DVD disks are commonly available from many different vendors and would have low specificity. A custom-made envelope that is padded and specially shaped to contain a specific item that is to be shipped would be an example of a high specificity item.

Commonly available products can be purchased using a relatively simple process. For low volume and inexpensive items purchased during the regular routine of work, a firm may order from an online catalog. Often, these online catalogs are customized for a customer. Special user identifications can be set up to authorize customer employees to purchase certain groups of items with spent limits. Other items require a more complex process.

A request for proposal (RFP) is commonly used for purchasing items that are more complex or expensive and where there may be a number of potential vendors. A detailed information packet describing what is to be purchased is prepared and distributed to potential vendors. The vendor then responds with a detailed proposal of how the company intends to meet the terms of the RFP. A request for bid or reverse auction is similar in terms of the information packet needed. A major difference is how the bid price is negotiated. In the RFP, the bid is included in the proposal whereas in a request for bid or reverse auction, vendors actually bid on the item in real time and often using Internet software.

Vendor managed inventory

Vendor managed inventory is when a customer actually allows the supplier to manage an item or group of items for them. In this case the supplier is given the freedom to replenish the item as they see fit. Typically, there are some constraints related to the maximum that the customer is willing to carry, required service levels, and other billing transaction processes. Selecting the proper process depends on minimizing the balance between the supplier's delivered costs of the item over a period of time; say a year, and the customer's costs of managing the inventory. This is discussed later in the chapter in the context of the "total cost of ownership" for a purchased item.

The Bullwhip Effect

Marshall Fisher[1] argues that in many cases there are adversarial relations between supply chain partners as well as dysfunctional industry practices such as a reliance on price promotions. Consider the common food industry practice of offering price promotions every January on a product. Retailers respond to the price cut by stocking up, in some cases buying a year's supply—a practice the industry calls *forward buying*. Nobody wins in the deal. Retailers have to pay to carry the year's supply, and the shipment bulge adds cost throughout the supplier's system. For example, the supplier plants must go on overtime starting in October to meet the bulge. Even the vendors that supply the manufacturing plants are affected because they must quickly react to the large surge in raw material requirements.

The impact of these types of practices has been studied at companies such as Procter & Gamble. Exhibit 8.2 shows typical order patterns faced by each node in a supply chain that

exhibit 8.2   Increasing Variability of Orders up the Supply Chain

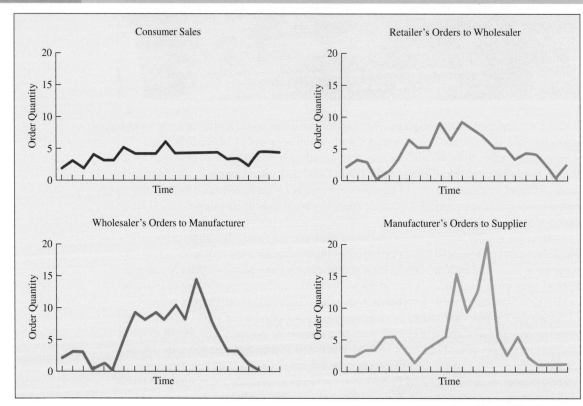

Supply Chain

consists of a manufacturer, a distributor, a wholesaler, and a retailer. In this case, the demand is for disposable baby diapers. The retailer's orders to the wholesaler display greater variability than the end-consumer sales; the wholesaler's orders to the manufacturer show even more oscillations; and, finally, the manufacturer's orders to its suppliers are the most volatile. This phenomenon of variability magnification as we move from the customer to the producer in the supply chain is often referred to as the **bullwhip effect**. The effect indicates a lack of synchronization among supply chain members. Even a slight change in consumer sales ripples backward in the form of magnified oscillations upstream, resembling the result of a flick of a bullwhip handle. Because the supply patterns do not match the demand patterns, inventory accumulates at various stages, and shortages and delays occur at others. This bullwhip effect has been observed by many firms in numerous industries, including Campbell Soup and Procter & Gamble in consumer products; Hewlett-Packard, IBM, and Motorola in electronics; General Motors in automobiles; and Eli Lilly in pharmaceuticals.

Bullwhip effect

Campbell Soup has a program called *continuous replenishment* that typifies what many manufacturers are doing to smooth the flow of materials through their supply chain. Here is how the program works. Campbell establishes electronic data interchange (EDI) links with retailers and offers an "everyday low price" that eliminates discounts. Every morning, retailers electronically inform the company of their demand for all Campbell products and of the level of inventories in their distribution centers. Campbell uses that information to forecast future demand and to determine which products require replenishment based on upper and lower inventory limits previously established with each supplier. Trucks leave the Campbell shipping plant that afternoon and arrive at the retailers' distribution centers with the required replenishments the same day. Using this system, Campbell can cut the retailers' inventories, which under the old system averaged four weeks of supply, to about two weeks of supply.

This solves some problems for Campbell Soup, but what are the advantages for the retailer? Most retailers figure that the cost to carry the inventory of a given product for a year equals at least 25 percent of what they paid for the product. A two-week inventory reduction represents a cost savings equal to nearly 1 percent of sales. The average retailer's profits equal about 2 percent of sales, so this saving is enough to increase profits by 50 percent. Because the retailer makes more money on Campbell products delivered through continuous replenishment, it has an incentive to carry a broader line of them and to give them more shelf space. Campbell Soup found that after it introduced the program, sales of its products grew twice as fast through participating retailers as they did through other retailers.

Fisher has developed a framework to help managers understand the nature of demand for their products and then devise the supply chain that can best satisfy that demand. Many aspects of a product's demand are important—for example, product life cycle, demand predictability, product variety, and market standards for lead times and service. Fisher has found that products can be categorized as either primarily functional or primarily innovative. Because each category requires a distinctly different kind of supply chain, the root cause of supply chain problems is a mismatch between the type of product and type of supply chain.

Functional products

Functional products include the staples that people buy in a wide range of retail outlets, such as grocery stores and gas stations. Because such products satisfy basic needs, which do not change much over time, they have stable, predictable demand and long life cycles. But their stability invites competition, which often leads to low profit margins. Specific criteria suggested by Fisher for identifying functional products include the following: product life cycle of more than two years, contribution margin of 5 to 20 percent, only 10 to 20 product variations, an average forecast error at time of production of only 10 percent, and a lead time for make-to-order products of from six months to one year.

To avoid low margins, many companies introduce innovations in fashion or technology to give customers an additional reason to buy their products. Fashionable clothes and personal computers are good examples. Although innovation can enable a company to achieve higher profit margins, the very newness of the innovative products makes demand for them unpredictable. These **innovative products** typically have a life cycle of just a few months. Imitators quickly erode the competitive advantage that innovative products enjoy, and companies are forced to introduce a steady stream of newer innovations. The short life cycles and the great variety typical of these products further increase unpredictability. Exhibit 8.3 summarizes the differences between functional and innovative products.

Innovative products

Hau Lee[2] expands on Fisher's ideas by focusing on the "supply" side of the supply chain. While Fisher has captured important demand characteristics, Lee points out that there are uncertainties revolving around the supply side that are equally important drivers for the right supply chain strategy.

Lee defines a *stable supply process* as one where the manufacturing process and the underlying technology are mature and the supply base is well established. In contrast, an *evolving supply process* is where the manufacturing process and the underlying technology are still under early development and are rapidly changing. As a result the supply base may be limited in both size and experience. In a stable supply process, manufacturing complexity tends to be low or manageable. Stable manufacturing processes tend to be highly automated, and long-term supply contracts are prevalent. In an evolving supply process, the

exhibit 8.3	Demand and Supply Uncertainty Characteristics

DEMAND CHARACTERISTICS		SUPPLY CHARACTERISTICS	
FUNCTIONAL	INNOVATIVE	STABLE	EVOLVING
Low demand uncertainty	High demand uncertainty	Less breakdowns	Vulnerable to breakdowns
More predictable demand	Difficult to forecast	Stable and higher yields	Variable and lower yields
Long product life	Short selling season	Less quality problems	Potential quality problems
Low inventory cost	High inventory cost	More supply sources	Limited supply sources
Low profit margin	High profit margin	Reliable suppliers	Unreliable suppliers
Low product variety	High product variety	Less process changes	More process changes
Higher volume	Low volume	Less capacity constraints	Potential capacity constrained
Low stockout cost	High stockout cost	Easier to change over	Difficult to change over
Low obsolescence	High obsolescence	Dependable lead times	Variable lead time

Hau Lee's Uncertainty Framework—Examples and Types of Supply Chain Needed

exhibit 8.4

		Demand Uncertainty	
		Low (Functional Products)	High (Innovative Products)
Supply Uncertainty	Low (Stable Process)	Grocery, basic apparel, food, oil and gas Efficient Supply Chain	Fashion apparel, computers, popular music Responsive Supply Chain
Supply Uncertainty	High (Evolving Process)	Hydroelectric power, some food produce Risk-Hedging Supply Chain	Telecom, high-end computers, semiconductor Agile Supply Chain

manufacturing process requires a lot of fine-tuning and is often subject to breakdowns and uncertain yields. The supply base may not be reliable, as the suppliers themselves are going through process innovations. Exhibit 8.3 summarizes some of the differences between stable and evolving supply processes.

Lee argues that while functional products tend to have a more mature and stable supply process, that is not always the case. For example, the annual demand for electricity and other utility products in a locality tend to be stable and predictable, but the supply of hydroelectric power, which relies on rainfall in a region, can be erratic year by year. Some food products also have a very stable demand, but the supply (both quantity and quality) of the products depends on yearly weather conditions. Similarly, there are also innovative products with a stable supply process. Fashion apparel products have a short selling season and their demand is highly unpredictable. However, the supply process is very stable, with a reliable supply base and a mature manufacturing process technology. Exhibit 8.4 gives some examples of products that have different demand and supply uncertainties.

According to Lee, it is more challenging to operate a supply chain that is in the right column of Exhibit 8.4 than in the left column, and similarly it is more challenging to operate a supply chain that is in the lower row of Exhibit 8.4 than in the upper row. Before setting up a supply chain strategy, it is necessary to understand the sources of the underlying uncertainties and explore ways to reduce these uncertainties. If it is possible to move the uncertainty characteristics of the product from the right column to the left or from the lower row to the upper; then the supply chain performance will improve.

Lee characterizes four types of supply chain strategies as shown in Exhibit 8.4. Information technologies play an important role in shaping such strategies.

Supply Chain

- **Efficient supply chains.** These are supply chains that utilize strategies aimed at creating the highest cost efficiency. For such efficiencies to be achieved, non-value-added activities should be eliminated, scale economies should be pursued, optimization techniques should be deployed to get the best capacity utilization in production and distribution, and information linkages should be established to ensure the most efficient, accurate, and cost-effective transmission of information across the supply chain.
- **Risk-hedging supply chains.** These are supply chains that utilize strategies aimed at pooling and sharing resources in a supply chain so that the risks in supply disruption can be shared. A single entity in a supply chain can be vulnerable to supply disruptions, but if there is more than one supply source or if alternative supply resources are available, then the risk of disruption is reduced. A company may, for

example, increase the safety stock of its key component to hedge against the risk of supply disruption, and by sharing the safety stock with other companies who also need this key component, the cost of maintaining this safety stock can be shared. This type of strategy is common in retailing, where different retail stores or dealerships share inventory. Information technology is important for the success of these strategies since real-time information on inventory and demand allows the most cost-effective management and transshipment of goods between partners sharing the inventory.

- **Responsive supply chains.**   These are supply chains that utilize strategies aimed at being responsive and flexible to the changing and diverse needs of the customers. To be responsive, companies use build-to-order and mass customization processes as a means to meet the specific requirements of customers.

- **Agile supply chains.**   These are supply chains that utilize strategies aimed at being responsive and flexible to customer needs, while the risks of supply shortages or disruptions are hedged by pooling inventory and other capacity resources. These supply chains essentially have strategies in place that combine the strengths of "hedged" and "responsive" supply chains. They are agile because they have the ability to be responsive to the changing, diverse, and unpredictable demands of customers on the front end, while minimizing the back-end risks of supply disruptions.

Demand and supply uncertainty is a good framework for understanding supply chain strategy. Innovative products with unpredictable demand and an evolving supply process face a major challenge. Because of shorter and shorter product life cycles, the pressure for dynamically adjusting and adopting a company's supply chain strategy is great. In the following we explore the concepts of outsourcing, green sourcing, and total cost of ownership. These are important tools for coping with demand and supply uncertainty.

OUTSOURCING

Outsourcing

Outsourcing is the act of moving some of a firm's internal activities and decision responsibility to outside providers. The terms of the agreement are established in a contract. Outsourcing goes beyond the more common purchasing and consulting contracts because not only are the activities transferred, but also resources that make the activities occur, including people, facilities, equipment, technology, and other assets, are transferred. The responsibilities for making decisions over certain elements of the activities are transferred as well. Taking complete responsibility for this is a specialty of contract manufacturers such as Flextronics.[3]

The reasons why a company decides to outsource can vary greatly. Exhibit 8.5 lists examples of reasons to outsource and the accompanying benefits. Outsourcing allows a firm to focus on activities that represent its core competencies. Thus, the company can create a competitive advantage while reducing cost. An entire function may be outsourced, or some elements of an activity may be outsourced, with the rest kept in-house. For example, some of the elements of information technology may be strategic, some may be critical, and some may be performed less expensively by a third party. Identifying a function as a potential outsourcing target, and then breaking that function into its components, allows decision makers to determine which activities are strategic or critical and should remain in-house and which can be outsourced like commodities. As an example, outsourcing the logistics function will be discussed.

exhibit 8.5

Reasons to Outsource and the Resulting Benefits

FINANCIALLY DRIVEN REASONS

Improve return on assets by reducing inventory and selling unnecessary assets.
Generate cash by selling low-return entities.
Gain access to new markets, particularly in developing countries.
Reduce costs through a lower cost structure.
Turn fixed costs into variable costs.

IMPROVEMENT-DRIVEN REASONS

Improve quality and productivity.
Shorten cycle time.
Obtain expertise, skills, and technologies that are not otherwise available.
Improve risk management.
Improve credibility and image by associating with superior providers.

ORGANIZATIONALLY DRIVEN REASONS

Improve effectiveness by focusing on what the firm does best.
Increase flexibility to meet changing demand for products and services.
Increase product and service value by improving response to customer needs.

Logistics

There has been dramatic growth in outsourcing in the logistics area. **Logistics** is a term that refers to the management functions that support the complete cycle of material flow: from the purchase and internal control of production materials; to the planning and control of work-in-process; to the purchasing, shipping, and distribution of the finished product. The emphasis on lean inventory means there is less room for error in deliveries. Trucking companies such as Ryder have started adding the logistics aspect to their businesses—changing from merely moving goods from point A to point B, to managing all or part of all shipments over a longer period, typically three years, and replacing the shipper's employees with their own. Logistics companies now have complex computer tracking technology that reduces the risk in transportation and allows the logistics company to add more value to the firm than it could if the function were performed in-house. Third-party logistics providers track freight using electronic data interchange technology and a satellite system to tell customers exactly where its drivers are and when deliveries will be made. Such technology is critical in some environments where the delivery window may be only 30 minutes long.

Federal Express has one of the most advanced systems available for tracking items being sent through its services. The system is available to all customers over the Internet. It tells the exact status of each item currently being carried by the company. Information on the exact time a package is picked up, when it is transferred between hubs in the company's network, and when it

DHL SMARTTRUCKS USE A TYPE OF ROUTE PLANNING SOFTWARE WHICH NAVIGATES AWAY FROM INNER CITY TRAFFIC JAMS AND CALCULATES THE BEST ROUTE TO DELIVER PACKAGES. THIS REDUCES TIME AND COSTS BUT ALSO FUEL CONSUMPTION AND CO_2 EMISSIONS. TRANSPORTED MAIL ITEMS USE RADIO FREQUENCY IDENTIFICATION (RFID) SMART TAGS ATTACHED TO THEM TO MONITOR VEHICLE LOADS.

is delivered is available on the system. You can access this system at the FedEx Web site (www.fedex.com). Select your country on the initial screen and then select "Track Shipments" in the Track box in the lower part of the page. Of course, you will need the actual tracking number for an item currently in the system to get information. Federal Express has integrated its tracking system with many of its customers' in-house information systems.

Another example of innovative outsourcing in logistics involves Hewlett-Packard. Hewlett-Packard turned over its inbound raw materials warehousing in Vancouver, Washington, to Roadway Logistics. Roadway's 140 employees operate the warehouse 24 hours a day, seven days a week, coordinating the delivery of parts to the warehouse and managing storage. Hewlett-Packard's 250 employees were transferred to other company activities. Hewlett-Packard reports savings of 10 percent in warehousing operating costs.

One of the drawbacks to outsourcing is the layoffs that often result. Even in cases where the outsourcing partner hires former employees, they are often hired back at lower wages with fewer benefits. Outsourcing is perceived by many unions as an effort to circumvent union contracts.

In theory, outsourcing is a no-brainer. Companies can unload noncore activities, shed balance sheet assets, and boost their return on capital by using third-party service providers. But in reality, things are more complicated. "It's really hard to figure out what's core and what's noncore today," says Jane Linder, senior research fellow and associate director of Accenture's Institute for Strategic Change in Cambridge, Massachusetts. "When you take another look tomorrow, things may have changed. On September 9, 2001, airport security workers were noncore; on September 12, 2001, they were core to the federal government's ability to provide security to the nation. It happens every day in companies as well."[4]

Exhibit 8.6 is a useful framework to help managers make appropriate choices for the structure of supplier relationships. The decision goes beyond the notion that "core

exhibit 8.6 A Framework for Structuring Supplier Relationships

	VERTICAL INTEGRATION (DO NOT OUTSOURCE)	ARM'S-LENGTH RELATIONSHIPS (OUTSOURCE)
Coordination	"Messy" interfaces; adjacent tasks involve a high degree of mutual adaptation, exchange of implicit knowledge, and learning-by-doing. Requisite information is highly particular to the task.	Standardized interfaces between adjacent tasks; requisite information is highly codified and standardized (prices, quantities, delivery schedules, etc.).
Strategic control	Very high: significant investments in highly durable relationship-specific assets needed for optimal execution of tasks. Investments cannot be recovered if relationship terminates: • Collocation of specialized facilities • Investment in brand equity • Large proprietary learning curves • Long-term investments in specialized R&D programs	Very low: assets applicable to businesses with a large number of other potential customers or suppliers.
Intellectual property	Unclear or weak intellectual property protection Easy-to-imitate technology "Messy" interfaces between different technological components	Strong intellectual property protection Difficult-to-imitate technology "Clean" boundaries between different technological components

Source: Robert Hayes, Gary Pisano, David Upton, and Steven Wheelwright, *Operations Strategy and Technology: Pursuing the Competitive Edge* (New York: John Wiley & Sons, 2005), p. 137. Copyright © 2005 John Wiley & Sons. Reprinted by permission.

competencies" should be maintained under the direct control of management of the firm and that other activities should be outsourced. In this framework, a continuum that ranges from vertical integration to arm's-length relationships forms the basis for the decision.

An activity can be evaluated using the following characteristics: required coordination, strategic control, and intellectual property. Required coordination refers to how difficult it is to ensure that the activity will integrate well with the overall process. Uncertain activities that require much back-and-forth exchange of information should not be outsourced whereas activities that are well understood and highly standardized can easily move to business partners who specialize in the activity. Strategic control refers to the degree of loss that would be incurred if the relationship with the partner were severed. There could be many types of losses that would be important to consider including specialized facilities, knowledge of major customer relationships, and investment in research and development. A final consideration is the potential loss of intellectual property through the partnership.

Global

Intel is an excellent example of a company that recognized the importance of this type of decision framework in the mid-1980s. During the early 1980s, Intel found itself being squeezed out of the market for the memory chips that it had invented by Japanese competitors such as Hitachi, Fujitsu, and NEC. These companies had developed stronger capabilities to develop and rapidly scale up complex semiconductor manufacturing processes. It was clear by 1985 that a major Intel competency was in its ability to design complex integrated circuits, not in manufacturing or developing processes for more standardized chips. As a result, faced with growing financial losses, Intel was forced to exit the memory chip market.

Learning a lesson from the memory market, Intel shifted its focus to the microprocessor market, a device that it had invented in the late 1960s. To keep from repeating the mistake with memory chips, Intel felt it was essential to develop strong capabilities in process development and manufacturing. A pure "core competency" strategy would have suggested that Intel focus on the design of microprocessors and use outside partners to manufacture them. Given the close connection between semiconductor product development and process development, however, relying on outside parties for manufacturing would likely have created costs in terms of longer development lead times. Over the late-1980s Intel invested heavily in building world-class capabilities in process development and manufacturing. These capabilities are one of the chief reasons it has been able to maintain approximately 90 percent of the personal computer microprocessor market, despite the ability of competitors like AMD to "clone" Intel designs relatively quickly. Expanding its capabilities beyond its original core capability of product design has been a critical ingredient in Intel's sustained success.

Good advice is to keep control of—or acquire—activities that are true competitive differentiators or leave the potential to yield a competitive advantage, and to outsource the rest. It is important to make a distinction between "core" and "strategic" activities. Core activities are key to the business, but do not confer a competitive advantage, such as a bank's information technology operations. Strategic activities are a key source of competitive advantage. Because the competitive environment can change rapidly, companies need to monitor the situation constantly, and adjust accordingly. As an example, Coca-Cola, which decided to stay out of the bottling business in the early 1900s, partnered instead with independent bottlers and quickly built market share. The company reversed itself in the 1980s when bottling became a key competitive element in the industry.

Capability Sourcing at 7-Eleven

The term *capability sourcing* was coined to refer to the way companies focus on the things they do best and outsource other functions to key partners. The idea is that owning capabilities may not be as important as having control of those capabilities. This allows many additional capabilities to be outsourced. Companies are under intense pressure to improve revenue and margins because of increased competition. An area where this has been particularly intense is the convenience store industry, where 7-Eleven is a major player.

Before 1991, 7-Eleven was one of the most vertically integrated convenience store chains. When it is vertically integrated, a firm controls most of the activities in its supply chain. In the case of 7-Eleven, the firm owned its own distribution network, which delivered gasoline to each store, made its own candy and ice, and required the managers to handle store maintenance, credit card processing, store payroll, and even the in-store information technology (IT) system. For a while 7-Eleven even owned the cows that produced the milk sold in the stores. It was difficult for 7-Eleven to manage costs in this diverse set of functions.

At that time 7-Eleven had a Japanese branch that was very successful but was based on a totally different integration model. Rather than using a company-owned and vertically integrated model, the Japanese stores had partnerships with suppliers that carried out many of the day-to-day functions.

Those suppliers specialized in each area, enhancing quality and improving service while reducing cost. The Japanese model involved outsourcing everything possible without jeopardizing the business by giving competitors critical information. A simple rule said that if a partner could provide a capability more effectively than 7-Eleven could itself, that capability should be outsourced. In the United States the company eventually outsourced activities such as human resources, finance, information technology, logistics, distribution, product development, and packaging. 7-Eleven still maintains control of all vital information and handles all merchandising, pricing, positioning, promotion of gasoline, and ready-to-eat food.

The following chart shows how 7-Eleven has structured key partnerships:

Activity	Outsourcing Strategy
Gasoline	Outsourced distribution to Citgo. Maintains control over pricing and promotion. These are activities that can differentiate its stores.
Snack foods	Frito-Lay distributes its products directly to the stores. 7-Eleven makes critical decisions about order quantities and shelf placement. 7-Eleven mines extensive data on local customer purchase patterns to make these decisions at each store.
Prepared foods	Joint venture with E.A. Sween: Combined Distribution Centers (CDC), a direct-store delivery operation that supplies 7-Eleven stores with sandwiches and other fresh goods two times a day.
Specialty products	Many are developed specially for 7-Eleven customers. For example, 7-Eleven worked with Hershey to develop an edible straw used with the popular Twizzler treat. Worked with Anheuser-Bush on special NASCAR and Major League Baseball promotions.
Data analysis	7-Eleven relies on an outside vendor, IRI, to maintain and format purchasing data while keeping the data proprietary. Only 7-Eleven can see the actual mix of products its customers purchase at each location.
New capabilities	American Express supplies automated teller machines. Western Union handles money wire transfers. CashWorks furnishes check-cashing capabilities. Electronic Data Systems (EDS) maintains network functions.

GREEN SOURCING

Being environmentally responsible has become a business imperative and many firms are looking to their supply chains to deliver "green" results. A significant area of focus relates to how a firm works with suppliers where the opportunity to save money and benefit the environment might not be a strict trade-off proposition. Financial results can often be improved through both cost reductions and boosting revenues.

Deloitte (www.deloitte.com) has developed a green strategic sourcing process that can be used with conventional sourcing techniques to enhance sourcing savings by taking advantage of environmental factors. Before looking at their six-step process, it is worth considering the long-term benefits of this type of approach. Green sourcing is not just about finding new environmentally friendly technologies or increasing the use of recyclable materials. It can also help drive cost reductions in a variety of ways including product content substitution, waste reduction, and lower usage.

A comprehensive green sourcing effort should assess how a company uses items that are purchased internally, in its own operations, or in its products and services. As costs of commodity items like steel, electricity, and fossil fuels continue to increase, properly designed green sourcing efforts should find ways to significantly reduce and possibly eliminate the need for these types of commodities. As an example, consider retrofitting internal lighting in a large office building to a modern energy efficient technology. Electricity cost savings of 10 to 12 percent per square foot can easily translate into millions of dollars in associated electricity cost savings.

Another important cost area in green sourcing is waste reduction opportunities. This includes everything from energy and water to packaging and transportation. A great example of this is the redesigned milk jug introduced recently by leading grocery retailers. Using the new jug, with more rectangular dimensions and a square base, cuts the associated water consumption of the jugs by 60 to 70 percent compared to earlier jug designs because the new design does not require the use of milk crates. Milk crates typically become filthy during use due to spillage and other natural factors; thus, they are usually hosed down before reuse, consuming thousands  of gallons of water. The new design also reduces fuel costs. Since crates are no longer used, they also do not have to be transported back to the dairy plant or farm distribution point for future shipments. Furthermore, the new jugs have the unexpected benefit of fitting better in modern home refrigerator doors and allow retailers to fit more of them in their in-store coolers. Breakthrough results like the new milk jug can result from comprehensive partnerships between users and their suppliers working to find innovative solutions.

A recent supply chain survey by Florida International University (see business.fiu.edu/greensupplychain) revealed that working with suppliers can result in opportunities that improve revenue. They can be the opportunity to turn waste products into sources of revenue. For example, a leading beverage manufacturer operates a recycling subsidiary that sources used aluminum cans from a large number of suppliers. The subsidiary actually processes more aluminum cans than are used in the company's own products, consequently developing a strong secondary revenue stream for the company.

In other cases, green sourcing can help establish entirely new lines of business to serve environmentally conscious customers. In the cleaning products aisle of a supermarket shoppers will find numerous options of "green" cleaning products from a variety of consumer products companies. These products typically use natural ingredients in lieu of chemicals, and many are in concentrated amounts to reduce overall packaging costs.

Green sourcing can also be essential for companies interested in winning high-profile deals. Being green can be the "order winner" for selection when many sourcing options are available. For example, the organizers of the 2008 U.S. Democratic National Convention (DNC) stipulated very stringent green procurement regulations for the convention's food suppliers. Suppliers that could source food from local and organic farms won the majority of the DNC's business.

Logistics suppliers could find business opportunities coming directly to them as a result of the green trend. A large automobile manufacturer completed a project to green its logistics/distribution network. The automaker analyzed the shipping carriers, locations, and overall efficiency of its distribution network both for parts and finished automobiles. By increasing the use of rail transportation for parts, consolidating shipments in fewer ports, and partnering with its logistics providers to increase fuel efficiency for both marine and road transportation, the company reduced its overall distribution-related carbon dioxide emissions by several thousand tons per year.

The following is an outline of a six-step process (see Exhibit 8.7) designed to transform a traditional process to a green sourcing process:

1. **Assess the opportunity.**   For a given category of expense, all relevant costs need to be taken into account. The five most common areas include electricity and other energy costs; disposal and recycling; packaging; commodity substitution (alternative materials to replace materials such as steel or plastic); and water (or other related resources). These costs are identified and incorporated into an analysis of total cost (sometimes referred to as "spend" cost analysis) at this step. From this analysis it is possible to prioritize the different costs based on the highest potential savings and criticality to the organization. This is important to directing effort to where it will likely have the most impact on the firm's financial position and cost reduction goals.

exhibit 8.7   Six-step Process for Green Sourcing

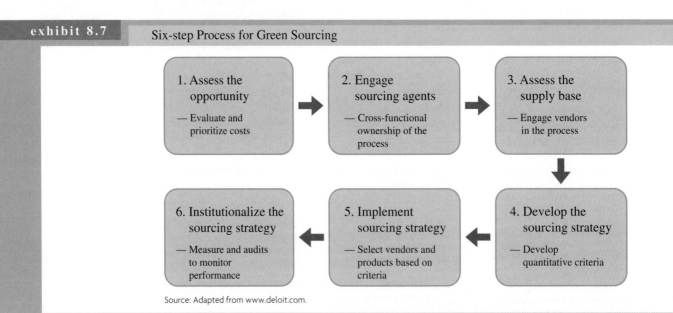

1. Assess the opportunity
— Evaluate and prioritize costs

2. Engage sourcing agents
— Cross-functional ownership of the process

3. Assess the supply base
— Engage vendors in the process

4. Develop the sourcing strategy
— Develop quantitative criteria

5. Implement sourcing strategy
— Select vendors and products based on criteria

6. Institutionalize the sourcing strategy
— Measure and audits to monitor performance

Source: Adapted from www.deloit.com.

Supply Chain

2. **Engage internal supply chain sourcing agents.** Internal sourcing agents are those within the firm that purchase items and have direct knowledge of business requirements, product specifications, and other internal perspectives inherent in the supply chain. These individuals and groups need to be "on-board" and partners in the improvement process to help set realistic green goals. The goal of generating no waste, for example, becomes a cross-functional supply chain effort that relies heavily on finding and developing the right suppliers. These internal managers need to identify the most significant opportunities. They can develop a robust baseline model of what should be possible for reducing current and ongoing costs. In the case of procuring new equipment, for example, the baseline model would include not just the initial price of the equipment as in traditional sourcing, but also energy, disposal, recycling, and maintenance costs.

3. **Assess the supply base.** A sustainable sourcing process requires engaging new and existing vendors. As in traditional sourcing, the firm needs to understand vendor capabilities, constraints, and product offering. The green process needs to be augmented with formal requirements that relate to green opportunities, including possible commodity substitutions and new manufacturing processes. These requirements need to be incorporated in vendor bid documents or the request for proposals (RFP).

A good example is concrete that uses fly ash, a by-product from coal-fired power plants. Fly ash can be substituted for Portland cement in ready-mix concrete or in concrete block to produce a stronger and lighter product with reduced water consumption. Fly ash substitution helped a company reduce its exposure to volatile and rapidly increasing prices for cement. At the same time, the reduced weight of the block lowered transportation costs to the company's new facilities. The company was also able to establish a specification incorporating fly ash for all new construction sites to follow. Finally, the substitution also helped the power plant, by providing a new market for the fly ash which previously had to be discarded.

4. **Develop the sourcing strategy.** The main goal with this step is to develop quantitative and qualitative criteria that will be used to evaluate the sourcing process. These are needed to properly analyze associated costs and benefits. These criteria need to be clearly articulated in bid documents and RFP when working with potential suppliers so that their proposals will address relevant goals related to sustainability.

FLY ASH IS GENERALLY STORED AT COAL POWER PLANTS OR PLACED IN LANDFILLS AS SHOWN HERE. ABOUT 43 PERCENT IS RECYCLED REDUCING THE HARMFUL IMPACT ON THE ENVIRONMENT FROM LANDFILLS.

5. **Implement the sourcing strategy.** The evaluation criteria developed in step 4 should help in the selection of vendors and products for each business requirement. The evaluation process should consider initial cost and the total cost of ownership for the items in the bid. So, for example, energy efficient equipment that is proposed with a higher initial cost may, over its productive life, actually result in a lower total cost due to energy savings and a related lower carbon footprint. Relevant green opportunities such as energy efficiency and waste reduction need to be modeled and then incorporated into the sourcing analysis to make it as comprehensive

as possible and to facilitate an effective vendor selection process that supports the firm's needs.

6. **Institutionalize the sourcing strategy.**   Once the vendor is selected and contracts finalized, the procurement process begins. Here the sourcing and procurement department needs to define a set of metrics against which the supplier will be measured for the contract's duration. These metrics should be based on performance, delivery, compliance with pricing guidelines, and similar factors. It is vital that metrics that relate to the company's sustainability goals are considered as well. Periodic audits may also need to be incorporated in the process to directly observe practices that relate to these metrics to ensure honest reporting of data.

A key aspect of green sourcing, compared to a traditional process, is the expanded view of the sourcing decision. This expanded view requires the incorporation of new criteria for evaluating alternatives. Further, it requires a wider range of internal integration such as designers, engineers, and marketers. Finally, visualizing and capturing the green sourcing savings often involves greater complexity and longer payback periods compared to a traditional process.

TOTAL COST OF OWNERSHIP

Total cost of ownership

The **total cost of ownership** (TCO) is an estimate of the cost of an item that includes all the costs related to the procurement and use of an item, including any related costs in disposing of the item after it is no longer useful. The concept can be applied to a company's internal costs or it can be viewed more broadly to consider costs throughout the supply chain. To fully appreciate the cost of purchasing an item from a particular vendor, an approach that captures the costs of the activities associated with purchasing and actually using the item should be considered. Depending on the complexity of the purchasing process, activities such as pre-bid conferences, visits by potential suppliers, and even visits to potential suppliers can significantly impact the total cost of the item.

A TCO analysis is highly dependent on the actual situation, in general though, the costs outlined in Exhibit 8.8 should be considered. The costs can be categorized into three broad areas: acquisition costs, ownership costs, and post-ownership costs.[5] Acquisition costs are the initial costs associated with the purchase of materials, products, and services. They are not long-term costs of ownership but represent an immediate cash outflow. Acquisition costs include the prepurchase costs associated with preparing documents to distribute to potential suppliers, identifying suppliers and evaluating suppliers, and other costs associated with actually procuring the item. The actual purchase prices, including taxes and transportation costs, are also included.

Ownership costs are incurred after the initial purchase and are associated with the ongoing use of the product or material. Examples of costs that are quantifiable include energy usage, scheduled maintenance, repair, and financing (leasing situation). There can also be qualitative costs such as aesthetic factors (e.g., the item is psychologically pleasing to the eye), and ergonomic factors (e.g., productivity improvement or reducing fatigue). These ownership costs can often exceed the initial purchase price and have an impact on cash flow, profitability, and even employee morale and productivity.

Major costs associated with post-ownership include salvage value and disposal costs. For many purchases, there are established markets that provide data to help estimate

| Total Cost of Ownership | exhibit 8.8 |

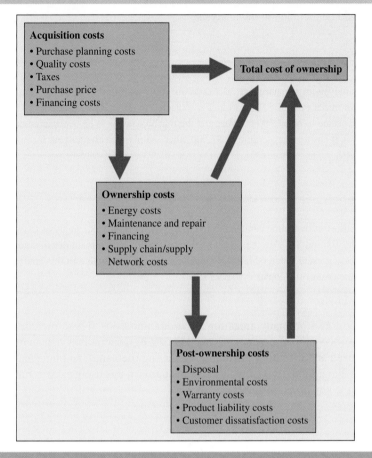

reasonable future values, such as the *Kelley Blue Book* for used automobiles. Other areas that can be included are the long-term environment impact (particularly when the firm has sustainability goals), warranty and product liabilities, and the negative marketing impact of low customer satisfaction with the item.

Overemphasis on acquisition cost or purchase price frequently results in failure to address other significant ownership and post-ownership costs. TCO is a philosophy for understating all relevant costs of doing business with a particular supplier for a good or service. It is not only relevant for a business that wants to reduce its cost of doing business but also for a firm that aims to design products or services that provide the lowest total cost of ownership to customers. For example, some automobile manufacturers have extended the tune-up interval on many models to 100,000 miles, thereby reducing vehicle operating cost for car owners. Viewing TCO in this way can lead to an increased value of the product to existing and potential customers.

These costs can be estimated as cash inflows (the sale of used equipment, etc.) or outflows (such as purchase prices, demolition of an obsolete facility, etc.). The following example shows how this analysis can be organized using a spreadsheet. Keep in mind that the costs considered need to be adapted to the decision being made. Costs that do not vary based on the decision need not be considered, but relevant costs that vary depending on the decision should be included in the analysis.

Step by Step

Example 8.1: Total Cost of Ownership Analysis

Consider the analysis of the purchase of a copy machine as might be used in a copy center. The machine has an initial cost of $120,000 and is expected to generate income of $40,000 per year.[6] Supplies are expected to be $7,000 per year and the machine needs to be overhauled during year 3 at a cost of $9,000. It has a salvage value of $7,500 when we plan to sell it at year 6.

SOLUTION

Laying these costs out over time can lead to the use of net present value analysis to evaluate the decision. Consider Exhibit 8.9. Are the present values of each yearly stream discounted to now.[7] (See Appendix D for a present value table.) As we can see, the present value in this analysis shows that the present value cost of the copier is $12,955. ●

TCO actually draws on many areas for a thorough analysis. These include finance (net present value), accounting (product pricing and costing), operations management (reliability, quality, need and inventory planning), marketing (demand), and information technology (systems integration). It is probably best to approach this using a cross-functional team representing the key functional areas.

---

exhibit 8.9   Analysis of the Purchase of an Office Copier

YEAR	Now	1	2	3	4	5	6
Cost of copier including installation	−$120,000						
Manufacturer required overhaul				$−9,000			
Cash inflows from using the machine		$ 40,000	$ 40,000	$ 40,000	$ 40,000	$ 40,000	$ 40,000
Supplies needed to use the machine		$−7,000	$−7,000	$−7,000	$−7,000	$−7,000	$−7,000
Salvage value							$ 7,500
Total of annual streams	−$120,000	$ 33,000	$ 33,000	$ 24,000	$ 33,000	$ 33,000	$ 40,500
Discount factor $(1+.2)^{-Year}$	1.000	0.833	0.694	0.579	0.482	0.402	0.335
Present value − yearly	−$120,000	$ 27,500	$ 22,917	$ 13,889	$ 15,914	$ 13,262	$ 13,563
Present value	$−12,955						

Discount factor = 20%.
Note: These calculations were done using the full precision of a spreadsheet.

MEASURING SOURCING PERFORMANCE

One view of sourcing is centered on the inventories that are positioned in the system. Exhibit 8.10 shows how hamburger meat and potatoes are stored in various locations in a typical fast-food restaurant chain. Here we see the steps that the beef and potatoes move through on their way to the local retail store and then to the customer. At each step inventory is carried, and this inventory has a particular cost to the company. Inventory serves as a buffer, thus allowing each stage to operate independently of the others. For example, the distribution center inventory allows the system that supplies the retail stores to operate independently of the meat and potato packing operations. Because the inventory at each stage ties up money, it is important that the operations at each stage are synchronized to minimize the size of these buffer inventories. The efficiency of the supply chain can be measured based on the size of the inventory investment in the supply chain. The inventory investment is measured relative to the total cost of the goods that are provided through the supply chain.

**Tutorial:
Strategic
Sourcing**

Two common measures to evaluate supply chain efficiency are *inventory turnover* and *weeks-of-supply*. These essentially measure the same thing and mathematically are the inverse of one another. **Inventory turnover** is calculated as follows:

Inventory turnover

$$\text{Inventory turnover} = \frac{\text{Cost of goods sold}}{\text{Average aggregate inventory value}} \qquad \textbf{[8.1]}$$

The **cost of goods sold** is the annual cost for a company to produce the goods or services provided to customers; it is sometimes referred to as the *cost of revenue*. This does not include the selling and administrative expenses of the company. The **average aggregate inventory value** is the total value of all items held in inventory for the firm valued at cost. It includes the raw material, work-in-process, finished goods, and distribution inventory considered owned by the company.

Cost of goods sold

**Average aggregate
inventory value**

Inventory in the Supply Chain—Fast-Food Restaurant

exhibit 8.10

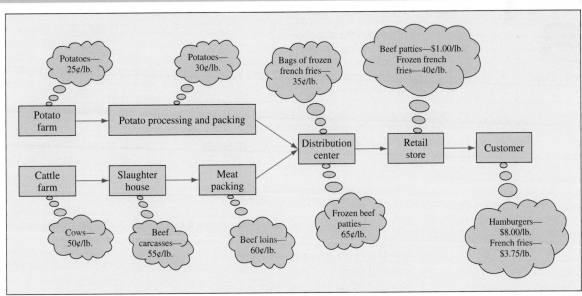

Good inventory turnover values vary by industry and the type of products being handled. At one extreme, a grocery store chain may turn inventory over 100 times per year. Values of six to seven are typical for manufacturing firms.

Weeks of supply   In many situations, particularly when distribution inventory is dominant, **weeks of supply** is the preferred measure. This is a measure of how many weeks' worth of inventory is in the system at a particular point in time. The calculation is as follows:

$$\text{Weeks of supply} = \left(\frac{\text{Average aggregate inventory value}}{\text{Cost of goods sold}}\right) \times 52 \text{ weeks} \qquad \textbf{[8.2]}$$

When company financial reports cite inventory turnover and weeks of supply, we can assume that the measures are being calculated firmwide. We show an example of this type of calculation in the example that follows using Dell Computer data. These calculations, though, can be done on individual entities within the organization. For example, we might be interested in the production raw materials inventory turnover or the weeks of supply associated with the warehousing operation of a firm. In these cases, the cost would be that associated with the total amount of inventory that runs through the specific inventory. In some very-low-inventory operations, days or even hours are a better unit of time for measuring supply.

A firm considers inventory an investment because the intent is for it to be used in the future. Inventory ties up funds that could be used for other purposes, and a firm may have to borrow money to finance the inventory investment. The objective is to have the proper amount of inventory and to have it in the correct locations in the supply chain. Determining the correct amount of inventory to have in each position requires a thorough analysis of the supply chain coupled with the competitive priorities that define the market for the company's products.

Example 8.2: Inventory Turnover Calculation

Dell Computer reported the following information in its 2005 annual report (all dollar amounts are expressed in millions):

Step by Step

Net revenue (fiscal year 2005)	$49,205
Cost of revenue (fiscal year 2005)	$40,190
Production materials on hand (28 January 2005)	$228
Work-in-process and finished goods on hand (28 January 2005)	$231
Days of supply in inventory	4 days

The cost of revenue corresponds to what we call cost of goods sold. One might think that U.S. companies, at least, would use a common accounting terminology, but this is not true. The inventory turnover calculation is

$$\text{Inventory turnover} = \frac{40{,}190}{228 + 231} = 87.56 \text{ turns per year}$$

This is amazing performance for a high-tech company, but it explains much of why the company is such a financial success.

The corresponding weeks of supply calculation is

$$\text{Weeks of supply} = \left(\frac{228 + 231}{40{,}190}\right) \times 52 = .59 \text{ week} \ \bullet$$

SUMMARY

Strategic sourcing is important in business today. Outsourcing is an important way to reduce cost while improving the strategic focus of a firm. Many companies have enjoyed significant success as a result of the unique ways in which they work with their suppliers. Many firms have adopted sourcing strategies that incorporate criteria that consider sustainable goals related to the environment and people.

Measures of sourcing efficiency are inventory turnover and weeks of supply. Efficient processes should be used for functional products, and responsive processes for innovative products. This alignment of sourcing strategy and product demand characteristics is extremely important to the operational success of a company.

Companies that face diverse sourcing, production, and distribution decisions need to weigh the costs associated with materials, transportation, production, warehousing, and distribution to develop a comprehensive network designed to minimize costs and preserve the environments.

Key Terms

Strategic sourcing The development and management of supplier relationships to acquire goods and services in a way that aids in achieving the immediate needs of a business.

Vendor managed inventory When a customer allows the supplier to manage an item or group of items.

Bullwhip effect The variability in demand is magnified as we move from the customer to the producer in the supply chain.

Functional products Staples that people buy in a wide range of retail outlets, such as grocery stores and gas stations.

Innovative products Products such as fashionable clothes and personal computers that typically have a life cycle of just a few months.

Outsourcing Moving some of a firm's internal activities and decision responsibility to outside providers.

Logistics Management functions that support the complete cycle of material flow: from the purchase and internal control of production materials; to the planning and control of work-in-process; to the purchasing, shipping, and distribution of the finished product.

Total cost of ownership (TCO) Estimate of the cost of an item that includes all the costs related to the procurement and use of the item including disposing the item after its useful life.

Inventory turnover and weeks of supply Measures of supply chain efficiency that are mathematically the inverse of one another.

Cost of goods sold The annual cost for a company to produce the goods or services provided to customers.

Average aggregate inventory value The total value of all items held in inventory for the firm, valued at cost.

Weeks of supply A measure of how many weeks' worth of inventory is in the system at a particular point in time.

Formula Review

$$\text{Inventory turnover} = \frac{\text{Cost of goods sold}}{\text{Average aggregate inventory value}} \qquad [8.1]$$

$$\text{Weeks of supply} = \left(\frac{\text{Average aggregate inventory value}}{\text{Cost of goods sold}} \right) \times 52 \text{ weeks} \qquad [8.2]$$

Review and Discussion Questions

1 What recent changes have caused supply chain management to gain importance?
2 With so much productive capacity and room for expansion in the United States, why would a company based in the United States choose to purchase items from a foreign firm? Discuss the pros and cons.
3 Describe the differences between functional and innovative products.
4 What are characteristics of efficient, responsive, risk-hedging, and agile supply chains? Can a supply chain be both efficient and responsive? Risk-hedging and agile? Why or why not?
5 As a supplier, which factors about a buyer (your potential customer) would you consider to be important in setting up a long-term relationship?
6 Describe how outsourcing works. Why would a firm want to outsource?

Problems

1 One of your Taiwanese suppliers has bid on a new line of molded plastic parts that is currently being assembled at your plant. The supplier has bid $0.10 per part, given a forecasted demand of 200,000 parts in year 1; 300,000 in year 2; and 500,000 in year 3. Shipping and handling of parts from the supplier's factory is estimated at $0.01 per unit. Additional inventory handling charges should amount to $0.005 per unit. Finally, administrative costs are estimated at $20 per month.

   Although your plant is able to continue producing the part, the plant would need to invest in another molding machine, which would cost $10,000. Direct materials can be purchased for $0.05 per unit. Direct labor is estimated at $0.03 per unit plus a 50 percent surcharge for benefits; indirect labor is estimated at $0.011 per unit plus 50 percent benefits. Up-front engineering and design costs will amount to $30,000. Finally, management has insisted that overhead be allocated if the parts are made in-house at a rate of 100 percent of direct labor cost. The firm uses a cost of capital of 15 percent per year.

   What should you do, continue to produce in-house or accept the bid from your Taiwanese supplier?

2 Your company assembles five different models of a motor scooter that is sold in specialty stores in the United States. The company uses the same engine for all five models. You have been given the assignment of choosing a supplier for these engines for the coming year. Due to the size of your warehouse and other administrative restrictions, you must order the engines in lot sizes of 1,000 each. Because of the unique characteristics of the engine, special tooling is needed during the manufacturing process which you agree to reimburse the supplier. Your assistant has obtained quotes from two reliable engine suppliers and you need to decide which to use. The following data has been collected:

Requirements (annual forecast)	12,000 units
Weight per engine	22 pounds
Order processing cost	$125 per order
Inventory carry cost	20 percent of the average value of inventory per year

Note: Assume that half of lot size is in inventory on average (1,000/2 = 500 units).

Two qualified suppliers have submitted the following quotations:

UNIT PRICE	SUPPLIER 1	SUPPLIER 2
1 to 999 units/order	$ 510.00	$505.00
1,000 to 2,999 units/order	500.00	498.00
3,000 + units/order	490.00	488.00
Tooling costs	$22,000	$20,000
Distance	125 miles	100 miles

Your assistant has obtained the following freight rates from your carrier:

| Truckload (40,000 each load): | $0.80 per ton-mile |
| Less-than-truckload: | $1.20 per ton-mile |

Note: Per ton-mile = 2,000 lbs. per mile

   a. Perform a total cost of ownership analysis and select a supplier.

   b. If you could move the lot size up to ship in truckload quantities would your supplier selection change?

3 The McDonald's fast-food restaurant on campus sells an average of 4,000 quarter-pound hamburgers each week. Hamburger patties are resupplied twice a week, and on average the store has 350 pounds of hamburger in stock. Assume that the hamburger costs $1.00 a pound. What is the inventory turnover for the hamburger patties? On average, how many days of supply are on hand?

4 The U.S. Airfilter company has hired you as a supply chain consultant. The company makes air filters for residential heating and air-conditioning systems. These filters are made in a single plant located in Louisville, Kentucky, in the United States. They are distributed to retailers through wholesale centers in 100 locations in the United States, Canada, and Europe. You have collected the following data relating to the value of inventory in the U.S. Airfilter supply chain:

	QUARTER 1 (JANUARY THROUGH MARCH)	QUARTER 2 (APRIL THROUGH JUNE)	QUARTER 3 (JULY THROUGH SEPTEMBER)	QUARTER 4 (OCTOBER THROUGH DECEMBER)
Sales (total quarter):				
United States	300	350	405	375
Canada	75	60	75	70
Europe	30	33	20	15
COST OF GOODS SOLD (TOTAL QUARTER)	280	295	340	350
RAW MATERIALS AT THE LOUISVILLE PLANT (END-OF-QUARTER)	50	40	55	60
WORK-IN-PROCESS AND FINISHED GOODS AT THE LOUISVILLE PLANT (END-OF-QUARTER)	100	105	120	150
DISTRIBUTION CENTER INVENTORY (END-OF-QUARTER):				
UNITED STATES	25	27	23	30
CANADA	10	11	15	16
EUROPE	5	4	5	5

ALL AMOUNTS IN MILLIONS OF U.S. DOLLARS

Excel: U.S. Airfilter

   a. What is the average inventory turnover for the firm?

   b. If you were given the assignment to increase inventory turnover, what would you focus on? Why?

   c. The company reported that it used $500M worth of raw material during the year. On average, how many weeks of supply of raw material are on hand at the factory?

CASE: Pepe Jeans

Pepe began to produce and sell denim jeans in the early 1970s in the United Kingdom and has achieved enormous growth. Pepe's success was the result of a unique approach in a product market dominated by strong brands and limited variety. Pepe presented a range of jeans styles that offered a better fit than traditional five-pocket Western jeans (such as those made by Levi Strauss in the United States)—particularly for female customers. The Pepe range of basic styles is modified each season, but each style keeps its identity with a slightly whimsical name featured prominently on the jeans and on the point-of-sale material. Variations such as modified washes, leather trim, and even designer wear marks are applied to respond to changing fashion trends. To learn more about Pepe and its products, visit its Web site at http://www.pepejeans.com.

Pepe's brand strength is such that the company can demand a retail price that averages about £45 (£1 = $1.8) for its standard products. A high percentage of Pepe sales are through about 1,500 independent outlets throughout the United Kingdom. The company maintains contact with its independent retailers via a group of approximately 10 agents, who are self-employed and work exclusively for Pepe. Each agent is responsible for retailers in a particular area of the country.

Pepe is convinced that a good relationship with the independent retailers is vital to its success. The agent meets with each independent retailer three to four times each year in order to present the new collections and to take sales orders. Because the number of accounts for each agent is so large, contact is often achieved by holding a presentation in a hotel for several retailers. Agents take orders from retailers for six-month delivery. After Pepe receives an order, the retailer has only one week in which to cancel because of the need to place immediate firm orders in Hong Kong to meet the delivery date. The company has had a long-standing policy of not holding any inventory of jeans in the United Kingdom.

After an order is taken and confirmed, the rest of the process up to delivery is administered from the Pepe office in Willesden. The status of orders can be checked from a Web site maintained by Pepe. The actual orders are sent to a sourcing agent in Hong Kong who arranges for manufacturing the jeans. The sourcing agent handles all the details associated with materials, fabrication, and shipping the completed jeans to the retailer. Pepe has an outstanding team of young in-house designers who are responsible for developing new styles and the accompanying point-of-sale material. Jeans are made to specifications provided by this team. The team works closely with the Hong Kong sourcing agent to ensure that the jeans are made properly and that the material used is of the highest quality.

A recent survey of the independent retailers indicated some growing problems. The independents praised the fit, quality, and variety of Pepe's jeans, although many thought that they had become much less of a trendsetter than in their early days. It was felt that Pepe's variety of styles and quality were the company's key advantage over the competition.

Global

Supply Chain

However, the independents were unhappy with Pepe's requirements to place firm orders six months in advance with no possibility of amendment, cancellation, or repeat ordering. Some claimed that the inflexible order system forced them to order less, resulting in stockouts of particular sizes and styles. The retailers estimated that Pepe's sales would increase by about 10 percent with a more flexible ordering system.

The retailers expected to have some slow-moving inventory, but the six-month order lead time made it difficult to accurately order and worsened the problem. Because the fashion market was so impulsive, the current favorites were often not in vogue six months in the future. On the other hand, when demand exceeded expectations, it took a long time to fill the gap. What the retailers wanted was some method of limited returns, exchange, or reordering to overcome the worst of these problems. Pepe was feeling some pressure to respond to these complaints because some of Pepe's smaller competitors offered delivery in only a few days.

Pepe has enjoyed considerable financial success with its current business model. Sales last year were approximately £200M. Cost of sales was approximately 40 percent, operating expenses 28 percent, and profit before taxes nearly 32 percent of sales. The company has no long-term debt and has a very healthy cash position.

Pepe was feeling considerable pressure and felt that a change was going to be needed soon. In evaluating alternatives the company found that the easiest would be to work with the Hong Kong sourcing agent to reduce the lead time associated with orders. The agent agreed that the lead time could be shortened, possibly to as little as six weeks, but costs would increase significantly. Currently, the agent collects orders over a period of time and about every two weeks puts these orders out on bid to about 1,000 potential suppliers. The sourcing agent estimated that costs might go up 30 percent if the lead time were shortened to six weeks. Even with the significant increase in cost, consistent delivery schedules would be difficult to keep.

The sourcing agent suggested that Pepe consider building a finishing operation in the United Kingdom. The agent indicated that a major retail chain in the United States had moved to this type of structure with considerable success. Basically, all the finishing operation did for the U.S. retail chain was apply different washes to the jeans to give them different "worn" looks. The U.S. operation also took orders for the retail stores and shipped the orders. The U.S. firm found that it could give two-day response time to the retail stores.

The sourcing agent indicated that costs for the basic jeans (jeans where the wash has not been applied) could probably be reduced by 10 percent because the volumes would be higher. In addition, lead time for the basic jeans could be reduced to approximately three months because the finishing step would be eliminated and the orders would be larger.

The Pepe designers found this an interesting idea, so they visited the U.S. operation to see how the system worked. They found that they would have to keep about six weeks' supply of basic jeans on hand in the United Kingdom and that they would have to invest in about £1,000,000 worth of equipment. They estimated that it would cost about £500,000 to operate the facility each year. They could locate the facility in the basement of the current Willesden office building, and the renovations would cost about £300,000.

Questions

1 Acting as an outside consultant, what would you recommend that Pepe do? Given the data in the case, perform a financial analysis to evaluate the alternatives that you have identified. (Assume that the new inventory could be valued at six weeks' worth of the yearly cost of sales. Use a 30 percent inventory carrying cost rate.) Calculate a payback period for each alternative.

2 Are there other alternatives that Pepe should consider?

Source: The idea for this case came from a case titled "Pepe Jeans" written by D. Bramley and C. John of the London Business School. Pepe Jeans is a real company, but the data given in the case do not represent actual company data.

Footnotes

1 M. L. Fisher, "What Is the Right Supply Chain for Your Product?" *Harvard Business Review,* March–April 1997, pp.105–16.

2 Hau L. Lee, "Aligning Supply Chain Strategies with Product Uncertainties," *California Management Review* 44, no. 3 (Spring 2002), pp. 105–19. Copyright © 2002 by the Regents of the University of California. By permission of the Regents.

3 "Have Factory Will Travel," *The Economist,* February 12–18, 2000, pp. 61–62.

4 Adapted from Martha Craumer, "How to Think Strategically about Outsourcing," *Harvard Management Update,* May 2002, p. 4.

5 See David Burt, et al. *Supply Management.* 8th ed. McGraw-Hill/Irwin, 2010, pp. 306–10.

6 Example is from David Burt, et al. *Supply Management.* 8th ed. McGraw-Hill/Irwin, 2010, p. 311.

Super Quiz

1 Refers to how common an item is or how many substitutes might be available.

2 When a customer allows the supplier to manage an item or group of items.

3 A phenomenon characterized by increased variation in ordering as we move from the customer to the manufacturer in the supply chain.

4 Products that satisfy basic needs and do not change much over time.

5 Products with short life cycles and typically high profit margins.

6 A supply chain that must deal with high levels of both supply and demand uncertainty.

7 In order to cope with high levels of supply uncertainty a firm would use this strategy to reduce risk.

8 Used to describe functions related to the flow of material in a supply chain.

9 When a firm works with suppliers to look for opportunities to save money and benefit the environment.

10 Refers to an estimate of the cost of an item that includes all costs related to the procurement and use of an item, including the costs of disposing after its useful life.

1. Specificity 2. Vendor managed inventory 3. Bullwhip effect 4. Functional products 5. Innovative products 6. Agile supply chain 7. Multiple sources of supply (pooling) 8. Logistics 9. Green sourcing 10. Total cost of ownership.

Selected Bibliography

Bowersox, D. J.; D. J. Closs; and M. B. Cooper. *Supply Chain and Logistics Management.* New York: Irwin/McGraw-Hill, 2002.

Burt, D. N.; D. W. Dobler; and S. L. Starling. *World Class Supply Management^SM: The Key to Supply Chain Management.* 7th ed. New York: McGraw-Hill/Irwin, 2003.

Chopra, S., and P. Meindl. *Supply Chain Management: Strategy, Planning, and Operations.* 2nd ed. Upper Saddle River, NJ: Prentice Hall, 2003.

Greaver II, M. F. *Strategic Outsourcing: A Structured Approach to Outsourcing Decisions and Initiatives.* New York: American Management Association, 1999.

Hayes, R.; G. Pisano; D. Upton; and S. Wheelwright. *Operations Strategy and Technology: Pursuing the Competitive Edge.* New York: John Wiley & Sons, 2005.

Simchi-Levi, D.; P. Kaminski; and E. Simchi-Levi. *Supply Chain Management.* 2nd ed. New York: McGraw-Hill, 2003.

Vollmann, T.; W. L. Berry; D. C. Whybark; and F. R. Jacobs. *Manufacturing Planning and Control Systems for Supply Chain Management: The Definitive Guide for Professionals.* New York: McGraw-Hill/Irwin, 2004.

CHAPTER 9

LOCATION, LOGISTICS, AND DISTRIBUTION

After reading the chapter you will:

- Describe what a third-party logistics provider is.
- Assess the major issues that need to be considered in locating a plant or warehouse facility.
- Set up the transportation model to analyze location problems and how to use Excel Solver to find solutions to these models.
- Understand the centroid method for locating entities such as cell phone communication towers.
- Know how a factor-rating system can be used to narrow potential location sites.

249	FedEx: A Leading Global Logistics Company	
250	Logistics	
		Logistics defined
		International logistics defined
		Third-party logistics company defined
251	Decisions Related to Logistics	
	Cross-Docking	Cross-docking defined
		Hub-and-spoke systems defined
253	Issues in Facility Location	
		Free trade zone defined
		Trading blocs defined
255	Plant Location Methods	
	Factor-Rating Systems	Factor-rating systems defined
	Transportation Method of Linear Programming	Transportation method defined
		Centroid method defined
	Centroid Method	
261	Locating Service Facilities	
263	Summary	

267   Case: Applichem—The Transportation Problem

268   Super Quiz

FedEx: A Leading Global Logistics Company

Service

Supply Chain

FedEx provides a host of logistics solutions to its customers. Those services are segmented on the basis of types of customer needs, ranging from turnkey distribution centers to full-scale logistics services that incorporate expedited delivery. Following are some of the major services provided to the business customer:

FedEx Distribution Centers: These centers provide turnkey warehousing services to businesses, using a network of warehouses in the United States and abroad. This service is targeted particularly at time-critical businesses. Goods stored in these centers are continuously available for 24-hour deliveries.

FedEx Returns Management: FedEx Return solutions are designed to streamline the return area of a company's supply chain. These process-intelligent tools give customers services that offer pickup, delivery, and online status tracking for items that need to be returned.

Other Value-Added Services: FedEx offers many other value-added services to its customers. One example is a merge-in-transit service offered to many customers that require rapid delivery. For example, under the merge-in-transit program, for a shipper of computers, FedEx could store peripheral products such as monitors and printers in its Memphis air hub and match those products up with the computer en route to a customer.

LOGISTICS

Supply Chain

A major issue in designing a great supply chain for manufactured goods is determining the way those items are moved from the manufacturing plant to the customer. For consumer products this often involves moving product from the manufacturing plant to a warehouse and then to a retail store. You probably do not think about this often, but consider all those items with "Made in China" on the label. That sweatshirt probably has made a trip longer than you may ever make. If you live in Chicago in the United States and the sweatshirt is made in the Fujian region of China, that sweatshirt traveled over 6,600 miles, or 10,600 kilometers, nearly halfway around the world, to get to the retail store where you bought it. To keep the price of the sweatshirt down, that trip must be made as efficiently as possible. There is no telling how that sweatshirt made the trip. It might have been flown in an airplane or might have traveled in a combination of vehicles, possibly going by truck part of the way and by boat or plane the rest. Logistics is about this movement of goods through the supply chain.

Logistics

The Association for Operations Management defines **logistics** as "the art and science of obtaining, producing, and distributing material and product in the proper place and in proper quantities." This is a fairly broad definition, and this chapter will focus on how to analyze where we locate warehouses and plants and how to evaluate the movement of materials to and from those locations. The term **international logistics** refers to managing these functions when the movement is on a global scale. Clearly, if the China-made sweatshirt is sold in the United States or Europe, this involves international logistics.

International logistics

There are companies that specialize in logistics, such as United Parcel Service (UPS), Federal Express (FedEx), and DHL. These global companies are in the business of moving everything from flowers to industrial equipment. Today a manufacturing company most often will contract with one of those companies to handle many of its logistics functions. In

this case, those transportation companies often are called a **third-party logistics company**. The most basic function would be simply moving the goods from one place to another. The logistics company also may provide additional services such as warehouse management, inventory control, and other customer service functions.

Logistics is big business, accounting for 8 to 9 percent of the U.S. gross domestic product, and growing. Today's modern, efficient warehouse and distribution centers are the heart of logistics. These centers are carefully managed and efficiently operated to ensure the secure storage and quick flow of goods, services, and related information from the point of origin to the point of consumption.

DECISIONS RELATED TO LOGISTICS

The problem of deciding how best to transport goods from plants to customers is a complex one that affects the cost of a product. Major trade-offs related to the cost of transporting the product, speed of delivery, and flexibility to react to changes are involved. Information systems play a major role in coordinating activities and include activities such as allocating resources, managing inventory levels, scheduling, and order tracking. A full discussion of these systems is beyond the scope of this book, but we cover basic inventory control and scheduling in later chapters.

A key decision area is deciding how material will be transported. The Logistics-System Design Matrix shown in Exhibit 9.1 depicts the basic alternatives. There are six widely recognized modes of transportation: highway (trucks), water (ships), air (aircraft), rail (trains), pipelines, and hand delivery. Each mode is uniquely suited to handle certain types of products, as described next:

- **Highway (truck).** Actually, few products are moved without some highway transportation. The highway offers great flexibility for moving goods to virtually any

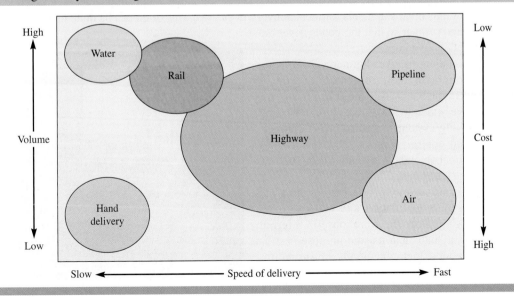

Logistics-System Design Matrix: Framework Describing Logistics Processes

exhibit 9.1

location not separated by water. Size of the product, weight, and liquid or bulk can all be accommodated with this mode.

- **Water (ship).** Very high capacity and very low cost, but transit times are slow, and large areas of the world are not directly accessible to water carriers. This mode is especially useful for bulk items such as oil, coal, and chemical products.
- **Air.** Fast but expensive. Small, light, expensive items are most appropriate for this mode of transportation.
- **Rail (trains).** This is a fairly low-cost alternative, but transit times can be long and may be subject to variability. The suitability of rail can vary depending on the rail infrastructure. The European infrastructure is highly developed, making this an attractive alternative compared to trucks, while in the United States, the infrastructure has declined over the last 50 years, making it less attractive.
- **Pipelines.** This is highly specialized and limited to liquids, gases, and solids in slurry forms. No packaging is needed and the costs per mile are low. The initial cost to build a pipeline is very high.
- **Hand Delivery.** This is the last step in many supply chains. Getting the product in the customer's hand is a relatively slow and costly activity due to the high labor content.

Few companies use a single mode of transportation. Multimodal solutions are the norm, and finding the correct multimode strategies can be a significant problem. The problem of coordination and scheduling the carriers requires comprehensive information systems capable of tracking goods through the system. Standardized containers often are used so that a product can be transferred efficiently from a truck to an airplane or ship.

Cross-Docking

Cross-docking

Special consolidation warehouses are used when shipments from various sources are pulled together and combined into larger shipments with a common destination. This improves the efficiency of the entire system. **Cross-docking** is an approach used in these consolidation warehouses, where rather than making larger shipments, large shipments are broken down into small shipments for local delivery in an area. This often can be done in a coordinated manner so that the goods never are stored in inventory.

Retailers receive shipments from many suppliers in their regional warehouses and immediately sort those shipments for delivery to individual stores by using cross-docking systems coordinated by computerized control systems. This results in a minimal amount of inventory being carried in the warehouses.

Hub-and-spoke systems

Hub-and-spoke systems combine the idea of consolidation and that of cross-docking. Here the warehouse is referred to as a "hub" and its sole purpose is sorting goods. Incoming goods are sorted immediately to consolidation areas, where each area is designated for shipment to a specific location. Hubs are located in strategic locations near the geographic center of the region they are to serve to minimize the distance a good must travel.

Designing a system is an interesting and complex task. The following section focuses on the plant and warehouse location problem as representative of the types of logistics decisions that need to be made. Logistics is a broad topic, and its elements evolve as the value-added services provided by major logistics vendors expand. Having the proper network design is fundamental to efficiency in the industry.

ISSUES IN FACILITY LOCATION

Global

The problem of facility location is faced by both new and existing businesses, and its solution is critical to a company's eventual success. An important element in designing a company's supply chain is the location of its facilities. For instance, 3M has moved a significant part of its corporate activity, including R&D, to the more temperate climate of Austin, Texas. Toys "Я" Us has opened a location in Japan as a part of its global strategy. Disney chose Paris, France, for its European theme park, and BMW assembles the Z3 sports car in South Carolina. Manufacturing and service companies' location decisions are guided by a variety of criteria defined by competitive imperatives. Criteria that influence manufacturing plant and warehouse location planning are discussed next.

Proximity to Customers   For example, Japan's NTN Drive shafts built a major plant in Columbus, Indiana, to be closer to major automobile manufacturing plants in the United States—whose buyers want their goods delivered yesterday. Such proximity also helps ensure that customer needs are incorporated into products being developed and built.

Business Climate   A favorable business climate can include the presence of similar-sized businesses, the presence of companies in the same industry, and, in the case of international locations, the presence of other foreign companies. Probusiness government legislation and local government intervention to facilitate businesses locating in an area via subsidies, tax abatements, and other support are also factors.

Total Costs   The objective is to select a site with the lowest total cost. This includes regional costs, inbound distribution costs, and outbound distribution costs. Land, construction, labor, taxes, and energy costs make up the regional costs. In addition, there are hidden costs that are difficult to measure. These involve (1) excessive moving of preproduction material between locations before final delivery to the customers and (2) loss of customer responsiveness arising from locating away from the main customer base.

Infrastructure   Adequate road, rail, air, and sea transportation is vital. Energy and telecommunications requirements also must be met. In addition, the local government's willingness to invest in upgrading infrastructure to the levels required may be an incentive to select a specific location.

Quality of Labor   The educational and skill levels of the labor pool must match the company's needs. Even more important are the willingness and ability to learn.

Suppliers   A high-quality and competitive supplier base makes a given location suitable. The proximity of important suppliers' plants also supports lean production methods.

Other Facilities   The location of other plants or distribution centers of the same company may influence a new facility's location in the network. Issues of product mix and capacity are strongly interconnected to the location decision in this context.

Free trade zone

Global

Free Trade Zones   A foreign trade zone or a **free trade zone** is typically a closed facility (under the supervision of the customs department) into which foreign goods can be brought without being subject to the normal customs requirements. There are about 260 such free trade zones in the United States today. Such specialized locations also exist in other countries. Manufacturers in free trade zones can use imported components in the final product and delay payment of customs duties until the product is shipped into the host country.

Political Risk   The fast-changing geopolitical scenes in numerous nations present exciting, challenging opportunities. But the extended phase of transformation that many countries are undergoing makes the decision to locate in those areas extremely difficult. Political risks in both the country of location and the host country influence location decisions.

Government Barriers   Barriers to enter and locate in many countries are being removed today through legislation. Yet many nonlegislative and cultural barriers should be considered in location planning.

Trading blocs

Trading Blocs   The Central America Free Trade Agreement (CAFTA) is one of the new **trading blocs** in our hemisphere. Such agreements influence location decisions, both within and outside trading bloc countries. Firms typically locate, or relocate, within a bloc to take advantage of new market opportunities or lower total costs afforded by the trading agreement. Other companies (those outside the trading bloc countries) decide on locations within the bloc so as not to be disqualified from competing in the new market. Examples include the location of various Japanese auto manufacturing plants in Europe before 1992 as well as recent moves by many communications and financial services companies into Mexico in a post-NAFTA environment.

Environmental Regulation   The environmental regulations that impact a certain industry in a given location should be included in the location decision. Besides measurable cost implications, these regulations influence the relationship with the local community.

Host Community   The host community's interest in having the plant in its midst is a necessary part of the evaluation process. Local educational facilities and the broader issue of quality of life are also important.

Competitive Advantage   An important decision for multinational companies is the nation in which to locate the home base for each distinct business. Porter suggests that a company can have different home bases for distinct businesses or segments. Competitive advantage is created at a home base where strategy is set, the core product and process technology are created, and a critical mass of production takes place. So a company should move its home base to a country that stimulates innovation and

Global

Honda announced that it will build its sixth assembly plant in Greensburg, Indiana. As the *Chicago Tribune* put it, the decision was based on "Location, location, location. Indiana had it. Illinois and Ohio didn't." Honda will invest $550 million to build the operation which will employ 2,000 workers when it starts producing 200,000 vehicles annually in 2008. What specific vehicles or models will be built in Greensburg was not announced, but it will be a "flex plant" capable of producing multiple models.

While Indiana officials confirmed promising Honda $141.5 million in incentives, Larry Jutte, a company executive, rejected the idea that handouts were a factor. "It wasn't a matter of incentives offered; that was never a consideration. It was a matter of logistics, the human factor, the infrastructure, and the location." He said the decision was based on being in close proximity to suppliers of parts, particularly the source of four-cylinder engines from Honda's operation in Anna, Ohio. The 1,700-acre Greensburg site is near I-74 and about 50 miles southwest of Indianapolis, and will be built with expansion as a possibility. Altogether, so far, Honda has invested $9 billion locating facilities in North America.

An interesting sidelight is that this plant will now be close to the Indy 500. "For more than 50 years, racing has been a key part of the Honda culture, and we use racing to help train our engineers," said Koichi Kondo, president and CEO of American Honda. "Last month the winning car at the Indy 500 was powered by a Honda engine. In fact all 33 cars in the race were powered by Honda engines." Amazingly, since Honda became the sole supplier of engines for the Indy 500 in 2006 and through the 2009 race, there have been no engine failures. Kondo said Honda and Indiana are beginning a long race together.

Sources: "Convenience Drives Indiana to Victory," *Chicago Tribune*—Business, June 29, 2006; http://blogs.edmunds.com/; http://corporate.honda.com/press; Motor Sport Forum, May 9, 2009.

provides the best environment for global competitiveness.[1] This concept can also be applied to domestic companies seeking to gain sustainable competitive advantage. It partly explains the southeastern states' recent emergence as the preferred corporate destination within the United States (that is, their business climate fosters innovation and low-cost production).

PLANT LOCATION METHODS

As we will see, there are many techniques available for identifying potential sites for plants or other types of facilities. The process required to narrow the decision down to a particular area can vary significantly depending on the type of business we are in and the competitive pressures that must be considered. As we have discussed, there are often many different criteria that need to be considered when selecting from the set of feasible sites.

In this section, we sample three different types of techniques that have proven to be very useful to many companies. The first is the *factor-rating system* that allows us to consider many different types of criteria using simple point-rating scales. Next, we consider the *transportation method of linear programming,* a powerful technique for estimating the cost of using a network of plants and warehouses. Following this, we consider the *centroid method,* a technique often used by communications companies (cell phone providers) to locate their transmission towers. Finally, later in the chapter we consider how service firms such as McDonald's and State Farm Insurance use statistical techniques to find desirable locations for their facilities.

Factor-Rating Systems

Factor-rating systems

Factor-rating systems are perhaps the most widely used of the general location techniques because they provide a mechanism to combine diverse factors in an easy-to-understand format.

By way of example, a refinery assigned the following range of point values to major factors affecting a set of possible sites:

	RANGE
Fuels in region	0 to 330
Power availability and reliability	0 to 200
Labor climate	0 to 100
Living conditions	0 to 100
Transportation	0 to 50
Water supply	0 to 10
Climate	0 to 50
Supplies	0 to 60
Tax policies and laws	0 to 20

Each site was then rated against each factor, and a point value was selected from its assigned range. The sums of assigned points for each site were then compared. The site with the most points was selected.

A major problem with simple point-rating schemes is that they do not account for the wide range of costs that may occur within each factor. For example, there may be only a few hundred dollars' difference between the best and worst locations on one factor and several thousands of dollars' difference between the best and the worst on another. The first factor may have the most points available to it but provide little help in making the location decision; the second may have few points available but potentially show a real difference in the value of locations. To deal with this problem, it has been suggested that points possible for each factor be derived using a weighting scale based on standard deviations of costs rather than simply total cost amounts. In this way, relative costs can be considered.

Transportation Method of Linear Programming

Transportation method

The **transportation method** is a special linear programming method. (Note that linear programming is developed in detail in Appendix A.) It gets its name from its application to problems involving transporting products from several sources to several destinations. The two common objectives of such problems are either (1) minimize the cost of shipping *n* units to *m* destinations or (2) maximize the profit of shipping *n* units to *m* destinations.

Example 9.1: U.S. Pharmaceutical Company

Suppose the U.S. Pharmaceutical Company has four factories supplying the warehouses of four major customers and its management wants to determine the minimum-cost shipping schedule for its monthly output to these customers. Factory supply, warehouse demands, and shipping costs per case for these drugs are shown in Exhibit 9.2.

The transportation matrix for this example appears in Exhibit 9.3, where supply availability at each factory is shown in the far right column and the warehouse demands are shown in the bottom row. The shipping costs are shown in the small boxes within the cells. For example, the cost to ship one unit from the Indianapolis factory to the customer warehouse in Columbus is $25. The actual flows would be shown in the cells intersecting the factory rows and warehouse columns.

Step by Step

Tutorial: Transportation Method Solver

---

exhibit 9.2

Data for U.S. Pharmaceutical Transportation Problem

					SHIPPING COSTS PER CASE (IN DOLLARS)			
FACTORY	SUPPLY	WAREHOUSE	DEMAND	FROM	To COLUMBUS	To ST. LOUIS	To DENVER	To LOS ANGELES
Indianapolis	15	Columbus	10	Indianapolis	$25	$35	$36	$60
Phoenix	6	St. Louis	12	Phoenix	55	30	25	25
New York	14	Denver	15	New York	40	50	80	90
Atlanta	11	Los Angeles	9	Atlanta	30	40	66	75

---

exhibit 9.3

Transportation Matrix for U.S. Pharmaceutical Problem

From \ To	Columbus	St. Louis	Denver	Los Angeles	Factory supply
Indianapolis	25	35	36	60	15
Phoenix	55	30	25	25	6
New York	40	50	80	90	14
Atlanta	30	40	66	75	11
Destination requirements	10	12	15	9	46 / 46

SOLUTION

This problem can be solved by using Microsoft Excel's Solver function. If you are not familiar with the Solver, you should study Appendix F, "Linear Programming Using the Excel Solver." Exhibit 9.4 shows how the problem can be set up in the spreadsheet. Cells B6 through E6 contain the requirement for each customer warehouse. Cells F2 through F5 contain the amount that can be supplied from each plant. Cells B2 through E5 are the cost of shipping one unit for each potential plant and warehouse combination.

Cells for the solution of the problem are B9 through E12. These cells can initially be left blank when setting up the spreadsheet. Column cells F9 through F12 are the sum of each row, indicating how much is actually being shipped from each factory in the candidate solution. Similarly, row cells B13 through E13 are sums of the amount being shipped to each customer in the candidate solution. The Excel Sum function can be used to calculate these values.

The cost of the candidate solution is calculated in cells B16 through E19. Multiplying the amount shipped in the candidate solution by the cost per unit of shipping over that particular route makes this calculation. For example, multiplying B2 by B9 in cell B16 gives the cost of shipping between Indianapolis and Columbus for the candidate solution. The total cost shown in cell F20 is the sum of all these individual costs.

To solve the problem, the Excel Solver application needs to be accessed. The Solver is found by selecting Tools and then Solver from the Excel menu. A screen similar to what is shown below should appear. If you cannot find Solver at that location, the required add-in might not have been added when Excel was initially installed on your computer. Solver can easily be added if you have your original Excel installation disk.

Solver parameters now need to be set. First set the target cell. This is the cell where the total cost associated with the solution is calculated. In our sample problem, this is cell F20. Next we need to indicate that we are minimizing this cell. Selecting the "Min" button does this. The location of our solution is indicated in the "Changing Cells." These cells are B9 through E12 in our example.

**Tutorial:
Intro to
Solver**

**Tutorial:
Intro to
Solver**

---

exhibit 9.4   Excel Screen Showing the U.S. Pharmaceutical Problem

**Excel: US
Pharmaceutical**

Microsoft Excel - US Pharmaceutical.xls

File Edit View Insert Format Tools Data Window Help

F20   = =SUM(B16:E19)

	A	B	C	D	E	F
1	From/To	Columbus	St. Louis	Denver	Los Angeles	Factory Supply
2	Indianapolis	25	35	36	60	15
3	Phoenix	55	30	25	25	6
4	New York	40	50	80	90	14
5	Atlanta	30	40	66	75	11
6	Requirements	10	12	15	9	
7						
8	Candidate Solution					Total Shipped
9	Indianapolis	0	0	15	0	15
10	Phoenix	0	0	0	6	6
11	New York	10	4	0	0	14
12	Atlanta	0	8	0	3	11
13	Total Supplied	10	12	15	9	
14						
15	Cost Calculations					
16	Indianapolis	0	0	540	0	
17	Phoenix	0	0	0	150	
18	New York	400	200	0	0	
19	Atlanta	0	320	0	225	
20					Total Cost	$1,835
21						
22						

US Pharmaceutical

Ready   NUM

Next we need to indicate the constraints for our problem. For our transportation problem we need to be sure that customer demand is met and that we do not exceed the capacity of our manufacturing plants. To ensure that demand is met, click on "Add" and highlight the range of cells where we have calculated the total amount being shipped to each customer. This range is B13 to E13 in our example. Next select "=" indicating that we want the amount shipped to equal demand. Finally, on the right side enter the range of cells where the actual customer demand is stated in our spreadsheet. This range is B6 to E6 in our example.

The second set of constraints that ensures that the capacity of our manufacturing plants is not exceeded is entered similarly. The range of cells that indicated how much is being shipped from each factory is F9 to F12. These values need to be less than or equal to (<=) the capacity of each factory, which is in cells F2 to F5. To set up the Solver, a few options need to be set as well. Click on the "Options" button and the following screen should appear:

Excel® Screen shots from Microsoft® Excel © 2007 Microsoft Corporation.

Two options need to be set for solving transportation problems. First we need "Assume Linear Model." This tells the Solver that there are no nonlinear calculations in our spreadsheet. This is important because the Solver can use a very efficient algorithm to calculate the optimal solution to this problem if this condition exists. Next the "Assume Non-Negative" box needs to be checked. This tells Solver that the values in our solution need to be greater than or equal to zero. In transportation problems, shipping negative quantities does not make any sense. Click "OK" to return to the main Solver box, and then click "Solve" to actually solve the problem. Solver will notify you that it found a solution. Indicate that you want that solution saved. Finally, click OK to go back to the main spreadsheet. The solution should be in cells B9 to E12.

The transportation method can be used to solve many different types of problems if it is applied innovatively. For example, it can be used to test the cost impact of different candidate locations on the entire production—distribution network. To do this we might add a new row that contains the unit shipping cost from a factory in a new location, say, Dallas, to the existing set of customer warehouses, along with the total amount it could supply.

We could then solve this particular matrix for minimum total cost. Next we would replace the factory located in Dallas in the same row of the matrix with a factory at a different location, Houston, and again solve for minimum total cost. Assuming the factories in Dallas and Houston would be identical in other important respects, the location resulting in the lowest total cost for the network would be selected.

For additional information about using the Solver, see Appendix A, "Linear Programming Using the Excel Solver." ●

Centroid Method

Centroid method

The **centroid method** is a technique for locating single facilities that considers the existing facilities, the distances between them, and the volumes of goods to be shipped. The technique is often used to locate intermediate or distribution warehouses. In its simplest form, this method assumes that inbound and outbound transportation costs are equal, and it does not include special shipping costs for less than full loads.

Another major application of the centroid method today is the location of communication towers in urban areas. Examples include radio, TV, and cell phone towers. In this application the goal is to find sites that are near clusters of customers, thus ensuring clear radio signals.

The centroid method begins by placing the existing locations on a coordinate grid system. Coordinates are usually based on longitude and latitude measures due to the rapid adoption of GPS systems for mapping locations. To keep it simple for our examples, we use arbitrary X, Y coordinates. Exhibit 9.5 shows an example of a grid layout.

The centroid is found by calculating the X and Y coordinates that result in the minimal transportation cost. We use the formulas

$$C_x = \frac{\Sigma d_{ix} V_i}{\Sigma V_i} \qquad C_y = \frac{\Sigma d_{iy} V_i}{\Sigma V_i} \qquad \text{[9.1]}$$

exhibit 9.5   Grid Map for Centroid Example

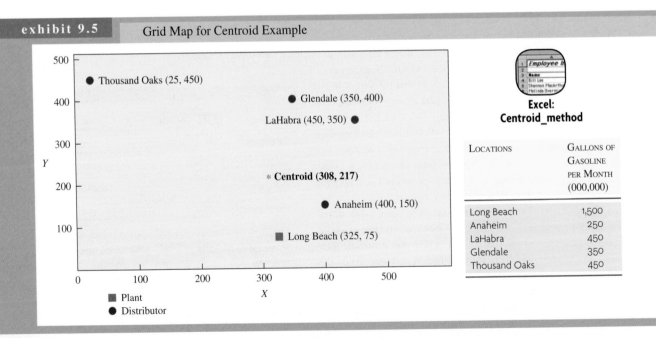

LOCATIONS	GALLONS OF GASOLINE PER MONTH (000,000)
Long Beach	1,500
Anaheim	250
LaHabra	450
Glendale	350
Thousand Oaks	450

where

C_x = X coordinate of the centroid
C_y = Y coordinate of the centroid
d_{ix} = X coordinate of the *i*th location
d_{iy} = Y coordinate of the *i*th location
V_i = Volume of goods moved to or from the *i*th location

Step by Step

Example 9.2: HiOctane Refining Company

The HiOctane Refining Company needs to locate an intermediate holding facility between its refining plant in Long Beach and its major distributors. Exhibit 9.5 shows the coordinate map and the amount of gasoline shipped to or from the plant and distributors.

In this example, for the Long Beach location (the first location), $d_{ix} = 325$, $d_{iy} = 75$, and $V_i = 1,500$.

SOLUTION

Using the information in Exhibit 9.5, we can calculate the coordinates of the centroid:

$$C_x = \frac{(325 \times 1,500) + (400 \times 250) + (450 \times 450) + (350 \times 350) + (25 \times 450)}{1,500 + 250 + 450 + 350 + 450}$$

$$= \frac{923,750}{3,000} = 307.9$$

$$C_y = \frac{(75 \times 1,500) + (150 \times 250) + (350 \times 450) + (400 \times 350) + (450 \times 450)}{1,500 + 250 + 450 + 350 + 450}$$

$$= \frac{650,000}{3,000} = 216.7$$

This gives management the X and Y coordinates of approximately 308 and 217, respectively, and provides an initial starting point to search for a new site. By examining the location of the calculated centroid on the grid map, we can see that it might be more cost-efficient to ship directly between the Long Beach plant and the Anaheim distributor than to ship via a warehouse near the centroid. Before a location decision is made, management would probably recalculate the centroid, changing the data to reflect this (that is, decrease the gallons shipped from Long Beach by the amount Anaheim needs and remove Anaheim from the formula). ●

LOCATING SERVICE FACILITIES

Service

Because of the variety of service firms and the relatively low cost of establishing a service facility compared to one for manufacturing, new service facilities are far more common than new factories and warehouses. Indeed, there are few communities in which rapid population growth has not been paralleled by concurrent rapid growth in retail outlets, restaurants, municipal services, and entertainment facilities.

Services typically have multiple sites to maintain close contact with customers. The location decision is closely tied to the market selection decision. If the target market is college-age groups, locations in retirement communities—despite desirability in terms of cost, resource availability, and so forth—are not viable alternatives. Market needs also affect the number of sites to be built and the size and characteristics of the sites. Whereas manufacturing location decisions are often made by minimizing costs, many service location decision techniques maximize the profit potential of various sites. Next we present a multiple regression model that can be used to help select good sites.

Step by Step

Example 9.3: Screening Hotel Location Sites

Selecting good sites is crucial to a hotel chain's success. Of the four major marketing considerations (price, product, promotion, and location), location and product have been shown to be most important for multisite firms. As a result, hotel chain owners who can pick good sites quickly have a distinct competitive advantage.

Exhibit 9.6 shows the initial list of variables included in a study to help a hotel chain screen potential locations for its new hotels. Data were collected on 57 existing sites. Analysis of the data identified the variables that correlated with operating profit in two years. (See Exhibit 9.7.)

exhibit 9.6 | Independent Variables Collected for the Initial Model-Building Stage

CATEGORY	NAME	DESCRIPTION
Competitive	INNRATE	Inn price
	PRICE	Room rate for the inn
	RATE	Average competitive room rate
	RMS 1	Hotel rooms within 1 mile
	RMSTOTAL	Hotel rooms within 3 miles
	ROOMSINN	Inn rooms
Demand generators	CIVILIAN	Civilian personnel on base
	COLLEGE	College enrollment
	HOSP1	Hospital beds within 1 mile
	HOSPTOTL	Hospital beds within 4 miles
	HVYIND	Heavy industrial employment
	LGTIND	Light industrial acreage
	MALLS	Shopping mall square footage
	MILBLKD	Military base blocked
	MILITARY	Military personnel
	MILTOT	MILITARY+CIVILIAN
	OFC1	Office space within 1 mile
	OFCTOTAL	Office space within 4 miles
	OFCCBD	Office space in Central Business District
	PASSENGR	Airport passengers enplaned
	RETAIL	Scale ranking of retail activity
	TOURISTS	Annual tourists
	TRAFFIC	Traffic count
	VAN	Airport van
Demographic	EMPLYPCT	Unemployment percentage
	INCOME	Average family income
	POPULACE	Residential population
Market awareness	AGE	Years inn has been open
	NEAREST	Distance to nearest inn
	STATE	State population per inn
	URBAN	Urban population per inn
Physical	ACCESS	Accessibility
	ARTERY	Major traffic artery
	DISTCBD	Distance to downtown
	SIGNVIS	Sign visibility

    a. Find the solution that minimizes moving costs using Microsoft Excel.

    b. What would you have to do to the costs to assure that *A* always sends a car to *D* as part of the optimal solution?

5   Moving resources efficiently from supplier to consumer is a challenging problem that can be solved using O.R. techniques. The figure below shows a map of blue factories that supply food to orange towns. The numbers below the factories and towns indicate how much food (in kg) each supplies and demands, respectively. Any factory can supply any amount of food to one or several towns. A new factory is being built that can supply 1,000 kg of food but the location of the factory has not yet been determined. The distance between adjacent cells on the map is 1 km. The cost to transport 1 kg of food 1 km is $10.

If the new factory is optimally located, what is the total transportation cost to satisfy the demand of all towns? The new factory cannot occupy a cell that already contains an existing factory or town.

Source: This problem taken from John Toczek, *ORMS Today*, February 2009, p. 16.

CASE: Applichem—The Transportation Problem

Applichem management is faced with the difficult problem of allocating to its customers the capacity of manufacturing plants that are located around the world. Management has long recognized that the manufacturing plants differ greatly in efficiency but has had little success in improving the operations of the inefficient plants. At this time, management has decided to focus on how best to use the capacity of its plants given the differences in manufacturing costs that currently exist. They recognize that this study may result in the significant reduction of output or possibly the shutting down of one or more of the existing plants.

Applichem makes a product called Release-ease. Plastics molding manufacturers use this chemical product. Plastic parts are made by injecting hot plastic into a mold made in the shape of the part. After the plastic has sufficiently cooled, the fresh part is removed from the mold and the mold is then reused to make subsequent parts. Release-ease is a dry

powder, applied as part of the manufacturing process, that makes it easy to remove the part from the mold.

Applichem has made the product since the early 1950s, and demand has been consistent over time. A recent study by Applichem's market research team has indicated that demand for Release-ease should be fairly steady for the next five years. Although Applichem does have some competition, particularly in the European markets, management feels that as long as they can provide a quality product at a competitive cost, customers should stick with Applichem. Release-ease sells at an average price of $1.00 per pound.

The company owns plants capable of making Release-ease in the following cities: Gary, Indiana; Windsor, Ontario, Canada; Frankfurt, Germany; Mexico City, Mexico; Caracas, Venezuela; and Osaka, Japan. Although the plants are focused on meeting demand for the immediate surrounding regions, there is considerable exporting and importing of product for various reasons. The following table contains data on how demand has been met during the past year:

PRODUCT MADE AND SHIPPED DURING PAST YEAR (× 100,000 POUNDS)

FROM/TO	MEXICO	CANADA	VENEZUELA	EUROPE	UNITED STATES	JAPAN
Mexico City	3.0		6.3			7.9
Windsor, Ontario		2.6				
Caracas			4.1			
Frankfurt			5.6	20.0	12.4	
Gary					14.0	
Osaka						4.0

Differences in the technologies used in the plants and in local raw material and labor costs created significant differences in the cost to produce Release-ease in the various locations. These costs may change dramatically due to currency valuation and labor law changes in some of the countries. This is especially true in Mexico and Venezuela. The capacity of each plant also differs at each location, and management has no interest in increasing capacity anywhere at this time. The following table gives details on the costs to produce and capacity of each plant:

PLANT PRODUCTION COSTS AND CAPACITY

PLANT	PRODUCTION COST (PER 1,000 LBS)	PLANT CAPACITY (× 100,000 LBS)
Mexico City	95.01	22.0
Windsor, Ontario	97.35	3.7
Caracas	116.34	4.5
Frankfurt	76.69	47.0
Gary	102.93	18.5
Osaka	153.80	5.0

In considering how best to use the capacity of its plants, Applichem management needs to consider the cost of shipping product from one customer region to another. Applichem now commonly ships product in bulk around the world, but it is expensive. The costs involved are not only the transportation costs but also import duties that are assessed by customs

in some countries. Applichem is committed to meeting demand, though, and sometimes this is done even though profit might not be made on all orders.

The following table details the demand in each country, the cost to transport product from each plant to each country, and the current import duty rate levied by each country. (These percentages do not reflect current duties.) Import duty is calculated on the approximate production plus transportation cost of product brought into the country. (For example, if the production and shipping cost for 1,000 pounds of Release-ease shipped into Venezuela were $100, the import duty would be $100 × .5 = $50.)

TRANSPORTATION COST (PER 1,000 LBS), IMPORT DUTIES, AND DEMANDS FOR RELEASE-EASE

PLANT/COUNTRY	MEXICO	CANADA	VENEZUELA	EUROPE	UNITED STATES	JAPAN
Mexico City	0	11.40	7.00	11.00	11.00	14.00
Windsor, Ontario	11.00	0	9.00	11.50	6.00	13.00
Caracas	7.00	10.00	0	13.00	10.40	14.30
Frankfurt	10.00	11.50	12.50	0	11.20	13.30
Gary	10.00	6.00	11.00	10.00	0	12.50
Osaka	14.00	13.00	12.50	14.20	13.00	0
Total demand (×100,000 lbs)	3.0	2.6	16.0	20.0	26.4	11.9
Import duty	0.0%	0.0%	50.0%	9.5%	4.5%	6.0%

Questions

Given all these data, set up a spreadsheet (Applichem.xls is a start) and answer the following questions for management:

Excel: Applichem

1   Evaluate the cost associated with the way Applichem's plant capacity is currently being used.

2   Determine the optimal use of Applichem's plant capacity using the Solver in Excel.

3   What would you recommend that Applichem management do? Why?

Source: This case is roughly based on data contained in "Applichem (A)," Harvard Business School, 9-685-051.

Footnote

1 M. E. Porter, "The Competitive Advantage of Nation," *Harvard Business Review,* March–April 1990.

Super Quiz

1   This is the art and science of obtaining, producing, and distributing material and product in the proper place and quantities.

2   A company that is hired to handle logistics functions.

3   A mode of transportation that is the most flexible relative to cost, volume, and speed of delivery.

4 When large shipments are broken down directly into smaller shipments for local delivery.

5 Sorting goods is the main purpose of this type of warehouse.

6 A place where foreign goods can be brought into the United States without being subject to normal customs requirements.

7 The main cost criterion used when a transportation model is used for analyzing a logistics network.

8 The Microsoft Excel function used to solve the transportation model.

9 For the transportation model to be able to find a feasible solution, this must always be greater than or equal to demand.

10 The "changing cells" in a transportation model represent this.

11 This is a method that locates facilities relative to an X, Y grid.

12 A technique that is useful for screening potential locations for services.

1. Logistics 2. Third-party logistics company 3. Highway 4. Cross-docking 5. Hub 6. Free trade zone 7. Cost of shipping 8. Solver 9. Total capacity 10. Allocation of demand to a plant or warehouse 11. Centroid method 12. Regression analysis

Selected Bibliography

Ballou, R. H. *Business Logistics Management.* 4th ed. Upper Saddle River, NJ: Prentice Hall, 1998.

Drezner, Z., and H. Hamacher. *Facility Location: Applications and Theory.* Berlin: Springer Verlag, 2002.

Klamroth, K. *Single Facility Location Problems with Barriers.* Berlin: Springer-Verlag Telos, 2002.

CHAPTER 10

LEAN AND SUSTAINABLE SUPPLY CHAINS

After reading this chapter you will:

- Describe how Green and Lean can complement each other.
- Explain how a production pull system works.
- Understand Toyota Production System concepts.
- Summarize important attributes of a lean supply chain.
- Analyze a supply chain process using value stream mapping.
- Know the principles of supply chain design.

271   Green Is the New Black

272   Lean Production

         Lean production defined
         Customer value defined
         Waste defined

273   Lean Logic

274   The Toyota Production System
         Elimination of Waste
         Respect for People

275   Lean Supply Chains

         Value stream defined
         Waste reduction defined

278   Value Stream Mapping

         Value stream mapping defined
         Kaizen defined

280   Lean Supply Chain Design Principles
         Lean Layouts   Preventive maintenance defined
         Lean Production Schedules   Group technology defined
         Lean Supply Chains   Quality at the source defined
                                  Level schedule defined
                                  Freeze window defined
                                  Backflush defined
                                  Uniform plant loading defined
                                  Kanban defined
                                  Kanban pull system defined

289   Lean Services

291   Summary

297   Case: Quality Parts Company

298   Case: Value Stream Mapping

300   Case: Pro Fishing Boats—A Value Stream Mapping Exercise

300   Super Quiz

GREEN IS THE NEW BLACK[1]

Survey Suggests that Enviro-Conscious Manufacturers are the Best Risk for Investors

Many manufacturers still have a long way to go to address the risks and opportunities posed by the push toward more environment-friendly production processes, according to a new study conducted by RiskMetrics Group, a provider of risk management services. Those risks include higher energy costs due to tighter greenhouse gas (GHG) emissions standards, and the opportunities include growing global demand for more energy-efficient products.

The report ranks large manufacturers and other companies on their effectiveness in such areas as reducing GHG emissions, energy efficiency projects, expanding renewable energy purchases, and integrating climate factors into product designs. However, perhaps reflecting the skepticism many people still have as to exactly what role, if any, manufacturing plays in global warming, many companies are largely ignoring climate change, particularly at the board and CEO level.

According to the report, which was sponsored by the Ceres Investor coalition, only 17 percent of the respondent companies say their boards

Top Ten Green
Manufacturers

1. IBM Corp.
2. Dell Inc.
3. Intel
4. Johnson & Johnson
5. Nike
6. Applied Materials
7. Coca-Cola
8. Sun Microsystems
9. Hewlett-Packard
10. Molson Coors

Source: RiskMetrics Group

**Supply
Chain**

receive climate-specific updates from management; 11 percent of the CEOs have taken leadership roles on climate change initiatives. The survey indicates that none of the companies have linked executive compensation directly to climate-related performance.

The survey indicates that green strategies that save energy and fight global warming have broad consumer appeal and political support. Companies that seize the initiative can gain market share, build investor confidence and insulate themselves against future energy shocks and climate change regulations. It's simply smart business to employ these governance practices today.

The highest ranking green manufacturers in the study tend to be high-tech, with IBM leading the way, followed by Dell, Intel, Johnson & Johnson and Nike (see chart, "Top Ten Green Manufacturers,"). High-tech companies were noteworthy for their product and service innovation, when it comes to making their operations, data centers, and product lines more energy efficient. IBM's energy conservation programs, for instance, helped save the company nearly $20 million last year.

Among other suggestions, the report recommends that companies raise supply chain awareness by including supply chain Green House Gas emissions—those emissions that result from raw material extraction, production, transport, and packaging—in emissions inventories, as well as setting emission standards for suppliers.

LEAN PRODUCTION

Lean production

**Supply
Chain**

Global

Customer value

Waste

The most significant operations and supply management approach of the past 50 years is **lean production**. In the context of supply chains, lean production refers to a focus on eliminating as much waste as possible. Moves that are not needed, unnecessary processing steps, and excess inventory in the supply chain are targets for improvement during the *learning* process. Some consultants in industry have coined the phrase *value chain* to refer to an emphasis that each step in the supply chain processes that delivers products and services to customers should create value. If a step does not create value it should be removed from the process. Lean production may be one of the best tools for implementing green strategies in manufacturing and service processes.

The basis of lean thinking came from the just-in-time (JIT) production concepts pioneered in Japan at Toyota. Even though JIT gained worldwide prominence in the 1970s, some of its philosophy can be traced to the early 1900s in the United States. Henry Ford used JIT concepts as he streamlined his moving assembly lines to make automobiles. For example, to eliminate waste, he used the bottom of the packing crates for car seats as the floor board of the car. Although elements of JIT were being used by Japanese industry as early as the 1930s, it was not fully refined until the 1970s when Tai-ichi Ohno of Toyota Motors used JIT to take Toyota's cars to the forefront of delivery time and quality.

Customer value, in the context of lean production, is defined as something for which the customer is willing to pay. Value-adding activities transform materials and information into something the customer wants. Non-value-adding activities consume resources and do not directly contribute to the end result desired by the customer. **Waste**, therefore, is defined as anything that does not add value from the customer's perspective. Examples of process wastes are defective products, overproduction, inventories, excess motion, processing steps, transportation, and waiting.

Lean concepts also apply to service industries. Consider the nonmanufacturing example of a flight to the Bahamas.[2] The value-adding part of that process is the actual flight itself. The non-value-added parts of that process are driving to the airport, parking, walking to the terminal, checking-in, waiting in line at check-in, walking to the security check, and so on. Many times the non-value-added time far exceeds the value-added time in this type of process. Where should improvement efforts be focused—on the non-value-added steps or on making the plane fly faster?

Understanding the difference between value and waste and value-added and non-value-added processes is critical to understanding lean production. Sometimes it is not easy to discern the difference when looking at the entire supply chain, The best way is to look at the individual components and apply lean thinking to each one. Then determine how to link the processes to reduce waste.

This chapter starts by reviewing the evolution of lean concepts from Japan and Toyota. We then expand this view to encompass a complete supply chain. The remainder of the chapter is devoted to value stream mapping, a tool that can be used to drive out waste and improve the efficiency of the supply chain.

Supply Chain

LEAN LOGIC

Lean production is an integrated set of activities designed to achieve production using minimal inventories of raw materials, work-in-process, and finished goods. Parts arrive at the next workstation "just-in-time" and are completed and move through the process quickly. Lean is also based on the logic that nothing will be produced until it is needed. Exhibit 10.1 illustrates the process. Production need is created by actual demand for the product. When an item is sold, in theory, the market pulls a replacement from the last position in the system—final assembly in this case. This triggers an order to the factory production line, where a worker then pulls another unit from an upstream station in the flow to replace the unit taken. This upstream station then pulls from the next station further upstream and so on back to the release of raw materials. To enable this pull process to work smoothly, lean production demands high levels of quality at each stage of the process, strong vendor relations, and a fairly predictable demand for the end product.

Lean Production Pull System

exhibit 10.1

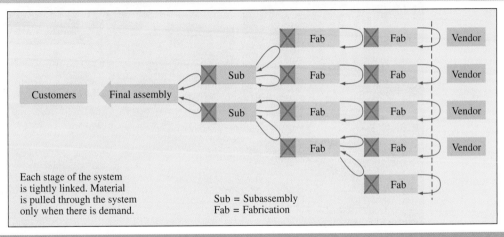

Each stage of the system is tightly linked. Material is pulled through the system only when there is demand.

Sub = Subassembly
Fab = Fabrication

THE TOYOTA PRODUCTION SYSTEM

In this section we develop the philosophy and elements of lean production developed in Japan and embodied in the Toyota Production System—the benchmark for lean manufacturing. The Toyota Production System was developed to improve quality and productivity and is predicated upon two philosophies that are central to the Japanese culture: elimination of waste and respect for people.[3]

Elimination of Waste

Global

Waste, as defined by Toyota's past president, Fujio Cho, is "anything other than the minimum amount of equipment, materials, parts, and workers (working time) which are absolutely essential to production." An expanded lean definition advanced by Fujio Cho identifies seven prominent types of waste to be eliminated from the supply chain: (1) waste from overproduction, (2) waste of waiting time, (3) transportation waste, (4) inventory waste, (5) processing waste, (6) waste of motion, and (7) waste from product defects.[4]

Respect for People

Global

Respect for people is a key to the Toyota Production System. They have traditionally strived to assure lifetime employment for permanent positions and to maintain level payrolls even when business conditions deteriorate. Permanent workers (about one-third of the total workforce of Japan) have job security and tend to be more flexible, remain with a company, and do all they can to help a firm achieve its goals. (Global recessions have caused many Japanese companies to move away from this ideal.)

Company unions at Toyota as well as elsewhere in Japan exist to foster a cooperative relationship with management. All employees receive two bonuses a year in good times. Employees know that if the company performs well, they will get a bonus. This encourages workers to improve productivity. Management views workers as assets, not as human

machines. Automation and robotics are used extensively to perform dull or routine jobs so employees are free to focus on important improvement tasks.

Toyota relies heavily on subcontractor networks. Indeed, more than 90 percent of all Japanese companies are part of the supplier network of small firms. Some suppliers are specialists in a narrow field, usually serving multiple customers. Firms have long-term partnerships with their suppliers and customers. Suppliers consider themselves part of a customer's family.

A study by Christer Karlsson of the Stockholm School of Economics points out that the lean ideas found here are not universally used in all manufacturing companies in Japan. Rather, they are applied situationally and where appropriate. However, the fundamental ideas of elimination of waste and respect for workers are still foundations of the exceptional productivity of most Japanese manufacturing companies.[5]

LEAN SUPPLY CHAINS

Supply Chain

The focus of the Toyota Production System is on elimination of waste and respect for people. The goals align well with the sustainability goals of profit, planet, and people discussed in Chapters 1, 2, and 8 in the book. As the concepts have evolved and become applied to the supply chain, the goal of maximizing customer value has been added. Customer value when considered from the entire supply chain should center on the perspective of the end customer with the goal being to maximize what the customer is willing to pay for a firm's goods or services. The **value stream** consists of the value-adding and non-value-adding activities required to design, order, and provide a product or service from concept to launch, order to delivery, and raw materials to customers. Exhibit 10.2 is a map that depicts the flow of an item through a supply chain. This all-inclusive view of the system is a significant expansion of the scope of application of the lean concepts pioneered by Toyota. When applied to supply chains, **waste reduction** relates to the optimization of the value-adding activities and the elimination of non-value-adding activities that are part of the value stream.

Value stream

Waste reduction

In the following we discuss the different components of a supply chain and what would be expected using a lean focus:

Lean Suppliers   Lean suppliers are able to respond to changes. Their prices are generally lower due to the efficiencies of lean processes, and their quality has improved to the point that incoming inspection at the next link is not needed. Lean suppliers deliver on time and their culture is one of continuous improvement. To develop lean suppliers, organizations should include them in their value stream planning. This will help them fix problems and share savings.

Lean Procurement   A key to lean procurement is automation. The term *e-procurement* relates to automatic transaction, sourcing, bidding and auctions using web-based applications, and the use of software that removes human interaction and integrates with the financial reporting of the firm. The key to lean procurement is visibility. Suppliers must be able to "see" into the customers' operations and customers must be able to "see" into their suppliers' operations. The overlap of these processes needs to be optimized to maximize value from the end customer perspective.

Lean Manufacturing   Lean manufacturing systems produce what the customer wants, in the quantity they want, when they want it, and with minimum resources. Applying lean concepts in manufacturing typically presents the greatest opportunities for cost reduction and quality improvement.

exhibit 10.2   ACME Fulfillment Stream Current State: SKU 918

Z010 — Assumptions

Inv Carrying Cost %	20	%

Z020 — Inventory

Total Inventory	88.00	Days
Total Value of Inventory	2750.00	K$
Total Inv Carrying Cost	550.00	K$

Z040 — Order Execution

Overall Perfect Order Execution	9.14	%

Z030 — Time

Min Processing Lead Time	57.00	Days
Max Processing Lead Time	138.00	Days
Min Order to Consumption Lead Time	145.00	Days
Max Order to Consumption Lead Time	226.00	Days

Frequency

Daily	Daily
5	21
Weekly	Monthly

Time

Wks	Months
5	21
Days	Days

(Starburst notes): Inventory significantly increasing lead times · Very low perfect order execution percent

Flow labels: Quarterly Forecast · Purchase Orders (weekly) · Master Production Schedule · Weekly Schedule · Weekly Customer Order · Sales & Service · Production Control

---

A010 — Suppliers

Min Order to Ship Time	10	Wks
Max Order to Ship Time	18	Wks
Inventory	15	Days
Inventory Value per Day	2	K$
Value of Inventory	30.00	K$
Inv Carrying Cost	6.00	K$
Batch Size	4000	Units
Min Order Qty	1000	Units

(Starburst): Large Batch Size · Large Inventory

A020 — Inbound Logistics

Min Transit Time	1	Days
Max Transit Time	3	Days
Inventory	5	Days
Inventory Value per Day	2	K$
Value of Inventory	10.00	K$
Inv Carrying Cost	2.00	K$
Order Frequency	1	Monthly
Delivery Frequency	1	Monthly

(Starburst): Infrequent shipments

A030 — Yard & Receiving

Min Yard to Line Time	1	Days
Max Yard to Line Time	15	Days
Inventory	15	Days
Inventory Value per Day	4	K$
Value of Inventory	60.00	K$
Inv Carrying Cost	12.00	K$
Standard Pack Size	250	Units
Delivery Frequency	4	Monthly

(Starburst): 5 to 15 trucks a day · Large variance

A040 — Shipping Operations

Min End of Line to Ship	0	Days
Max End of Line to Ship	6	Days
Inventory	3	Days
Inventory Value per Day	50	K$
Value of Inventory	150.00	K$
Inv Carrying Cost	30.00	K$
Avg Shipment Size	100	Units
Batch Size	100	Units

A050 — Interplant Logistics

Min Transit Time	1	Days
Max Transit Time	6	Days
Inventory	3	Days
Inventory Value per Day	50	K$
Value of Inventory	150.00	K$
Inv Carrying Cost	30.00	K$
Avg Shipment Size	100	Units
Delivery Frequency	2	Monthly

A060 — Distribution Centers

Min Processing Time	2	Days
Max Processing Time	7	Days
Inventory	30	Days
Inventory Value per Day	50	K$
Value of Inventory	1500.00	K$
Inv Carrying Cost	300.00	K$
Min Order Qty	250	Units
Planned Order Frequency	1	Weekly

(Starburst): Low Fill Rates

A070 — Outbound Logistics

Min Transit Time	1	Days
Max Transit Time	5	Days
Inventory	2	Days
Inventory Value per Day	50	K$
Value of Inventory	100.00	K$
Inv Carrying Cost	20.00	K$
Avg Shipment Size	250	Units
Delivery Frequency	1	Monthly

(Starburst): Poor visibility of shipments. Unexpected truck arrivals

A080 — Customer

Min Processing Time	1	Days
Max Processing Time	6	Days
Inventory	15	Days
Inventory Value per Day	50	K$
Value of Inventory	750.00	K$
Inv Carrying Cost	150.00	K$
Standard Pack Size	1	Units
Consumption	50	Daily

(Starburst): Rarely deliver a full order to customer

Lean Warehousing   This relates to eliminating non-value-added steps and waste in product storage processes. Typical functions include the following: receiving of material; put-away/storing; replenishment of inventory; picking inventory; packing for shipment; and shipping. Waste can be found in many warehousing processes including: shipping defects, which create returns; overproduction or overshipment of products; excess inventory, which requires extra space and reduces warehouse efficiency; excess motion and handling; waiting for parts; and inadequate information systems.

VOICE DIRECTED ORDER FULFILLMENT ALLOWS WORKERS HANDS-FREE OPERATION FOR FASTER, SAFER, AND MORE ACCURATE INVENTORY PICKING. IT ALSO SUPPORTS THE USE OF MULTIPLE LANGUAGES.

Lean Logistics   Lean concepts can be applied to the functions associated with the movement of material through the system. Some of the key areas include: optimized mode selection and pooling orders; combined multistop truckloads; optimized routing; cross docking; import/export transportation processes; and backhaul minimization. Just as with the other areas, these logistics functions need to be optimized by eliminating non-value-adding activities while improving the value-adding activities.

POST LOGISTICS IN AUSTRALIA DISTRIBUTES THE SPEEDO SWIMWEAR BRAND. THREE LEVELS OF STORAGE ARE CONNECTED BY A SPIRAL CONVEYOR LINKED TO A "SMART" HORIZONTAL CONVEYOR SYSTEM THAT INTERCONNECTS PICKING ZONES ON EACH OF THE THREE LEVELS AND CARRIES THROUGH TO A SIX-LANE PACKING AND DISTRIBUTION AREA.

Lean Customers   Lean customers have a great understanding of their business needs and specify meaningful requirements. They value speed and flexibility and expect high levels of delivery performance. Lean customers are interested in establishing effective partnerships with their suppliers. Lean customers expect value from the products they purchase and provide value to their customers.

The benefits of a lean supply chain primarily are in the improved responsiveness to the customer. As business conditions change, the supply chain adapts to dynamic needs. The ideal is a culture of rapid change with a bias for change when it is needed. The reduced inventory inherent in a lean supply chain reduces obsolescence and reduces flow time through the value-added processes. The reduced cost along with improved customer service allows the firms using a lean supply chain a significant competitive advantage when competing in the global marketplace.

VALUE STREAM MAPPING

Value stream mapping

Value stream mapping (VSM) is a special type of flowcharting tool that is valuable for the development of lean processes. The technique is used to visualize product flows through various processing steps. The tool also illustrates information flows that result from the process as well as information used to control flow through the process. The aim of this section is to provide a brief introduction to VSM and to illustrate its use with an example.

To create a lean process, one needs to have a full understanding of the business, including production processes, material flows, and information flows. In this section we discuss this in the context of a production process where a product is being made. VSM is not limited to this context and can be readily applied to service, logistics, distribution, or virtually any type of process.

In the context of a production process such as a manufacturing plant, the technique is used to identify all of the value-adding as well as non-value-adding processes that materials are subjected to within a plant, from raw material coming into the plant through delivery to the customer. Exhibit 10.3 is a sample map that depicts a production process. With this map, identification of wasteful processes and flows can be made so that they can be modified or eliminated, and the manufacturing system made more productive.

Details explaining the symbols will be discussed later in the section but here it is useful to discuss what the information in the map depicted in Exhibit 10.3 actually means.[6] Starting from the left, we see that material is supplied on a weekly basis and deposited in a raw material inventory indicated by the triangle. The average level for this inventory is 2,500 units. This material is run through a five-step process consisting of machining, honing, cleaning, inspection, and packaging. The machining, honing, inspection, and packaging process all use a single operator. Under each of these process symbols is the activity cycle time (CT), changeover time (c/o time to switch from one type of item to another), lot size, available number of seconds per day, and percent uptime. The cleaning/duburring activity is a multistep process where items are handled on a first-come-first-served basis. In between each process are inventory buffers with the average inventory in these buffers depicted in the exhibit.

Information flows are shown on the map. In Exhibit 10.3 we see that production control issues monthly demand forecasts, weekly orders to the supplier, and a weekly production schedule that is managed by the supervisor on a daily basis. Monthly forecasts are provided by the customer and they place their order on a weekly basis. The time line at the bottom shows the processing time for each production activity (in seconds) together with the

Manufacturing Process Map

exhibit 10.3

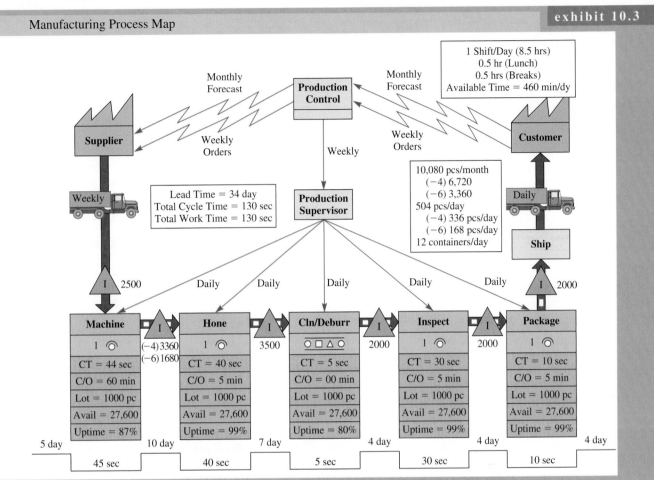

average inventory wait time. Adding these times together gives an estimate of the lead time through the entire system.

VSM symbols are somewhat standardized but there are many variations. Several common symbols are depicted in Exhibit 10.4. These are categorized as Process, Material, Information, and General symbols.

Value stream mapping is a two part process—first depicting the "current state" of the process, and second a possible "future state." Exhibit 10.5 depicts another map of the same process with suggested improvements. The map has been annotated using Kaizen bursts that suggest the areas for improvement. **Kaizen** is the Japanese philosophy that focuses on continuous improvement. In this exhibit we see a totally redesigned process where the individual production operations have been combined into a workcell operated by three employees. In addition, rather than "pushing" material through the system based on weekly schedules generated by production control, the entire process is converted to a pull system that is operated directly in response to customer demand. Note that the lead time in the new system is only 5 days, compared to the 34-day lead time with the old system.

To study another example using value stream mapping (VSM), consider the Solved Problem at the end of the chapter. VSM is a great visual way to analyze an existing system and to find areas where waste can be eliminated. Value stream maps are simple to

Kaizen

exhibit 10.4   Value Stream Mapping Symbols

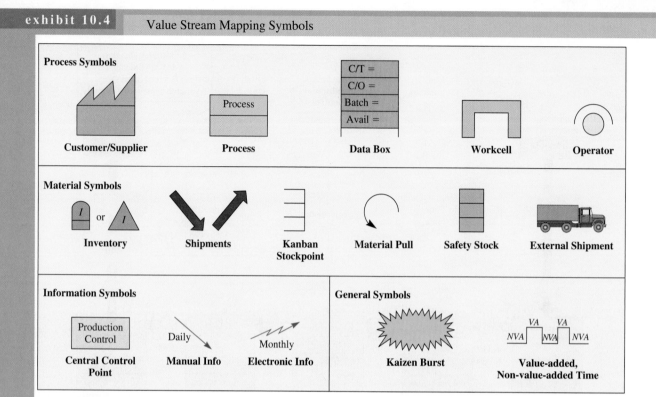

draw and it is possible to construct the maps totally on paper and pencil. These maps can, however, be more easily constructed using standard office software or graphics packages. Additionally, dedicated VSM software is available from Strategos (www.strategosinc.com) and System2win (www.Systems2win.com).

LEAN SUPPLY CHAIN DESIGN PRINCIPLES

Supply Chain

Value stream mapping is a great way to analyze existing processes. Looking for ways to improve supply chain processes should be based on ideas that have been proven over time. In the following we review a set of key principles which can guide the design of lean supply chains. We divide our design principles into three major categories. The first two sets of principles relate to internal production processes. These are the processes that actually create the goods and services within a firm. The third category applies lean concepts to the entire supply chain. These principles include:

1. Lean Layouts
   a. Group technology
   b. Quality at the source
   c. JIT production
2. Lean Production Schedules
   a. Uniform plant loading
   b. Kanban production control system

Analysis Showing Potential Areas for Improving a Process

exhibit 10.5

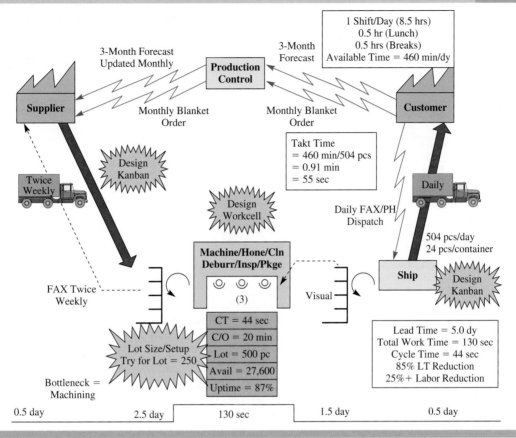

c. Determine number of Kanbans needed
d. Minimized setup times
3. Lean supply chains
a. Specialized plants
b. Work with suppliers
c. Building a lean supply chain

Lean Layouts

Lean requires the plant layout to be designed to ensure balanced work flow with a minimum of work-in-process inventory. Each workstation is part of a production line, whether or not a physical line actually exists. Capacity is balanced using the same logic for an assembly line, and operations are linked through a pull system. In addition, the system designer must visualize how all aspects of the internal and external logistics system tie to the layout.

Preventive maintenance is emphasized to ensure that flows are not interrupted by downtime or malfunctioning equipment. Preventive maintenance involves periodic inspection and repair designed to keep a machine reliable. Operators perform much of the maintenance because they are most familiar with their machines and because machines are easier to repair, as lean operations favor several simple machines rather than one large complex one.

Preventive maintenance

exhibit 10.6   Group Technology versus Departmental Specialty

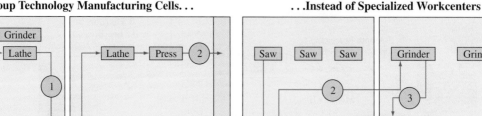

Group technology

Group Technology Group technology (GT) is a philosophy in which similar parts are grouped into families, and the processes required to make the parts are arranged in a manufacturing cell. Instead of transferring jobs from one specialized department to another, GT considers all operations required to make a part and groups those machines together. Exhibit 10.6 illustrates the difference between the clusters of different machines grouped into cells versus departmental layouts. The group technology cells eliminate movement and queue (waiting) time between operations, reduce inventory, and reduce the number of employees required. Workers, however, must be flexible to run several machines and processes. Due to their advanced skill level, these workers have increased job security.

Quality at the source

Quality at the Source Quality at the source means do it right the first time and, when something goes wrong, stop the process or assembly line immediately. Factory workers become their own inspectors, personally responsible for the quality of their output. Workers concentrate on one part of the job at a time so quality problems are uncovered. If the pace is too fast, if the worker finds a quality problem, or if a safety issue is discovered, the worker is obligated to push a button to stop the line and turn on a visual signal. People from other areas respond to the alarm and the problem. Workers are empowered to do their own maintenance and housekeeping until the problem is fixed.

JIT Production JIT (Just-in-Time) means producing what is needed when needed and no more. Anything over the minimum amount necessary is viewed as waste, because effort and material expended for something not needed now cannot be utilized now. This is in contrast to relying on extra material just in case something goes wrong.

JIT is typically applied to repetitive manufacturing, which is when the same or similar items are made one after another. JIT does not require large volumes and can be applied to any repetitive segments of a business regardless of where they appear. Under JIT the ideal lot size or production batch is one. Although workstations may be geographically dispersed, it is important to minimize transit time and keep transfer quantities small—typically one-tenth of a day's production. Vendors even ship several times a day to their customers

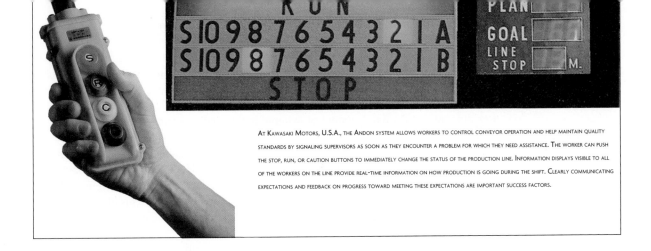

to keep lot sizes small and inventory low. The goal is to drive all inventory queues to zero, thus minimizing inventory investment and shortening lead times.

When inventory levels are low, quality problems become very visible. Exhibit 10.7 illustrates this idea. If the water in a pond represents inventory, the rocks represent problems that could occur in a firm. A high level of water hides the problems (rocks). Management assumes everything is fine, but as the water level drops in an economic downturn, problems are presented. If you deliberately force the water level down (particularly in good economic times), you can expose and correct problems before they cause worse

exhibit 10.7

Inventory Hides Problems

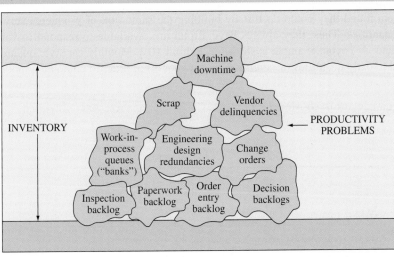

problems. JIT manufacturing exposes problems otherwise hidden by excess inventories and staff.

Lean Production Schedules

Level schedule

As noted earlier, lean production requires a stable schedule over a lengthy time horizon. This is accomplished by level scheduling, freeze windows, and underutilization of capacity. A **level schedule** is one that requires material to be pulled into final assembly in a pattern uniform enough to allow the various elements of production to respond to pull signals. It does not necessarily mean that the usage of every part on an assembly line is identified hour by hour for days on end; it does mean that a given production system equipped with flexible setups and a fixed amount of material in the pipelines can respond.[7]

Freeze window

Backflush

The term **freeze window** refers to that period of time during which the schedule is fixed and no further changes are possible. An added benefit of the stable schedule is seen in how parts and components are accounted for in a pull system. Here, the concept of **backflush** is used where the parts that go into each unit of the product are periodically removed from inventory and accounted for based on the number of units produced. This eliminates much of the shop-floor data collection activity, which is required if each part must be tracked and accounted for during production.

Underutilization and overutilization of capacity are controversial features of lean production. Conventional approaches use safety stocks and early deliveries as a hedge against production problems like poor quality, machine failures, and unanticipated bottlenecks in traditional manufacturing. Under lean production, excess labor, machines, and overtime provide the hedge. The excess capacity in labor and equipment that results is much cheaper than carrying excess inventory. When demand is greater than expected, overtime must be used. Often part-time labor is used when additional capacity is needed. During idle periods, personnel can be put to work on other activities such as special projects, work group activities, and workstation housekeeping.

Uniform plant loading

Uniform Plant Loading Smoothing the production flow to dampen the reaction waves that normally occur in response to schedule variations is called **uniform plant loading**. When a change is made in a final assembly, the changes are magnified throughout the line and the supply chain. The only way to eliminate the problem is to make adjustments as small as possible by setting a firm monthly production plan for which the output rate is frozen.

Toyota found they could do this by building the same mix of products every day in small quantities. Thus, they always have a total mix available to respond to variations in demand. A Toyota example is shown in Exhibit 10.8. Monthly car style quantities are reduced to daily quantities (assuming a 20-day month) in order to compute a model *cycle*

---

exhibit 10.8   Toyota Example of Mixed-Model Production Cycle in a Japanese Assembly Plant

MODEL	MONTHLY QUANTITY	DAILY QUANTITY	MODEL CYCLE TIME (MINUTES)
Sedan	5,000	250	2
Hardtop	2,500	125	4
Wagon	2,500	125	4

Sequence: Sedan, hardtop, sedan, wagon, sedan, hardtop, sedan, wagon, and so on (one minute apart)

exhibit 10.9

Flow of Two Kanbans

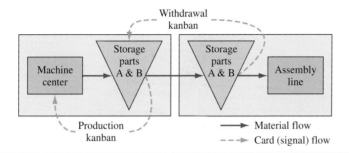

time (defined here as the time between two identical units being completed on the line). The cycle time figure is used to adjust resources to produce the precise quantity needed. The speed of equipment or of the production line is adjusted so only the needed quantity is produced each day. JIT strives to produce on schedule, on cost, and on quality.

Kanban Production Control Systems   A kanban control system uses a signaling device to regulate JIT flows. **Kanban** means "sign" or "instruction card" in Japanese. In a paperless control system, containers can be used instead of cards. The cards or containers make up the **kanban pull system**. The authority to produce or supply additional parts comes from downstream operations. Consider Exhibit 10.9, where we show an assembly line that is supplied with parts by a machine center. The machine center makes two parts, A and B. These two parts are stored in containers that are located next to the assembly line and next to the machine center. Each container next to the assembly line has a withdrawal kanban, and each container next to the machine center has a production kanban. This is often referred to as a two-card kanban system.

When the assembly line takes the first part A from a full container, a worker takes the withdrawal kanban from the container, and takes the card to the machine center storage area. In the machine center area, the worker finds a container of part A, removes the production kanban, and replaces it with the withdrawal kanban. Placement of this card on the container authorizes the movement of the container to the assembly line. The freed production kanban is placed on a rack by the machine center, which authorizes the production of another lot of material. A similar process is followed for part B. The cards on the rack become the dispatch list for the machine center. Cards are not the only way to signal the need for production of a part; other visual methods are possible, as shown in Exhibit 10.10.

The following are some other possible approaches:

Kanban squares.   Some companies use marked spaces on the floor or on a table to identify where material should be stored. When the square is empty, the supplying operations are authorized to produce; when the square is full, no parts are needed.

Container system.   Sometimes the container itself can be used as a signal device. In this case, an empty container on the factory floor visually signals the need to fill it. The amount of inventory is adjusted by simply adding or removing containers.

Colored golf balls.   At a Kawasaki engine plant, when a part used in a subassembly is down to its queue limit, the assembler rolls a colored golf ball down a pipe to the

Kanban

Kanban pull system

Global

Global

exhibit 10.10   Diagram of Outbound Stockpoint with Warning Signal Marker

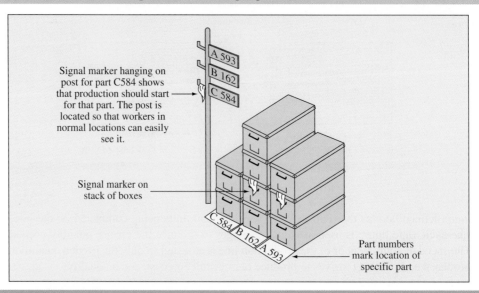

Signal marker hanging on post for part C584 shows that production should start for that part. The post is located so that workers in normal locations can easily see it.

Signal marker on stack of boxes

A 593
B 162
C 584

C 584 / B 162 / A 593

Part numbers mark location of specific part

replenishment machine center. This tells the operator which part to make next. Many variations have been developed on this approach.

The kanban pull approach can be used not only within a manufacturing facility but also between manufacturing facilities (pulling engines and transmissions into an automobile assembly operation, for example) and between manufacturers and external suppliers.

Determining the Number of Kanbans Needed   Setting up a kanban control system requires determination of the number of kanban cards (or containers) needed. In a two-card system, we are finding the number of sets of withdrawal and production cards. The kanban cards represent the number of containers of material that flow back and forth between the supplier and the user areas. Each container represents the minimum production lot size to be supplied. The number of containers, therefore, directly controls the amount of work-in-process inventory in the system.

Accurately estimating the lead time needed to produce a container of parts is the key to determining the number of containers. This lead time is a function of the processing time for the container, any waiting time during the production process, and the time required to transport the material to the user. Enough kanbans are needed to cover the expected demand during this lead time plus some additional amount for safety stock. The number of kanban card sets is

$$k = \frac{\text{Expected demand during lead time} + \text{Safety stock}}{\text{Size of the container}}$$

$$= \frac{DL(1 + S)}{C}$$ [10.1]

where

k = Number of kanban card sets

D = Average number of units demanded per period (lead time and demand must be expressed in the same time units)

L = Lead time to replenish an order (expressed in the same units as demand)

S = Safety stock expressed as a percentage of demand during the lead time (This can be based on a service level and variance as shown in Chapter 13.)

C = Container size

Observe that a kanban system does not produce zero inventory; rather, it controls the amount of material that can be in process at a time—the number of containers of each item. The kanban system can be easily adjusted to fit the current way the system is operating, because card sets can be easily added or removed from the system. If the workers find that they are not able to consistently replenish the item on time, an additional container of material, with the accompanying kanban cards, can be added. If it is found that excess containers of material accumulate, card sets can be easily removed, thus reducing the amount of inventory.

Step by Step

Example 10.1: Determining the Number of Kanban Card Sets

Arvin Automotive, a company that makes muffler assemblies for the Big Three, is committed to the use of kanban to pull material through its manufacturing cells. Arvin has designed each cell to fabricate a specific family of muffler products. Fabricating a muffler assembly involves cutting and bending pieces of pipe that are welded to a muffler and a catalytic converter. The mufflers and catalytic converters are pulled into the cell based on current demand. The catalytic converters are made in a specialized cell.

Catalytic converters are made in batches of 10 units and are moved in special hand carts to the fabrication cells. The catalytic converter cell is designed so that different types of catalytic converters can be made with virtually no setup loss. The cell can respond to an order for a batch of catalytic converters in approximately four hours. Because the catalytic converter cell is right next to the muffler assembly fabrication cell, transportation time is virtually zero.

The muffler assembly fabrication cell averages approximately eight assemblies per hour. Each assembly uses the same catalytic converter. Due to some variability in the process, management has decided to have safety stock equivalent to 10 percent of the needed inventory.

How many kanban sets are needed to manage the replenishment of the catalytic converters?

SOLUTION

In this case, the lead time for replenishment of the converters (L) is four hours. The demand (D) for the catalytic converters is eight per hour. Safety stock (S) is 10 percent of the expected demand, and the container size (C) is 10 units.

$$k = \frac{8 \times 4(1 + .1)}{10} = \frac{35.2}{10} = 3.52$$

In this case, we would need four kanban card sets, and we would have four containers of converters in the system. In all cases, when we calculate k, we will round the number up because we always need to work with full containers of parts. ●

Minimized Setup Times The reductions in setup and changeover times are necessary to achieve a smooth flow. Exhibit 10.11 shows the relationship between lot size and setup costs. Under a traditional approach, setup cost is treated as a constant, and the optimal order quantity is shown as six. Under the kanban approach, setup cost is significantly reduced and the corresponding optimal order quantity is reduced. In the exhibit, the order quantity has been reduced from six to two under lean methods by employing setup-time–saving procedures. This organization will ultimately strive for a lot size of one.

exhibit 10.11   Relationship between Lot Size and Setup Cost

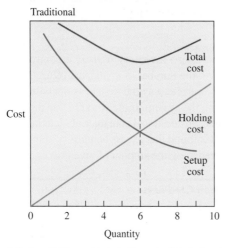

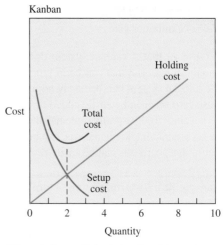

Definitions: *Holding* cost includes the costs of storing inventory and the cost of money tied up in inventory. Setup cost includes the wage costs attributable to workers making the setup, and various administrative and supplies costs. (These are defined in total in Chapter 13, "Inventory Control.")

Global

In a widely cited example from the late 1970s, Toyota teams of press operators producing car hoods and fenders were able to change an 800-ton press in 10 minutes, compared with the average of six hours for U.S. workers and four hours for German workers. (Now, however, such speed is common in most U.S. auto plants.) To achieve such setup time reduction, setups are divided into internal and external activities. Internal setups must be done while a machine is stopped. External setups can be done while the machine is running. Other time-saving devices such as duplicate tool holders also are used to speed setups.

Lean Supply Chains

Building a lean supply chain involves taking a systems approach to integrating the partners. Supply must be coordinated with the need of the production facilities and production must be tied directly to the demand of the customers for products. The importance of speed and steady consistent flow that is responsive to actual customer demand cannot be overemphasized. Concepts that relate to lean network design are discussed next.

Supply Chain

Specialized plants   Small specialized plants rather than large vertically integrated manufacturing facilities are important. Large operations and their inherent bureaucracies are difficult to manage and not in line with the lean philosophy. Plants designed for one purpose can be constructed and operated more economically. These plants need to be linked together so they can be synchronized to one another and to the actual need of the market. Speed and quick response to changes are keys to the success of a lean supply chain.

Work with Suppliers   Just as customers and employees are key components of lean systems, suppliers are also important to the process. If a firm shares its projected usage requirements with its vendors, they have a long-run picture of the demands that will be placed on their production and distribution systems. Some vendors are linked online with a customer to share production scheduling and input needs data. This permits them to develop level production systems. Confidence in the supplier or vendor's delivery commitment allows reductions of buffer inventories. Maintaining stock at a lean level requires frequent deliveries during the day. Some suppliers even deliver directly to a location on the production line and not at a receiving dock. When vendors adopt quality practices, incoming receiving inspections of their products can be bypassed.

Building a Lean Supply Chain   As we discussed in Chapter 8, a supply chain is the sum total of organizations involved—from raw materials firms through tiers of suppliers to original equipment manufacturers, onward to the ultimate distribution and delivery of the finished product to the customer. Womack and Jones, in their seminal work *Lean Thinking,* provide the following guidelines for implementing a lean supply chain:[8]

Supply Chain

- Value must be defined jointly for each product family along with a target cost based on the customer's perception of value.
- All firms along the value stream must make an adequate return on their investments related to the value stream.
- The firms must work together to identify and eliminate *muda* (waste) to the point where the overall target cost and return-on-investment targets of each firm are met.
- When cost targets are met, the firms along the stream will immediately conduct new analyses to identify remaining *muda* and set new targets.
- Every participating firm has the right to examine every activity in every firm relevant to the value stream as part of the joint search for waste.

To summarize: To be lean, everyone's got to be on the same page!

LEAN SERVICES

Many lean techniques have been successfully applied by service firms. Just as in manufacturing, the suitability of each technique and the corresponding work steps depend on the characteristics of the firm's markets, production and equipment technology, skill sets, and corporate culture. Service firms are not different in this respect. Here are 10 of the more successful techniques applied to service companies:

Service

Global

1. **Organize Problem-Solving Groups**   Honeywell is extending its use of quality teams from manufacturing into its service operations. Other corporations as diverse as First Bank/Dallas, Standard Meat Company, and Miller Brewing Company are using similar approaches to improve service. British Airways used quality teams as a fundamental part of its strategy to implement new service practices.

2. **Upgrade Housekeeping**   Good housekeeping means more than winning the clean broom award. It means that only the necessary items are kept in a work area, that there is a place for everything, and that everything is clean and in a constant state of readiness. The employees clean their own areas.

    Service organizations such as McDonald's, Disneyland, and Speedi-Lube have recognized the critical nature of housekeeping. Their dedication to housekeeping has meant that service processes work better, the attitude of continuous improvement is easier to develop, and customers perceive that they are receiving better service.

3. **Upgrade Quality**   The only cost-effective way to improve quality is to develop reliable process capabilities. Process quality is quality at the source—it guarantees first-time production of consistent and uniform products and services.

    McDonald's is famous for building quality into its service delivery process. It literally "industrialized" the service delivery system so that part-time, casual workers could provide the same eating experience anywhere in the world. Quality doesn't mean producing the best; it means consistently producing products and services that give the customers their money's worth.

4. **Clarify Process Flows**   Clarification of flows, based on JIT themes, can dramatically improve the process performance. Here are three examples.

First, Federal Express Corporation changed air flight patterns from origin-to-destination to origin-to-hub, where the freight is transferred to an outbound plane heading for the destination. This revolutionized the air transport industry. Second, the order-entry department of a manufacturing firm converted from functional subdepartments to customer-centered work groups and reduced the order processing lead time from eight to two days. Finally, Supermaids sends in a team of house cleaners, each with a specific responsibility, to clean a part of each house quickly with parallel processes. Changes in process flows can literally revolutionize service industries.

5. **Revise Equipment and Process Technologies**   Revising technologies involves evaluation of the equipment and processes for their ability to meet the process requirements, to process consistently within tolerance, and to fit the scale and capacity of the work group.

Speedi-Lube converted the standard service station concept to a specialized lubrication and inspection center by changing the service bays from drive-in to drive-through and by eliminating the hoists and instead building pits under the cars where employees have full access to the lubrication areas on the vehicle.

A hospital reduced operating room setup time so that it had the flexibility to perform a wider range of operations without reducing the operating room availability.

6. **Level the Facility Load**   Service firms synchronize production with demand. They have developed unique approaches to leveling demand so they can avoid making customers wait for service. McDonald's offers a special breakfast menu in the morning. Retail stores use take-a-number systems. The post office charges more for next-day delivery. These are all examples of the service approach for creating uniform facility loads.

7. **Eliminate Unnecessary Activities**   A step that does not add value is a candidate for elimination. A step that does add value may be a candidate for reengineering

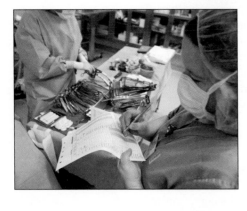

to improve the process consistency or to reduce the time to perform the tasks.

A hospital discovered that significant time was spent during an operation waiting for an instrument that was not available when the operation began. It developed a checklist of instruments required for each category of operation. Speedi-Lube eliminated steps, but also added steps that did not improve the lubrication process but did make customers feel more assured about the work being performed.

8. **Reorganize Physical Configuration**   Work area configurations frequently require reorganization during a lean implementation. Often manufacturers accomplish this by setting up manufacturing cells to produce items in small lots, synchronous to demand. These cells amount to microfactories inside the plant.

Most service firms are far behind manufacturers in this area. However, a few interesting examples do come out of the service sector. Some hospitals—instead of routing patients all over the building for tests, exams, X-rays, and injections—are reorganizing their services into work groups based on the type of problem. Teams that treat only trauma are common, but other work groups have been formed to treat less immediate conditions like hernias. These amount to microclinics within the hospital facility.

9. **Introduce Demand-Pull Scheduling**   Due to the nature of service production and consumption, demand-pull (customer-driven) scheduling is necessary for operating a service business. Moreover, many service firms are separating their operations into "back room" and "customer contact" facilities. This approach creates new problems in coordinating schedules between the facilities. The original Wendy's restaurants were set up so cooks could see cars enter the parking lot. They put a preestablished number of hamburger patties on the grill for each car. This pull system was designed to have a fresh patty on the grill before the customer even placed an order.

10. **Develop Supplier Networks**   The term *supplier networks* in the lean context refers to the cooperative association of suppliers and customers working over the long term for mutual benefit. Service firms have not emphasized supplier networks for materials because the service costs are often predominantly labor. Notable exceptions include service organizations like McDonald's, one of the biggest food products purchasers in the world, which has been developing lean practices. Manpower and other employment agencies have established lean-type relationships with a temporary employment service and a trade school to develop a reliable source of trained assemblers.

SUMMARY

Lean production has proven its value to thousands of companies throughout the world. The idea behind *lean* is achieving high volume with minimal inventory. Toyota pioneered the ideas associated with *lean* production with the Toyota Production System. Lean concepts are best applied in environments where the same products are produced over and over at relatively high volume. Value stream mapping is a useful tool for visualizing supply chains and for applying lean concepts.

Key Terms

Lean production Integrated activities designed to achieve high-volume, high-quality production using minimal inventories of raw materials, work-in-process, and finished goods.

Customer value In the context of lean, something for which the customer is willing to pay.

Waste Something that does not add value from the customer's perspective.

Value stream These are the value-adding and non-value-adding activities required to design, order, and provide a product from concept to launch, order to delivery, and raw materials to customers.

Waste reduction The optimization of value-adding activities and elimination of non-value-adding activities that are part of the value stream.

Value stream mapping A graphical way to analyze where value is or is not being added as material flows through a process.

Kaizen Japanese philosophy that focuses on continuous improvement.

Preventive maintenance Periodic inspection and repair designed to keep equipment reliable.

Group technology A philosophy in which similar parts are grouped into families, and the processes required to make the parts are arranged in a specialized work cell.

Quality at the source Philosophy of making factory workers personally responsible for the quality of their output. Workers are expected to make the part correctly the first time and to stop the process immediately if there is a problem.

Level schedule A schedule that pulls material into final assembly at a constant rate.

Freeze window The period of time during which the schedule is fixed and no further changes are possible.

Backflush Calculating how many of each part were used in production and using these calculations to adjust actual on-hand inventory balances. This eliminates the need to actually track each part used in production.

Uniform plant loading Smoothing the production flow to dampen schedule variation.

Kanban and the kanban pull system An inventory or production control system that uses a signaling device to regulate flows.

Formula Review

Determining the number of kanbans

$$k = \frac{DL(1 + S)}{C}$$ [10.1]

Solved Problem 1

Value Stream Mapping Example: Bolt Manufacturing[9]

A simple example will illustrate the use of value stream mapping. Exhibit 10.12 depicts a bolt manufacturing operation that ships 7,500 bolts per week. The current state map provides cycle time and setup time information for each of the 15 processes used, and it provides inventory levels at each location. The map also depicts, information flow between the steel supplier, the bolt customer, and management via production scheduling. The total value-added time, denoted as processing time, is obtained by summing all of the individual value-added contributions at each processing step on the time line. For the example, it equals 28.88 seconds. At each inventory location, lead time is calculated by dividing inventory level by daily production demand, which is 1,500 bolts. Summing all of the lead time produces an overall production lead time of 66.1 days, which is the entire time it takes an individual bolt to make its way through the plant.

There are several possibilities to optimize the current production scenario. Exhibit 10.13 provides a few of these, shown as Kaizen bursts, including eliminating several processing steps, modifying some of the existing processes, and reducing travel distances between processes. Exhibit 10.14, the future state map, illustrates the incorporation of these modifications. As shown, the changes reduce production lead time to 50.89 days, which is a 23 percent reduction. The production scenario could be enhanced even more if pull systems were incorporated at various locations.

Solved Problem 2

A local hospital wants to set up a kanban system to manage its supply of blood with the regional blood bank. The regional blood bank delivers blood to the hospital each day with a one-day order lead time (an order placed by 6 P.M. today will be delivered tomorrow afternoon). Internally, the hospital purchasing group places orders for blood each day at 5 P.M. Blood is measured by the pint and is shipped in containers that contain six pints. For a particular blood type, the hospital uses an average of 12 pints per day. Due to the critical nature of a blood shortage, the hospital wants to carry a safety stock of two days' expected supply. How many kanban card sets should the hospital prepare?

Solution

This problem is typical of how a real application might look. Using the data given, the variables for this problem are as follows:

$D = 12$ pints per day (average demand)
$L = 1$ day (lead time)
$S = 200$ percent (safety stock, as a fraction this is 2.0)

exhibit 10.12   Current State Map for Bolt Manufacturing Example

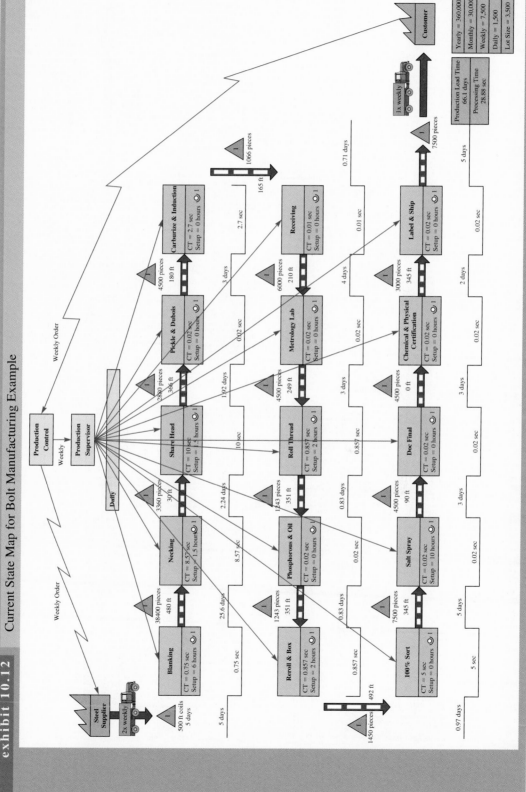

exhibit 10.13 Potential Process Changes for Bolt Manufacturing Example

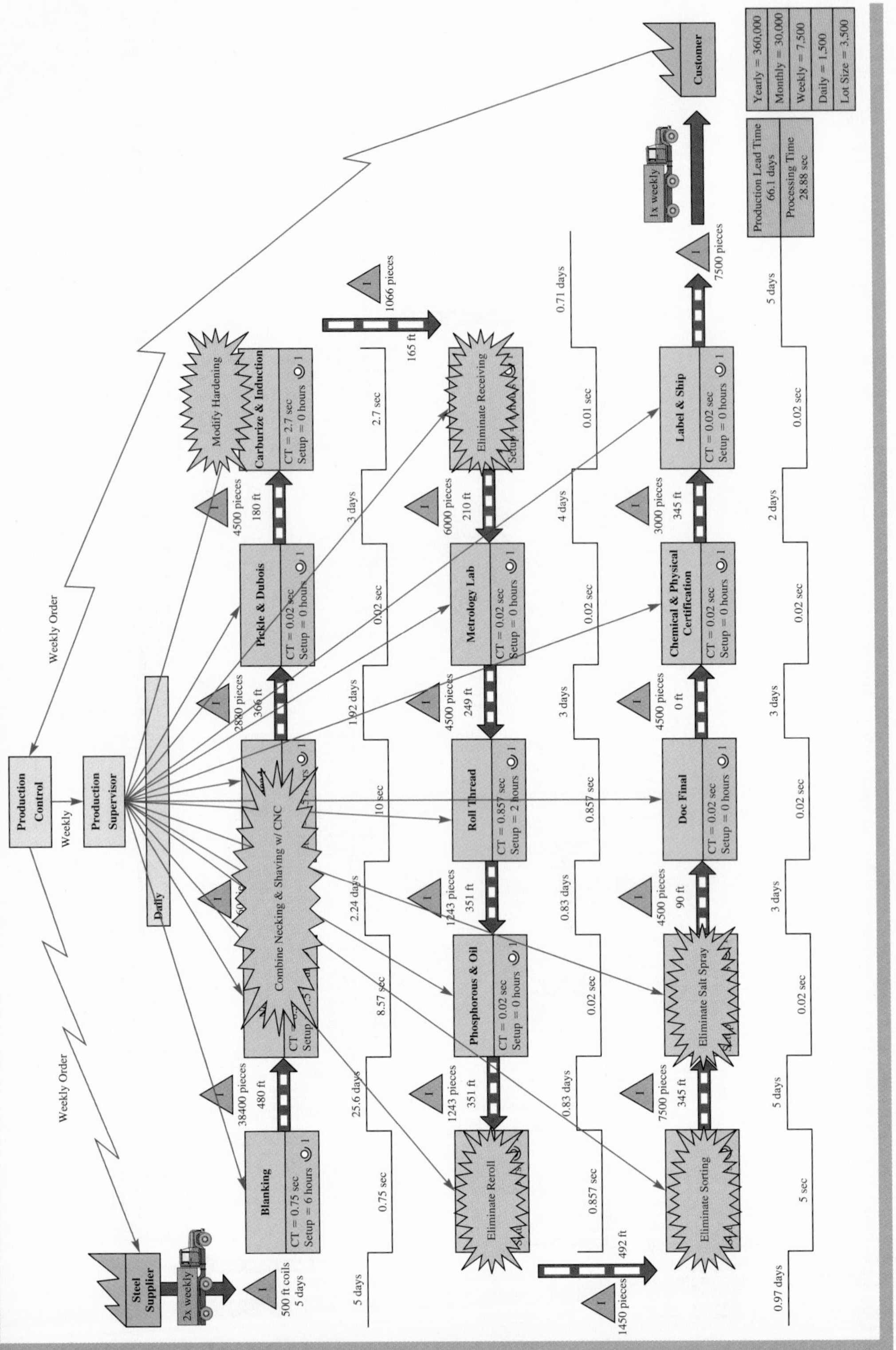

Production Control
Production Supervisor
Weekly Order
Weekly
Weekly Order
Daily
Steel Supplier
2x weekly
500 ft coils
5 days
Customer
1x weekly
Blanking
CT = 0.75 sec
Setup = 6 hours
38400 pieces
480 ft
Combine Necking & Shaving w/ CNC
2880 pieces
366 ft
Pickle & Dubois
CT = 0.02 sec
Setup = 0 hours
4500 pieces
180 ft
Carburize & Induction
CT = 2.7 sec
Setup = 0 hours
Modify Hardening
1066 pieces
165 ft
Eliminate Reroll
1243 pieces
351 ft
Phosphorous & Oil
CT = 0.02 sec
Setup = 0 hours
1243 pieces
351 ft
Roll Thread
CT = 0.857 sec
Setup = 2 hours
4500 pieces
249 ft
Metrology Lab
CT = 0.02 sec
Setup = 0 hours
6000 pieces
210 ft
Eliminate Receiving
1450 pieces
492 ft
Eliminate Sorting
7500 pieces
345 ft
Eliminate Salt Spray
4500 pieces
90 ft
Doc Final
CT = 0.02 sec
Setup = 0 hours
4500 pieces
0 ft
Chemical & Physical Certification
CT = 0.02 sec
Setup = 0 hours
3000 pieces
345 ft
Label & Ship
CT = 0.02 sec
Setup = 0 hours
7500 pieces
5 days
0.75 sec
25.6 days
8.57 sec
2.24 days
10 sec
1.92 days
0.02 sec
3 days
2.7 sec
0.857 sec
0.83 days
0.02 sec
0.83 days
0.857 sec
3 days
0.02 sec
4 days
0.01 sec
0.71 days
0.97 days
5 sec
5 days
0.02 sec
3 days
0.02 sec
3 days
0.02 sec
2 days
0.02 sec
5 days
Production Lead Time 66.1 days
Processing Time 28.88 sec
Yearly = 360,000
Monthly = 30,000
Weekly = 7,500
Daily = 1,500
Lot Size = 3,500

Map of the Current State

exhibit 10.17

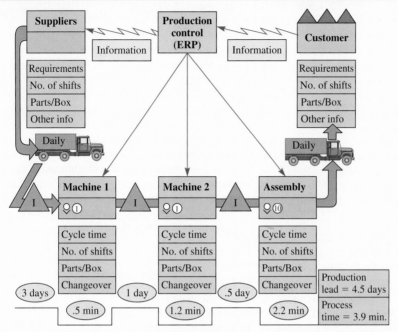

Source: Jared Lovelle, "Mapping the Value Stream," *IIE Solutions* 33, no. 2 (February 2001), p. 32.

Map of the Future State

exhibit 10.18

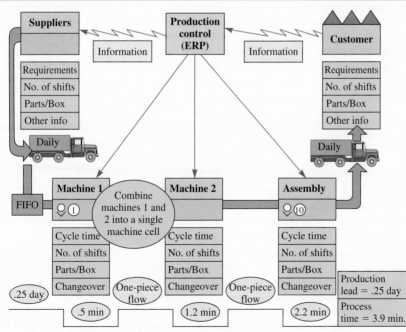

Source: Jared Lovelle, "Mapping the Value Stream," *IIE Solutions* 33, no. 2 (February 2001), p. 30.

Questions

1   Eliminating the queue of work dramatically quickens the time it takes a part to flow through the system. What are the disadvantages of removing those queues?

2   How do you think the machine operators would react to the change?

3   What would you do to ensure that the operators were kept busy?

CASE: Pro Fishing Boats—A Value Stream Mapping Exercise

A fishing boat manufacturer, Pro Fishing Boats, is having many problems with critical globally sourced parts. Pro Fishing has two manufacturing facilities in the United States. The firm's reliance on efficient global supply chain operations is increasing as the manufacturer is sourcing more and more parts overseas, including critical components. Recent problems with a number of these critical parts have caused line shutdowns. In response, Pro Fishing has *mandated* a six-week inventory on all globally sourced parts. Management has asked you to evaluate whether this is the right decision.

First, you must understand Pro Fishing's supply chain. Currently, there is very little visibility (knowledge of the current status) of inventory in the supply chain and communication with the supply base is minimal. In fact, the boat manufacturer does not have *any* visibility past the Tier I suppliers. Adding to the complexity of this problem, each part of the supply chain is handled by different departments within the company.

In order to understand the supply chain, Pro Fishing has asked you to map their supply chain. In order to do so, they have identified a critical component to follow in the supply chain. After having the opportunity to interview supply chain participants, including suppliers, you have collected the following information.

The component is manufactured overseas in China by the Tier I supplier, Manufacturing Inc. The Manufacturing Inc. production schedule is based on orders sent via fax from the Pro Fishing warehouse. They operate on a 90-60-30 day forecast along with a weekly order. Upon completion of the component, Manufacturing Inc. sends the component via truck to the Shanghai Port where it is loaded onto a ship heading to the United States. Loading at the port takes 1 week and truck

transport takes 3 days. Manufacturing Inc. holds a 9-week finished goods buffer inventory. Manufacturing time for each component is only about 3 days. The ship bound to the United States takes about 14 days to travel overseas. Upon arrival in the United States the component is unloaded at the Los Angeles port. This takes about 5 days and customs inspects in Los Angeles. The goods travel by train to Chicago, which takes about 7 days. Goods are held in Chicago for about half a week. From there, the component is trucked to a Pro Fishing warehouse where the 6-week inventory buffer has been mandated. Shipment to the Pro Fishing warehouse takes 2 days. From the warehouse, the components are trucked to plants in the United States triggered by electronic orders from each of the Pro Fishing plants.

In talking to Manufacturing Inc., Pro Fishing has learned that their component is made up of two main raw materials: one from China and the other from the United States. Due to the risk of running out of these raw materials, Manufacturing Inc. maintains a 4-week buffer on the China-based raw materials and a 12-week buffer in the U.S. based raw material. These Tier II supplier orders are by formal purchase order only. It is interesting to note that Manufacturing Inc. uses these suppliers due to Pro Fishing's strict supplier qualification requirements.

Questions

1   Create a value stream map (VSM) of this supply chain. What other information is needed?
2   Where is there risk for supply chain disruptions or stoppages to the flow of materials?
3   Where do opportunities reside in improving supply chain operations and how has VSM helped to reveal these?

Super Quiz

1   Anything that does not add value from the customer's perspective.
2   An integrated set of activities designed to achieve production using minimal inventories of raw materials, work-in-process, and finished goods.

3   The Toyota Production System is founded in these two philosophies.
4   The set of value and non-value-adding activities required to design, order, and provide a product from

concept to launch, order to delivery, and raw materials to customers.

5 The Japanese philosophy that focuses on continuous improvement.

6 A philosophy in which similar parts are brought together in families for production purposes.

7 Means only producing what is needed when needed and no more.

8 A period of time during which the production schedule cannot be changed.

9 Producing a mix of products that matches demand as closely as possible.

10 A production control system that uses a signaling device to regulate the flow of material.

11 If the lead time for an item is exactly five days, the demand is a constant four units per day, and the shipment container contains two units; how many kanban card sets would be needed?

12 A firm wants to justify smaller lot sizes economically. Management knows that it cannot change the cost to carry one unit in inventory since this is largely based on the value of the item. To justify a smaller lot size what must they do?

1. Waste 2. Lean production 3. Elimination of waste and respect for people 4. Value stream
5. Kaizen 6. Group technology 7. JIT (just-in-time) production 8. Freeze window 9. Uniform plant loading 10. Kanban 11. 10 card sets 12. Reduce setup cost

Selected Bibliography

Allen, M. "Picture-Perfect Manufacturing [Using Value Stream Mapping]." *Modern Machine Shop Magazine Online,* August 2004.

George, M. L. *Lean Six Sigma.* New York: McGraw-Hill, 2002.

Gross, J. M., and K. R. McInnis. *Kanban Made Simple: Demystifying and Applying Toyota's Legendary Manufacturing Process.* New York: AMACOM, 2003.

Monden, Y. *Toyota Production System: An Integrated Approach to Just-in-Time.* Atlanta, GA: Institute of Industrial Engineers, 1998.

Phelps, T.; M. Smith; and T. Hoenes. "Building a Lean Supply Chain." *Manufacturing Engineering* 132, no. 5 (May 2004), pp. 107–13.

Womack, J. P., and D. T. Jones. *Lean Thinking: Banish Waste and Create Wealth in Your Corporation.* New York: Simon & Schuster, 1996.

Womack, J. P.; D. T. Jones; and D. Roos. *The Machine That Changed the World.* New York: R. A. Rawston Associates, 1990.

Footnotes

1 Adapted from D. Blanchard, *Green Is the New Black,* March 1, 2009, IndustryWeek.com.

2 Adapted from B. Tompkins, *Lean Thinking for the Supply Chain,* from www.tompkinsinc.com.

3 K. A. Wantuck, *The Japanese Approach to Productivity* (Southfield, MI: Bendix Corporation, 1983).

4 K. Suzaki, *The New Manufacturing Challenge: Techniques for Continuous Improvement* (New York: Free Press, 1987), pp. 7–25.

5 C. Karlsson, *Japanese Production Management in Sunrise or Sunset* (Stockholm, Sweden: Stockholm School of Economics, EFI/The Economic Research Institute. 1999).

6 This was adapted from material from Strategos Consultants. See www.strategosinc.com.

7 R. H. Hall, *Zero Inventories* (Homewood, IL: Dow Jones-Irwin, 1983), p. 64.

8 J. P. Womack and D. T. Jones, *Lean Thinking* (New York: Simon & Shuster, 1996), p. 277.

9 K. A. Rosentrater and R. Balamuralikrishna, *Value Stream Mapping—A Tool for Engineering and Technology Education and Practice.* ASEE Illinois-Indiana Sectional Conference, Fort Wayne, IN. American Society for Engineering Education. Presented April 1, 2006.

10 J. Lovelle, "Mapping the Value Stream," *IIE Solutions* 33, no. 2 (February 2001), pp. 26–33.

SECTION FOUR

SUPPLY AND DEMAND PLANNING

11. Demand Management and Forecasting

12. Sales and Operations Planning

13. Inventory Control

14. Material Requirements Planning

IN RUNNING A BUSINESS, COMPUTERS CAN DO MORE THAN JUST WORD PROCESSING AND E-MAIL

Running a business requires a great planning system. What do we expect to sell in the future? How many people should we hire to handle the Christmas rush? How much inventory do we need? What should we make today? This section discusses various approaches used to answer these questions. The use of comprehensive software packages is common practice but it is important to understand the basic planning concepts that underlie them so that the right software can be purchased and configured correctly. Moreover, given this basic understanding a spreadsheet can be created for simple production planning situations.

CHAPTER 11

DEMAND MANAGEMENT AND FORECASTING

After reading this chapter you will:

- Understand the role of forecasting as a basis for supply chain planning.
- Compare the differences between independent and dependent demand.
- Identify the basic components of independent demand: average, trend, seasonal, and random variation.
- Describe the common qualitative forecasting techniques such as the Delphi method and Collaborative Forecasting.
- Show how to make a time series forecast using regression, moving averages, and exponential smoothing.
- Use decomposition to forecast when trend and seasonality is present.

305	Walmart's Data Warehouse	
		Strategic forecasts defined
		Tactical forecasts defined
307	Demand Management	
		Dependent demand defined
		Independent demand defined
308	Types of Forecasting	
		Time series analysis defined
308	Components of Demand	
310	Time Series Analysis	
	Linear Regression Analysis	Linear regression forecasting defined
	Decomposition of a Time Series	Exponential smoothing defined
	Simple Moving Average	Smoothing constant alpha (α) defined
	Weighted Moving Average	Smoothing constant delta (δ) defined
	Exponential Smoothing	Mean absolute deviation (MAD) defined
	Forecast Errors	Mean absolute percent error (MAPE) defined
	Sources of Error	Tracking signal defined
	Measurement of Error	

331 **Causal Relationship Forecasting**
Multiple Regression Analysis   Causal relationship defined

333 **Qualitative Techniques in Forecasting**
Market Research
Panel Consensus
Historical Analogy
Delphi Method

335 **Web-Based Forecasting: Collaborative Planning, Forecasting, and Replenishment (CPFR)**
Collaborative Planning, Forecasting, and Replenishment (CPFR) defined

336 **Summary**

352 **Case: Altavox Electronics**

352 **Super Quiz**

WALMART'S DATA WAREHOUSE

Walmart's size and power in the retail industry is having a huge influence in the database industry. Walmart manages one of the world's largest data warehouses with more than 35 terabytes of data. A terabyte is equal to 1,024 gigabytes or a trillion bytes. Your computer is probably 40–80 gigabytes. Walmart's formula for success—getting the right product on the appropriate shelf at the lowest price—owes much to the company's multimillion-dollar investment in data warehousing. Walmart has more detail than most of its competitors on what's going on by product, by store, and by day.

The systems track point of sale data at each store, inventory levels by store, products in transit, market statistics, customer demographics, finance, product returns, and supplier performance. The data are used for three broad areas of decision support: analyzing trends, managing inventory, and understanding customers. What emerges are "personality traits" for each of Walmart's 3,000

or so outlets, which Walmart managers use to determine product mix and presentation for each store.

Data mining is next. Walmart has developed a demand-forecasting application that looks at individual items for individual stores to decide the seasonal sales profile of each item. The system keeps a year's worth of data on the sales of 100,000 products and predicts which items will be needed in each store.

Walmart is now doing market-basket analysis. Data are collected on items that make up a shopper's total purchase so that the company can analyze relationships and patterns in customer purchases. The data warehouse is made available over the Web to its store managers and suppliers.

Forecasts are vital to every business organization and for every significant management decision. Forecasting is the basis of corporate long-run planning. In the functional areas of finance and accounting, forecasts provide the basis for budgetary planning and cost control. Marketing relies on sales forecasting to plan new products, compensate sales personnel, and make other key decisions. Production and operations personnel use forecasts to make periodic decisions involving supplier selection, process selection, capacity planning, and facility layout, as well as for continual decisions about purchasing, production planning, scheduling, and inventory.

Strategic forecasts

In considering what forecasting approach to use it is important to consider the purpose of the forecast. Some forecasts are for very high-level demand analysis. What do we expect the demand to be for a group of products over the next year, for example? Some forecasts are used to help set the strategy of how, in an aggregate sense, we will meet demand. We will call these **strategic forecasts**. Relative to the material in the book, strategic forecasts are most appropriate when making decisions related to overall strategy (Chapter 2), capacity (Chapter 3), production process design (Chapter 4), service process design (Chapter 5), sourcing (Chapter 8), location and distribution design (Chapter 9), and in aggregate

operations planning (Chapter 12). These all involve relatively long-term decisions that relate to how demand will be met strategically.

Forecasts are also needed for how a firm operates processes on a day-to-day basis. For example, when should the inventory for an item be replenished, or how much production should we schedule for an item next week? These are **tactical forecasts** where the goal is to estimate demand in the relative short term, a few weeks or months. These forecasts are important to ensure that in the short term we are able to meet customer lead time expectations and other criteria related to the availability of our products and services.

Tactical forecasts

Supply Chain

In Chapter 4, the concept of decoupling points was discussed. These are points within the supply chain where inventory is positioned to allow processes or entities in the supply chain to operate independently. For example, if a product is stocked at a retailer, the customer pulls the item from the shelf and the manufacturer never sees a customer order. Inventory acts as a buffer to separate the customer from the manufacturing process. Selection of decoupling points is a strategic decision that determines customer lead times and can greatly impact inventory investment. The closer this point is to the customer, the quicker the customer can be served. Typically, a trade-off is involved where quicker response to customer demand comes at the expense of greater inventory investment, because finished goods inventory is more expensive than raw material inventory.

Forecasting is needed at these decoupling points to set appropriate inventory levels for these buffers. The actual setting of these levels is the topic of Chapter 13, Inventory Control, but an essential input into those decisions is a forecast of expected demand and the expected error associated with that demand. If, for example, we are able to forecast demand very accurately then inventory levels can be set precisely to expected customer demand. On the other hand, if predicting short-term demand is difficult, then extra inventory to cover this uncertainty will be needed.

The same is true relative to service settings where inventory is not used to buffer demand. Here capacity availability relative to expected demand is the issue. If we can predict demand in a service setting very accurately, then tactically all we need to do is ensure that we have the appropriate capacity in the short term. When demand is not predictable then excess capacity may be needed if servicing customers quickly is important.

Service

Bear in mind that a perfect forecast is virtually impossible. Too many factors in the business environment cannot be predicted with certainty. Therefore, rather than search for the perfect forecast, it is far more important to establish the practice of continual review of forecasts and to learn to live with inaccurate forecasts. This is not to say that we should not try to improve the forecasting model or methodology or even to try to influence demand in a way that reduces demand uncertainty. When forecasting, a good strategy is to use two or three methods and look at them for the commonsense view. Will expected changes in the general economy affect the forecast? Are there changes in our customers' behaviors that will impact demand that is not being captured by our current approaches? In this chapter we look at both *qualitative* techniques that use managerial judgment and also *quantitative* techniques that rely on mathematical models. It is our view that combining these techniques is essential to a good forecasting process that is appropriate to the decisions being made.

DEMAND MANAGEMENT

The purpose of demand management is to coordinate and control all sources of demand so the supply chain can be run efficiently and the product delivered on time.

Where does demand for a firm's product or service come from, and what can a firm do to manage it? There are two basic sources of demand: dependent demand and independent demand. **Dependent demand** is the demand for a product or service caused by the

Dependent demand

Independent demand

demand for other products or services. For example, if a firm sells 1,000 tricycles, then 1,000 front wheels and 2,000 rear wheels are needed. This type of internal demand needs not a forecast, just a tabulation. As to how many tricycles the firm might sell, this is called **independent demand** because its demand cannot be derived directly from that of other products.[1] We discuss dependence and independence more fully in Chapters 13 and 14.

There is not much a firm can do about dependent demand. It must be met (although the product or service can be purchased rather than produced internally). But there is a lot a firm can do about independent demand—if it wants to. The firm can:

1. **Take an active role to influence demand.**   The firm can apply pressure on its sales force, it can offer incentives both to customers and to its own personnel, it can wage campaigns to sell products, and it can cut prices. These actions can increase demand. Conversely, demand can be decreased through price increases or reduced sales efforts.

2. **Take a passive role and simply respond to demand.**   There are several reasons a firm may not try to change demand but simply accept what happens. If a firm is running at full capacity, it may not want to do anything about demand. Other reasons are a firm may be powerless to change demand because of the expense to advertise; the market may be fixed in size and static; or demand is beyond its control (such as in the case of sole supplier). There are other competitive, legal, environmental, ethical, and moral reasons that market demand is passively accepted.

A great deal of coordination is required to manage these dependent, independent, active, and passive demands. These demands originate both internally and externally in the form of new product sales from marketing, repair parts for previously sold products from product service, restocking from the factory warehouses, and supply items for manufacturing. In this chapter, our primary interest is in forecasting for independent items.

TYPES OF FORECASTING

Forecasting can be classified into four basic types: *qualitative, time series analysis, causal relationships,* and *simulation.*

Time series analysis

Qualitative techniques are subjective or judgmental and are based on estimates and opinions. **Time series analysis**, the primary focus of this chapter, is based on the idea that data relating to past demand can be used to predict future demand. Past data may include several components, such as trend, seasonal, or cyclical influences, and are described in the following section. Causal forecasting, which we discuss using the linear regression technique, assumes that demand is related to some underlying factor or factors in the environment. Simulation models allow the forecaster to run through a range of assumptions about the condition of the forecast. In this chapter we focus on qualitative and time series techniques since these are most often used in supply chain planning and control.

COMPONENTS OF DEMAND

In most cases, demand for products or services can be broken down into six components: average demand for the period, a trend, seasonal element, cyclical elements, random variation, and autocorrelation. Exhibit 11.1 illustrates a demand over a four-year period, showing the average, trend, and seasonal components and randomness around the smoothed demand curve.

exhibit 11.1

Historical Product Demand Consisting of a Growth Trend and Seasonal Demand

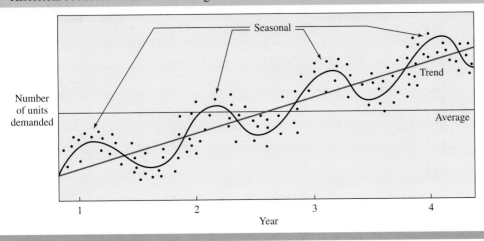

**Excel:
Components of
Demand**

Cyclical factors are more difficult to determine because the time span may be unknown or the cause of the cycle may not be considered. Cyclical influence on demand may come from such occurrences as political elections, war, economic conditions, or sociological pressures.

Random variations are caused by chance events. Statistically, when all the known causes for demand (average, trend, seasonal, cyclical, and autocorrelative) are subtracted from total demand, what remains is the unexplained portion of demand. If we cannot identify the cause of this remainder, it is assumed to be purely random chance.

Autocorrelation denotes the persistence of occurrence. More specifically, the value expected at any point is highly correlated with its own past values. In waiting line theory, the length of a waiting line is highly autocorrelated. That is, if a line is relatively long at one time, then shortly after that time, we would expect the line still to be long.

When demand is random, it may vary widely from one week to another. Where high autocorrelation exists, demand is not expected to change very much from one week to the next.

Trend lines are the usual starting point in developing a forecast. These trend lines are then adjusted for seasonal effects, cyclical elements, and any other expected events that may influence the final forecast. Exhibit 11.2 shows four of the most common types of trends. A linear trend is obviously a straight continuous relationship. An S-curve is typical of a product growth and maturity cycle. The most important point in the S-curve is where the trend changes from slow growth to fast growth, or from fast to slow. An asymptotic trend starts with the highest demand growth at the beginning but then tapers off. Such a curve could happen when a firm enters an existing market with the objective of saturating and capturing a large share of the market. An exponential curve is common in products with explosive growth. The exponential trend suggests that sales will continue to increase—an assumption that may not be safe to make.

A widely used forecasting method plots data and then searches for the curve pattern (such as linear, S-curve, asymptotic, or exponential) that fits best. The attractiveness of this method is that because the mathematics for the curve are known, solving for values for future time periods is easy.

Sometimes our data do not seem to fit any standard curve. This may be due to several causes essentially beating the data from several directions at the same time. For these cases, a simplistic but often effective forecast can be obtained by simply plotting data.

exhibit 11.2
Common Types of Trends

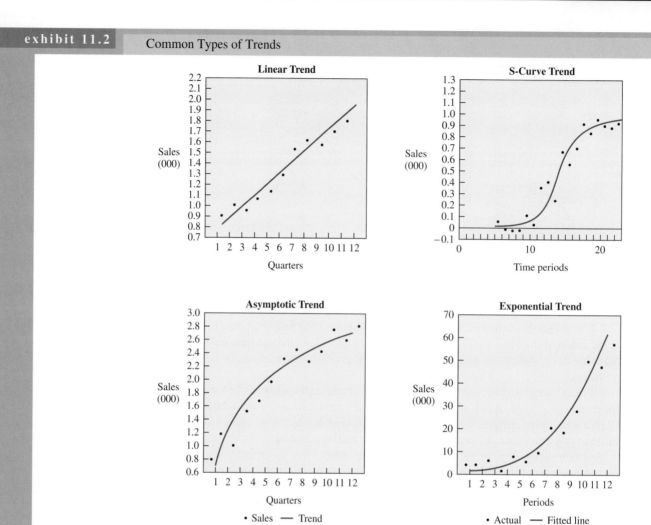

TIME SERIES ANALYSIS

Time series forecasting models try to predict the future based on past data. For example, sales figures collected for the past six weeks can be used to forecast sales for the seventh week. Quarterly sales figures collected for the past several years can be used to forecast future quarters. Even though both examples contain sales, different forecasting time series models would likely be used.

Exhibit 11.3 shows the time series models discussed in the chapter and some of their characteristics. Terms such as *short, medium,* and *long* are relative to the context in which they are used. However, in business forecasting *short term* usually refers to under three months; *medium term,* three months to two years; and *long term,* greater than two years. We would generally use short-term forecasts for tactical decisions such as replenishing inventory or scheduling employees in the near term and medium-term forecasts for planning a strategy for meeting demand over the next six months to a year and a half. In general, the short-term models compensate for random variation and adjust for short-term changes (such as consumers' responses to a new product). They are especially good for measuring the current variability

Least Squares Regression Line

exhibit 11.4

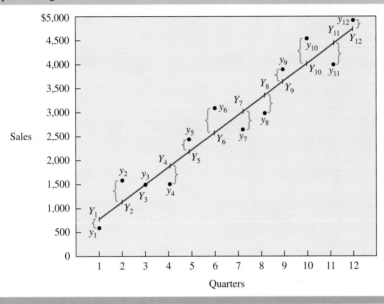

Excel: Forecasting

$$b = \frac{\sum xy - n\bar{x} \cdot \bar{y}}{\sum x^2 - n\bar{x}^2}$$

[11.3]

where

$a = Y$ intercept
$b =$ Slope of the line
$\bar{y} =$ Average of all ys
$\bar{x} =$ Average of all xs
$x = x$ value at each data point
$y = y$ value at each data point
$n =$ Number of data points
$Y =$ Value of the dependent variable computed with the regression equation

Exhibit 11.5 shows these computations carried out for the 12 data points in the problem. Note that the final equation for Y shows an intercept of 441.6 and a slope of 359.6. The slope shows that for every unit change in X, Y changes by 359.6.

Strictly based on the equation, forecasts for periods 13 through 16 would be

$$Y_{13} = 441.6 + 359.6(13) = 5,116.4$$
$$Y_{14} = 441.6 + 359.6(14) = 5,476.0$$
$$Y_{15} = 441.6 + 359.6(15) = 5,835.6$$
$$Y_{16} = 441.6 + 359.6(16) = 6,195.2$$

The standard error of estimate, or how well the line fits the data, is[2]

$$S_{yx} = \sqrt{\frac{\sum_{i=1}^{n}(y_i - Y_i)^2}{n-2}}$$

[11.4]

Least Squares Regression Analysis

(1) x	(2) y	(3) xy	(4) x^2	(5) y^2	(6) Y
1	600	600	1	360,000	801.3
2	1,550	3,100	4	2,402,500	1,160.9
3	1,500	4,500	9	2,250,000	1,520.5
4	1,500	6,000	16	2,250,000	1,880.1
5	2,400	12,000	25	5,760,000	2,239.7
6	3,100	18,600	36	9,610,000	2,599.4
7	2,600	18,200	49	6,760,000	2,959.0
8	2,900	23,200	64	8,410,000	3,318.6
9	3,800	34,200	81	14,440,000	3,678.2
10	4,500	45,000	100	20,250,000	4,037.8
11	4,000	44,000	121	16,000,000	4,397.4
12	4,900	58,800	144	24,010,000	4,757.1
78	33,350	268,200	650	112,502,500	

$\bar{x} = 6.5 \quad b = 359.6153$

$\bar{y} = 2,779.17 \quad a = 441.6666$

Therefore, $Y = 441.66 + 359.6x$

$\qquad S_{yx} = 363.9$

Excel:
Forecasting

The standard error of estimate is computed from the second and last columns of Exhibit 11.5:

$$S_{yx} = \sqrt{\frac{(600 - 801.3)^2 + (1,550 - 1,160.9)^2 + (1,500 - 1,520.5)^2 + \cdots + (4,900 - 4,757.1)^2}{10}}$$

$$= 363.9$$

Microsoft Excel has a very powerful regression tool designed to perform these calculations. To use the tool, a table is needed that contains data relevant to the problem (see Exhibit 11.6). The tool is part of the Data Analysis ToolPak that is accessed from the Tools menu (or Data tab in Excel 2007) (you may need to add this to your Tools options by using the Add-In option under Tools).

To use the tool, first input the data in two columns in your spreadsheet, then access the Regression option from the Tools → Data Analysis menu. Next, specify the Y Range, which is B2:B13, and the X-Range, which is A2:A13 in our example. Finally, an Output Range is specified. This is where you would like the results of the regression analysis placed in your spreadsheet. In the example, A16 is entered. There is some information provided that goes beyond what we have covered, but what you are looking for is the Intercept and X Variable coefficients that correspond to the intercept and slope values in the linear equation. These are in rows 32 and 33 in Exhibit 11.6. ●

We discuss the possible existence of seasonal components in the next section on decomposition of a time series.

Decomposition of a Time Series

A *time series* can be defined as chronologically ordered data that may contain one or more components of demand: trend, seasonal, cyclical, autocorrelation, and random. *Decomposition* of a time series means identifying and separating the time series data into these components. In practice, it is relatively easy to identify the trend (even without mathematical

exhibit 11.6

Excel Regression Tool

	A	B	C	D	E	F	G	H	I
1	Qtr	Demand							
2	1	600							
3	2	1550							
4	3	1500							
5	4	1500							
6	5	2400							
7	6	3100							
8	7	2600							
9	8	2900							
10	9	3800							
11	10	4500							
12	11	4000							
13	12	4900							
14									
15									
16	SUMMARY OUTPUT								
17									
18	Regression Statistics								
19	Multiple R	0.96601558							
20	R Square	0.933186102							
21	Adjusted R Square	0.926504712							
22	Standard Error	363.8777972							
23	Observations	12							
24									
25	ANOVA								
26		df	SS	MS	F	Significance F			
27	Regression	1	18493221.15	18493221	139.6695	3.37202E-07			
28	Residual	10	1324070.513	132407.1					
29	Total	11	19817291.67						
30									
31		Coefficients	Standard Error	t Stat	P-value	Lower 95%	Upper 95%	Lower 95.0%	Upper 95.0%
32	Intercept	441.6666667	223.9513029	1.972155	0.076869	-57.3279302	940.661264	-57.3279302	940.6612636
33	X Variable 1	359.6153846	30.42899005	11.81818	3.37E-07	291.8153699	427.415399	291.81537	427.4153993
34									

Regression

Input
Input Y Range: $B$2:$B$13
Input X Range: $A$2:$A$13
☐ Labels   ☐ Constant is Zero
☐ Confidence Level: 95 %

Output options
⦿ Output Range: $A$16
○ New Worksheet Ply:
○ New Workbook
Residuals
☐ Residuals   ☐ Residual Plots
☐ Standardized Residuals   ☐ Line Fit Plots
Normal Probability
☐ Normal Probability Plots

OK   Cancel   Help

Excel: Forecasting

analysis, it is usually easy to plot and see the direction of movement) and the seasonal component (by comparing the same period year to year). It is considerably more difficult to identify the cycles (these may be many months or years long), autocorrelation, and random components. (The forecaster usually calls random anything left over that cannot be identified as another component.)

When demand contains both seasonal and trend effects at the same time, the question is how they relate to each other. In this description, we examine two types of seasonal variation: *additive* and *multiplicative*.

Additive Seasonal Variation Additive seasonal variation simply assumes that the seasonal amount is a constant no matter what the trend or average amount is.

$$\text{Forecast including trend and seasonal} = \text{Trend} + \text{Seasonal}$$

Exhibit 11.7A shows an example of increasing trend with constant seasonal amounts.

Multiplicative Seasonal Variation In multiplicative seasonal variation, the trend is multiplied by the seasonal factors.

$$\text{Forecast including trend and seasonal} = \text{Trend} \times \text{Seasonal factor}$$

Exhibit 11.7B shows the seasonal variation increasing as the trend increases because its size depends on the trend.

The multiplicative seasonal variation is the usual experience. Essentially, this says that the larger the basic amount projected, the larger the variation around this that we can expect.

exhibit 11.7   Additive and Multiplicative Seasonal Variation Superimposed on Changing Trend

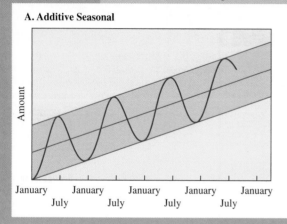

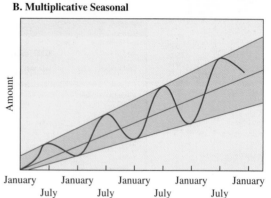

**Excel:
Forecasting**

COMPANIES SUCH AS TORO
MANUFACTURE LAWNMOWERS AND
SNOW BLOWERS TO MATCH SEASONAL
DEMAND. USING THE SAME EQUIPMENT
AND ASSEMBLY LINES PROVIDES BETTER
CAPACITY UTILIZATION, WORKFORCE
STABILITY, PRODUCTIVITY, AND REVENUE.

Seasonal Factor (or Index)   A seasonal factor is the amount of correction
needed in a time series to adjust for the season of the year.

We usually associate *seasonal* with a period of the year characterized by some particular activity. We use the word *cyclical* to indicate other than annual recurrent periods of
repetitive activity.

The following examples show how seasonal indexes are determined and used to forecast (1) a simple calculation based on past seasonal data and (2) the trend and seasonal
index from a hand-fit regression line. We follow this with a more formal procedure for the
decomposition of data and forecasting using least squares regression.

EXAMPLE 11.2: Simple Proportion

Assume that in past years, a firm sold an average of 1,000 units of a particular product line each year.
On the average, 200 units were sold in the spring, 350 in the summer, 300 in the fall, and 150 in the
winter. The seasonal factor (or index) is the ratio of the amount sold during each season divided by
the average for all seasons.

Step by Step

SOLUTION

In this example, the yearly amount divided equally over all seasons is $1,000 \div 4 = 250$. The seasonal factors therefore are

	PAST SALES	AVERAGE SALES FOR EACH SEASON (1,000/4)	SEASONAL FACTOR
Spring	200	250	200/250 = 0.8
Summer	350	250	350/250 = 1.4
Fall	300	250	300/250 = 1.2
Winter	150	250	150/250 = 0.6
Total	1,000		

Using these factors, if we expected demand for next year to be 1,100 units, we would forecast the demand to occur as

	EXPECTED DEMAND FOR NEXT YEAR	AVERAGE SALES FOR EACH SEASON (1,100/4)		SEASONAL FACTOR		NEXT YEAR'S SEASONAL FORECAST
Spring		275	×	0.8	=	220
Summer		275	×	1.4	=	385
Fall		275	×	1.2	=	330
Winter		275	×	0.6	=	165
Total	1,100					●

The seasonal factor may be periodically updated as new data are available. The following example shows the seasonal factor and multiplicative seasonal variation.

EXAMPLE 11.3: Computing Trend and Seasonal Factor from a Hand-Fit Straight Line

Here we must compute the trend as well as the seasonal factors.

Step by Step

SOLUTION

We solve this problem by simply hand fitting a straight line through the data points and measuring the trend and intercept from the graph. Assume the history of data is

QUARTER	AMOUNT	QUARTER	AMOUNT
I–2008	300	I–2009	520
II–2008	200	II–2009	420
III–2008	220	III–2009	400
IV–2008	530	IV–2009	700

First, we plot as in Exhibit 11.8 and then visually fit a straight line through the data. (Naturally, this line and the resulting equation are subject to variation. We show how to do this using regression in the next section.) The equation for the line is

$$\text{Trend}_t = 170 + 55t$$

Our equation was derived from the intercept 170 plus a rise of $(610 - 170) \div 8$ periods. Next we can derive a seasonal index by comparing the actual data with the trend line as in Exhibit 11.8. The seasonal factor was developed by averaging the same quarters in each year.

exhibit 11.8   Computing a Seasonal Factor from the Actual Data and Trend Line

Excel:
Forecasting

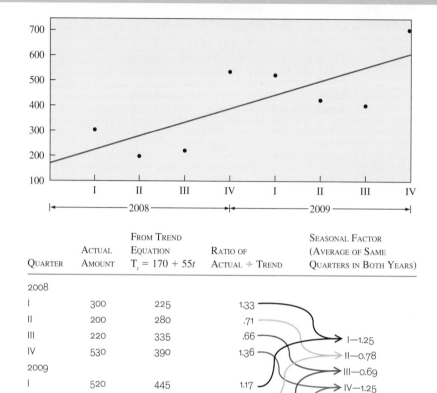

Quarter	Actual Amount	From Trend Equation $T_t = 170 + 55t$	Ratio of Actual ÷ Trend	Seasonal Factor (Average of Same Quarters in Both Years)
2008				
I	300	225	1.33	
II	200	280	.71	I—1.25
III	220	335	.66	II—0.78
IV	530	390	1.36	III—0.69
2009				IV—1.25
I	520	445	1.17	
II	420	500	.84	
III	400	555	.72	
IV	700	610	1.15	

We can compute the 2010 forecast including trend and seasonal factors (FITS) as follows:

$$\text{FITS}_t = \text{Trend} \times \text{Seasonal}$$
$$\text{I—2010 FITS}_9 = [170 + 55(9)]1.25 = 831$$
$$\text{II—2010 FITS}_{10} = [170 + 55(10)]0.78 = 562$$
$$\text{III—2010 FITS}_{11} = [170 + 55(11)]0.69 = 535$$
$$\text{IV—2010 FITS}_{12} = [170 + 55(12)]1.25 = 1,038 \; \bullet$$

Decomposition Using Least Squares Regression   Decomposition of a time series means finding the series' basic components of trend, seasonal, and cyclical. Indexes are calculated for seasons and cycles. The forecasting procedure then reverses the process by projecting the trend and adjusting it by the seasonal and cyclical indexes, which were determined in the decomposition process. More formally, the process is:

1.   Decompose the time series into its components.
    a. Find seasonal component.
    b. Deseasonalize the demand.
    c. Find trend component.

2. Forecast future values of each component.
   a. Project trend component into the future.
   b. Multiply trend component by seasonal component.

Note that the random component is not included in this list. We implicitly remove the random component from the time series when we average as in step 1. It is pointless to attempt a projection of the random component in step 2 unless we have information about some unusual event, such as a major labor dispute, that could adversely affect product demand (and this would not really be random).

Exhibit 11.9 shows the decomposition of a time series using least squares regression and the same basic data we used in our first regression example. Each data point corresponds to using a single three-month quarter of the three-year (12-quarter) period. Our objective is to forecast demand for the four quarters of the fourth year.

Step 1. Determine the seasonal factor (or index). Exhibit 11.9 summarizes the calculations needed. Column 4 develops an average for the same quarters in the three-year period. For example, the first quarters of the three years are added together and divided by three. A seasonal factor is then derived by dividing that average by the general average for all 12 quarters $\left(\dfrac{33,350}{12}, \text{ or } 2,779\right)$. For example, this first quarter seasonal factor

---

exhibit 11.9

Deseasonalized Demand

(1) PERIOD (x)	(2) QUARTER	(3) ACTUAL DEMAND (y)	(4) AVERAGE OF THE SAME QUARTERS OF EACH YEAR	(5) SEASONAL FACTOR	(6) DESEASONALIZED DEMAND (y_d) COL. (3) ÷ COL. (5)	(7) x^2 (COL. 1)^2	(8) $x \times y_d$ COL. (1) × COL. (6)
1	I	600	(600 + 2,400 + 3,800)/3 = 2,266.7	0.82	735.7	1	735.7
2	II	1,550	(1,550 + 3,100 + 4,500)/3 = 3,050	1.10	1,412.4	4	2,824.7
3	III	1,500	(1,500 + 2,600 + 4,000)/3 = 2,700	0.97	1,544.0	9	4,631.9
4	IV	1,500	(1,500 + 2,900 + 4,900)/3 = 3,100	1.12	1,344.8	16	5,379.0
5	I	2,400		0.82	2,942.6	25	14,713.2
6	II	3,100		1.10	2,824.7	36	16,948.4
7	III	2,600		0.97	2,676.2	49	18,733.6
8	IV	2,900		1.12	2,599.9	64	20,798.9
9	I	3,800		0.82	4,659.2	81	41,932.7
10	II	4,500		1.10	4,100.4	100	41,004.1
11	III	4,000		0.97	4,117.3	121	45,290.1
12	IV	4,900		1.12	4,392.9	144	52,714.5
78		33,350		12.03	33,350.1*	650	265,706.9

$$\bar{x} = \frac{78}{12} = 6.5 \qquad b = \frac{\sum xy_d - n\bar{x}\bar{y}_d}{\sum \bar{x}^2 - n\bar{x}^2} = \frac{265,706.9 - 12(6.5)2,779.2}{650 - 12(6.5)^2} = 342.2$$

$$\bar{y}_d = 33,350/12 = 2,779.2 \qquad a = \bar{y}_d - b\bar{x} = 2,779.2 - 342.2(6.5) = 554.9$$

Therefore, $Y = a + bx = 554.9 + 342.2x$

*Column 3 and column 6 totals should be equal at 33,350. Differences are due to rounding. Column 5 was rounded to two decimal places.

is $\dfrac{2,266.7}{2,779} = 0.82$. These are entered in column 5. Note that the seasonal factors are identical for similar quarters in each year.

Step 2. Deseasonalize the original data. To remove the seasonal effect on the data, we divide the original data by the seasonal factor. This step is called the deseasonalization of demand and is shown in column 6 of Exhibit 11.9.

Step 3. Develop a least squares regression line for the deseasonalized data. The purpose here is to develop an equation for the trend line Y, which we then modify with the seasonal factor. The procedure is the same as we used before:

$$Y = a + bx$$

where

y_d = Deseasonalized demand (see Exhibit 11.9)

x = Quarter

Y = Demand computed using the regression equation $Y = a + bx$

a = Y intercept

b = Slope of the line

The least squares calculations using columns 1, 7, and 8 of Exhibit 11.9 are shown in the lower section of the exhibit. The final deseasonalized equation for our data is $Y = 554.9 + 342.2x$. This straight line is shown in Exhibit 11.10.

Step 4. Project the regression line through the period to be forecast. Our purpose is to forecast periods 13 through 16. We start by solving the equation for Y at each of these periods (shown in step 5, column 3).

Step 5. Create the final forecast by adjusting the regression line by the seasonal factor. Recall that the Y equation has been deseasonalized. We now reverse the procedure by multiplying the quarterly data we derived by the seasonal factor for that quarter:

PERIOD	QUARTER	Y FROM REGRESSION LINE	SEASONAL FACTOR	FORECAST ($Y \times$ SEASONAL FACTOR)
13	1	5,003.5	0.82	4,102.87
14	2	5,345.7	1.10	5,880.27
15	3	5,687.9	0.97	5,517.26
16	4	6,030.1	1.12	6,753.71

exhibit 11.10   Straight Line Graph of Deseasonalized Equation

**Excel:
Forecasting**

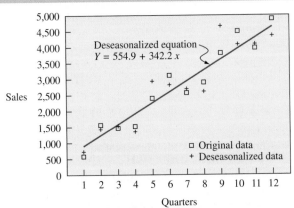

exhibit 11.11

Prediction Intervals for Linear Trend

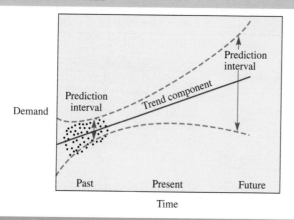

Our forecast is now complete. The procedure is generally the same as what we did in the hand-fit previous example. In the present example, however, we followed a more formal procedure and computed the least squares regression line as well.

Error Range   When a straight line is fitted through data points and then used for forecasting, errors can come from two sources. First, there are the usual errors similar to the standard deviation of any set of data. Second, there are errors that arise because the line is wrong. Exhibit 11.11 shows this error range. Instead of developing the statistics here, we will briefly show why the range broadens. First, visualize that one line is drawn that has some error such that it slants too steeply upward. Standard errors are then calculated for this line. Now visualize another line that slants too steeply downward. It also has a standard error. The total error range, for this analysis, consists of errors resulting from both lines as well as all other possible lines. We included this exhibit to show how the error range widens as we go further into the future.

Simple Moving Average

When demand for a product is neither growing nor declining rapidly, and if it does not have seasonal characteristics, a moving average can be useful in removing the random fluctuations for forecasting. Although *moving averages* are frequently centered, it is more convenient to use past data to predict the following period directly. To illustrate, a centered five-month average of January, February, March, April, and May gives an average centered on March. However, all five months of data must already exist. If our objective is to forecast for June, we must project our moving average—by some means—from March to June. If the average is not centered but is at the forward end, we can forecast more easily, though we may lose some accuracy. Thus, if we want to forecast June with a five-month moving average, we can take the average of January, February, March, April, and May. When June passes, the forecast for July would be the average of February, March, April, May, and June. This is how Exhibit 11.12 was computed.

Although it is important to select the best period for the moving average, there are several conflicting effects of different period lengths. The longer the moving average period, the more the random elements are smoothed (which may be desirable in many cases). But if there is a trend in the data—either increasing or decreasing—the moving average has the adverse characteristic of lagging the trend. Therefore, while a shorter time span produces

exhibit 11.12   Forecast Demand Based on a Three- and a Nine-Week Simple Moving Average

**Excel:
Forecasting**

WEEK	DEMAND	3 WEEK	9 WEEK	WEEK	DEMAND	3 WEEK	9 WEEK
1	800			16	1,700	2,200	1,811
2	1,400			17	1,800	2,000	1,800
3	1,000			18	2,200	1,833	1,811
4	1,500	1,067		19	1,900	1,900	1,911
5	1,500	1,300		20	2,400	1,967	1,933
6	1,300	1,333		21	2,400	2,167	2,011
7	1,800	1,433		22	2,600	2,233	2,111
8	1,700	1,533		23	2,000	2,467	2,144
9	1,300	1,600		24	2,500	2,333	2,111
10	1,700	1,600	1,367	25	2,600	2,367	2,167
11	1,700	1,567	1,467	26	2,200	2,367	2,267
12	1,500	1,567	1,500	27	2,200	2,433	2,311
13	2,300	1,633	1,556	28	2,500	2,333	2,311
14	2,300	1,833	1,644	29	2,400	2,300	2,378
15	2,000	2,033	1,733	30	2,100	2,367	2,378

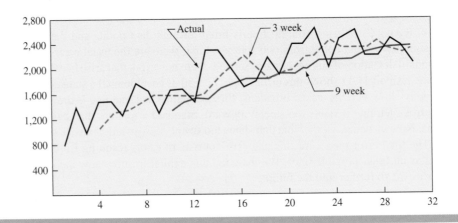

more oscillation, there is a closer following of the trend. Conversely, a longer time span gives a smoother response but lags the trend.

The formula for a simple moving average is

$$F_t = \frac{A_{t-1} + A_{t-2} + A_{t-3} + \cdots + A_{t-n}}{n}$$ [11.5]

where

$$F_t = \text{Forecast for the coming period}$$

$$n = \text{Number of periods to be averaged}$$

$$A_{t-1} = \text{Actual occurrence in the past period}$$

$$A_{t-2}, A_{t-3}, \text{ and } A_{t-n} = \text{Actual occurrences two periods ago, three periods ago, and so on}$$
up to n periods ago

A plot of the data in Exhibit 11.12, shows the effects of various lengths of the period of a moving average. We see that the growth trend levels off at about the 23rd week. The three-week moving average responds better in following this change than the nine-week average, although overall, the nine-week average is smoother.

The main disadvantage in calculating a moving average is that all individual elements must be carried as data because a new forecast period involves adding new data and dropping the earliest data. For a three- or six-period moving average, this is not too severe. But plotting a 60-day moving average for the usage of each of 20,000 items in inventory would involve a significant amount of data.

Weighted Moving Average

Whereas the simple moving average gives equal weight to each component of the moving average database, a weighted moving average allows any weights to be placed on each element, providing, of course, that the sum of all weights equals 1. For example, a department store may find that in a four-month period, the best forecast is derived by using 40 percent of the actual sales for the most recent month, 30 percent of two months ago, 20 percent of three months ago, and 10 percent of four months ago. If actual sales experience was

Month 1	Month 2	Month 3	Month 4	Month 5
100	90	105	95	?

the forecast for month 5 would be

$$F_5 = 0.40(95) + 0.30(105) + 0.20(90) + 0.10(100)$$
$$= 38 + 31.5 + 18 + 10$$
$$= 97.5$$

The formula for a weighted moving average is

$$F_t = w_1 A_{t-1} + w_2 A_{t-2} + \cdots + w_n A_{t-n} \qquad \textbf{[11.6]}$$

where

w_1 = Weight to be given to the actual occurrence for the period $t - 1$
w_2 = Weight to be given to the actual occurrence for the period $t - 2$
w_n = Weight to be given to the actual occurrence for the period $t - n$
n = Total number of periods in the forecast

Although many periods may be ignored (that is, their weights are zero) and the weighting scheme may be in any order (for example, more distant data may have greater weights than more recent data), the sum of all the weights must equal 1.

$$\sum_{i=1}^{n} w_i = 1$$

Suppose sales for month 5 actually turned out to be 110. Then the forecast for month 6 would be

$$F_6 = 0.40(110) + 0.30(95) + 0.20(105) + 0.10(90)$$
$$= 44 + 28.5 + 21 + 9$$
$$= 102.5$$

Choosing Weights Experience and trial and error are the simplest ways to choose weights. As a general rule, the most recent past is the most important indicator of what to expect in the future, and, therefore, it should get higher weighting. The past month's revenue or plant capacity, for example, would be a better estimate for the coming month than the revenue or plant capacity of several months ago.

However, if the data are seasonal, for example, weights should be established accordingly. Bathing suit sales in July of last year should be weighted more heavily than bathing suit sales in December (in the Northern Hemisphere).

The weighted moving average has a definite advantage over the simple moving average in being able to vary the effects of past data. However, it is more inconvenient and costly to use than the exponential smoothing method, which we examine next.

Exponential Smoothing

In the previous methods of forecasting (simple and weighted moving averages), the major drawback is the need to continually carry a large amount of historical data. (This is also true for regression analysis techniques, which we soon will cover.) As each new piece of data is added in these methods, the oldest observation is dropped, and the new forecast is calculated. In many applications (perhaps in most), the most recent occurrences are more indicative of the future than those in the more distant past. If this premise is valid—that the importance of data diminishes as the past becomes more distant—then **exponential smoothing** may be the most logical and easiest method to use.

Exponential smoothing

The reason this is called exponential smoothing is that each increment in the past is decreased by $(1 - \alpha)$. If α is 0.05, for example, weights for various periods would be as follows (α is defined below):

	WEIGHTING AT $\alpha = 0.05$
Most recent weighting $= \alpha(1 - \alpha)^0$	0.0500
Data one time period older $= \alpha(1 - \alpha)^1$	0.0475
Data two time periods older $= \alpha(1 - \alpha)^2$	0.0451
Data three time periods older $= \alpha(1 - \alpha)^3$	0.0429

Therefore, the exponents 0, 1, 2, 3, . . . , and so on give it its name.

Exponential smoothing is the most used of all forecasting techniques. It is an integral part of virtually all computerized forecasting programs, and it is widely used in ordering inventory in retail firms, wholesale companies, and service agencies.

Exponential smoothing techniques have become well accepted for six major reasons:

1 Exponential models are surprisingly accurate.
2. Formulating an exponential model is relatively easy.
3. The user can understand how the model works.
4. Little computation is required to use the model.
5. Computer storage requirements are small because of the limited use of historical data.
6. Tests for accuracy as to how well the model is performing are easy to compute.

In the exponential smoothing method, only three pieces of data are needed to forecast the future: the most recent forecast, the actual demand that occurred for that forecast period, and a **smoothing constant alpha** (α). This smoothing constant determines the level of smoothing and the speed of reaction to differences between forecasts and actual

Smoothing constant alpha (α)

occurrences. The value for the constant is determined both by the nature of the product and by the manager's sense of what constitutes a good response rate. For example, if a firm produced a standard item with relatively stable demand, the reaction rate to differences between actual and forecast demand would tend to be small, perhaps just 5 or 10 percentage points. However, if the firm were experiencing growth, it would be desirable to have a higher reaction rate, perhaps 15 to 30 percentage points, to give greater importance to recent growth experience. The more rapid the growth, the higher the reaction rate should be. Sometimes users of the simple moving average switch to exponential smoothing but like to keep the forecasts about the same as the simple moving average. In this case, α is approximated by $2 \div (n + 1)$, where n is the number of time periods.

The equation for a single exponential smoothing forecast is simply

$$F_t = F_{t-1} + \alpha(A_{t-1} - F_{t-1})$$ [11.7]

where

F_t = The exponentially smoothed forecast for period t

F_{t-1} = The exponentially smoothed forecast made for the prior period

A_{t-1} = The actual demand in the prior period

α = The desired response rate, or smoothing constant

This equation states that the new forecast is equal to the old forecast plus a portion of the error (the difference between the previous forecast and what actually occurred).[3]

To demonstrate the method, assume that the long-run demand for the product under study is relatively stable and a smoothing constant (α) of 0.05 is considered appropriate. If the exponential method were used as a continuing policy, a forecast would have been made for last month.[4] Assume that last month's forecast (F_{t-1}) was 1,050 units. If 1,000 actually were demanded, rather than 1,050, the forecast for this month would be

$$F_t = F_{t-1} + \alpha(A_{t-1} - F_{t-1})$$
$$= 1,050 + 0.05(1,000 - 1,050)$$
$$= 1,050 + 0.05(-50)$$
$$= 1,047.5 \text{ units}$$

Because the smoothing coefficient is small, the reaction of the new forecast to an error of 50 units is to decrease the next month's forecast by only $2\frac{1}{2}$ units.

Single exponential smoothing has the shortcoming of lagging changes in demand. Exhibit 11.13 presents actual data plotted as a smooth curve to show the lagging effects of the exponential forecasts. The forecast lags during an increase or decrease but overshoots when a change in direction occurs. Note that the higher the value of alpha, the more closely the forecast follows the actual. To more closely track actual demand, a trend factor may be added. Adjusting the value of alpha also helps. This is termed *adaptive forecasting*. Both trend effects and adaptive forecasting are briefly explained in following sections.

Trend Effects in Exponential Smoothing   Remember that an upward or downward trend in data collected over a sequence of time periods causes the exponential forecast to always lag behind (be above or below) the actual occurrence. Exponentially smoothed forecasts can be corrected somewhat by adding in a trend adjustment. To correct the trend, we need two smoothing constants. Besides the smoothing constant α, the trend

| exhibit 11.13 | Exponential Forecasts versus Actual Demand for Units of a Product over Time Showing the Forecast Lag |

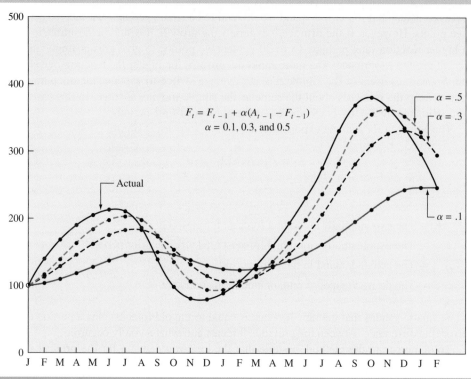

$$F_t = F_{t-1} + \alpha(A_{t-1} - F_{t-1})$$
$$\alpha = 0.1, 0.3, \text{ and } 0.5$$

Smoothing constant delta (δ)

equation also uses a **smoothing constant delta (δ)**. The delta reduces the impact of the error that occurs between the actual and the forecast. If both alpha and delta are not included, the trend overreacts to errors.

To get the trend equation going, the first time it is used the trend value must be entered manually. This initial trend value can be an educated guess or a computation based on observed past data.

The equation to compute the forecast including trend (FIT) is

$$\text{FIT}_t = F_t + T_t \tag{11.8}$$
$$F_t = \text{FIT}_{t-1} + \alpha(A_{t-1} - \text{FIT}_{t-1}) \tag{11.9}$$
$$T_t = T_{t-1} + \delta(F_t - \text{FIT}_{t-1}) \tag{11.10}$$

where

F_t = The exponentially smoothed forecast for period t

T_t = The exponentially smoothed trend for period t

FIT_t = The forecast including trend for period t

FIT_{t-1} = The forecast including trend made for the prior period

A_{t-1} = The actual demand for the prior period

α = Smoothing constant

δ = Smoothing constant

EXAMPLE 11.4: Forecast Including Trend

Assume an initial starting F_t of 100 units, a trend of 10 units, an alpha of .20, and a delta of .30. If actual demand turned out to be 115 rather than the forecast 100, calculate the forecast for the next period.

Step by Step

SOLUTION

Adding the starting forecast and the trend, we have

$$\text{FIT}_{t-1} = F_{t-1} + T_{t-1} = 100 + 10 = 110$$

The actual A_{t-1} is given as 115. Therefore,

$$F_t = \text{FIT}_{t-1} + \alpha(A_{t-1} - \text{FIT}_{t-1})$$
$$= 110 + .2(115 - 110) = 111.0$$
$$T_t = T_{t-1} + \delta(F_t - \text{FIT}_{t-1})$$
$$= 10 + .3(111 - 110) = 10.3$$
$$\text{FIT}_t = F_t + T_t = 111.0 + 10.3 = 121.3$$

If, instead of 121.3, the actual turned out to be 120, the sequence would be repeated and the forecast for the next period would be

$$F_{t+1} = 121.3 + .2(120 - 121.3) = 121.04$$
$$T_{t+1} = 10.3 + .3(121.04 - 121.3) = 10.22$$
$$\text{FIT}_{t+1} = 121.04 + 10.22 = 131.26 \bullet$$

Choosing the Appropriate Value for Alpha   Exponential smoothing requires that the smoothing constant alpha (α) be given a value between 0 and 1. If the real demand is stable (such as demand for electricity or food), we would like a small alpha to lessen the effects of short-term or random changes. If the real demand is rapidly increasing or decreasing (such as in fashion items or new small appliances), we would like a large alpha to try to keep up with the change. It would be ideal if we could predict which alpha we should use. Unfortunately, two things work against us. First, it would take some passage of time to determine the alpha that would best fit our actual data. This would be tedious to follow and revise. Second, because demands do change, the alpha we pick this week may need to be revised soon. Therefore, we need some automatic method to track and change our alpha values.

There are two approaches to controlling the value of alpha. One uses various values of alpha. The other uses a tracking signal.

1. **Two or more predetermined values of alpha.**   The amount of error between the forecast and the actual demand is measured. Depending on the degree of error, different values of alpha are used. If the error is large, alpha is 0.8; if the error is small, alpha is 0.2.
2. **Computed values for alpha.**   A tracking alpha computes whether the forecast is keeping pace with genuine upward or downward changes in demand (as opposed to random changes). In this application, the tracking alpha is defined as the exponentially smoothed actual error divided by the exponentially smoothed absolute error. Alpha changes from period to period within the possible range of 0 to 1.

Forecast Errors

In using the word *error,* we are referring to the difference between the forecast value and what actually occurred. In statistics, these errors are called *residuals.* As long as the forecast value is within the confidence limits, as we discuss later in "Measurement of Error," this is not really an error. But common usage refers to the difference as an error.

Demand for a product is generated through the interaction of a number of factors too complex to describe accurately in a model. Therefore, all forecasts certainly contain some error. In discussing forecast errors, it is convenient to distinguish between *sources of error* and the *measurement of error.*

Sources of Error

Errors can come from a variety of sources. One common source that many forecasters are unaware of is projecting past trends into the future. For example, when we talk about statistical errors in regression analysis, we are referring to the deviations of observations from our regression line. It is common to attach a confidence band (that is, statistical control limits) to the regression line to reduce the unexplained error. But when we then use this regression line as a forecasting device by projecting it into the future, the error may not be correctly defined by the projected confidence band. This is because the confidence interval is based on past data; it may not hold for projected data points and therefore cannot be used with the same confidence. In fact, experience has shown that the actual errors tend to be greater than those predicted from forecast models.

Errors can be classified as bias or random. *Bias errors* occur when a consistent mistake is made. Sources of bias include the failure to include the right variables; the use of the wrong relationships among variables; employing of the wrong trend line; a mistaken shift in the seasonal demand from where it normally occurs; and the existence of some undetected secular trend. *Random errors* can be defined as those that cannot be explained by the forecast model being used.

Measurement of Error

Several common terms used to describe the degree of error are *standard error, mean squared error* (or *variance*), and *mean absolute deviation.* In addition, tracking signals may be used to indicate any positive or negative bias in the forecast.

Standard error is discussed in the section on linear regression in this chapter. Because the standard error is the square root of a function, it is often more convenient to use the function itself. This is called the mean square error or variance.

Mean absolute deviation (MAD)

The **mean absolute deviation (MAD)** was in vogue in the past but subsequently was ignored in favor of standard deviation and standard error measures. In recent years, MAD has made a comeback because of its simplicity and usefulness in obtaining tracking signals. MAD is the average error in the forecasts, using absolute values. It is valuable because MAD, like the standard deviation, measures the dispersion of some observed value from some expected value.

MAD is computed using the differences between the actual demand and the forecast demand without regard to sign. It equals the sum of the absolute deviations divided by the number of data points, or, stated in equation form,

$$\text{MAD} = \frac{\sum\limits_{i=1}^{n} |A_t - F_t|}{n}$$

[11.11]

where

t = Period number

A = Actual demand for the period

F = Forecast demand for the period

n = Total number of periods

$||$ = A symbol used to indicate the absolute value disregarding positive and negative signs

When the errors that occur in the forecast are normally distributed (the usual case), the mean absolute deviation relates to the standard deviation as

$$1 \text{ standard deviation} = \sqrt{\frac{\pi}{2}} \times \text{MAD, or approximately 1.25 MAD}$$

Conversely,

$$1 \text{ MAD} = 0.8 \text{ standard deviation}$$

The standard deviation is the larger measure. If the MAD of a set of points was found to be 60 units, then the standard deviation would be 75 units. In the usual statistical manner, if control limits were set at plus or minus 3 standard deviations (or ± 3.75 MADs), then 99.7 percent of the points would fall within these limits.

An additional measure of error that is often useful is the **mean absolute percent error (MAPE)**. This measure gauges the error relative to the average demand. For example, if the MAD is 10 units and average demand is 20 units, the error is large and significant, but relatively insignificant on an average demand of 1,000 units. MAPE is calculated by taking the MAD and dividing by the average demand,

Mean absolute percent error (MAPE)

$$\text{MAPE} = \frac{\text{MAD}}{\text{Average demand}} \qquad \text{[11.12]}$$

This is a useful measure because it is an estimate of how much error to expect with a forecast. So if the MAD were 10 and average demand 20, the MAPE would be 50 percent $\left(\frac{10}{20} = 50\right)$. In the case of an average demand of 1,000 units, the MAPE would be only 1 percent $\left(\frac{10}{1,000} = 1\right)$.

A **tracking signal** is a measurement that indicates whether the forecast average is keeping pace with any genuine upward or downward changes in demand. As used in forecasting, the tracking signal is the *number* of mean absolute deviations that the forecast value is above or below the actual occurrence. Exhibit 11.14 shows a normal distribution with a mean of 0 and a MAD equal to 1. Thus, if we compute the tracking signal and find it equal to minus 2, we can see that the forecast model is providing forecasts that are quite a bit above the mean of the actual occurrences.

Tracking signal

A tracking signal (TS) can be calculated using the arithmetic sum of forecast deviations divided by the mean absolute deviation:

$$\text{TS} = \frac{\text{RSFE}}{\text{MAD}} \qquad \text{[11.13]}$$

where

RSFE = The running sum of forecast errors, considering the nature of the error. (For example, negative errors cancel positive errors and vice versa.)

MAD = The average of all the forecast errors (disregarding whether the deviations are positive or negative). It is the average of the absolute deviations.

Exhibit 11.15 illustrates the procedure for computing MAD and the tracking signal for a six-month period where the forecast had been set at a constant 1,000 and the actual

exhibit 11.14   A Normal Distribution with Mean = 0 and MAD = 1

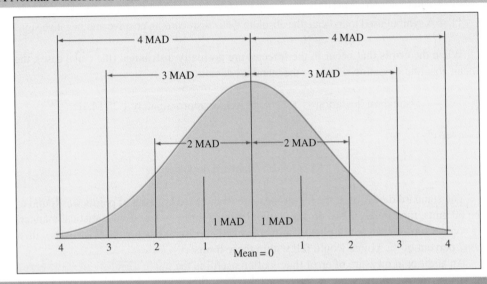

exhibit 11.15   Computing the Mean Absolute Deviation (MAD), the Running Sum of Forecast Errors (RSFE), and the Tracking Signal (TS) from Forecast and Actual Data

Excel: Forecasting

MONTH	DEMAND FORECAST	ACTUAL	DEVIATION	RSFE	ABS. DEV.	SUM OF ABS. DEV.	MAD*	TS = $\frac{RSFE^{\dagger}}{MAD}$
1	1,000	950	−50	−50	50	50	50	−1
2	1,000	1,070	+70	+20	70	120	60	.33
3	1,000	1,100	+100	+120	100	220	73.3	1.64
4	1,000	960	−40	+80	40	260	65	1.2
5	1,000	1,090	+90	+170	90	350	70	2.4
6	1,000	1,050	+50	+220	50	400	66.7	3.3

*For month 6, MAD = 400 ÷ 6 = 66.7.

†For month 6, TS = $\frac{RSFE}{MAD} = \frac{220}{66.7} = 3.3$ MADs.

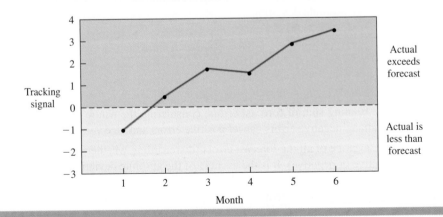

demands that occurred are as shown. In this example, the forecast, on the average, was off by 66.7 units and the tracking signal was equal to 3.3 mean absolute deviations.

We can get a better feel for what the MAD and tracking signal mean by plotting the points on a graph. Though this is not completely legitimate from a sample-size standpoint, we plotted each month in Exhibit 11.15 to show the drift of the tracking signal. Note that it drifted from minus 1 MAD to plus 3.3 MADs. This happened because actual demand was greater than the forecast in four of the six periods. If the actual demand does not fall below the forecast to offset the continual positive RSFE, the tracking signal would continue to rise and we would conclude that assuming a demand of 1,000 is a bad forecast.

CAUSAL RELATIONSHIP FORECASTING

Causal relationship forecasting involves using independent variables other than time to predict future demand. To be of value for the purpose of forecasting, any independent variable must be a leading indicator. For example, we can expect that an extended period of rain will increase sales of umbrellas and raincoats. The rain causes the sale of rain gear. This is a **causal relationship**, where one occurrence causes another. If the causing element is known far enough in advance, it can be used as a basis for forecasting.

Causal relationship

The first step in causal relationship forecasting is to find those occurrences that are really the causes. Often leading indicators are not causal relationships, but in some indirect way, they may suggest that some other things might happen. Other noncausal relationships just seem to exist as a coincidence. The following shows one example of a forecast using a causal relationship.

EXAMPLE 11.5: Forecasting Using a Causal Relationship

The Carpet City Store in Carpenteria has kept records of its sales (in square yards) each year, along with the number of permits for new houses in its area.

Step by Step

	NUMBER OF HOUSING STARTS	
YEAR	PERMITS	SALES (IN SQ. YDS.)
1999	18	13,000
2000	15	12,000
2001	12	11,000
2002	10	10,000
2003	20	14,000
2004	28	16,000
2005	35	19,000
2006	30	17,000
2007	20	13,000

Carpet City's operations manager believes forecasting sales is possible if housing starts are known for that year. First, the data are plotted in Exhibit 11.16, with

x = Number of housing start permits

y = Sales of carpeting

Because the points appear to be in a straight line, the manager decides to use the linear relationship $Y = a + bx$. We solve this problem by hand fitting a line. We also could solve for this equation using least squares regression as we did earlier.

---

exhibit 11.16

Causal Relationship: Sales to Housing Starts

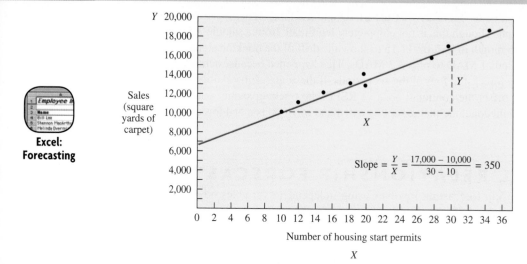

Excel:
Forecasting

Slope $= \dfrac{Y}{X} = \dfrac{17{,}000 - 10{,}000}{30 - 10} = 350$

SOLUTION

Projecting the hand-fit line causes it to intercept the Y axis at about 7,000 yards. This could be interpreted as the demand when no new houses are built; that is, probably as replacement for old carpeting. To estimate the slope, two points are selected, such as

YEAR	x	y
2004	10	10,000
2008	30	17,000

From algebra the slope is calculated as

$$b = \frac{y(2008) - y(2004)}{x(2008) - x(2004)} = \frac{17{,}000 - 10{,}000}{30 - 10} = \frac{7{,}000}{20} = 350$$

The manager interprets the slope as the average number of square yards of carpet sold for each new house built in the area. The forecasting equation is therefore

$$Y = 7{,}000 + 350x$$

Now suppose that there are 25 permits for houses to be built in 2010. The 2010 sales forecast would therefore be

$$7{,}000 + 350(25) = 15{,}750 \text{ square yards}$$

In this problem, the lag between filing the permit with the appropriate agency and the new homeowner coming to Carpet City to buy carpet makes a causal relationship feasible for forecasting. ●

Multiple Regression Analysis

Another forecasting method is multiple regression analysis, in which a number of variables are considered, together with the effects of each on the item of interest. For example, in the home furnishings field, the effects of the number of marriages, housing starts, disposable income, and the trend can be expressed in a multiple regression equation as

$$S = B + B_m(M) + B_h(H) + B_i(I) + B_t(T)$$

where

S = Gross sales for year

B = Base sales, a starting point from which other factors have influence

M = Marriages during the year

H = Housing starts during the year

I = Annual disposable personal income

T = Time trend (first year = 1, second = 2, third = 3, and so forth)

B_m, B_h, B_i, and B_t represent the influence on expected sales of the numbers of marriages and housing starts, income, and trend.

Forecasting by multiple regression is appropriate when a number of factors influence a variable of interest—in this case, sales. Its difficulty lies with the mathematical computation. Fortunately, standard computer programs for multiple regression analysis are available, relieving the need for tedious manual calculation.

Microsoft Excel supports the time series analysis techniques described in this section. These functions are available under the Data Analysis tools for exponential smoothing, moving averages, and regression.

QUALITATIVE TECHNIQUES IN FORECASTING

Qualitative forecasting techniques generally take advantage of the knowledge of experts and require much judgment. These techniques typically involve processes that are well defined to those participating in the forecasting exercise. For example, in the case of forecasting the demand for new fashions merchandise in a retail store, the firm can include a combination of typical customers to express preferences and store managers who understand product mix and store volumes, where they view the merchandise and run through a series of exercises designed to bring the group to a consensus estimate. The point is that these are not wild guesses as to the expected demand but rather involve a well thought-out and structured decision-making approach.

These techniques are most useful when the product is new or there is little experience with selling into a new region. Here such information as knowledge of similar products, the habits of customers in the area, and how the product will be advertized and introduced may be important to estimate demand successfully. In some cases it may even be useful to consider industry data and the experience of competing firms in making estimates of expected demand.

The following are samples of qualitative forecasting techniques.

Market Research

Firms often hire outside companies that specialize in *market research* to conduct this type of forecasting. You may have been involved in market surveys through a marketing class.

A NUMBER OF FIRMS, INCLUDING THE GILMORE RESEARCH GROUP, NOW OFFER MARKETERS SOFTWARE OR DATABASES TO HELP THEM MORE ACCURATELY FORECAST SALES FOR SPECIFIC MARKET AREAS, PRODUCTS, OR SEGMENTS.

Certainly you have not escaped telephone calls asking you about product preferences, your income, habits, and so on.

Market research is used mostly for product research in the sense of looking for new product ideas, likes and dislikes about existing products, which competitive products within a particular class are preferred, and so on. Again, the data collection methods are primarily surveys and interviews.

Panel Consensus

In a *panel consensus,* the idea that two heads are better than one is extrapolated to the idea that a panel of people from a variety of positions can develop a more reliable forecast than a narrower group. Panel forecasts are developed through open meetings with free exchange of ideas from all levels of management and individuals. The difficulty with this open style is that lower employee levels are intimidated by higher levels of management. For example, a salesperson in a particular product line may have a good estimate of future product demand but may not speak up to refute a much different estimate given by the vice president of marketing. The Delphi technique (which we discuss shortly) was developed to try to correct this impairment to free exchange.

When decisions in forecasting are at a broader, higher level (as when introducing a new product line or concerning strategic product decisions such as new marketing areas), the term *executive judgment* is generally used. The term is self-explanatory: a higher level of management is involved.

Historical Analogy

In trying to forecast demand for a new product, an ideal situation would be where an existing product or generic product could be used as a model. There are many ways to classify such analogies—for example, complementary products, substitutable or competitive products, and products as a function of income. Again, you have surely gotten a deluge of mail advertising products in a category similar to a product purchased via catalog, the Internet, or mail order. If you buy a DVD through the mail, you will receive more mail about new DVDs and DVD players. A causal relationship would be that demand for compact discs is caused by demand for DVD players. An analogy would be forecasting the demand for digital videodisc players by analyzing the historical demand for VCRs. The products are in the same general category of electronics and may be bought by consumers at similar rates. A simpler example would be toasters and coffee pots. A firm that already produces toasters and wants to produce coffee pots could use the toaster history as a likely growth model.

Delphi Method

As we mentioned under panel consensus, a statement or opinion of a higher-level person will likely be weighted more than that of a lower-level person. The worst case is where lower-level people feel threatened and do not contribute their true beliefs. To prevent this problem, the *Delphi method* conceals the identity of the individuals participating in the study. Everyone has the same weight. Procedurally, a moderator creates a questionnaire and distributes it to participants. Their responses are summed and given back to the entire group along with a new set of questions.

The step-by-step procedure for the Delphi method is:

1. Choose the experts to participate. There should be a variety of knowledgeable people in different areas.

2. Through a questionnaire (or e-mail), obtain forecasts (and any premises or qualifications for the forecasts) from all participants.

3. Summarize the results and redistribute them to the participants along with appropriate new questions.

4. Summarize again, refining forecasts and conditions, and again develop new questions.

5. Repeat step 4 if necessary. Distribute the final results to all participants.

The Delphi technique can usually achieve satisfactory results in three rounds. The time required is a function of the number of participants, how much work is involved for them to develop their forecasts, and their speed in responding.

WEB-BASED FORECASTING: COLLABORATIVE PLANNING, FORECASTING, AND REPLENISHMENT (CPFR)[5]

Collaborative Planning, Forecasting, and Replenishment (CPFR) is a Web-based tool used to coordinate demand forecasting, production and purchase planning, and inventory replenishment between supply chain trading partners. CPFR is being used as a means of integrating all members of an *n*-tier supply chain, including manufacturers, distributors, and retailers. As depicted in Exhibit 11.17, the ideal point of collaboration utilizing CPFR is the retail-level demand forecast, which is successively used to synchronize forecasts, production, and replenishment plans upstream through the supply chain.

Collaborative Planning, Forecasting, and Replenishment (CPFR)

Although the methodology is applicable to any industry, CPFR applications to date have largely focused on the food, apparel, and general merchandise industries. The potential benefits of sharing information for enhanced planning visibility in any supply chain are enormous. Various estimates for cost savings attributable to improved supply chain coordination have been proposed, including $30 billion annually in the food industry alone.[6]

CPFR's objective is to exchange selected internal information on a shared Web server in order to provide for reliable, longer-term future views of demand in the supply chain. CPFR uses a cyclic and iterative approach to derive consensus supply chain forecasts. It consists of the following five steps:

Supply Chain

Step 1. Creation of a front-end partnership agreement. This agreement specifies (1) objectives (e.g., inventory reductions, lost sale elimination, lower product obsolescence) to be gained through collaboration, (2) resource requirements (e.g., hardware, software, performance metrics) necessary for the collaboration, and (3) expectations of confidentiality concerning the prerequisite trust necessary to share sensitive company information, which represents a major implementation obstacle.

Step 2. Joint business planning. Typically partners create partnership strategies, design a joint calendar identifying the sequence and frequency of planning activities to follow that affect product flows, and specify exception criteria for handling planning variances between the trading partners' demand forecasts.

Step 3. Development of demand forecasts. Forecast development may follow preexisting company procedures. Retailers should play a critical role as shared *point-of-sale* (POS) data permit the development of more accurate and timely expectations (compared with extrapolated warehouse withdrawals or aggregate store orders) for both retailers and vendors. Given the frequency of forecast generation and the potential for vast numbers of items requiring forecast preparation, a simple forecast procedure such

exhibit 11.17   *n*-Tier Supply Chain with Retail Activities

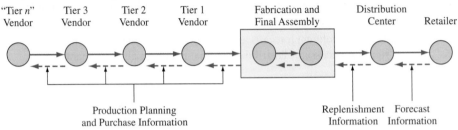

Note: Solid arrows represent material flows; dashed arrows represent information flows.

as a moving average is commonly used within CPFR. Simple techniques are easily used in conjunction with expert knowledge of promotional or pricing events to modify forecast values accordingly.

Step 4. Sharing forecasts.   Retailer (order forecasts) and vendor (sales forecasts) then electronically post their latest forecasts for a list of products on a shared, dedicated server. The server examines pairs of corresponding forecasts and issues an exception notice for any forecast pair where the difference exceeds a preestablished safety margin (e.g., 5 percent). If the safety margin is exceeded, planners from both firms may collaborate electronically to derive a consensus forecast.

Step 5. Inventory replenishment.   Once the corresponding forecasts are in agreement, the order forecast becomes an actual order, which commences the replenishment process. Each of these steps is then repeated iteratively in a continuous cycle, at varying times, by individual products and the calendar of events established between trading partners. For example, partners may review the front-end partnership agreement annually, evaluate the joint business plans quarterly, develop forecasts weekly to monthly, and replenish daily.

The early exchange of information between trading partners provides for reliable, longer-term future views of demand in the supply chain. The forward visibility based upon information sharing leads to a variety of benefits within supply chain partnerships.

As with most new corporate initiatives, there is skepticism and resistance to change. One of the largest hurdles hindering collaboration is the lack of trust over complete information sharing between supply chain partners. The conflicting objective between the profit-maximizing vendor and the cost-minimizing customer gives rise to adversarial supply chain relationships. Sharing sensitive operating data may enable one trading partner to take advantage of the other. Similarly, there is the potential loss of control as a barrier to implementation. Some companies are rightfully concerned about the idea of placing strategic data such as financial reports, manufacturing schedules, and inventory values online. Companies open themselves to security breaches. The front-end partnership agreements, nondisclosure agreements, and limited information access may help overcome these fears.

SUMMARY

Developing a forecasting system is not easy. However, it must be done because forecasting is fundamental to any planning effort. In the short run, a forecast is needed to predict the requirements for materials, products, services, or other resources to respond to changes in demand. Forecasts permit adjusting schedules and varying labor and materials. In the long run, forecasting is required as a basis for strategic changes, such as developing new markets, developing new products or services, and expanding or creating new facilities.

For medium and long-term strategic forecasts that lead to heavy financial commitments, great care should be taken to derive the forecast. Several approaches should be used. Regression analysis or multiple regression analysis are best suited for these problems. These provide a basis for discussion. Economic factors, product trends, growth factors, and competition, as well as myriad other possible variables, need to be considered and the forecast adjusted to reflect the influence of each.

Short- and intermediate-term forecasting (such as required for inventory control as well as staffing and material scheduling) may be satisfied with simpler models, such as exponential smoothing with perhaps an adaptive feature or a seasonal index. In these applications, thousands of items are usually being forecast. The forecasting routine should therefore be simple and run quickly on a computer. The routines also should detect and respond rapidly to definite short-term changes in demand while at the same time ignoring the occasional spurious demands. Exponential smoothing, when monitored by management to control the value of alpha, is an effective technique.

Web-based collaborative forecasting systems that use combinations of the forecasting methods will be the wave of the future in many industries. Information sharing between trading partners with direct links into each firm's ERP system ensures rapid and error-free information, at very low cost.

In summary, forecasting is tough. A perfect forecast is like a hole in one in golf: great to get but we should be satisfied just to get close to the cup—or, to push the analogy, just to land on the green. The ideal philosophy is to create the best forecast that you reasonably can and then hedge by maintaining flexibility in the system to account for the inevitable forecast error.

Key Terms

Strategic forecasts Medium and long-term forecasts that are used to make decisions related to design and plans for meeting demand.

Tactical forecasts Short-term forecasts used as input for making day-to-day decisions related to meeting demand.

Dependent demand Requirements for a product or service caused by the demand for other products or services. This type of internal demand does not need a forecast, but can be calculated based on the demand for the other products or services.

Independent demand Demand that cannot be directly derived from the demand for other products.

Time series analysis A type of forecast in which data relating to past demand are used to predict future demand.

Linear regression forecasting A forecasting technique that assumes that past data and future projections fall around a straight line.

Exponential smoothing A time series forecasting technique in which each increment of past demand data is decreased by $(1 = \alpha)$.

Smoothing constant alpha (α) The parameter in the exponential smoothing equation that controls the speed of reaction to differences between forecasts and actual demand.

Smoothing constant delta (δ) An additional parameter used in an exponential smoothing equation that includes an adjustment for trend.

Mean absolute deviation (MAD) The average forecast error using absolute values of the error of each past forecast.

Mean absolute percent error (MAPE) The mean absolute deviation divided by the average demand. The average error expressed as a percentage of demand.

Tracking signal A measure that indicates whether the forecast average is keeping pace with any genuine upward or downward changes in demand.

Causal relationship A situation in which one event causes another. If the event is far enough in the future, it can be used as a basis for forecasting.

Collaborative Planning, Forecasting, and Replenishment (CPFR) An Internet tool to coordinate forecasting, production, and purchasing in a firm's supply chain.

Formula Review

Least squares regression

$$Y = a + bx \qquad [11.1]$$

$$a = \bar{y} - b\bar{x} \qquad [11.2]$$

$$b = \frac{\Sigma xy - n\bar{x} \cdot \bar{y}}{\Sigma x^2 - n\bar{x}^2} \qquad [11.3]$$

Standard error of estimate

$$S_{yx} = \sqrt{\frac{\sum_{i=1}^{n}(y_i - Y_i)^2}{n - 2}} \qquad [11.4]$$

Simple moving average

$$F_t = \frac{A_{t-1} + A_{t-2} + A_{t-3} + \cdots + A_{t-n}}{n} \qquad [11.5]$$

Weighted moving average

$$F_t = w_t A_{t-1} + w_2 A_{t-2} + \cdots + w_n A_{t-n} \qquad [11.6]$$

Single exponential smoothing

$$F_t = F_{t-1} + \alpha(A_{t-1} - F_{t-1}) \qquad [11.7]$$

Exponential smoothing with trend

$$\text{FIT}_t = F_t + T_t \qquad [11.8]$$

$$F_t = \text{FIT}_{t-1} + \alpha(A_{t-1} - \text{FIT}_{t-1}) \qquad [11.9]$$

$$T_t = T_{t-1} + \delta(F_t - \text{FIT}_{t-1}) \qquad [11.10]$$

Mean absolute deviation

$$\text{MAD} = \frac{\sum_{i=1}^{n}|A_t - F_t|}{n} \qquad [11.11]$$

$$\text{MAP} = \frac{\text{MAD}}{\text{Average Demand}} \qquad [11.12]$$

Tracking signal

$$\text{TS} = \frac{\text{RSFE}}{\text{MAD}} \qquad [11.13]$$

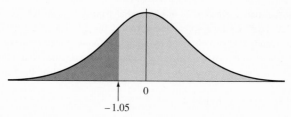

There is not enough evidence to reject the forecasting model, so we accept its recommendations.

Review and Discussion Questions

1   Examine Exhibit 11.3 and suggest which model you might use for (*a*) bathing suit demand, (*b*) demand for new houses, (*c*) electrical power usage, (*d*) new plant expansion plans.
2   What is the logic in the least squares method of linear regression analysis?
3   Explain the procedure to create a forecast using the decomposition method of least squares regression.
4   Give some very simple rules you might use to manage demand for a firm's product. (An example is "limited to stock on hand.")
5   What strategies are used by supermarkets, airlines, hospitals, banks, and cereal manufacturers to influence demand?
6   All forecasting methods using exponential smoothing, adaptive smoothing, and exponential smoothing including trend require starting values to get the equations going. How would you select the starting value for, say, F_{t-1}?
7   From the choice of simple moving average, weighted moving average, exponential smoothing, and linear regression analysis, which forecasting technique would you consider the most accurate? Why?
8   Give some examples that have a multiplicative seasonal trend relationship.
9   What is the main disadvantage of daily forecasting using regression analysis?
10   What are the main problems with using adaptive exponential smoothing in forecasting?
11   How is a seasonal index computed from a regression line analysis?
12   Discuss the basic differences between the mean absolute deviation and the standard deviation.
13   What implications do forecast errors have for the search for ultrasophisticated statistical forecasting models?
14   Causal relationships are potentially useful for which component of a time series?

Problems

1   Demand for stereo headphones and CD players for joggers has caused Nina Industries to grow almost 50 percent over the past year. The number of joggers continues to expand, so Nina expects demand for headsets to also expand, because, as yet, no safety laws have been passed to prevent joggers from wearing them. Demand for the stereo units for last year was as follows:

Month	Demand (Units)	Month	Demand (Units)
January	4,200	July	5,300
February	4,300	August	4,900
March	4,000	September	5,400
April	4,400	October	5,700
May	5,000	November	6,300
June	4,700	December	6,000

    a. Using least squares regression analysis, what would you estimate demand to be for each month next year? Using a spreadsheet, follow the general format in Exhibit 11.5. Compare your results to those obtained by using the forecast spreadsheet function.

    b. To be reasonably confident of meeting demand, Nina decides to use three standard errors of estimate for safety. How many additional units should be held to meet this level of confidence?

2   Historical demand for a product is

	DEMAND
January	12
February	11
March	15
April	12
May	16
June	15

    a. Using a weighted moving average with weights of 0.60, 0.30, and 0.10, find the July forecast.

    b. Using a simple three-month moving average, find the July forecast.

    c. Using single exponential smoothing with $\alpha = 0.2$ and a June forecast $= 13$, find the July forecast. Make whatever assumptions you wish.

    d. Using simple linear regression analysis, calculate the regression equation for the preceding demand data.

    e. Using the regression equation in *d*, calculate the forecast for July.

3   The following tabulations are actual sales of units for six months and a starting forecast in January.

    a. Calculate forecasts for the remaining five months using simple exponential smoothing with $\alpha = 0.2$.

    b. Calculate MAD for the forecasts.

	ACTUAL	FORECAST
January	100	80
February	94	
March	106	
April	80	
May	68	
June	94	

4   Zeus Computer Chips, Inc., used to have major contracts to produce the Centrino-type chips. The market has been declining during the past three years because of the dual-core chips, which it cannot produce, so Zeus has the unpleasant task of forecasting next year. The task is unpleasant because the firm has not been able to find replacement chips for its product lines. Here is demand over the past 12 quarters:

2007		2008		2009	
I	4,800	I	3,500	I	3,200
II	3,500	II	2,700	II	2,100
III	4,300	III	3,500	III	2,700
IV	3,000	IV	2,400	IV	1,700

Use the decomposition technique to forecast the four quarters of 2010.

5   Sales data for two years are as follows. Data are aggregated with two months of sales in each "period."

MONTHS	SALES	MONTHS	SALES
January–February	109	January–February	115
March–April	104	March–April	112
May–June	150	May–June	159
July–August	170	July–August	182
September–October	120	September–October	126
November–December	100	November–December	106

a. Plot the data.

b. Fit a simple linear regression model to the sales data.

c. In addition to the regression model, determine multiplicative seasonal index factors. A full cycle is assumed to be a full year.

d. Using the results from parts *b* and *c,* prepare a forecast for the next year.

6   The tracking signals computed using past demand history for three different products are as follows. Each product used the same forecasting technique.

	TS 1	TS 2	TS 3
1	−2.70	1.54	0.10
2	−2.32	−0.64	0.43
3	−1.70	2.05	1.08
4	−1.1	2.58	1.74
5	−0.87	−0.95	1.94
6	−0.05	−1.23	2.24
7	0.10	0.75	2.96
8	0.40	−1.59	3.02
9	1.50	0.47	3.54
10	2.20	2.74	3.75

Discuss the tracking signals for each and what the implications are.

7   The following table shows the past two years of quarterly sales information. Assume that there are both trend and seasonal factors and that the seasonal cycle is one year. Use time series decomposition to forecast quarterly sales for the next year.

QUARTER	SALES	QUARTER	SALES
1	160	5	215
2	195	6	240
3	150	7	205
4	140	8	190

8   Tucson Machinery, Inc., manufactures numerically controlled machines, which sell for an average price of $0.5 million each. Sales for these NCMs for the past two years were as follows:

QUARTER	QUANTITY (UNITS)	QUARTER	QUANTITY (UNITS)
2008		2009	
I	12	I	16
II	18	II	24
III	26	III	28
IV	16	IV	18

a. Hand fit a line (or do a regression using Excel).

b. Find the trend and seasonal factors.

c. Forecast sales for 2010.

9   Not all the items in your office supply store are evenly distributed as far as demand is concerned, so you decide to forecast demand to help plan your stock. Past data for legal-sized yellow tablets for the month of August are

Week 1	300	Week 3	600
Week 2	400	Week 4	700

a. Using a three-week moving average, what would you forecast the next week to be?
b. Using exponential smoothing with $\alpha = 0.20$, if the exponential forecast for week 3 was estimated as the average of the first two weeks $[(300 + 400)/2 = 350]$, what would you forecast week 5 to be?

10   Given the following history, use focus forecasting to forecast the third quarter of this year. Use three focus forecasting strategies.

	JAN	FEB	MAR	APR	MAY	JUN	JUL	AUG	SEP	OCT	NOV	DEC
Last year	100	125	135	175	185	200	150	140	130	200	225	250
This year	125	135	135	190	200	190						

11   Here are the actual tabulated demands for an item for a nine-month period (January through September). Your supervisor wants to test two forecasting methods to see which method was better over this period.

MONTH	ACTUAL	MONTH	ACTUAL
January	110	June	180
February	130	July	140
March	150	August	130
April	170	September	140
May	160		

a. Forecast April through September using a three-month moving average.
b. Use simple exponential smoothing with an alpha of .3 to estimate April through September.
c. Use MAD to decide which method produced the better forecast over the six-month period.

12   A particular forecasting model was used to forecast a six-month period. Here are the forecasts and actual demands that resulted:

	FORECAST	ACTUAL
April	250	200
May	325	250
June	400	325
July	350	300
August	375	325
September	450	400

Find the tracking signal and state whether you think the model being used is giving acceptable answers.

13   Harlen Industries has a simple forecasting model: Take the actual demand for the same month last year and divide that by the number of fractional weeks in that month. This gives the average weekly demand for that month. This weekly average is used as the weekly forecast for the same month this year. This technique was used to forecast eight weeks for this year, which are shown below along with the actual demand that occurred.

The following eight weeks show the forecast (based on last year) and the demand that actually occurred:

WEEK	FORECAST DEMAND	ACTUAL DEMAND	WEEK	FORECAST DEMAND	ACTUAL DEMAND
1	140	137	5	140	180
2	140	133	6	150	170
3	140	150	7	150	185
4	140	160	8	150	205

a. Compute the MAD of forecast errors.

b. Using the RSFE, compute the tracking signal.

c. Based on your answers to *a* and *b*, comment on Harlen's method of forecasting.

14 The following table contains the demand from the last 10 months:

MONTH	ACTUAL DEMAND	MONTH	ACTUAL DEMAND
1	31	6	36
2	34	7	38
3	33	8	40
4	35	9	40
5	37	10	41

a. Calculate the single exponential smoothing forecast for these data using an α of .30 and an initial forecast (F_1) of 31.

b. Calculate the exponential smoothing with trend forecast for these data using an α of .30, a δ of .30, an initial trend forecast (T_1) of 1, and an initial exponentially smoothed forecast (F_1) of 30.

c. Calculate the mean absolute deviation (MAD) for each forecast. Which is best?

15 In this problem, you are to test the validity of your forecasting model. Here are the forecasts for a model you have been using and the actual demands that occurred:

WEEK	FORECAST	ACTUAL
1	800	900
2	850	1,000
3	950	1,050
4	950	900
5	1,000	900
6	975	1,100

Use the method stated in the text to compute the MAD and tracking signal. Then decide whether the forecasting model you have been using is giving reasonable results.

16 Assume that your stock of sales merchandise is maintained based on the forecast demand. If the distributor's sales personnel call on the first day of each month, compute your forecast sales by each of the three methods requested here.

	ACTUAL
June	140
July	180
August	170

a. Using a simple three-month moving average, what is the forecast for September?

b. Using a weighted moving average, what is the forecast for September with weights of .20, .30, and .50 for June, July, and August, respectively?

c. Using single exponential smoothing and assuming that the forecast for June had been 130, forecast sales for September with a smoothing constant alpha of .30.

17 Historical demand for a product is as follows:

	DEMAND
April	60
May	55
June	75
July	60
August	80
September	75

  a. Using a simple four-month moving average, calculate a forecast for October.
  b. Using single exponential smoothing with $\alpha = 0.2$ and a September forecast $= 65$, calculate a forecast for October.
  c. Using simple linear regression, calculate the trend line for the historical data. Say the X axis is April $= 1$, May $= 2$, and so on, while the Y axis is demand.
  d. Calculate a forecast for October.

18 Sales by quarter for last year and the first three quarters of this year were as follows:

	QUARTER			
	I	II	III	IV
Last year	23,000	27,000	18,000	9,000
This year	19,000	24,000	15,000	

Using the focus forecasting procedure described in the text, forecast expected sales for the fourth quarter of this year.

19 The following table shows predicted product demand using your particular forecasting method along with the actual demand that occurred:

FORECAST	ACTUAL
1,500	1,550
1,400	1,500
1,700	1,600
1,750	1,650
1,800	1,700

  a. Compute the tracking signal using the mean absolute deviation and running sum of forecast errors.
  b. Discuss whether your forecasting method is giving good predictions.

20 Your manager is trying to determine what forecasting method to use. Based upon the following historical data, calculate the following forecast and specify what procedure you would utilize.

MONTH	ACTUAL DEMAND	MONTH	ACTUAL DEMAND
1	62	7	76
2	65	8	78
3	67	9	78
4	68	10	80
5	71	11	84
6	73	12	85

  a. Calculate the simple three-month moving average forecast for periods 4–12.
  b. Calculate the weighted three-month moving average using weights of 0.50, 0.30, and 0.20 for periods 4–12.

  c. Calculate the single exponential smoothing forecast for periods 2–12 using an initial forecast (F_1) of 61 and an α of 0.30.

  d. Calculate the exponential smoothing with trend component forecast for periods 2–12 using an initial trend forecast (T_1) of 1.8, an initial exponential smoothing forecast (F_1) of 60, an α of 0.30, and a δ of 0.30.

  e. Calculate the mean absolute deviation (MAD) for the forecasts made by each technique in periods 4–12. Which forecasting method do you prefer?

21 Use regression analysis on deseasonalized demand to forecast demand in summer 2010, given the following historical demand data:

YEAR	SEASON	ACTUAL DEMAND
2008	Spring	205
	Summer	140
	Fall	375
	Winter	575
2009	Spring	475
	Summer	275
	Fall	685
	Winter	965

22 Here are the data for the past 21 months for actual sales of a particular product:

	2006	2007
January	300	275
February	400	375
March	425	350
April	450	425
May	400	400
June	460	350
July	400	350
August	300	275
September	375	350
October	500	
November	550	
December	500	

Develop a forecast for the fourth quarter using three different focus forecasting rules. (Note that to correctly use this procedure, the rules are first tested on the third quarter; the best-performing one is used to forecast the fourth quarter.) Do the problem using quarters, as opposed to forecasting separate months.

23 Actual demand for a product for the past three months was

Three months ago	400 units
Two months ago	350 units
Last month	325 units

  a. Using a simple three-month moving average, make a forecast for this month.

  b. If 300 units were actually demanded this month, what would your forecast be for next month?

  c. Using simple exponential smoothing, what would your forecast be for this month if the exponentially smoothed forecast for three months ago was 450 units and the smoothing constant was 0.20?

24 After using your forecasting model for six months, you decide to test it using MAD and a tracking signal. Here are the forecast and actual demands for the six-month period:

PERIOD	FORECAST	ACTUAL
May	450	500
June	500	550
July	550	400
August	600	500
September	650	675
October	700	600

a. Find the tracking signal.

b. Decide whether your forecasting routine is acceptable.

25 Here are earnings per share for two companies by quarter from the first quarter of 2006 through the second quarter of 2009. Forecast earnings per share for the rest of 2009 and 2010. Use exponential smoothing to forecast the third period of 2009, and the time series decomposition method to forecast the last two quarters of 2009 and all four quarters of 2010. (It is much easier to solve this problem on a computer spreadsheet so you can see what is happening.)

EARNINGS PER SHARE

	QUARTER	COMPANY A	COMPANY B
2006	I	$1.67	$0.17
	II	2.35	0.24
	III	1.11	0.26
	IV	1.15	0.34
2007	I	1.56	0.25
	II	2.04	0.37
	III	1.14	0.36
	IV	0.38	0.44
2008	I	0.29	0.33
	II	−0.18 (loss)	0.40
	III	−0.97 (loss)	0.41
	IV	0.20	0.47
2009	I	−1.54 (loss)	0.30
	II	0.38	0.47

a. For the exponential smoothing method, choose the first quarter of 2006 as the beginning forecast. Make two forecasts: one with $\alpha = 0.10$ and one with $\alpha = 0.30$.

b. Using the MAD method of testing the forecasting model's performance, plus actual data from 2006 through the second quarter of 2009, how well did the model perform?

c. Using the decomposition of a time series method of forecasting, forecast earnings per share for the last two quarters of 2009 and all four quarters of 2010. Is there a seasonal factor in the earnings?

d. Using your forecasts, comment on each company.

26 The following are sales revenues for a large utility company for 1999 through 2009. Forecast revenue for 2010 through 2013. Use your own judgment, intuition, or common sense concerning which model or method to use, as well as the period of data to include.

	REVENUE (MILLIONS)		REVENUE (MILLIONS)
1999	$4,865.9	2005	$5,094.4
2000	5,067.4	2006	5,108.8
2001	5,515.6	2007	5,550.6
2002	5,728.8	2008	5,738.9
2003	5,497.7	2009	5,860.0
2004	5,197.7		

27 Mark Price, the new productions manager for Speakers and Company, needs to find out which
variable most affects the demand for their line of stereo speakers. He is uncertain whether the
unit price of the product or the effects of increased marketing are the main drivers in sales
and wants to use regression analysis to figure out which factor drives more demand for their
particular market. Pertinent information was collected by an extensive marketing project that
lasted over the past 10 years and was reduced to the data that follow:

Year	Sales/Unit (Thousands)	Price/Unit	Advertising ($000)
1998	400	280	600
1999	700	215	835
2000	900	211	1,100
2001	1,300	210	1,400
2002	1,150	215	1,200
2003	1,200	200	1,300
2004	900	225	900
2005	1,100	207	1,100
2006	980	220	700
2007	1,234	211	900
2008	925	227	700
2009	800	245	690

a. Perform a regression analysis based on these data using Excel. Answer the following
questions based on your results.
b. Which variable, price or advertising, has a larger effect on sales and how do you know?
c. Predict average yearly speaker sales for Speakers and Company based on the regression
results if the price was $300 per unit and the amount spent on advertising (in thousands)
was $900.

28 Assume an initial starting F_t of 300 units, a trend of eight units, an alpha of 0.30, and a delta
of 0.40. If actual demand turned out to be 288, calculate the forecast for the next period.

29 The following table contains the number of complaints received in a department store for the
first 6 months of operation.

Month	Complaints	Month	Complaints
January	36	April	90
February	45	May	108
March	81	June	144

If a three-month moving average is used to smooth this series, what would have been the
forecast for May?

30 The number of cases of merlot wine sold by the Connor Owen winery in an eight-year period
is as follows:

Year	Cases of Merlot Wine	Year	Cases of Merlot Wine
2002	270	2006	358
2003	356	2007	500
2004	398	2008	410
2005	456	2009	376

Using an exponential smoothing model with an alpha value of 0.20, estimate the smoothed
value calculated as of the end of 2009. Use the average demand for 2002 through 2004 as
your initial forecast, then smooth the forecast forward to 2009.

CASE: Altavox Electronics

Altavox is a manufacturer and distributor of many different electronic instruments and devices, including digital/analog multimeters, function generators, oscilloscopes, frequency counters, and other test and measuring equipment. Altavox sells a line of test meters that are popular with professional electricians. The model VC202 is sold through six distributors to retail stores in the United States. These distributors are located in Atlanta, Boston, Chicago, Dallas, and Los Angeles and have been selected to serve different regions in the country.

The model VC202 has been a steady seller over the years due to its reliability and rugged construction. Altavox does not consider this a seasonal product, but there is some variability in demand. Demand for the product over the past 13 weeks is shown in the following table.

These data are contained in an Excel spreadsheet *Altavox Data* included on the DVD with the book. The demand in the regions varies between a high of 40 units on average per week in Atlanta and 48 units in Dallas. This quarter's data are pretty close to the demand last quarter.

Management would like you to experiment with some forecasting models to determine what should be used in a new system being implemented. The new system is programmed to use one of two models: simple moving average or exponential smoothing.

WEEK	1	2	3	4	5	6	7	8	9	10	11	12	13	AVERAGE
Atlanta	33	45	37	38	55	30	18	58	47	37	23	55	40	40
Boston	26	35	41	40	46	48	55	18	62	44	30	45	50	42
Chicago	44	34	22	55	48	72	62	28	27	95	35	45	47	47
Dallas	27	42	35	40	51	64	70	65	55	43	38	47	42	48
LA	32	43	54	40	46	74	40	35	45	38	48	56	50	46
Total	162	199	189	213	246	288	245	204	236	257	174	248	229	222

**Excel:
Altavox Data**

Questions

1 Consider using a simple moving average model. Experiment with models using five weeks' and three weeks' past data. The past data in each region is given below (week −1 is the week before week 1 in the table, −2 is two weeks before week 1, etc.). Evaluate the forecasts that would have been made over the 13 weeks using the mean absolute deviation, mean absolute percent error, and tracking signal as criteria.

WEEK	−5	−4	−3	−2	−1
Atlanta	45	38	30	58	37
Boston	62	18	48	40	35
Chicago	62	22	72	44	48
Dallas	42	35	40	64	43
LA	43	40	54	46	35
Total	254	153	244	252	198

2 Next, consider using a simple exponential smoothing model. In your analysis, test two alpha values, .2 and .4. Use the same criteria for evaluating the model as in part 1. Assume that the initial previous forecast for the model using an alpha value of .2 is the past three-week average. For the model using an alpha of .4, assume that the previous forecast is the past five-week average.

3 Altavox is considering a new option for distributing the model VC202 where, instead of using five vendors, only a single vendor would be used. Evaluate this option by analyzing how accurate the forecast would be based on the demand aggregated across all regions. Use the model that you think is best from your analysis of parts 1 and 2. What are the advantages and disadvantages of aggregating demand from a forecasting view? Are there other things that should be considered when going from multiple distributors to a single distributor?

Super Quiz

1 This is a type of forecast used to make long-term decisions such as where to locate a warehouse or how many employees to have in a plant next year.

2 This is the type of demand that is most appropriate for using forecasting models.

3 This is a term used for actually influencing the sale of a product or service.

4 These are the six major components of demand.

5 This type of analysis is most appropriate when the past is a good predictor of the future.

6 This is identifying and separating time series data into components of demand.

7 If the demand in the current week was 102 units and we had forecast it to be 125, what would be next week's forecast using an exponential smoothing model with an alpha of 0.3?

8 Assume that you are using exponential smoothing with an adjustment for trend. Demand is increasing at a very steady rate of about five units per week. Would you expect your alpha and delta parameters to be closer to one or zero?

9 Your forecast is, on average, incorrect by about 10 percent. The average demand is 130 units. What is the MAD?

10 If the tracking signal for your forecast were consistently positive, you could then say this about your forecasting technique.

11 What would you suggest to improve the forecast described in question 10?

12 You know that sales are greatly influenced by the amount your firm advertises in the local paper. What forecasting technique would you suggest trying?

13 What forecasting tool is most appropriate when closely working with customers dependent on your products?

1. Strategic forecast 2. Independent demand 3. Demand management 4. Average demand for the period, trend, seasonal elements, cyclical elements, random variation, and autocorrelation 5. Time series analysis 6. Decomposition 7. 118 units 8. Zero 9. 13 10. Bias, consistently too low 11. Add a trend component 12. Causal relationship forecasting (using regression) 13. Collaborative planning, forecasting, and replenishment (CPFR)

Selected Bibliography

Diebold, F. X. *Elements of Forecasting.* 4th ed. Mason, OH: South-Western College Publishing, 2006.

Hanke, J. E.; A. G. Reitsch; and D. W. Wichem. *Business Forecasting.* 8th ed. Upper Saddle River, NJ : Prentice Hall, 2004.

Makridakis, S; S. C. Wheelwright; and R. J. Hyndman. *Forecasting: Methods for Management.* New York: John Wiley & Sons, 1998.

Footnotes

1 In addition to dependent and independent demands, other relationships include complementary products and causal relationships where demand for one causes the demand for another.

2 An equation for the standard error that is often easier to compute is $S_{yx} = \sqrt{\dfrac{\Sigma y^2 - a\Sigma y - b\Sigma xy}{n-2}}$.

3 Some writers prefer to call F_t a smoothed average.

4 When exponential smoothing is first introduced, the initial forecast or starting point may be obtained by using a simple estimate or an average of preceding periods such as the average of the first two or three periods.

5 Special thanks to Gene Fliedner for help with this section. Gene Fliedner, "Hierarchical Forecasting: Issues and Use Guidelines," *Industrial Management & Data Systems* 101, no. 1 (2001), pp. 5–12.

6 Marshall L. Fisher, "What Is the Right Supply Chain for Your Product?" *Harvard Business Review,* March–April 1997, pp. 105–16.

CHAPTER 12

SALES AND OPERATIONS PLANNING

After reading the chapter you will:

- Understand what sales and operations planning is and how it coordinates manufacturing, logistics, service, and marketing plans.
- Construct aggregate plans that employ different strategies for meeting demand.
- Describe what yield management is and why it is an important strategy for leveling demand.

Aggregate operations plan defined

356   What Is Sales and Operations Planning?

356   Overview of Sales and Operations Planning Activities
Sales and operations planning defined
Long-range planning defined
Intermediate-range planning defined
Short-range planning defined

358   The Aggregate Operations Plan
Production Planning Environment
Relevant Costs
Production rate defined
Workforce level defined
Inventory on hand defined
Production planning strategies defined
Pure strategy defined
Mixed strategy defined

362   Aggregate Planning Techniques
A Cut-and-Try Example: The JC Company
Aggregate Planning Applied to Services: Tucson Parks and Recreation Department

370   Level Scheduling

372   Yield Management
Operating Yield Management Systems
Yield management defined

374   Summary

381   Case: Bradford Manufacturing—Planning Plant Production

382   Super Quiz

Let's eavesdrop on an executive staff meeting at the Acme Widget Company. The participants are not happy campers.

President: This shortage situation is terrible. When will we ever get our act together? Whenever business gets good, we run out of product and our customer service is lousy.

VP Operations: I'll tell you when. When we start to get some decent forecasts from the Sales Department . . .

VP Sales (interrupting): Wait a minute. We forecasted this upturn.

VP Operations: . . . in time to do something about it. Yeah, we got the revised forecast—four days after the start of the month. By then it was too late.

VP Sales: I could have told you months ago. All you had to do was ask.

VP Finance: I'd like to be in on those conversations. We've been burned more than once by building inventories for a business upturn that doesn't happen. Then we get stuck with tons of inventory and run out of cash.

And the beat goes on. Back orders, dissatisfied customers, high inventories, late shipments, finger-pointing, cash-flow problems, demand and supply out of balance, missing the business plan. This is the norm in many companies.

It does not, however, have to be that way. Today many companies are using a business process called sales and operations planning (S&OP) to help avoid such problems. To learn what it is, and how to make it work, read on.

Source: Adapted from Thomas F. Wallace, *Sales and Operations Planning: The How-To Handbook* (Cincinnati, OH: T. F. Wallace & Co., 2000), p. 3. Copyright © 2000 Thomas Wallace. Used with permission.

Aggregate operations plan

In this chapter, we focus on the **aggregate operations plan**, which translates annual and quarterly business plans into broad labor and output plans for the intermediate term (3 to 18 months). The objective of the aggregate operations plan is to minimize the cost of resources required to meet demand over that period.

WHAT IS SALES AND OPERATIONS PLANNING?

Sales and operations planning is a process that helps firms provide better customer service, lower inventory, shorten customer lead times, stabilize production rates, and give top management a handle on the business. The process is designed to coordinate activities in the field with the manufacturing and service functions that are required to meet demand over time. Depending on the situation, activities in the field may include the supply of warehouse distribution centers, retail sales outlets, or direct sales channels. The process is designed to help a company get demand and supply in balance and keep them in balance over time. The process requires teamwork among sales, distribution and logistics, operations, finance, and product development.

The sales and operations planning process consists of a series of meetings, finishing with a high-level meeting where key intermediate-term decisions are made. The end goal is an agreement between various departments on the best course of action to achieve the optimal balance between supply and demand. The idea is to put the operational plan in line with the business plan.

This balance must occur at an aggregate level and also at the detailed individual product level. By *aggregate* we mean at the level of major groups of products. Over time, we need to ensure that we have enough total capacity. Since demand is often quite dynamic, it is important that we monitor our expected needs 3 to 18 months or further in the future. When planning this far into the future, it is difficult to know exactly how many of a particular product we will need, but we should be able to know how a larger group of similar products should sell. The term *aggregate* refers to this group of products. Given that we have enough aggregate capacity, our individual product schedulers, working within aggregate capacity constraints, can handle the daily and weekly launching of individual product orders to meet short-term demand.

OVERVIEW OF SALES AND OPERATIONS PLANNING ACTIVITIES

Sales and operations planning

Exhibit 12.1 positions sales and operations planning relative to other major operations planning activities. The term **sales and operations planning** was coined by companies to refer to the process that helps firms keep demand and supply in balance. In operations

Overview of Major Operations and Supply Planning Activities

exhibit 12.1

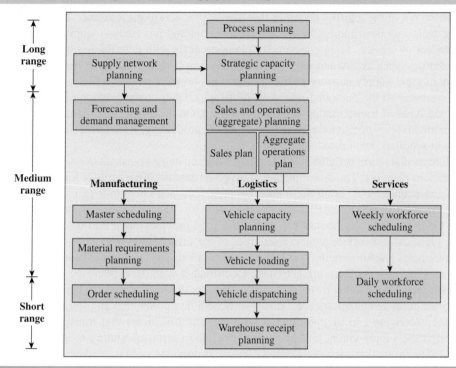

management this process traditionally was called *aggregate planning*. The new terminology is meant to capture the importance of cross-functional work. Typically, this activity requires an integrated effort with cooperation from sales, distribution and logistics, operations, finance, and product development.

Within sales and operations planning, marketing develops a sales plan that extends through the next 3 to 18 months. This sales plan typically is stated in units of aggregate product groups and often is tied into sales incentive programs and other marketing activities. The operations side develops an operations plan as an output of the process, which is discussed in depth in this chapter. By focusing on aggregate product and sales volumes, the marketing and operations functions are able to develop plans for the way demand will be met. This is a particularly difficult task when there are significant changes in demand over time as a result of market trends or other factors.

Aggregation on the supply side is done by product families, and on the demand side it is done by groups of customers. Individual product production schedules and matching customer orders can be handled more readily as a result of the sales and operations planning process. Typically, sales and operations planning occurs on a monthly cycle. Sales and operations planning links a company's strategic plans and business plan to its detailed operations and supply processes. These detailed processes include manufacturing, logistics, and service activities, as shown in Exhibit 12.1.

In Exhibit 12.1 the time dimension is shown as long, intermediate, and short range. **Long-range planning** generally is done annually, focusing on a horizon greater than one year. **Intermediate-range planning** usually covers a period from 3 to 18 months, with time increments that are weekly, monthly, or sometimes quarterly. **Short-range planning** covers a period from one day to six months, with daily or weekly time increments.

Long-range planning

Intermediate-range planning

Short-range planning

Supply Chain

Service

Long-range planning activities are done in two major areas. The first is the design of the manufacturing and service processes that produce the products of the firm, and the second is the design of the logistics activities that deliver products to the customer. Process planning deals with determining the specific technologies and procedures required to produce a product or service. Strategic capacity planning deals with determining the long-term capabilities (such as size and scope) of the production systems. Similarly, from a logistics point of view, supply network planning determines how the product will be distributed to the customer on the outbound side, with decisions relating to the location of warehouses and the types of transportation systems to be used. On the inbound side, supply network planning involves decisions relating to outsourcing production, selection of parts and component suppliers, and related decisions.

Intermediate-term activities include forecasting and demand management and sales and operations planning. The determination of expected demand is the focus of forecasting and demand management. From these data, detailed sales and operations plans for meeting these requirements are made. The sales plans are inputs to sales force activities, which are the focus of marketing books. The operations plan provides input into the manufacturing, logistics, and service planning activities of the firm. Master scheduling and material requirements planning are designed to generate detailed schedules that indicate when parts are needed for manufacturing activities. Coordinated with these plans are the logistics plans needed to move the parts and finished products through the supply chain.

Short-term details are focused mostly on scheduling production and shipment orders. These orders need to be coordinated with the actual vehicles that transport material through the supply chain. On the service side, short-term scheduling of employees is needed to ensure that adequate customer service is provided and fair worker schedules are maintained.

THE AGGREGATE OPERATIONS PLAN

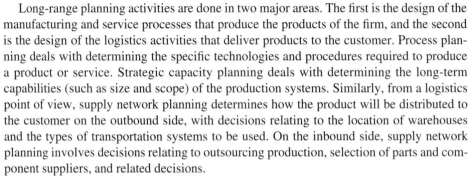

Production rate

Workforce level

Inventory on hand

The aggregate operations plan is concerned with setting production rates by product group or other broad categories for the intermediate term (3 to 18 months). Note again from Exhibit 12.1 that the aggregate plan precedes the master schedule. *The main purpose of the aggregate plan is to specify the optimal combination of production rate, workforce level, and inventory on hand.* **Production rate** refers to the number of units completed per unit of time (such as per hour or per day). **Workforce level** is the number of workers needed for production (production = production rate × workforce level). **Inventory on hand** is unused inventory carried over from the previous period.

Here is a formal statement of the aggregate planning problem: Given the demand forecast F_t for each period t in the planning horizon that extends over T periods, determine the production level P_t, inventory level I_t, and workforce level W_t for periods $t = 1, 2, \ldots, T$ that minimize the relevant costs over the planning horizon.

The form of the aggregate plan varies from company to company. In some firms, it is a formalized report containing planning objectives and the planning premises on which it is based. In other companies, particularly smaller ones, the owner may make simple calculations of workforce needs that reflect a general staffing strategy.

The process by which the plan itself is derived also varies. One common approach is to derive it from the corporate annual plan, as shown in Exhibit 12.1. A typical corporate plan contains a section on manufacturing that specifies how many units in each major product line need to be produced over the next 12 months to meet the sales forecast. The planner takes this information and attempts to determine how best to meet these requirements with available resources. Alternatively, some organizations combine output requirements into equivalent units and use this as the basis for the aggregate plan. For example, a division of General Motors may be asked to produce a certain number of cars of all types at a particular facility. The production planner would then take the average labor hours required for all models as a basis for the overall aggregate plan. Refinements to this plan, specifically model types to be produced, would be reflected in shorter-term production plans.

Another approach is to develop the aggregate plan by simulating various master production schedules and calculating corresponding capacity requirements to see if adequate labor and equipment exist at each work center. If capacity is inadequate, additional requirements for overtime, subcontracting, extra workers, and so forth are specified for each product line and combined into a rough-cut plan. This plan is then modified by cut-and-try or mathematical methods to derive a final and (one hopes) lower-cost plan.

Production Planning Environment

Exhibit 12.2 illustrates the internal and external factors that constitute the production planning environment. In general, the external environment is outside the production planner's direct control, but in some firms, demand for the product can be managed. Through close cooperation between marketing and operations, promotional activities and price cutting can be used to build demand during slow periods. Conversely, when demand is strong, promotional activities can be curtailed and prices raised to maximize the revenues from those products or services that the firm has the capacity to provide. The current practices in managing demand will be discussed later in the section titled "Yield Management."

Complementary products may work for firms facing cyclical demand fluctuations. For instance, lawnmower manufacturers will have strong demand for spring and summer, but weak demand during fall and winter. Demands on the production system can be smoothed out by producing a complementary product with high demand during fall and winter, and low demand during spring and summer (for instance, snowmobiles, snowblowers, or leafblowers). With services, cycles are more often measured in hours than months. Restaurants with strong demand during lunch and dinner will often add a breakfast menu to increase demand during the morning hours.

Service

WATER SKIS AND SNOW SKIS ARE GREAT EXAMPLES OF COMPLEMENTARY PRODUCTS.

exhibit 12.2   Required Inputs to the Production Planning System

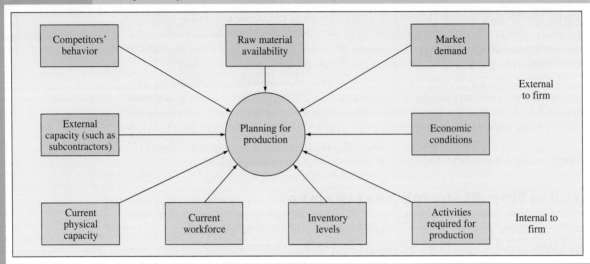

But even so, there are limits to how much demand can be controlled. Ultimately, the production planner must live with the sales projections and orders promised by the marketing function, leaving the internal factors as variables that can be manipulated in deriving a production plan. A new approach to facilitate managing these internal factors is termed *accurate response*. This entails refined measurement of historical demand patterns blended with expert judgment to determine when to begin production of particular items. The key element of the approach is clearly identifying those products for which demand is relatively predictable from those for which demand is relatively unpredictable.[1]

The internal factors themselves differ in their controllability. Current physical capacity (plant and equipment) is usually nearly fixed in the short run; union agreements often constrain what can be done in changing the workforce; physical capacity cannot always be increased; and top management may limit the amount of money that can be tied up in inventories. Still, there is always some flexibility in managing these factors, and production planners can implement one or a combination of the **production planning strategies** discussed here.

Production planning strategies

Production Planning Strategies   There are essentially three production planning strategies. These strategies involve trade-offs among the workforce size, work hours, inventory, and backlogs.

1. **Chase strategy.** Match the production rate to the order rate by hiring and laying off employees as the order rate varies. The success of this strategy depends on having a pool of easily trained applicants to draw on as order volumes increase. There are obvious motivational impacts. When order backlogs are low, employees may feel compelled to slow down out of fear of being laid off as soon as existing orders are completed.

2. **Stable workforce—variable work hours.** Vary the output by varying the number of hours worked through flexible work schedules or overtime. By varying the

number of work hours, you can match production quantities to orders. This strategy provides workforce continuity and avoids many of the emotional and tangible costs of hiring and firing associated with the chase strategy.

3. **Level strategy.** Maintain a stable workforce working at a constant output rate. Shortages and surpluses are absorbed by fluctuating inventory levels, order backlogs, and lost sales. Employees benefit from stable work hours at the costs of potentially decreased customer service levels and increased inventory costs. Another concern is the possibility of inventoried products becoming obsolete.

When just one of these variables is used to absorb demand fluctuations, it is termed a **pure strategy**; two or more used in combination constitute a **mixed strategy**. As you might suspect, mixed strategies are more widely applied in industry.

Pure strategy

Mixed strategy

Subcontracting In addition to these strategies, managers also may choose to subcontract some portion of production. This strategy is similar to the chase strategy, but hiring and laying off are translated into subcontracting and not subcontracting. Some level of subcontracting can be desirable to accommodate demand fluctuations. However, unless the relationship with the supplier is particularly strong, a manufacturer can lose some control over schedule and quality.

Relevant Costs

Four costs are relevant to the aggregate production plan. These relate to the production cost itself as well as the cost to hold inventory and to have unfilled orders. More specifically, these are

1. **Basic production costs.** These are the fixed and variable costs incurred in producing a given product type in a given time period. Included are direct and indirect labor costs and regular as well as overtime compensation.
2. **Costs associated with changes in the production rate.** Typical costs in this category are those involved in hiring, training, and laying off personnel. Hiring temporary help is a way of avoiding these costs.
3. **Inventory holding costs.** A major component is the cost of capital tied up in inventory. Other components are storing, insurance, taxes, spoilage, and obsolescence.
4. **Backordering costs.** Usually these are very hard to measure and include costs of expediting, loss of customer goodwill, and loss of sales revenues resulting from backordering.

Budgets To receive funding, operations managers are generally required to submit annual, and sometimes quarterly, budget requests. The aggregate plan is key to the success of the budgeting process. Recall that the goal of the aggregate plan is to minimize the total production-related costs over the planning horizon by determining the optimal combination of workforce levels and inventory levels. Thus, the aggregate plan provides justification for the requested budget amount. Accurate medium-range planning increases the likelihood of (1) receiving the requested budget and (2) operating within the limits of the budget.

In the next section we provide an example of medium-range planning in a manufacturing setting. This example illustrates the trade-offs associated with different production planning strategies.[2]

It's All in the Planning

You're sitting anxiously in the suddenly assembled general manager's staff meeting. Voices are nervously subdued. The rumor mill is in high gear about another initiative-of-the-month about to be loosed among the leery survivors of the last purge. The meeting begins. Amid the tricolor visuals and 3D spreadsheets, the same old message is skeptically received by managers scrambling for politically correct responses in an endless game of shoot the messenger.

This is a familiar scene in corporations around the world. But interestingly, firms such as Advanced Optical Components, a division of Finisar, formerly VCSEL, have learned how to manage the process of successfully matching supply and demand. Advanced Optical Components has developed a new semiconductor laser used in computing, networking, and sensing applications. Forecasting and managing production capacity is a unique challenge for companies with a stream of new and innovative products coming to market. Using a monthly sales and operations planning process, Advanced Optical Components has been able to improve their short- and long-term forecasting accuracy from 60 percent to consistently hitting 95 percent or better. The specific steps within their plan focus the executive team on (1) the demand opportunities for current and new products and (2) the constraints on the organization's ability to produce product to meet this demand. The plan, developed in a monthly sales and operations planning executive meeting, ensures that demand is synchronized with supply, so customers get the product they want, when they want it, while inventory and costs are kept to a minimum.

Advanced Optical Components managers indicated that a critical step was getting the general manager to champion the process. The second step was achieving a complete understanding of required behavior from the team, including committing to a balanced and synchronized demand/supply plan, being accountable for meeting the performance standards, having open and honest communication, not promising what cannot be delivered, and making the decisions needed to address the identified opportunities and constraints.

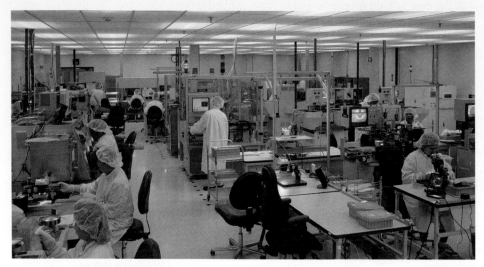

Source: Adapted from http://www.themanufacturer.com.

AGGREGATE PLANNING TECHNIQUES

Companies commonly use simple cut-and-try charting and graphic methods to develop aggregate plans. A cut-and-try approach involves costing out various production planning alternatives and selecting the one that is best. Elaborate spreadsheets are developed to facilitate the decision process. Sophisticated approaches involving linear programming and simulation are often incorporated into these spreadsheets. In the following, we demonstrate a spreadsheet approach to evaluate four strategies for meeting demand for the JC Company. Later we discuss more sophisticated approaches using linear programming (see Appendix A).

A Cut-and-Try Example: The JC Company

A firm with pronounced seasonal variation normally plans production for a full year to capture the extremes in demand during the busiest and slowest months. But we can illustrate the general principles involved with a shorter horizon. Suppose we wish to set up a production plan for the JC Company for the next six months. We are given the following information:

Service

DEMAND AND WORKING DAYS

	JANUARY	FEBRUARY	MARCH	APRIL	MAY	JUNE	TOTALS
Demand forecast	1,800	1,500	1,100	900	1,100	1,600	8,000
Number of working days	22	19	21	21	22	20	125

COSTS

Materials	$100.00/unit
Inventory holding cost	$1.50/unit/month
Marginal cost of stockout	$5.00/unit/month
Marginal cost of subcontracting	$20.00/unit ($120 subcontracting cost less $100 material savings)
Hiring and training cost	$200.00/worker
Layoff cost	$250.00/worker
Labor hours required	5/unit
Straight-time cost (first eight hours each day)	$4.00/hour
Overtime cost (time and a half)	$6.00/hour

INVENTORY

Beginning inventory	400 units
Safety stock	25% of month demand

In solving this problem, we can exclude the material costs. We could have included this $100 cost in all our calculations, but if we assume that a $100 cost is common to each demanded unit, then we need only concern ourselves with the marginal costs. Because the subcontracting cost is $120, our true cost for subcontracting is just $20 because we save the materials.

Note that many costs are expressed in a different form than typically found in the accounting records of a firm. Therefore, do not expect to obtain all these costs directly from such records, but obtain them indirectly from management personnel, who can help interpret the data.

Inventory at the beginning of the first period is 400 units. Because the demand forecast is imperfect, the JC Company has determined that a *safety stock* (buffer inventory) should be established to reduce the likelihood of stockouts. For this example, assume the safety stock should be one-quarter of the demand forecast. (Chapter 13 covers this topic in depth.)

Before investigating alternative production plans, it is often useful to convert demand forecasts into *production requirements,* which take into account the safety stock estimates. In Exhibit 12.3, note that these requirements implicitly assume that the safety stock is

exhibit 12.3

Aggregate Production Planning Requirements

**Excel:
Aggregate
Planning**

	JANUARY	FEBRUARY	MARCH	APRIL	MAY	JUNE
Beginning inventory	400	450	375	275	225	275
Demand forecast	1,800	1,500	1,100	900	1,100	1,600
Safety stock (.25 × Demand forecast)	450	375	275	225	275	400
Production requirement (Demand forecast + Safety stock − Beginning inventory)	1,850	1,425	1,000	850	1,150	1,725
Ending inventory (Beginning inventory + Production requirement − Demand forecast)	450	375	275	225	275	400

never actually used, so that the ending inventory each month equals the safety stock for that month. For example, the January safety stock of 450 (25 percent of January demand of 1,800) becomes the inventory at the end of January. The production requirement for January is demand plus safety stock minus beginning inventory (1,800 + 450 − 400 = 1,850).

Now we must formulate alternative production plans for the JC Company. Using a spreadsheet, we investigate four different plans with the objective of finding the one with the lowest total cost.

Plan 1. Produce to exact monthly production requirements using a regular eight-hour day by varying workforce size.

Plan 2. Produce to meet expected average demand over the next six months by maintaining a constant workforce. This constant number of workers is calculated by finding the average number of workers required each day over the horizon. Take the total production requirements and multiply by the time required for each unit. Then divide by the total time that one person works over the horizon [(8,000 units × 5 hours per unit) ÷ (125 days × 8 hours per day) = 40 workers]. Inventory is allowed to accumulate, with shortages filled from next month's production by backordering. Negative beginning inventory balances indicate that demand is backordered. In some cases, sales may be lost if demand is not met. The lost sales can be shown with a negative ending inventory balance followed by a zero beginning inventory balance in the next period. Notice that in this plan we use our safety stock in January, February, March, and June to meet expected demand.

Plan 3. Produce to meet the minimum expected demand (April) using a constant workforce on regular time. Subcontract to meet additional output requirements. The number of workers is calculated by locating the minimum monthly production requirement and determining how many workers would be needed for that month [(850 units × 5 hours per unit) ÷ (21 days × 8 hours per day) = 25 workers] and subcontracting any monthly difference between requirements and production.

Plan 4. Produce to meet expected demand for all but the first two months using a constant workforce on regular time. Use overtime to meet additional output requirements. The number of workers is more difficult to compute for this plan, but the goal is to finish June with an ending inventory as close as possible to the June safety stock. By trial and error it can be shown that a constant workforce of 38 workers is the closest approximation.

The next step is to calculate the cost of each plan. This requires the series of simple calculations shown in Exhibit 12.4. Note that the headings in each row are different for each plan because each is a different problem requiring its own data and calculations.

Costs of Four Production Plans

exhibit 12.4

Excel: Aggregate Planning

PRODUCTION PLAN 1: EXACT PRODUCTION; VARY WORKFORCE

	JANUARY	FEBRUARY	MARCH	APRIL	MAY	JUNE	TOTAL
Production requirement (from Exhibit 12.3)	1,850	1,425	1,000	850	1,150	1,725	
Production hours required (Production requirement × 5 hr./unit)	9,250	7,125	5,000	4,250	5,750	8,625	
Working days per month	22	19	21	21	22	20	
Hours per month per worker (Working days × 8 hrs./day)	176	152	168	168	176	160	
Workers required (Production hours required/Hours per month per worker)	53	47	30	25	33	54	
New workers hired (assuming opening workforce equal to first month's requirement of 53 workers)	0	0	0	0	8	21	
Hiring cost (New workers hired × $200)	$0	$0	$0	$0	$1,600	$4,200	$5,800
Workers laid off	0	6	17	5	0	0	
Layoff cost (Workers laid off × $250)	$0	$1,500	$4,250	$1,250	$0	$0	$7,000
Straight-time cost (Production hours required × $4)	$37,000	$28,500	$20,000	$17,000	$23,000	$34,500	$160,000
						Total cost	$172,800

PRODUCTION PLAN 2: CONSTANT WORKFORCE; VARY INVENTORY AND STOCKOUT

	JANUARY	FEBRUARY	MARCH	APRIL	MAY	JUNE	TOTAL
Beginning inventory	400	8	−276	−32	412	720	
Working days per month	22	19	21	21	22	20	
Production hours available (Working days per month × 8 hr./day × 40 workers)*	7,040	6,080	6,720	6,720	7,040	6,400	
Actual production (Production hours available/5 hr./unit)	1,408	1,216	1,344	1,344	1,408	1,280	
Demand forecast (from Exhibit 12.3)	1,800	1,500	1,100	900	1,100	1,600	
Ending inventory (Beginning inventory + Actual production − Demand forecast)	8	−276	−32	412	720	400	
Shortage cost (Units short × $5)	$0	$1,380	$160	$0	$0	$0	$1,540
Safety stock (from Exhibit 12.3)	450	375	275	225	275	400	
Units excess (Ending inventory − Safety stock) only if positive amount	0	0	0	187	445	0	
Inventory cost (Units excess × $1.50)	$0	$0	$0	$281	$668	$0	$948
Straight-time cost (Production hours available × $4)	$28,160	$24,320	$26,880	$26,880	$28,160	$25,600	$160,000
						Total cost	$162,488

*(Sum of production requirement in Exhibit 12.3 × 5 hr./unit)/(Sum of production hours available × 8 hr./day) = (8,000 × 5)/(125 × 8) = 40.

(continued)

exhibit 12.4   Costs of Four Production Plans (*Concluded*)

PRODUCTION PLAN 3: CONSTANT LOW WORKFORCE; SUBCONTRACT

	JANUARY	FEBRUARY	MARCH	APRIL	MAY	JUNE	TOTAL
Production requirement (from Exhibit 12.3)	1,850	1,425	1,000	850	1,150	1,725	
Working days per month	22	19	21	21	22	20	
Production hours available (Working days × 8 hrs./day × 25 workers)*	4,400	3,800	4,200	4,200	4,400	4,000	
Actual production (Production hours available/5 hr. per unit)	880	760	840	840	880	800	
Units subcontracted (Production requirement − Actual production)	970	665	160	10	270	925	
Subcontracting cost (Units subcontracted × $20)	$19,400	$13,300	$3,200	$200	$5,400	$18,500	$60,000
Straight-time cost (Production hours available × $4)	$17,600	$15,200	$16,800	$16,800	$17,600	$16,000	$100,000
						Total cost	$160,000

*Minimum production requirement. In this example, April is minimum of 850 units. Number of workers required for April is (850 × 5)/(21 × 8) = 25.

PRODUCTION PLAN 4: CONSTANT WORKFORCE; OVERTIME

	JANUARY	FEBRUARY	MARCH	APRIL	MAY	JUNE	TOTAL
Beginning inventory	400	0	0	177	554	792	
Working days per month	22	19	21	21	22	20	
Production hours available (Working days × 8 hr./day × 38 workers)*	6,688	5,776	6,384	6,384	6,688	6,080	
Regular shift production (Production hours available/5 hrs. per unit)	1,338	1,155	1,277	1,277	1,338	1,216	
Demand forecast (from Exhibit 12.3)	1,800	1,500	1,100	900	1,100	1,600	
Units available before overtime (Beginning inventory + Regular shift production − Demand forecast). This number has been rounded to the nearest integer.	−62	−345	177	554	792	408	
Units overtime	62	375	0	0	0	0	
Overtime cost (Units overtime × 5 hr./unit × $6/hr.)	$1,860	$10,350	$0	$0	$0	$0	$12,210
Safety stock (from Exhibit 12.3)	450	375	275	225	275	400	
Units excess (Units available before overtime − Safety stock) only if positive amount	0	0	0	329	517	8	
Inventory cost (Units excessive × $1.50)	$0	$0	$0	$494	$776	$12	$1,281
Straight-time cost (Production hours available × $4)	$26,752	$23,104	$25,536	$25,536	$26,752	$24,320	$152,000
						Total cost	$165,491

*Workers determined by trial and error. See text for explanation.

exhibit 12.5

Comparison of Four Plans

Costs	Plan 1: Exact Production; Vary Workforce	Plan 2: Constant Workforce; Vary Inventory and Stockout	Plan 3: Constant Low Workforce; Subcontract	Plan 4: Constant Workforce; Overtime
Hiring	$ 5,800	$ 0	$ 0	$ 0
Layoff	7,000	0	0	0
Excess inventory	0	948	0	1,281
Shortage	0	1,540	0	0
Subcontract	0	0	60,000	0
Overtime	0	0	0	12,210
Straight time	160,000	160,000	100,000	152,000
	$172,800	$162,488	$160,000	$165,491

Excel: Aggregate Planning

The final step is to tabulate and graph each plan and compare their costs. From Exhibit 12.5 we can see that using subcontractors resulted in the lowest cost (Plan 3). Exhibit 12.6 shows the effects of the four plans. This is a cumulative graph illustrating the expected results on the total production requirement.

Note that we have made one other assumption in this example: The plan can start with any number of workers with no hiring or layoff cost. This usually is the case because an aggregate plan draws on existing personnel, and we can start the plan that way. However, in an actual application, the availability of existing personnel transferable from other areas of the firm may change the assumptions.

Plan 1 is the "S" curve when we chase demand by varying workforce. Plan 2 has the highest average production rate (the line representing cumulative demand has the greatest slope). Using subcontracting in Plan 3 results in it having the lowest production rate. Limits on the amount of overtime available results in Plan 4 being similar to Plan 2.

Each of these four plans focused on one particular cost, and the first three were simple pure strategies. Obviously, there are many other feasible plans, some of which would use a combination of workforce changes, overtime, and subcontracting. The problems at the end of this chapter include examples of such mixed strategies. In practice, the final plan chosen would come from searching a variety of alternatives and future projections beyond the six-month planning horizon we have used.

Keep in mind that the cut-and-try approach does not guarantee finding the minimum-cost solution. However, spreadsheet programs, such as Microsoft Excel, can perform cut-and-try cost estimates in seconds and have elevated this kind of what-if analysis to a fine art. More sophisticated programs can generate much better solutions without the user having to intercede, as in the cut-and-try method.

Aggregate Planning Applied to Services: Tucson Parks and Recreation Department

Charting and graphic techniques are also useful for aggregate planning in service applications. The following example shows how a city's parks and recreation department could use the alternatives of full-time employees, part-time employees, and subcontracting to meet its commitment to provide a service to the city.

Service

exhibit 12.6 Four Plans for Satisfying a Production Requirement over the Number of Production Days Available

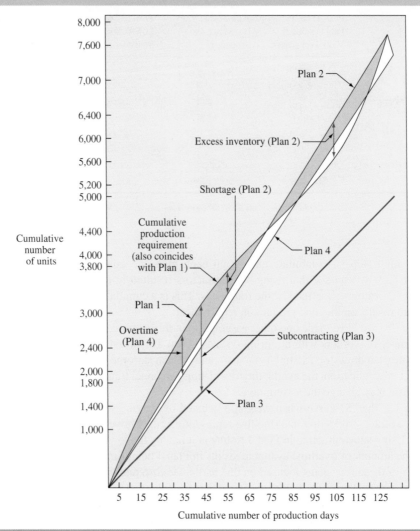

Tucson Parks and Recreation Department has an operation and maintenance budget of $9,760,000. The department is responsible for developing and maintaining open space, all public recreational programs, adult sports leagues, golf courses, tennis courts, pools, and so forth. There are 336 full-time-equivalent employees (FTEs). Of these, 216 are full-time permanent personnel who provide the administration and year-round maintenance to all areas. The remaining 120 FTE positions are staffed with part-timers; about three-quarters of them are used during the summer, and the remaining quarter in the fall, winter, and spring seasons. The three-fourths (or 90 FTE positions) show up as approximately 800 part-time summer jobs: lifeguards, baseball umpires, and instructors in summer programs for children. Eight hundred part-time jobs came from 90 FTEs because many last only for a month or two, while the FTEs are a year long.

Currently, the only parks and recreation work subcontracted amounts to less than $100,000. This is for the golf and tennis pros and for grounds maintenance at the libraries and veterans' cemetery.

Because of the nature of city employment, the probable bad public image, and civil service rules, the option to hire and fire full-time help daily or weekly to meet seasonal demand is out of the question. However, temporary part-time help is authorized and traditional. Also, it is virtually impossible to have regular (full-time) staff for all the summer jobs. During the summer months, the approximately 800 part-time employees are staffing many programs that occur simultaneously, prohibiting level scheduling over a normal 40-hour week. A wider variety of skills are required (such as umpires, coaches, lifeguards, and teachers of ceramics, guitar, karate, belly dancing, and yoga) than can be expected from full-time employees.

Three options are open to the department in its aggregate planning:

1.   The present method, which is to maintain a medium-level full-time staff and schedule work during off-seasons (such as rebuilding baseball fields during the winter months) and to use part-time help during peak demands.
2.   Maintain a lower level of staff over the year and subcontract all additional work presently done by full-time staff (still using part-time help).
3.   Maintain an administrative staff only and subcontract all work, including part-time help. (This would entail contracts to landscaping firms and pool maintenance companies as well as to newly created private firms to employ and supply part-time help.)

The common unit of measure of work across all areas is full-time equivalent jobs or employees. For example, assume in the same week that 30 lifeguards worked 20 hours each, 40 instructors worked 15 hours each, and 35 baseball umpires worked 10 hours each. This is equivalent to $(30 \times 20) + (40 \times 15) + (35 \times 10) = 1{,}550 \div 40 = 38.75$ FTE positions for that week. Although a considerable amount of workload can be shifted to off-season, most of the work must be done when required.

Full-time employees consist of three groups: (1) the skeleton group of key department personnel coordinating with the city, setting policy, determining budgets, measuring performance, and so forth; (2) the administrative group of supervisory and office personnel who are responsible for or whose jobs are directly linked to the direct-labor workers; and (3) the direct-labor workforce of 116 full-time positions. These workers physically maintain the department's areas of responsibility, such as cleaning up, mowing golf greens and ballfields, trimming trees, and watering grass.

Cost information needed to determine the best alternative strategy is

Full-time direct-labor employees	
Average wage rate	$4.45 per hour
Fringe benefits	17% of wage rate
Administrative costs	20% of wage rate
Part-time employees	
Average wage rate	$4.03 per hour
Fringe benefits	11% of wage rate
Administrative costs	25% of wage rate
Subcontracting all full-time jobs	$1.6 million
Subcontracting all part-time jobs	$1.85 million

June and July are the peak demand seasons in Tucson. Exhibit 12.7 shows the high requirements for June and July personnel. The part-time help reaches 576 FTE positions (although, in actual numbers, this is approximately 800 different employees). After a low fall and winter staffing level, the demand shown as "full-time direct" reaches 130 in March

exhibit 12.7

Actual Demand Requirement for Full-Time Direct Employees and Full-Time Equivalent (FTE) Part-Time Employees

**Excel:
Aggregate
Planning**

	JAN.	FEB.	MAR.	APR.	MAY	JUNE	JULY	AUG.	SEPT.	OCT.	NOV.	DEC.	TOTAL
Days	22	20	21	22	21	20	21	21	21	23	18	22	252
Full-time employees	66	28	130	90	195	290	325	92	45	32	29	60	
Full-time days*	1,452	560	2,730	1,980	4,095	5,800	6,825	1,932	945	736	522	1,320	28,897
Full-time equivalent part-time employees	41	75	72	68	72	302	576	72	0	68	84	27	
FTE days	902	1,500	1,512	1,496	1,512	6,040	12,096	1,512	0	1,564	1,512	594	30,240

*Full-time days are derived by multiplying the number of days in each month by the number of workers.

Monthly Requirement for Full-Time Direct-Labor Employees (Other Than Key Personnel) and Full-Time Equivalent Part-Time Employees

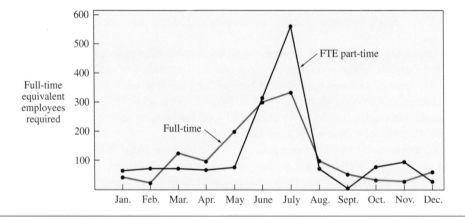

(when grounds are reseeded and fertilized) and then increases to a high of 325 in July. The present method levels this uneven demand over the year to an average of 116 full-time year-round employees by early scheduling of work. As previously mentioned, no attempt is made to hire and lay off full-time workers to meet this uneven demand.

Exhibit 12.8 shows the cost calculations for all three alternatives and compares the total costs for each alternative. From this analysis, it appears that the department is already using the lowest-cost alternative (Alternative 1).

LEVEL SCHEDULING

In this chapter we looked at four primary strategies for production planning: vary workforce size to meet demand, work overtime and part-time, vary inventory through excesses and shortages, and subcontract.

A level schedule holds production constant over a period of time. It is something of a combination of the strategies we have mentioned here. For each period, it keeps the workforce

exhibit 12.8

Three Possible Plans for the Parks and Recreation Department

Alternative 1: Maintain 116 full-time regular direct workers. Schedule work during off-seasons to level workload throughout the year. Continue to use 120 full-time equivalent (FTE) part-time employees to meet high demand periods.

Costs	Days per Year (Exhibit 12.7)	Hours (Employees × Days × 8 Hours)	Wages (Full-Time, $4.45; Part-Time, $4.03)	Fringe Benefits (Full-Time, 17%; Part-Time, 11%)	Administrative Cost (Full-Time, 20%; Part-Time, 25%)
116 full-time regular employees	252	233,856	$1,040,659	$176,912	$208,132
120 part-time employees	252	241,920	974,938	107,243	243,735
Total cost = $2,751,619			$2,015,597	$284,155	$451,867

Alternative 2: Maintain 50 full-time regular direct workers and the present 120 FTE part-time employees. Subcontract jobs releasing 66 full-time regular employees. Subcontract cost, $1,100,000.

Cost	Days per Year (Exhibit 12.7)	Hours (Employees × Days × 8 Hours)	Wages (Full-Time, $4.45; Part-Time, $4.03)	Fringe Benefits (Full-Time, 17%; Part-Time, 11%)	Administrative Cost (Full-Time, 20%; Part-Time, 25%)	Subcontract Cost
50 full-time employees	252	100,800	$ 448,560	$ 76,255	$ 89,712	
120 FTE part-time employees	252	241,920	974,938	107,243	243,735	
Subcontracting cost						$1,100,000
Total cost = $3,040,443			$1,423,498	$183,498	$333,447	$1,100,000

Alternative 3: Subcontract all jobs previously performed by 116 full-time regular employees. Subcontract cost $1,600,000. Subcontract all jobs previously performed by 120 FTE part-time employees. Subcontract cost $1,850,000.

Cost	Subcontract Cost
0 full-time employees 0 part-time employees	
Subcontract full-time jobs	$1,600,000
Subcontract part-time jobs	1,850,000
Total cost	$3,450,000

Excel: Aggregate Planning

---

constant and inventory low, and depends on demand to pull products through. Level production has a number of advantages, which makes it the backbone of JIT production:

1. The entire system can be planned to minimize inventory and work-in-process.
2. Product modifications are up-to-date because of the low amount of work-in-process.
3. There is a smooth flow throughout the production system.
4. Purchased items from vendors can be delivered when needed, and, in fact, often directly to the production line.

Toyota Motor Corporation, for example, creates a yearly production plan that shows the total number of cars to be made and sold. The aggregate production plan creates the system

Global

requirements to produce this total number with a level schedule. The secret to success in the Japanese level schedule is *production smoothing.* The aggregate plan is translated into monthly and daily schedules that *sequence* products through the production system. The procedure is essentially this: Two months in advance, the car types and quantities needed are established. This is converted to a detailed plan one month ahead. These quantities are given to subcontractors and vendors so that they can plan on meeting Toyota's needs. The monthly needs of various car types are then translated into daily schedules. For example, if 8,000 units of car type A are needed in one month, along with 6,000 type B, 4,000 type C, and 2,000 type D, and if we assume the line operates 20 days per month, then this would be translated to a daily output of 400, 300, 200, and 100, respectively. Further, this would be sequenced as four units of A, three of B, two of C, and one of D each 9.6 minutes of a two-shift day (960 minutes).

Each worker operates a number of machines, producing a sequence of products. To use this level scheduling technique,

1. Production should be repetitive (assembly-line format).
2. The system must contain excess capacity.
3. Output of the system must be fixed for a period of time (preferably a month).
4. There must be a smooth relationship among purchasing, marketing, and production.
5. The cost of carrying inventory must be high.
6. Equipment costs must be low.
7. The workforce must be multiskilled.

For more about level scheduling, see lean production schedules in Chapter 10. Also see the discussion on mixed-model line balancing in Chapter 4.

YIELD MANAGEMENT

Yield management

Why is it that the guy sitting next to you on the plane paid half the price you paid for your ticket? Why was a hotel room you booked more expensive when you booked it six months in advance than when you checked in without a reservation (or vice versa)? The answers lie in the practice known as yield management. **Yield management** can be defined as the process of allocating the right type of capacity to the right type of customer at the right price and time to maximize revenue or yield. Yield management can be a powerful approach to making demand more predictable, which is important to aggregate planning.

Service

Yield management has existed as long as there has been limited capacity for serving customers. However, its widespread scientific application began with American Airlines' computerized reservation system (SABRE), introduced in the mid-1980s. The system allowed the airline to change ticket prices on any routes instantaneously as a function of forecast demand. Peoples' Express, a no-frills, low-cost competitor airline, was one of the most famous victims of American's yield management system. Basically, the system enabled hour-by-hour updating on competing routes so that American could match or better prices wherever Peoples' Express was flying. The president of Peoples' Express realized that the game was lost when his mother flew on American to Peoples' hub for a lower price than Peoples' could offer!

From an operational perspective, yield management is most effective when

1. Demand can be segmented by customer.
2. Fixed costs are high and variable costs are low.

3. Inventory is perishable.
4. Product can be sold in advance.
5. Demand is highly variable.

Hotels illustrate these five characteristics well. They offer one set of rates during the week for the business traveler and another set during the weekend for the vacationer. The variable costs associated with a room (such as cleaning) are low in comparison to the cost of adding rooms to the property. Available rooms cannot be transferred from night to night, and blocks of rooms can be sold to conventions or tours. Finally, potential guests may cut short their stay or not show up at all.

Most organizations (such as airlines, rental car agencies, cruise lines, and hotels) manage yield by establishing decision rules for opening or closing rate classes as a function of expected demand and available supply. The methodologies for doing this can be quite sophisticated. A common approach is to forecast demand over the planning horizon and then use marginal analysis to determine the rates that will be charged if demand is forecast as being above or below set control limits around the forecast mean.

Operating Yield Management Systems

A number of interesting issues arise in managing yield. One is that pricing structures must appear logical to the customer and justify the different prices. Such justification, commonly called *rate fences*, may have either a physical basis (such as a room with a view) or a nonphysical basis (like unrestricted access to the Internet). Pricing also should relate to addressing specific capacity problems. If capacity is sufficient for peak demand, price reductions stimulating off-peak demand should be the focus. If capacity is insufficient, offering deals to customers who arrive during nonpeak periods (or creating alternative service locations) may enhance revenue generation.

A second issue is handling variability in arrival or starting times, duration, and time between customers. This entails employing maximally accurate forecasting methods (the greater the accuracy in forecasting demand, the more likely yield management will succeed); coordinated policies on overbooking, deposits, and no-show or cancellation penalties; and well-designed service processes that are reliable and consistent.

A third issue relates to managing the service process. Some strategies include scheduling additional personnel to meet peak demand; increasing customer coproduction; creating adjustable capacity; utilizing idle capacity for complementary services; and cross-training employees to create reserves for peak periods.

Service

The fourth and perhaps most critical issue is training workers and managers to work in an environment where overbooking and price changes are standard occurrences that directly impact the customer. Companies have developed creative ways of mollifying overbooked customers. A golf course company offers $100 putters to players who have been overbooked at a popular tee time. Airlines, of course, frequently give overbooked passengers free tickets for other flights.

The essence of yield management is the ability to manage demand. Kimes and Chase suggest that two strategic levers can be used to accomplish this goal: pricing and duration control.[3] If these two levers are thought of in matrix form (see Exhibit 12.9) with price being either fixed or variable and duration being either predictable or unpredictable, then traditional applications of yield management have been by firms located in the variable price/predictable duration quadrant. This type of matrix provides a framework for a firm to identify its position and the necessary actions to manage yield. For example, an action controlling duration would be to convert the service offering from an event of indeterminate

exhibit 12.9	Price/Service Duration Matrix: Positioning of Selected Service Industries

		PRICE	
		FIXED	VARIABLE
DURATION	PREDICTABLE	Movies Stadiums/arenas Convention centers	Hotels Airlines Rental cars Cruise lines
	UNPREDICTABLE	Restaurants Golf courses Internet service providers	Continuing care hospitals

Source: S. Kimes and R. B. Chase, "The Strategic Levers of Yield Management," *Journal of Service Research* 1, no. 2 (1998), pp. 298–308. Copyright © 1998 by Sage Publishers. Used by permission of Sage Publications, Inc.

time to an offering that is time-based. This improves reservation planning and hence allocation of resources. An example would be having diners reserve a fixed block of time for dining at a restaurant (e.g., 7–8 P.M.) rather than an open-ended table reservation for 7 P.M.

SUMMARY

Sales and operations planning and the aggregate plan translate corporate strategic and capacity plans into broad categories of workforce size, inventory quantity, and production levels.

Demand variations are a fact of life, so the planning system must include sufficient flexibility to cope with such variations. Flexibility can be achieved by developing alternative sources of supply, cross-training workers to handle a wide variety of orders, and engaging in more frequent replanning during high-demand periods.

Decision rules for production planning should be adhered to once they have been selected. However, they should be carefully analyzed prior to implementation by checks such as simulation of historical data to see what really would have happened if the decision rules had operated in the past.

Yield management is an important tool that can be used to shape demand patterns so a firm can operate more efficiently.

Key Terms

Aggregate operations plan Translating annual and quarterly business plans into labor and production output plans for the intermediate term. The objective is to minimize the cost of resources required to meet demand.

Sales and operations planning A term that refers to the process that helps companies keep demand and supply in balance. The terminology is meant to capture the importance of cross-functional work.

Long-range planning Activity typically done annually and focusing on a horizon of a year or more.

Intermediate-range planning Activity that usually covers a period from 3 to 18 months with weekly, monthly, or quarterly time increments.

Short-range planning Planning that covers a period less than six months with either daily or weekly increments of time.

Production rate The number of units completed per unit of time.

Workforce level The number of production workers needed each period.

Inventory on hand Unused inventory carried from a previous period.

Production planning strategies Plans that involve trade-offs among workforce size, work hours, inventory, and backlogs.

Pure strategy A plan that uses just one of the options available for meeting demand. Typical options include chasing demand, using a stable workforce with overtime or part-time work, and constant production with shortages and overages absorbed by inventory.

Mixed strategy A plan that combines options available for meeting demand.

Yield management Allocating the right type of capacity to the right type of customer at the right price and time to maximize revenue or yield.

Solved Problem

Excel: Aggregate Planning Solved Problem

Jason Enterprises (JE) produces video telephones for the home market. Quality is not quite as good as it could be at this point, but the selling price is low and Jason can study market response while spending more time on R&D.

At this stage, however, JE needs to develop an aggregate production plan for the six months from January through June. You have been commissioned to create the plan. The following information should help:

DEMAND AND WORKING DAYS

	JANUARY	FEBRUARY	MARCH	APRIL	MAY	JUNE	TOTALS
Demand forecast	500	600	650	800	900	800	4,250
Number of working days	22	19	21	21	22	20	125

COSTS

Materials	$100.00/unit
Inventory holding cost	$10.00/unit/month
Marginal cost of stockout	$20.00/unit/month
Marginal cost of subcontracting	$100.00/unit ($200 subcontracting cost less $100 material savings)
Hiring and training cost	$50.00/worker
Layoff cost	$100.00/worker
Labor hours required	4/unit
Straight-time cost (first eight hours each day)	$12.50/hour
Overtime cost (time and a half)	$18.75/hour

INVENTORY

Beginning inventory	200 units
Safety stock required	0% of month demand

What is the cost of each of the following production strategies?

a. Produce exactly to meet demand; vary workforce (assuming opening workforce equal to first month's requirements).

b. Constant workforce; vary inventory and allow shortages only (assuming a starting workforce of 10).

c. Constant workforce of 10; use subcontracting.

Solution

AGGREGATE PRODUCTION PLANNING REQUIREMENTS

	JANUARY	FEBRUARY	MARCH	APRIL	MAY	JUNE	TOTAL
Beginning inventory	200	0	0	0	0	0	
Demand forecast	500	600	650	800	900	800	
Safety stock (0.0 × Demand forecast)	0	0	0	0	0	0	
Production requirement (Demand forecast + Safety stock − Beginning inventory)	300	600	650	800	900	800	
Ending inventory (Beginning inventory + Production requirement − Demand forecast)	0	0	0	0	0	0	

PRODUCTION PLAN 1: EXACT PRODUCTION; VARY WORKFORCE

	JANUARY	FEBRUARY	MARCH	APRIL	MAY	JUNE	TOTAL
Production requirement	300	600	650	800	900	800	
Production hours required (Production requirement × 4 hr./unit)	1,200	2,400	2,600	3,200	3,600	3,200	
Working days per month	22	19	21	21	22	20	
Hours per month per worker (Working days × 8 hrs./day)	176	152	168	168	176	160	
Workers required (Production hours required/Hours per month per worker)	7	16	15	19	20	20	
New workers hired (assuming opening workforce equal to first month's requirement of 7 workers)	0	9	0	4	1	0	
Hiring cost (New workers hired × $50)	$0	$450	$0	$200	$50	$0	$700
Workers laid off	0	0	1	0	0	0	
Layoff cost (Workers laid off × $100)	$0	$0	$100	$0	$0	$0	$100
Straight-time cost (Production hours required × $12.50)	$15,000	$30,000	$32,500	$40,000	$45,000	$40,000	$202,500

Total Cost $203,300

PRODUCTION PLAN 2: CONSTANT WORKFORCE; VARY INVENTORY AND STOCKOUT

	JANUARY	FEBRUARY	MARCH	APRIL	MAY	JUNE	TOTAL
Beginning inventory	200	140	−80	−310	−690	−1150	
Working days per month	22	19	21	21	22	20	
Production hours available (Working days per month × 8 hr./day × 10 workers)*	1,760	1,520	1,680	1,680	1,760	1,600	

*Assume a constant workforce of 10.

(continued)

	JANUARY	FEBRUARY	MARCH	APRIL	MAY	JUNE	TOTAL
Actual production (Production hours available/4 hr./unit)	440	380	420	420	440	400	
Demand forecast	500	600	650	800	900	800	
Ending inventory (Beginning inventory + Actual production − Demand forecast)	140	−80	−310	−690	−1150	−1550	
Shortage cost (Units short × $20)	$0	$1,600	$6,200	$13,800	$23,000	$31,000	$75,600
Safety stock	0	0	0	0	0	0	
Units excess (Ending inventory − Safety stock; only if positive amount)	140	0	0	0	0	0	
Inventory cost (Units excess × $10)	$1,400	$0	$0	$0	$0	$0	$1,400
Straight-time cost (Production hours available × $12.50)	$22,000	$19,000	$21,000	$21,000	$22,000	$20,000	$125,000
						Total cost	$202,000

PRODUCTION PLAN 3: CONSTANT WORKFORCE; SUBCONTRACT

	JANUARY	FEBRUARY	MARCH	APRIL	MAY	JUNE	TOTAL
Production requirement	300	460[†]	650	800	900	800	
Working days per month	22	19	21	21	22	20	
Production hours available (Working days × 8 hrs./day × 10 workers)*	1,760	1,520	1,680	1,680	1,760	1,600	
Actual production (Production hours available/4 hr. per unit)	440	380	420	420	440	400	
Units subcontracted (Production requirements − Actual production)	0	80	230	380	460	400	
Subcontracting cost (Units subcontracted × $100)	$0	$8,000	$23,000	$38,000	$46,000	$40,000	$155,000
Straight-time cost (Production hours available × $12.50)	$22,000	$19,000	$21,000	$21,000	$22,000	$20,000	$125,000
						Total cost	$280,000

*Assume a constant workforce of 10.
[†]600 − 140 units of beginning inventory in February.

SUMMARY

PLAN DESCRIPTION	HIRING	LAYOFF	SUBCONTRACT	STRAIGHT TIME	SHORTAGE	EXCESS INVEN-TORY	TOTAL COST
1. Exact production; vary workforce	$700	$100		$202,500			$203,300
2. Constant workforce; vary inventory and shortages				$125,000	$75,600	$1,400	$202,000
3. Constant workforce; subcontract			$155,000	$125,000			$280,000

Review and Discussion Questions

1 What are the major differences between aggregate planning in manufacturing and aggregate planning in services?

2 What are the basic controllable variables of a production planning problem? What are the four major costs?

3 Distinguish between pure and mixed strategies in production planning.

4 Define level scheduling. How does it differ from the pure strategies in production planning?

5 How does forecast accuracy relate, in general, to the practical application of the aggregate planning models discussed in the chapter?

6 In which way does the time horizon chosen for an aggregate plan determine whether it is the best plan for the firm?

7 Review the opening vignette. How does sales and operations planning help resolve product shortage problems?

8 How would you apply yield management concepts to a barbershop? A soft drink vending machine?

Problems

1 For the solved problem, devise the least costly plan you can. You may choose your starting workforce level.

2 Develop a production plan and calculate the annual cost for a firm whose demand forecast is fall, 10,000; winter, 8,000; spring, 7,000; summer, 12,000. Inventory at the beginning of fall is 500 units. At the beginning of fall you currently have 30 workers, but you plan to hire temporary workers at the beginning of summer and lay them off at the end of the summer. In addition, you have negotiated with the union an option to use the regular workforce on overtime during winter or spring if overtime is necessary to prevent stockouts at the end of those quarters. Overtime is *not* available during the fall. Relevant costs are: hiring, $100 for each temp; layoff, $200 for each worker laid off; inventory holding, $5 per unit-quarter; backorder, $10 per unit; straight time, $5 per hour; overtime, $8 per hour. Assume that the productivity is 0.5 unit per worker hour, with eight hours per day and 60 days per season.

3 Plan production for a four-month period: February through May. For February and March, you should produce to exact demand forecast. For April and May, you should use overtime and inventory with a stable workforce; *stable* means that the number of workers needed for March will be held constant through May. However, government constraints put a maximum of 5,000 hours of overtime labor per month in April and May (zero overtime in February and March). If demand exceeds supply, then backorders occur. There are 100 workers on January 31. You are given the following demand forecast: February, 80,000; March, 64,000; April, 100,000; May, 40,000. Productivity is four units per worker hour, eight hours per day, 20 days per month. Assume zero inventory on February 1. Costs are hiring, $50 per new worker; layoff, $70 per worker laid off; inventory holding, $10 per unit-month; straight-time labor, $10 per hour; overtime, $15 per hour; backorder, $20 per unit. Find the total cost of this plan.

4 Plan production for the next year. The demand forecast is spring, 20,000; summer, 10,000; fall, 15,000; winter, 18,000. At the beginning of spring you have 70 workers and 1,000 units in inventory. The union contract specifies that you may lay off workers only once a year, at the beginning of summer. Also, you may hire new workers only at the end of summer to begin regular work in the fall. The number of workers laid off at the beginning of summer and the number hired at the end of summer should result in planned production levels for summer and fall that equal the demand forecasts for summer and fall, respectively. If demand exceeds supply, use overtime in spring only, which means that backorders could occur

in winter. You are given these costs: hiring, $100 per new worker; layoff, $200 per worker laid off; holding, $20 per unit-quarter; backorder cost, $8 per unit; straight-time labor, $10 per hour; overtime, $15 per hour. Productivity is 0.5 unit per worker hour, eight hours per day, 50 days per quarter. Find the total cost.

5   DAT, Inc., needs to develop an aggregate plan for its product line. Relevant data are

Production time	1 hour per unit	Beginning inventory	500 units
Average labor cost	$10 per hour	Safety stock	One-half month
Workweek	5 days, 8 hours each day	Shortage cost	$20 per unit per month
Days per month	Assume 20 work days per month	Carrying cost	$5 per unit per month

The forecast for next year is

Jan.	Feb.	Mar.	Apr.	May	June	July	Aug.	Sept.	Oct.	Nov.	Dec.
2,500	3,000	4,000	3,500	3,500	3,000	3,000	4,000	4,000	4,000	3,000	3,000

Management prefers to keep a constant workforce and production level, absorbing variations in demand through inventory excesses and shortages. Demand not met is carried over to the following month.

Develop an aggregate plan that will meet the demand and other conditions of the problem. Do not try to find the optimum; just find a good solution and state the procedure you might use to test for a better solution. Make any necessary assumptions.

6   Old Pueblo Engineering Contractors creates six-month "rolling" schedules, which are re-computed monthly. For competitive reasons (they would need to divulge proprietary design criteria, methods, and so on), Old Pueblo does not subcontract. Therefore, its only options to meet customer requirements are (1) work on regular time; (2) work on overtime, which is limited to 30 percent of regular time; (3) do customers' work early, which would cost an additional $5 per hour per month; and (4) perform customers' work late, which would cost an additional $10 per hour per month penalty, as provided by their contract.

Old Pueblo has 25 engineers on its staff at an hourly rate of $30. The overtime rate is $45. Customers' hourly requirements for the six months from January to June are

January	February	March	April	May	June
5,000	4,000	6,000	6,000	5,000	4,000

Develop an aggregate plan using a spreadsheet. Assume 20 working days in each month.

7   Alan Industries is expanding its product line to include new models: Model A, Model B, and Model C. These are to be produced on the same production equipment, and the objective is to meet the demands for the three products using overtime where necessary. The demand forecast for the next four months, in required hours, is

Product	April	May	June	July
Model A	800	600	800	1,200
Model B	600	700	900	1,100
Model C	700	500	700	850

Because the products deteriorate rapidly, there is a high loss in quality and, consequently, a high carryover cost into subsequent periods. Each hour's production carried into future months costs $3 per productive hour of Model A, $4 for Model B, and $5 for Model C.

Production can take place during either regular working hours or overtime. Regular time is paid at $4 when working on Model A, $5 for Model B, and $6 for Model C. Overtime premium is 50 percent.

The available production capacity for regular time and overtime is

	APRIL	MAY	JUNE	JULY
Regular time	1,500	1,300	1,800	1,700
Overtime	$700	650	900	850

a. Set up the problem in matrix form and show appropriate costs.
b. Show a feasible solution.

8 Shoney Video Concepts produces a line of videodisc players to be linked to personal computers for video games. Videodiscs have much faster access time than tape. With such a computer/video link, the game becomes a very realistic experience. In a simple driving game where the joystick steers the vehicle, for example, rather than seeing computer graphics on the screen, the player is actually viewing a segment of a videodisc shot from a real moving vehicle. Depending on the action of the player (hitting a guard rail, for example), the disc moves virtually instantaneously to that segment and the player becomes part of an actual accident of real vehicles (staged, of course).

Shoney is trying to determine a production plan for the next 12 months. The main criterion for this plan is that the employment level is to be held constant over the period. Shoney is continuing in its R&D efforts to develop new applications and prefers not to cause any adverse feeling with the local workforce. For the same reason, all employees should put in full workweeks, even if this is not the lowest-cost alternative. The forecast for the next 12 months is

MONTH	FORECAST DEMAND	MONTH	FORECAST DEMAND
January	600	July	200
February	800	August	200
March	900	September	300
April	600	October	700
May	400	November	800
June	300	December	900

Manufacturing cost is $200 per set, equally divided between materials and labor. Inventory storage cost is $5 per month. A shortage of sets results in lost sales and is estimated to cost an overall $20 per unit short.

The inventory on hand at the beginning of the planning period is 200 units. Ten labor hours are required per videodisc player. The workday is eight hours.

Develop an aggregate production schedule for the year using a constant workforce. For simplicity, assume 22 working days each month except July, when the plant closes down for three weeks' vacation (leaving seven working days). Assume that total production capacity is greater than or equal to total demand.

9 Develop a production schedule to produce the exact production requirements by varying the workforce size for the following problem. Use the example in the chapter as a guide (Plan 1).

The monthly forecasts for Product X for January, February, and March are 1,000, 1,500, and 1,200, respectively. Safety stock policy recommends that half of the forecast for that month be defined as safety stock. There are 22 working days in January, 19 in February, and 21 in March. Beginning inventory is 500 units.

Manufacturing cost is $200 per unit, storage cost is $3 per unit per month, standard pay rate is $6 per hour, overtime rate is $9 per hour, cost of stockout is $10 per unit per month, marginal cost of subcontracting is $10 per unit, hiring and training cost is $200 per worker, layoff cost is $300 per worker, and worker productivity is 0.1 unit per hour. Assume that you start off with 50 workers and that they work 8 hours per day.

10 Helter Industries, a company that produces a line of women's bathing suits, hires temporaries to help produce its summer product demand. For the current four-month rolling schedule, there are three temps on staff and 12 full-time employees. The temps can be hired when

needed and can be used as needed, whereas the full-time employees must be paid whether they are needed or not. Each full-time employee can produce 205 suits, while each part-time employee can produce 165 suits per month.

Demand for bathing suits for the next four months is as follows:

MAY	JUNE	JULY	AUGUST
3,200	2,800	3,100	3,000

Beginning inventory in May is 403 complete (a complete two-piece includes both top and bottom) bathing suits. Bathing suits cost $40 to produce and carrying cost is 24 percent per year. Develop an aggregate plan using a spreadsheet.

CASE: Bradford Manufacturing— Planning Plant Production

The Situation

You are the operations manager for a manufacturing plant that produces pudding food products. One of your important responsibilities is to prepare an aggregate plan for the plant. This plan is an important input into the annual budget process. The plan provides information on production rates, manufacturing labor requirements, and projected finished goods inventory levels for the next year.

You make those little boxes of pudding mix on packaging lines in your plant. A packaging line has a number of machines that are linked by conveyors. At the start of the line the pudding is mixed; it is then placed in small packets. These packets are inserted into the small pudding boxes, which are collected and placed in cases that hold 48 boxes of pudding. Finally, 160 cases are collected and put on a pallet. The pallets are staged in a shipping area from which they are sent to four distribution centers. Over the years, the technology of the packaging lines has improved so that all the different flavors can be made in relatively small batches with no setup time to switch between flavors. The plant has 15 of these lines, but currently only 10 are being used. Six employees are required to run each line.

The demand for this product fluctuates from month to month. In addition, there is a seasonal component, with peak sales before Thanksgiving, Christmas, and Easter each year. To complicate matters, at the end of the first quarter of each year the marketing group runs a promotion in which special deals are made for large purchases. Business is going well, and the company has been experiencing a general increase in sales.

The plant sends product to four large distribution warehouses strategically located in the United States. Trucks move product daily. The amounts shipped are based on maintaining target inventory levels at the warehouses. These targets are calculated based on anticipated weeks of supply at each warehouse. Current targets are set at two weeks of supply.

In the past, the company has had a policy of producing very close to what it expects sales to be because of limited

Excel: Bradford Manufacturing

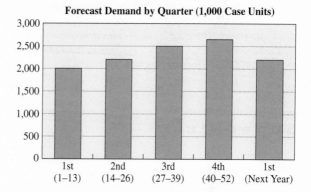

Forecast Demand by Quarter (1,000 Case Units)

capacity for storing finished goods. Production capacity has been adequate to support this policy.

A sales forecast for next year has been prepared by the marketing department. The forecast is based on quarterly sales quotas, which are used to set up an incentive program for the salespeople. Sales are mainly to the large U.S. retail grocers. The pudding is shipped to the grocers from the distribution warehouses based on orders taken by the salespeople.

Your immediate task is to prepare an aggregate plan for the coming year. The technical and economic factors that must be considered in this plan are shown next.

Technical and Economic Information

1   Currently the plant is running 10 lines with no overtime. Each line requires six people to run. For planning purposes, the lines are run for 7.5 hours each normal shift. Employees, though, are paid for eight

hours' work. It is possible to run up to two hours of overtime each day, but it must be scheduled for a week at a time, and all the lines must run overtime when it is scheduled. Workers are paid $20.00/hour during a regular shift and $30.00/hour on overtime. The standard production rate for each line is 450 cases/hour.

2   The marketing forecast for demand is as follows: Q1—2,000; Q2—2,200; Q3—2,500; Q4—2,650; and Q1 (next year)—2,200. These numbers are in 1,000-case units. Each number represents a 13-week forecast.

3   Management has instructed manufacturing to maintain a two-week supply of pudding inventory in the warehouses. The two-week supply should be based on future expected sales. The following are ending inventory target levels for each quarter: Q1—338; Q2—385; Q3—408; Q4—338.

4   Inventory carrying cost is estimated by accounting to be $1.00 per case per year. This means that if a case of pudding is held in inventory for an entire year, the cost to just carry that case in inventory is $1.00. If a case is carried for only one week, the cost is $1.00/52, or $.01923. The cost is proportional to the time carried in inventory. There are 200,000 cases in inventory at the beginning of Q1 (this is 200 cases in the 1,000-case units that the forecast is given in).

5   If a stockout occurs, the item is backordered and shipped at a later date. The cost when a backorder occurs is $2.40 per case due to the loss of goodwill and the high cost of emergency shipping.

6   The human resource group estimates that it costs $5,000 to hire and train a new production employee. It costs $3,000 to lay off a production worker.

Questions

1   Prepare an aggregate plan for the coming year, assuming that the sales forecast is perfect. Use the spreadsheet "Bradford Manufacturing". In the spreadsheet an area has been designated for your aggregate plan solution. Supply the number of packaging lines to run and the number of overtime hours for each quarter. You will need to set up the cost calculations in the spreadsheet.

You may want to try using the Excel Solver to find a solution. Remember that your final solution needs an integer number of lines and an integer number of overtime hours for each quarter. (Solutions that require 8.9134 lines and 1.256 hours of overtime are not feasible.)

2   Review your solution carefully and be prepared to defend it. Bring a printout of your solution to class.

Super Quiz

1   Term used to refer to the process a firm uses to balance supply and demand.

2   When doing aggregate planning, these are the three general operations–related variables that can be varied.

3   A strategy where the production rate is set to match expected demand.

4   When overtime is used to meet demand and avoid the costs associated with hiring and firing.

5   A strategy that uses inventory and backorders as part of the strategy to meet demand.

6   Sometimes a firm may choose to have all or part of the work done by an outside vendor. This is the term used for the approach.

7   If expected demand during the next four quarters were 150, 125, 100, 75 thousand units and each worker can produce 1,000 units per quarter; how many workers should be used if a level strategy were being employed?

8   Given the data from question 7, how many workers would be needed for a chase strategy?

9   In a service setting, what general operations–related variable is not available compared to a production setting?

10   The practice of allocating capacity and manipulating demand to make it more predictable.

1. Sales and operations planning 2. Production rate, workforce level, inventory 3. Chase 4. Stable workforce – variable work hours 5. Level strategy 6. Subcontracting 7. 113 8. 150, 125, 100, 75 9. Inventory 10. Yield management

Selected Bibliography

Brandimarte, P., and A. Villa (eds.). *Modeling Manufacturing Systems: From Aggregate Planning to Real-Time Control.* New York: Springer, 1999.

Fisher, M. L.; J. H. Hammond; W. R. Obermeyer; and A. Raman. "Making Supply Meet Demand in an Uncertain World." *Harvard Business Review* 72, no. 3 (May–June 1994), pp. 83–93.

Narasimhan, S.; D. W. McLeavey; and P. J. Billington. *Production Planning and Inventory Control.* Englewood Cliffs, NJ: Prentice Hall, 1995.

Silver, E. A.; D. F. Pyke; and R. Peterson. *Inventory Management and Production Planning and Scheduling.* New York: Wiley, 1998.

Vollmann, T. E.; W. L. Berry; D. C. Whybark; and F. R. Jacobs. *Manufacturing Planning and Control for Supply Chain Management.* 5th ed. New York: Irwin/McGraw-Hill, 2004.

Wallace, T. F. *Sales and Operations Planning: The How-To Handbook.* Cincinnati, OH: T. F. Wallace & Company, 2000.

Footnotes

1 M. L. Fisher, J. H. Hammond, W. R. Obermeyer, and A. Raman, "Making Supply Meet Demand in an Uncertain World," *Harvard Business Review* 72, no. 3 (May–June 1994), p. 84.

2 For an interesting application of aggregate planning in nonprofit humanitarian organizations, see C. Sheu and J. G. Wacker, "A Planning and Control Framework for Nonprofit Humanitarian Organizations," *International Journal of Operations and Production Management* 14, no. 4 (1994), pp. 64–77.

3 S. Kimes and R. B. Chase, "The Strategic Levers of Yield Management," *Journal of Service Research* 1, no. 2 (1998), pp. 298–308.

CHAPTER 13

INVENTORY CONTROL

After reading the chapter you will:

- Explain the different purposes for keeping inventory.
- Understand that the type of inventory system logic that is appropriate for an item depends on the type of demand for that item.
- Calculate the appropriate order size when a one-time purchase must be made.
- Describe what the economic order quantity is and how to calculate it.
- Summarize fixed–order quantity and fixed–time period models, including ways to determine safety stock when there is variability in demand.
- Discuss why inventory turn is directly related to order quantity and safety stock.

385   **Direct to Store—The UPS Vision**
     The UPS Direct Approach

389   **Definition of Inventory**
         Inventory defined

389   **Purposes of Inventory**

390   **Inventory Costs**

391   **Independent versus Dependent Demand**
         Independent and dependent demand defined

392   **Inventory Systems**
     A Single-Period Inventory Model   *Fixed–order quantity models*
     Multiperiod Inventory Systems   *(Q-model) defined*
         Fixed–time period models (P-model) defined

398   **Fixed–Order Quantity Models**
     Establishing Safety Stock Levels   *Inventory position defined*
     Fixed–Order Quantity Model with Safety Stock   *Safety stock defined*

405   **Fixed–Time Period Models**
     Fixed–Time Period Model with Safety Stock

407   **Inventory Control and Supply Chain Management**

408   Price-Break Models

410   ABC Inventory Planning
          ABC Classification

412   Inventory Accuracy and Cycle Counting
                                         Cycle counting defined

414   Summary

425   Case: Hewlett-Packard—Supplying the DeskJet Printer in Europe

428   Super Quiz

DIRECT TO STORE—THE UPS VISION

Logistics visionaries have talked for years about eliminating—or, at least, drastically reducing—the role of inventory in modern supply chains. The most efficient, slack-free supply chains, after all, wouldn't require any inventory buffer, because supply and demand would be in perfect sync. This vision certainly has its appeal: The death of inventory would mean dramatically reduced logistics costs and simplified fulfillment.

Supply Chain

There's no need to write a eulogy for inventory just yet. Most companies haven't honed their networks and technologies well enough to eliminate the need for at least minimal inventory. Logistics managers have to perform a daily, delicate balancing act, balancing

- Transportation costs against fulfillment speed
- Inventory costs against the cost of stock-outs
- Customer satisfaction against cost to serve
- New capabilities against profitability

What's more, two accelerating business trends are making it even harder to synchronize supply chains.

Global

First, global sourcing is forcing supply chains to stretch farther across borders. The goods people consume are increasingly made in some other part of the world, particularly in Asia. This acceleration in global sourcing changes the logistics equation. When goods cross borders, considerations such as fulfillment speed (these are the activities performed once an order is received) and inventory costs get more complicated. Second, powerful retailers and other end customers with clout are starting to push value-added supply chain responsibilities further up the supply chain. More customers are asking manufacturers or third-party logistics providers to label and prepare individual items so the products are ready to go directly to store shelves. With added responsibilities, of course, come added costs. Upstream suppliers are always looking for ways to squeeze more costs out of other areas of the supply chain, such as transportation and distribution.

The UPS Direct Approach

A growing number of companies are overcoming these barriers by taking a more direct approach to global fulfillment. This direct-to-store approach—also known as distribution center bypass or direct distribution—keeps inventory moving from manufacturer to end customer by eliminating stops at warehouses along the way. Because companies can shrink the fulfillment cycle and eliminate inventory costs, direct-to-store can offer a good balance between fulfillment speed and logistics costs.

What accounts for the emergence of the direct-to-store model?

Global sourcing and the upstream migration of value-added logistics services are certainly primary drivers. But other pieces of the puzzle have fallen into place in recent years to make direct-to-store shipments feasible.

Internet-enabled electronic links between supply chain partners have allowed better coordination and collaboration among the various supply chain segments. Meanwhile, at the front of the supply chain, increasingly sophisticated point-of-sale systems can capture product demand patterns. This information can then be fed up the supply chain to manufacturers and components suppliers. More accurate sales-forecasting tools take some of the guesswork out of production and reduce the need for large inventory safety stocks. Tracking and tracing tools are also available to follow orders across borders and through the hands of different supply partners.

In short, companies no longer need as much inventory gathering dust in warehouses because they can better synchronize production and distribution with demand. Direct-to-store lets them keep inventory in motion—across borders and around the world.

See United Parcel Service of America (UPS) Supply Chain Solutions for more information about these types of services: www.ups.com.

You should visualize inventory as stacks of money sitting on forklifts, on shelves, and in trucks and planes while in transit. That's what inventory is—money. For many businesses, inventory is the largest asset on the balance sheet at any given time, even though it is often not very liquid. It is a good idea to try to get your inventory down as far as possible.

A few years ago, Heineken, the Netherlands beer company, figured it could save a whole bunch of money on inventory-in-transit if it could just shorten the forecasting lead time. They expected two things to happen. First, they expected to reduce the need for inventory in the pipeline, therefore cutting down the amount of money devoted to inventory itself. Second, they figured that with a shorter forecasting time, forecasts would be more accurate, reducing emergencies and waste. The Heineken system, called HOPS, cut overall inventory in the system from 16 to 18 weeks to 4 to 6 weeks—a huge drop in time, and a big gain in cash. Forecasts were more accurate, and there was another benefit, too.

Global

Heineken found that its salespeople were suddenly more productive. That is because they were not dealing with all those calls where they had to check on inventory or solve bad forecasting problems, or change orders that were already in process. Instead, they could concentrate on good customer service and helping distributors do better. It was a "win" all the way around.

The key here involves doing things that decrease your inventory order cycle time and increase the accuracy of your forecast. Look for ways to use automated systems and electronic communication to substitute the rapid movement of electrons for the cumbersome movement of masses of atoms.

The economic benefit from inventory reduction is evident from the following statistics: The average cost of inventory in the United States is 30 to 35 percent of its value. For example, if a firm carries an inventory of $20 million, it costs the firm more than $6 million per year. These costs are due mainly to obsolescence, insurance, and opportunity costs. If the amount of inventory could be reduced to $10 million, for instance, the firm would save over $3 million, which goes directly to the bottom line. That is, the savings from reduced inventory results in increased profit.

This chapter and Chapter 14 present techniques designed to manage inventory in different supply chain settings. In this chapter, the focus is on settings where the desire is to maintain a stock of inventory that can be delivered to our customers on demand. Recall in Chapter 4 the concept of *customer order decoupling point,* which is a point where inventory is positioned to allow processes or entities in the supply chain to operate independently. For example, if a product is stocked at a retailer, the customer pulls the item from the shelf and the manufacturer never sees a customer order. In this case, inventory acts as a buffer to separate the customer from the manufacturing process. Selection of decoupling points is a strategic decision that determines customer lead times and can greatly impact inventory investment. The closer this point is to the customer, the quicker the customer can be served.

Supply Chain

The techniques described in this chapter are suited for managing the inventory at these decoupling points. Typically, there is a trade-off where quicker response to customer demand comes at the expense of greater inventory investment. This is because finished goods inventory is more expensive than raw material inventory. In practice, the idea of a single decoupling point in a supply chain is unrealistic. There may actually be multiple points where buffering takes place.

Good examples of where the models described in this chapter are used include retail stores, grocery stores, wholesale distributors, hospital suppliers, and suppliers of repair parts needed to fix or maintain equipment quickly. Situations in which it is necessary to have the item "in-stock" are ideal candidates for the models described in this chapter. A distinction that needs to be made with the models included in this chapter is whether this

exhibit 13.1   Supply Chain Inventories—Make-to-Stock Environment

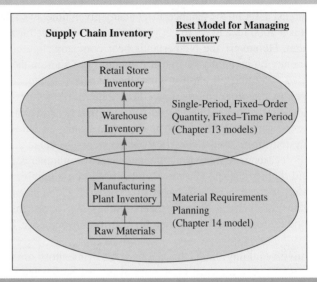

is a one-time purchase, for example, for a seasonal item or for use at a special event, or whether the item will be stocked on an ongoing basis.

Exhibit 13.1 depicts different types of supply chain inventories that would exist in a make-to-stock environment, typical of items directed at the consumer. In the upper echelons of the supply chain, which are supply points closer to the customer, stock usually is kept so that an item can be delivered quickly when a customer need occurs. Of course, there are many exceptions, but in general this is the case. The raw materials and manufacturing plant inventory held in the lower echelon potentially can be managed in a special way to take advantage of the planning and synchronization that are needed to efficiently operate this part of the supply chain. In this case, the models in this chapter are most appropriate for the upper echelon inventories (retail and warehouse), and the lower echelon should use the Material Requirements Planning (MRP) technique described in Chapter 14. The applicability of these models could be different for other environments such as when we produce directly to customer order as in the case of an aircraft manufacturer.

The techniques described here are most appropriate when demand is difficult to predict with great precision. In these models, we characterize demand by using a probability distribution and maintain stock so that the risk associated with stock out is managed. For these applications, the following three models are discussed:

1. **The single-period model.**   This is used when we are making a one-time purchase of an item. An example might be purchasing T-shirts to sell at a one-time sporting event.
2. **Fixed–order quantity model.**   This is used when we want to maintain an item "in-stock," and when we resupply the item, a certain number of units must be ordered each time. Inventory for the item is monitored until it gets down to a level where the risk of stocking out is great enough that we are compelled to order.
3. **Fixed–time period model.**   This is similar to the fixed–order quantity model; it is used when the item should be in-stock and ready to use. In this case, rather than monitoring the inventory level and ordering when the level gets down to a critical

quantity, the item is ordered at certain intervals of time, for example, every Friday morning. This is often convenient when a group of items is ordered together. An example is the delivery of different types of bread to a grocery store. The bakery supplier may have 10 or more products stocked in a store, and rather than delivering each product individually at different times, it is much more efficient to deliver all 10 together at the same time and on the same schedule.

In this chapter, we want to show not only the mathematics associated with great inventory control but also the "art" of managing inventory. Ensuring accuracy in inventory records is essential to running an efficient inventory control process. Techniques such as ABC analysis and cycle counting are essential to the actual management of the system since they focus attention on the high-value items and ensure the quality of the transactions that affect the tracking of inventory levels.

DEFINITION OF INVENTORY

Inventory is the stock of any item or resource used in an organization. An *inventory system* is the set of policies and controls that monitor levels of inventory and determine what levels should be maintained, when stock should be replenished, and how large orders should be.

    By convention, *manufacturing inventory* generally refers to items that contribute to or become part of a firm's product output. Manufacturing inventory is typically classified into *raw materials, finished products, component parts, supplies,* and *work-in-process.* In services, *inventory* generally refers to the tangible goods to be sold and the supplies necessary to administer the service.

    The basic purpose of inventory analysis in manufacturing and stockkeeping services is to specify (1) when items should be ordered and (2) how large the order should be. Many firms are tending to enter into longer-term relationships with vendors to supply their needs for perhaps the entire year. This changes the "when" and "how many to order" to "when" and "how many to deliver."

Inventory

PURPOSES OF INVENTORY

All firms (including JIT operations) keep a supply of inventory for the following reasons:

1. **To maintain independence of operations.** A supply of materials at a work center allows that center flexibility in operations. For example, because there are costs for making each new production setup, this inventory allows management to reduce the number of setups.

   Independence of workstations is desirable on assembly lines as well. The time that it takes to do identical operations will naturally vary from one unit to the next. Therefore, it is desirable to have a cushion of several parts within the workstation so that shorter performance times can compensate for longer performance times. This way the average output can be fairly stable.

2. **To meet variation in product demand.** If the demand for the product is known precisely, it may be possible (though not necessarily economical) to produce the product to exactly meet the demand. Usually, however, demand is not completely known, and a safety or buffer stock must be maintained to absorb variation.

3. **To allow flexibility in production scheduling.**   A stock of inventory relieves the pressure on the production system to get the goods out. This causes longer lead times, which permit production planning for smoother flow and lower-cost operation through larger lot-size production. High setup costs, for example, favor producing a larger number of units once the setup has been made.

4. **To provide a safeguard for variation in raw material delivery time.**   When material is ordered from a vendor, delays can occur for a variety of reasons: a normal variation in shipping time, a shortage of material at the vendor's plant causing backlogs, an unexpected strike at the vendor's plant or at one of the shipping companies, a lost order, or a shipment of incorrect or defective material.

5. **To take advantage of economic purchase order size.**   There are costs to place an order: labor, phone calls, typing, postage, and so on. Therefore, the larger each order is, the fewer the orders that need be written. Also, shipping costs favor larger orders—the larger the shipment, the lower the per-unit cost.

For each of the preceding reasons (especially for items 3, 4, and 5), be aware that inventory is costly and large amounts are generally undesirable. Long cycle times are caused by large amounts of inventory and are undesirable as well.

INVENTORY COSTS

In making any decision that affects inventory size, the following costs must be considered.

1. **Holding (or carrying) costs.**   This broad category includes the costs for storage facilities, handling, insurance, pilferage, breakage, obsolescence, depreciation, taxes, and the opportunity cost of capital. Obviously, high holding costs tend to favor low inventory levels and frequent replenishment.

2. **Setup (or production change) costs.**   To make each different product involves obtaining the necessary materials, arranging specific equipment setups, filling out the required papers, appropriately charging time and materials, and moving out the previous stock of material.

    If there were no costs or loss of time in changing from one product to another, many small lots would be produced. This would reduce inventory levels, with a resulting savings in cost. One challenge today is to try to reduce these setup costs to permit smaller lot sizes. (This is the goal of a JIT system.)

3. **Ordering costs.**   These costs refer to the managerial and clerical costs to prepare the purchase or production order. Ordering costs include all the details, such as counting items and calculating order quantities. The costs associated with maintaining the system needed to track orders are also included in ordering costs.

4. **Shortage costs.**   When the stock of an item is depleted, an order for that item must either wait until the stock is replenished or be canceled. There is a trade-off between carrying stock to satisfy demand and the costs resulting from stockout. This balance is sometimes difficult to obtain, because it may not be possible to estimate lost profits, the effects of lost customers, or lateness penalties. Frequently, the assumed shortage cost is little more than a guess, although it is usually possible to specify a range of such costs.

Establishing the correct quantity to order from vendors or the size of lots submitted to the firm's productive facilities involves a search for the minimum total cost resulting from

TOYOTA PRIUSES AND OTHER VEHICLES CLAD IN PROTECTIVE COVERING AWAIT SHIPMENT TO U.S. DEALERS AT THE LONG BEACH, CA, PORT. IN 2008 THE VALUE OF THE COMPANY'S INVENTORY TOTALED ABOUT ¥1.83 TRILLION AND THE COST OF GOODS SOLD WAS ¥21.5 TRILLION. SO TOYOTA'S INVENTORY TURNED OVER ABOUT 11.7 TIMES PER YEAR, OR ROUGHLY 31 DAYS OF INVENTORY ON HAND.

Global

the combined effects of four individual costs: holding costs, setup costs, ordering costs, and shortage costs. Of course, the timing of these orders is a critical factor that may impact inventory cost.

INDEPENDENT VERSUS DEPENDENT DEMAND

In inventory management, it is important to understand the trade-offs involved in using different types of inventory control logic. Exhibit 13.2 is a framework that shows how characteristics of demand, transaction cost, and the risk of obsolete inventory map into different types of systems. The systems in the upper left of the exhibit are described in this chapter, and those in the lower right in Chapter 14.

Transaction cost is dependent on the level of integration and automation incorporated in the system. Manual systems such as simple *two-bin* logic depend on human posting of the transactions to replenish inventory, which is relatively expensive compared to using a computer to automatically detect when an item needs to be ordered. Integration relates to how connected systems are. For example, it is common for orders for material to be automatically transferred to suppliers electronically and for these orders to be automatically captured by the supplier inventory control system. This type of integration greatly reduces transaction cost.

The risk of obsolescence is also an important consideration. If an item is used infrequently or only for a very specific purpose, there is considerable risk in using inventory control logic that does not track the specific source of demand for the item. Further, items

exhibit 13.2 Inventory Control-System Design Matrix: Framework Describing Inventory Control Logic

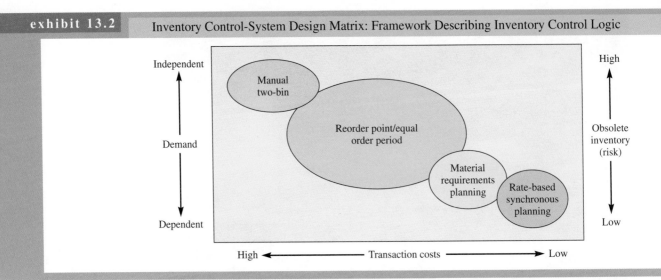

that are sensitive to technical obsolescence, such as computer memory chips, and processors, need to be managed carefully based on actual need to reduce the risk of getting stuck with inventory that is outdated.

An important characteristic of demand relates to whether demand is derived from an end item or is related to the item itself. We use the terms **independent and dependent demand** to describe this characteristic. Briefly, the distinction between independent and dependent demand is this. In independent demand, the demands for various items are unrelated to each other. For example, a workstation may produce many parts that are unrelated but meet some external demand requirement. In dependent demand, the need for any one item is a direct result of the need for some other item, usually a higher-level item of which it is part.

Independent and dependent demand

In concept, dependent demand is a relatively straightforward computational problem. Needed quantities of a dependent-demand item are simply computed, based on the number needed in each higher-level item in which it is used. For example, if an automobile company plans on producing 500 cars per day, then obviously it will need 2,000 wheels and tires (plus spares). The number of wheels and tires needed is *dependent* on the production levels and is not derived separately. The demand for cars, on the other hand, is *independent*—it comes from many sources external to the automobile firm and is not a part of other products; it is unrelated to the demand for other products.

To determine the quantities of independent items that must be produced, firms usually turn to their sales and market research departments. They use a variety of techniques, including customer surveys, forecasting techniques, and economic and sociological trends, as we discussed in Chapter 11 on forecasting. Because independent demand is uncertain, extra units must be carried in inventory. This chapter presents models to determine how many units need to be ordered, and how many extra units should be carried to reduce the risk of stocking out.

INVENTORY SYSTEMS

An inventory system provides the organizational structure and the operating policies for maintaining and controlling goods to be stocked. The system is responsible for ordering and receipt of goods: timing the order placement and keeping track of what has been ordered, how much, and from whom. The system also must follow up to answer such questions as, Has the supplier received the order? Has it been shipped? Are the dates correct? Are the procedures established for reordering or returning undesirable merchandise?

This section divides systems into single-period systems and multiple-period systems. The classification is based on whether the decision is just a one-time purchasing decision where the purchase is designed to cover a fixed period of time and the item will not be re-ordered, or the decision involves an item that will be purchased periodically where inventory should be kept in stock to be used on demand. We begin with a look at the one-time purchasing decision and the single-period inventory model.

**Tutorial:
Inventory**

Service

A Single-Period Inventory Model

Certainly, an easy example to think about is the classic single-period "newsperson" problem. For example, consider the problem that the newsperson has in deciding how many newspapers to put in the sales stand outside a hotel lobby each morning. If the person does not put enough papers in the stand, some customers will not be able to purchase a paper and the newsperson will lose the profit associated with these sales. On the other hand, if too many papers are placed in the stand, the newsperson will have paid for papers that were not sold during the day, lowering profit for the day.

Actually, this is a very common type of problem. Consider the person selling T-shirts promoting a championship basketball or football game. This is especially difficult, since the person must wait to learn what teams will be playing. The shirts can then be printed with the proper team logos. Of course, the person must estimate how many people will actually want the shirts. The shirts sold prior to the game can probably be sold at a premium price, whereas those sold after the game will need to be steeply discounted.

A simple way to think about this is to consider how much risk we are willing to take for running out of inventory. Let's consider that the newsperson selling papers in the sales stand had collected data over a few months and had found that on average each Monday 90 papers were sold with a standard deviation of 10 papers (assume that during this time the papers were purposefully overstocked in order not to run out, so they would know what "real" demand was). With these data, our newsperson could simply state a service rate that is felt to be acceptable. For example, the newsperson might want to be 80 percent sure of not running out of papers each Monday.

Recall from your study of statistics, assuming that the probability distribution associated with the sales of the paper is normal, then if we stocked exactly 90 papers each Monday morning, the risk of stocking out would be 50 percent, since 50 percent of the time we expect demand to be less than 90 papers and 50 percent of the time we expect demand to be greater than 90. To be 80 percent sure of not stocking out, we need to carry a few more papers. From the "cumulative standard normal distribution" table given in Appendix F, we see that we need approximately 0.85 standard deviation of extra papers to be 80 percent sure of not stocking out. A quick way to find the exact number of standard deviations needed for a given probability of stocking out is with the NORMSINV(probability) function in Microsoft Excel (NORMSINV(0.8) = 0.84162). Given our result from Excel, which is more accurate than what we can get from the tables, the number of extra papers would be $0.84162 \times 10 = 8.416$, or 9 papers (there is no way to sell 0.4 paper!).

To make this more useful, it would be good to actually consider the potential profit and loss associated with stocking either too many or too few papers on the stand. Let's say that our newspaper person pays \$0.20 for each paper and sells the papers for \$0.50. In this case the marginal cost associated with underestimating demand is \$0.30, the lost profit. Similarly, the marginal cost of overestimating demand is \$0.20, the cost of buying too many papers. The optimal stocking level, using marginal analysis, occurs at the point where the expected benefits derived from carrying the next unit are less than the expected costs for that unit. Keep in mind that the specific benefits and costs depend on the problem.

In symbolic terms, define

$$C_o = \text{Cost per unit of demand overestimated}$$
$$C_u = \text{Cost per unit of demand underestimated}$$

By introducing probabilities, the expected marginal cost equation becomes

$$P(C_o) \le (1 - P)C_u$$

where P is the probability that the unit will not be sold and $1 - P$ is the probability of it being sold, because one or the other must occur. (The unit is sold or is not sold.)[1]

Then, solving for P, we obtain

$$P \le \frac{C_u}{C_o + C_u} \qquad \text{[13.1]}$$

This equation states that we should continue to increase the size of the order so long as the probability of selling what we order is equal to or less than the ratio $C_u/(C_o + C_u)$.

Returning to our newspaper problem, our cost of overestimating demand (C_o) is $0.20 per paper and the cost of underestimating demand (C_u) is $0.30. The probability therefore is $0.3/(0.2 + 0.3) = 0.6$. Now, we need to find the point on our demand distribution that corresponds to the cumulative probability of 0.6. Using the NORMSINV function to get the number of standard deviations (commonly referred to as the Z-score) of extra newspapers to carry, we get 0.253, which means that we should stock $0.253(10) = 2.53$ or 3 extra papers. The total number of papers for the stand each Monday morning, therefore, should be 93 papers.

This model is very useful and, as we will see in our solved sample problem, can even be used for many service sector problems, such as the number of seats to book on a full airline flight or the number of reservations to book on a full night at a hotel.

Step by Step

Service

Example 13.1: Hotel Reservations

A hotel near the university always fills up on the evening before football games. History has shown that when the hotel is fully booked, the number of last-minute cancellations has a mean of 5 and standard deviation of 3. The average room rate is $80. When the hotel is overbooked, policy is to find a room in a nearby hotel and to pay for the room for the customer. This usually costs the hotel approximately $200 since rooms booked on such late notice are expensive. How many rooms should the hotel overbook?

SOLUTION

The cost of underestimating the number of cancellations is $80 and the cost of overestimating cancellations is $200.

$$P \le \frac{C_u}{C_o + C_u} = \frac{\$80}{\$200 + \$80} = 0.2857$$

Using NORMSINV(.2857) from Excel gives a Z-score of -0.56599. The negative value indicates that we should overbook by a value less than the average of 5. The actual value should be

$-0.56599(3) = -1.69797$, or 2 reservations less than 5. The hotel should overbook three reservations on the evening prior to a football game.

Another common method for analyzing this type of problem is with a discrete probability distribution found using actual data and marginal analysis. For our hotel, consider that we have collected data and our distribution of no-shows is as follows:

NUMBER OF NO-SHOWS	PROBABILITY	CUMULATIVE PROBABILITY
0	0.05	0.05
1	0.08	0.13
2	0.10	0.23
3	0.15	0.38
4	0.20	0.58
5	0.15	0.73
6	0.11	0.84
7	0.06	0.90
8	0.05	0.95
9	0.04	0.99
10	0.01	1.00

Using these data, a table showing the impact of overbooking is created. Total expected cost of each overbooking option is then calculated by multiplying each possible outcome by its probability and summing the weighted costs. The best overbooking strategy is the one with minimum cost.

No-Shows	Probability	NUMBER OF RESERVATIONS OVERBOOKED										
		0	1	2	3	4	5	6	7	8	9	10
0	0.05	0	200	400	600	800	1,000	1,200	1,400	1,600	1,800	2,000
1	0.08	80	0	200	400	600	800	1,000	1,200	1,400	1,600	1,800
2	0.1	160	80	0	200	400	600	800	1,000	1,200	1,400	1,600
3	0.15	240	160	80	0	200	400	600	800	1,000	1,200	1,400
4	0.2	320	240	160	80	0	200	400	600	800	1,000	1,200
5	0.15	400	320	240	160	80	0	200	400	600	800	1,000
6	0.11	480	400	320	240	160	80	0	200	400	600	800
7	0.06	560	480	400	320	240	160	80	0	200	400	600
8	0.05	640	560	480	400	320	240	160	80	0	200	400
9	0.04	720	640	560	480	400	320	240	160	80	0	200
10	0.01	800	720	640	560	480	400	320	240	160	80	0
Total cost		337.6	271.6	228	212.4	238.8	321.2	445.6	600.8	772.8	958.8	1,156

Excel: Inventory Control

From the table, the minimum total cost is when three extra reservations are taken. This approach using discrete probability is useful when valid historic data are available. ●

Single-period inventory models are useful for a wide variety of service and manufacturing applications. Consider the following:

1. **Overbooking of airline flights.**   It is common for customers to cancel flight reservations for a variety of reasons. Here the cost of underestimating the number of cancellations is the revenue lost due to an empty seat on a flight. The cost of

Service

overestimating cancellations is the awards, such as free flights or cash payments, that are given to customers unable to board the flight.

2. **Ordering of fashion items.** A problem for a retailer selling fashion items is that often only a single order can be placed for the entire season. This is often caused by long lead times and limited life of the merchandise. The cost of underestimating demand is the lost profit due to sales not made. The cost of overestimating demand is the cost that results when it is discounted.

3. **Any type of one-time order.** For example, ordering T-shirts for a sporting event or printing maps that become obsolete after a certain period of time.

Multiperiod Inventory Systems

Fixed–order quantity models (Q-model)

Fixed–time period models (P-model)

There are two general types of multiperiod inventory systems: **fixed–order quantity models** (also called the *economic order quantity,* EOQ, and **Q-model**) and **fixed–time period models** (also referred to variously as the *periodic* system, *periodic review* system, *fixed-order interval* system, and **P-model**). Multiperiod inventory systems are designed to ensure that an item will be available on an ongoing basis throughout the year. Usually the item will be ordered multiple times throughout the year where the logic in the system dictates the actual quantity ordered and the timing of the order.

The basic distinction is that fixed–order quantity models are "event triggered" and fixed–time period models are "time triggered." That is, a fixed–order quantity model initiates an order when the event of reaching a specified reorder level occurs. This event may take place at any time, depending on the demand for the items considered. In contrast, the fixed–time period model is limited to placing orders at the end of a predetermined time period; only the passage of time triggers the model.

To use the fixed–order quantity model (which places an order when the remaining inventory drops to a predetermined order point, R), the inventory remaining must be continually monitored. Thus, the fixed–order quantity model is a *perpetual* system, which requires that every time a withdrawal from inventory or an addition to inventory is made, records must be updated to reflect whether the reorder point has been reached. In a fixed–time period model, counting takes place only at the review period. (We will discuss some variations of systems that combine features of both.)

Some additional differences tend to influence the choice of systems (also see Exhibit 13.3):

Tutorial: Inventory

- The fixed–time period model has a larger average inventory because it must also protect against stockout during the review period, T; the fixed–order quantity model has no review period.
- The fixed–order quantity model favors more expensive items because average inventory is lower.
- The fixed–order quantity model is more appropriate for important items such as critical repair parts because there is closer monitoring and therefore quicker response to potential stockout.
- The fixed–order quantity model requires more time to maintain because every addition or withdrawal is logged.

Exhibit 13.4 shows what occurs when each of the two models is put into use and becomes an operating system. As we can see, the fixed–order quantity system focuses on order quantities and reorder points. Procedurally, each time a unit is taken out of stock, the withdrawal is logged and the amount remaining in inventory is immediately compared to

exhibit 13.3

Fixed–Order Quantity and Fixed–Time Period Differences

FEATURE	Q-MODEL FIXED–ORDER QUANTITY MODEL	P-MODEL FIXED–TIME PERIOD MODEL
Order quantity	Q—constant (the same amount ordered each time)	q—variable (varies each time order is placed)
When to place order	R—when inventory position drops to the reorder level	T—when the review period arrives
Recordkeeping	Each time a withdrawal or addition is made	Counted only at review period
Size of inventory	Less than fixed–time period model	Larger than fixed–order quantity model
Time to maintain	Higher due to perpetual recordkeeping	
Type of items	Higher-priced, critical, or important items	

exhibit 13.4

Comparison for Fixed–Order Quantity and Fixed–Time Period Reordering Inventory Systems

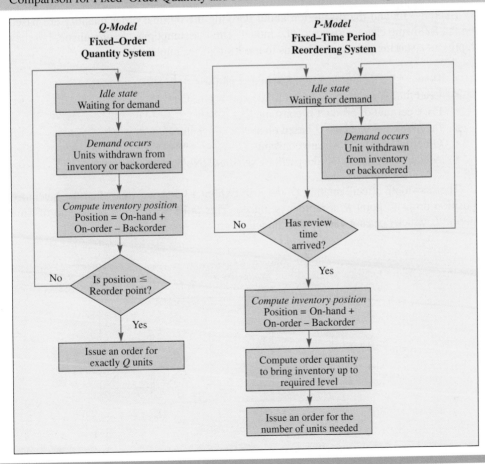

the reorder point. If it has dropped to this point, an order for Q items is placed. If it has not, the system remains in an idle state until the next withdrawal.

In the fixed–time period system, a decision to place an order is made after the stock has been counted or reviewed. Whether an order is actually placed depends on the inventory position at that time.

FIXED–ORDER QUANTITY MODELS

Fixed–order quantity models attempt to determine the specific point, R, at which an order will be placed and the size of that order, Q. The order point, R, is always a specified number of units. An order of size Q is placed when the inventory available (currently in stock and on order) reaches the point R. **Inventory position** is defined as the on-hand plus on-order minus backordered quantities. The solution to a fixed–order quantity model may stipulate something like this: When the inventory position drops to 36, place an order for 57 more units.

Inventory position

The simplest models in this category occur when all aspects of the situation are known with certainty. If the annual demand for a product is 1,000 units, it is precisely 1,000—not 1,000 plus or minus 10 percent. The same is true for setup costs and holding costs. Although the assumption of complete certainty is rarely valid, it provides a good basis for our coverage of inventory models.

Exhibit 13.5 and the discussion about deriving the optimal order quantity are based on the following characteristics of the model. These assumptions are unrealistic, but they represent a starting point and allow us to use a simple example.

- Demand for the product is constant and uniform throughout the period.
- Lead time (time from ordering to receipt) is constant.
- Price per unit of product is constant.
- Inventory holding cost is based on average inventory.
- Ordering or setup costs are constant.
- All demands for the product will be satisfied. (No backorders are allowed.)

The "sawtooth effect" relating Q and R in Exhibit 13.5 shows that when the inventory position drops to point R, a reorder is placed. This order is received at the end of time period L, which does not vary in this model.

exhibit 13.5	Basic Fixed–Order Quantity Model

Excel:
Inventory
Control

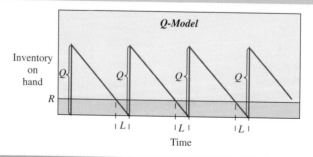

In constructing any inventory model, the first step is to develop a functional relationship between the variables of interest and the measure of effectiveness. In this case, because we are concerned with cost, the following equation pertains:

$$\text{Total annual cost} = \text{Annual purchase cost} + \text{Annual ordering cost} + \text{Annual holding cost}$$

or

$$TC = DC + \frac{D}{Q}S + \frac{Q}{2}H \qquad\qquad \text{[13.2]}$$

where

TC = Total annual cost

D = Demand (annual)

C = Cost per unit

Q = Quantity to be ordered (the optimal amount is termed the *economic order quantity*—EOQ—or Q_{opt})

S = Setup cost or cost of placing an order

R = Reorder point

L = Lead time

H = Annual holding and storage cost per unit of average inventory (often holding cost is taken as a percentage of the cost of the item, such as $H = iC$, where i is the percent carrying cost)

On the right side of the equation, DC is the annual purchase cost for the units, $(D/Q)S$ is the annual ordering cost (the actual number of orders placed, D/Q, times the cost of each order, S), and $(Q/2)H$ is the annual holding cost (the average inventory, $Q/2$, times the cost per unit for holding and storage, H). These cost relationships are graphed in Exhibit 13.6.

The second step in model development is to find that order quantity Q_{opt} at which total cost is a minimum. In Exhibit 13.5, the total cost is minimal at the point where the slope of

exhibit 13.6

Annual Product Costs, Based on Size of the Order

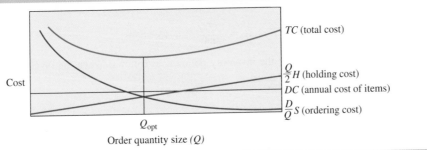

Cost

TC (total cost)

$\frac{Q}{2}H$ (holding cost)

DC (annual cost of items)

$\frac{D}{Q}S$ (ordering cost)

Q_{opt}

Order quantity size (Q)

Excel: Inventory Control

the curve is zero. Using calculus, we take the derivative of total cost with respect to Q and set this equal to zero. For the basic model considered here, the calculations are

$$TC = DC + \frac{D}{Q}S + \frac{Q}{2}H$$

$$\frac{dTC}{dQ} = 0 + \left(\frac{-DS}{Q^2}\right) + \frac{H}{2} = 0$$

$$Q_{opt} = \sqrt{\frac{2DS}{H}}$$

[13.3]

Because this simple model assumes constant demand and lead time, neither safety stock nor stockout cost are necessary, and the reorder point, R, is simply

$$R = \bar{d}L$$

[13.4]

where

$\bar{d}$ = Average daily demand (constant)

L = Lead time in days (constant)

Example 13.2: Economic Order Quantity and Reorder Point

Find the economic order quantity and the reorder point, given

Annual demand (D) = 1,000 units
Average daily demand $(\bar{d})$ = 1,000/365
Ordering cost (S) = $5 per order
Holding cost (H) = $1.25 per unit per year
Lead time (L) = 5 days
Cost per unit (C) = $12.50

What quantity should be ordered?

**Excel:
Inventory
Control**

Step by Step

SOLUTION

The optimal order quantity is

$$Q_{opt} = \sqrt{\frac{2DS}{H}} = \sqrt{\frac{2(1,000)5}{1.25}} = \sqrt{8,000} = 89.4 \text{ units}$$

The reorder point is

$$R = \bar{d}L = \frac{1,000}{365}(5) = 13.7 \text{ units}$$

Rounding to the nearest unit, the inventory policy is as follows: When the inventory position drops to 14, place an order for 89 more.

The total annual cost will be

$$TC = DC + \frac{D}{Q}S + \frac{Q}{2}H$$

$$= 1,000(12.50) + \frac{1,000}{89}(5) + \frac{89}{2}(1.25)$$

$$= \$12,611.81$$

Note that in this example, the purchase cost of the units was not required to determine the order quantity and the reorder point because the cost was constant and unrelated to order size. ●

Establishing Safety Stock Levels

The previous model assumed that demand was constant and known. In the majority of cases, though, demand is not constant but varies from day to day. Safety stock must therefore be maintained to provide some level of protection against stock outs. **Safety stock** can be defined as the amount of inventory carried in addition to the expected demand. In a normal distribution, this would be the mean. For example, if our average monthly demand is 100 units and we expect next month to be the same, if we carry 120 units, then we have 20 units of safety stock.

Safety stock

Safety stock can be determined based on many different criteria. A common approach is for a company to simply state that a certain number of weeks of supply be kept in safety stock. It is better, though, to use an approach that captures the variability in demand.

For example, an objective may be something like "set the safety stock level so that there will only be a 5 percent chance of stocking out if demand exceeds 300 units." We call this approach to setting safety stock the probability approach.

The Probability Approach   Using the probability criterion to determine safety stock is pretty simple. With the models described in this chapter, we assume that the demand over a period of time is normally distributed with a mean and a standard deviation. *Again, remember that this approach considers only the probability of running out of stock, not how many units we are short.* To determine the probability of stocking out over the time period, we can simply plot a normal distribution for the expected demand and note where the amount we have on hand lies on the curve.

Let's take a few simple examples to illustrate this. Say we expect demand to be 100 units over the next month, and we know that the standard deviation is 20 units. If we go into the month with just 100 units, we know that our probability of stocking out is 50 percent. Half of the months we would expect demand to be greater than 100 units; half of the months we would expect it to be less than 100 units. Taking this further, if we ordered a month's worth of inventory of 100 units at a time and received it at the beginning of the month, over the long run we would expect to run out of inventory in six months of the year.

If running out this often was not acceptable, we would want to carry extra inventory to reduce this risk of stocking out. One idea might be to carry an extra 20 units of inventory for the item. In this case, we would still order a month's worth of inventory at a time, but we would schedule delivery to arrive when we still have 20 units remaining in inventory. This would give us that little cushion of safety stock to reduce the probability of stocking out. If the standard deviation associated with our demand was 20 units, we would then be carrying one standard deviation worth of safety stock. Looking at the Cumulative Standard Normal Distribution (Appendix F), and moving one standard deviation to the right of the mean, gives a probability of 0.8413. So approximately 84 percent of the time we would not expect to stock out, and 16 percent of the time we would. Now if we order every month, we would expect to stock out approximately two months per year ($0.16 \times 12 = 1.92$). For those using Excel, given a z value, the probability can be obtained with the NORMSDIST function.

It is common for companies using this approach to set the probability of not stocking out at 95 percent. This means we would carry about 1.64 standard deviations of safety stock, or 33 units ($1.64 \times 20 = 32.8$) for our example. Once again, keep in mind that this does

exhibit 13.7   Fixed–Order Quantity Model

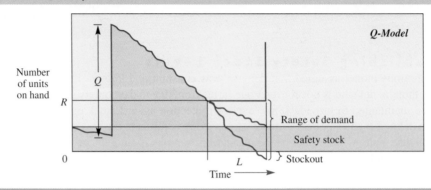

not mean that we would order 33 units extra each month. Rather, it means that we would still order a month's worth each time, but we would schedule the receipt so that we could expect to have 33 units in inventory when the order arrives. In this case, we would expect to stock out approximately 0.6 month per year, or that stockouts would occur in 1 of every 20 months.

Fixed–Order Quantity Model with Safety Stock

A fixed–order quantity system perpetually monitors the inventory level and places a new order when stock reaches some level, R. The danger of stock out in this model occurs only during the lead time, between the time an order is placed and the time it is received. As shown in Exhibit 13.7, an order is placed when the inventory position drops to the reorder point, R. During this lead time L, a range of demands is possible. This range is determined either from an analysis of past demand data or from an estimate (if past data are not available).

The amount of safety stock depends on the service level desired, as previously discussed. The quantity to be ordered, Q, is calculated in the usual way considering the demand, shortage cost, ordering cost, holding cost, and so forth. A fixed–order quantity model can be used to compute Q, such as the simple Q_{opt} model previously discussed. The reorder point is then set to cover the expected demand during the lead time plus a safety stock determined by the desired service level. Thus, *the key difference between a fixed–order quantity model where demand is known and one where demand is uncertain is in computing the reorder point. The order quantity is the same in both cases.* The uncertainty element is taken into account in the safety stock.

The reorder point is

$$R = \bar{d}L + z\sigma_L \qquad \textbf{[13.5]}$$

where

R = Reorder point in units

$\bar{d}$ = Average daily demand

L = Lead time in days (time between placing an order and receiving the items)

z = Number of standard deviations for a specified service probability

σ_L = Standard deviation of usage during lead time

The term $z\sigma_L$ is the amount of safety stock. Note that if safety stock is positive, the effect is to place a reorder sooner. That is, R without safety stock is simply the average demand during the lead time. If lead time usage was expected to be 20, for example, and safety stock was computed to be 5 units, then the order would be placed sooner, when 25 units remained. The greater the safety stock, the sooner the order is placed.

Computing $\bar{d}$, σ_L, and z Demand during the replenishment lead time is really an estimate or forecast of expected use of inventory from the time an order is placed to when it is received. It may be a single number (for example, if the lead time is a month, the demand may be taken as the previous year's demand divided by 12), or it may be a summation of expected demands over the lead time (such as the sum of daily demands over a 30-day lead time). For the daily demand situation, d can be a forecast demand using any of the models in Chapter 11 on forecasting. For example, if a 30-day period was used to calculate d, then a simple average would be

$$\bar{d} = \frac{\sum_{i=1}^{n} d_i}{n}$$

$$= \frac{\sum_{i=1}^{30} d_i}{30}$$

[13.6]

where n is the number of days.

The standard deviation of the daily demand is

$$\sigma_d = \sqrt{\frac{\sum_{i=1}^{n}(d_i - \bar{d})^2}{n}}$$

$$= \sqrt{\frac{\sum_{i=1}^{30}(d_i - \bar{d})^2}{30}}$$

[13.7]

Because σ_d refers to one day, if lead time extends over several days, we can use the statistical premise that the standard deviation of a series of independent occurrences is equal to the square root of the sum of the variances. That is, in general,

$$\sigma_L = \sqrt{\sigma_1^2 + \sigma_2^2 + \cdots + \sigma_L^2}$$

[13.8]

For example, suppose we computed the standard deviation of demand to be 10 units per day. If our lead time to get an order is five days, the standard deviation for the five-day period, assuming each day can be considered independent, is

$$\sigma_5 = \sqrt{(10)^2 + (10)^2 + (10)^2 + (10)^2 + (10)^2} = 22.36$$

Next we need to find z, the number of standard deviations of safety stock.

Suppose we wanted our probability of not stocking out during the lead time to be 0.95. The z value associated with a 95 percent probability of not stocking out is 1.64 (see Appendix F or use the Excel NORMSINV function). Given this, safety stock is calculated as follows:

$$SS = z\sigma_L$$

[13.9]

$$= 1.64 \times 22.36$$

$$= 36.67$$

We now compare two examples. The difference between them is that in the first, the variation in demand is stated in terms of standard deviation over the entire lead time, while in the second, it is stated in terms of standard deviation per day.

Step by Step

Example 13.3: Reorder Point

Consider an economic order quantity case where annual demand $D = 1,000$ units, economic order quantity $Q = 200$ units, the desired probability of not stocking out $P = .95$, the standard deviation of demand during lead time $\sigma_L = 25$ units, and lead time $L = 15$ days. Determine the reorder point. Assume that demand is over a 250-workday year.

SOLUTION

In our example, $\bar{d} = \frac{1000}{250} = 4$, and lead time is 15 days. We use the equation

$$R = \bar{d}L + z\sigma_L$$
$$= 4(15) + z(25)$$

In this case z is 1.64.

Completing the solution for R, we have

$$R = 4(15) + 1.64(25) = 60 + 41 = 101 \text{ units}$$

This says that when the stock on hand gets down to 101 units, order 200 more. ●

Step by Step

Excel: Inventory Control

Example 13.4: Order Quantity and Reorder Point

Daily demand for a certain product is normally distributed with a mean of 60 and standard deviation of 7. The source of supply is reliable and maintains a constant lead time of six days. The cost of placing the order is $10 and annual holding costs are $0.50 per unit. There are no stock out costs, and unfilled orders are filled as soon as the order arrives. Assume sales occur over the entire 365 days of the year. Find the order quantity and reorder point to satisfy a 95 percent probability of not stocking out during the lead time.

SOLUTION

In this problem we need to calculate the order quantity Q as well as the reorder point R.

$$\bar{d} = 60 \qquad S = \$10$$
$$\sigma_d = 7 \qquad H = \$0.50$$
$$D = 60(365) \qquad L = 6$$

The optimal order quantity is

$$Q_{opt} = \sqrt{\frac{2DS}{H}} = \sqrt{\frac{2(60)365(10)}{0.50}} = \sqrt{876,000} = 936 \text{ units}$$

To compute the reorder point, we need to calculate the amount of product used during the lead time and add this to the safety stock.

The standard deviation of demand during the lead time of six days is calculated from the variance of the individual days. Because each day's demand is independent[2]

$$\sigma_L = \sqrt{\sum_{i=1}^{L} \sigma_d^2} = \sqrt{6(7)^2} = 17.15$$

Once again, z is 1.64.

$$R = \bar{d}L + z\sigma_L = 60(6) + 1.64(17.15) = 388 \text{ units}$$

To summarize the policy derived in this example, an order for 936 units is placed whenever the number of units remaining in inventory drops to 388. ●

FIXED–TIME PERIOD MODELS

In a fixed–time period system, inventory is counted only at particular times, such as every week or every month. Counting inventory and placing orders periodically is desirable in situations such as when vendors make routine visits to customers and take orders for their complete line of products, or when buyers want to combine orders to save transportation costs. Other firms operate on a fixed time period to facilitate planning their inventory count; for example, Distributor X calls every two weeks and employees know that all Distributor X's product must be counted.

Fixed–time period models generate order quantities that vary from period to period, depending on the usage rates. These generally require a higher level of safety stock than a fixed–order quantity system. The fixed–order quantity system assumes continual tracking of inventory on hand, with an order immediately placed when the reorder point is reached. In contrast, the standard fixed–time period models assume that inventory is counted only at the time specified for review. It is possible that some large demand will draw the stock down to zero right after an order is placed. This condition could go unnoticed until the next review period. Then the new order, when placed, still takes time to arrive. Thus, it is possible to be out of stock throughout the entire review period, T, and order lead time, L. Safety stock, therefore, must protect against stockouts during the review period itself as well as during the lead time from order placement to order receipt.

Fixed–Time Period Model with Safety Stock

In a fixed–time period system, reorders are placed at the time of review (T), and the safety stock that must be reordered is

$$\text{Safety stock} = z\sigma_{T+L} \qquad \textbf{[13.10]}$$

Exhibit 13.8 shows a fixed–time period system with a review cycle of T and a constant lead time of L. In this case, demand is randomly distributed about a mean d. The quantity to order, q, is

$$\begin{matrix} \text{Order} \\ \text{quantity} \end{matrix} = \begin{matrix} \text{Average demand} \\ \text{over the} \\ \text{vulnerable period} \end{matrix} + \begin{matrix} \text{Safety} \\ \text{stock} \end{matrix} - \begin{matrix} \text{Inventory currently} \\ \text{on hand (plus on} \\ \text{order, if any)} \end{matrix} \qquad \textbf{[13.11]}$$

$$q = \bar{d}(T + L) + z\sigma_{T+L} - I$$

Tutorial:
Inventory

Fixed–Time Period Inventory Model

exhibit 13.8

Inventory on hand (in units)

Place order

Place order

Place order

Place order

Place order

P-Model

Safety stock

Stockout

L T L T L T

Time

where

q = Quantity to be ordered

T = The number of days between reviews

L = Lead time in days (time between placing an order and receiving it)

$\bar{d}$ = Forecast average daily demand

z = Number of standard deviations for a specified service probability

σ_{T+L} = Standard deviation of demand over the review and lead time

I = Current inventory level (includes items on order)

Note: The demand, lead time, review period, and so forth can be any time units such as days, weeks, or years so long as they are consistent throughout the equation.

In this model, demand $(\bar{d})$ can be forecast and revised each review period if desired or the yearly average may be used if appropriate. We assume that demand is normally distributed.

The value of z is dependent on the probability of stocking out and can be found using Appendix F or by using the Excel NORMSINV function.

Step by Step

**Excel:
Inventory
Control.xls**

Example 13.5: Quantity to Order

Daily demand for a product is 10 units with a standard deviation of 3 units. The review period is 30 days, and lead time is 14 days. Management has set a policy of satisfying 98 percent of demand from items in stock. At the beginning of this review period, there are 150 units in inventory.

How many units should be ordered?

SOLUTION

The quantity to order is

$$q = \bar{d}(T + L) + z\sigma_{T+L} - I$$
$$= 10(30 + 14) + z\sigma_{T+L} - 150$$

Before we can complete the solution, we need to find σ_{T+L} and z. To find σ_{T+L}, we use the notion, as before, that the standard deviation of a sequence of independent random variables equals the square root of the sum of the variances. Therefore, the standard deviation during the period $T + L$ is the square root of the sum of the variances for each day:

$$\sigma_{T+L} = \sqrt{\sum_{i=1}^{T+L} \sigma_d^2} \qquad \text{[13.12]}$$

Because each day is independent and σ_d is constant,

$$\sigma_{T+L} = \sqrt{(T + L)\sigma_d^2} = \sqrt{(30 + 14)(3)^2} = 19.90$$

The z value for $P = 0.98$ is 2.05.

The quantity to order, then, is

$$q = \bar{d}(T + L) + z\sigma_{T+L} - I = 10(30 + 14) + 2.05(19.90) - 150 = 331 \text{ units}$$

To ensure a 98 percent probability of not stocking out, order 331 units at this review period. ●

A SALES CLERK AT TOKYO'S MITSUKOSHI DEPARTMENT STORE READS AN RFID TAB ON JEANS TO CHECK STOCK. MITSUKOSHI AND JAPAN'S ELECTRONIC GIANT FUJITSU PARTNERED TO USE RFID TO IMPROVE STOCK CONTROL AND CUSTOMER SERVICE.

allows items to be removed for both legitimate and unauthorized purposes. The legitimate removal may have been done in a hurry and simply not recorded. Sometimes parts are misplaced, turning up months later. Parts are often stored in several locations, but records may be lost or the location recorded incorrectly. Sometimes stock replenishment orders are recorded as received, when in fact they never were. Occasionally, a group of parts is recorded as removed from inventory, but the customer order is canceled and the parts are replaced in inventory without canceling the record. To keep the production system flowing smoothly without parts shortages and efficiently without excess balances, records must be accurate.

How can a firm keep accurate, up-to-date records? Using bar codes and RFID tags is important to minimizing errors caused by inputting wrong numbers in the system. It is also important to keep the storeroom locked. If only storeroom personnel have access, and one of their measures of performance for personnel evaluation and merit increases is record accuracy, there is a strong motivation to comply. Every location of inventory storage, whether in a locked storeroom or on the production floor, should have a recordkeeping mechanism. A second way is to convey the importance of accurate records to all personnel and depend on them to assist in this effort. (This all boils down to this: Put a fence that goes all the way to the ceiling around the storage area so that workers cannot climb over to get parts; put a lock on the gate and give one person the key. Nobody can pull parts without having the transaction authorized and recorded.)

Another way to ensure accuracy is to count inventory frequently and match this against records. A widely used method is called *cycle counting*.

Cycle counting is a physical inventory-taking technique in which inventory is counted frequently rather than once or twice a year. The key to effective cycle counting and, therefore, to accurate records lies in deciding which items are to be counted, when, and by whom.

Cycle counting

Virtually all inventory systems these days are computerized. The computer can be programmed to produce a cycle count notice in the following cases:

1. When the record shows a low or zero balance on hand. (It is easier to count fewer items.)
2. When the record shows a positive balance but a backorder was written (indicating a discrepancy).
3. After some specified level of activity.
4. To signal a review based on the importance of the item (as in the ABC system) such as in the following table:

ANNUAL DOLLAR USAGE	REVIEW PERIOD
$10,000 or more	30 days or less
$3,000–$10,000	45 days or less
$250–3,000	90 days or less
Less than $250	180 days or less

The easiest time for stock to be counted is when there is no activity in the stockroom or on the production floor. This means on the weekends or during the second or third shift, when the facility is less busy. If this is not possible, more careful logging and separation of items are required to count inventory while production is going on and transactions are occurring.

The counting cycle depends on the available personnel. Some firms schedule regular stockroom personnel to do the counting during lulls in the regular working day. Other companies hire private firms that come in and count inventory. Still other firms use full-time cycle counters who do nothing but count inventory and resolve differences with the records. Although this last method sounds expensive, many firms believe that it is actually less costly than the usual hectic annual inventory count generally performed during the two- or three-week annual vacation shutdown.

The question of how much error is tolerable between physical inventory and records has been much debated. Some firms strive for 100 percent accuracy, whereas others accept 1, 2, or 3 percent error. The accuracy level often recommended by experts is ± 0.2 percent for A items, ± 1 percent for B items, and ± 5 percent for C items. Regardless of the specific accuracy decided on, the important point is that the level be dependable so that safety stocks may be provided as a cushion. Accuracy is important for a smooth production process so that customer orders can be processed as scheduled and not held up because of unavailable parts.

SUMMARY

This chapter introduced the two main classes of demand: (1) independent demand, referring to the external demand for a firm's end product, and (2) dependent demand, usually referring—within the firm—to the demand for items created because of the demand for more complex items of which they are a part. Most industries have items in both classes. In manufacturing, for example, independent demand is common for finished products, service and repair parts, and operating supplies; and dependent demand is common for those parts and materials needed to produce the end product. In wholesale and retail sales of consumer goods, most demand is independent—each item is an end item, with the wholesaler or retailer doing no further assembly or fabrication.

Independent demand, the focus of this chapter, is based on statistics. In the fixed–order quantity and fixed–time period models, the influence of service level was shown on safety stock and reorder point determinations. One special-purpose model—the single-period model—was also presented.

To distinguish among item categories for analysis and control, the ABC method was offered. The importance of inventory accuracy was also noted, and cycle counting was described.

In this chapter, we also pointed out that inventory reduction requires a knowledge of the operating system. It is not simply a case of selecting an inventory model off the shelf and plugging in some numbers. In the first place, a model might not even be appropriate. In the second case, the numbers might be full of errors or even based on erroneous data. Determining order quantities is often referred to as a trade-off problem; that is, trading off holding costs for setup costs. Note that companies really want to reduce both.

The simple fact is that firms have very large investments in inventory, and the cost to carry this inventory runs from 25 to 35 percent of the inventory's worth annually. Therefore, a major goal of most firms today is to reduce inventory.

A caution is in order, though. The formulas in this chapter try to minimize cost. Bear in mind that a firm's objective should be something like "making money"—so be sure that reducing inventory cost does, in fact, support this. Usually, correctly reducing inventory lowers cost, improves quality and performance, and enhances profit.

Key Terms

Inventory The stock of any item or resource used in an organization.

Independent demand The demands for various items are unrelated to each other.

Dependent demand The need for any one item is a direct result of the need for some other item, usually an item of which it is a part.

Fixed–order quantity model (or Q-model) An inventory control model where the amount requisitioned is fixed and the actual ordering is triggered by inventory dropping to a specified level of inventory.

Fixed–time period model (or P-model) An inventory control model that specifies inventory is ordered at the end of a predetermined time period. The interval of time between orders is fixed and the order quantity varies.

Inventory position The amount on-hand plus on-order minus backordered quantities. In the case where inventory has been allocated for special purposes, the inventory position is reduced by these allocated amounts.

Safety stock The amount of inventory carried in addition to the expected demand.

Cycle counting A physical inventory-taking technique in which inventory is counted on a frequent basis rather than once or twice a year.

Formula Review

Single-period model. Cumulative probability of not selling the last unit. Ratio of marginal cost of underestimating demand and marginal cost of overestimating demand.

$$P \le \frac{C_u}{C_o + C_u}$$

[13.1]

Q-model. Total annual cost for an order Q, a per-unit cost C, setup cost S, and per-unit holding cost H.

$$TC = DC + \frac{D}{Q}S + \frac{Q}{2}H \qquad [13.2]$$

Q-model. Optimal (or economic) order quantity.

$$Q_{opt} = \sqrt{\frac{2DS}{H}} \qquad [13.3]$$

Q-model. Reorder point R based on average daily demand $\bar{d}$ and lead time L in days.

$$R = \bar{d}L \qquad [13.4]$$

Q-model. Reorder point providing a safety stock of $z\sigma_L$.

$$R = \bar{d}L + z\sigma_L \qquad [13.5]$$

Average daily demand over a period of n days.

$$\bar{d} = \frac{\sum_{i=1}^{n} d_i}{n} \qquad [13.6]$$

Standard deviation of demand over a period of n days.

$$\sigma_d = \sqrt{\frac{\sum_{i=1}^{n}(d_i - \bar{d})^2}{n}} \qquad [13.7]$$

Standard deviation of a series of independent demands.

$$\sigma_s = \sqrt{\sigma_1^2 + \sigma_2^2 + \cdots + \sigma_i^2} \qquad [13.8]$$

Q-model. Safety stock calculation.

$$SS = z\sigma_L \qquad [13.9]$$

P-model. Safety stock calculation.

$$SS = z\sigma_{T+L} \qquad [13.10]$$

P-model. Optimal order quantity in a fixed-period system with a review period of T days and lead time of L days.

$$q = \bar{d}(T + L) + z\sigma_{T+L} - I \qquad [13.11]$$

P-model. Standard deviation of a series of independent demands over the review period T and lead time L.

$$\sigma_{T+L} = \sqrt{\sum_{i=1}^{T+L}\sigma_{d_i}^2} \qquad [13.12]$$

$$\text{Average inventory value} = (Q/2 + SS)C \qquad [13.13]$$

$$\text{Inventory turn} = \frac{DC}{(Q/2 + SS)C} = \frac{D}{Q/2 + SS} \qquad [13.14]$$

$$Q = \sqrt{\frac{2DS}{iC}} \qquad [13.15]$$

Solved Problems

SOLVED PROBLEM 1

A product is priced to sell at $100 per unit, and its cost is constant at $70 per unit. Each unsold unit has a salvage value of $20. Demand is expected to range between 35 and 40 units for the period; 35 definitely can be sold and no units over 40 will be sold. The demand probabilities and the associated cumulative probability distribution (P) for this situation are shown below.

NUMBER OF UNITS DEMANDED	PROBABILITY OF THIS DEMAND	CUMULATIVE PROBABILITY
35	0.10	0.10
36	0.15	0.25
37	0.25	0.50
38	0.25	0.75
39	0.15	0.90
40	0.10	1.00

**Excel:
Inventory
Control**

How many units should be ordered?

Solution

The cost of underestimating demand is the loss of profit, or $C_u = \$100 - \$70 = \$30$ per unit. The cost of overestimating demand is the loss incurred when the unit must be sold at salvage value, $C_o = \$70 - \$20 = \$50$.

The optimal probability of not being sold is

$$P \leq \frac{C_u}{C_o + C_u} = \frac{30}{50 + 30} = .375$$

From the distribution data above, this corresponds to the 37th unit.

The following is a full marginal analysis for the problem. Note that the minimum cost is when 37 units are purchased.

UNITS DEMANDED	PROBABILITY	NUMBER OF UNITS PURCHASED					
		35	36	37	38	39	40
35	0.1	0	50	100	150	200	250
36	0.15	30	0	50	100	150	200
37	0.25	60	30	0	50	100	150
38	0.25	90	60	30	0	50	100
39	0.15	120	90	60	30	0	50
40	0.1	150	120	90	60	30	0
Total cost		75	53	43	53	83	125

SOLVED PROBLEM 2

Items purchased from a vendor cost $20 each, and the forecast for next year's demand is 1,000 units. If it costs $5 every time an order is placed for more units and the storage cost is $4 per unit per year, what quantity should be ordered each time?

a. What is the total ordering cost for a year?

b. What is the total storage cost for a year?

Solution

The quantity to be ordered each time is

$$Q = \sqrt{\frac{2DS}{H}} = \sqrt{\frac{2(1,000)5}{4}} = 50 \text{ units}$$

a. The total ordering cost for a year is

$$\frac{D}{Q}S = \frac{1,000}{50}(\$5) = \$100$$

b. The storage cost for a year is

$$\frac{Q}{2}H = \frac{50}{2}(\$4) = \$100$$

SOLVED PROBLEM 3

Daily demand for a product is 120 units, with a standard deviation of 30 units. The review period is 14 days and the lead time is 7 days. At the time of review, 130 units are in stock. If only a 1 percent risk of stocking out is acceptable, how many units should be ordered?

**Excel:
Inventory
Control**

Solution

$$\sigma_{T+L} = \sqrt{(14 + 7)(30)^2} = \sqrt{18,900} = 137.5$$
$$z = 2.33$$
$$q = \bar{d}(T + L) + z\sigma_{T+L} - I$$
$$= 120(14 + 7) + 2.33(137.5) - 130$$
$$= 2,710 \text{ units}$$

SOLVED PROBLEM 4

A company currently has 200 units of a product on hand that it orders every two weeks when the salesperson visits the premises. Demand for the product averages 20 units per day with a standard deviation of 5 units. Lead time for the product to arrive is seven days. Management has a goal of a 95 percent probability of not stocking out for this product.

**Excel:
Inventory
Control**

  The salesperson is due to come in late this afternoon when 180 units are left in stock (assuming that 20 are sold today). How many units should be ordered?

Solution

Given $I = 180, T = 14, L = 7, d = 20$
$$\sigma_{T+L} = \sqrt{21(5)^2} = 23$$
$$z = 1.64$$
$$q = \bar{d}(T + L) + z\sigma_{T+L} - I$$
$$= 20(14 + 7) + 1.64(23) - 180$$
$$q = 278 \text{ units}$$

Review and Discussion Questions

1 Distinguish between dependent and independent demand in a McDonald's restaurant, in an integrated manufacturer of personal copiers, and in a pharmaceutical supply house.
2 Distinguish between in-process inventory, safety stock inventory, and seasonal inventory.
3 Discuss the nature of the costs that affect inventory size.

4 Under which conditions would a plant manager elect to use a fixed–order quantity model as opposed to a fixed–time period model? What are the disadvantages of using a fixed–time period ordering system?

5 What two basic questions must be answered by an inventory-control decision rule?

6 Discuss the assumptions that are inherent in production setup cost, ordering cost, and carrying costs. How valid are they?

7 "The nice thing about inventory models is that you can pull one off the shelf and apply it so long as your cost estimates are accurate." Comment.

8 Which type of inventory system would you use in the following situations?

   a. Supplying your kitchen with fresh food.

   b. Obtaining a daily newspaper.

   c. Buying gas for your car.

   To which of these items do you impute the highest stockout cost?

9 Why is it desirable to classify items into groups, as the ABC classification does?

Problems

1 The local supermarket buys lettuce each day to ensure really fresh produce. Each morning any lettuce that is left from the previous day is sold to a dealer that resells it to farmers who use it to feed their animals. This week the supermarket can buy fresh lettuce for $4.00 a box. The lettuce is sold for $10.00 a box and the dealer that sells old lettuce is willing to pay $1.50 a box. Past history says that tomorrow's demand for lettuce averages 250 boxes with a standard deviation of 34 boxes. How many boxes of lettuce should the supermarket purchase tomorrow?

2 Next week, Super Discount Airlines has a flight from New York to Los Angeles that will be booked to capacity. The airline knows from past history that an average of 25 customers (with a standard deviation of 15) cancel their reservation or do not show for the flight. Revenue from a ticket on the flight is $125. If the flight is overbooked, the airline has a policy of getting the customer on the next available flight and giving the person a free round-trip ticket on a future flight. The cost of this free round-trip ticket averages $250. Super Discount considers the cost of flying the plane from New York to Los Angeles a sunk cost. By how many seats should Super Discount overbook the flight?

3 Ray's Satellite Emporium wishes to determine the best order size for its best-selling satellite dish (model TS111). Ray has estimated the annual demand for this model at 1,000 units. His cost to carry one unit is $100 per year per unit, and he has estimated that each order costs $25 to place. Using the EOQ model, how many should Ray order each time?

4 Dunstreet's Department Store would like to develop an inventory ordering policy of a 95 percent probability of not stocking out. To illustrate your recommended procedure, use as an example the ordering policy for white percale sheets.

   Demand for white percale sheets is 5,000 per year. The store is open 365 days per year. Every two weeks (14 days) inventory is counted and a new order is placed. It takes 10 days for the sheets to be delivered. Standard deviation of demand for the sheets is five per day. There are currently 150 sheets on hand.

   How many sheets should you order?

5 Charlie's Pizza orders all of its pepperoni, olives, anchovies, and mozzarella cheese to be shipped directly from Italy. An American distributor stops by every four weeks to take orders. Because the orders are shipped directly from Italy, they take three weeks to arrive.

   Charlie's Pizza uses an average of 150 pounds of pepperoni each week, with a standard deviation of 30 pounds. Charlie's prides itself on offering only the best-quality ingredients and a high level of service, so it wants to ensure a 98 percent probability of not stocking out on pepperoni.

   Assume that the sales representative just walked in the door and there are currently 500 pounds of pepperoni in the walk-in cooler. How many pounds of pepperoni would you order?

6   Given the following information, formulate an inventory management system. The item is demanded 50 weeks a year.

Item cost	$10.00	Standard deviation of	
Order cost	$250.00	weekly demand	25 per week
Annual holding cost (%)	33% of item cost	Lead time	1 week
Annual demand	25,750	Service probability	95%
Average demand	515 per week		

   a. State the order quantity and reorder point.
   b. Determine the annual holding and order costs.
   c. If a price break of $50 per order was offered for purchase quantities of over 2,000, would you take advantage of it? How much would you save annually?

7   Lieutenant Commander Data is planning to make his monthly (every 30 days) trek to Gamma Hydra City to pick up a supply of isolinear chips. The trip will take Data about two days. Before he leaves, he calls in the order to the GHC Supply Store. He uses chips at an average rate of five per day (seven days per week) with a standard deviation of demand of one per day. He needs a 98 percent service probability. If he currently has 35 chips in inventory, how many should he order? What is the most he will ever have to order?

8   Jill's Job Shop buys two parts (Tegdiws and Widgets) for use in its production system from two different suppliers. The parts are needed throughout the entire 52-week year. Tegdiws are used at a relatively constant rate and are ordered whenever the remaining quantity drops to the reorder level. Widgets are ordered from a supplier who stops by every three weeks. Data for both products are as follows:

ITEM	TEGDIW	WIDGET
Annual demand	10,000	5,000
Holding cost (% of item cost)	20%	20%
Setup or order cost	$150.00	$25.00
Lead time	4 weeks	1 week
Safety stock	55 units	5 units
Item cost	$10.00	$2.00

   a. What is the inventory control system for Tegdiws? That is, what is the reorder quantity and what is the reorder point?
   b. What is the inventory control system for Widgets?

9   Demand for an item is 1,000 units per year. Each order placed costs $10; the annual cost to carry items in inventory is $2 each. In what quantities should the item be ordered?

10   The annual demand for a product is 15,600 units. The weekly demand is 300 units with a standard deviation of 90 units. The cost to place an order is $31.20, and the time from ordering to receipt is four weeks. The annual inventory carrying cost is $0.10 per unit. Find the reorder point necessary to provide a 98 percent service probability.

   Suppose the production manager is asked to reduce the safety stock of this item by 50 percent. If she does so, what will the new service probability be?

11   Daily demand for a product is 100 units, with a standard deviation of 25 units. The review period is 10 days and the lead time is 6 days. At the time of review there are 50 units in stock. If 98 percent service probability is desired, how many units should be ordered?

12   Item X is a standard item stocked in a company's inventory of component parts. Each year the firm, on a random basis, uses about 2,000 of item X, which costs $25 each. Storage costs, which include insurance and cost of capital, amount to $5 per unit of average inventory. Every time an order is placed for more item X, it costs $10.
   a. Whenever item X is ordered, what should the order size be?
   b. What is the annual cost for ordering item X?
   c. What is the annual cost for storing item X?

13   Annual demand for a product is 13,000 units; weekly demand is 250 units with a standard deviation of 40 units. The cost of placing an order is $100, and the time from ordering to receipt is four weeks. The annual inventory carrying cost is $0.65 per unit. To provide a 98 percent service probability, what must the reorder point be?

   Suppose the production manager is told to reduce the safety stock of this item by 100 units. If this is done, what will the new service probability be?

14   In the past, Taylor Industries has used a fixed–time period inventory system that involved taking a complete inventory count of all items each month. However, increasing labor costs are forcing Taylor Industries to examine alternative ways to reduce the amount of labor involved in inventory stockrooms, yet without increasing other costs, such as shortage costs. Here is a random sample of 20 of Taylor's items.

ITEM NUMBER	ANNUAL USAGE	ITEM NUMBER	ANNUAL USAGE
1	$ 1,500	11	$13,000
2	12,000	12	600
3	2,200	13	42,000
4	50,000	14	9,900
5	9,600	15	1,200
6	750	16	10,200
7	2,000	17	4,000
8	11,000	18	61,000
9	800	19	3,500
10	15,000	20	2,900

   a. What would you recommend Taylor do to cut back its labor cost? (Illustrate using an ABC plan.)

   b. Item 15 is critical to continued operations. How would you recommend it be classified?

15   Gentle Ben's Bar and Restaurant uses 5,000 quart bottles of an imported wine each year. The effervescent wine costs $3 per bottle and is served only in whole bottles because it loses its bubbles quickly. Ben figures that it costs $10 each time an order is placed, and holding costs are 20 percent of the purchase price. It takes three weeks for an order to arrive. Weekly demand is 100 bottles (closed two weeks per year) with a standard deviation of 30 bottles.

   Ben would like to use an inventory system that minimizes inventory cost and will provide a 95 percent service probability.

   a. What is the economic quantity for Ben to order?

   b. At what inventory level should he place an order?

16   Retailers Warehouse (RW) is an independent supplier of household items to department stores. RW attempts to stock enough items for a 98 percent service probability.

   A stainless steel knife set is one item it stocks. Demand (2,400 sets per year) is relatively stable over the entire year. Whenever new stock is ordered, a buyer must assure that numbers are correct for stock on hand and then phone in a new order. The total cost involved to place an order is about $5. RW figures that holding inventory in stock and paying for interest on borrowed capital, insurance, and so on, adds up to about $4 holding cost per unit per year.

   Analysis of the past data shows that the standard deviation of demand from retailers is about four units per day for a 365-day year. Lead time to get the order is seven days.

   a. What is the economic order quantity?

   b. What is the reorder point?

17   Daily demand for a product is 60 units with a standard deviation of 10 units. The review period is 10 days, and lead time is 2 days. At the time of review there are 100 units in stock. If 98 percent service probability is desired, how many units should be ordered?

18   University Drug Pharmaceuticals orders its antibiotics every two weeks (14 days) when a salesperson visits from one of the pharmaceutical companies. Tetracycline is one of its most prescribed antibiotics, with average daily demand of 2,000 capsules. The standard deviation of daily demand was derived from examining prescriptions filled over the past three months and was found to be 800 capsules. It takes five days for the order to arrive. University Drug would like to satisfy 99 percent of the prescriptions. The salesperson just arrived, and there are currently 25,000 capsules in stock.

How many capsules should be ordered?

19   Sally's Silk Screening produces specialty T-shirts that are primarily sold at special events. She is trying to decide how many to produce for an upcoming event. During the event itself, which lasts one day, Sally can sell T-shirts for $20 apiece. However, when the event ends, any unsold T-shirts are sold for $4 apiece. It costs Sally $8 to make a specialty T-shirt. Using Sally's estimate of demand that follows, how many T-shirts should she produce for the upcoming event?

DEMAND	PROBABILITY
300	.05
400	.10
500	.40
600	.30
700	.10
800	.05

20   Famous Albert prides himself on being the Cookie King of the West. Small, freshly baked cookies are the specialty of his shop. Famous Albert has asked for help to determine the number of cookies he should make each day. From an analysis of past demand he estimates demand for cookies as

DEMAND	PROBABILITY OF DEMAND
1,800 dozen	0.05
2,000	0.10
2,200	0.20
2,400	0.30
2,600	0.20
2,800	0.10
3,000	0.05

Each dozen sells for $0.69 and costs $0.49, which includes handling and transportation. Cookies that are not sold at the end of the day are reduced to $0.29 and sold the following day as day-old merchandise.

a. Construct a table showing the profits or losses for each possible quantity.

b. What is the optimal number of cookies to make?

c. Solve this problem by using marginal analysis.

21   Sarah's Muffler Shop has one standard muffler that fits a large variety of cars. Sarah wishes to establish a reorder point system to manage inventory of this standard muffler. Use the following information to determine the best order size and the reorder point:

Annual demand	3,500 mufflers	Ordering cost	$50 per order
Standard deviation of daily demand	6 mufflers per working day	Service probability	90%
Item cost	$30 per muffler	Lead time	2 working days
Annual holding cost	25% of item value	Working days	300 per year

22   Alpha Products, Inc., is having a problem trying to control inventory. There is insufficient time to devote to all its items equally. Here is a sample of some items stocked, along with the annual usage of each item expressed in dollar volume.

ITEM	ANNUAL DOLLAR USAGE	ITEM	ANNUAL DOLLAR USAGE
a	$ 7,000	k	$80,000
b	1,000	l	400
c	14,000	m	1,100
d	2,000	n	30,000
e	24,000	o	1,900
f	68,000	p	800
g	17,000	q	90,000
h	900	r	12,000
i	1,700	s	3,000
j	2,300	t	32,000

   a. Can you suggest a system for allocating control time?
   b. Specify where each item from the list would be placed.

23   After graduation, you decide to go into a partnership in an office supply store that has existed for a number of years. Walking through the store and stockrooms, you find a great discrepancy in service levels. Some spaces and bins for items are completely empty; others have supplies that are covered with dust and have obviously been there a long time. You decide to take on the project of establishing consistent levels of inventory to meet customer demands. Most of your supplies are purchased from just a few distributors that call on your store once every two weeks.

   You choose, as your first item for study, computer printer paper. You examine the sales records and purchase orders and find that demand for the past 12 months was 5,000 boxes. Using your calculator you sample some days' demands and estimate that the standard deviation of daily demand is 10 boxes. You also search out these figures:

   Cost per box of paper: $11.
   Desired service probability: 98 percent.
   Store is open every day.
   Salesperson visits every two weeks.
   Delivery time following visit is three days.

   Using your procedure, how many boxes of paper would be ordered if, on the day the salesperson calls, 60 boxes are on hand?

24   A distributor of large appliances needs to determine the order quantities and reorder points for the various products it carries. The following data refer to a specific refrigerator in its product line:

Cost to place an order	$100
Holding cost	20 percent of product cost per year
Cost of refrigerator	$500 each
Annual demand	500 refrigerators
Standard deviation during lead time	10 refrigerators
Lead time	7 days

   Consider an even daily demand and a 365-day year.
   a. What is the economic order quantity?
   b. If the distributor wants a 97 percent service probability, what reorder point, R, should be used?

25 It is your responsibility, as the new head of the automotive section of Nichols Department Store, to ensure that reorder quantities for the various items have been correctly established. You decide to test one item and choose Michelin tires, XW size 185 × 14 BSW. A perpetual inventory system has been used, so you examine this as well as other records and come up with the following data:

Cost per tire	$35 each
Holding cost	20 percent of tire cost per year
Demand	1,000 per year
Ordering cost	$20 per order
Standard deviation of daily demand	3 tires
Delivery lead time	4 days

Because customers generally do not wait for tires but go elsewhere, you decide on a service probability of 98 percent. Assume the demand occurs 365 days per year.

  a. Determine the order quantity.
  b. Determine the reorder point.

26 UA Hamburger Hamlet (UAHH) places a daily order for its high-volume items (hamburger patties, buns, milk, and so on). UAHH counts its current inventory on hand once per day and phones in its order for delivery 24 hours later. Determine the number of hamburgers UAHH should order for the following conditions:

Average daily demand	600
Standard deviation of demand	100
Desired service probability	99%
Hamburger inventory	800

27 DAT, Inc., produces digital audiotapes to be used in the consumer audio division. DAT lacks sufficient personnel in its inventory supply section to closely control each item stocked, so it has asked you to determine an ABC classification. Here is a sample from the inventory records:

ITEM	AVERAGE MONTHLY DEMAND	PRICE PER UNIT	ITEM	AVERAGE MONTHLY DEMAND	PRICE PER UNIT
1	700	$6.00	6	100	10.00
2	200	4.00	7	3,000	2.00
3	2,000	12.00	8	2,500	1.00
4	1,100	20.00	9	500	10.00
5	4,000	21.00	10	1,000	2.00

Develop an ABC classification for these 10 items.

28 A local service station is open 7 days per week, 365 days per year. Sales of 10W40 grade premium oil average 20 cans per day. Inventory holding costs are $0.50 per can per year. Ordering costs are $10 per order. Lead time is two weeks. Backorders are not practical—the motorist drives away.

  a. Based on these data, choose the appropriate inventory model and calculate the economic order quantity and reorder point. Describe in a sentence how the plan would work. Hint: Assume demand is deterministic.
  b. The boss is concerned about this model because demand really varies. The standard deviation of demand was determined from a data sample to be 6.15 cans per day. The manager wants a 99.5 percent service probability. Determine a new inventory plan based on this information and the data in *a.* Use Q_{opt} from *a.*

29 Dave's Auto Supply custom mixes paint for its customers. The shop performs a weekly inventory count of the main colors that are used for mixing paint. Determine the amount of white paint that should be ordered using the following information:

Average weekly demand	20 gallons
Standard deviation of demand	5 gallons/week
Desired service probability	98%
Current inventory	25 gallons
Lead time	1 week

30   A particular raw material is available to a company at three different prices, depending on the size of the order:

Less than 100 pounds	$20 per pound
100 pounds to 1,000 pounds	$19 per pound
More than 1,000 pounds	$18 per pound

The cost to place an order is $40. Annual demand is 3,000 units. Holding (or carrying) cost is 25 percent of the material price.

What is the economic order quantity to buy each time?

31   CU, Incorporated (CUI), produces copper contacts that it uses in switches and relays. CUI needs to determine the order quantity, Q, to meet the annual demand at the lowest cost. The price of copper depends on the quantity ordered. Here are price-break and other data for the problem:

Price of copper	$0.82 per pound up to 2,499 pounds
	$0.81 per pound for orders between 2,500 and 5,000 pounds
	$0.80 per pound for orders greater than 5,000 pounds
Annual demand	50,000 pounds per year
Holding cost	20 percent per unit per year of the price of the copper
Ordering cost	$30

Which quantity should be ordered?

CASE: Hewlett-Packard—Supplying the DeskJet Printer in Europe

The DeskJet printer was introduced in 1988 and has become one of Hewlett-Packard's (HP's) most successful products. Sales have grown steadily, now reaching a level of over 600,000. Unfortunately, inventory growth has tracked sales growth closely. HP's distribution centers are filled with pallets of the DeskJet printer. Worse yet, the organization in Europe claims that inventory levels there need to be raised even further to maintain satisfactory product availability.

The DeskJet Supply Chain

The network of suppliers, manufacturing sites, distribution centers (DCs), dealers, and customers for the DeskJet product make up the DeskJet supply chain (see Exhibit 13.12).

HP in Vancouver does manufacturing. There are two key stages in the manufacturing process: (1) printed circuit assembly and test (PCAT) and (2) final assembly and test (FAT). PCAT involves the assembly and testing of electronic components (like integrated circuits, read-only memories, and raw printed circuit boards) to make logic boards used in the printer. FAT involves the assembly of other subassemblies (like motors, cables, keypads, plastic chassis, gears, and the printed circuit assemblies from PCAT) to produce a working printer, as well as the final testing of the printer. The components needed for PCAT and FAT are sourced from other HP divisions as well as from external suppliers worldwide.

exhibit 13.12   HP DeskJet Supply Chain

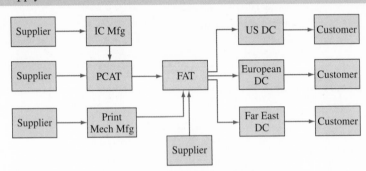

Key: IC Mfg—Integrated Circuit Manufacturing
PCAT—Printed Circuit Assembly and Test
FAT—Final Assembly and Test
Print Mech Mfg—Print Mechanism Manufacturing

Selling the DeskJet in Europe requires customizing the printer to meet the language and power supply requirements of the local countries, a process known as "localization." Specifically, the localization of the DeskJet of different countries involves assembling the appropriate power supply module, which reflects the correct voltage requirements (110 or 220) and power cord plug, and packaging it with the working printer and a manual written in the appropriate language. Currently, the final test is done with the actual power supply module included with the printer. Hence, the finished products of the factory are "localized" versions of the printer destined for all the different countries. For the European Market six different versions are currently produced. These are designated A, AA, AB, AQ, AU, and AY as indicated in the Bills of Materials shown in Exhibit 13.13.

The total factory throughput time through the PCAT and FAT stages is about one week. The transportation time from Vancouver to the European DC is five weeks. The long shipment time to Europe is due to ocean transit and the time to clear customs and duties at port of entry. The plant sends a weekly shipment of printers to the DC in Europe.

The printer industry is highly competitive. Resellers want to carry as little inventory as possible. Consequently there has been increasing pressure for HP as a manufacturer to provide high levels of availability at the DC. In response, management has decided to stock the DCs so that a high level of availability is maintained.

Global

Supply Chain

exhibit 13.13   HP DeskJet Bill of Materials

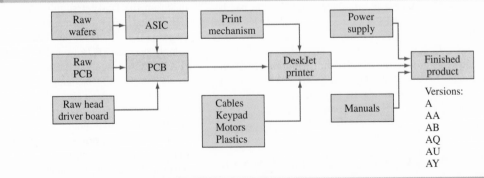

The Inventory Service Crisis

To limit the amount of inventory throughout the DeskJet supply chain and at the same time provide the high level of service needed has been quite a challenge to Vancouver's management. The manufacturing group has been very successful in reducing the uncertainties caused by delivery to the European DC. Forecasting demand in Europe, though, is a significant problem. It has become common to have product shortages for model demands from some countries, while inventory of other models keeps piling up. In the past, the target inventory levels at the DCs were based on safety stocks that were a result of some judgmental rule of thumb. Specifically, target inventory levels, equal to one-month average sales, were set for each model carried in the DC. Now, however, it seems that the increasing difficulty of getting accurate forecasts means the safety stock rules should be revisited.

HP has put together a team of employees to help implement a scientifically based safety stock system that will be responsive to forecast errors and replenishment lead times. They are to recommend a method for calculating appropriate safety stock levels for the various DeskJet models carried in the European DC. The team has a good sample of demand data that can be used for developing the safety stock methodology (see Exhibit 13.14). HP hopes this new methodology will solve the inventory and service problem.

One issue that continually comes up is the choice of inventory carrying cost to be used in safety stock analyses. Estimates within the company range from 12 percent (HP's cost of debt plus some warehousing expenses) to 60 percent (based on the ROI expected of new product development projects). Management has decided to use 25 percent for this study. Assume that all printers cost an average of approximately $250 each to produce and ship to Europe. Another issue is the choice of safety stock probability for the model.

The company has decided to use a probability of 98 percent, a number that marketing feels is appropriate.

The Distribution Process

The DCs have traditionally envisioned their process as a simple, straight-line, standardized process. There are four process stops:

1. Receive (complete) products from various suppliers and stock them.
2. Pick the various products needed to fill a customer order.
3. Shrink-wrap the complete order and label it.
4. Ship the order via the appropriate carrier.

The DeskJet printer fits well into the standard process. In contrast, other products, such as personal computers and monitors, require special processing called "integration," which includes addition of an appropriate keyboard and manual for the destination country. Although this extra processing does not require much extra labor, it is difficult to accommodate in the standard process and disrupts the material flow. There is considerable frustration within DC management regarding the support of assembly processes. In general, DC management stresses the DCs' role as warehouses and the need to continue to do what they are best at—distribution.

Top management, though, feels that integration of the product at the warehouse is extremely valuable because it allows generic products to be sent to the DC with final configuration of the product done just prior to shipment to the customer. Rather than the factory making products specific to a country, generic products could be produced and shipped to Europe. Management is very interested in studying the value of this approach as it could be applied to the DeskJet printers.

DeskJet Demand Data from Europe

exhibit 13.14

EUROPE OPTIONS	NOV.	DEC.	JAN.	FEB.	MAR.	APR.	MAY	JUN.	JUL.	AUG.	SEP.	OCT.
A	80	—	60	90	21	48	—	9	20	54	84	42
AB	20,572	20,895	19,252	11,052	19,864	20,316	13,336	10,578	6,095	14,496	23,712	9,792
AU	4,564	3,207	7,485	4,908	5,295	90	—	5,004	4,385	5,103	4,302	6,153
AA	400	255	408	645	210	87	432	816	430	630	456	273
AQ	4,008	2,196	4,761	1,953	1,008	2,358	1,676	540	2,310	2,046	1,797	2,961
AY	248	450	378	306	219	204	248	484	164	363	384	234
Total	29,872	27,003	32,344	18,954	26,617	23,103	15,692	17,431	13,405	22,692	30,735	19,455

**Excel:
HP Deskjet**

Questions

1 Develop an inventory model for managing the DeskJet printers in Europe assuming that the Vancouver plant continues to produce the six models sold in Europe. Using the data in Exhibit 13.13, apply your model and calculate the expected yearly investment in DeskJet printer inventory in the Europe DC.

2 Compare your results from question 1 to the current policy of carrying one month's average inventory at the DC.

3 Evaluate the idea of supplying generic printers to the Europe DC and integrating the product by packaging the power supply and the instruction manual at the DC just prior to delivery to the European resellers. Focus on the impact on DC inventory investment in this analysis.

4 What is your recommendation to HP?

Super Quiz

1 Model most appropriate for making a one-time purchase of an item.

2 Model most appropriate when inventory is replenished only in fixed intervals of time, for example, on the first Monday of each month.

3 Model most appropriate when a fixed amount must be purchased each time an order is placed.

4 Based on an EOQ-type ordering criterion, what cost must be taken to zero if the desire is to have an order quantity of a single unit?

5 Term used to describe demand that can be accurately calculated to meet the need of a production schedule, for example.

6 Term used to describe demand that is uncertain and needs to be forecast.

7 We are ordering T-shirts for the spring party and are selling them for twice what we paid for them. We expect to sell 100 shirts and the standard deviation associated with our forecast is 10 shirts. How many shirts should we order?

8 We have an item that we stock in our store that has fairly steady demand. Our supplier insists that we buy 1,200 units at a time. The lead time is very short on the item, since the supplier is only a few blocks away and we can pick up another 1,200 units when we run out. How many units do you expect to have in inventory on average?

9 For the item described in question 8, if we expect to sell approximately 15,600 units next year, how many trips will we need to make to the supplier over the year?

10 If we decide to carry 10 units of safety stock for the item described in questions 8 and 9, and we implemented this by going to our supplier when we had 10 units left, how much inventory would you expect to have on average now?

11 We are being evaluated based on the percentage of total demand met in a year (not the probability of stocking out as used in the chapter). Consider an item that we are managing using a fixed-order quantity model with safety stock. We decide to double the order quantity, but leave the reorder point the same. Would you expect the percent of total demand met next year to go up or down? Why?

12 Consider an item that we have 120 units currently in inventory. The average demand for the item is 60 units per week. The lead time for the item is exactly 2 weeks and we carry 16 units for safety stock. What is the probability of running out of the item if we order right now?

13 If we take advantage of a quantity discount would you expect your average inventory to go up or down? Assume that the probably of stocking out criterion stays the same.

14 This is an inventory auditing technique where inventory levels are checked more frequently than one time a year.

1. Single-period model 2. Fixed—time period model 3. Fixed—order quantity model 4. Setup or ordering cost 5. Dependent demand 6. Independent demand 7. 100 shirts 8. 600 units 9. 13 times 10. 610 units 11. Go up (we are taking fewer chances of running out) 12. 50 percent 13. Will probably go up if the probability of stocking out stays the same 14. Cycle counting

Selected Bibliography

Brooks, R. B., and L. W. Wilson. *Inventory Record Accuracy: Unleashing the Power of Cycle Counting.* Essex Junction, VT: Oliver Wight, 1993.

Silver, E.; D. Pyke; and R. Peterson. *Decision Systems for Inventory Management and Production Planning and Control.* 3rd ed. New York: Wiley, 1998.

Sipper, D., and R. L. Bulfin Jr. *Production Planning, Control, and Integration.* New York: McGraw-Hill, 1997.

Tersine, R. J. *Principles of Inventory and Materials Management.* 4th ed. New York: North-Holland, 1994.

Vollmann, T. E.; W. L. Berry; D. C. Whybark; and F. R. Jacobs. *Manufacturing Planning and Control Systems for Supply Chain Management.* 5th ed. New York: McGraw-Hill, 2004.

Wild, T. *Best Practices in Inventory Management.* New York: Wiley, 1998.

Zipkin, P. H. *Foundations of Inventory Management.* New York: Irwin/McGraw-Hill, 2000.

Footnotes

1 P is actually a cumulative probability because the sale of the nth unit depends not only on exactly n being demanded but also on the demand for any number greater than n.

2 As previously discussed, the standard deviation of a sum of independent variables equals the square root of the sum of the variances.

3 The Pareto principle is also widely applied in quality problems through the use of Pareto charts. (See Chapter 6.)

CHAPTER 14

MATERIAL REQUIREMENTS PLANNING

After reading the chapter you will:

- Describe what MRP is and where it is best applied.
- Understand the source of the information used by the system.
- Demonstrate how to do an MRP "explosion."
- Explain how order quantities are calculated in MRP systems.

431   **From Push to Pull**

Enterprise resource planning (ERP) defined
Material requirements planning (MRP) defined

433   **Master Production Scheduling**

Time Fences   Master production schedule (MPS) defined

Available to promise defined

435   **Where MRP Can Be Used**

436   **Material Requirements Planning System Structure**

Demand for Products   Bill of materials (BOM) defined
Bill of Materials   Net change system defined
Inventory Records
MRP Computer Program

441   **An Example Using MRP**

Forecasting Demand
Developing a Master Production Schedule
Bill of Materials (Product Structure)
Inventory Records
Performing the MRP Calculations

447   **Lot Sizing in MRP Systems**

Lot-for-Lot
Economic Order Quantity
Least Total Cost
Least Unit Cost
Choosing the Best Lot Size

451   Summary

457   Case: Brunswick Motors, Inc.—An Introductory
Case for MRP

458   Super Quiz

FROM PUSH TO PULL

In the 1980s manufacturing led the national economy in the move from batch-oriented data processing systems to online transaction processing systems. The focus was MRP (initially material requirements planning, evolving to manufacturing resource planning), which later evolved into enterprise resource planning (ERP). It has been a long ride, and anyone who has been there for the duration deserves a rest.

However, the winds of change are blowing again as yet another new paradigm comes roaring through manufacturing. Specifically, we are speaking of the change in our economy from a build-to-stock to a build-to-order model of doing business.

The weak link in the build-to-stock model is inventory management, and this can be traced to an even weaker link, reliance upon sales forecasts. A build-to-order model begins with the order, not the forecast. The old problem of coordinating the procurement of parts, production of the product, and shipping the product still exists.

Today the term *flow management* is used to describe new hybrid production planning systems that combine the information integration and planning capability of MRP with the response of a JIT kanban system. Major ERP software vendors such as Oracle, SAP, and i2 Technologies are selling these new systems.

Essentially, the idea with flow management is to produce a constantly changing mix of products, a mix that is based on current orders, using a stream of parts that are sup-plied just-in-time. It's important not to be tricked into thinking that all these new words really rep-resent something new. Actually, flow manufacturing just combines things that have been used for years. In this case the combination is JIT kanban logic, MRP logic for planning material requirements, and client–server ERP.

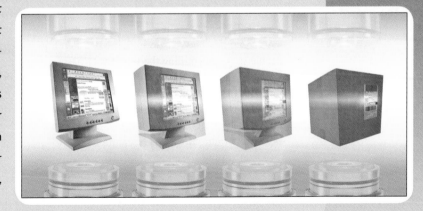

Enterprise resource planning (ERP)

Supply Chain

Enterprise resource planning (ERP) is a computer system that integrates application programs in accounting, sales, manufacturing, and the other functions in a firm. This integration is accomplished through a database shared by all the application programs. Current ERP vendors have set new standards in information integration that can significantly benefit a company. When implemented correctly, ERP links all areas of the business. Manufacturing knows about new orders as soon as they are entered into the system. Sales knows the exact status of a customer order. Purchasing knows what manufacturing needs to the minute, and the accounting system is updated as all relevant transactions occur. The potential benefits of ERP are huge.

The operations and supply functions in an ERP system include many applications. In Exhibit 14.1 we see a diagram that depicts typical operations and supply chain functions.

- In sales and distribution (SD), products or services are sold to customers. All the details of shipping to the customer and invoices are handled in these modules.
- Production planning (PP) supports both discrete and process manufacturing processes and includes the material requirements planning (MRP) application, which is the topic of this chapter.
- Quality management (QM) plans and implements procedures for inspection and quality assurance. It is integrated with the procurement and production processes so that the user can identify inspection points both for incoming materials and for products during the manufacturing process.
- Material management (MM) covers all tasks within the supply chain, including purchasing, vendor evaluation, invoice verification, and material use planning. It also includes inventory and warehouse management.
- Plant maintenance (PM) supports the activities associated with planning and performing repairs and preventive maintenance. Completion and cost reports are available and maintenance activities can be managed and measured.

Material requirements planning (MRP)

Our emphasis here is on **material requirements planning (MRP)**, which is the key piece of logic that ties the production functions together from a material planning and control view. MRP has been installed almost universally in manufacturing firms, even those considered small. The reason is that MRP is a logical, easily understandable approach to the problem of determining the number of parts, components, and materials needed to produce each end item. MRP also provides the schedule specifying when each of these items should be order or produced.

MRP is based on dependent demand. Dependent demand is caused by the demand for a higher-level item. Tires, wheels, and engines are dependent demand items based on the demand for automobiles, for example.

Determining the number of dependent demand items needed is essentially a straightforward multiplication process. If one Part A takes five parts of B to make, then five parts of A require 25 parts of B. The basic difference in independent demand covered in the previous chapter and dependent demand covered in this chapter is as follows: If Part A is sold outside the firm, the amount of Part A that we sell is uncertain. We need to create a forecast using past data or do something like a market analysis. Part A is an independent item. However, Part B is a dependent part and its use depends on Part A. The number of B

exhibit 14.1

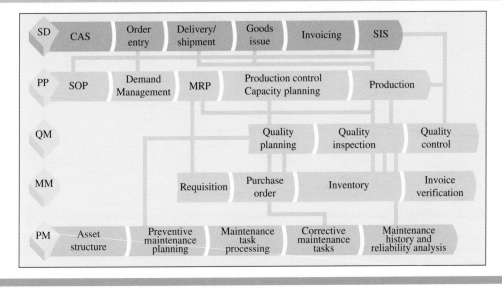

Supply Chain

needed is simply the number of A times five. As a result of this type of multiplication, the requirements of other dependent demand items tend to become more and more lumpy as we go farther down into the product creation sequence. Lumpiness means that the requirements tend to bunch or lump rather than having an even dispersal. This is also caused by the way manufacturing is done. When manufacturing occurs in lots (or batches), items needed to produce the lot are withdrawn from inventory in quantities (perhaps all at once) rather than one at a time.

MASTER PRODUCTION SCHEDULING

Generally, the master schedule deals with end items and is a major input to the MRP process. If the end item is quite large or quite expensive, however, the master schedule may schedule major subassemblies or components instead.

All production systems have limited capacity and limited resources. This presents a challenging job for the master scheduler. Although the aggregate plan provides the general range of operation, the master scheduler must specify exactly what is to be produced. These decisions are made while responding to pressures from various functional areas such as the sales department (meet the customer's promised due date), finance (minimize inventory), management (maximize productivity and customer service, minimize resource needs), and manufacturing (have level schedules and minimize setup time).

To determine an acceptable feasible schedule to be released to the shop, trial master production schedules are run through the MRP program, which is described in the next section. The resulting planned order releases (the detailed production schedules) are checked to make sure that resources are available and that the completion times are reasonable. What appears to be a feasible master schedule may turn out to require excessive resources once the product explosion has taken place and materials, parts, and components from lower levels are determined. If this does happen (the usual case), the master production

exhibit 14.2   The Aggregate Plan and the Master Production Schedule for Mattresses

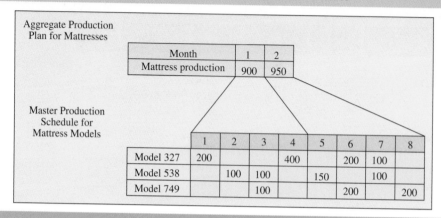

schedule is then modified with these limitations and the MRP program is run again. To ensure good master scheduling, the master scheduler (the human being) must

- Include all demands from product sales, warehouse replenishment, spares, and inter-plant requirements.
- Never lose sight of the aggregate plan.
- Be involved with customer order promising.
- Be visible to all levels of management.
- Objectively trade off manufacturing, marketing, and engineering conflicts.
- Identify and communicate all problems.

The upper portion of Exhibit 14.2 shows an aggregate plan for the total number of mattresses planned per month, without regard for mattress type. The lower portion shows a master production schedule specifying the exact type of mattress and the quantity planned for production by week. The next level down (not shown) would be the MRP program that develops detailed schedules showing when cotton batting, springs, and hardwood are needed to make the mattresses.

To again summarize the planning sequence, the aggregate operations plan, discussed in Chapter 12, specifies product groups. It does not specify exact items. The next level down in the planning process is the master production schedule. The **master production schedule (MPS)** is the time-phased plan specifying how many and when the firm plans to build each end item. For example, the aggregate plan for a furniture company may specify the total volume of mattresses it plans to produce over the next month or next quarter. The MPS goes the next step down and identifies the exact size mattresses and their qualities and styles. All of the mattresses sold by the company would be specified by the MPS. The MPS also states period by period (usually weekly) how many and when each of these mattress types is needed.

Still further down the disaggregation process is the MRP program, which calculates and schedules all raw materials, parts, and supplies needed to make the mattress specified by the MPS.

Master production schedule (MPS)

Time Fences

The question of flexibility within a master production schedule depends on several factors: production lead time, commitment of parts and components to a specific end item,

exhibit 14.3

Master Production Schedule Time Fences

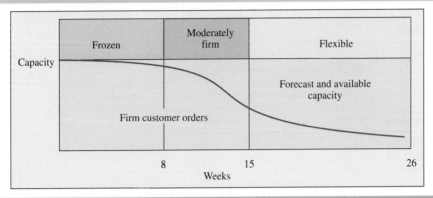

relationship between the customer and vendor, amount of excess capacity, and the reluctance or willingness of management to make changes.

The purpose of time fences is to maintain a reasonably controlled flow through the production system. Unless some operating rules are established and adhered to, the system could be chaotic and filled with overdue orders and constant expediting.

Exhibit 14.3 shows an example of a master production schedule time fence. Management defines *time fences* as periods of time having some specified level of opportunity for the customer to make changes. (The customer may be the firm's own marketing department, which may be considering product promotions, broadening variety, or the like.) Note in the exhibit that for the next eight weeks, this particular master schedule is frozen. Each firm has its own time fences and operating rules. Under these rules, *frozen* could be defined as anything from absolutely no changes in one company to only the most minor of changes in another. *Moderately firm* may allow changes in specific products within a product group so long as parts are available. *Flexible* may allow almost any variations in products, with the provisions that capacity remains about the same and that there are no long lead time items involved.

Some firms use a feature known as **available to promise** for items that are master scheduled. This feature identifies the difference between the number of units currently included in the master schedule and firm customer orders. For example, assume the master schedule indicates that 100 units of Model 538 mattress are going to be made during week seven. If firm customer orders now only indicate that 65 of those mattresses have actually been sold, the sales group has another 35 mattresses "available to promise" for delivery during that week. This can be a powerful tool for coordinating sales and production activities.

Available to promise

WHERE MRP CAN BE USED

MRP is most valuable in industries where a number of products are made in batches using the same productive equipment. The list in Exhibit 14.4 includes examples of different industry types and the expected benefit from MRP. As you can see in the exhibit, MRP is most valuable to companies involved in assembly operations and least valuable to those in fabrication. One more point to note: MRP does not work well in companies that produce a low number of units annually. Especially for companies producing complex, expensive products requiring advanced research and design, experience has shown that lead times

exhibit 14.4   Industry Applications and Expected Benefits of MRP

INDUSTRY TYPE	EXAMPLES	EXPECTED BENEFITS
Assemble-to-stock	Combines multiple component parts into a finished product, which is then stocked in inventory to satisfy customer demand. Examples: watches, tools, appliances.	High
Fabricate-to-stock	Items are manufactured by machine rather than assembled from parts. These are standard stock items carried in anticipation of customer demand. Examples: piston rings, electrical switches.	Low
Assemble-to-order	A final assembly is made from standard options that the customer chooses. Examples: trucks, generators, motors.	High
Fabricate-to-order	Items are manufactured by machine to customer order. These are generally industrial orders. Examples: bearings, gears, fasteners.	Low
Manufacture-to-order	Items are fabricated or assembled completely to customer specification. Examples: turbine generators, heavy machine tools.	High
Process	Includes industries such as foundries, rubber and plastics, specialty paper, chemicals, paint, drug, food processors.	Medium

tend to be too long and too uncertain, and the product configuration too complex. Such companies need the control features that network scheduling techniques offer. These project management methods are covered in Chapter 7.

MATERIAL REQUIREMENTS PLANNING SYSTEM STRUCTURE

The material requirements planning portion of manufacturing activities most closely interacts with the master schedule, bill of materials file, inventory records file, and the output reports as shown in Exhibit 14.5.

Each facet of Exhibit 14.5 is detailed in the following sections, but essentially, the MRP system works as follows: the master production schedule states the number of items to be produced during specific time periods. A *bill of materials* file identifies the specific materials used to make each item and the correct quantities of each. The inventory records file contains data such as the number of units on hand and on order. These three sources—master production schedule, bill of materials file, and inventory records file—become the data sources for the material requirements program, which expands the production schedule into a detailed order scheduling plan for the entire production sequence.

Demand for Products

Product demand for end items comes primarily from two main sources. The first is known customers who have placed specific orders, such as those generated by sales personnel, or from interdepartment transactions. These orders usually carry promised delivery dates. There is no forecasting involved in these orders—simply add them up. The second source is forecast demand. These are the normal independent-demand orders; the forecasting models presented in Chapter 11 can be used to predict the quantities. The demand from the known customers and the forecast demand are combined and become the input for the master production schedule, as described in the previous section.

Overall View of the Inputs to a Standard Material Requirements Planning Program and the Reports Generated by the Program

exhibit 14.5

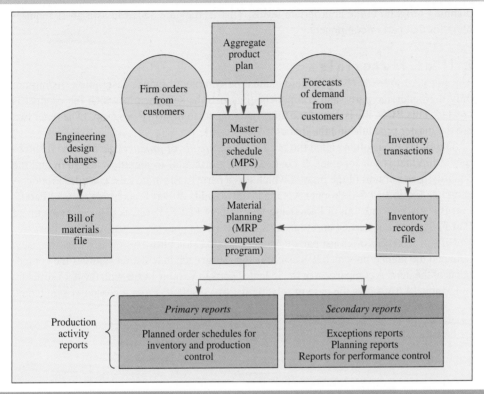

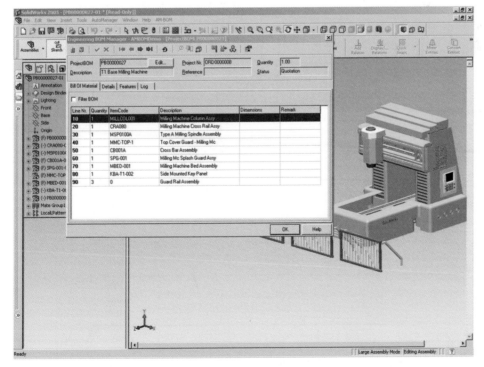

BLUECIELO ECM SOLUTIONS' ENTERPRISE SOFTWARE, SOLIDWORKS, INTERACTS WITH VARIOUS SYSTEMS TO LINK CAD DESIGNS TO THE BILL OF MATERIALS FOR ENGINEERING PROJECTS. THE ERP SYSTEMS ALLOW COMPANIES TO SHARE INFORMATION ACROSS THE ORGANIZATION TO PREVENT ERRORS AND OMIT REDUNDANCY, THUS IMPROVING EFFICIENCY.

In addition to the demand for end products, customers also order specific parts and components either as spares or for service and repair. These demands are not usually part of the master production schedule; instead, they are fed directly into the material requirements planning program at the appropriate levels. That is, they are added in as a gross requirement for that part or component.

Bill of Materials

Bill of materials (BOM)

The **bill of materials (BOM)** file contains the complete product description, listing not only the materials, parts, and components but also the sequence in which the product is created. This BOM file is one of the three main inputs to the MRP program. (The other two are the master schedule and the inventory records file.)

The BOM file is often called the *product structure file* or *product tree* because it shows how a product is put together. It contains the information to identify each item and the quantity used per unit of the item of which it is a part. To illustrate this, consider Product A shown in Exhibit 14.6A. Product A is made of two units of Part B and three units of Part C. Part B is made of one unit of Part D and four units of Part E. Part C is made of two units of Part F, five units of Part G, and four units of Part H.

Bills of materials often list parts using an indented structure. This clearly identifies each item and the manner in which it is assembled because each indentation signifies the components of the item. A comparison of the indented parts in Exhibit 14.6B with the item structure in Exhibit 14.6A shows the ease of relating the two displays. From a computer standpoint,

exhibit 14.6   A. Bill of Materials (Product Structure Tree) for Product A

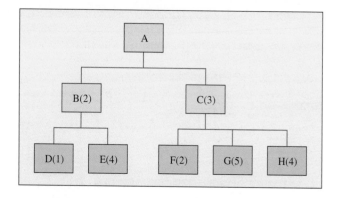

B. Parts List in an Indented Format and in a Single-Level List

INDENTED PARTS LIST	SINGLE-LEVEL PARTS LIST
A	A
B(2)	B(2)
D(1)	C(3)
E(4)	B
C(3)	D(1)
F(2)	E(4)
G(5)	C
H(4)	F(2)
	G(5)
	H(4)

exhibit 14.7

Product L Hierarchy in (A) Expanded to the Lowest Level of Each Item in (B)

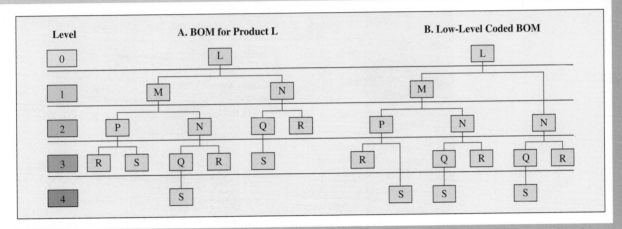

however, storing items in indented parts lists is very inefficient. To compute the amount of each item needed at the lower levels, each item would need to be expanded ("exploded") and summed. A more efficient procedure is to store parts data in simple single-level lists. That is, each item and component is listed showing only its parent and the number of units needed per unit of its parent. This avoids duplication because it includes each assembly only once. Exhibit 14.6B shows both the indented parts list and the single-level parts list for Product A.

A *modular* bill of materials is the term for a buildable item that can be produced and stocked as a subassembly. It is also a standard item with no options within the module. Many end items that are large and expensive are better scheduled and controlled as modules (or subassemblies). It is particularly advantageous to schedule subassembly modules when the same subassemblies appear in different end items. For example, a manufacturer of cranes can combine booms, transmissions, and engines in a variety of ways to meet a customer's needs. Using a modular bill of materials simplifies the scheduling and control and also makes it easier to forecast the use of different modules. Another benefit in using modular bills is that if the same item is used in a number of products, then the total inventory investment can be minimized.

A *super* bill of materials includes items with fractional options. (A super bill can specify, for example, 0.3 of a part. What that means is that 30 percent of the units produced contain that part and 70 percent do not.) Modular and super bills of materials are often referred to as planning bills of materials since they simplify the planning process.

Low-Level Coding If all identical parts occur at the same level for each end product, the total number of parts and materials needed for a product can be computed easily. Consider Product L shown in Exhibit 14.7A. Notice that Item N, for example, occurs both as an input to L and as an input to M. Item N, therefore, needs to be lowered to level 2 (Exhibit 14.7B) to bring all Ns to the same level. If all identical items are placed at the same level, it becomes a simple matter for the computer to scan across each level and summarize the number of units of each item required.

Inventory Records

The inventory records file can be quite lengthy. Exhibit 14.8 shows the variety of information contained in the inventory records. The MRP program accesses the *status* segment of

exhibit 14.8   The Inventory Status Record for an Item in Inventory

Item master data segment	Part no.		Description			Lead time			Std. cost		Safety stock		
	Order quantity			Setup		Cycle		Last year's usage			Class		
	Scrap allowance			Cutting data			Pointers			Etc.			

				Control balance	Period									Totals
					1	2	3	4	5	6	7	8		
Inventory status segment	Allocated													
	Gross requirements													
	Scheduled receipts													
	Projected available balance													
	Planned order releases													
Subsidiary data segment	Order details													
	Pending action													
	Counters													
	Keeping track													

the record according to specific time periods (called *time buckets* in MRP slang). These records are accessed as needed during the program run.

As we will see, the MRP program performs its analysis from the top of the product structure downward, calculating requirements level by level. There are times, however, when it is desirable to identify the parent item that caused the material requirement. The MRP program allows the creation of a *peg record* file either separately or as part of the inventory record file. Pegging requirements allows us to retrace a material requirement upward in the product structure through each level, identifying each parent item that created the demand.

Inventory Transactions File   The inventory status file is kept up to date by posting inventory transactions as they occur. These changes occur because of stock receipts and disbursements, scrap losses, wrong parts, canceled orders, and so forth.

MRP Computer Program

The material requirements planning program operates using information from the inventory records, the master schedule, and the bill of materials. The process of calculating the exact requirements for each item managed by the system is often referred to as the "explosion" process. Working from the top level downward in the bill of materials, requirements from parent items are used to calculate the requirements for component items. Consideration is taken of current on-hand balances and orders that are scheduled for receipt in the future.

The following is a general description of the MRP explosion process:

1. The requirements for level 0 items, typically referred to as "end items," are retrieved from the master schedule. These requirements are referred to as "gross requirements" by the MRP program. Typically, the gross requirements are scheduled in weekly time buckets.

2. Next, the program uses the current on-hand balance together with the schedule of orders that will be received in the future to calculate the "net requirements." Net

requirements are the amounts that are needed week by week in the future over and above what is currently on hand or committed to through an order already released and scheduled.

3. Using net requirements, the program calculates when orders should be received to meet these requirements. This can be a simple process of just scheduling orders to arrive according to the exact net requirements or a more complicated process where requirements are combined for multiple periods. This schedule of when orders should arrive is referred to as "planned-order receipts."

4. Since there is typically a lead time associated with each order, the next step is to find a schedule for when orders are actually released. Offsetting the "planned-order receipts" by the required lead time does this. This schedule is referred to as the "planned-order release."

5. After these four steps have been completed for all the level zero items, the program moves to level 1 items.

6. The gross requirements for each level 1 item are calculated from the planned-order release schedule for the parents of each level 1 item. Any additional independent demand also needs to be included in the gross requirements.

7. After the gross requirements have been determined, net requirements, planned-order receipts, and planned-order releases are calculated as described in steps 2–4 above.

8. This process is then repeated for each level in the bill of materials.

The process of doing these calculations is much simpler than the description, as you will see in the example that follows. Typically, the explosion calculations are performed each week or whenever changes have been made to the master schedule. Some MRP programs have the option of generating immediate schedules, called *net change* schedules. **Net change systems** are "activity" driven and requirements and schedules are updated whenever a transaction is processed that has an impact on the item. Net change enables the system to reflect in "real time" the exact status of each item managed by the system.

Net change systems

AN EXAMPLE USING MRP

Ampere, Inc., produces a line of electric meters installed in residential buildings by electric utility companies to measure power consumption. Meters used on single-family homes are of two basic types for different voltage and amperage ranges. In addition to complete meters, some subassemblies are sold separately for repair or for changeovers to a different voltage or power load. The problem for the MRP system is to determine a production schedule to identify each item, the period it is needed, and the appropriate quantities. The schedule is then checked for feasibility, and the schedule is modified if necessary.

Forecasting Demand

Demand for the meters and components originates from two sources: regular customers that place firm orders and unidentified customers that make the normal random demands for these items. The random requirements were forecast using one of the usual techniques described in Chapter 11 and past demand data. Exhibit 14.9 shows the requirements for meters A and B and Subassembly D for a three-month period (months three

Tutorial:
SAP R13

exhibit 14.9

Future Requirements for Meters A and B and Subassembly D Stemming from Specific Customer Orders and from Random Sources

Month	METER A		METER B		SUBASSEMBLY D	
	KNOWN	RANDOM	KNOWN	RANDOM	KNOWN	RANDOM
3	1,000	250	410	60	200	70
4	600	250	300	60	180	70
5	300	250	500	60	250	70

through five). There are some "other parts" used to make the meters. In order to keep our example manageable, we are not including them in this example.

Developing a Master Production Schedule

For the meter and component requirements specified in Exhibit 14.9, assume that the quantities to satisfy the known and random demands must be available during the first week of the month. This assumption is reasonable because management (in our example) prefers to produce meters in a single batch each month rather than a number of batches throughout the month.

Exhibit 14.10 shows the trial master schedule that we use under these conditions, with demand for months 3, 4, and 5 listed in the first week of each month, or as Weeks 9, 13, and 17. For brevity, we will work with demand through Week 9. The schedule we develop should be examined for resource availability, capacity availability, and so on, and then revised and run again. We will stop with our example at the end of this one schedule, however.

Bill of Materials (Product Structure)

The product structure for meters A and B is shown in Exhibit 14.11A in the typical way using low-level coding, in which each item is placed at the lowest level at which it appears in the structure hierarchy. Meters A and B consist of a common subassembly C and some parts that include part D. To keep things simple, we will focus on only one of the parts, part D, which is a transformer.

From the product structure, notice that part D (the transformer) is used in subassembly C (which is used in both meters A and B). In the case of meter A, an additional part D (transformer) is needed. The "2" in parentheses next to D when used to make a C indicates that

exhibit 14.10

A Master Schedule to Satisfy Demand Requirements as Specified in Exhibit 14.9

	Week								
	9	10	11	12	13	14	15	16	17
Meter A	1,250				850				550
Meter B	470				360				560
Subassembly D	270				250				320

exhibit 14.11

A. Product Structure for Meters A and B

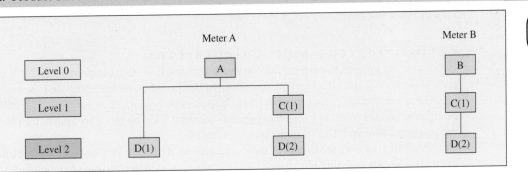

B. Indented Parts List for Meter A and Meter B, with the Required Number of Items per Unit of Parent Listed in Parentheses

METER A		METER B	
A		B	
D(1)		C(1)	
C(1)			D(2)
	D(2)		

Exhibit shows the subassemblies and parts that make up the meters and shows the numbers of units required per unit of parent in parentheses.

two D's are required for every C that is made. The product structure, as well as the indented parts list in Exhibit 14.11B, indicates how the meters are actually made. First, subassembly C is made, and potentially these are carried in inventory. In a final assembly process, meters A and B are put together, and in the case of meter A an additional part D is used.

Inventory Records

The inventory records data would be similar to that shown in Exhibit 14.8. As shown earlier in the chapter, additional data such as vendor identity, cost, and lead time also would be included in these data. For this example, the pertinent data include the on-hand inventory at the start of the program run, safety stock requirements, and the current status of orders that have already been released (see Exhibit 14.12). Safety stock is a minimum amount of inventory that we always want to keep on hand for an item. For example, for subassembly C, we never want the inventory to get below 5 units. We also see that we have

exhibit 14.12

Number of Units on Hand and Lead Time Data That Would Appear on the Inventory Record File

ITEM	ON-HAND INVENTORY	LEAD TIME (WEEKS)	SAFETY STOCK	ON ORDER
A	50	2	0	
B	60	2	0	10 (week 5)
C	40	1	5	
D	200	1	20	100 (week 4)

an order for 10 units of meter B that is scheduled for receipt at the beginning of Week 5. Another order for 100 units of part D (the transformer) is scheduled to arrive at the beginning of Week 4.

Performing the MRP Calculations

Conditions are now set to perform the MRP calculations: End-item requirements have been presented in the master production schedule, while the status of inventory and the order lead times are available, and we also have the pertinent product structure data. The MRP calculations (often referred to as an explosion) are done level by level, in conjunction with the inventory data and data from the master schedule.

Exhibit 14.13 shows the details of these calculations. The following analysis explains the logic in detail. We will limit our analysis to the problem of meeting the gross requirements for 1,250 units of meter A, 470 units of meter B, and 270 units of transformer D, all in Week 9.

An MRP record is kept for each item managed by the system. The record contains *gross requirements, scheduled receipts, projected available balance, net requirements, planned order receipts,* and *planned order releases* data. *Gross requirements* are the total amount

exhibit 14.13   Material Requirements Planning Schedule for Meters A and B, and Subassemblies C and D

Item		Week					
		4	5	6	7	8	9
A LT = 2 weeks On hand = 50 Safety stock = 0 Order qty = lot-for-lot	Gross requirements Scheduled receipts Projected available balance Net requirements Planned order receipts Planned order releases	50	50	50	50 1200	50	1250 50 1200 1200
B LT = 2 weeks On hand = 60 Safety stock = 0 Order qty = lot-for-lot	Gross requirements Scheduled receipts Projected available balance Net requirements Planned order receipts Planned order releases	60	10 60	70	70 400	70	470 70 400 400
C LT = 1 week On hand = 40 Safety stock = 5 Order qty = 2000	Gross requirements Scheduled receipts Projected available balance Net requirements Planned order receipts Planned order releases	35	35	35	400+ 1200 35 1565 2000	435	435
D LT = 1 week On hand = 200 Safety stock = 20 Order qty = 5000	Gross requirements Scheduled receipts Projected available balance Net requirements Planned order receipts Planned order releases	100 180	280 5000	4000 280 3720 5000	1200 1280	80 5000	270 80 190 5000

Tutorial: MRP

required for a particular item. These requirements can be from external customer demand and also from demand calculated due to manufacturing requirements. *Scheduled receipts* represent orders that have already been released and that are scheduled to arrive as of the beginning of the period. Once the paperwork on an order has been released, what was prior to that event a "planned" order now becomes a *scheduled receipt*. *Projected available balance* is the amount of inventory that is expected as of the end of a period. This can be calculated as follows:

$$\begin{array}{c} \text{Projected} \\ \text{available} \\ \text{balance}_t \end{array} = \begin{array}{c} \text{Projected} \\ \text{available} \\ \text{balance}_{t-1} \end{array} - \begin{array}{c} \text{Gross} \\ \text{requirements}_t \end{array} + \begin{array}{c} \text{Scheduled} \\ \text{receipts}_t \end{array} + \begin{array}{c} \text{Planned} \\ \text{order} \\ \text{receipts}_t \end{array} - \begin{array}{c} \text{Safety} \\ \text{stock} \end{array}$$

A *net requirement* is the amount needed when the *projected available* balance plus the *scheduled receipts* in a period are not sufficient to cover the *gross requirement*. The *planned order receipt* is the amount of an order that is required to meet a net requirement in the period. Finally, the *planned order release* is the planned order receipt offset by the lead time.

Beginning with meter A, the projected available balance is 50 units and there are no net requirements until Week 9. In Week 9, an additional 1,200 units are needed to cover the demand of 1,250 generated from the order scheduled through the master schedule. The order quantity is designated "lot-for-lot," which means that we can order the exact quantity needed to meet net requirements. An order, therefore, is planned for receipt of 1,200 units for the beginning of Week 9. Since the lead time is two weeks, this order must be released at the beginning of Week 7.

Meter B is similar to A, although an order for 10 units is scheduled for receipt in period 5. We project that 70 units will be available at the end of week 5. There is a net requirement for 400 additional units to meet the gross requirement of 470 units in Week 9. This requirement is met with an order for 400 units that must be released at the beginning of Week 7.

Item C is the subassembly used in both meters A and B. We only need additional C's when either A or B is being made. Our analysis of A indicates that an order for 1,200 will be released in Week 7. An order for 400 B's also will be released in Week 7, so total demand for C is 1,600 units in Week 7. The projected available balance is the 40 units on hand minus the safety stock of 5 units that we have specified, or 35 units. In Week 7, the net requirement is 1,565 units. The order policy for C indicates an order quantity of 2,000 units, so an order receipt for 2,000 is planned for Week 7. This order needs to be released in Week 6 due to the one-week lead time. Assuming this order is actually processed in the future, the projected available balance is 435 units in Weeks 7, 8, and 9.

Item D, the transformer, has demand from three different sources. The demand in Week 6 is due to the requirement to put D's into subassembly C. In this case two D's are needed for every C, or 4,000 units (the product structure indicates this two-to-one relationship). In the seventh week, 1,200 D's are needed for the order for 1,200 A's that are scheduled to be released in Week 7. Another 270 units are needed in Week 9 to meet the independent demand that is scheduled through the master schedule. Projected available balance at the end of Week 4 is 280 units (200 on hand plus the scheduled receipt of 100 units minus the safety stock of 20 units) and 280 units in Week 5. There is a net requirement for an additional 3,720 units in Week 6, so we plan to receive an order for 5,000 units (the order quantity). This results in a projected balance of 80 in Week 7 since 1,200 are used to meet demand. Eighty units are projected to be available in Week 8. Due to the demand for 270 in Week 9, a net requirement of 190 units in Week 9 results in planning the receipt of an additional 5,000-unit order in Week 9.

Example 14.1: MRP Explosion Calculations

Juno Lighting makes special lights that are popular in new homes. Juno expects demand for two popular lights to be the following over the next eight weeks.

	WEEK							
	1	2	3	4	5	6	7	8
VH1-234	34	37	41	45	48	48	48	48
VH2-100	104	134	144	155	134	140	141	145

A key component in both lights is a socket that the bulb is screwed into in the base fixture. Each light has one of these sockets. Given the following information, plan the production of the lights and purchases of the socket.

	VH1-234	VH2-100	LIGHT SOCKET
On hand	85	358	425
Q	200 (the production lot size)	400 (to production lot size)	500 (purchase quantity)
Lead time	1 week	1 week	3 weeks
Safety stock	0 units	0 units	20 units

SOLUTION

ITEM		WEEK							
		1	2	3	4	5	6	7	8
VH1-234	Gross requirement	34	37	41	45	48	48	48	48
Q = 200	Scheduled receipts								
LT = 1	Projected available balance	51	14	173	128	80	32	184	136
OH = 85	Net requirements			27				16	
SS = 0	Planned order receipts			200				200	
	Planned order releases		200				200		
VH2-100	Gross requirement	104	134	144	155	134	140	141	145
Q = 400	Scheduled receipts								
LT = 1	Projected available balance	254	120	376	221	87	347	206	61
OH = 358	Net requirements			24			53		
SS = 0	Planned order receipts			400			400		
	Planned order releases		400			400			
Socket	Gross requirement		600			400	200		
Q = 500	Scheduled receipts	500							
LT = 3	Projected available balance	905	305	305	305	405	205	205	205
OH = 425	Net requirements					95			
SS = 20	Planned order receipts					500			
	Planned order releases		500						●

The best way to proceed is to work period by period by focusing on the projected available balance calculation. Whenever the available balance goes below zero, a net requirement is generated. When this happens, plan an order receipt to meet the requirement. For example, for VH1 we start with 85 units in inventory and need 34 to meet Week 1 production requirements. This brings our available balance at the end of Week 1 to 51 units. Another 37 units are used during Week 2, dropping inventory to 14. In Week 3, our project balance drops to 0 and we have a net requirement of 27 units that needs to be covered with an order scheduled to be received in Week 3. Since the lead time is one week, this order needs to be released in Week 2. Week 4 projected available balance is 128, calculated by taking the 200 units that are received in Week 3 and subtracting the Week 3 net requirement of 27 units and the 45 units needed for Week 4.

Since sockets are used in both VH1 and VH2, the gross requirements come from the planned order releases for these items: 600 are needed in Week 2 (200 for VH1s and 400 for VH2s), 400 in Week 5, and 200 in Week 6. Projected available balance is beginning inventory of 425 plus the scheduled receipts of 500 units minus the 20 units of safety stock.

LOT SIZING IN MRP SYSTEMS

The determination of lot sizes in an MRP system is a complicated and difficult problem. Lot sizes are the part quantities issued in the planned order receipt and planned order release sections of an MRP schedule. For parts produced in-house, lot sizes are the production quantities of batch sizes. For purchased parts, these are the quantities ordered from the supplier. Lot sizes generally meet part requirements for one or more periods.

Most lot-sizing techniques deal with how to balance the setup or order costs and holding costs associated with meeting the net requirements generated by the MRP planning process. Many MRP systems have options for computing lot sizes based on some of the more commonly used techniques. The use of lot-sizing techniques increases the complexity of running MRP schedules in a plant. In an attempt to save setup costs, the inventory generated with the larger lot sizes needs to be stored making the logistics in the plant much more complicated.

Next we explain four lot-sizing techniques using a common example. The lot-sizing techniques presented are lot-for-lot (L4L), economic order quantity (EOQ), least total cost (LTC), and least unit cost (LUC).

Consider the following MRP lot-sizing problem; the net requirements are shown for eight scheduling weeks:

Cost per item	$10.00
Order or setup cost	$47.00
Inventory carrying cost/week	0.5%

Weekly net requirements:							
1	2	3	4	5	6	7	8
50	60	70	60	95	75	60	55

Lot-for-Lot

Lot-for-lot (L4L) is the most common technique. It

- Sets planned orders to exactly match the net requirements.
- Produces exactly what is needed each week with none carried over into future periods.
- Minimizes carrying cost.
- Does not take into account setup costs or capacity limitations.

Exhibit 14.14 shows the lot-for-lot calculations. The net requirements are given in column 2. Because the logic of lot-for-lot says the production quantity (column 3) will exactly match the required quantity (column 2), there will be no inventory left at the end (column 4). Without any inventory to carry over into the next week, there is zero holding

exhibit 14.14   Lot-for-Lot Run Size for an MRP Schedule

(1) WEEK	(2) NET REQUIREMENTS	(3) PRODUCTION QUANTITY	(4) ENDING INVENTORY	(5) HOLDING COST	(6) SETUP COST	(7) TOTAL COST
1	50	50	0	$0.00	$47.00	$ 47.00
2	60	60	0	0.00	47.00	94.00
3	70	70	0	0.00	47.00	141.00
4	60	60	0	0.00	47.00	188.00
5	95	95	0	0.00	47.00	235.00
6	75	75	0	0.00	47.00	282.00
7	60	60	0	0.00	47.00	329.00
8	55	55	0	0.00	47.00	376.00

cost (column 5). However, lot-for-lot requires a setup cost each week (column 6). Incidentally, there is a setup cost each week because this is a work center where a variety of items are worked on each week. This is not a case where the work center is committed to one product and sits idle when it is not working on that product (in which case only one setup would result). Lot-for-lot causes high setup costs.

Economic Order Quantity

In Chapter 13 we already discussed the EOQ model that explicitly balances setup and holding costs. In an EOQ model, either fairly constant demand must exist or safety stock must be kept to provide for demand variability. The EOQ model uses an estimate of total annual demand, the setup or order cost, and the annual holding cost. EOQ was not designed for a system with discrete time periods such as MRP. The lot-sizing techniques used for MRP assume that part requirements are satisfied at the start of the period. Holding costs are then charged only to the ending inventory for the period, not to the average inventory as in the case of the EOQ model. EOQ assumes that parts are used continuously during the period. The lot sizes generated by EOQ do not always cover the entire number of periods. For example, the EOQ might provide the requirements for 4.6 periods. Using the same data as in the lot-for-lot example, the economic order quantity is calculated as follows:

$$\text{Annual demand based on the 8 weeks} = D = \frac{525}{8} \times 52 = 3{,}412.5 \text{ units}$$

$$\text{Annual holding cost} = H = 0.5\% \times \$10 \times 52 \text{ weeks} = \$2.60 \text{ per unit}$$

$$\text{Setup cost} = S = \$47 \text{ (given)}$$

$$\therefore \text{EOQ} = \sqrt{\frac{2DS}{H}} = \sqrt{\frac{2(3{,}412.5)(\$47)}{\$2.60}} = 351 \text{ units}$$

Exhibit 14.15 shows the MRP schedule using an EOQ of 351 units. The EOQ lot size in Week 1 is enough to meet requirements for Weeks 1 through 5 and a portion of Week 6. Then, in Week 6 another EOQ lot is planned to meet the requirements for Weeks 6 through 8. Notice that the EOQ plan leaves some inventory at the end of Week 8 to carry forward into Week 9.

Least Total Cost

The least total cost method (LTC) is a dynamic lot-sizing technique that calculates the order quantity by comparing the carrying cost and the setup (or ordering) costs for various lot sizes and then selects the lot in which these are most nearly equal.

Economic Order Quantity Run Size for an MRP Schedule

exhibit 14.15

WEEK	NET REQUIREMENTS	PRODUCTION QUANTITY	ENDING INVENTORY	HOLDING COST	SETUP COST	TOTAL COST
1	50	351	301	$15.05	$47.00	$ 62.05
2	60	0	241	12.05	0.00	74.10
3	70	0	171	8.55	0.00	82.65
4	60	0	111	5.55	0.00	88.20
5	95	0	16	0.80	0.00	89.00
6	75	351	292	14.60	47.00	150.60
7	60	0	232	11.60	0.00	162.20
8	55	0	177	8.85	0.00	171.05

Least Total Cost Run Size for an MRP Schedule

exhibit 14.16

WEEKS	QUANTITY ORDERED	CARRYING COST	ORDER COST	TOTAL COST	
1	50	$0.00	$47.00	$47.00	
1–2	110	3.00	47.00	50.00	
1–3	180	10.00	47.00	57.00	
1–4	240	19.00	47.00	66.00	1st order
1–5	335	38.00	47.00	85.00 ← Least total cost	
1–6	410	56.75	47.00	103.75	
1–7	470	74.75	47.00	121.75	
1–8	525	94.00	47.00	141.00	
6	75	0.00	47.00	47.00	
6–7	135	3.00	47.00	50.00	2nd order
6–8	190	8.50	47.00	55.50 ← Least total cost	

WEEK	NET REQUIREMENTS	PRODUCTION QUANTITY	ENDING INVENTORY	HOLDING COST	SETUP COST	TOTAL COST
1	50	335	285	$14.25	$47.00	$ 61.25
2	60	0	225	11.25	0.00	72.50
3	70	0	155	7.75	0.00	80.25
4	60	0	95	4.75	0.00	85.00
5	95	0	0	0.00	0.00	85.00
6	75	190	115	5.75	47.00	137.75
7	60	0	55	2.75	0.00	140.50
8	55	0	0	0.00	0.00	140.05

The top half of Exhibit 14.16 shows the least cost lot size results. The procedure to compute least total cost lot sizes is to compare order costs and holding costs for various numbers of weeks. For example, costs are compared for producing in Week 1 to cover the requirements for Week 1; producing in Week 1 for Weeks 1 and 2; producing in Week 1 to cover Weeks 1, 2, and 3, and so on. The correct selection is the lot size where the ordering costs and holding costs are approximately equal. In Exhibit 14.16 the best lot size is 335 because a $38 carrying cost and a $47 ordering cost are closer than $56.75 and $47 ($9 versus $9.75). This lot size covers requirements for Weeks 1 through 5. Unlike EOQ, the lot size covers only whole numbers of periods.

Based on the Week 1 decision to place an order to cover five weeks, we are now located in Week 6, and our problem is to determine how many weeks into the future we can provide for from here. Exhibit 14.16 shows that holding and ordering costs are closest in the quantity that covers requirements for Weeks 6 through 8. Notice that the holding and ordering costs here are far apart. This is because our example extends only to Week 8. If the planning horizon were longer, the lot size planned for Week 6 would likely cover more weeks into the future beyond Week 8. This brings up one of the limitations of both LTC and LUC (discussed below). Both techniques are influenced by the length of the planning horizon. The bottom half of Exhibit 14.16 shows the final run size and total cost.

Least Unit Cost

The least unit cost method is a dynamic lot-sizing technique that adds ordering and inventory carrying cost for each trial lot size and divides by the number of units in each lot size, picking the lot size with the lowest unit cost. The top half of Exhibit 14.17 calculates the unit cost for ordering lots to meet the needs of Weeks 1 through 8. Note that the minimum occurred when the quantity 410, ordered in Week 1, was sufficient to cover Weeks 1 through 6. The lot size planned for Week 7 covers through the end of the planning horizon.

The least unit cost run size and total cost are shown in the bottom half of Exhibit 14.17.

exhibit 14.17   Least Unit Cost Run Size for an MRP Schedule

WEEKS	QUANTITY ORDERED	CARRYING COST	ORDER COST	TOTAL COST	UNIT COST	
1	50	$ 0.00	$ 47.00	$ 47.00	$0.9400	
1–2	110	3.00	47.00	50.00	0.4545	
1–3	180	10.00	47.00	57.00	0.3167	
1–4	240	19.00	47.00	66.00	0.2750	
1–5	335	38.00	47.00	85.00	0.2537	1st order
1–6	410	56.75	47.00	103.75	0.2530	← Least unit cost
1–7	470	74.75	47.00	121.75	0.2590	
1–8	525	94.00	47.00	141.00	0.2686	
?	60	0.00	47.00	47.00	0.7833	2nd order
7–8	115	2.75	47.00	49.75	0.4326	← Least unit cost

WEEK	NET REQUIREMENTS	PRODUCTION QUANTITY	ENDING INVENTORY	HOLDING COST	SETUP COST	TOTAL COST
1	50	410	360	$18.00	$ 47.00	$ 65.00
2	60	0	300	15.00	0.00	80.00
3	70	0	230	11.50	0.00	91.50
4	60	0	170	8.50	0.00	100.00
5	95	0	75	3.75	0.00	103.75
6	75	0	0	0	0	103.75
7	60	115	55	2.75	47.00	153.50
8	55	0	0	0	0	$ 153.50

Choosing the Best Lot Size

Using the lot-for-lot method, the total cost for the eight weeks is $376; the EOQ total cost is $171.05; the least total cost method is $140.50; and the least unit cost is $153.50. The lowest cost was obtained using the least total cost method of $140.50. If there were more than eight weeks, the lowest cost could differ.

The advantage of the least unit cost method is that it is a more complete analysis and would take into account ordering or setup costs that might change as the order size increases. If the ordering or setup costs remain constant, the lowest total cost method is more attractive because it is simpler and easier to compute; yet it would be just as accurate under that restriction.

SUMMARY

Since the 1970s, MRP has grown from its original purpose of determining simple time schedules for production and material procurement to its present use as an integral part of enterprise resource planning that ties together all the major functions of a firm. MRP has proved to be a flexible platform that has been adapted to many different situations, including repetitive manufacturing using just-in-time systems.

In this chapter the basic concepts needed to understand MRP have been covered. The MRP engine takes information from a master schedule that is a detailed plan for future production. Depending on the needs of the firm, the master schedule can be stated in terms of individual products, generic products, or modules and subassemblies. Master scheduling is part of the sales and operations planning process that is critical to implementing the firm's operations strategy successfully.

The bill of materials depicts exactly how a firm makes the items in the master schedule. The "structure" of the bill of materials (sometimes referred to as the "product structure") captures how raw materials and purchased parts come together to form subassemblies and how those subassembles are brought together to make the items in the master schedule.

The MRP "explosion" process is the heart of the system. Using the master schedule and bill of materials, together with the current inventory status (amount on-hand and on-order) of each part in the bill of materials, detailed schedules are calculated that show the exact timing of needed parts in the future. In a typical company, this process can require a significant computation effort involving literally thousands of detailed schedules.

In this chapter, the important topic of how to consider inventory-related costs was addressed. A number of common MRP lot-sizing rules were described that consider the fixed cost and variable cost trade-off that can be significant in minimizing inventory costs.

Key Terms

Enterprise resource planning (ERP) A computer system that integrates application programs in accounting, sales, manufacturing, and the other functions in a firm. This integration is accomplished through a database shared by all the application programs.

Material requirements planning (MRP) The logic for determining the number of parts, components, and materials needed to produce a product. MRP also provides the schedule specifying when each of these materials, parts, and components should be ordered or produced.

Master production schedule (MPS) A time-phased plan specifying how many and when the firm plans to build each end item.

Available to promise A feature of MRP systems that identifies the difference between the number of units currently included in the master schedule and the actual (firm) customer orders.

Bill of materials (BOM) A computer file that contains the complete product description, listing the materials, parts, and components and the sequence in which the product is created.

Net change system An MRP system that calculates the impact of a change in the MRP data (the inventory status, BOM, or master schedule) immediately. This is a common feature in current systems.

Solved Problems

SOLVED PROBLEM 1

Product X is made of two units of Y and three of Z. Y is made of one unit of A and two units of B. Z is made of two units of A and four units of C.

Lead time for X is one week; Y, two weeks; Z, three weeks; A, two weeks; B, one week; and C, three weeks.

a. Draw the bill of materials (product structure tree).

b. If 100 units of X are needed in week 10, develop a planning schedule showing when each item should be ordered and in what quantity.

Solution

a.

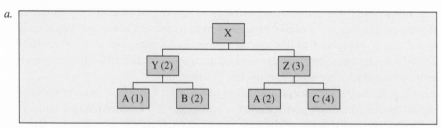

b.

		3	4	5	6	7	8	9	10
X	LT = 1							100	100
Y	LT = 2					200		200	
Z	LT = 3				300			300	
A	LT = 2			600	600	200			
					200				
B	LT = 1				400	400			
C	LT = 3	1200			1200				

SOLVED PROBLEM 2

Product M is made of two units of N and three of P. N is made of two units of R and four units of S. R is made of one unit of S and three units of T. P is made of two units of T and four units of U.

a. Show the bill of materials (product structure tree).

b. If 100 M are required, how many units of each component are needed?

c. Show both a single-level parts list and an indented parts list.

Solution

a.

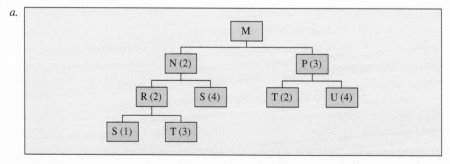

b. M = 100   S = 800 + 400 = 1,200
    N = 200   T = 600 + 1,200 = 1,800
    P = 300   U = 1,200
    R = 400

c.

SINGLE-LEVEL PARTS LIST		INDENTED PARTS LIST	
M		M	
	N (2)	N(2)	
	P (3)		R(2)
N			S (1)
	R (2)		T (3)
	S (4)	S (4)	
R		P (3)	
	S (1)		T (2)
	T (3)		U (4)
P			
	T (2)		
	U (4)		

Review and Discussion Questions

1 Discuss the meaning of MRP terms such as *planned order release* and *scheduled order receipt.*
2 Many practitioners currently update MRP weekly or biweekly. Would it be more valuable if it were updated daily? Discuss.
3 What is the role of safety stock in an MRP system?
4 Contrast the significance of the term *lead time* in the traditional EOQ context and in an MRP system.
5 Discuss the importance of the master production schedule in an MRP system.
6 "MRP just prepares shopping lists. It does not do the shopping or cook the dinner." Comment.
7 What are the sources of demand in an MRP system? Are these dependent or independent, and how are they used as inputs to the system?
8 State the types of data that would be carried in the bill of materials file and the inventory record file.

Problems

1 Semans is a manufacturer that produces bracket assemblies. Demand for bracket assemblies (X) is 130 units. The following is the BOM in indented form:

ITEM	DESCRIPTION	USAGE
X	Bracket assembly	1
A	Wall board	4
B	Hanger subassembly	2
D	Hanger casting	3
E	Ceramic knob	1
C	Rivet head screw	3
F	Metal tong	4
G	Plastic cap	2

Below is a table indicating current inventory levels:

Item	X	A	B	C	D	E	F	G
Inventory	25	16	60	20	180	160	1000	100

a. Using Excel, create the MRP using the product tree structure.

b. What are the net requirements of each item in the MPS?

2 In the following MRP planning schedule for Item J, indicate the correct net requirements, planned order receipts, and planned order releases to meet the gross requirements. Lead time is one week.

ITEM J	WEEK NUMBER					
	0	1	2	3	4	5
Gross requirements			75		50	70
On-hand	40					
Net requirements						
Planned order receipt						
Planned order release						

3 Repeat Solved Problem 1 using current on-hand inventories of 20 X, 40 Y, 30 Z, 50 A, 100 B, and 900 C.

4 Assume that Product Z is made of two units of A and four units of B. A is made of three units of C and four D. D is made of two units of E.

Lead times for purchase or fabrication of each unit to final assembly are: Z takes two weeks; A, B, C, and D take one week each; and E takes three weeks.

Fifty units are required in Period 10. (Assume that there is currently no inventory on hand of any of these items.)

a. Show the bill of materials (product structure tree).

b. Develop an MRP planning schedule showing gross and net requirements and order release and order receipt dates.

5 *Note:* For Problems 5 through 10, to simplify data handling to include the receipt of orders that have actually been placed in previous periods, the following six-level scheme can be used. (A number of different techniques are used in practice, but the important issue is to keep track of what is on hand, what is expected to arrive, what is needed, and what size orders should be placed.) One way to calculate the numbers is as follows:

WEEK
Gross requirements
Scheduled receipts
Projected available balance
Net requirements
Planned order receipt
Planned order release

One unit of A is made of three units of B, one unit of C, and two units of D. B is composed of two units of E and one unit of D. C is made of one unit of B and two units of E. E is made of one unit of F.

Items B, C, E, and F have one-week lead times; A and D have lead times of two weeks.

Assume that lot-for-lot (L4L) lot sizing is used for Items A, B, and F; lots of size 50, 50, and 200 are used for Items C, D, and E, respectively. Items C, E, and F have on-hand (beginning) inventories of 10, 50, and 150, respectively; all other items have zero beginning inventory. We are scheduled to receive 10 units of A in Week 2, 50 units of E in Week 1, and also 50 units of F in Week 1. There are no other scheduled receipts. If 30 units of A are required in Week 8, use the low-level-coded bill of materials to find the necessary planned order releases for all components.

6 One unit of A is made of two units of B, three units of C, and two units of D. B is composed of one unit of E and two units of F. C is made of two units of F and one unit of D. E is made of two units of D. Items A, C, D, and F have one-week lead times; B and E have lead times of two weeks. Lot-for-lot (L4L) lot sizing is used for Items A, B, C, and D; lots of size 50 and 180 are used for Items E and F, respectively. Item C has an on-hand (beginning) inventory of 15; D has an on-hand inventory of 50; all other items have zero beginning inventory. We are scheduled to receive 20 units of Item E in Week 2; there are no other scheduled receipts.

Construct simple and low-level-coded bills of materials (product structure tree) and indented and summarized parts lists.

If 20 units of A are required in Week 8, use the low-level-coded bill of materials to find the necessary planned order releases for all components. (See the note in Problem 5.)

7 One unit of A is made of one unit of B and one unit of C. B is made of four units of C and one unit each of E and F. C is made of two units of D and one unit of E. E is made of three units of F. Item C has a lead time of one week; Items A, B, E, and F have two-week lead times; and Item D has a lead time of three weeks. Lot-for-lot lot sizing is used for Items A, D, and E; lots of size 50, 100, and 50 are used for Items B, C, and F, respectively. Items A, C, D, and E have on-hand (beginning) inventories of 20, 50, 100, and 10, respectively; all other items have zero beginning inventory. We are scheduled to receive 10 units of A in Week 1, 100 units of C in Week 1, and 100 units of D in Week 3; there are no other scheduled receipts. If 50 units of A are required in Week 10, use the low-level-coded bill of materials (product structure tree) to find the necessary planned order releases for all components. (See the note in Problem 5.)

8 One unit of A is made of two units of B and one unit of C. B is made of three units of D and one unit of F. C is composed of three units of B, one unit of D, and four units of E. D is made of one unit of E. Item C has a lead time of one week; Items A, B, E, and F have two-week lead times; and Item D has a lead time of three weeks. Lot-for-lot lot sizing is used for Items C, E, and F; lots of size 20, 40, and 160 are used for Items A, B, and D, respectively. Items A, B, D, and E have on-hand (beginning) inventories of 5, 10, 100, and 100, respectively; all other items have zero beginning inventories. We are scheduled to receive 10 units of A in Week 3, 20 units of B in Week 7, 40 units of F in Week 5, and 60 units of E in Week 2; there are no other scheduled receipts. If 20 units of A are required in Week 10, use the low-level-coded bill of materials (product structure tree) to find the necessary planned order releases for all components. (See the note in Problem 5.)

9 One unit of A is composed of 2 units of B and three units of C. Each B is composed of one unit of F. C is made of one unit of D, one unit of E, and two units of F. Items A, B, C, and D have 20, 50, 60, and 25 units of on-hand inventory. Items A, B, and C use lot-for-lot (L4L) as their lot-sizing technique, while D, E, and F require multiples of 50, 100, and 100, respectively, to be purchased. B has scheduled receipts of 30 units in Period 1. No other scheduled receipts exist. Lead times are one period for Items A, B, and D, and two periods for Items C, E, and F. Gross requirements for A are 20 units in Period 1, 20 units in Period 2, 60 units in Period 6, and 50 units in Period 8. Find the planned order releases for all items.

10 Each unit of A is composed of one unit of B, two units of C, and one unit of D. C is composed of two units of D and three units of E. Items A, C, D, and E have on-hand inventories of 20, 10, 20, and 10 units, respectively. Item B has a scheduled receipt of 10 units in Period 1, and C has a scheduled receipt of 50 units in Period 1. Lot-for-lot (L4L) is used for Items A and B. Item C requires a minimum lot size of 50 units. D and E are required to be purchased in multiples of 100 and 50, respectively. Lead times are one period for Items A, B, and C, and two periods for Items D and E. The gross requirements for A are 30 in Period 2, 30 in Period 5, and 40 in Period 8. Find the planned order releases for all items.

11   The MRP gross requirements for Item A are shown here for the next 10 weeks. Lead time for A is three weeks and setup cost is $10. There is a carrying cost of $0.01 per unit per week. Beginning inventory is 90 units.

						WEEK					
	1	2	3	4	5	6	7	8	9	10
Gross requirements	30	50	10	20	70	80	20	60	200	50

Use the least total cost or the least unit cost lot-sizing method to determine when and for what quantity the first order should be released.

12   Product A is an end item and is made from two units of B and four of C. B is made of three units of D and two of E. C is made of two units of F and two of E.

A has a lead time of one week. B, C, and E have lead times of two weeks, and D and F have lead times of three weeks.

a. Show the bill of materials (product structure tree).

b. If 100 units of A are required in Week 10, develop the MRP planning schedule, specifying when items are to be ordered and received. There are currently no units of inventory on hand.

13   Product A consists of two units of Subassembly B, three units of C, and one unit of D. B is composed of four units of E and three units of F. C is made of two units of H and three units of D. H is made of five units of E and two units of G.

a. Construct a simple bill of materials (product structure tree).

b. Construct a product structure tree using low-level coding.

c. Construct an indented parts list.

d. To produce 100 units of A, determine the numbers of units of B, C, D, E, F, G, and H required.

14   The MRP gross requirements for Item X are shown here for the next 10 weeks. Lead time for A is two weeks, and setup cost is $9. There is a carrying cost of $0.02 per unit per week. Beginning inventory is 70 units.

						WEEK					
	1	2	3	4	5	6	7	8	9	10
Gross requirements	20	10	15	45	10	30	100	20	40	150

Use the least total cost or the least unit cost lot-sizing method to determine when and for what quantity the first order should be released.

15   Audio Products, Inc., produces two AM/FM/CD players for cars. The radio/CD units are identical, but the mounting hardware and finish trim differ. The standard model fits intermediate and full-size cars, and the sports model fits small sports cars.

Audio Products handles the production in the following way. The chassis (radio/CD unit) is assembled in Mexico and has a manufacturing lead time of two weeks. The mounting hardware is purchased from a sheet steel company and has a three-week lead time. The finish trim is purchased from a Taiwan electronics company with offices in Los Angeles as prepackaged units consisting of knobs and various trim pieces. Trim packages have a two-week lead time. Final assembly time may be disregarded because adding the trim package and mounting are performed by the customer.

Audio Products supplies wholesalers and retailers, who place specific orders for both models up to eight weeks in advance. These orders, together with enough additional units to satisfy the small number of individual sales, are summarized in the following demand schedule:

MODEL	WEEK							
	1	2	3	4	5	6	7	8
Standard model				300				400
Sports model					200			100

There are currently 50 radio/CD units on hand but no trim packages or mounting hardware.

Prepare a material requirements plan to meet the demand schedule exactly. Specify the gross and net requirements, on-hand amounts, and the planned order release and receipt periods for the radio/CD chassis, the standard trim and sports car model trim, and the standard mounting hardware and the sports car mounting hardware.

CASE: Brunswick Motors, Inc.— An Introductory Case for MRP

Recently, Phil Harris, the production control manager at Brunswick, read an article on time-phased requirements planning. He was curious about how this technique might work in scheduling Brunswick's engine assembly operations and decided to prepare an example to illustrate the use of time-phased requirements planning.

Phil's first step was to prepare a master schedule for one of the engine types produced by Brunswick: the Model 1000 engine. This schedule indicates the number of units of the Model 1000 engine to be assembled each week during the last 12 weeks and is shown below. Next, Phil decided to simplify his requirements planning example by considering only two of the many components that are needed to complete the assembly of the Model 1000 engine. These two components, the gear box and the input shaft, are shown in the product structure diagram shown on the next page. Phil noted that the gear box is assembled by the Subassembly Department and subsequently is sent to the main engine assembly line. The input shaft is one of several component parts manufactured by Brunswick that are needed to produce a gear box subassembly. Thus, levels 0, 1, and 2 are included in the product structure diagram to indicate the three manufacturing stages that are involved in producing an engine: the Engine Assembly Department, the Subassembly Department, and the Machine Shop.

The manufacturing lead times required to produce the gear box and input shaft components are also indicated in the product structure diagram. Note that two weeks are required to produce a batch of gear boxes and that all the gear boxes must be delivered to the assembly line parts stockroom before Monday morning of the week in which they are to be used. Likewise, it takes three weeks to produce a lot of input shafts, and all the shafts that are needed for the production of gear boxes in a given week must be delivered to the Subassembly Department stockroom before Monday morning of that week.

In preparing the MRP example Phil planned to use the worksheets shown on the next page and make the following assumptions:

1. Seventeen gear boxes are on hand at the beginning of week 1, and five gear boxes are currently on order to be delivered at the start of week 2.
2. Forty input shafts are on hand at the start of week 1, and 22 are scheduled for delivery at the beginning of week 2.

Assignment

1. Initially, assume that Phil wants to minimize his inventory requirements. Assume that each order will be only for what is required for a single period. Using the following forms, calculate the net requirements and planned order releases for the gear boxes and input shafts. Assume that lot sizing is done using lot-for-lot.
2. Phil would like to consider the costs that his accountants are currently using for inventory carrying and setup for the gear boxes and input shafts. These costs are as follows:

PART	COST
Gear Box	Setup = $90/order
	Inventory carrying cost = $2/unit/week
Input Shaft	Setup = $45/order
	Inventory carrying cost = $1/unit/week

Given the cost structure, evaluate the cost of the schedule from (1). Assume inventory is valued at the end of each week.

3. Calculate a schedule using least-total-cost lot sizing. What are the savings with this new schedule?

Model 1000 master schedule

Week	1	2	3	4	5	6	7	8	9	10	11	12
Demand	15	5	7	10		15	20	10		8	2	16

Model 1000 product structure

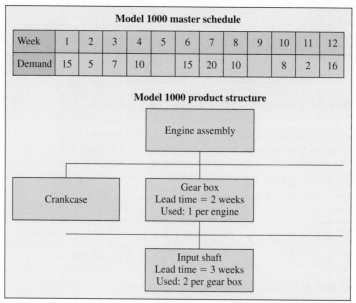

Engine assembly master schedule

Week	1	2	3	4	5	6	7	8	9	10	11	12
Quantity												

Gear box requirements

Week	1	2	3	4	5	6	7	8	9	10	11	12
Gross requirements												
Scheduled receipts												
Projected available balance												
Net requirements												
Planned order release												

Input shaft requirements

Week	1	2	3	4	5	6	7	8	9	10	11	12
Gross requirements												
Scheduled receipts												
Projected available balance												
Net requirements												
Planned order release												

S u p e r   Q u i z

1 Term used for a computer system that integrates application programs for the different functions in a firm.

2 Logic used to calculate the needed parts, components, and other materials needed to produce an end item.

3 This drives the MRP calculations and is a detailed plan for how we expect to meet demand.

4 Period of time during which a customer has a specified level of opportunity to make changes.

5 This identifies the specific materials used to make each item and the correct quantities of each.

6 If an item is used in two places in a bill of material, say level 3 and level 4, what low-level code would be assigned to the item?

7 One unit of Part C is used in item A and in item B. Currently, we have 10 A's, 20 B's, and 100 C's in inventory. We want to ship 60 A's and 70 B's. How many additional C's do we need to purchase?

8 These are orders that have already been released and are to arrive in the future.

9 This is the total amount required for a particular item.

10 This is the amount needed after considering what we currently have in inventory and what we expect to arrive in the future.

11 The planned order receipt and planned order release are offset by this amount of time.

12 These are the part quantities issued in the planned order release section of an MRP report.

13 Ordering exactly what is needed each period without regard to economic considerations.

14 None of the techniques for determining order quantity consider this important noneconomic factor that could make the order quantity infeasible.

1. Enterprise resource planning (ERP) 2. Material requirements planning (MRP) 3. Master schedule 4. Time fence 5. Bill of materials 6. Level 4 7. Zero 8. Scheduled receipts 9. Gross requirements 10. Net requirements 11. Lead time 12. Lot sizes 13. Lot-for-lot ordering 14. Capacity

Selected Bibliography

Orlicky, J. *Materials Requirements Planning*. 2nd ed. New York: McGraw-Hill, 1994. (This is the classic book on MRP)

Sheikh, K. *Manufacturing Resource Planning (MRP II) with Introduction to ERP, SCM, and CRM*. New York: McGraw-Hill, 2002.

Vollmann, T. E.; W. L. Berry; D. C. Whybark; and F. R. Jacobs. *Manufacturing Planning and Control Systems for Supply Chain Management*. 5th ed. Burr Ridge, IL: McGraw-Hill, 2004.

LINEAR PROGRAMMING USING THE EXCEL SOLVER

462   Introduction

Linear programming (LP) defined

463   The Linear Programming Model

464   Graphical Linear Programming

Graphical linear programming defined

466   Linear Programming Using Microsoft Excel

The key to profitable operations is making the best use of available resources of people, material, plant and equipment, and money. Today's manager has a powerful mathematical modeling tool available for this purpose with linear programming. In this appendix, we will show how the use of the Microsoft Excel Solver to solve LP problems opens a whole new world to the innovative manager and provides an invaluable addition to the technical skill set for those who seek careers in consulting. We introduce the use of this tool using a product-planning problem. Here we find the optimal mix of products that have different costs and resource requirements. This problem is certainly relevant to today's competitive market. Truly successful companies provide a mix of products, from standard to high-end luxury models. All these products compete for the use of limited production and other capacity. Maintaining the proper mix of these products over time can significantly bolster earnings and the return on a firm's assets.

We begin with a quick introduction to linear programming and conditions under which the technique is applicable. Then we solve a simple product-mix problem.

INTRODUCTION

Linear programming (or simply **LP**) refers to several related mathematical techniques used to allocate limited resources among competing demands in an optimal way. LP is the most popular of the approaches falling under the general heading of mathematical optimization techniques and has been applied to many operations management problems. The following are typical applications:

Aggregate sales and operations planning: Finding the minimum-cost production schedule. The problem is to develop a three- to six-month plan for meeting expected demand given constraints on expected production capacity and workforce size. Relevant costs considered in the problem include regular and overtime labor rates, hiring and firing, subcontracting, and inventory carrying cost.

Service/manufacturing productivity analysis: Comparing how efficiently different service and manufacturing outlets are using their resources compared to the best-performing unit. This is done using an approach called data envelopment analysis.

Product planning: Finding the optimal product mix where several products have different costs and resource requirements. Examples include finding the optimal blend of chemicals for gasoline, paints, human diets, and animal feeds. Examples of this problem are covered in this appendix.

Product routing: Finding the optimal way to produce a product that must be processed sequentially through several machine centers, with each machine in the center having its own cost and output characteristics.

Vehicle/crew scheduling: Finding the optimal way to use resources such as aircraft, buses, or trucks and their operating crews to provide transportation services to customers and materials to be moved between different locations.

Process control: Minimizing the amount of scrap material generated by cutting steel, leather, or fabric from a roll or sheet of stock material.

Inventory control: Finding the optimal combination of products to stock in a network of warehouses or storage locations.

Distribution scheduling: Finding the optimal shipping schedule for distributing products between factories and warehouses or between warehouses and retailers.

Plant location studies: Finding the optimal location of a new plant by evaluating shipping costs between alternative locations and supply and demand sources.

Material handling: Finding the minimum-cost routings of material handling devices (such as forklift trucks) between departments in a plant, or hauling materials from a supply yard to work sites by trucks, for example. Each truck might have different capacity and performance capabilities.

Linear programming is gaining wide acceptance in many industries due to the availability of detailed operating information and the interest in optimizing processes to reduce cost. Many software vendors offer optimization options to be used with enterprise resource planning systems. Some firms refer to these as *advanced planning option, synchronized planning,* and *process optimization.*

There are five essential conditions in a problem situation for linear programming to pertain. First, there must be *limited resources* (such as a limited number of workers, equipment, finances, and material); otherwise there would be no problem. Second, there must be an *explicit objective* (such as maximize profit or minimize cost). Third, there must be *linearity* (two is twice as much as one; if it takes three hours to make a part, then two parts would take six hours and three parts would take nine hours). Fourth, there must be *homogeneity* (the products produced on a machine are identical, or all the hours available from a worker are equally productive). Fifth, there must be *divisibility:* Normal linear programming assumes products and resources can be subdivided into fractions. If this subdivision is not possible (such as flying half an airplane or hiring one-fourth of a person), a modification of linear programming, called *integer programming,* can be used.

When a single objective is to be maximized (like profit) or minimized (like costs), we can use linear programming. When multiple objectives exist, *goal programming* is used. If a problem is best solved in stages or time frames, *dynamic programming* is employed. Other restrictions on the nature of the problem may require that it be solved by other variations of the technique, such as *nonlinear programming* or *quadratic programming.*

THE LINEAR PROGRAMMING MODEL

Stated formally, the linear programming problem entails an optimizing process in which nonnegative values for a set of decision variables $X_1, X_2,\ldots, X_n$ are selected so as to maximize (or minimize) an objective function in the form

$$\text{Maximize (minimize) } Z = C_1X_1 + C_2X_2 + \cdots + C_nX_n$$

subject to resource constraints in the form

$$A_{11}X_1 + A_{12}X_2 + \cdots + A_{1n}X_n \le B_1$$
$$A_{21}X_1 + A_{22}X_2 + \cdots + A_{2n}X_n \le B_2$$
$$\vdots$$
$$A_{m1}X_1 + A_{m2}X_2 + \cdots + A_{mn}X_n \le B_m$$

where C_n, A_{mn}, and B_m are given constants.

Depending on the problem, the constraints also may be stated with equal signs ($=$) or greater-than-or-equal-to signs ($\ge$).

Example A.1: Puck and Pawn Company

We describe the steps involved in solving a simple linear programming model in the context of a sample problem, that of Puck and Pawn Company, which manufactures hockey sticks and chess sets. Each hockey stick yields an incremental profit of $2, and each chess set, $4. A hockey stick requires 4 hours of processing at machine center A and 2 hours at machine center B. A chess set requires 6 hours at machine center A, 6 hours at machine center B, and 1 hour at machine center C. Machine center A has a maximum of 120 hours of available capacity per day, machine center B has 72 hours, and machine center C has 10 hours.

If the company wishes to maximize profit, how many hockey sticks and chess sets should be produced per day?

**Tutorial:
Intro to
Solver**

Step by Step

SOLUTION

Formulate the problem in mathematical terms. If H is the number of hockey sticks and C is the number of chess sets, to maximize profit the objective function may be stated as

$$\text{Maximize } Z = \$2H + \$4C$$

The maximization will be subject to the following constraints:

$$4H + 6C \leq 120 \text{ (machine center A constraint)}$$
$$2H + 6C \leq 72 \text{ (machine center B constraint)}$$
$$1C \leq 10 \text{ (machine center C constraint)}$$
$$H, C \geq 0 \bullet$$

This formulation satisfies the five requirements for standard LP stated in the first section of this appendix:

1. There are limited resources (a finite number of hours available at each machine center).
2. There is an explicit objective function (we know what each variable is worth and what the goal is in solving the problem).
3. The equations are linear (no exponents or cross-products).
4. The resources are homogeneous (everything is in one unit of measure, machine hours).
5. The decision variables are divisible and nonnegative (we can make a fractional part of a hockey stick or chess set; however, if this were deemed undesirable, we would have to use integer programming).

GRAPHICAL LINEAR PROGRAMMING

Graphical linear programming

Though limited in application to problems involving two decision variables (or three variables for three-dimensional graphing), **graphical linear programming** provides a quick insight into the nature of linear programming. We describe the steps involved in the graphical method in the context of Puck and Pawn Company. The following steps illustrate the graphical approach:

1. **Formulate the problem in mathematical terms.** The equations for the problem are given above.
2. **Plot constraint equations.** The constraint equations are easily plotted by letting one variable equal zero and solving for the axis intercept of the other. (The inequality portions of the restrictions are disregarded for this step.) For the machine center A constraint equation, when $H = 0$, $C = 20$, and when $C = 0$, $H = 30$. For the machine center B constraint equation, when $H = 0$, $C = 12$, and when $C = 0$, $H = 36$. For the machine center C constraint equation, $C = 10$ for all values of H. These lines are graphed in Exhibit A.1.
3. **Determine the area of feasibility.** The direction of inequality signs in each constraint determines the area where a feasible solution is found. In this case, all inequalities are of the less-than-or-equal-to variety, which means it would be impossible to produce any combination of products that would lie to the right of any constraint line on the graph. The region of feasible solutions is unshaded on the graph and forms a convex polygon. A convex polygon exists when a line drawn between any two points in the polygon stays within the boundaries of that polygon. If this condition of convexity does not exist, the problem is either incorrectly set up or is not amenable to linear programming.
4. **Plot the objective function.** The objective function may be plotted by assuming some arbitrary total profit figure and then solving for the axis coordinates, as was done for the constraint equations. Other terms for the objective function when used

Graph of Hockey Stick and Chess Set Problem

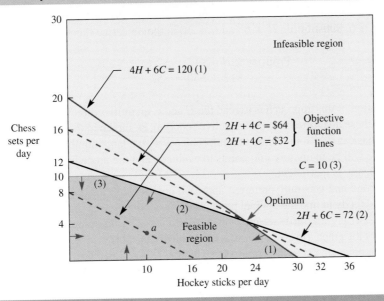

in this context are the *iso-profit* or *equal contribution line,* because it shows all possible production combinations for any given profit figure. For example, from the dotted line closest to the origin on the graph, we can determine all possible combinations of hockey sticks and chess sets that yield $32 by picking a point on the line and reading the number of each product that can be made at that point. The combination yielding $32 at point *a* would be 10 hockey sticks and three chess sets. This can be verified by substituting $H = 10$ and $C = 3$ in the objective function:

$$\$2(10) + \$4(3) = \$20 + \$12 = \$32$$

H	C	EXPLANATION
0	120/6 = 20	Intersection of Constraint (1) and C axis
120/4 = 30	0	Intersection of Constraint (1) and H axis
0	72/6 = 12	Intersection of Constraint (2) and C axis
72/2 = 36	0	Intersection of Constraint (2) and H axis
0	10	Intersection of Constraint (3) and C axis
0	32/4 = 8	Intersection of $32 iso-point line (objective function) and C axis
32/2 = 16	0	Intersection of $32 iso-profit line and H axis
0	64/4 = 16	Intersection of $64 iso-profit line and C axis
64/2 = 32	0	Intersection of $64 iso-profit line and H axis

5. **Find the optimal point.**   It can be shown mathematically that the optimal combination of decision variables is always found at an extreme point (corner point) of the convex polygon. In Exhibit A.1 there are four corner points (excluding the origin), and we can determine which one is the optimum by either of two approaches. The first approach is to find the values of the various corner solutions algebraically. This entails simultaneously solving the equations of various pairs of intersecting lines and substituting the quantities of the resultant variables in the objective

function. For example, the calculations for the intersection of $2H + 6C = 72$ and $C = 10$ are as follows:

Substituting $C = 10$ in $2H + 6C = 72$ gives $2H + 6(10) = 72$, $2H = 12$, or $H = 6$. Substituting $H = 6$ and $C = 10$ in the objective function, we get

$$\text{Profit} = \$2H + \$4C = \$2(6) + \$4(10)$$
$$= \$12 + \$40 = \$52$$

A variation of this approach is to read the H and C quantities directly from the graph and substitute these quantities into the objective function, as shown in the previous calculation. The drawback in this approach is that in problems with a large number of constraint equations, there will be many possible points to evaluate, and the procedure of testing each one mathematically is inefficient.

The second and generally preferred approach entails using the objective function or iso-profit line directly to find the optimal point. The procedure involves simply drawing a straight line *parallel* to any arbitrarily selected initial iso-profit line so the iso-profit line is farthest from the origin of the graph. (In cost minimization problems, the objective would be to draw the line through the point closest to the origin.) In Exhibit A.1, the dashed line labeled $\$2H + \$4C = \$64$ intersects the most extreme point. Note that the initial arbitrarily selected iso-profit line is necessary to display the slope of the objective function for the particular problem.[1] This is important since a different objective function (try profit $= 3H + 3C$) might indicate that some other point is farthest from the origin. Given that $\$2H + \$4C = \$64$ is optimal, the amount of each variable to produce can be read from the graph: 24 hockey sticks and four chess sets. No other combination of the products yields a greater profit.

LINEAR PROGRAMMING USING MICROSOFT EXCEL

Spreadsheets can be used to solve linear programming problems. Microsoft Excel has an optimization tool called *Solver* that we will demonstrate by solving the hockey stick and chess problem. We invoke the Solver from the Tools menu. A dialogue box requests information required by the program. The following example describes how our sample problem can be solved using Excel.

If the Solver option does not appear in your Tools menu, click on Add-Ins, select the Solver Add-In, and then click OK. Solver should then be available directly from the Tools menu for future use.

In the following example, we work in a step-by-step manner, setting up a spreadsheet and then solving our Puck and Pawn Company problem. Our basic strategy is to first define the problem within the spreadsheet. Following this, we invoke the Solver and feed it required information. Finally, we execute the Solver and interpret results from the reports provided by the program.

Step 1: Define Changing Cells A convenient starting point is to identify cells to be used for the decision variables in the problem. These are H and C, the number of hockey sticks and number of chess sets to produce. Excel refers to these cells as changing cells in Solver. Referring to our Excel screen (Exhibit A.2), we have designated B4 as the location for the number of hockey sticks to produce and C4 for the number of chess sets. Note that we have set these cells equal to 2 initially. We could set these cells to anything, but it is good to use some value other than zero to help verify that our calculations are correct.

Microsoft Excel Screen for Puck and Pawn Company

Microsoft Excel - Solver_LP.xls					
File Edit View Insert Format Tools Data Window Help					
D5		fx =+B4*B5+C4*C5			
	A	B	C	D	E	F
1						
2						
3		Hockey Sticks	Chess Sets	Total		
4	Changing Cells	2	2			
5	Profit	$2	$4	$12		
6						
7				Resources		
8		Hockey Sticks	Chess Sets	Used		Capacity
9	Machine A	4	6	20	<=	120
10	Machine B	2	6	16	<=	72
11	Machine C	0	1	2	<=	10
12						
13						
14						

Hockey Stocks and Chess Sets

Ready   NUM

Step 2: Calculate Total Profit (or Cost) This is our objective function and is calculated by multiplying profit associated with each product by the number of units produced. We have placed the profits in cells B5 and C5 ($2 and $4), so the profit is calculated by the following equation: B4*B5 + C4*C5, which is calculated in cell D5. Solver refers to this as the Target Cell, and it corresponds to the objective function for a problem.

Step 3: Set Up Resource Usage Our resources are machine centers A, B, and C as defined in the original problem. We have set up three rows (9, 10, and 11) in our spreadsheet, one for each resource constraint. For machine center A, 4 hours of processing time are used for each hockey stick produced (cell B9) and 6 hours for each chess set (cell C9). For a particular solution, the total amount of the machine center A resource used is calculated in D9 (B9*B4 + C9*C4). We have indicated in cell E9 that we want this value to be less than the 120-hour capacity of machine center A, which is entered in F9. Resource usage for machine centers B and C are set up in the exact same manner in rows 10 and 11.

Step 4: Set Up Solver Go to the Tools menu and select the Solver option.

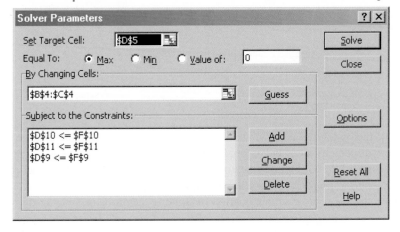

1. Set Target Cell: is set to the location where the value that we want to optimize is calculated. This is the profit calculated in D5 in our spreadsheet.
2. Equal To: is set to Max since the goal is to maximize profit.
3. By Changing Cells: are the cells that Solver can change to maximize profit. Cells B4 through C4 are the changing cells in our problem.
4. Subject to the Constraints: correspond to our machine center capacity. Here we click on Add and indicate that the total used for a resource is less than or equal to the capacity available. A sample for machine center A follows. Click OK after each constraint is specified.

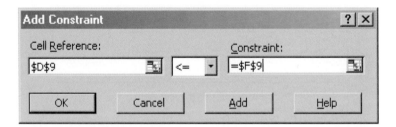

5. Clicking on Options allows us to tell Solver what type of problem we want it to solve and how we want it solved. Solver has numerous options, but we will need to use only a few. The screen is shown below.

Most of the options relate to how Solver attempts to solve nonlinear problems. These can be very difficult to solve and optimal solutions difficult to find. Luckily our problem is a linear problem. We know this since our constraints and our objective function are all calculated using linear equations. Click on Assume Linear Model to tell Solver that we want to use the linear programming option for solving the problem. In addition, we know

Excel Solver Answer and Sensitivity Reports

Answer Report

TARGET CELL (MAX)

CELL	NAME	ORIGINAL VALUE	FINAL VALUE
$D$5	Profit Total	$12	$64

ADJUSTABLE CELLS

CELL	NAME	ORIGINAL VALUE	FINAL VALUE
$B$4	Changing Cells Hockey Sticks	2	24
$C$4	Changing Cells Chess Sets	2	4

CONSTRAINTS

CELL	NAME	CELL VALUE	FORMULA	STATUS	SLACK
$D$11	Machine C Used	4	$D$11<=$F$11	Not Binding	6
$D$10	Machine B Used	72	$D$10<=$F$10	Binding	0
$D$9	Machine A Used	120	$D$9<=$F$9	Binding	0

Sensitivity Report

ADJUSTABLE CELLS

CELL	NAME	FINAL VALUE	REDUCED COST	OBJECTIVE COEFFICIENT	ALLOWABLE INCREASE	ALLOWABLE DECREASE
$B$4	Changing Cells Hockey Sticks	24	0	2	0.666666667	0.666666667
$C$4	Changing Cells Chess Sets	4	0	4	2	1

CONSTRAINT

CELL	NAME	FINAL VALUE	SHADOW PRICE	CONSTRAINT R.H. SIDE	ALLOWABLE INCREASE	ALLOWABLE DECREASE
$D$11	Machine C Used	4	0	10	1E+30	6
$D$10	Machine B Used	72	0.333333333	72	18	12
$D$9	Machine A Used	120	0.333333333	120	24	36

our changing cells (decision variables) must be numbers that are greater than or equal to zero since it makes no sense to make a negative number of hockey sticks or chess sets. We indicate this by selecting Assume Non-Negative as an option. We are now ready to actually solve the problem. Click OK to return to the Solver Parameters box.

Step 5: Solve the Problem Click Solve. We immediately get a Solver Results acknowledgment like that shown below.

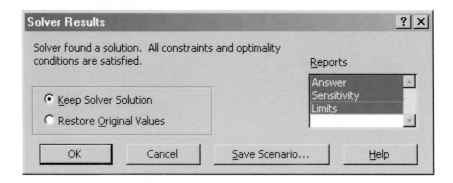

Solver acknowledges that a solution was found that appears to be optimal. On the right side of this box are options for three reports: an Answer Report, a Sensitivity Report, and a Limits Report. Click on each report to have Solver provide these. After highlighting the reports, click OK to exit back to the spreadsheet. Three new tabs have been created that correspond to these reports.

The most interesting reports for our problem are the Answer Report and the Sensitivity Report, both of which are shown in Exhibit A.3. The Answer Report shows the final answers for the total profit ($64) and the amounts produced (24 hockey sticks and 4 chess sets). In the constraints section of the Answer Report, the status of each resource is given. All of machine A and machine B are used, and there are six units of slack for machine C.

The Sensitivity Report is divided into two parts. The first part, titled "Adjustable Cells," corresponds to objective function coefficients. The profit per unit for the hockey sticks can be either up or down $.67 (between $2.67 and $1.33) without having an impact on the solution. Similarly, the profit of the chess sets could be between $6 and $3 without changing the solution. In the case of machine A, the right-hand side could increase to 144 (120 + 24) or decrease to 84 with a resulting $.33 increase or decrease per unit in the objective function. The right-hand side of machine B can increase to 90 units or decrease to 60 units with the same $.33 change for each unit in the objective function. For machine C, the right-hand side could increase to infinity (1E+30 is scientific notation for a very large number) or decrease to 4 units with no change in the objective function.

Key Terms

Linear programming (LP) Refers to several related mathematical techniques used to allocate limited resources among competing demands in an optimal way.

Graphical linear programming Provides a quick insight into the nature of linear programming.

Solved Problems

SOLVED PROBLEM 1

A furniture company produces three products: end tables, sofas, and chairs. These products are processed in five departments: the saw lumber, fabric cutting, sanding, staining, and assembly departments. End tables and chairs are produced from raw lumber only, and the sofas require lumber and fabric. Glue and thread are plentiful and represent a relatively insignificant cost that is included in operating expense. The specific requirements for each product are as follows:

RESOURCE OR ACTIVITY (QUANTITY AVAILABLE PER MONTH)	REQUIRED PER END TABLE	REQUIRED PER SOFA	REQUIRED PER CHAIR
Lumber (4,300 board feet)	10 board feet @ $10/foot = $100/table	7.5 board feet @ $10/foot = $75	4 board feet @ $10/foot = $40
Fabric (2,500 yards)	None	10 yards @ $17.50/yard = $175	None
Saw lumber (280 hours)	30 minutes	24 minutes	30 minutes
Cut fabric (140 hours)	None	24 minutes	None
Sand (280 hours)	30 minutes	6 minutes	30 minutes
Stain (140 hours)	24 minutes	12 minutes	24 minutes
Assemble (700 hours)	60 minutes	90 minutes	30 minutes

The company's direct labor expenses are $75,000 per month for the 1,540 hours of labor, at $48.70 per hour. Based on current demand, the firm can sell 300 end tables, 180 sofas, and 400 chairs per month. Sales prices are $400 for end tables, $750 for sofas, and $240 for chairs. Assume that labor cost is fixed and the firm does not plan to hire or fire any employees over the next month.

  a. What is the most limiting resource to the furniture company?
  b. Determine the product mix needed to maximize profit at the furniture company. What is the optimal number of end tables, sofas, and chairs to produce each month?

Solution

Define X_1 as the number of end tables, X_2 as the number of sofas, and X_3 as the number of chairs to produce each month. Profit is calculated as the revenue for each item minus the cost of materials (lumber and fabric), minus the cost of labor. Since labor is fixed, we subtract this out as a total sum. Mathematically we have $(400 - 100) + (750 - 75 - 175) + (240 - 40) - 75,000$. Profit is calculated as follows:

$$\text{Profit} = 400X_1 + 750X_2 + 240X_3 - 75,000$$

Constraints are the following:

Lumber:	$10X_1 + 7.5X_2 + 4X_3 \le 4,350$
Fabric:	$10X_2 \le 2,500$
Saw:	$.5X_1 + .4X_2 + .5X_3 \le 280$
Cut:	$.4X_2 \le 140$
Sand:	$.5X_1 + .1X_2 + .5X_3 \le 280$
Stain:	$.4X_1 + .2X_2 + .4X_3 \le 140$
Assemble:	$1X_1 + 1.5X_2 + .5X_3 \le 700$
Demand:	
Table:	$X_1 \le 300$
Sofa:	$X_2 \le 180$
Chair:	$X_3 \le 400$

Step 1: Define changing cells These are B3, C3, and D3. Note that these cells have been set equal to zero.

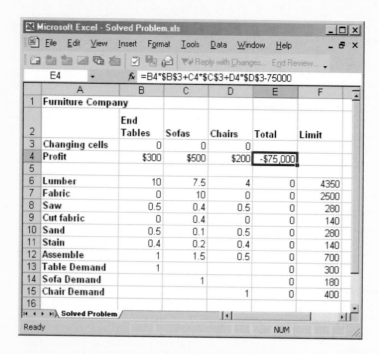

Step 2: Calculate total profit This is E4 (this is equal to B3 times the $300 revenue associated with each end table, plus C3 times the $500 revenue for each sofa, plus D3 times the $200 revenue associated with each chair). Note the $75,000 fixed expense that has been subtracted from revenue to calculate profit.

Step 3: Set up resource usage In cells E6 through E15, the usage of each resource is calculated by multiplying B3, C3, and D3 by the amount needed for each item and summing the product (for example, E6 = B3*B6 + C3*C6 + D3*D6). The limits on these constraints are entered in cells F6 to F15.

Step 4: Set up Solver Go to Tools and select the Solver option.

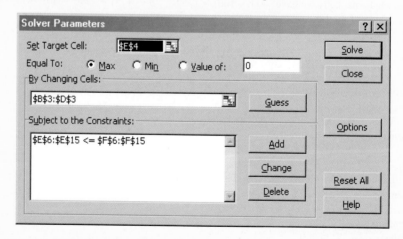

a. Set Target Cell: is set to the location where the value that we want to optimize is calculated. This is the profit calculated in E4 in this spreadsheet.
b. Equal To: is set to Max since the goal is to maximize profit.
c. By Changing Cells: are the cells that Solver can change to maximize profit (cells B3 through D3 in this problem).

d. Subject to the Constraints: is where a constraint set is added; we indicate that the range E6 to E15 must be less than or equal to F6 to F15.

Add Constraint

Cell Reference:

$E$6:$E$15   <=   =$F$6:$F$15

OK   Cancel   Add   Help

Step 5: Set Options There are many options here, but for our purposes we just need to indicate Assume Linear Model and Assume Non-Negative. Assume Linear Model means all of our formulas are simple linear equations. Assume Non-Negative indicates that changing cells must be greater than or equal to zero. Click OK and we are ready to solve our problem.

Solver Options

Max Time:	100 seconds	OK
Iterations:	100	Cancel
Precision:	0.000001	Load Model...
Tolerance:	5 %	Save Model...
Convergence:	0.0001	Help

☑ Assume Linear Model   ☐ Use Automatic Scaling
☑ Assume Non-Negative   ☐ Show Iteration Results

Estimates
⊙ Tangent
○ Quadratic

Derivatives
⊙ Forward
○ Central

Search
⊙ Newton
○ Conjugate

Step 6: Solve the Problem Click Solve. We can see the solution and two special reports by highlighting items on the Solver Results acknowledgment that is displayed after a solution is found. Note that in the following report, Solver indicates that it has found a solution and all constraints and optimality conditions are satisfied. In the Reports box on the right, the Answer, Sensitivity, and Limits options have been highlighted, indicating that we would like to see these items. After highlighting the reports, click OK to exit back to the spreadsheet.

Solver Results

Solver found a solution. All constraints and optimality conditions are satisfied.

Reports

Answer
Sensitivity
Limits

⊙ Keep Solver Solution
○ Restore Original Values

OK   Cancel   Save Scenario...   Help

Note that three new tabs have been created: an Answer Report, a Sensitivity Report, and a Limits Report. The Answer Report indicates in the Target Cell section that the profit associated with this solution is $93,000 (we started at −$75,000). From the Target Cell section, we should make 260 end tables, 180 sofas, and no chairs. From the Constraints section, notice that the only constraints limiting profit are the staining capacity and the demand for sofas. We can see this from the column indicating whether a constraint is binding or nonbinding. Nonbinding constraints have slack, as indicated in the last column.

Target Cell (Max)

Cell	Name	Original Value	Final Value
$E$4	Profit Total	−$75,000	$93,000

Adjustable Cells

Cell	Name	Original Value	Final Value
$B$3	Changing cells End Tables	0	260
$C$3	Changing cells Sofas	0	180
$D$3	Changing cells Chairs	0	0

Constraints

Cell	Name	Cell Value	Formula	Status	Slack
$E$6	Lumber Total	3950	$E$6<=$F$6	Not Binding	400
$E$7	Fabric Total	1800	$E$7<=$F$7	Not Binding	700
$E$8	Saw Total	202	$E$8<=$F$8	Not Binding	78
$E$9	Cut fabric Total	72	$E$9<=$F$9	Not Binding	68
$E$10	Sand Total	148	$E$10<=$F$10	Not Binding	132
$E$11	Stain Total	140	$E$11<=$F$11	Binding	0
$E$12	Assemble Total	530	$E$12<=$F$12	Not Binding	170
$E$13	Table Demand Total	260	$E$13<=$F$13	Not Binding	40
$E$14	Sofa Demand Total	180	$E$14<=$F$14	Binding	0
$E$15	Chair Demand Total	0	$E$15<=$F$15	Not Binding	400

Of course, we may not be too happy with this solution since we are not meeting all the demand for tables, and it may not be wise to totally discontinue the manufacturing of chairs.

The Sensitivity Report (shown below) gives additional insight into the solution. The Adjustable Cells section of this report shows the final value for each cell and the reduced cost. The reduced cost indicates how much the target cell value would change if a cell that was currently set to zero were brought into the solution. Since the end tables (B3) and sofas (C3) are in the current solution, their reduced cost is zero. For each chair (D3) that we make, our target cell would be reduced $100 (just round these numbers for interpretation purposes). The final three columns in the adjustable cells section of the report are the Objective Coefficient from the original spreadsheet and columns titled Allowable Increase and Allowable Decrease. Allowable Increase and Decrease show by how much the value of the corresponding coefficient could change so there would not be a change in the changing cell values (of course, the target cell value would change). For example, revenue for each end table could be as high as $1,000 ($300 + $700) or as low as $200 ($300 − $100), and we would still want to produce 260 end tables. Keep in mind that these values assume nothing else is changing in the problem. For the allowable increase value for sofas, note the value 1E+30. This is a very large number, essentially infinity, represented in scientific notation.

Adjustable Cells

Cell	Name	Final Value	Reduced Cost	Objective Coefficient	Allowable Increase	Allowable Decrease
$B$3	Changing cells End Tables	260	0	299.9999997	700.0000012	100.0000004
$C$3	Changing cells Sofas	180	0	500.0000005	1E+30	350.0000006
$D$3	Changing cells Chairs	0	−100.0000004	199.9999993	100.0000004	1E+30

Constraints

Cell	Name	Final Value	Shadow Price	Constraint R.H. Side	Allowable Increase	Allowable Decrease
$E$6	Lumber Total	3950	0	4350	1E+30	400
$E$7	Fabric Total	1800	0	2500	1E+30	700
$E$8	Saw Total	202	0	280	1E+30	78
$E$9	Cut fabric Total	72	0	140	1E+30	68
$E$10	Sand Total	148	0	280	1E+30	132
$E$11	Stain Total	140	749.9999992	140	16	104
$E$12	Assemble Total	530	0	700	1E+30	170
$E$13	Table Demand Total	260	0	300	1E+30	40
$E$14	Sofa Demand Total	180	350.0000006	180	70	80
$E$15	Chair Demand Total	0	0	400	1E+30	400

For the Constraints section of the report, the actual final usage of each resource is given in Final Value. The Shadow Price is the value to our target cell for each unit increase in the resource. If we could increase staining capacity, it would be worth $750 per hour. The Constraint Right-Hand Side is the current limit on the resource. Allowable Increase is the amount the resource could be increased while the shadow price is still valid. Another 16 hours' work of staining capacity could be added with a value of $750 per hour. Similarly, the Allowable Decrease column shows the amount the resource could be reduced without changing the shadow price. There is some valuable information available in this report.

The Limits Report provides additional information about our solution.

Cell	Target Name	Value
$E$4	Profit Total	$93,000

Cell	Adjustable Name	Value	Lower Limit	Target Result	Upper Limit	Target Result
$B$3	Changing cells End Tables	260	0	15000	260.0000002	93000
$C$3	Changing cells Sofas	180	0	3000	180	93000
$D$3	Changing cells Chairs	0	0	93000	0	93000

Total profit for the current solution is $93,000. Current value for B3 (end tables) is 260 units. If this were reduced to 0 units, profit would be reduced to $15,000. At an upper limit of 260, profit is $93,000 (the current solution). Similarly, for C3 (sofas), if this were reduced to 0, profit would be reduced to $3,000. At an upper limit of 180, profit is $93,000. For D3 (chairs), if this were reduced to 0, profit is $93,000 (current solution), and in this case the upper limit on chairs is also 0 units.

Acceptable answers to the questions are as follows:

a. *What is the most limiting resource to the furniture company?*
   In terms of our production resources, staining capacity is really hurting profit at this time. We could use another 16 hours of capacity.
b. *Determine the product mix needed to maximize profit at the furniture company.*
   The product mix would be to make 260 end tables, 180 sofas, and no chairs.

Of course, we have only scratched the surface with this solution. We could actually experiment with increasing staining capacity. This would give insight into the next most limiting resource. We also could run scenarios where we are required to produce a minimum number of each product, which is probably a more realistic scenario. This could help us determine how we could possibly reallocate the use of labor in our shop.

SOLVED PROBLEM 2

It is 2:00 on Friday afternoon and Joe Bob the head chef (grill cook) at Bruce's Diner is trying to decide the best way to allocate the available raw material to the four Friday night specials. The decision has to be made in the early afternoon because three of the items must be started now (Sloppy Joes, Tacos, and Chili). The table below contains the information on the food in inventory and the amounts required for each item.

Food	Cheeseburger	Sloppy Joes	Taco	Chili	Available
Ground Beef (lbs.)	0.3	0.25	0.25	0.4	100 lbs.
Cheese (lbs.)	0.1	0	0.3	0.2	50 lbs.
Beans (lbs.)	0	0	0.2	0.3	50 lbs.
Lettuce (lbs.)	0.1	0	0.2	0	15 lbs.
Tomato (lbs.)	0.1	0.3	0.2	0.2	50 lbs.
Buns	1	1	0	0	80 buns
Taco Shells	0	0	1	0	80 shells

There is one other fact relevant to Joe Bob's decision. That is the estimated market demand and selling price.

	Cheeseburger	Sloppy Joes	Taco	Chili
Demand	75	60	100	55
Selling Price	$2.25	$2.00	$1.75	$2.50

Joe Bob wants to maximize revenue since he has already purchased all the materials that are sitting in the cooler.

Required:

1. What is the best mix of the Friday night specials to maximize Joe Bob's revenue?
2. If a supplier offered to provide a rush order of buns at $1.00 a bun, is it worth the money?

Solution

Define X_1 as the number of cheeseburgers, X_2 as the number of sloppy joes, X_3 as the number of tacos, and X_4 as the number of bowls of chili made for the Friday night specials.

$$\text{Revenue} = \$2.25\,X_1 + \$2.00\,X_2 + \$1.75\,X_3 + \$2.50\,X_4$$

Constraints are the following:

Ground Beef:	$0.30\,X_1 + 0.25\,X_2 + 0.25\,X_3 + 0.40\,X_4 \le 100$
Cheese:	$0.10\,X_1 + 0.30\,X_3 + 0.20\,X_4 \le 50$
Beans:	$0.20\,X_3 + 0.30\,X_4 \le 50$
Lettuce:	$0.10\,X_1 + 0.20\,X_3 \le 15$
Tamato:	$0.10\,X_1 + 0.30\,X_2 + 0.20\,X_3 + 0.20\,X_4 \le 50$
Buns:	$X_1 + X_2 \le 80$
Taco Shells:	$X_3 \le 80$

Demand:

Cheeseburger	$X_1 \le 75$
Sloppy Joes	$X_2 \le 603$
Taco	$X_3 \le 100$
Chili	$X_4 \le 55$

Step 1: Define the changing cells—These are B3, C3, D3, and E3. Note the values in the changing cells are set to 10 each so the formulas can be checked.

Step 2: Calculate total revenue—This is in cell F7 (this is equal to B3 times the $2.25 for each cheeseburger, plus C3 times the $2.00 for a sloppy joe, plus D3 times the $1.75 for each taco, plus E3 times the $2.50 for each bowl of chili, the SUMPRODUCT function in Excel was used to make this calculation faster). Note that the current value is $85, which is a result of selling 10 of each item.

Step 3: Setup the usage of the food—In cells F11 to F17 the usage of each food is calculated by multiplying the changing cells row times the per item use in the table and then summing the result. The limits on each of these food types are given in H11 through H17.

Step 4: Set up Solver and select the Solver option.

a. Set Target Cell to the location where the value that we want to optimize is calculated. The revenue is calculated in F7 in this spreadsheet.
b. Equal to: is set to Max since the goal is to maximize revenue.
c. By Changing Cells: are the cells that tell how many of each special to produce.
d. Subject to the Constraints: here we added two separate constraints, one for demand and one for the usage of food.

Step 5: Set Options: clicking on "Options" we will leave all the settings as the default values and we only need to make sure of two changes: (1) we need to make sure that there is a check under the Assume Linear Model option and (2) we must check the Assume Non-Negative option. These two options make sure that Solver knows that this is a linear programming problem and that all changing cells should be non-negative. Click OK to return to the Solver Parameters screen.

Step 6: Solve the Problem—Click Solve. We will get a solver results box. Make sure it says, "Solver found a solution. All constraints and optimality conditions are satisfied."

On the right-hand side of the box there is an option for three reports: Answer, Sensitivity, and Limit. Click on all three reports and then click OK, and this will exit you back to the spreadsheet, but you will have three new worksheets on your work book.

The Answer Report indicates that the target cell has a final solution of $416.50 and started at $85. From the adjustable cells area we can see that we should make 20 cheeseburgers, 60 sloppy joes, 65 tacos, and 55 bowls of chili. This answers the first requirement from the problem of what the mix of Friday night specials should be.

TARGET CELL (MAX)

CELL	NAME	ORIGINAL VALUE	FINAL VALUE
$F$7	Revenue Total	$85.00	$416.25

ADJUSTABLE CELLS

CELL	NAME	ORIGINAL VALUE	FINAL VALUE
$B$3	Changing Cells Cheeseburger	10	20
$C$3	Changing Cells Sloppy Joes	10	60
$D$3	Changing Cells Taco	10	65
$E$3	Changing Cells Chili	10	55

CONSTRAINTS

CELL	NAME	CELL VALUE	FORMULA	STATUS	SLACK
$F$11	Ground Beef (lbs.) Total	59.25	$F$11<=$H$11	Not Binding	40.75
$F$12	Cheese (lbs.) Total	32.50	$F$12<=$H$12	Not Binding	17.5
$F$13	Beans (lbs.) Total	29.50	$F$13<=$H$13	Not Binding	20.5
$F$14	Lettuce (lbs.) Total	15.00	$F$14<=$H$14	Binding	0
$F$15	Tomato (lbs.) Total	44.00	$F$15<=$H$15	Not Binding	6
$F$16	Buns Total	80.00	$F$16<=$H$16	Binding	0
$F$17	Taco Shells Total	65.00	$F$17<=$H$17	Not Binding	15
$B$3	Changing Cells Cheeseburger	20	$B$3<=$B$5	Not Binding	55
$C$3	Changing Cells Sloppy Joes	60	$C$3<=$C$5	Binding	0
$D$3	Changing Cells Taco	65	$D$3<=$D$5	Not Binding	35
$E$3	Changing Cells Chili	55	$E$3<=$E$5	Binding	0

The second required answer was whether it is worth it to pay a rush supplier $1 a bun for additional buns. The answer report shows us that the buns constraint was binding. This means that if we had more buns we could make more money. However, the Answer Report does not tell us whether a rush order of buns at $1 a bun is worthwhile. In order to answer that question we have to look at the Sensitivity Report.

ADJUSTABLE CELLS

CELL	NAME	FINAL VALUE	REDUCED COST	OBJECTIVE COEFFICIENT	ALLOWABLE INCREASE	ALLOWABLE DECREASE
$B$3	Changing Cells Cheeseburger	20	0	2.25	0.625	1.375
$C$3	Changing Cells Sloppy Joes	60	0.625	2	1E+30	0.625
$D$3	Changing Cells Taco	65	0	1.75	2.75	1.25
$E$3	Changing Cells Chili	55	2.5	2.5	1E+30	2.5

CONSTRAINTS

CELL	NAME	FINAL VALUE	SHADOW PRICE	CONSTRAINT R.H. SIDE	ALLOWABLE INCREASE	ALLOWABLE DECREASE
$F$11	Ground Beef (lbs.) Total	59.25	0.00	100	1E+30	40.75
$F$12	Cheese (lbs.) Total	32.50	0.00	50	1E+30	17.5
$F$13	Beans (lbs.) Total	29.50	0.00	50	1E+30	20.5
$F$14	Lettuce (lbs.) Total	15.00	8.75	15	3	13
$F$15	Tomato (lbs.) Total	44.00	0.00	50	1E+30	6
$F$16	**Buns Total**	80.00	1.38	80	55	20
$F$17	Taco Shells Total	65.00	0.00	80	1E+30	15

We have highlighted the buns row to answer the question. We can see that buns have a shadow price of $1.38. This shadow price means that each additional bun will generate $1.38 of profit. We can also see that other foods such as ground beef have a shadow price of $0. The items with a shadow price add nothing to profit since there we are currently not using all that we have now. The other important piece of information that we have on the buns is that they are only worth $1.38 up until the next 55 buns and that is why the allowable increase is 55. We can also see that a pound of lettuce is worth $8.75. It might be wise to also look for a rush supplier of lettuce so we can increase our profit on Friday nights.

Acceptable answers to the questions are as follows:

1   *What is the best mix of the Friday night specials to maximize Joe Bob's revenue?* 20 cheeseburgers, 60 sloppy joes, 65 tacos, and 55 bowls of chili.

2   *If a supplier offered to provide a rush order of buns at $1.00 a bun is it worth the money?* Yes, each additional bun brings in $1.38 so if they cost us $1 then we will net $0.38 per bun. However, this is only true up to 55 additional buns.

Problems

1   Solve the following problem with Excel Solver:

$$\text{Maximize } Z = 3X + Y.$$
$$12X + 14Y \le 85$$
$$3X + 2Y \le 18$$
$$Y \le 4$$

2   Solve the following problem with Excel Solver:

$$\text{Minimize } Z = 2A + 4B.$$
$$4A + 6B \ge 120$$
$$2A + 6B \ge 72$$
$$B \ge 10$$

3   A manufacturing firm has discontinued production of a certain unprofitable product line. Considerable excess production capacity was created as a result. Management is considering devoting this excess capacity to one or more of three products: X_1, X_2, and X_3.

Machine hours required per unit are

| | PRODUCT | | |
MACHINE TYPE	X_1	X_2	X_3
Milling machine	8	2	3
Lathe	4	3	0
Grinder	2	0	1

The available time in machine hours per week is

	MACHINE HOURS PER WEEK
Milling machines	800
Lathes	480
Grinders	320

The salespeople estimate they can sell all the units of X_1 and X_2 that can be made. But the sales potential of X_3 is 80 units per week maximum.

Unit profits for the three products are

	UNIT PROFITS
X_1	$20
X_2	6
X_3	8

a. Set up the equations that can be solved to maximize the profit per week.

b. Solve these equations using the Excel Solver.

c. What is the optimal solution? How many of each product should be made, and what should the resultant profit be?

d. What is this situation with respect to the machine groups? Would they work at capacity, or would there be unused available time? Will X_3 be at maximum sales capacity?

e. Suppose that an additional 200 hours per week can be obtained from the milling machines by working overtime. The incremental cost would be $1.50 per hour. Would you recommend doing this? Explain how you arrived at your answer.

4 A diet is being prepared for the University of Arizona dorms. The objective is to feed the students at the least cost, but the diet must have between 1,800 and 3,600 calories. No more than 1,400 calories can be starch, and no fewer than 400 can be protein. The varied diet is to be made of two foods: A and B. Food A costs $0.75 per pound and contains 600 calories, 400 of which are protein and 200 starch. No more than 2 pounds of food A can be used per resident. Food B costs $0.15 per pound and contains 900 calories, of which 700 are starch, 100 are protein, and 100 are fat.

a. Write the equations representing this information.

b. Solve the problem graphically for the amounts of each food that should be used.

5 Do problem 4 with the added constraint that not more than 150 calories shall be fat and that the price of food has escalated to $1.75 per pound for food A and $2.50 per pound for food B.

6 Logan Manufacturing wants to mix two fuels, A and B, for its trucks to minimize cost. It needs no fewer than 3,000 gallons to run its trucks during the next month. It has a maximum fuel storage capacity of 4,000 gallons. There are 2,000 gallons of fuel A and 4,000 gallons of fuel B available. The mixed fuel must have an octane rating of no less than 80.

When fuels are mixed, the amount of fuel obtained is just equal to the sum of the amounts put in. The octane rating is the weighted average of the individual octanes, weighted in proportion to the respective volumes.

The following is known: Fuel A has an octane of 90 and costs $1.20 per gallon. Fuel B has an octane of 75 and costs $0.90 per gallon.

a. Write the equations expressing this information.

b. Solve the problem using the Excel Solver, giving the amount of each fuel to be used. State any assumptions necessary to solve the problem.

7 You are trying to create a budget to optimize the use of a portion of your disposable income. You have a maximum of $1,500 per month to be allocated to food, shelter, and entertainment. The amount spent on food and shelter combined must not exceed $1,000. The amount spent

on shelter alone must not exceed $700. Entertainment cannot exceed $300 per month. Each dollar spent on food has a satisfaction value of 2, each dollar spent on shelter has a satisfaction value of 3, and each dollar spent on entertainment has a satisfaction value of 5.

Assuming a linear relationship, use the Excel Solver to determine the optimal allocation of your funds.

8   C-town brewery brews two beers: Expansion Draft and Burning River. Expansion draft sells for $20 per barrel while Burning River sells for $8 per barrel. Producing a barrel of Expansion Draft takes 8 pounds of corn and 4 pounds of hops. Producing a barrel of Burning River requires 2 pounds of corn, 6 pounds of rice, and 3 pounds of hops. The brewery has 500 pounds of corn, 300 pounds of rice, and 400 pounds of hops. Assuming a linear relationship, use the Excel Solver to determine the optimal mix of Expansion Draft and Burning River that maximizes C-town's revenue.

9   BC Petrol manufactures three chemicals at their chemical plant in Kentucky: BCP1, BCP2, and BCP3. These chemicals are produced in two production processes known as zone and man. Running the zone process for an hour costs $48 and yields three units of BCP1, one unit of BCP2, and one unit of BCP3. Running the man process for one hour costs $24 and yields one unit of BCP1 and one unit of BCP2. To meet customer demands, at least twenty units of BCP1, ten units of BCP2, and six units of BCP3 must be produced daily. Assuming a linear relationship, use the Excel Solver to determine the optimal mix of processes zone and man to minimize costs and meet BC Petrol daily demands.

10   A farmer in Wood County has 900 acres of land. She is going to plant each acre with corn, soybeans, or wheat. Each acre planted with corn yields a $2,000 profit; each with soybeans yields $2,500 profit; and each with wheat yields $3,000 profit. She has 100 workers and 150 tons of fertilizer. The table below shows the requirement per acre of each of the crops. Assuming a linear relationship, use the Excel Solver to determine the optimal planting mix of corn, soybeans, and wheat to maximize her profits.

	CORN	SOYBEANS	WHEAT
Labor (workers)	0.1	0.3	0.2
Fertilizer (tons)	0.2	0.1	0.4

SELECTED BIBLIOGRAPHY

Anderson, D. R.; D. J. Sweeney; and T. A. Williams. *An Introduction to Management Science*. 10th ed. Cincinnati: South-Western, 2002.

Winston, W. L., and S. C. Albright. *Practical Management Science*. 3rd ed. Belmont, CA: Duxbury Press, 2002.

FOOTNOTE

1   The slope of the objective function is -2. If P = profit, $P = \$2H + \$4C$; $\$2H = P - \$4C$; $H = P/2 - 2C$. Thus the slope is -2.

LEARNING CURVES

481   The Learning Curve
         Plotting Learning Curves   Learning curve defined
         Logarithmic Analysis
         Learning Curve Tables

THE LEARNING CURVE

Learning curve

A well-known concept is the learning curve. A **learning curve** is a line displaying the relationship between unit production and the cumulative number of units produced. As plants produce more, they gain experience in the best production methods, which reduce their costs of production in a predictable manner. Every time a plant's cumulative production doubles, its production costs decline by a specific percentage depending on the nature of the business. Exhibit B.1 demonstrates the effect of a learning curve on the production costs of hamburgers.

The learning curve percentage varies across industries. To apply this concept to the restaurant industry, consider a hypothetical fast-food chain that has produced 5 million hamburgers. Given a current variable cost of $0.55 per burger, what will the cost per burger be when cumulative production reaches 10 million burgers? If the firm has a 90 percent learning curve, costs will fall to 90 percent of $0.55, or $0.495, when accumulated production reaches 10 million. At 1 billion hamburgers, the variable cost drops to less than $0.25.

Note that sales volume becomes an important issue in achieving cost savings. If firm A serves twice as many hamburgers daily as firm B, it will accumulate "experience" twice as fast.

Learning curve theory is based on three assumptions:

1. The amount of time required to complete a given task or unit of a product will be less each time the task is undertaken.
2. The unit time will decrease at a decreasing rate.
3. The reduction in time will follow a predictable pattern.

The Learning Curve   **exhibit B.1**

a. Costs per unit produced fall by a specific percentage each time cumulative production doubles. This relationship can be expressed through a linear scale as shown in this graph of 90 percent learning curve:

b. It can also be expressed through logarithms:

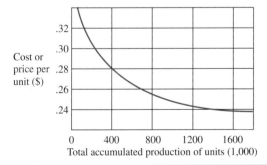

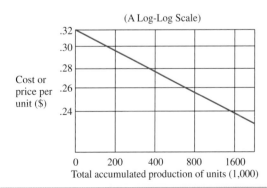

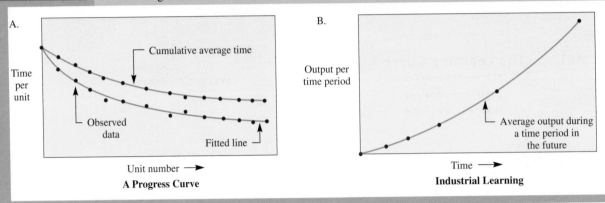

A Progress Curve

Industrial Learning

Each of these assumptions was found to hold true in the airplane industry, where learning curves were first applied. In this application, it was observed that, as output doubled, there was a 20 percent reduction in direct production worker-hours per unit between doubled units. Thus, if it took 100,000 hours for Plane 1, it would take 80,000 hours for Plane 2, 64,000 hours for Plane 4, and so forth. Because the 20 percent reduction meant that, say, Unit 4 took only 80 percent of the production time required for Unit 2, the line connecting the coordinates of output and time was referred to as an "80 percent learning curve." (By convention, the percentage learning rate is used to denote any given exponential learning curve.)

A learning curve may be developed from an arithmetic tabulation, by logarithms, or by some other curve-fitting method, depending on the amount and form of the available data.

There are two ways to think about the improved performance that comes with learning curves: time per unit (as in Exhibit B.2A) or units of output per time period (as in B.2B). *Time per unit* shows the decrease in time required for each successive unit. *Cumulative average time* shows the cumulative average performance times as the total number of units increases. Time per unit and cumulative average times are also called *progress curves* or *product learning* and are useful for complex products or products with a longer cycle time. *Units of output per time period* is also called *industry learning* and is generally applied to high-volume production (short cycle time).

Note in Exhibit B.2A that the cumulative average curve does not decrease as fast as the time per unit because the time is being averaged. For example, if the time for Units 1, 2, 3, and 4 were 100, 80, 70, and 64, they would be plotted that way on the time per unit graph, but would be plotted as 100, 90, 83.3, and 78.5 on the cumulative average time graph.

Plotting Learning Curves

There are many ways to analyze past data to fit a useful trend line. We will use the simple exponential curve first as an arithmetic procedure and then by a logarithmic analysis. In an arithmetical tabulation approach, a column for units is created by doubling, row by row, as 1, 2, 4, 8, 16. . . . The time for the first unit is multiplied by the learning percentage to obtain the time for the second unit. The second unit is multiplied by the learning percentage for the fourth unit, and so on. Thus, if we are developing an 80 percent learning curve, we would arrive at the figures listed in column 2 of Exhibit B.3. Because it is often desirable for planning purposes to know the cumulative direct labor hours, column 4, which lists this information, is also provided. The calculation of these figures is straightforward; for example, for Unit 4, cumulative average direct labor hours would be found by dividing cumulative direct labor hours by 4, yielding the figure given in column 4.

Unit, Cumulative, and Cumulative Average Direct Labor Worker-Hours Required for an 80 Percent Learning Curve

(1) UNIT NUMBER	(2) UNIT DIRECT LABOR HOURS	(3) CUMULATIVE DIRECT LABOR HOURS	(4) CUMULATIVE AVERAGE DIRECT LABOR HOURS
1	100,000	100,000	100,000
2	80,000	180,000	90,000
4	64,000	314,210	78,553
8	51,200	534,591	66,824
16	40,960	892,014	55,751
32	32,768	1,467,862	45,871
64	26,214	2,392,453	37,382
128	20,972	3,874,395	30,269
256	16,777	6,247,318	24,404

Excel: Learning Curves

Exhibit B.4A shows three curves with different learning rates: 90 percent, 80 percent, and 70 percent. Note that if the cost of the first unit was $100, the 30th unit would cost $59.63 at the 90 percent rate and $17.37 at the 70 percent rate. Differences in learning rates can have dramatic effects.

In practice, learning curves are plotted using a graph with logarithmic scales. The unit curves become linear throughout their entire range and the cumulative curve becomes linear after the first few units. The property of linearity is desirable because it facilitates extrapolation and permits a more accurate reading of the cumulative curve. This type of scale is an option in Microsoft Excel. Simply generate a regular scatter plot in your spreadsheet and then select each axis and format the axis with the logarithmic option. Exhibit B.4B

B.4A—Arithmetic Plot of 70, 80, and 90 Percent Learning Curves
B.4B—Logarithmic Plot of an 80 Percent Learning Curve

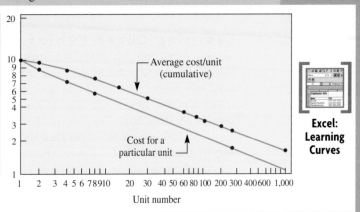

Excel: Learning Curves

shows the 80 percent unit cost curve and average cost curve on a logarithmic scale. Note that the cumulative average cost is essentially linear after the eighth unit.

Although the arithmetic tabulation approach is useful, direct logarithmic analysis of learning curve problems is generally more efficient because it does not require a complete enumeration of successive time–output combinations. Moreover, where such data are not available, an analytical model that uses logarithms may be the most convenient way of obtaining output estimates.

Logarithmic Analysis

The normal form of the learning curve equation is

$$Y_x = Kx^n \tag{B.1}$$

where

x = Unit number
Y_x = Number of direct labor hours required to produce the xth unit
K = Number of direct labor hours required to produce the first unit
n = log b/log 2 where b = Learning percentage

We can solve this mathematically or by using a table, as shown in the next section. Mathematically, to find the labor-hour requirement for the eighth unit in our example (Exhibit B.3), we would substitute as follows:

$$Y_8 = (100,000)(8)^n$$

Using logarithms:

$$Y_8 = 100,000(8)^{\log 0.8/\log 2}$$

$$= 100,000(8)^{-0.322} = \frac{100,000}{(8)^{0.322}}$$

$$= \frac{100,000}{1.9535} = 51,192$$

Therefore, it would take 51,192 hours to make the eighth unit. (See the spreadsheet "Learning Curves.")

Learning Curve Tables

When the learning percentage is known, the tables in Exhibit B.5 can be easily used to calculate estimated labor hours for a specific unit or for cumulative groups of units. We need only multiply the initial unit labor hour figure by the appropriate tabled value.

To illustrate, suppose we want to double-check the figures in Exhibit B.3 for unit and cumulative labor hours for Unit 16. From Exhibit B.5, the unit improvement factor for Unit 16 at 80 percent is .4096. This multiplied by 100,000 (the hours for Unit 1) gives 40,960, the same as in Exhibit B.3. From Exhibit B.6, the cumulative improvement factor for cumulative hours for the first 16 units is 8.920. When multiplied by 100,000, this gives 892,000, which is reasonably close to the exact value of 892,014 shown in Exhibit B.3.

The following is a more involved example of the application of a learning curve to a production problem.

**Excel:
Learning
Curves**

Step by Step

EXAMPLE B.1: Sample Learning Curve Problem

Captain Nemo, owner of the Suboptimum Underwater Boat Company (SUB), is puzzled. He has a contract for 11 boats and has completed 4 of them. He has observed that his production manager, young Mr. Overick, has been reassigning more and more people to torpedo assembly after the construction of the first four boats. The first boat, for example, required 225 workers, each working a 40-hour week, while 45 fewer workers were required for the second boat. Overick has told them that "this is just the beginning" and that he will complete the last boat in the current contract with only 100 workers!

Overick is banking on the learning curve, but has he gone overboard?

SOLUTION

Because the second boat required 180 workers, a simple exponential curve shows that the learning percentage is 80 percent (180 ÷ 225). To find out how many workers are required for the 11th boat, we look up unit 11 for an 80 percent improvement ratio in Exhibit B.5 and multiply this value by the number required for the first sub. By interpolating between Unit 10 and Unit 12 we find the improvement ratio is equal to .4629. This yields 104.15 workers (.4269 interpolated from table × 225). Thus, Overick's estimate missed the boat by four people. ●

Step by Step

EXAMPLE B.2: Estimating Cost Using Learning Curves

SUB has produced the first unit of a new line of minisubs at a cost of $500,000—$200,000 for materials and $300,000 for labor. It has agreed to accept a 10 percent profit, based on cost, and it is willing to contract on the basis of a 70 percent learning curve. What will be the contract price for three minisubs?

SOLUTION

Cost of first sub		$ 500,000
Cost of second sub		
Materials	$200,000	
Labor: $300,000 × .70	210,000	410,000
Cost of third sub		
Materials	200,000	
Labor: $300,000 × .5682	170,460	370,460
Total cost		1,280,460
Markup: $1,280,460 × .10		128,046
Selling price		$1,408,506

If the operation is interrupted, then some relearning must occur. How far to go back up the learning curve can be estimated in some cases. ●

Managerial Considerations in Using Learning Curves Managers should be aware of the following factors when using and interpreting learning curves.

1. **Individual learning and incentives.** Extensive research indicates a rather obvious fact: in order to enhance worker learning, there must be adequate incentives for the worker and the organization. (It should be noted, however, that the concept of incentives may be broadened to include any of the positive or negative administrative options available to managers.)

2. **Learning on new jobs versus old jobs.** The newer the job, the greater will be the improvement in labor hours and cost. Conversely, when production has been underway for a long time, improvement will be less discernible. For example, for an 80 percent learning curve situation, the improvement between the first and second units will be 20 percent. However, if the product has been manufactured for 50 years, it will take another 50 years to reduce labor hours by 20 percent.

3. **Improvement comes from working smarter, not harder.** While incentives must be included to motivate the individual worker, most improvement in output comes from better methods and effective support systems rather than simply increased worker effort.

4. **Built-in production bias through suggesting any learning rate.** If a manager expects an 80 percent improvement factor, he or she may treat this percentage as a goal rather than as an unbiased measure of actual learning. In short, it may be a "self-fulfilling prophecy." This, however, is not necessarily undesirable. What is wrong with setting a target improvement factor and then attempting to control production to achieve it?

5. **Preproduction versus postproduction adjustments.** The amount of learning shown by the learning curve depends both on the initial unit(s) of output and on the learning percentage. If there is much preproduction planning, experimentation, and adjustment, the early units will be produced more rapidly than if improvements are made after the first few units—other things being equal. In the first case, therefore, the apparent learning will, be less than in the second case, even though subsequent "actual" learning may be the same in each instance.

6. **Changes in indirect labor and supervision.** Learning curves represent direct labor output, but if the mix of indirect labor and supervision changes, it is likely that the productivity of direct labor will be altered. We expect, for example, that more supervisors, repairpersons, and material handlers would speed up production, whereas a reduction in their numbers would slow it down.

7. **Changes in purchasing practices, methods, and organization structure.** Obviously, significant adjustments in any of these factors will affect the production rate and, hence, the learning curve. Likewise, the institution of preventive maintenance programs, zero defect programs, and other schemes designed to improve efficiency or product quality generally would have some impact on the learning phenomenon.

8. **Contract phase-out.** Though not relevant to all contract situations, the point should be made that the learning curve may begin to turn upward as a contract nears completion. This may result from transferring trained workers to other projects, nonreplacement of worn tooling, and reduced attention to efficiency on the part of management.

Key Terms

Learning curve A line displaying the relationship between unit production time and the cumulative number of units produced.

Formula Review

Logarithmic curve:

$$Y_x = Kx^n \tag{B.1}$$

Solved Problems

SOLVED PROBLEM 1

A job applicant is being tested for an assembly line position. Management feels that steady-state times have been approximately reached after 1,000 performances. Regular assembly line workers are expected to perform the task within four minutes.

a. If the job applicant performed the first test operation in 10 minutes and the second one in 9 minutes, should this applicant be hired?

b. What is the expected time that the job applicant would take to finish the 10th unit?

c. What is a significant limitation of this analysis?

Solution

a. Learning rate = 9 minutes/10 minutes = 90%
   From Exhibit B.5, the time for the 1,000th unit is .3499 × 10 minutes = 3.499 minutes. Yes, hire the person.

b. From Exhibit B.5, unit 10 at 90% is .7047. Therefore, the time for the 10th unit = .7047 × 10 = 7.047 minutes.

c. Extrapolating based on just the first two units is unrealistic. More data should be collected to evaluate the job applicant's performance.

SOLVED PROBLEM 2

Boeing Aircraft collected the following cost data on the first 8 units of their new business jet.

UNIT NUMBER	COST ($ MILLIONS)	UNIT NUMBER	COST ($ MILLIONS)
1	$100	5	60
2	83	6	57
3	73	7	53
4	62	8	51

Excel: Learning Curves

a. Estimate the learning curve for the new business jet.

b. Estimate the average cost for the first 1,000 units of the jet.

c. Estimate the cost to produce the 1,000th jet.

Solution

a. First, estimate the learning curve rate by calculating the average learning rate with each doubling of production.

$$\text{Units 1 to 2} = 83/100 = 83\%$$
$$\text{Units 2 to 4} = 62/83 = 74.7\%$$
$$\text{Units 4 to 8} = 51/62 = 82.26\%$$
$$\text{Average} = (83 + 74.7 + 82.3)/3 = 80\%$$

b. The average cost of the first 1,000 units can be estimated using Exhibit B.6. The cumulative improvement factor for the 1,000th unit at 80 percent learning is 158.7. The cost to produce the first 1,000 units is

$$\$100M \times 158.7 = \$15,870M$$

The average cost for each of the first 1,000 units is

$$\$15,870M/1,000 = \$15.9M$$

c. To estimate the cost to produce the 1,000th unit use Exhibit B.5.
   The unit improvement factor for the 1,000th unit at 80 percent is .1082.
   The cost to produce the 1,000th unit is

$$\$100M \times .1082 = \$10.82M$$

Problems

1   A time standard was set as 0.20 hour per unit based on the 50th unit produced. If the task has a 90 percent learning curve, what would be the expected time of the 100th, 200th, and 400th units?

2   You have just received 10 units of a special subassembly from an electronics manufacturer at a price of $250 per unit. A new order has also just come in for your company's product that uses these subassemblies, and you wish to purchase 40 more to be shipped in lots of 10 units each. (The subassemblies are bulky, and you need only 10 a month to fill your new order.)

   a. Assuming a 70 percent learning curve by your supplier on a similar product last year, how much should you pay for each lot? Assume that the learning rate of 70 percent applies to each lot of 10 units, not each unit.

   b. Suppose you are the supplier and can produce 20 units now but cannot start production on the second 20 units for two months. What price would you try to negotiate for the last 20 units?

3   Johnson Industries received a contract to develop and produce four high-intensity long-distance receiver/transmitters for cellular telephones. The first took 2,000 labor hours and $39,000 worth of purchased and manufactured parts; the second took 1,500 labor hours and $37,050 in parts; the third took 1,450 labor hours and $31,000 in parts; and the fourth took 1,275 labor hours and $31,492 in parts.

   Johnson was asked to bid on a follow-on contract for another dozen receiver/transmitter units. Ignoring any forgetting factor effects, what should Johnson estimate time and parts costs to be for the dozen units? (Hint: There are two learning curves—one for labor and one for parts.)

4   Lambda Computer Products competed for and won a contract to produce two prototype units of a new type of computer that is based on laser optics rather than on electronic binary bits.

   The first unit produced by Lambda took 5,000 hours to produce and required $250,000 worth of material, equipment usage, and supplies. The second unit took 3,500 hours and used $200,000 worth of materials, equipment usage, and supplies. Labor is $30 per hour.

   a. Lambda was asked to present a bid for 10 additional units as soon as the second unit was completed. Production would start immediately. What would this bid be?

   b. Suppose there was a significant delay between the contracts. During this time, personnel and equipment were reassigned to other projects. Explain how this would affect the subsequent bid.

5   You've just completed a pilot run of 10 units of a major product and found the processing time for each unit was as follows:

UNIT NUMBER	TIME (HOURS)
1	970
2	640
3	420
4	380
5	320
6	250
7	220
8	207
9	190
10	190

   a. According to the pilot run, what would you estimate the learning rate to be?

   b. Based on *a*, how much time would it take for the next 190 units, assuming no loss of learning?

   c. How much time would it take to make the 1,000th unit?

6   Lazer Technologies Inc. (LTI) has produced a total of 20 high-power laser systems that could be used to destroy any approaching enemy missiles or aircraft. The 20 units have been

produced, funded in part as private research within the research and development arm of LTI, but the bulk of the funding came from a contract with the U.S. Department of Defense (DoD).

Testing of the laser units has shown that they are effective defense weapons, and through redesign to add portability and easier field maintenance, the units could be truck-mounted.

DoD has asked LTI to submit a bid for 100 units.

The 20 units that LTI has built so far cost the following amounts and are listed in the order in which they were produced:

UNIT NUMBER	COST ($ MILLIONS)	UNIT NUMBER	COST ($ MILLIONS)
1	$12	11	$3.9
2	10	12	3.5
3	6	13	3.0
4	6.5	14	2.8
5	5.8	15	2.7
6	6	16	2.7
7	5	17	2.3
8	3.6	18	3.0
9	3.6	19	2.9
10	4.1	20	2.6

a. Based on past experience, what is the learning rate?

b. What bid should LTI submit for the total order of 100 units, assuming that learning continues?

c. What is the cost expected to be for the last unit under the learning rate you estimated?

7 Jack Simpson, contract negotiator for Nebula Airframe Company, is currently involved in bidding on a follow-up government contract. In gathering cost data from the first three units, which Nebula produced under a research and development contract, he found that the first unit took 2,000 labor hours, the second took 1,800 labor hours, and the third took 1,692 hours.

In a contract for three more units, how many labor hours should Simpson plan for?

8 Honda Motor Company has discovered a problem in the exhaust system of one of its automobile lines and has voluntarily agreed to make the necessary modifications to conform with government safety requirements. Standard procedure is for the firm to pay a flat fee to dealers for each modification completed.

Honda is trying to establish a fair amount of compensation to pay dealers and has decided to choose a number of randomly selected mechanics and observe their performance and learning rate. Analysis demonstrated that the average learning rate was 90 percent, and Honda then decided to pay a $60 fee for each repair (3 hours × $20 per flat-rate hour).

Southwest Honda, Inc., has complained to Honda Motor Company about the fee. Six mechanics, working independently, have completed two modifications each. All took 9 hours on the average to do the first unit and 6.3 hours to do the second. Southwest refuses to do any more unless Honda allows at least 4.5 hours. The dealership expects to perform the modification to approximately 300 vehicles.

What is your opinion of Honda's allowed rate and the mechanics' performance?

9 United Research Associates (URA) had received a contract to produce two units of a new cruise missile guidance control. The first unit took 4,000 hours to complete and cost $30,000 in materials and equipment usage. The second took 3,200 hours and cost $21,000 in materials and equipment usage. Labor cost is charged at $18 per hour.

The prime contractor has now approached URA and asked to submit a bid for the cost of producing another 20 guidance controls.

a. What will the last unit cost to build?

b. What will be the average time for the 20 missile guidance controls?

c. What will the average cost be for guidance control for the 20 in the contract?

LEARNING CURVE TABLES

exhibit B.5   Learning Curves: Table of Unit Values

**Excel:
Learning
Curves**

	UNIT IMPROVEMENT FACTOR							
UNIT	60%	65%	70%	75%	80%	85%	90%	95%
1	1.0000	1.0000	1.0000	1.0000	1.0000	1.0000	1.0000	1.0000
2	.6000	.6500	.7000	.7500	.8000	.8500	.9000	.9500
3	.4450	.5052	.5682	.6338	.7021	.7729	.8462	.9219
4	.3600	.4225	.4900	.5625	.6400	.7225	.8100	.9025
5	.3054	.3678	.4368	.5127	.5956	.6857	.7830	.8877
6	.2670	.3284	.3977	.4754	.5617	.6570	.7616	.8758
7	.2383	.2984	.3674	.4459	.5345	.6337	.7439	.8659
8	.2160	.2746	.3430	.4219	.5120	.6141	.7290	.8574
9	.1980	.2552	.3228	.4017	.4930	.5974	.7161	.8499
10	.1832	.2391	.3058	.3846	.4765	.5828	.7047	.8433
12	.1602	.2135	.2784	.3565	.4493	.5584	.6854	.8320
14	.1430	.1940	.2572	.3344	.4276	.5386	.6696	.8226
16	.1290	.1785	.2401	.3164	.4096	.5220	.6561	.8145
18	.1188	.1659	.2260	.3013	.3944	.5078	.6445	.8074
20	.1099	.1554	.2141	.2884	.3812	.4954	.6342	.8012
22	.1025	.1465	.2038	.2772	.3697	.4844	.6251	.7955
24	.0961	.1387	.1949	.2674	.3595	.4747	.6169	.7904
25	.0933	.1353	.1908	.2629	.3548	.4701	.6131	.7880
30	.0815	.1208	.1737	.2437	.3346	.4505	.5963	.7775
35	.0728	.1097	.1605	.2286	.3184	.4345	.5825	.7687
40	.0660	.1010	.1498	.2163	.3050	.4211	.5708	.7611
45	.0605	.0939	.1410	.2060	.2936	.4096	.5607	.7545
50	.0560	.0879	.1336	.1972	.2838	.3996	.5518	.7486
60	.0489	.0785	.1216	.1828	.2676	.3829	.5367	.7386
70	.0437	.0713	.1123	.1715	.2547	.3693	.5243	.7302
80	.0396	.0657	.1049	.1622	.2440	.3579	.5137	.7231
90	.0363	.0610	.0987	.1545	.2349	.3482	.5046	.7168
100	.0336	.0572	.0935	.1479	.2271	.3397	.4966	.7112
120	.0294	.0510	.0851	.1371	.2141	.3255	.4830	.7017
140	.0262	.0464	.0786	.1287	.2038	.3139	.4718	.6937
160	.0237	.0427	.0734	.1217	.1952	.3042	.4623	.6869
180	.0218	.0397	.0691	.1159	.1879	.2959	.4541	.6809
200	.0201	.0371	.0655	.1109	.1816	.2887	.4469	.6757
250	.0171	.0323	.0584	.1011	.1691	.2740	.4320	.6646
300	.0149	.0289	.0531	.0937	.1594	.2625	.4202	.6557
350	.0133	.0262	.0491	.0879	.1517	.2532	.4105	.6482
400	.0121	.0241	.0458	.0832	.1453	.2454	.4022	.6419
450	.0111	.0224	.0431	.0792	.1399	.2387	.3951	.6363
500	.0103	.0210	.0408	.0758	.1352	.2329	.3888	.6314
600	.0090	.0188	.0372	.0703	.1275	.2232	.3782	.6229
700	.0080	.0171	.0344	.0659	.1214	.2152	.3694	.6158
800	.0073	.0157	.0321	.0624	.1163	.2086	.3620	.6098
900	.0067	.0146	.0302	.0594	.1119	.2029	.3556	.6045
1,000	.0062	.0137	.0286	.0569	.1082	.1980	.3499	.5998
1,200	.0054	.0122	.0260	.0527	.1020	.1897	.3404	.5918
1,400	.0048	.0111	.0240	.0495	.0971	.1830	.3325	.5850
1,600	.0044	.0102	.0225	.0468	.0930	.1773	.3258	.5793
1,800	.0040	.0095	.0211	.0446	.0895	.1725	.3200	.5743
2,000	.0037	.0089	.0200	.0427	.0866	.1683	.3149	.5698
2,500	.0031	.0077	.0178	.0389	.0806	.1597	.3044	.5605
3,000	.0027	.0069	.0162	.0360	.0760	.1530	.2961	.5530

Learning Curves: Table of Cumulative Values

UNIT	CUMULATIVE IMPROVEMENT FACTOR							
	60%	65%	70%	75%	80%	85%	90%	95%
1	1.000	1.000	1.000	1.000	1.000	1.000	1.000	1.000
2	1.600	1.650	1.700	1.750	1.800	1.850	1.900	1.950
3	2.045	2.155	2.268	2.384	2.502	2.623	2.746	2.872
4	2.405	2.578	2.758	2.946	3.142	3.345	3.556	3.774
5	2.710	2.946	3.195	3.459	3.738	4.031	4.339	4.662
6	2.977	3.274	3.593	3.934	4.299	4.688	5.101	5.538
7	3.216	3.572	3.960	4.380	4.834	5.322	5.845	6.404
8	3.432	3.847	4.303	4.802	5.346	5.936	6.574	7.261
9	3.630	4.102	4.626	5.204	5.839	6.533	7.290	8.111
10	3.813	4.341	4.931	5.589	6.315	7.116	7.994	8.955
12	4.144	4.780	5.501	6.315	7.227	8.244	9.374	10.62
14	4.438	5.177	6.026	6.994	8.092	9.331	10.72	12.27
16	4.704	5.541	6.514	7.635	8.920	10.38	12.04	13.91
18	4.946	5.879	6.972	8.245	9.716	11.41	13.33	15.52
20	5.171	6.195	7.407	8.828	10.48	12.40	14.61	17.13
22	5.379	6.492	7.819	9.388	11.23	13.38	15.86	18.72
24	5.574	6.773	8.213	9.928	11.95	14.33	17.10	20.31
25	5.668	6.909	8.404	10.19	12.31	14.80	17.71	21.10
30	6.097	7.540	9.305	11.45	14.02	17.09	20.73	25.00
35	6.478	8.109	10.13	12.72	15.64	19.29	23.67	28.86
40	6.821	8.631	10.90	13.72	17.19	21.43	26.54	32.68
45	7.134	9.114	11.62	14.77	18.68	23.50	29.37	36.47
50	7.422	9.565	12.31	15.78	20.12	25.51	32.14	40.22
60	7.941	10.39	13.57	17.67	22.87	29.41	37.57	47.65
70	8.401	11.13	14.74	19.43	25.47	33.17	42.87	54.99
80	8.814	11.82	15.82	21.09	27.96	36.80	48.05	62.25
90	9.191	12.45	16.83	22.67	30.35	40.32	53.14	69.45
100	9.539	13.03	17.79	24.18	32.65	43.75	58.14	76.59
120	10.16	14.11	19.57	27.02	37.05	50.39	67.93	90.71
140	10.72	15.08	21.20	29.67	41.22	56.78	77.46	104.7
160	11.21	15.97	22.72	32.17	45.20	62.95	86.80	118.5
180	11.67	16.79	24.14	34.54	49.03	68.95	95.96	132.1
200	12.09	17.55	25.48	36.80	52.72	74.79	105.0	145.7
250	13.01	19.28	28.56	42.05	61.47	88.83	126.9	179.2
300	13.81	20.81	31.34	46.94	69.66	102.2	148.2	212.2
350	14.51	22.18	33.89	51.48	77.43	115.1	169.0	244.8
400	15.14	23.44	36.26	55.75	84.85	127.6	189.3	277.0
450	15.72	24.60	38.48	59.80	91.97	139.7	209.2	309.0
500	16.26	25.68	40.58	63.68	98.85	151.5	228.8	340.6
600	17.21	27.67	44.47	70.97	112.0	174.2	267.1	403.3
700	18.06	29.45	48.04	77.77	124.4	196.1	304.5	465.3
800	18.82	31.09	51.36	84.18	136.3	217.3	341.0	526.5
900	19.51	32.60	54.46	90.26	147.7	237.9	376.9	587.2
1,000	20.15	31.01	57.40	96.07	158.7	257.9	412.2	647.4
1,200	21.30	36.59	62.85	107.0	179.7	296.6	481.2	766.6
1,400	22.32	38.92	67.85	117.2	199.6	333.9	548.4	884.2
1,600	23.23	41.04	72.49	126.8	218.6	369.9	614.2	1001
1,800	24.06	43.00	76.85	135.9	236.8	404.9	678.8	1116
2,000	24.83	44.84	80.96	144.7	254.4	438.9	742.3	1230
2,500	26.53	48.97	90.39	165.0	296.1	520.8	897.0	1513
3,000	27.99	52.62	98.90	183.7	335.2	598.9	1047	1791

Excel: Learning Curves

APPENDIX C

ANSWERS TO SELECTED PROBLEMS

Chapter 2
1   2.06
2   3.69

Chapter 3
3   No, must consider demand in the fourth year.
5   Expected NPV – Small = $4.8 million
    Expected NPV – Large = $2.6 million

Chapter 4
3   *a.* 20,000 books
    b. higher
    c. lower
11 *a.* 33.6 seconds
    b. 3.51; therefore, 4 workstations
    d. AB, DF, C, EG, H
    e. Efficiency = 70.2%
    f. Reduce cycle time to 32 seconds and work
        $6\frac{2}{3}$ minutes overtime
    g. 1.89 hours overtime; may be better to
        rebalance

Chapter 5
9   $W_s = 4.125$ minutes
    $L_q' = 4.05$ cars
    $L_s = 4.95$ car
13 *a.* 2 people
    b. 6 minutes
    c. .2964
    d. 67%
    e. 0.03375 hour
19 *a.* 0.833
    b. 5 documents
    c. 0.2 hour
    d. 0.4822
    e. L_1 = tends to infinity

Chapter 6
2   *a.* Not inspecting cost = $20/hr. Cost to
        inspect = $9/hr. Therefore, inspect.
    b. $.18 each
    c. $.22 per unit
8   $\overline{\overline{X}} = 999.1$
    $UCL = 1014.965$
    $LCL = 983.235$
    $\overline{R} = 21.733$
    $UCL = 49.551$
    $LCL = 0$
    Process is in control

11 *a.* $n = 31.3$ (round sample size to 32)
    b. Random sample 32; reject if more than 8 are
        defective.
14 $\overline{\overline{X}} = .499$
    $UCL = .520$
    $LCL = .478$
    $R = .037$
    $UCL = .078$
    $LCL = .000$
    Process is in control

Chapter 7
5   *b.* A-C-F-G-I and A-D-F-G-I
    c. C: one week
        D: one week
        G: one week
    d. Two paths: A-C-F-G-I and A-D-F-G-I;
        16 weeks
10 *a.* Critical path is A-E-G-C-D
    b. 26 weeks
    c. No difference in completion date
11 *a.* Critical path is A-C-D-F-G
    b.

Day	Cost	Activity
First	$1,000	A
Second	1,200	C
Third	1,500	D (or F)
Fourth	1,500	F (or D)
	$5,200	

Chapter 8
1   PV $84K versus $149K, purchasing from
    Taiwan looks attractive
3   Inventory turns = 148.6
    .35 weeks or 2.45 days

Chapter 9
1   $C_X = 176.7$
    $C_Y = 241.5$
2   $C_X = 374$
    $C_Y = 357$
3   Total profit = $4,240,000

Chapter 10
1   5 kanban card sets

Chapter 11

3 *a.* February 84
       March 86
       April 90
       May 88
       June 84
    b. MAD = 15

11 *a.* April to September = 130, 150, 160, 170,
        160, 150
    b. April to September = 136, 146, 150, 159,
        153, 146
    c. Exponential smoothing performed better.

15 MAD = 104
    TS = 3.1
    The high TS value indicates the model is unac-
    ceptable.

19 *a.* MAD = 90
        TS = −1.67
    b. Model okay since tracking is −1.67

Chapter 12

2 Total cost = $413,600
5 Total cost = $413,750

Chapter 13

5 *q* = 713
8 *a.* Q = 1,225
       R = 824
    b. *q* = 390 − Inventory on hand
12 *a.* Q = 89
    b. $224.72
    c. $222.50
14 *a.* A (4, 13, 18);
       B (2, 5, 8, 10, 11, 14, 16);
       C (remainder)
    b. Classify as A.

17 *q* = 691
26 729 hamburgers

Chapter 14

4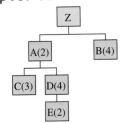

11 Least total cost method: Order 250 units in
    Period 1 for Periods 1–8;
    Least unit cost method: Order 450 units in
    Period 1 for Periods 1–9.

13 *c.* .A
        .B(2)
            .E(4)
            .F(3)
        .C(3)
            .D(3)
            .H(2)
                .E(5)
                .G(2)
        .D(1)
    d. Level 0   100 units of A
        Level 1   200 units of B
                   300 units of C
        Level 2   600 units of F
                   600 units of H
                   1,000 units of D
        Level 3   3,800 units of E
                   1,200 units of G

APPENDIX D

PRESENT VALUE TABLE

table D.1 Present Value of $1

YEAR	1%	2%	3%	4%	5%	6%	7%	8%	9%	10%	12%	14%	15%
1	.990	.980	.971	.962	.952	.943	.935	.926	.917	.909	.893	.877	.870
2	.980	.961	.943	.925	.907	.890	.873	.857	.842	.826	.797	.769	.756
3	.971	.942	.915	.889	.864	.840	.816	.794	.772	.751	.712	.675	.658
4	.961	.924	.889	.855	.823	.792	.763	.735	.708	.683	.636	.592	.572
5	.951	.906	.863	.822	.784	.747	.713	.681	.650	.621	.567	.519	.497
6	.942	.888	.838	.790	.746	.705	.666	.630	.596	.564	.507	.456	.432
7	.933	.871	.813	.760	.711	.665	.623	.583	.547	.513	.452	.400	.376
8	.923	.853	.789	.731	.677	.627	.582	.540	.502	.467	.404	.351	.327
9	.914	.837	.766	.703	.645	.592	.544	.500	.460	.424	.361	.308	.284
10	.905	.820	.744	.676	.614	.558	.508	.463	.422	.386	.322	.270	.247
11	.896	.804	.722	.650	.585	.527	.475	.429	.388	.350	.287	.237	.215
12	.887	.788	.701	.625	.557	.497	.444	.397	.356	.319	.257	.208	.187
13	.879	.773	.681	.601	.530	.469	.415	.368	.326	.290	.229	.182	.163
14	.870	.758	.661	.577	.505	.442	.388	.340	.299	.263	.205	.160	.141
15	.861	.743	.642	.555	.481	.417	.362	.315	.275	.239	.183	.140	.123
16	.853	.728	.623	.534	.458	.394	.339	.292	.252	.218	.163	.123	.107
17	.844	.714	.605	.513	.436	.371	.317	.270	.231	.198	.146	.108	.093
18	.836	.700	.587	.494	.416	.350	.296	.250	.212	.180	.130	.095	.081
19	.828	.686	.570	.475	.396	.331	.276	.232	.194	.164	.116	.083	.070
20	.820	.673	.554	.456	.377	.312	.258	.215	.178	.149	.104	.073	.061
25	.780	.610	.478	.375	.295	.233	.184	.146	.116	.092	.059	.038	.030
30	.742	.552	.412	.308	.231	.174	.131	.099	.075	.057	.033	.020	.015

YEAR	16%	18%	20%	24%	28%	32%	36%	40%	50%	60%	70%	80%	90%
1	.862	.847	.833	.806	.781	.758	.735	.714	.667	.625	.588	.556	.526
2	.743	.718	.694	.650	.610	.574	.541	.510	.444	.391	.346	.309	.277
3	.641	.609	.579	.524	.477	.435	.398	.364	.296	.244	.204	.171	.146
4	.552	.516	.482	.423	.373	.329	.292	.260	.198	.153	.120	.095	.077
5	.476	.437	.402	.341	.291	.250	.215	.186	.132	.095	.070	.053	.040
6	.410	.370	.335	.275	.227	.189	.158	.133	.088	.060	.041	.029	.021
7	.354	.314	.279	.222	.178	.143	.116	.095	.059	.037	.024	.016	.011
8	.305	.266	.233	.179	.139	.108	.085	.068	.039	.023	.014	.009	.006
9	.263	.226	.194	.144	.108	.082	.063	.048	.026	.015	.008	.005	.003
10	.227	.191	.162	.116	.085	.062	.046	.035	.017	.009	.005	.003	.002
11	.195	.162	.135	.094	.066	.047	.034	.025	.012	.006	.003	.002	.001
12	.168	.137	.112	.076	.052	.036	.025	.018	.008	.004	.002	.001	.001
13	.145	.116	.093	.061	.040	.027	.018	.013	.005	.002	.001	.001	.000
14	.125	.099	.078	.049	.032	.021	.014	.009	.003	.001	.001	.000	.000
15	.108	.084	.065	.040	.025	.016	.010	.006	.002	.001	.000	.000	.000
16	.093	.071	.054	.032	.019	.012	.007	.005	.002	.001	.000	.000	
17	.080	.060	.045	.026	.015	.009	.005	.003	.001	.000	.000		
18	.069	.051	.038	.021	.012	.007	.004	.002	.001	.000	.000		
19	.060	.043	.031	.017	.009	.005	.003	.002	.000	.000			
20	.051	.037	.026	.014	.007	.004	.002	.001	.000	.000			
25	.024	.016	.010	.005	.002	.001	.000	.000					
30	.012	.007	.004	.002	.001	.000	.000						

Using Microsoft Excel®, these are calculated with the equation: $(1 + \text{interest})^{-\text{years}}$.

APPENDIX E

NEGATIVE EXPONENTIAL DISTRIBUTION: VALUES OF e^{-x} [1]

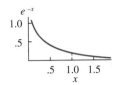

X	e^{-x} (VALUE)	X	e^{-x} (VALUE)	X	e^{-x} (VALUE)	X	e^{-x} (VALUE)
0.00	1.00000	0.50	0.60653	1.00	0.36788	1.50	0.22313
0.01	0.99005	0.51	.60050	1.01	.36422	1.51	.22091
0.02	.98020	0.52	.59452	1.02	.36060	1.52	.21871
0.03	.97045	0.53	.58860	1.03	.35701	1.53	.21654
0.04	.96079	0.54	.58275	1.04	.35345	1.54	.21438
0.05	.95123	0.55	.57695	1.05	.34994	1.55	.21225
0.06	.94176	0.56	.57121	1.06	.34646	1.56	.21014
0.07	.93239	0.57	.56553	1.07	.34301	1.57	.20805
0.08	.92312	0.58	.55990	1.08	.33960	1.58	.20598
0.09	.91393	0.59	.55433	1.09	.33622	1.59	.20393
0.10	.90484	0.60	.54881	1.10	.33287	1.60	.20190
0.11	.89583	0.61	.54335	1.11	.32956	1.61	.19989
0.12	.88692	0.62	.53794	1.12	.32628	1.62	.19790
0.13	.87809	0.63	.53259	1.13	.32303	1.63	.19593
0.14	.86936	0.64	.52729	1.14	.31982	1.64	.19398
0.15	.86071	0.65	.52205	1.15	.31664	1.65	.19205
0.16	.87514	0.66	.51685	1.16	.31349	1.66	.19014
0.17	.84366	0.67	.51171	1.17	.31037	1.67	.18825
0.18	.83527	0.68	.50662	1.18	.30728	1.68	.18637
0.19	.82696	0.69	.50158	1.19	.30422	1.69	.18452
0.20	.81873	0.70	.49659	1.20	.30119	1.70	.18268
0.21	.81058	0.71	.49164	1.21	.29820	1.71	.18087
0.22	.80252	0.72	.48675	1.22	.29523	1.72	.17907
0.23	.79453	0.73	.48191	1.23	.29229	1.73	.17728
0.24	.78663	0.74	.47711	1.24	.28938	1.74	.17552
0.25	.77880	0.75	.47237	1.25	.28650	1.75	.17377
0.26	.77105	0.76	.46767	1.26	.28365	1.76	.17204
0.27	.76338	0.77	.46301	1.27	.28083	1.77	.17033
0.28	.75578	0.78	.45841	1.28	.27804	1.78	.16864
0.29	.74826	0.79	.45384	1.29	.27527	1.79	.16696
0.30	.74082	0.80	.44933	1.30	.27253	1.80	.16530
0.31	.73345	0.81	.44486	1.31	.26982	1.81	.16365
0.32	.72615	0.82	.44043	1.32	.26714	1.82	.16203
0.33	.71892	0.83	.43605	1.33	.26448	1.83	.16041
0.34	.71177	0.84	.43171	1.34	.26185	1.84	.15882
0.35	.70469	0.85	.42741	1.35	.25924	1.85	.15724
0.36	.69768	0.86	.42316	1.36	.25666	1.86	.15567
0.37	.69073	0.87	.41895	1.37	.25411	1.87	.15412
0.38	.68386	0.88	.41478	1.38	.25158	1.88	.15259
0.39	.67706	0.89	.41066	1.39	.24908	1.89	.15107
0.40	.67032	0.90	.40657	1.40	.24660	1.90	.14957
0.41	.66365	0.91	.40252	1.41	.24414	1.91	.14808
0.42	.65705	0.92	.39852	1.42	.24171	1.92	.14661
0.43	.65051	0.93	.39455	1.43	.23931	1.93	.14515
0.44	.64404	0.94	.39063	1.44	.23693	1.94	.14370
0.45	.63763	0.95	.38674	1.45	.23457	1.95	.14227
0.46	.63128	0.96	.38289	1.46	.23224	1.96	.14086
0.47	.62500	0.97	.37908	1.47	.22993	1.97	.13946
0.48	.61878	0.98	.37531	1.48	.22764	1.98	.13807
0.49	.61263	0.99	.37158	1.49	.22537	1.99	.13670
0.50	.60653	1.00	.36788	1.50	.22313	2.00	.13534

[1] Using Microsoft Excel, these values are calculated with the equation: $1 - EXPONDIST(x, 1, TRUE)$.

APPENDIX F

AREAS OF THE CUMULATIVE STANDARD NORMAL DISTRIBUTION[1]

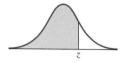

An entry in the table is the proportion under the curve cumulated from the negative tail.

z	G(z)	z	G(z)	z	G(z)
−4.00	0.00003	−1.30	0.09680	1.40	0.91924
−3.95	0.00004	−1.25	0.10565	1.45	0.92647
−3.90	0.00005	−1.20	0.11507	1.50	0.93319
−3.85	0.00006	−1.15	0.12507	1.55	0.93943
−3.80	0.00007	−1.10	0.13567	1.60	0.94520
−3.75	0.00009	−1.05	0.14686	1.65	0.95053
−3.70	0.00011	−1.00	0.15866	1.70	0.95543
−3.65	0.00013	−0.95	0.17106	1.75	0.95994
−3.60	0.00016	−0.90	0.18406	1.80	0.96407
−3.55	0.00019	−0.85	0.19766	1.85	0.96784
−3.50	0.00023	−0.80	0.21186	1.90	0.97128
−3.45	0.00028	−0.75	0.22663	1.95	0.97441
−3.40	0.00034	−0.70	0.24196	2.00	0.97725
−3.35	0.00040	−0.65	0.25785	2.05	0.97982
−3.30	0.00048	−0.60	0.27425	2.10	0.98214
−3.25	0.00058	−0.55	0.29116	2.15	0.98422
−3.20	0.00069	−0.50	0.30854	2.20	0.98610
−3.15	0.00082	−0.45	0.32636	2.25	0.98778
−3.10	0.00097	−0.40	0.34458	2.30	0.98928
−3.05	0.00114	−0.35	0.36317	2.35	0.99061
−3.00	0.00135	−0.30	0.38209	2.40	0.99180
−2.95	0.00159	−0.25	0.40129	2.45	0.99286
−2.90	0.00187	−0.20	0.42074	2.50	0.99379
−2.85	0.00219	−0.15	0.44038	2.55	0.99461
−2.80	0.00256	−0.10	0.46017	2.60	0.99534
−2.75	0.00298	−0.05	0.48006	2.65	0.99598
−2.70	0.00347	0.00	0.50000	2.70	0.99653
−2.65	0.00402	0.05	0.51994	2.75	0.99702
−2.60	0.00466	0.10	0.53983	2.80	0.99744
−2.55	0.00539	0.15	0.55962	2.85	0.99781
−2.50	0.00621	0.20	0.57926	2.90	0.99813
−2.45	0.00714	0.25	0.59871	2.95	0.99841
−2.40	0.00820	0.30	0.61791	3.00	0.99865
−2.35	0.00939	0.35	0.63683	3.05	0.99886
−2.30	0.01072	0.40	0.65542	3.10	0.99903
−2.25	0.01222	0.45	0.67364	3.15	0.99918
−2.20	0.01390	0.50	0.69146	3.20	0.99931
−2.15	0.01578	0.55	0.70884	3.25	0.99942
−2.10	0.01786	0.60	0.72575	3.30	0.99952
−2.05	0.02018	0.65	0.74215	3.35	0.99960
−2.00	0.02275	0.70	0.75804	3.40	0.99966
−1.95	0.02559	0.75	0.77337	3.45	0.99972
−1.90	0.02872	0.80	0.78814	3.50	0.99977
−1.85	0.03216	0.85	0.80234	3.55	0.99981
−1.80	0.03593	0.90	0.81594	3.60	0.99984
−1.75	0.04006	0.95	0.82894	3.65	0.99987
−1.70	0.04457	1.00	0.84134	3.70	0.99989
−1.65	0.04947	1.05	0.85314	3.75	0.99991
−1.60	0.05480	1.10	0.86433	3.80	0.99993
−1.55	0.06057	1.15	0.87493	3.85	0.99994
−1.50	0.06681	1.20	0.88493	3.90	0.99995
−1.45	0.07353	1.25	0.89435	3.95	0.99996
−1.40	0.08076	1.30	0.90320	4.00	0.99997
−1.35	0.08851	1.35	0.91149		

[1]Using Microsoft Excel, these probabilities are generated with the NORMSDIST(z) function.

NAME INDEX

A

Abernathy, William, 16
Albright, S. C., 131, 482
Allen, M., 301
Anderson, D. R., 482

B

Balamuralikrishna, R., 301
Ballou, R. H., 269
Barone, J. E., 130
Berry, W. L., 247, 383, 429, 459
Billington, P. J., 383
Blabey, R. G., 130
Blanchard, David, 39, 301
Bowersox, D. J., 247
Bramley, D., 247
Brandimarte, P., 383
Brooks, R. B., 429
Bulfin, R. L., Jr., 429
Burt, David, 247

C

Caltani, Kyle, 39
Cecere, J., 130
Chase, R. B., 373, 374, 383
Cho, Fujio, 274
Chopra, S., 247
Clark, Kim, 16
Closs, D. J., 247
Cooper, M. B., 247
Craumer, Martha, 247
Crosby, Philip, 16, 135, 138, 176

D

Deming, W. Edwards, 16, 135
Dobler, D. W., 247
Dodge, Harold F., 16, 176
Drezner, Z., 269

E

Elkington, J., 39
Evans, James R., 177

F

Fisher, M. L., 226, 227, 247, 353, 383
Fitzsimmons, J. A., 131
Fitzsimmons, M. A., 131
Fliedner, Gene, 353
Fogarty, D., 77
Ford, Henry, 16, 272
Friedman, Thomas L., 224

G

Gail, R., 131
Gantt, Henry L., 186
Garvin, D. A., 176
Geddes, Patrick, 24
George, M. L., 301
Gilbreth, Frank, 17
Gilbreth, Lillian, 17
Grant, E. L., 176
Gray, C., 219
Greaver, M. F., 247
Gross, D., 131
Gross, J. M., 301
Gryna, F. M., 163
Gustofsson, Anders, 12

H

Hall, R. H., 301
Hall, R. W., 83
Hamacher, H., 269
Hammer, Michael, 16–17
Hammond, J. H., 383
Hamper, B., 78
Hanke, J. E., 353
Harris, C. M., 131
Hayes, Robert, 16, 39, 232, 247
Haywood-Farmer, J., 55
Heragu, S., 97
Hill, Terry, 30, 39
Hillier, F. S., 131
Hoenas, T., 301
Hoffman, T., 77
Hyer, N., 97
Hyndman, R. J., 353

I

Icenogel, M. L., 177

J

Jacobs, F. R., 247, 383, 429, 459
John, C., 247
Johnson, Michael D., 12
Jones, D. T., 289, 301
Juran, Joseph M., 16, 135, 138, 163
Jutte, Larry, 255

K

Kaminski, P., 247
Karlsson, C., 301
Kerzner, H., 219
Kimes, S., 373, 374, 383
Klamroth, K., 269
Kleinrock, L., 131
Kopczak, L., 428

L

Larson, E. W., 219
Leader, C., 176
Leavenworth, R. S., 176
Lee, Hau, 228–229, 247, 428
Leonard, Frank S., 176
Lewis, James P., 219
Lewis, M., 39
Linder, Jane, 232
Lindsay, William M., 177
Lovelle, Jared, 299, 301

M

Makridakis, S., 353
McInnis, K. R., 301
McLeavey, D. W., 383
Meindl, P., 247
Monden, Yasuhiro, 84, 301

N

Nakamura, Toshihiro, 66
Narasimhan, S., 383
Neely, A., 20
Nersesian, R. L., 20
Nollet, J., 55

O

Obermeyer, W. R., 383
O'Donnell, Jayne, 5
O'Halloran, D., 176
Ohno, Tai-ichi, 272
Orlicky, J., 459

P

Pareto, Villefredo, 411
Peters, Tom, 182
Peterson, R., 383, 429
Phelps, T., 301
Pisano, Gary, 39, 232, 247
Porter, M. E., 31, 254, 268
Pyke, D. F., 383, 429

R

Raman, A., 383
Reitsch, A. G., 353
Rha, C. K., 130
Romig, Harry, 16, 176
Roos, D., 301
Rosentrater, K. A., 301
Ruck, Bill, 36

S

Sampson, Scott, 103
Sheikh, K., 459
Shewhart, Walter, 16
Shouldice, Edward Earle, 43
Silver, E. A., 383, 429
Simchi-Levi, D., 247
Simchi-Levi, E., 247
Sipper, D., 429
Skinner, Wickham, 16
Slack, N., 20, 39
Small, B. B., 177
Smith, M., 301
Spohrer, Jim, 17, 21
Starling, S. L., 247
Suzaki, K., 301
Sweeney, D. J., 482

T

Taguchi, Genichi, 148–149
Taylor, Frederick W., 17

Tersine, R. J., 429
Tompkins, B., 301
Tompkins, J. A., 97
Tucker, J. B., 130

U

Upton, David, 39, 232, 247

V

Villa, A., 383
Vollman, T. E., 247, 383, 429, 459

W

Wallace, Thomas F., 356, 383
Walleck, S., 176
Wantuck, K. A., 301
Welch, Jack, 133
Wemmerlöv, U., 97

Wheelwright, Steven, 16, 39, 232, 247, 353
White, J. A., 97
Whybark, D. C., 247, 383, 429, 459
Wichem, D. W., 353
Wild, T., 429
Williams, T. A., 482
Wilson, J., 21
Wilson, L. W., 429
Winchester, Simon, 8
Winston, W. L., 131, 482
Womack, J. P., 289, 301
Wright, T. P., 63

Y

Yu-Lee, R. T., 63

Z

Zimmerman, S. M., 177
Zipkin, P. H., 429

SUBJECT INDEX

A

ABC classification, 410–412
Abercrombie & Fitch, 5
Acceptable quality level (AQL), 164
Acceptance sampling, 162–166
Accuracy, of inventory control, 412–414
Accurate response, 360
Acquisition costs, 238–239
Activities, 186, 206
Activity direct costs, 199–200
Activity-system maps, 31, 35
Actual customer contact, 103
Adaptive forecasting, 325
Additive seasonal variation, 315–316
Advanced Optical Components, 362
Advanced planning option, 462
Aéropostale, 5
Aggregate operations plan, 356, 358–362,
    374, 434; See also Sales and
    operations planning
Aggregate plan
    applied to services, 367–370
    costs, 361
    cut-and-try approach, 363–368
    defined, 356, 374
    forecasting demand; See Forecasting
    internal/external variables, 359–360
    level scheduling, 370–372
    linear programming and, 462
    master production schedule, 434
    production planning environment,
        359–361
    purpose, 358
    yield management, 359, 372–374, 375
Agile supply chains, 230
Air, as a mode of transportation, 252
Airbus, 13
Amazon, 17
AMD, 233
America West, 13
Appraisal costs, 138, 140
AQL, 164
ARPANET, 17
Arrival
    batch, 112
    distribution of, 109–112
    impatient, 112
    patient, 112
    single, 112
Arrival rate, 109, 123
Assemble-to-order, 67–68, 85, 436
Assemble-to-stock, 436
Assembly lines; See also Production
        processes
    balancing, 72, 78–84, 85
    defined, 72, 76, 85
    design of, 78–84

flexible layouts, 82, 83
Ford Co., 16
    splitting tasks, 82
    U-shaped layouts, 82
Assignable variation, 146, 167
Association of Operations
        Management, 250
Attributes, 154, 167
Available to promise, 435, 451
Average, 167
Average aggregate inventory value,
    241–242, 243
Awards, for quality, 16, 134–135, 166

B

Backflush, 284, 292
Backordering costs, 261
Balance, system, 47–48
Balancing, of assembly lines, 72, 78–84, 85
Baldrige National Quality Award, 16, 134
Balking, 112
Bar chart, 186–187
Bar coding, 413
Batch arrival, 112
Best operating level, 45, 57
Best practices, 140
Bias errors, 328
Bill of materials (BOM), 438–439,
    442–443, 451
Black belts, 17
Blueprinting, service, 103–105, 123
BMW, 27, 46, 253
Boeing Co., 13, 69
Bottlenecks, 48
Brainwork, 182
Break-even analysis, 73–75
Breakthrough projects, 180–181
British Airways, 289
Budgeted cost of work performed (BCWP),
    188–191
Budgets, 361
Buffer inventory, 363; See also Safety stock
Buffered core, 101–102
Bullwhip effect, 226–227, 243
Business process reengineering, 16–17

C

C charts, 157–158
Call center management, 99
Campbell Soup, 227
Capability index (C_{pk}), 151–154, 167
Capability sourcing, 234
Capacity, 284
Capacity cushion, 49, 57
Capacity focus, 46

Capacity management, 42–63
    best operating level, 45, 57
    changes in, 47–48
    decision trees, 51–54
    defined, 44, 57
    determining requirements, 48–51
    economies/diseconomies of scale,
        45–46, 57
    flexibility, 46–47
    forecasting, 48–50
    imbalances in, 48
    intermediate-range, 44, 357–358, 374
    long-range, 44, 357–358, 374
    objective of, 45
    outsourcing and, 48
    service versus manufacturing, 54–56
    services, 101
    short-range, 44, 357–358, 374
    underutilization of, 284
    utilization rate, 45, 55–56, 57
Careers, in OSM, 14–15
Cases
    Altavox Electronics, 352
    Applichem—The Transportation Problem,
        267–268
    Bradford Manufacturing—Planning Plant
        Production, 381–382
    Brunswick Motors, Inc.—An Introductory
        Case for MRP, 457–458
    Cell Phone Design Project, 217–218
    Community Hospital Evening Operating
        Room, 130
    Designing Toshiba's Notebook Computer
        Line, 93–96
    Hank Kolb, Director of Quality Assurance,
        174–176
    Hewlett-Packard—Supplying the Deskjet
        Printer in Europe, 425–428
    Pepe Jeans, 246–247
    Pro Fishing Boats—A Value Stream
        Mapping Exercise, 300
    Quality Parts Company, 297–298
    Shouldice Hospital—A Cut Above, 60–62
    The Tao of Timbuk2*, 38–39
    Value Stream Mapping, 298–299
Causal relationship forecasting, 331–333, 338
Cause-and-effect diagrams, 143, 145
Central America Free Trade Agreement
    (CAFTA), 254
Centroid method, 260–261, 264
Certification, of quality, 16
Change management, 28
Changeover time, 47
Chase strategy, 360
Checksheets, 143
Chief Operating Officer, 15
Chrysler, 30, 34

Closed-loop strategy process, 26
CNN, 17
Coca-Cola, 233
Collaborative planning, forecasting and replenishment (CPFR), 335–336, 338
Common variation, 146–147, 167
Competitive dimensions, 27–29
Computer simulation, 122
Concept-to-cash, 5
Conformance quality, 137, 166
Consolidated billing services, 99
Consolidated warehouses, 252
Constant arrival rate, 109
Consumer's risk, 164
Continental Airlines, 29–30
Continuous process layouts, 72, 76, 78, 85
Continuous replenishment, 227
Contract manufacturers, 18
Control charts, 155, 186–191
Core competencies, 233
Corporate annual plan, 358
Cost
    acquisition, 238–239
    activity direct, 199–200
    adding capacity, 48
    aggregate production plan, 361–362
    appraisal, 138, 140
    backordering, 261
    failure, 138–140
    holding, 261, 390
    inventory, 390–391
    ordering, 390
    ownership, 238–239
    post-ownership, 238–239
    prevention, 138–140
    versus price, 27
    production, 361
    production change, 390
    project indirect, 199–200
    of quality, 138–140, 166
    revenue, 241
    salvage, 238
    setup, 390
    shortage, 390
    total, 238–240, 243
    transaction, 391
    variability, 148–149
Cost of goods sold (COGS), 241–242, 243
Cost schedule status reports (CSSR), 188
Cost scheduling, 199–201
CPFR, 335–336, 338
C_{pk}, 151–154
Cradle-to-grave, 25
Crash cost (CC), 200–202
Crash time (CT), 200–202
Crashing, project, 199–203
Critical customer requirement (CCR), 141–142
Critical path method, 191–199, 206
Cross-docking, 252–253, 264

Cumulative Standard Normal Distribution, 401
Customer arrivals, 108
Customer contact, 100–103
Customer order decoupling point, 67, 85, 307, 387
Customer touch points, 18
Customer value, 272, 291
Customers, lean, 278
Customization, mass, 17, 19
Cut-and-try approach, 363–368
Cycle counting, 412–414, 415
Cycle time, 85, 284–285

D
DaimlerChrysler, 34
Data mining, 306
Data warehouse, 305–306
Days-of-supply, 70, 85
Decision rules, 374
Decision trees, 51–54
Decomposition, of a time series, 314–321
Decoupling points, 67, 85, 307, 387
Defects per million opportunities (DPMO), 141, 167
Define, measure, analyze, improve, control (DMAIC), 142–145, 167
Delivering process, 10
Delivery speed, 28
Dell Computer, 18, 48, 66, 68, 272
Deloitte, 235
Delphi method, 334–335
Demand
    changes in, 28
    components of, 308–310
    dependent, 307–308, 337, 391–392, 415, 432
    forecasting, 436, 438, 441–442
    independent, 308, 337, 391–392, 415
    management of, 307–308
    product, 436, 438
    seasonal, 315–321
    volatility of, 55
Demand planning, 8–9
Dependent demand, 307–308, 337, 391–392, 415, 432
Derivative projects, 180–181
Design of experiments (DOE), 143
Design quality, 27–28, 136, 166
DHL, 99, 250
Dimensions of quality, 136–137
Direct costs, 199–200
Direct distribution, 386
Direct-to-store, 385–386
Discipline, in a queue, 113
Discounts, 227
Diseconomies of scale, 45–46
Disneyland, 289
Distribution center bypass, 386
Distribution of arrivals, 109–111

DMAIC, 142–145, 167
DPMO, 141, 167
Du Pont, 191
Dynamic programming, 463

E
Early start schedule, 193–194, 196, 206
Earned value management (EVM), 188–191, 206
eBay, 17
Economic order quantity (EOQ), 396, 399–400, 404, 448
Economic prosperity, 24
Economies of scale, 45–46, 57
Economies of scope, 47, 57
EDI, 227
Effectiveness, 13, 19, 25
Efficiency, 13, 19
Efficient supply chains, 229
Electronic commerce, 17
Electronic data interchange, 227
Eli Lilly, 227
Engineer-to-order, 67, 69, 85
Enterprise resource planning (ERP), 432, 451; *See also* Material requirements planning (MRP)
Environment
    activities, 221
    green sourcing, 235–238
    stewardship of, 24–25
    top green manufacturers, 271–272
    waste reduction, 235, 272, 274, 275, 291
Environmental footprint, 221
ERP, 432, 451
Errors, in forecasts, 313–314, 328–331
Event triggered models, 396
Everyday low price, 227
Executive judgment, 334
Explicit objective, 462
Explosion process, 440–441
Exponential distribution, 109–110, 123
Exponential smoothing, 324–327, 337
External failure costs, 139, 140

F
Fabricate-to-order, 436
Fabricate-to-stock, 436
Face-to-face contact, 101–102
Facility layout, 72–73, 281–283
Facility location; *See* Plant location
Factor-rating systems, 256, 264
Fail-safing, 103–105
Failure costs, 138–140
Failure mode and effect analysis (FMEA), 143, 146
Federal Express, 17, 231–232, 249, 250, 290
Finished products inventory, 389
Finite population, 108–109

First Bank/Dallas, 289
First come, first served (FCFS), 113
Fishbone diagrams, 143, 145
Fitness for use, 137
Fixed-order quantity model, 388, 396–404, 415
Fixed-time period model, 388–389, 396–398, 405–406, 415
Flexibility
   capacity, 46–47
   in workers, 47
Flexible line layouts, 82, 83
Flextronics, 230
Flow management, 431
Flow time, 70, 85
Flowcharts, 103–105, 143–145
FMEA, 143, 146
Focused factory, 46–47, 57
Folk, Work, and Place, 24
Ford, 27, 30, 34, 46
Forecasting, 304–353
   adaptive, 325
   capacity planning and, 48–50
   causal relationship, 331–333, 338
   components of demand, 308–310
   CPFR, 335–336, 338
   demand management, 307–308, 441–442
   errors in, 313–314, 328–331
   long term, 310
   multiple regression analysis, 332–333
   purpose of, 306
   qualitative techniques
      Delphi method, 334–335
      historical analogy, 334
      market research, 333–334
      panel consensus, 334
   short term, 310
   strategic, 306, 337
   tactical, 307, 337
   time series analysis
      decomposition of, 314–321
      defined, 308, 337
      exponential smoothing, 324–327, 337
      linear regression, 311–314, 337
      selecting a model, 311
      simple moving average, 321–323
      weighted moving average, 323–324
   web-based, 335–336
Foreign trade zone, 254
Forward buying, 226
Free trade zones, 254, 264
Freeze window, 284, 291
Fujitsu, 233
Functional products, 228–229, 243
Functional projects, 182–184, 206

G
Gantt chart, 186–187, 192, 205, 206
Gap, 5

General Electric, 133, 141, 142
General Motors, 30, 34, 78, 227, 359
General purpose equipment, 73
Global enterprise resource planning, 18
Global sourcing
   free trade zones, 254, 264
   logistics of, 250, 254, 264
   offshoring and, 223–224
   strategic sourcing, 224–230
Global supply chains, 8
Goal programming, 463
Goods versus services, 11–13
Google, 17
Graphical linear programming, 464–466
Green belts, 17
Green manufacturing, 271–272
Green sourcing, 235–238
Green supply chain management, 221
Gross requirements, 445
Group technology (GT), 282, 291

H
Hand delivery, as a mode of transportation, 252
Harley-Davidson, 3, 19–20
Hedging, 229–230
Heineken, 387
Hewlett-Packard, 227, 232
High degree of customer contact, 100, 123
Highway, as a mode of transportation, 251–252
Histograms, 143
Historical analogy, 334
Hitachi, 233
Holding costs, 261, 390
Honda, 46, 84, 255
Honeywell, 289
Host community, 254
Hub-and-spoke systems, 252–253, 264

I
IBM, 12, 17, 227, 272
IDEO, 100
IKEA, 23, 30–31
Immediate predecessor, 193, 206
Impatient arrival, 112
In-transit inventory, 69
Independent demand, 308, 337, 391–392, 415
Indirect costs, 199–200
Industry learning, 484
Infinite population, 109
Infinite potential length, 112
Information technology, 17
Initiatives, 26–27
Innovative products, 228–229, 243
Inspection, 163
Intel, 233, 272

Intermediate-range planning, 44, 357–358, 374
Internal failure costs, 138, 140
International logistics, 250, 254, 264
International Organization for Standardization, 16, 140
Internet
   EDI, 227
   electronic commerce, 17
   virtual customer contact, 103
   web based forecasting, 335–336
Inventory
   buffer, 363
   costs, 261, 390–391
   defined, 389, 415
   finished products, 389
   in-transit, 69
   obsolescence of, 391–392
   purpose of, 389–390
   raw material, 389
   total value of, 69–70, 85
   turnover of, 70, 85, 241–242, 243, 407–408
   types of, 388
Inventory control, 384–429; See also Production processes
   ABC classification, 410–412
   accuracy, 412–414
   benefits of, 387
   bullwhip effect, 226–227, 243
   continuous replenishment, 227
   cycle counting, 412–414, 415
   EOQ, 396, 399–400, 404, 448
   fixed-order quantity model, 388, 396–404, 415
   fixed-time period model, 388–389, 396–398, 405–406, 415
   independent versus dependent demand, 391–392
   Little's Law, 70, 85
   multiperiod systems, 396–397
   performance measurement, 241–242
   price-break models, 408–410
   RFID, 413
   safety stock; See Safety stock
   single-period model, 388, 393–396
   vendor managed, 226, 243
Inventory on hand, 358, 375
Inventory position, 398, 415
Inventory records, 439–440, 443–444
ISO 9000, 16, 140–141
ISO 14000, 140–141

J
J. Crew, 5
J. D. Power and Associates, 137
Jaguar, 46
JC Company, 363
JC Penney, 5

Job shop, 72
Johnson & Johnson, 272
Just-in-time (JIT), 15–16, 272, 282–284;
      See also Lean production

K
Kaizen, 279, 291
Kanban, 285–287, 292
Kohl's, 5

L
Land's End, 6
Late start schedule, 193–194, 196, 206
Lead time, 67, 85, 441, 443–447
Lean layouts, 281–283
Lean manufacturing, 15–16, 68, 85, 275
Lean procurement, 275
Lean production, 270–301
   defined, 272, 291
   design principles, 280–289
   JIT, 272, 282–284
   kanban, 285–287, 292
   pull system, 273
   schedules, 284–288
   supply chains and, 275–278, 288–289
   Toyota Production System, 274–275
   value stream mapping, 278–280, 291
Lean services, 289–291
Lean suppliers, 275
Learning curve, 483–493
Least squares method, 312–314, 318–321
Least total cost (LTC), 448–450
Least unit cost, 450
Level schedule, 284, 291, 370–372
Level strategy, 361
Leveling, 205
Life cycle, product, 227
Limited line capacity, 112
Line balancing, 72, 78–84, 85; *See also*
      Assembly lines
Linear programming, 256–260, 264, 461–470
Linear regression forecasting, 311–314, 337
Little's Law, 70, 85
L.L. Bean, 6
Location, 54
Lockheed Martin, 69
Logistics, 248–269
   cross-docking, 252–253, 264
   defined, 243, 250, 264
   hub-and-spoke systems, 252–253, 264
   international, 250, 254, 264
   lean, 277
   linear programming, 256–260, 264
   modes of transportation, 251–252
   outsourcing of, 231–232
   plant location
      centroid method, 260–261, 264
      criteria, 253–255

   factor-rating systems, 256, 264
      transportation method, 256–260, 264
   processes, 10
   service facility locations, 261–263
   third-party providers, 231, 251, 264
Logistics-System Design Matrix, 251
Long range capacity management, 44
Long-range planning, 357–358, 374
Long term forecasting, 310
Lot-for-lot (L4L), 447–448
Lot sizing, 166, 447–451
Lot tolerance percent defective (LTPD), 164
Low degree of customer contact, 100, 123
Low-level coding, 439
Lower control limits (LCL), 156
Lower specification limits, 148–149, 167

M
MAD, 328–331, 337
Maintenance, preventive, 281, 291
Make-to-order, 67, 69, 85
Make-to-stock, 67–68, 69, 85, 388
Making process, 10
Malcolm Baldrige National Quality Award,
      135, 166
Management by exception, 205
Manufacturing; *See also* Production processes
   assembly lines; *See* Assembly lines
   break-even analysis, 73–75
   capacity planning; *See* Capacity
      management
   contract, 18
   focused factory, 46–47, 57
   green, 271–272
   JIT, 15–16, 272, 282–284
   lean, 68, 85
   plant location; *See* Plant location
   repetitive, 282
Manufacturing cell layout, 72, 76, 77, 85
Manufacturing inventory, 389
MAPE, 329, 337
Mapping, process, 69–71
Market-basket analysis, 306
Market research, 333–334
Marketing function, 357
Marketing–operations link, 30
Mass customization, 17, 19
Master production schedule (MPS), 433–435,
      442, 451
Material requirements planning (MRP),
      430–459
   benefits, 436
   bill of materials, 438–439, 442–443, 451
   computer programs for, 440–441
   defined, 432, 451
   ERP, 432, 451
   evolution of, 431
   example using, 441–447
   inputs to, 437

   inventory records, 439–440, 443–444
   lot sizing, 166, 447–451
   MPS, 433–435, 442, 451
   planned order release, 445
   scheduled receipts, 445
   system structure, 436–441
   where to use, 435–436
Materials management, 432
Matrix projects, 184, 206
Mayo Clinic, 100
McDonald's, 16, 289
Mean, 167
Mean absolute deviation (MAD),
      328–331, 337
Mean absolute percent error (MAPE),
      329, 337
Mean squared error, 328
Merck, 34
Milestone chart, 186–188
Miller Brewing Company, 289
Minimum-cost scheduling, 199–203
Mixed line, 115
Mixed-model line balancing, 82–84
Mixed-model production cycle, 284
Mixed strategy, 361, 375
Mixed virtual customer contact, 103
M&M Mars, 46
Modular bill of materials, 439
Motorola, 141, 149, 182–183, 227
Moving average
   simple, 321–323
   weighted, 323–324
MPS, 433–435, 442, 451
MRP; *See* Material requirements planning
      (MRP)
Muda, 289
Multichannel
   multiphase line, 115
   single phase line, 114–115
Multifactor productivity measure, 32–33
Multiperiod inventory systems, 396–397
Multiple lines, 112
Multiple regression analysis, 332–333
Multiplicative seasonal variation, 315–316
Multivariate testing, 143

N
NASA, 179–180
National Institute of Standards and
      Technology, 16
NEC, 233
Negative capacity cushion, 49
Net change system, 441, 451
Network planning models
   critical path method, 191–199, 206
   PERT, 192, 197
   project crashing, 199–203
   three activity time estimates, 196–199
   time–cost models, 199–203, 206

Networks, supply, 6–7, 291
Newsperson problem, 393
Nike, 272
Nissan, 46
Nonlinear programming, 463
Normal cost (NC), 200–202
Normal time (NT), 200–202

O

Objective function, 464–466
Obsolescence, 391–392
Offshoring, 223–224
Operating characteristic curve, 165–166
Operations, defined, 8
Operations and supply management (OSM)
  careers, 14–15
  current issues, 18
  defined, 6, 19
  development of, 15–17
Operations and supply strategy
  competitive dimensions, 27–29
  defined, 25, 35
  fitting activities to strategy, 30–32
  order winners/qualifiers, 30, 35, 236
  trade-offs, 29–30
  triple bottom line, 18, 19, 24–25, 35
Operations effectiveness, 13, 25
Opportunity flow diagram, 143, 145
Order management, 99
Order winners/qualifiers, 30, 35, 236
Ordering costs, 390
Outsourcing
  benefits of, 230–231
  capability sourcing, 234
  capacity management and, 48
  contract manufacturers, 18
  core competencies and, 233
  defined, 223–224, 230, 243
  drawbacks, 232
  logistics, 231–232
  reasons to, 230–231
  supplier relationship structure, 232–233
  trend toward, 17
Ownership costs, 238–239

P

P charts, 156–157
P-model, 396–397, 415
Panel consensus, 334
Pareto charts, 143–144
Pareto principle, 411
Part families, 76
Partial productivity measure, 32–33
Patient arrival, 112
Peg record, 440
People, Planet, and Profit, 24
Peoples' Express, 372

Performance measurement
  inventory control, 241–242
  of the production process, 69–71
  productivity and, 32–34
Periodic review system, 396
Permeable system, 101–102
Perpetual system, 396
PERT, 192, 197
Pfizer, 34
PIMS, 205
Pipelines, as a mode of transportation, 252
Piper Jaffray, 5
Planned order release, 445
Planned value (PV), 188
Planning process, 10
Plant layouts, 281–283
Plant location
  centroid method, 260–261, 264
  criteria, 253–255
  factor-rating systems, 256, 264
  transportation method, 256–260, 264
Plant maintenance, 432
Plant within a plant (PWP), 46–47, 57
Platform projects, 181
PMIS, 205
Point-of-sale, 335
Poisson distribution, 110–112, 123, 157–158
Poka-yokes, 104–105, 123
Post-ownership costs, 238–239
Precedence relationship, 78, 85
Prevention costs, 138–140
Preventive maintenance, 281, 291
Price
  versus cost, 27
  everyday low, 227
Price-break inventory models, 408–410
Price promotions, 226
Priority rules, 113
Probability analysis, 200
Probability approach, 401–402
Process capability, 149–151
Process control, 154–162
Process control chart, 143, 145
Process mapping, 69–71
Process optimization, 462
Process quality, 27–28
Process selection, 72
Procter & Gamble, 226–227
Producer's risk, 164
Product life cycle, 227
Product–process matrix, 72–73, 85
Product structure file, 438, 442–443
Product tree, 438
Production change costs, 390
Production costs, 361
Production planning, 359–361, 432
Production processes, 64–97
  assembly lines
    balancing, 72, 78–84, 85
    defined, 72, 76, 85

  design of, 78–84
  flexible layouts, 82, 83
  Ford Co., 16
  splitting tasks, 82
  U-shaped layouts, 82
break-even analysis, 73–75
continuous process layout, 72, 76, 78, 85
customer order decoupling point, 67, 85, 307, 387
facility layout, 72–73, 281–283
manufacturing cell layout, 72, 76, 77, 85
mapping, 69–71
mixed-model line balancing, 82–84
organization of, 72–73
product–process matrix, 72–73, 85
project layout, 72, 75, 85
steps in, 66–67
workcenter layout, 72, 75–76, 85
Production rate, 358, 375
Production requirements, 363–364
Production schedules, lean, 284–288
Production smoothing, 372
Productivity, 32–34
Program Evaluation and Review technique (PERT), 192, 197
Progress curves, 484
Project, 205
Project crashing, 199–203
Project indirect costs, 199–200
Project layout, 72, 75, 85
Project management, 178–219
  breakthrough projects, 180–181
  control charts for, 186–191
  defined, 181, 205
  derivative projects, 180–181
  EVM, 188–191, 206
  functional projects, 182–184, 206
  information systems for, 204–205
  matrix projects, 184, 206
  minimum-cost scheduling, 199–203
  network planning models, 191–203
    critical path method, 191–199, 206
    PERT, 192, 197
    project crashing, 199–203
    three activity time estimates, 196–199
    time–cost models, 199–203, 206
  platform projects, 181
  probability analysis, 200
  pure projects, 182, 206
  resource management, 203–205
  using teams, 182
  work breakdown structure, 185–186, 206
Project management information system (PMIS), 205
Project milestones, 185, 206
Projected available balance, 445
Pull system, 273
Pure projects, 182, 206
Pure strategy, 361, 375
Pure virtual customer contact, 103

Q

Q-Model, 396–397, 415
Quadratic programming, 463
Qualitative forecasting techniques
Delphi method, 334–335
historical analogy, 334
market research, 333–334
panel consensus, 334
Quality, 132–177
acceptance sampling, 162–166
analytical tools for, 142–146
awards for, 16, 134–135, 166
certification of, 16
conformance, 137
control charts, 155, 186–191
costs, 138–140, 166
defined, 137
design, 27–28, 166
dimensions of, 136–137
gurus, 135
inspection, 163
ISO 9000/14000, 16, 140–141
kaizen, 279, 291
kanban, 285–287
process, 27–28
six sigma
concept of, 133–134
defined, 141, 166
DPMO, 141, 167
methodology, 142
tools for, 17, 142–146
SPC, 154–162, 167
specification development, 136–137
SQC, 146–154
TQC, 15–16
TQM, 16, 134–136, 166
Quality at the source, 137, 166, 282, 291
Quality circles, 289
Quality management, 432
Queuing system; See also Waiting lines
arrival rates, 109, 123
components of, 107–108
customer arrivals, 108
defined, 123
distribution of arrivals, 109–111
exiting, 115
exponential distribution, 109–110, 123
factors to consider, 112–115
finite population, 108–109
infinite population, 109
line structure, 113–115
poisson distribution, 110–112, 123
queue discipline, 113
service time distribution, 113

R

R charts, 158–162
Rail, as a mode of transportation, 252
Random errors, 328

Random variation, 147, 309
Rate fences, 373
Raw material inventory, 389
Reactive system, 101–102
Reengineering, business process, 16–17
Regression, linear, 311–314, 337
Regression analysis, 332–333
Regression model, 263
Relative measure, 32
Reliability, of delivery, 28
Reneging, 112
Reorder point, 396–404; See also Economic
order quantity (EOQ)
Repetitive manufacturing, 282
Request for proposal (RFP), 225, 237
Residuals, 328
Resource management, 203–205
Respect for people, 274–275
Responsive supply chains, 230
Returning process, 10
Revenue, cost of, 241
Reverse pyramid, 13
RFID, 413
Risk, 164
Risk-hedging supply chains, 229–230
Risk priority number (RPN), 143
RiskMetrics Group, 271
Roadway Logistics, 232
Run charts, 143–144
Ryder, 231

S

Safety stock
aggregate planning, 363–364
defined, 401, 415, 443
fixed-order quantity model, 402–404
fixed-time period model, 405–406
probability approach, 401–402
Sales and distribution, 432
Sales and operations planning, 354–383
aggregate plan
applied to services, 367–370
costs, 361
cut-and-try approach, 363–368
defined, 356, 374
forecasting demand; See Forecasting
internal/external variables,
359–360
level scheduling, 370–372
linear programming and, 462
master production schedule, 434
production planning environment,
359–361
purpose of, 358
yield management, 359,
372–374, 375
defined, 356, 374
intermediate range, 357–358, 374
long-range, 357–358, 374

overview of, 356–358
production planning, 359–361
short-range, 357–358, 374
Salvage costs, 238
Sampling, 147, 162–166
Sawtooth effect, 398
Scheduled receipts, 445
Schedules, lean, 284–288
Scheduling
critical path method, 191–199
early start, 193–194, 196, 206
late start, 193–194, 196, 206
level, 284, 291, 370–372
master production, 433–435, 442, 451
minimum-cost, 199–203
time–cost models, 199–203, 206
Schwab, 17
Scientific management, 17
Seasonal factor, 316–317
Seasonal variation, 315–321
Self-contained teams, 182
Service blueprint, 103–105, 123
Service encounters, 101–103
Service processes, 98–131
blueprinting and fail-safing,
103–105, 123
capacity planning, 101
classification of services, 100
customer contact, 100–103, 123
designing, 101
queuing system, 107–115
service encounters, 101–103
service system design matrix, 101–103
waiting line economics, 106–107
Service rate, 113, 123
Service Science Management and
Engineering (SSME), 17
Service system design matrix, 101–103
Service time distribution, 113
Service utilization, 55
Services
aggregate planning and, 367–370
capacity planning and, 54–56
facility location, 261–263
versus goods, 11–13
lean, 289–291
specifications of, 11
Servitization, 12, 19
Setup costs, 390
Setup times, 287
7-Eleven, 234
Shared capacity, 48
Shareholders, 24
Shell Oil Company, 24
Shibaura Seisaku-sho, 65
Short-range planning, 44,
357–358, 374
Short-term forecasting, 310
Shortage costs, 390
Sigma, 148

Simple moving average, 321–323
Simulation, computer, 122
Single arrival, 112
Single channel
  multiphase line, 114
  single phase lines, 113–114
Single exponential smoothing, 325
Single-period inventory model, 388, 393–396
Single phase line, 114–115
Single sampling plan, 162–165
SIPOC, 143
Six sigma; See also Quality
  concept of, 133–134
  defined, 141, 166
  DPMO, 141, 167
  methodology, 142
  tools for, 17, 142–146
Skunkworks, 182
Skype, 17
Slack time, 193, 206
Slipping filter, 205
Smoothing
  exponential, 324–327, 337
  production, 372
Smoothing constant alpha, 324, 337
Smoothing constant delta, 326, 337
Social responsibility, 24
Sourcing; See Strategic sourcing
Sourcing/purchasing design matrix, 224
Southwest Airlines, 13, 18, 29
SOW, 185
SPC; See Statistical process control (SPC)
Special purpose equipment, 73
Specifications
  development of, 136–137
  of services, 11
  upper and lower limits, 148–149, 167
Specificity, 225
Speed of delivery, 28
Speedi-Lube, 289–290
Splitting tasks, 82
SQC; See Statistical quality control (SQC)
Stable supply process, 228
Stable workforce, 360–361
Stakeholders, 24
Standard deviation, 147
Standard errors, 313–314, 328
Standard Meat Company, 289
Statement of work (SOW), 185
Statistical process control (SPC), 154–162
  attributes, 154, 167
  defined, 154, 167
  using c charts, 157–158
  using p charts, 156–157
  using X and R charts, 158–162
Statistical quality control (SQC)
  applications, 146
  capability index (Cpk), 151–154, 167
  process capability, 149–151

upper and lower specification limits, 148–149, 167
  variation, 146–149
Straddling, 29, 35
Strategic analysis, 26
Strategic capacity planning, 45, 57
Strategic forecasts, 306, 337
Strategic planning, 26
Strategic sourcing
  bullwhip effect, 226–227, 243
  defined, 224, 243
  functional products, 228–229, 243
  global, 224–230
  green sourcing, 235–238
  innovative products, 228–229, 243
  outsourcing; See Outsourcing
  performance measurement, 241–242
  supply chain strategies, 229–230
  supply uncertainty, 228–229
  TCO, 238–240, 243
Subcontracting, 361
Subtask, 185
Super bill of materials, 439; See also Bill of materials (BOM)
Suppliers, lean, 275
Supply, defined, 8
Supply and demand planning, 8–9
Supply chain management, 17
Supply chains
  agile, 230
  bullwhip effect, 226–227, 243
  efficient, 229
  global, 8
  lean, 275–278, 288–289
  responsive, 230
Supply management, 6; See also Operations and supply management (OSM)
Supply networks, 6–7, 291
Supply strategy
  competitive dimensions, 27–29
  defined, 25, 35
  fitting activities to strategy, 30–32
  order winners/qualifiers, 30, 35, 236
  trade-offs, 29–30
  triple bottom line, 18, 19, 24–25, 35
Supply uncertainty, 228–229
Sustainability, 18, 19
Sustainable strategy, 24–25
Synchronized planning, 462
System balance, 47–48

T
T-Mobile, 17
Taco Bell, 18
Tactical forecasts, 307, 337
Task ordering, 75
Tasks, 82, 185
Teams, self-contained, 182
Third-party logistics providers, 231, 251, 264

Three T's, 104
3M, 253
Throughput, 70, 85
Time, 54
Time and motion studies, 17
Time buckets, 440
Time–cost models, 199–203, 206
Time fences, 434–435
Time series analysis
  decomposition of, 314–321
  defined, 308, 337
  exponential smoothing, 324–327, 337
  linear regression, 311–314, 337
  selecting a model, 311
  simple moving average, 321–323
  weighted moving average, 323–324
Time to market, 5
Time triggered models, 396
Tokyo Electric Company, 65
Tokyo Shibaura Denki, 65
Toshiba, 65–66, 72
Total average value of inventory, 69–70, 85
Total cost of ownership (TCO), 238–240, 243
Total factor measure of productivity, 32–33
Total quality control (TQC), 15–16
Total quality management (TQM), 16, 134–136, 166; See also Quality
Touch points, customer, 18
Toyota, 8, 18, 34, 46, 84, 272, 284, 288, 371
Toyota Production System, 274–275
Tracking Gantt chart, 205
Tracking signal, 329, 337
Trade-offs, 29–30
Trading blocs, 254, 264
Transaction cost, 391
Transportation method of linear programming, 256–260, 264
Transportation modes, 251–252; See also Logistics
Trend lines, 309–310
Triple bottom line, 18, 19, 24–25, 35
Trucking, 251–252
Turnover, of inventory, 70, 85, 241–242, 243, 407–408

U
U-shaped line layouts, 82
Uncertainty, of supply, 228–229
Underutilization of capacity, 284
Uniform plant loading, 284–285, 292
United Parcel Service (UPS), 250
Upper control limits (UCL), 156
Upper specification limits, 148–149, 167
UPS, 385–386
US Airways, 13
Utilization rate, 45, 55–56, 57

V

Value, 13, 19
Value chain, 272
Value stream, 275, 291
Value stream mapping (VSM),
    278–280, 291
Variability costs, 148–149
Variable arrival rates, 109
Variation
    assignable, 146, 167
    common, 146–147, 167
    random, 147, 309
    seasonal, 315–321
    SQC, 146–149
Vendor managed inventory, 226, 243
Virtual service, 103
Volatility of demand, 55
Volvo, 46

W

Waiting lines
    computer simulation, 122
    economics of, 106–107
    line structure, 113–115
    models, 115–122
    queuing systems; *See* Queuing system
Walmart, 27, 305–306, 412
Warehousing
    consolidated, 252
    cross-docking, 252–253, 264
    lean, 277
Waste reduction, 235, 272, 274, 275, 291
Water, as a mode of transportation, 252
Web based forecasting, 335–336
Weeks-of-supply, 241–242, 243
Weighted moving average, 323–324
Work breakdown structure, 185–186, 206

Work-in-process inventory, 389
Work package, 185
Workcenter layout, 72, 75–76, 85
Workforce level, 358, 375
Workstation cycle time, 78, 85
World Trade Organization, 223

X

X charts, 158–162

Y

Yield management, 359, 372–374, 375

Z

Zero-changeover time, 47

STUDENT OPERATIONS MANAGEMENT VIDEO DVD

Fourteen Full Length Video Segments

- Project Management at Six Flags, New Jersey

- Service Processing at BuyCostumes.com

- Six Sigma at Caterpillar

- Green Manufacturing at Xerox

- Burton Snowboards - Manufacturing Design

- Honda - Green Product Design and PHILL

- FedEx - Logistics and Customer Service

- DHL - Global Delivery Service

- Ford - Total Supply Chain Management

- Ford - Supplier Relationships - Fords CAP Supplier Campus featuring SY

- Flexible Manufacturing: Featuring Ford - Chicago Assembly Plant

- The Product Process Matrix

- Queuing - Featuring Disney World

- Louisville Slugger Aluminum Bats - Plant Tour